THE ROBBER BARONS

Matthew Josephson

THE ROBBER BARONS

There are never wanting some persons
of violent and undertaking natures,
who, so they may have power and
business, will take it at any cost.

—FRANCIS BACON

A HARVEST BOOK • HARCOURT, INC.
SAN DIEGO   NEW YORK   LONDON

To Charles A. Beard
and Mary R. Beard

www.hmhco.com

Library of Congress Cataloging-in-Publication Data
Josephson, Matthew, 1899-1978.
The robber barons: the great American capitalists,
1861-1901 by Matthew Josephson.
p. cm.—(Harvest book)
Includes bibliographical references and index.
ISBN 0-15-676790-2
1. Capitalists and financiers—United States. 2. Railroads—United
States—History. 3. Industries—United States—History. I. Title.
HG181.J6 1995
332′.0973′09034—dc20 95-30125

Printed in the United States of America

DOH 50 49 48 47 46 45 44 43

4500638568

FOREWORD

The Robber Barons was written during that Great Slump which, beginning in 1929, reached its lowest depths in 1929–1933. The New Era of Prosperity had ended; the captains and the kings of industry were, some of them, departing; and we were asking ourselves insistently how we, as a nation, had got into such a pass. In the twenties I had worked for a few years in Wall Street and learned a few things about the "Men Who Rule America," according to James W. Gerard. Some time later, after 1929, I did a number of biographical studies of them for a well-known satirical magazine. Yet, what I gathered from these experts and from readings in our financial history led me to consider the money men of the twenties as mere epigones compared with their mighty forebears, the economic dinosaurians who flourished during the latter part of the nineteenth century and gave a special character to their period, so aptly named by Mark Twain the Gilded Age. Thus the idea was conceived of writing a history of the earlier generation of capitalists who had put their stamp so deeply upon our business society. It was my purpose to give an account not only of their lives and their manners and morals, but also of how they got the money.

At that season in 1933 when money itself was disappearing (all the banks having been closed for a while) it seemed as if this whole breed might disappear, or perhaps be reformed beyond recognition. Would such fearsome bulls and bears ever again range over the marketplace as anarchs of all they surveyed? Then, the old barons had such great panache!—with their private "palace cars" on rails, their imitation-Renaissance castles, and their pleasure yachts, one of which J. P. Morgan defiantly christened *The Corsair*. Those "kings" of railways, those monopolists of iron or pork, moreover, founded dynastic families which Charles A. Beard once likened to the old ducal families of feudal England.

The expanding America of the post–Civil War era was the paradise of freebooting capitalists, untrammeled and untaxed. They demanded always a free hand in the market, promising that in enriching themselves they would "build up the country" for the benefit of all the people. The Americans of those days had no time for the arts of civilization, as Henry Adams observed, but turned as with a single impulse to the huge tasks of developing their half-empty continent, spanning it with a railway net, and constructing the heavy industrial plant requisite for the new scale of power. All of this was achieved in a climactic quarter-century of our industrial revolution, with much haste, much public scandal, and without plan—under the leadership of a small class of *parvenus*. These were the aggressive and acquisitive types (much censured by our classic writers and historians) who believed they constituted "the survival of the fittest."

Theirs is the story of a well-nigh irresistible drive toward monopoly, which the plain citizens, Congresses, and Presidents opposed—seemingly in vain. The captains or barons of industry were, nevertheless, *agents of progress*—in the words of their contemporary Marx; under their command our mainly agrarian-mercantile society was swiftly transformed into a mass-production economy. I have tried to give a candid description of their most ruthless actions, their conspiracies and their plunderings; for they accepted no ethics of business conduct; but I have also spoken of their constructive virtues, and sought to picture them as human beings living in their time.

In the crisis years of the 1930's, economic intervention by the Federal Government was employed on an unprecedented scale, not only in the interests of human welfare, but also to regulate and control the masters of capital who, by their excesses and bad leadership, had helped to bring about the debacle of 1929–1933. At that period a critical literature also arose (of which the present work may perhaps be taken as an example), providing background material to the men of the New Deal.

Of late years, however, a group of academic historians have constituted themselves what may be called a revisionist school, which reacts against the critical spirit of the 1930's. They reject the idea that our nineteenth-century barons-of-the-bags may have been inspired by the same motives animating the ancient barons-of-the-crags—who, by force of arms, instead of corporate combinations, monopolized strategic valley roads or mountain passes through which commerce flowed. To the revisionists of our history our old-time moneylords "were not robber barons but architects of material progress," and, in some ways, "saviors" of our country. They have proposed rewriting parts of America's history so that the image of the old-school capitalists should be retouched and restored, like rare pieces of antique furniture.

This business of rewriting our history—perhaps in conformity to current fashions in intellectual reaction—has unpleasant connotations to my mind, recalling the propaganda schemes used in authoritarian societies, and the "truth factories" in George Orwell's anti-utopian novel *1984*.

A surprising number of the old family dynasties have survived up to the third generation and, despite the tax burdens of the Welfare State, flourish better than ever. The later Rockefellers, Harrimans, Mellons, Whitneys, and Fords are generally more public spirited than their ancestors; their estates have sometimes mounted into the billions, instead of mere millions, during this half-century of great foreign wars and cold war, accompanied by inflation and prosperity. Certain of our revisionist historians seem to have become reconciled to the presence of these monolithic family fortunes as permanent features of our democratic American landscape. The founders of those fortunes were often men of heroic stature, and their days were charged with drama; but though they were often envied they were not loved by the American people. It was not I, but the embattled farmers of Kansas, who, in one of their anti-monopoly pamphlets of 1880, first applied the nomenclature of Robber Barons to the masters of railway systems.

MATTHEW JOSEPHSON
Sherman, Conn.
September, 1962

CONTENTS

PART ONE

I. THE NATIONAL SCENE: THE NATIONAL CHARACTER   3

The Civil War: flowering of our industrial revolution • The early republic as an agrarian-mercantile democracy • Calvinism and the pecuniary spirit • Benjamin Franklin • Legend of the Self-made Man • Slater, Astor, Vanderbilt, Drew • The Yankee Trader at the frontier • Perpetual land boom • California: a parable • The new barons confront the democracy.

II. WHAT THE YOUNG MEN DREAM   32

Childhood and youth of captains of industry • The race for fortune • Environment of poverty and optimism • The training for ruse • Beginnings of Jay Cooke, Jay Gould, Andrew Carnegie, Pierpont Morgan, John D. Rockefeller and others.

III. OF EMPIRE-BUILDERS   50

The young entrepreneurs stay behind the lines • The new order and the new business chances • Partition of the public domain • Jay Cooke as the government's banker • His new financial technique • The war profiteers • Morgan's speculations in carbines • Jay Gould's dealings in gold • Rise of the Erie ring • Vanderbilt's rotten ships • His entrance into railroads • The Harlem corner • Vanderbilt's conflicts with Erie.

IV. THE WINNING OF THE WEST   75

Manifest destiny in the Great West • Coming of the Iron Horse • Wartime railroad grants • A "national plan" for railways to the Pacific • Festival of the Golden Spike • The Western land and town booms • Jay Cooke's "Banana Belt" • Cooke's Northern Pacific project.

V. TWO CAPTAINS OF INDUSTRY   100

The new tempo of business enterprise • Carnegie becomes an ironmaster • Skill in promotion • In using others • His large ven-

ture in Bessemer steel • Rockefeller enters the oil trade • Disorder
of the oil market • Expansion of Rockefeller's company • Founding of Standard Oil • Use of freight rebates • Birth of a great
monopoly: "The South Improvement Company."

VI. THE FIGHT FOR ERIE   121

*Vanderbilt's contests with Erie for key positions • His buying of
Erie stock • Treachery of Drew, Gould and Fisk • Vanderbilt
prosecutes • Flight of the Erie ring to New Jersey • The "boodle
war," in Albany • Triumph of Gould and Fisk • The Albany &
Susquehanna incident • Morgan wins his spurs • Jay Gould's gold
conspiracy • "Black Friday," 1869.*

VII. GRANDEURS AND MISERIES OF EMPIRE-BUILDING   149

*The golden age of speculation • The alliance of undertakers with
politicians • Rumblings of scandal: the Erie Revolution • Assassination of Jim Fisk • Ejection of Gould • Uprisings against Rockefeller in the Oil Regions • The Crédit Mobilier exposures • The
vulnerability of Jay Cooke • The Northern Pacific bubble • Failure of Jay Cooke & Co. • Panic of 1873.*

PART TWO

VIII. RISING FROM THE RUINS   177

*Gains of the strongest undertakers during panic • Reign of un-
bridled competition • Concentrated struggle for railway lines •
Advance of the Vanderbilt dynasty • Death of the Commodore •
New York Central under Billy Vanderbilt • "The public be
damned!" • Blackmail of the railroad barons.*

IX. MEPHISTOPHELES   192

*Gould's tactics: blockage of the industrial system • Encirclement
of Union Pacific • Its purchase of Gould's rival trunk lines • Rise
of the Missouri-Pacific • Raiding the telegraph field • Capture of
Western Union • Seizure of New York elevated lines • Betrayal
of Cyrus Field • Gould's empire in the United States • Its decline • The great railway strike: 1886 • The gathering of enemies •
Near-catastrophe.*

X. CAESAR BORGIA IN CALIFORNIA   216

*The sack of California • Entrenchment of the Pacific Associates •
Seizure of the Sierra passes • Huntington's lobbying in Washing-*

ton • *Triumph of the Southern Pacific monopoly* • *Rule of the "Octopus" over the Pacific states.*

XI. GIANTS OF THE NORTHWEST   231

The Northwest opens to all comers • *James Hill and Henry Villard scan the field* • *Hill's operations in Minnesota* • *His technical skill and ruthlessness* • *Rise of the Great Northern system* • *Henry Villard preëmpts the Oregon coast ships and railways* • *Stops the westward approach of Northern Pacific* • *Capture of Northern Pacific by the "blind pool"* • *Its completion to the sea* • *Sapping action of Hill* • *Triumph and downfall of Villard* • *Failure of popular rebellions against the Railway Barons.*

XII. CERTAIN INDUSTRIALISTS AROSE   253

The coming of large-scale industry • *The fortune of Carnegie's steel works* • *His rapacity and enthusiasm* • *Carnegie as "business pirate"* • *Henry Frick, baron of coke* • *His "efficiency"* • *Union with Carnegie: a "vertical" combination* • *Renewed campaigns of Rockefeller for monopoly* • *Terrorism in oil* • *The pipe-line war* • *The completion of the great Trust* • *The industrial pools: their weakness and strength* • *Success of the meat-packers' combination* • *The cavemen of capital.*

XIII. MORGAN AND THE RAILWAYS   290

The banker old and new • *Disastrous railroad financing* • *An appeal to the House of Morgan* • *The Pennsylvania's squabbles with Vanderbilt* • *Morgan as arbiter* • *New disorders fomented by Harriman and others* • *Passage of Interstate Commerce Act, 1887* • *Conspiracy of the Railway Barons to nullify the Act* • *"Gentlemen's Agreement" effected by Morgan* • *Morgan's drive for supreme control.*

XIV. THE ROBBER BARONS   315

"Popular consent" won by the new-rich • *Religious piety of the barons* • *Wooing of the barons by the churchmen* • *Conquest of the school* • *The new gold rush to the social heights* • *Acceptance of the pecuniary standard* • *Merger of the parvenus Vanderbilts and the "old" Astors* • *Varieties of conspicuous consumption* • *Pursuit of titles and culture* • *Mr. Maecenas in the New World.*

XV. AGAIN THE ROBBER BARONS   347

Toward the capture of popular political institutions • *Machiavellian technique of barons* • *Indifference to parties* • *Populist revolts of the*

'90's • *The superior strategy of Mark Hanna* • *The attitude toward labor remains medieval* • *Implacable resistance to unions* • *Jay Gould defeats the Knights of Labor* • *Henry Frick and the steel-workers Bloody Homestead* • *Doctrine of "divine right" of capital.*

XVI.   CONCENTRATION: THE GREAT TRUSTS   375

1893: renewal of panic • *Expropriation of the lesser capitalists* • *Expansion of the great monopolies in depression* • *The craze for Trusts after Standard Oil* • *Framing of Trusts by lawyers and bankers* • *Strength and inherent weaknesses of the Trusts* • *Consolidation of Carnegie's steel kingdom* • *The materials of conflict in steel* • *Penetration of the Standard Oil monopoly into new industries* • *The "money machine" at 26 Broadway* • *The Rockefeller alliance with Harriman* • *Preparations for final conflicts by three dominant financial groups.*

XVII.   THE EMPIRE OF MORGAN   404

Morgan as investment banker • *His rule of the money Trust* • *Organization of the House of Morgan—Its campaign for "Community of interest"* • *Its chain of industrial and railway combinations* • *Anxieties of Carnegie* • *His quarrel with the "disloyal" Frick* • *Carnegie makes war upon the Morgan steel combinations* • *The demoralization of heavy industry.*

XVIII.   BATTLE OF GIANTS   424

Termination of the steel war • *Purchase of Carnegie Steel company by Morgan* • *Formation of the United States Steel Trust* • *Frenzied finance* • *Expansion of Morgan-Hill combination in the Northwest* • *Fierce opposition of Rockefeller-Harriman group* • *The Northern Pacific panic* • *A last "battle of titans"* • *The peace conference at the Metropolitan Club* • *Formation of the Northern Securities Company* • *Achievement of "community of interest"* • *Roosevelt attacks the Morgan-Rockefeller holding company* • *Dissolution of Northern Securities* • *Lasting harmony and dissimulation of the combined monopolists* • *The end of the tether.*

BIBLIOGRAPHY   455

INDEX   461

PART ONE

CHAPTER ONE

THE NATIONAL SCENE:
THE NATIONAL CHARACTER

THE cannonading that began at Charleston with the dawn of April 12, 1861, sounded the tocsin for the men of the new American union. The fatal clash of the two economic nations within the republic could no longer be escaped; the "irrepressible conflict" was at hand. When the trivial siege of Sumter was over, the North rallied from its stupor, its breathless waiting. A people who had barely known themselves a nation were unified at last by danger. The North, with a passion no less bitter than the South's, moved to crush the rebel who had ruled the national policy for generations, and stubbornly barred the way of industrial growth as if he would halt inevitability itself.

In legions, the recruits, the young men of '61, marched away to Bull Run for the three months' war. On both sides they were the soldiers of a people without tradition or gift for military heroics; a people which had come out to attend three earlier wars only in small numbers, with remarkable apathy. The frontier democracy had known as little of the rule of the military captain as of the feudal noble or the prince of the Church. Its sons were no soldiers, yet possessed deathless courage; it had few battle leaders; most of these must rise up from disaster. Therefore the conflict would be long, the most stubborn, the most sanguinary in all the history of the West, and colossal in its scale of operations.

If the South did not truly estimate its powers for such a contest, neither did the North know its strength, its wealth, its destiny. Not many in either camp could have pictured the incredible transformations which would accompany those thundering years. And fewer still knew or sensed what the Civil War was really fought for.

The epoch of martial glory and martial stupidity need concern

3

us but little here. We observe only that its grand blood-letting fixes a turning point at which the trend of our history declares itself: the opening of the Second American Revolution, that "industrial revolution" which worked upon society with far greater effect than the melodramatic battles. After Appomattox, in 1865, it is widely and conveniently assumed, the Old Order was ended.

"Had they been Tyrian traders of the year 1000 B.C., landing from a galley fresh from Gibraltar," writes Henry Adams concerning his family's return from diplomatic duties abroad, "they could hardly have been stranger on the shore of a world so changed from what it had been ten years before." All this is true figuratively. But literally the symptoms of the future order of things, all the new shapes and forces existed vigorously in the days of Jefferson, side by side with the institutions and conditions of pre-capitalist or feudal eras. The process of change, the departure from the old ways toward large-scale industry, toward giant capitalism, toward a centralized, national economy, was long in preparing, gradual, and not too imperceptible. When the abyss of the Civil War suddenly yawned before men's eyes it but registered a "lag" which had existed already during the whole of the preceding generation. Where England had officially recognized its economic transition peacefully by the repeal of the Corn Laws, America, through blood and iron, consecrated its own industrial revolution by the end of what had been comparatively free trade....

All this we see in retrospect. But besides the young men who marched to Bull Run, there were other young men of '61 whose instinctive sense of history proved to be unerring. Loving not the paths of glory they slunk away quickly, bent upon business of their own. They were warlike enough and pitiless yet never risked their skin: they fought without military rules or codes of honor or any tactics or weapons familiar to men: they were the strange, new mercenary soldiers of economic life. The plunder and trophies of victory would go neither to the soldier nor the statesman, but to these other young men of '61, who soon figured as "massive interests moving obscurely in the background" of wars. Hence these, rather than the military captains or tribunes, are the subject of this history.

2

Shortly before or very shortly after 1840 were born nearly all the galaxy of uncommon men who were to be the overlords of the future society. They were born at a historical moment when by an easy effort one could as well look back at the mellow past as scan the eventful future. Their parents could remember the disturbed but very simple and light-hearted times of Mr. Jefferson, when pigs wandered unmolested at the steps of the Capitol; and it was only a comparatively few years since Mr. Jackson had "driven the money-changers from the temple."

It was not true of course that the early Republic was a millennium of free farmers and artisans; yet in the simplicity of its organization and of its mercantile economy, the nation belonged almost to a pre-capitalist age. Over great regions of the country men still worked for a "livelihood" rather than for "money." This man of the mercantile age, certainly contrasted with his successor, a few generations later, "did not stand on his head or run on all fours," but was a "natural man" and in himself was "the meteyard of all things." The handicrafts were widespread; little shops and factories were interspersed among the farms of New England. And it was still true, in many parts of the earlier America, that the artisan, as in olden times, loved his work and feared more that it might not be worthy of him than that he might not put a high enough price upon it. It was also true that goods circulated at a slow rate. The ingenious Yankee and his wife wove their cloth, turned their own furniture, molded their own pottery, in a manner now considered quaint but then truly economical. As their traffic in goods and moneys, while limited to narrow regions, was carried on at the pace of the horse-drawn post, the ox-cart, the river or canal vessel, so their opportunities were narrowed, while differences in station were correspondingly moderate. Thus although there were instances enough of large inequalities of wealth and power, there was more individual equality than in other countries. And of the possessors of great fortunes we note that their wealth was based on ownership of land. This was true of New York as of Virginia. In New England and elsewhere along the coast, the shipping trade was the medium of great fortune;

but in this commerce too the pace of trade was long-breathed, temperate, at first.

In such spacious and leisurely days the art of politics and the art of rhetoric tended to flourish. Many documents testify to the charm of ideas and talk in the circle of Jefferson, Madison, Gallatin and Marshall, who held forth almost daily in the incompleted presidential "palace" of the village of Washington. These statesmen were latter-day Romans; in their own eyes, at least, their rôle was high. With an acrid passion, they, and behind them the mass in town dwellings and log cabins, the lowliest immigrants from Scotland and Germany, upheld the notions of the free republic upon which Napoleonic Europe and even English opinion habitually heaped its contempt. Proud of having cast off the incubus of feudal and aristocratic institutions, each toiler with "every stroke of the ax and the hoe" knew himself a gentleman and his children gentlemen. Where monarchies clerical and temporal and theatrical military adventurers sucked the nourishment of Europe, here was a land where government was simply to be a judicature and a police. In the mind of the tall, negligently dressed but eloquent statesman from Virginia, little more was necessary to make the happiness and prosperity of the people than

> a wise and frugal government which shall restrain men from injuring one another, which shall leave them otherwise free to regulate their own pursuits of industry and improvement, and shall not take from the mouth of labor the bread it has earned. This is the sum of good government, and this is necessary to close the circle of our felicities.

Thus, under the lax political institutions, society would be wholly directed by *interest*, rather than by outworn traditions, or by the appetites of autocrats. Under favoring circumstances the Americans threw themselves into their tasks with a revolutionary zeal. And though Jefferson had hoped that only the "agricultural capacities of our country" would be furthered, rather than industry which would lead to "the mimicry of an Amsterdam, a Hamburg, a city of London," it was soon evident that the outcome was to be a different and unattended one. It was the qualities of trade and industry, in most predatory form, and not the "agricultural capacities" that flourished in the turbulent laissez-faire society of the frontier democracy. This was one of the first effects that struck the eye of visiting foreigners, such as Alexis de Tocqueville.

The Americans, and no less the newly arrived immigrants, were soon living in the future, filled with a large excitement over solid mountains of salt and iron, of lead, copper, silver and gold; over cornfields waving and rustling in the sun, over "limitless riches, unimaginable stores of wealth and power"—none of which the cultured satirists who frequently journeyed here could see. But the poor who came here saw those mountains of gold. These wandering Yankee traders, these "projectors," these pioneers and immigrants remembered only how hungry and naked their forbears had been through the centuries, and were ravished by the future. To their minds, every new method which led by a shorter road to wealth, every machine which spared labor, diminished the cost of production, facilitated or augmented pleasure, seemed the grandest effort of the human intellect. Hence the two strains in the national character: political freedom and idealism, abetting a "sordid and practical" materialism, which asked nothing of ideas, of the arts, and of science, but their application toward ends of use and profit.

When we search for the springs of the national character we can never long forget that the original settlers were English Protestants. In the worshipers of the Reformed Church the individual conscience had been liberated from Catholic and Anglican formula and tradition; was freer to adjust itself flexibly to new hazards and opportunities. Among the New Englanders, for a time, and among the widely scattered Scotch-Irish, Calvinism was dominant and its influence was widespread in nearly all the colonies. And though it was not true that Calvin had introduced usury, as so many suppose, he had recognized its existence more candidly than the Catholic Church; and, as shown by R. H. Tawney, in his "Religion and the Rise of Capitalism," Calvin liberated the economic energies of the rising bourgeoisie of Europe by his teachings. By the Calvinist scale of moral values, the true Christian "must conduct his business with a high seriousness as in itself a kind of religion." By his sober ideal of social conduct the members of the merchant and artisan class, the roturiers, found their "soul"; saw all careers "open to character" rather than to the well-born; became wielded into a disciplined social force. Hence the combination of business address and discipline noted among the early New Englanders, as in similar milieux of the mother country whence they came. So many sayings of the time show how "among the Reformed, the greater their zeal, the greater was their inclination to trade and industry, as holding idleness unlawful." Others commemorate the amalgam of piety and ruse which made the best of both worlds: "*The tradesman meek and much a liar. . . .*" We feel in the Puritan type that the will is organized, disciplined, nerved to the utmost, as Tawney concludes; and if his personal life is sober, then it is also true that he enjoys freedom in the deepest sense; he ends by utterly opposing the authority even of church officers to police him; in the end his own individual conscience is his final authority.

For the people of the Reformed Church (as for the Jews) money was long ago the sole means to power. We find early economists in the time of Charles II saying of the nonconformists that "none are of more importance than they in the trading part of the people and those that live by industry, upon whose hands the business of the nation lies so much."

The first colonists, then, were brimming with the developed "middle-class virtues"; their strict sumptuary laws and domestic habits seemed to lead always to diligence, to cheerless self-restraint, and finally culminated in the parsimony and "holy economy" of the Quakers.[1]

Among those who won notable triumphs by pursuing the Puritan

[1]Werner Sombart in his treatise "*Der Bourgeois*" speaks of the emergence of the "middle-class spirit" wherever conditions favored it, apparently a force shaping religious and political institutions rather than otherwise. Thus the need for a new social attitude brings the shift in emphasis by a Calvin, whom Tawney calls "the Marx" of the bourgeoisie. . . . The Complete Citizen in fifteenth-century Florence, as in seventeenth-century Scotland, Sombart tells us, practiced that "holy thrift" which Franklin was later to sing. Idleness and extravagance were the two cardinal sins for the trading class; thrift betokened not only economy of money or goods, but also the profitable expenditure of time. "Beware of unnecessary expenditure as a deadly foe," exclaims the Florentine sage Alberti. Leonardo da Vinci recalls his grandfather exhorting his children to take the busy ants as their models. "To whom shall I compare a prosperous householder or a good paterfamilias? I will liken him to a spider, sitting in the center of her widespread web, yet ever on the alert to strengthen and repair if any one thread tremble ever so lightly." The same themes are developed in Defoe's "Compleat English Tradesman": "The tradesman should also avoid all pleasures and diversions, even of the most harmless kind; they are a cause of disaster." Expensive living is "a kind of slow fever . . . a secret enemy that feeds upon the vitals, it feeds upon the life and blood of the tradesman."

economic virtues was no other than the free-thinking Benjamin Franklin who was the son of Puritans; and none more than he was the representative and container of the national character in the early period of the republic. He was Defoe's wise shopman, his "Compleat English Tradesman," for whom "trade was not a ball where people appear in masque and act a part to make sport ... but 'tis a plain, visible scene of honest life ... supported by prudence and frugality." It was not for nothing that Franklin, even more than Washington, was held up as model for succeeding generations; indeed he was a paragon for the entire bourgeois world, inasmuch as no man of his time was more widely read than he, millions of copies of his "Poor Richard" and his "Autobiography" circulating in scores of languages, in all continents, at the outset of the nineteenth century.[2] In him, as a result of the long slow process of economic and religious liberation there had crystallized what we may call the "bourgeois spirit," as opposed to the feudal; he was the *homo economicus* of the new times. The usefulness of his virtue and thrift are all the more significant inasmuch as we now have the strongest reasons to believe they were public; for the rest he showed strong tendencies to relapse into little uninjurious vices in private, or when abroad in foreign land....

It was Franklin, philosopher of the new middle class, inventor of a stove and the lightning rod, who lamented that we lose so much time in sleep; who framed the immortal dictum: "Time is money";

[2]The very literary Judge Thomas Mellon, father of Andrew Mellon, and founder of the famous banking house, always recalled the joy with which he came upon a dilapidated copy of Dr. Franklin's autobiography for the first time, in 1828, at the age of fourteen. "It delighted me," he writes, "with a wider view of life and inspired me with new ambition.... For so poor and friendless a boy to be able to become a merchant or a professional man had before seemed an impossibility; but here was Franklin, poorer than myself, *who by industry, thrift and frugality* had become learned and wise, and elevated to wealth and fame. The maxims of 'Poor Richard' exactly suited my sentiments.... I regard the reading of Franklin's 'Autobiography' as the turning point of my life." (*My italics.*) The foregoing is cited by Mr. Harvey O'Connor from "Thomas Mellon and His Times," by Thomas Mellon; privately printed, Pittsburgh, 1886. Thomas Mellon determined once and for all to leave his father's farm at Poverty Point and establish himself in the near-by city of Pittsburgh, where owing to the sternest self-denial he prospered first as lawyer and later as money-lender. A statue of Franklin overlooks the great banking room of the Mellon National Bank, according to Harvey O'Connor, author of "Mellon's Millions."

whose whole life was one long worship of "holy economy." It
was he who wrote:

> ... *The way to wealth, if you desire it, is as plain as the way to
> market. It depends chiefly on two words, industry and frugality;
> that is, waste neither time nor money, but make the best use of both.
> Without industry and frugality nothing will do, and with them
> everything. He that gets all he can honestly and saves all he gets
> will certainly become rich, if that Being who governs the world,
> to whom all should look for a blessing on their honest endeavors;
> doth not, in His wise providence, otherwise determine.*

Franklin believed that given personal restraint and prudence in
the conduct of his affairs, God would oversee the rest. This Yankee
was avid of novelty and invention, free of prejudices, ingenious
mechanically, skillful with his hands, quick of wit. And, finally, he
was respectable, his respectability being designed, as he said candidly,
to impress his clients.

> *In order to secure my character and credit as a tradesman, I took
> care not only to be in reality industrious and frugal, but to avoid
> the appearance to the contrary. I dressed plain, and was seen at no
> places of idle diversion; I never went out a-fishing or shooting.*

This respectability, this honesty toward customers, this conservatism, in good quality, small volume, high prices, was also a
strong trait of the earlier capitalism which was already departing
toward 1840. The keeping of clients, the avoidance of encroachment
upon others' trade, was part of the atmosphere of those unhurried
times which referred back to a world already passing, in which man
and his life were "the measure of all things" and, to a greater extent
than ever afterward, of his business.

Franklin, the historic Yankee, the legendary Self-made Man, owed
his success as a printer as much to his strict attention to new
machinery studied in London as to his good and prudent business
management; just as in journalism he owed his success to enterprise
in the current of new ideas. Typical of the old order of early
capitalism, he was in his own person a man of enterprise, a skilled
artisan of nimble and strong hands; he was also a "small master" who
having made his "primary accumulations," held command over a
little troop of apprentices and craftsmen whose associated toil

represented the "division of labor" which was the momentous contribution of his century.

As in the case of Franklin, so in the other early Self-made Men of the young Republic we may study the naked process of change from the early stages of industrialism to the more advanced. We see Samuel Slater removing from England to the United States at the close of the eighteenth century, carrying in his brain the memory of Richard Arkwright's machinery designs. Bounties had been offered for power-carding machinery by our government and the ingenious British craftsman by his skill and of course his want of scruples about the pirating and exporting of patents-then forbidden by English law-sets up at Pawtucket the first successful cotton-spinning mill. He is aided, to be sure, by local capital in the person of the pious Moses Brown of Providence who had written to him in 1790:

> If thou canst do this thing, I invite thee to come to Rhode Island, and have the credit of introducing cotton-manufacture into America.

So with his own hands the Derbyshire master craftsman had set up numerous mills, employing numerous companies of workmen (whose labor as far as possible in those days was carefully divided into simple, routine motions), and had become by his technical talent a man of great wealth. Together with Moses and Obadiah Brown, the philanthropic Quakers, he had finally become a commander of armies of workmen whose mechanized and accelerated labor produced mountains of cotton and woolen cloth. But note how, while diligent and aggressive, these early masters of capital are godly men as well, giving their tithe to the Lord. Slater established in one of his mills in 1796 a Sunday-school for the improvement of his work people, "the first, or among the first, in the United States"; while Obadiah Brown, dying childless, left the stupendous sum of $100,000 to Quaker charities.

Thus at a time when most of the great fortunes were yet derived from the ownership of large landholdings, as in the Virginia of Washington or even along the Hudson River Valley, where the descendants of the Dutch patroons lived in feudal state, the first successes in manufacture and in use of natural resources revealed the significant symptoms of the new order of society.

The history of John Jacob Astor, legend of the poor boy risen to riches, was immortalized by Washington Irving in his romance of "Astoria" and was in everyone's eye. With empty hands the German butcher's son had arrived in New York in 1783 and apprenticed himself to a furrier; then with alternate boldness and parsimony made his first important accumulations. He himself had gone up the Mohawk Valley to trade with the Indians; then he had lived in frugal style over his own shop at Broadway and Vesey Street for two decades, he and his wife laboring over the stinking furs and skins, close-fisted, weighing every penny, secretive of his plans as of his possessions, until with his great means he was enabled to expand his trading to the wildest outposts of the frontier. The American Fur Company of Astor ranged in its quest of furs from Missouri to Oregon and farthest Canada. It was not only said that its canny agents were vendors of liquor demoralizing the Indians who brought skins, but according to Congressional reports of 1821–22, even debased the liquors they sold to the aborigines!

Out of the trading posts of drunkenness and misery came much of the great accumulations of an Astor. Then his wealth had been translated into city land, into bonds, into banks, above all, land— so that his heir, William B. Astor, after 1848, was called "the land-lord of New York." Thenceforth tens of thousands of city dwellers collectively paid tribute to the grandees of the Astor family, which was likened to that of the Rothschilds of Europe.

There were other famous nouveaux riches. Had not Alexander Stewart, arrived in 1823 from Belfast, and dealer in Irish laces and linens, become within several years the lord of a great marble emporium which towered above Broadway and dispensed dry goods of every sort to the multitude? Soon two thousand persons labored in association for the modern merchant prince whose income was above a million a year!

And finally when had the world ever seen the like of "Commodore" Cornelius Vanderbilt, most astonishing of all the famous parvenus of the 1840's and 1850's? The hulking, Silenus-like figure of an old man, in his eternal fur coat and "plug hat," winter and summer, with the handsome, bald head, and the profane language of a sea-dog, was known and liked by all New York. Remembered as a Staten Island ferry-boy, untutored, unable to spell correctly, he was the pure type of the modern captain of industry flourishing along the frontier of a new world. He was born of poor Dutch peasants in 1794, when a landed baron and a soldier commanded the republic, and his career spanned the flight of time into a new epoch. At his death, the steamship, the railroad, the magnetic telegraph, the iron and steel industry had worked their changes upon society; changes which even if he did not comprehend them, he had the good fortune to turn to his use eventually, so that he would prosper to a grand old age, to a time that the Jeffersons and Gallatins of his youth could never have dreamed, with his hands always at the levers of the new power. But if Vanderbilt had much of Franklin's parsimony, he had something of John Hawkins's ferocity too. Engaged in the shipping trade of New York harbor from boyhood, Cornelius Vanderbilt had known no other school than that of the dock and the forecastle. His herculean strength, his dexterity, his mixture of fierce courage and shiftiness had gradually brought him to the fore as a master of river and coastwise sailing vessels. His early years were filled with long, savage struggle against the dominant Eastern shipping interests, the Fulton-Livingston group, whom he would underbid perpetually in the competition for freight. And since they often had the law on their side in the dispute, Vanderbilt was driven to many wiles at times to avoid process-servers; at others to sudden violent aggressions, worthy of an old-time corsair, whereby his enemies and their minions were overwhelmed.

Possessed of a sharp wharf-rat's tongue and a rough wit, according to his early biographers, he took joy in combat. "His foible was opposition," we are told. "Wherever his keen eye detected a line that was making a large profit . . . he swooped down and drove it to the wall, by offering a better service and lower rates"— for a time. Then with the opposition driven out, he would raise his rates without pity, to the lasting misery of his clients.

The career of Vanderbilt shows little of that triumphant enterprise or "vision" for which he has been applauded so long. As a master of sailing vessels, he despised the newly arrived paddle-wheelers of 1807, holding that they were merely good enough for Sunday picnics. When they proved their value for passenger service, he was among those who insisted that the new steamboats could never be used for freight "because the machinery would take up too much room." But when the hazardous experimental period had been survived by the steamship, then he judged the time ripe for intrusion; he had the best steamboats built for his lines and became a dominant factor in the ocean and coastwise trade. In waiting for the steamboat to be perfected, he showed the shrewd capacity of the great entrepreneur whose undertakings are always larger, but tardier, safer and more profitable than those of the early inventor or pioneer.

The "heroic period" of Vanderbilt was undoubtedly the time of the California gold rush, when he moved heaven and earth to throw a competing line—against the Collins line—by ship and stagecoach across Nicaragua. Here he overcame unheard-of dangers of tide, of native revolutions and filibusters, of tropical heat and plague. In person he drove his men to the breaking point, setting the example for fourteen to sixteen hours a day of sleepless vigilance and labor. In an emergency he once took the helm of the side-wheel steamboat which must be sent up the San Juan River rapids to Lake Nicaragua, firing up the boiler to the utmost. His biographer, Croffut, relates:

> Sometimes he got over the rapids by putting on all steam; sometimes ... he extended a heavy cable to great trees up stream and warped the boat over. ... The engineers reported that he "tied down the safety-valve and 'jumped' the obstructions, to the great terror of the whole party."

But out of the traffic to California he drew the bulk of his sudden fortune, in the ripeness of age. In the 1850's when American shipping was supreme, he had over a hundred vessels afloat, and earned $100,000 each month. At the time of the "shipping subsidy" scandals, aired in the Senate in 1858, it was seen that Vanderbilt and E. K. Collins of the Pacific Mail Steamship Line were the chief plunderers, sometimes conciliating, sometimes blackmailing each other. To keep Vanderbilt silent and inactive, while he drew a government mail subsidy of $900,000 a year, and quadrupled steerage rates, Collins paid Vanderbilt the large sum of $56,000 a month. Thus the vigorous old privateer was enabled to boast in 1853 of a fortune of $11,000,000, which he kept invested at 25 per cent.[3]

But though fabulously rich and engaged in numerous complex undertakings the Commodore carried all his bookkeeping accounts

---

[3] It was to "blackmail" that Gustavus Myers, historian of the "Great American Fortunes," attributes the tremendous leap of Vanderbilt's fortune. The general citizenry good-humoredly paid him tribute in government subsidies; but then one looks in vain, at the period, for a sign of another form of conscience or morality in the general public.

in his own head and trusted no one with them. His own son, William
H. Vanderbilt, declared that he knew nothing of his father's
methods. He clung to his wealth. The carpet in his small home on
Washington Place was long threadbare; his long-suffering wife,
who had lived in a terrible frugality with him, was for a long time
denied anything resembling luxury. The nine children she had borne
him grew up under a parent now brutally indifferent, now cruel
with a fierce parsimony. His eldest son, William Henry, who was
to be his heir, a meek and sluggish character, was consigned to a
farm on Staten Island until he was of middle age: his father thought
him an idiot and often told him so to his face. Another less patient
and calculating son, Cornelius, was disowned for his extravagance.
His pathetic wife, who at last became permanently distracted, the
Commodore finally committed to Bloomingdale Asylum; while at
the age of senility he pursued young women insatiably.

In an age of free struggle and fierce competition for power, this
old buccaneer, who was almost a septuagenarian at the outbreak of
the Civil War, was admired most of all for his unflagging aggressiveness. One incident was generally known of, in which associates had
tried to take advantage of his absence upon a European journey to
seize control of one of his properties. He wrote them:

Gentlemen:
You have undertaken to cheat me. I will not sue you, for law
takes too long. I will ruin you.
                          Sincerely yours,
                          Cornelius Van Derbilt.

And he did.

A characteristic expression of his, in another emergency, also became celebrated. "What do I care about the law?" he had exclaimed. "Hain't I got the power?"

In one respect, Vanderbilt foreshadowed the new conceptions
of large-scale capitalism in his shipping business. His tactics were
often directed to obtaining a great volume of traffic at lower rates
than his competitors gave—in any case, until he obtained the upper
hand, when he might safely give way to greed again. Once the great
shipper Collins reproached Vanderbilt for making the federal government a lower offer for the mail-carrying privilege than seemed
necessary. "I can't make it pay as it is," Collins had concluded.

"Then you are probably in a business that you don't understand," rejoined the Commodore.

Vanderbilt, then, combined in himself the new and the old social traits at once. Something of a sea-dog and a pioneer, endowed with physical courage and high energy as well as craftiness, he was the Self-made Man, for whom the earlier, ruder frontier America was the native habitat. At the same time his individual conscience was already free of those prescriptive, restraining codes, as of the habitual prudence of Franklin's age of early capitalism. Though he kept no complicated books he had the taste for ever larger affairs such as men used to undertake only under the patronage of monarchs. In seeking quickened activity, great volume and lower prices —instead of honest but limited services at high tariffs—he gave intimations of a new personal departure from the older bourgeois order. And though he had succeeded earlier as a craggy pioneer, he learned to employ the capital he possessed in the vast labyrinth of the modern marketplace. In short, he became originally a leader of men and undertakings, an owner of capital, because he was strong; but he learned to thrive in an age when men became commanders of industry because of their command of capital itself.

3

In the arts of buying and selling capital itself men grew both more subtle and more daring. Progress was registered not only in water power and steam engines, but in the rise and spread of "joint-stock companies" before 1840, in the growth of bourses or exchanges which dealt in such capital. The most notable of these at the time of the Civil War was the Stock Exchange of the City of New York, which by its natural advantages became the seaport and commercial metropolis of the nation. A century earlier, Wall and Water Streets were the haunt of pirates and slave-traders, and especially of the immortal William Kidd; here a market flourished already which differed in no ways from the old 'changes of Amsterdam, Frankfurt, Paris and London. Out of the neighboring coffee-houses where merchants of the shiftier kind, gamblers, lottery-players, touts and politicians had been wont to gather, the personnel of the marketplace was recruited in the days of the Revolutionary War. Under the shade of a famous old buttonwood tree at

68 Wall Street there congregated those shrewd, lynx-eyed, slit-mouthed speculator-politicians who participated in the "bull" movement in "continentals" of the 1790's—a crowd bearing a close enough resemblance to the grave, secretive traders who walked in the florence of the Medicis or in seventeenth-century Edinburgh, or on the London Exchange whose "stock-jobbers" Defoe has described.

Robert Morris had been the leader of the first manipulative campaign for selling dear the rescued government scrip and securities which had been bought so cheap. The "stock-jobbers" who dealt in these peculiar wares were a perennial, hardy and resourceful race. In good times they did a flourishing business; even before the War of 1812 it often seemed that "stock and scrip were the sole subject of conversation" among the commercial-minded freemen, as Madison complainingly wrote to Jefferson. The press of the early republic spoke of the "raving madness bordering on insanity" of the mercantile public. And when the exaltation was succeeded by the cathartic cycle of depression, of tragic disillusionment, the society of brokers which had formed itself in Wall Street showed, ever since 1791, a wonderful poise, a "calm detachment toward the public ruin" which was to be one of the undying traditions of Wall Street.

The character of the Wall Street market had become definitely fixed after it had housed itself indoors in the Merchants' Exchange Building at Wall and William Street, with solemn rules, initiation fees, and regular charges to outsiders. All its swift, smooth-running machinery—especially after the introduction of the telegraph—for dealing in pieces or shares of capital, as an "open and free securities market" were much as they are now, and had the same function. Even the "bear" had appeared in Jacob Little, who sold stocks "short" on six months' options in 1837. And as it is now so Wall Street was then a huge whispering gallery, vibrant with a thousand rumors, fears and passions, emotional and mercurial, or now impassive and inscrutable; a place of restless tides and bewitching calms, or howling hurricanes, a place as unfathomable as the sea, as impenetrable as the jungle.

In the 1850's another of the picturesque, weather-beaten figures who ruled as a king of the marketplace was Daniel Drew ("The Great Bear"), sometimes an associate, sometimes rival of Vanderbilt, and no less celebrated than the hardy Commodore. Tall, thin, bearded, rustic and "negligently dressed like a drover," Drew was renowned both for his piety and for his terrible market prowess, by which he dominated stock-gambling for almost a generation. This "Sphinx of the Stock Market" was as suspicious as Vanderbilt, also kept all his accounts in his head and considered the whole paraphernalia of bookkeeping a confounded fraud. Timid and mistrustful, he always believed the worst of men and their business ventures. He said: "Never tell nobody what yer goin' ter do, till ye do it."

Born in 1797, in the village of Carmel, New York, in the rural fastnesses of Putnam County, he had grown up to be a cattle-drover and lived a life of terrible privation in youth, which may have contributed to his "bearish" view of life. The cattle that he gathered up from farmers to drive to New York, purchased on credit, he often never settled for, according to the natives of Carmel; a practice which was the cause of his removing the base of his operations as far as Ohio. To him is also credited the invention of "watered stock," his cattle being kept thirsty throughout the journey, and only given drink immediately before arrival at the drovers' market uptown. Once, in bringing cattle at night over the Allegheny Mountains during a lightning storm, a tree had fallen upon Daniel Drew, killing his horse under him. But as Henry Clews relates, "No hardships or privations could deter him from the pursuit of money."

After having prospered in the cattle trade by his particular methods he had become the owner of the Bull's Head Tavern in the Third Avenue drovers' center; then a moneylender, an owner of Hudson River steamboats, and finally a stockbroker, head of the house of Drew, Robinson & Co., which bought and sold not only bank and steamboat shares, but also the new railroad shares which were already immensely popular in the '50's. In 1854 he had loaned the Erie Railroad, of which he was a director, $1,500,000 in return for a chattel mortgage on its rolling stock.

The Erie was then a great trunk line, nearly 500 miles long, plying between the harbor of New York and the Great Lakes. It had been built at a cost of $15,000,000, partly through state subsidies; great celebrations, tremendous barbecues, had attended its completion, which was considered an enormous boon for the economy of the country at large as well as one of the marvels of modern science.

But its capital had soon been watered until it stood at $26,000,000. Its rickety, lamp-lit trains, its weak iron rails had brought disaster and scandal, such as clung to its whole career; and when Daniel Drew, by virtue of his loans to the company, became its treasurer and master after the panic of 1857, it was soon clear that the flinty old speculator was not in the least interested in the Erie Railroad as a public utility or highway of traffic.

His strategic position gave him intimate knowledge of the large railroad's affairs which he used only to advance his private speculations. The very decrepitude of the rolling stock, the occurrence of horrendous accidents, were a financial "good" to the Speculative Director, who used even the treasury of his railroad to augment his short-selling of its own stock.

Nevertheless Drew, like Vanderbilt, became a character of renown, possessing a fortune of many millions, a model for the rising generation. His sayings were repeated everywhere and his more famous tricks were rehearsed by younger disciples. There was for instance the "handkerchief trick." In an uptown club one hot day, at a moment when he was supposed to be hard pressed in the market, Old Daniel pulled out his proverbial red bandanna handkerchief to mop his brow before sitting down with some fellow speculators. A slip of paper bearing a "point," or tip, fell to the floor; a bystander put his foot on it. As Drew left, apparently not noticing the incident, the others pounced upon the piece of paper, which proved to be an order. They bought Erie stock in large quantities, and were soon gulled. This is the "handkerchief trick."

According to Clews he cared not a fig what people thought of him, or what newspapers said. "He holds the honest people of the world to be a pack of fools. . . . When he has been unusually lucky in his trade of fleecing other men, he settles accounts with his conscience by subscribing toward a new chapel or attending a prayer meeting." And when unlucky, he would retreat to his house in Bleecker Street, "shut himself up, stuff up all the windows, bar all the doors, go to bed, swathe himself in blankets, pray and begin drinking."

For Drew was devoutly religious; and against the view held in money quarters that he never hesitated to sacrifice a friend, illustrated by innumerable anecdotes, his admirers pointed to his "genuine piety" as refuting his "closeness." Had he not given the immense sum of $250,000 to found a Methodist theological seminary in New Jersey? But in truth, it turned out in the end that he had given only his note, which after many years, in the shifting fortunes of new times, was never to be honored. . . .

At any rate "Uncle Daniel" Drew, like Vanderbilt, remained a hero, and a mystery to his contemporaries because of his "daring, subtle and obscure speculations" by which he excelled all others.

4

Upon the customs of the market, upon its principles of negotiation and trading which an Astor, a Vanderbilt, a Drew exemplified, other decisive influences were at work to give them their special American character. Immigrants or natives, these masters of the market soon absorbed the genius of the Yankee. But the Yankee was changing. We must look for him elsewhere than in the foot-worn marketplaces of the "civilized" East; we must observe the Yankee in process of transformation under the particular climate of the untamed frontier.

The legend of the Yankee Trader also formed a significant part of the composite national portrait, in which the mellow features of Franklin are prominent. . . . He was Uncle Jonathan, or Jonathan Slick or Sam Slick, as Miss Constance Rourke describes him in her recent inquiries into American folklore. He was long and lean and weather-beaten; never passive, he was "noticeably out in the world; it was a prime part of his character to be 'a-doin'.'" He pulled strings, he made shrewd and caustic comments; he ridiculed old values; "the persistent contrast with the British showed part of his intention." And to the British especially he had always appeared homely and "rapacious," but never slow-witted. If you met him in a tavern and he drew you into a trade, he soon quietly stripped you of everything you had. In the South, superstitious colored folks and even white folks, according to tradition, locked their doors piously at the approach of the long, flapping peddler's figure.

This ingenious Yankee, quick to adapt himself everywhere, easily extricating himself from situations, and by religion and training profoundly rational, his passions under control, his reason dominating his natural inclinations, "plain and pawky," overassertive, self-assured, moving everywhere, had left his mark upon the society and leavened it. But in the give and take of the frontier he was at home naturally; he easily bested all others.

Those who looked for "noble savages" at the frontier looked in vain. (Two or three appeared in the most sophisticated region of the country, in Concord, outside of Boston, the products of much book-learning.) Freed of the restraints of organized society, at liberty to possess himself of all the riches of nature, the far-wandering Yankee or immigrant pioneer was deeply transformed, but now ennobled. The effect of the frontier movement was a "constant" in the conditioning of the nation, its recurrent waves and upheavals deeply marking the national character along with the low-church religion and the democratic institutions, until its cycle was ended in 1893.

The American frontier, as Frederick J. Turner holds, was as the outer edge of a wave, "the meeting place of civilization and savagery." Here the wilderness mastered the colonist. "It finds him a European. . . . It strips away the garments of civilization." So periodically, in the Old Northwest (Ohio, Indiana, Illinois), in the Mississippi Valley, the farther Western prairies and the Pacific Slope, the frontier worked deeply upon the national character. It gave its measure of independence and optimism through the continued advantage of free land and the opportunity of a competency to all.

The immigrant (who came in a swarm of seven millions, between 1820 and 1870, chiefly from Great Britain and Germany), blended his character with that of the far-wandered New England Ulysses. The immigrant, in general, was the most aggressive, the coolest head, the least sentimental among his people, the least fettered by superstition or authority; he had no ties with any place or with the past, but lived only in the future. Having risked all, and crossed the ocean in search of pecuniary gain, he was stayed by few scruples, he feared no loss from a bold stroke. A stranger, like the others all about him, whose past, whose credit was unknown, he often dealt with the others as strangers. Thus, in the rude, loosely controlled commonwealths of the frontier, the pioneer became, as Turner concludes, "strong in selfishness and individualism, intolerant of . . . experience and education, and pressing individual liberty beyond its proper bounds." Here the national character assumed traits of "coarseness and strength"; it was "rooted strongly in material prosperity"; it tended toward a unity, a nationalism or Federalism rather than intense sectionalism of spirit; it would be lax in its business honor, its government affairs; it set at a premium acquisitiveness (crying always anew for free land) under a Jackson, a Lincoln, a Grant; it showed an inventive grasp of material things, it ranged to lawlessness and violence in the predations of those who sought either to "brave" the natural elements or to best each other.

The Yankee Trader, puritan though he was, and imbued with the "Poor Richard" principles of a mercantile capitalism, underwent a sea-change at the frontier, as Turner suggests. Civilized yesterday, he became half-savage in the wilderness, the deserts, the mountain gullies. To the traits of parsimony and prudence and calculation must be added those protective ones of force, swiftness and animal cunning, something of the "muffled bound of the wild beast." Else he was lost, trampled over, in the rush for the gold fields or the town-site claims.

In the recurrent, frenzied waves of land speculation, gold rushes and railroad booms, you saw the American at work, at his best and at his worst, prospector, pioneer, trader and settler.

"Were I to characterize the United States," writes an English traveler, William Priest, as early as 1796, "it would be by the appellation of the land of speculations." The very Fathers of the Republic, Washington, Franklin, Robert Morris and Livingston and most of the others, were busy buying land at one shilling or less the acre and selling it out at $2, in parcels of 10,000 acres or more. The very occasion of choosing a site for a National Capitol had been the outcome of collusion between the great land-grabbers, securities speculators, and the statesmen. Even before 1800 "land offices" were opened up, orators harangued the populace and sold shares or scrip, lots and subdivisions to settlers, often without deed or title. Cities like Cincinnati and Cleveland were laid out in the trackless wilderness and "jobbed." "Remember that lot in Buffalo!" cried the land-jobbers. "Remember that acre in Cleveland! that quarter-section in Chicago!" Only promptness, speed, enthusiasm, vision were needed to wrest such a fortune as an Astor had taken from his acres in Putnam County, New York.

But though it was true that land speculations had given rise to the greatest fortunes in America up to about 1840, it was also true, as another distinguished foreigner remarked toward 1800, that "they

have ... been the cause of total ruin and disastrous bankruptcy."
In 1795 the first great and typical panic had swept through the
country with the failure of Robert Morris's colossal land projects.
Such cruel disillusionments were to occur again and again. Yet
mindless of all this the roving Americans, as Emerson wrote to
Carlyle, were bent only upon their "sections and quarter sections
of swamp-land," kept "the country growing furiously, town and
state ... new Kansas, new Nebraskas, looming these days ...
vicious politicians seething a wretched destiny for them already in
Washington." The pioneer kept moving westward toward the
moving frontier, much as Mark Twain's Si Hawkins and his family,
shiftless, voluble and happy-go-lucky, moved along, from Kentucky
to Missouri, where numberless acres could be bought at $2 apiece.

*But some day people would be glad to get it for twenty dollars,
fifty dollars, a hundred dollars an acre! What should you say to
(here he dropped his voice to a whisper and looked anxiously
around to see that there were no eavesdroppers) a thousand dollars
an acre!*

Such was the legend of the land boom, faithfully caught in "The
Gilded Age" by Mark Twain and Charles Dudley Warner.

The sequel to the Mexican War was an orgy of land-grabbing
and speculation in which the origin of the war is not hard to trace.
A young army-officer of engineers, Grenville Dodge, later to be a
distinguished general and railroad-builder, writes: "I can double any
amount of money you've got in six months.... To start with buy
a couple of Mexican War land warrants."

More illuminating still was it to see the frontiersman in the railroad boom of the '40's and '50's. You saw him scheming, sometimes
in collusion with men of capital, or with men of politics, to open the
markets of inexhaustible coal fields or untold millions of feet of
lumber. Along the right of way of the new railroad line, as along
the canal lines a decade or so earlier, the directors would purchase
town sites in the prairies. Thus when in 1850 the Illinois Central
Railroad was awarded a vast land grant by the federal government
of 2,600,000 acres in alternate sections between Chicago and Mobile,
the affair was looked upon primarily as a land-jobbing project,
Abraham Lincoln, heading a Western group of promoters, contended in vain against a ring of Massachusetts capitalists, who seizing

the affair were able to sell land to their friends at $2.50 an acre along the line, while the public fought for town sites, to be had only at ten or fifteen times the price tomorrow. . . .

Anthony Trollope, visiting America during the Civil War, commented that the railroad companies "were in fact companies combined for the purchase of land . . . looking to increase the value of it five-fold by the opening of the railroad. It is in this way that the thousands of miles of railroads have been opened." And Mark Twain accurately pictures the process in his "Gilded Age": as Mr. Bigler unfolds his scheme for the "Tunkhannock, Rattlesnake & Youngstown Railroad":

> We'll buy the land on long time . . . and then mortgage . . . for enough money to get the road well on. Then get the towns on the line to issue their bonds for stock. . . . We can then sell the rest of the stock on the prospects of the business of the road . . . and also sell the land on the strength of the road at a big advance.

But the furor of Si Hawkins, as he looks toward the unknown and trackless Missouri, is even more instructive:

> Nancy, you've heard of steamboats, and maybe you believed in them—they're going to make a revolution in this world's affairs that will make men dizzy to contemplate. . . . And this is not all, Nancy—it isn't even half! There's a bigger wonder—the railroad! Coaches that fly over the ground twenty miles an hour—heavens and earth, think of that, Nancy! It makes a man's brain whirl. . . .

He saw not only farm lands and towns. He saw

> mountains of ore there, Nancy—whole mountains of it. . . . Pine forests, wheat lands, corn land, iron, copper, coal—wait till the railroads come, and the steamboats!

But in 1849 mountains of gold had suddenly surged up before the avid eyes of these restless people—such as the Spanish Conquerors had dreamed. In the gold rush, in the mining camp, the frontiersman, certainly by protective coloration, lost the historic, conservative bourgeois traits; created the morale of violent speculation with his possessions and life itself. You saw him, as Mark Twain again reveals in "Roughing It":

It was a driving, restless population, in those days. There were none of your simpering, dainty, kid-glove weaklings, but stalwart, muscular, dauntless young braves, brimful of push and energy.... For all the slow, sleepy, sluggish-brained sloths stayed at home—you never find that sort of people among pioneers.

The frenzy and thunder of gold rushes, silver rushes, oil rushes, were to repeat themselves decade after decade, as this richest continent of the world opened up its underground to all comers, to the swift and the strong, to *fourrer dans le sac*, to take what he willed, till his arms tired. In the history of the frontier, the gaudy and tragic drama of the settlement of California is the eternal parable of the nation of pioneers.

5

Before 1849, the Pacific Slope is a garden of paradise. Hearing of its blessed climate, its soil and fruits, the mild Sutter, after long wanderings, enters the bay of San Francisco. He settles not far away in the Sacramento Valley, to dwell upon his ranch as a hidalgo, among his happy natives and Indians, in the peace of a medieval sleep.

Suddenly a man stumbles upon the glittering quartz in the brook gravel; the alarm is given. The gold lust sweeps not only the United States but the remotest corners of the civilized world. The bookkeeper in New York, the farmer of Pennsylvania, the Yankee tinpeddler, the waiter in New Orleans, all rush toward California, by land and by sea, around Cape Horn, or over Panama and Nicaragua, or the Great American desert. The mob of gold-seekers come in tens of thousands; Sutter's enchanted ranch is overrun by the desperadoes, his land is seized, his claims derided.

San Francisco, the beautiful Spanish port, is turned overnight into a shambles by the latter-day Argonauts. Within a year or two, literally, it is a "metropolis" of the Pacific, holding some 25,000 souls. From its wharves along the water front there stretches out an endless expanse of unpainted, rude frame dwellings, ramshackle warehouses, false-fronted shops and saloons, marked off by woodenplanked streets which straggle up toward Telegraph Hill.

A strange world; a strange social order. At night there are few lamps, burning whale-oil; only the "rum-holes" send out a dull glow of light. A man arrives—it is more rare now—with buckskin poke heavy with gold dust; he drinks like a god, stakes his whole bag on a single throw of cards; there is a stabbing affray, and quickly he is taken and strung up. Before he has ceased kicking, two men of the mob steal away, leap upon horses, and go galloping off to "jump" the unfortunate's claim. Those who owned provisions or land must watch them with unremitting vigilance against the rough squatters or Sydneymen who might expropriate them at any moment, with the help of gunplay by officers of the peace or justice no less unscrupulous or violent than they. And when the expropriations, the knifing or gunplay become intolerable, the great fire-bell is rung, sounding alarm to the thousands of Vigilantes secretly banded together to preserve "law and order." They come running, armed, disciplined, impassive. Sometimes they err: but on the whole it is better so.

Soon the first rich placer claims on the western slope of the Sierra seem stripped, and deeper mining, needing both capital and technical skill, must now be attempted. The golden flood seems exhausted; and since the region offers at first nothing but its ore, the spoilers fall upon each other, in a kind of despair, robbing, fighting, cheating each other. An exodus begins; many more leave, broken in spirit and pocket, than those who come in.

Misery rises. The local gazette (*Alta California*) by February 12, 1853, comments:

> *There has never been so deplorable an exhibition of mendicancy in our streets as may be witnessed daily at this time . . . hundreds of destitute men and scores of women . . . little girls are to be found in front of the city saloons at all hours of the day, going through their graceless performances.*

And eggs are still three dollars a dozen, milk 50 cents a quart; a rude dinner of fried pork and fried potatoes and molasses may be had at the heavy cost of a whole dollar. Civilization and the existing forms of capitalism have come to Eldorado—a swarm of shrewd, rough-joking entrepreneurs, tapsters, horse-traders, madames, dance-hall girls, dry-goods merchants have come to serve and to feed voraciously upon the care-free, high-hearted gold-seekers. As in San Francisco and Sacramento, so in the neighboring mining camps or communities, civilization has bloomed mushroom-like, in "Jackass Gulch," or "Hangtown," or "Slum Gullions" where the names give the moral tone. Here the heritage of puritanism has shrunk to its original core; only the puritan economic philosophy remains "strong in selfishness and individualism, intolerant of administrative experience," or tradition, or learning or social values, as Turner has noted, "and pressing individual liberty beyond its proper bounds," breeding new and incalculable dangers.

These sunbaked mining towns of the western slope, upon which the economic civilization of the time fixed itself, their single sandy street sprawling up the side of the Sierra Nevada, their unpainted, weather-beaten shacks already grown old, their weary population of some two thousand red-and blue-shirted miners, bartenders, blacksmiths, gamblers, Chinamen and Mexicans, dance-hall girls and tired mothers and unkempt, scrawny children—how often and untruthfully they have been pictured by the native historians. The frontier evolution, romanticized by a Bret Harte, was caught with a shrewd, veritably poetic vision by a Mark Twain. Out of the cycle of perpetual feverish gold-rushes, in the years after the Forty-niners, there was the renewed stampede to the Comstock Lode, at the western edge of Nevada. Here Mark Twain pictures to us the historical process of "Hell-On-Wheels." The "van-leader of civilization" is always whiskey.

> Look history over and you will see. The missionary comes after the whiskey—I mean, he arrives after the whiskey has arrived. Next comes the poor immigrant with ax and hoe and rifle; next, the trader, next the miscellaneous rush; next the gambler, the desperado, the highwayman, and all their kindred in sin of both sexes; and next the smart chap who has bought up an old grant that covers all the land; this brings in the lawyer tribe; the vigilance committee brings the undertaker. All these interests bring the newspaper; the newspaper starts up politics and a railroad; all hands turn to and build a church and a jail—and behold, civilization is established forever in the land.

So in the second decade of the Pacific Slope's terrestrial paradise, the cycle is already completed, the arc defined. Out of the strenuous milling of free frontiersmen, two or three Yankee shopkeepers emerge, a derelict lawyer from the East, a pair of practical Irish miners in collaboration with a pair of Irish saloonkeepers, an English invalid gambler, a land-jobber, a drover and innkeeper from Indiana —these have banded together to form a ruling class, by something equivalent to an imperceptible process of *coup d'état* have seized all power, all economic control. For them the gold and silver flood of the Comstock; for them a great railroad leaps the Sierras and in spreading network penetrates into every smiling valley to levy toll and carry off the produce of the deep rich soil. The banking institution which dominates the Pacific Slope is in their hands; the mines, the water front, the terminals, a vast section of the land as right-of-way grant; also invaluable franchises, a heavy portion of all tax receipts in the communities are theirs. An industrial society is established; but under the ruder, simpler frontier conditions, it is done as if overnight, in the twinkling of an eye. The human mass of free pioneers who came yesterday plodding over the desert route, with its trail of ox and horse skeletons and wrecked wagons, its numerous mounds of graves, braving storms, flooded rivers, thirst, hunger, heat, and Indian raiders—these and their children and their children's children are all in subjection to princely and dynastic overlords, who rule by "use" and "wont," who "own" because they own, and are well seized of so much land, forest, mineral deposits, harbor rights and franchises and rights of way because they have seized.

The story of this seizure of power—mightier than all the transient gains of hilarious and rudderless gold-seekers—a power and authority, a seizure, to remain vested forever, consecrated by law and custom, legalized by statute, confirmed by long undisturbed possession, this story has scarcely been told; though in parable, almost in caricature form and concentrated within a brief generation of California life, it epitomizes dramatically the historic process through which the nation in general passed over a somewhat longer period.

6

In a brief cycle, the laissez-faire political philosophy of a Jefferson, having given free reign to self-interest, would stimulate the acquisitive appetites of the citizen above all. These, whetted by an incredibly rich soil, checked by no institutions or laws, would determine the pattern of American destiny. The idealism of Jefferson's Declaration of Independence, as of his Inaugural Address of

1801, would be caricatured in the predatory liberty of the "Valley of Democracy" where, as Vernon Parrington has said, Americans democratic in professions, became "middle-class in spirit and purpose"; where freedom came to mean "the natural right of every citizen to satisfy his acquisitive instinct by exploiting the national resources in the measure of his shrewdness." And the strong, as in the Dark Ages of Europe, and like the military captains of old, having preëmpted more than others, having been well seized of land and highways and strong places, would own because they owned. Chieftains would arise, in the time-honored way, to whom the crowd would look for leadership, for protection, finally for their very existence. They would be the nobles of a new feudal system, for whom the great mass of men toiled willingly. These barons resembled their forerunners, since they traced their ownership back, as Veblen has said, to the "ancient feudalistic ground of privilege and prescriptive tenure . . . to the right of seizure by force and collusion."

Only the material conditions, the instruments of such sovereignty, would be changed owing to the advanced material standards of the society. Instead of armament, mercenary soldiers, serfs, the weapons of offense and defense might be a fleet of ships as with the Merchant Adventurers), fur-trading stations in the frontier, finally railways which were to be the arteries of trade, mines, factories laboring for a continental or a world market.

All this transformation and "progress" the young men of '61 could look back upon as a momentous part of their history while the democratic spirit of the laws still blessed them: the conquest of the Frontier was always in their eye, whether it was the virgin prairies of the Mississippi Valley, the mineral deposits of the Sierras, or the "Frontier" of new industries and of projects and speculations in the East, all about them. If the doctrine of the nation favored an ideal of free and equal opportunity for all, so its current folklore glorified the freebooting citizen who by his own efforts, by whatever methods feasible, had wrested for himself a power that flung its shadow upon the liberties and privileges of all the others.

It was not surprising that a Livingston in New York, a Washington in Virginia should wield great influence in the republic. That men who were penniless, ignorant, without antecedents or influential connections, who knew neither the arts of war nor those of the forum, but only of the marketplace and counting-house should have acquired grandiose wealth within their own lifetime, which the human imagination then could scarcely spend, this was one of the wonders of the time, and the favorite legend held up before the new generations, the young men of '61. It bespoke also the new structure of society—finally crystallized—the triumph of bourgeoisdom. In olden days, mercenary captains, hereditary princes, landed nobles or mighty prelates of the Church would have preyed on the tradesman, held him down with their contempt; now all society protected him, government policed his property, paid him homage— and tomorrow in the sequel to the national crisis the country would change its laws, its Constitution, sacrifice a million lives for him and the economic force he represented.

In the meantime the paddle-wheels of Progress which typify the age were turning as always; steaming up the river valleys busily— though sometimes "snags" were struck and overheated boilers without safety valves blew up all hands. Then in all directions upon iron rails held by wooden "sleepers" the first Iron Horses, red and black, brass-ornamented, puffing and rattling, named "Old Ironsides" or "Best Friend" or "Stourbridge Lion," were cutting their trail of destiny. By 1840, over 9,000 miles of railroad had been constructed, and they had climbed the difficult barrier of the Alleghenies, which had so long separated the settlers of Ohio, Indiana and Illinois from the Eastern market they panted for. Abandoning the river, the turnpike and canal the farmers of the West turned to using the railroad, as they would soon turn to use McCormick's horse-drawn reaper and thresher. Thus the whole tier of Northern states was linked closer than ever in a vast intercourse. The axis of trade had shifted away from the Mississippi by 1860, when 30,000 miles of railroad existed; so that with the river closed the following year there was little hardship. The settler was part of the orbit of a national market, in which goods circulated at a new speed. He found prosperity in free labor rather than in the routine effort of slaves. His spirit called for national unity, for freely circulating capital, and above all for a Pacific Railroad. The new political party clamored against the blockade of its future prosperity held by the South, as the Manchester industrialists of yesterday had clamored for the repeal of the Corn Laws in England. Its leader, a lawyer for Western railroads, included a Pacific Railroad bill and a protective tariff for native industries in his platform. Such overwhelming economic needs, confronted with the alarmed passionate resistance of the agrarian, slave-owning, static South, must burst the dam at last in the inevitable social cataclysm of the Civil War.

CHAPTER TWO

WHAT THE YOUNG MEN DREAM

T HE young men who were to form the new nobility of industry and banking had, most of them, reached their prime
of youth or manhood when Lincoln issued his first call for
volunteers. Jay Gould, Jim Fisk, J. P. Morgan, Philip Armour,
Andrew Carnegie, James Hill and John Rockefeller were all in their
early twenties: Collis Huntington and Leland Stanford were over
thirty; while Jay Cooke was not yet forty. In the ensuing years all
of the members of this band of youth would have met with their
first "windfalls"; sure-footed, they would take their part, they would
take their posts in the economic revolution which rose to a climax
in the war; and the end of the war would see them masters of money,
capitalists equipped to increase their capital. In the hour of danger
and confusion it was as if *they alone were prepared.* It was as if the
Second American Revolution were fought for them.

Most of these young men, whose fortunes will be the special subject of this history, were drawn from the aggressive Yankee race
which had thrived in New England. Collis Huntington and J. P.
Morgan were literally Connecticut Yankees by birth, Gould and
Cooke by descent; Jim Fisk was the son of a Vermont peddler.
Carnegie and Hill were Scotch, of the race called "the Florentines
of the north," instinctively apt and shrewd in trade. In general, they
were puritanical and pious, with the exception of Carnegie, a child
of radical Scotch weavers. Only one of them, Fisk, was given to
free living, drinking and fleshpots in youth; in private life they were
generally discreet, sober, well-controlled, their strongest lust being
the pecuniary appetite. The poverty which darkened the childhood
of all of them save Morgan, son of a banker, lent them sobriety, and
the Protestant teachings they received disciplined their will and
guaranteed them rewards in this world for their self-denial. Even

32

when they drifted to the frontier they remained cool-headed and continent. For instance, James Hill, migrating to the Northwest territory in the 1850's, seems prudent and methodical in the extreme among the first rough settlers of St. Paul. At least one of their number, involved in the gold rush to the Comstock Lode on the Pacific Slope, incurred the displeasure of his companions because he never drank! Not to drink, to forego the gaming tables and red-lit bordelloes of the frontier camps, to be calculating forever, silently, furtively poring over books and accounts, scheming projects all night—while others drank, laughed, danced, brawled and died—this was the method and principle of the young men who were to conquer both the wild frontier and the pioneers alike.

But if they grew up in poverty, for the most part, they also absorbed thoroughly the restless hope which pervaded the very air they breathed. They listened to all the cheerful, hammering sounds of the booming world around them; saw the settlement of new lands, the opening of new resources, the planning of new towns, each a future "metropolis" of the wilderness, a Paris of the interior plain, a London of the Great Lakes. They saw the new machines and processes taking shape, and with the continued advance of the "level of technical culture" acquired the fixed idea that everything, towns, ships, locomotives, mills, must grow bigger—an idea that like an infantile obsession rooted itself deeply in the American mind. But those whose vision then "projected" the populous cities, the mountains of coal and iron, were not wrong; and there was nothing illusory about their quick rewards.

It is noteworthy also that most of these young men left the paternal shelter early in youth, to wander alone and make their own way. Some of them had been taught close trading in infancy, like Jim Fisk, who traveled all the roads of Vermont in the wagon of his father, the tin-peddler. They showed promising signs of shiftiness and self-reliance in boyhood, as did Collis Huntington, who "secured his freedom from his father when fourteen years old by promising to support himself" and then, as a peddler of watch findings, wandered about the world for ten years learning to survive violent conditions, or to best wild and lawless companions. Marooned for three months while en route to San Francisco with a band of Forty-niners at the Isthmus of Panama, Collis Huntington as a youth outtraded all his fellow voyagers, until he had multiplied his little capital over threefold to some $4,000. Verily the gold in the Sierras must have trembled at the distant approach of this tall, crooked-nosed Yankee. But he, like his fellows, Stanford and Armour, would be too wise to dig the wide, mysterious earth with his own hands. Believing with Simon Suggs that "it's good to be shifty in a new country," they would choose rather to pit their nimble brains, their power of calculation against the gold-dust bags of the lucky prospectors.

But there were many other illuminating traits besides strength of will, ruse and violence in the young men of '61 which are yielded by a more detailed examination of the leading members of their company, those upon whose early life we have most information. With varying accents and voices they sound a common refrain; from different corners of the country, each in his own devious, particular manner, each one expresses the same aspirations, approaches the same goal.

2

"Arise, ye men of Sandusky! Shake off your apathy! Risk all for her, and I trust she will yet reward you for your care." Thus in stirring tones did Jay Cooke as a boy of sixteen appeal to his fellows —not to save their frontier village from menacing Chippewas or Wyandottes but, as the historian Oberholtzer tells us, to boom her real estate. It was in 1837, and the first Iron Horse, running over the twelve-mile length of the Lake Erie & Mad River line had at last reached Sandusky amid the jubilation of her settlers. Jay Cooke, who was born as the first or nearly the first baby-boy in this outpost of civilization, shared almost from birth all the speculative enthusiasm of the frontiersmen, and would never quite outgrow it.

He was the son of Eleutheros Cooke, who was something of a lawyer as well as a settler, eventually a Congressman, noted for his rodomontades on behalf of "the material interests of Sandusky." His father, a man who long eschewed tobacco and a leader of temperance societies, reared Jay strictly according to the precepts of his New England ancestors. The boy at the age of sixteen was fated to leave Sandusky (overshadowed by the rival town of Cleveland), penetrating as far as St. Louis in order to learn to trade there with the pioneers and trappers. But wherever he went he would continue to be abstemious and prudent.

In the pioneering city of St. Louis, the young man of sixteen complains because there "is but few respectable persons" there; he is happy over the "splendid assortment of goods" (dry goods) he trades in, regretting only the dullness of business in the winter season. Within a year he has saved a little capital of $200, and goes to the Eastern metropolis of Philadelphia to join relatives of his family in the shipping and transport business, giving his "solemn oath to keep clear of vicious habits . . . not to associate with any of the young rakes of the city until I am certain of their good character."

Here all is "business and bustle"; but this boy who had wished no other schooling except that of trade made himself remarked for his cool resourcefulness as well as his industry. Violence does not shake him; even in Philadelphia of 1838, "fires and mobs and abolition squabbles" are to him "everyday occurrences." As a ticket agent, shipping immigrants and goods by wagon, canal boat and railroad toward Pittsburgh, he comes in conflict every day with the agents of rival lines, whom he must outmaneuver or balk. In the course of his business he runs the risk of being thrown into the Delaware River. But undiscouraged he hews to his line steadfastly; the business is immensely lucrative, and the young clerk reports with delight: "We shall clear 50 per cent. . . ."

A year later and Cooke has become a clerk in the large banking house of Clark & Dodge. It is a promising, a "most enviable position." Pleasing of person, zestful in business, he makes an apt pupil of money-changing. His clients remembered long afterward how the notes used to pass through his delicate fingers as a smoothly flowing stream of noiseless water, "the wilde-cats and all, just as equally and uninterruptedly counted." He soon boasted of knowing the counterfeits at sight, all the broken banks in America; an education which, in those days of hazardous currencies, he candidly reckoned was "worth a mint to him." Advanced to posts of responsibility, and appointed a junior partner after a few years, when only twenty-one, he began to build castles in the air for himself, castles filled with money, of course, such as he stared at wistfully along the banks of the Schuylkill.

In the meantime, a quality of iron enters the soul of this young man; we feel that, like his contemporaries, he acquires a philosophy suited to opportunities. The crush of Yankees, Quakers, Southerners, Spanish noblemen with their servants and slaves, who pass in an endless line before his money-changing counter, he views now with the cold scrutiny of the banker, in which as Balzac has said, "there is something of the vulture, something of the attorney, at once covetous and cold, clear and inscrutable, somber and ablaze with light." Cooke, at an early stage of his experience, commented shrewdly, in the picturesque letters which Oberholtzer has gathered, "Through all the grades I see the same all-pervading, all-engrossing anxiety to grow rich. This is the only thing for which men live here." Money, as Cooke wrote, was "chiefly the object for which all men contend," and he no less than the others, but with a better knowledge of "its true worth and character." He lived in "funny times" he wrote home and, "we nearly double our capital in a year." His firm discounted checks and commercial paper at from 9 to 18 per cent! Or it dealt in gold, and by its especially intimate knowledge of the affairs of the United States Bank (then of Pennsylvania) realized a premium of above 20 per cent. Or at other times, as in the period of the Mexican War, when the annexation of Texas was being agitated, Cooke and his associates worked in collusion with politicians who knew in advance what disposition would be made of the existing Texas bonds after annexation by the federal government. "Large sums were realized," Cooke relates candidly, "by those who were directly and indirectly interested in obtaining the legislation for final settlement" of the bondholders' claims. Now, as in after years, Cooke would have, by his own principles, not the slightest doubt or scruple in combining forces with the statesmen to pursue that one "object for which all men contend." It was the early knowledge of such tactics, which he utilized more extensively than any other man, that gave Cooke the boundless optimism, the serene confidence that accounts for his smooth progress in accumulation. His were among the many hands busy in ministering to the growing banking machinery of the country by financing packers, millers, speculators in grains and produce, all of which was affecting the flow of trade and seasonal movements of goods as visibly as the new canals and railways; that is, increasing its tempo and hastening its circulation. This tall young man, handsome, with clear, ruddy complexion and keen blue eyes, saw himself living in "palaces and castles which kings might own." He said to himself: "I shall be rich. Go into business myself...."

3

The early formative period of Jay Gould's life was passed in a kind of naked poverty, which he remembered afterward with horror. He was born in 1836, in the village of Roxbury, Delaware County, New York, the son of a poor farmer of Yankee stock— and not of Jewish race, as Henry Adams supposed when he called Gould "the complex Jew." As a boy he was compelled to wake up before dawn to tend the cows. Frail and undersized, he dreaded the cold darkness; he would recall, thirty years later, in defending his character publicly, how the thistles hurt his bare feet; he spoke with vibrant bitterness of his boyhood. He had had to plead with his father to be permitted even to attend the village school; and he had been enabled to enter the near-by Hobart academy only by living with the village blacksmith and keeping his books for him.

He would be no farmer. At twelve or thirteen he studied geometry and logarithms, prepared himself to be a surveyor or engineer. In 1849, he was thinking, his sister relates, of building a railroad across the continent "so that California might be nearer to us."

"If you give me time," he once cried to his father, "I'll make my fortune."

This outcry is symptomatic; one after another of the young men of '61 voiced the same dream. At the center of the stirring, shifting drama of material progress toward new railroads or gold fields, was the notion of individual fortune and change of station. No longer to remain fixed in an inherited calling or estate, an eternal part of the eternal social organism, that had come down from feudal times, but to be "a-doin'," to be on the alert for new opportunity. Hence the young Gould instinctively sought information that would arm him for the struggle. An old letter of his boyhood gives us clearly his notion of education; it is a means of "placing one where he is capable of speaking and acting for himself without being bargained away and deceived by his more enlightened brothers." What could be more illuminating? As a schoolboy Gould actually wrote— though posterity will scarcely believe it—a composition entitled: "Honesty Is the Best Policy."

But such axioms had been learned by rote, and must soon have seemed as meaningless as they proved to be. For at the very same time the young Jay Gould consummated his first important business "deal," an operation of the most promising artfulness which could not have succeeded without the collaboration of his father. While employed as a clerk by the village storekeeper, he had learned that his master was negotiating for a good property in the neighborhood which happened to be in chancery, and had offered $2,000 for it. The boy of sixteen quickly made some investigations of his own, then went to his father and by the most urgent pleading got a loan of $2,500 toward purchasing the property himself. In two weeks, thanks to the connivance of his parent, he had been able to sell it out for $4,000. But his employer, it appears, was highly incensed at what he saw as trickery or duplicity in his assistant and summarily dismissed him. It is to this incident perhaps that another early letter of Gould's refers, when he speaks further of continuing his interrupted education, and voices the hope that "a kind Providence that has thus far sheltered me under her wing will crown my, at least, honest exertions with a sphere of usefulness."

However that might be, Jay Gould, small, dark, of a somewhat furtive and melancholy cast, left home and set to wandering about from place to place, after the age of sixteen, upon his own, making "noon-marks" for farmers, surveys and maps, and living frugally by one fertile device after another. In these obscure years of struggle this gifted youth would be trained in cunning rather than direct aggression; he would learn to use the rapier rather than the bludgeon. Promptness of action, speed in flight, would make him immune even to the more violent hazards among which he thrived.

His mind teemed with "projects" by which he hoped to win his fortune quickly. Once he came to New York with a most curious invention for which he had the fondest hopes. "I was ambitious," he related, "and had brought a little thing with me which I was sure was to make my fortune and revolutionize the world, and you will smile when I tell you it was a mousetrap." Arriving in the great city, he boarded a street car, and every now and then ran out to the rear platform to stare at the buildings six or seven stories high, leaving the mahogany case containing his mousetrap on his seat. A thief stole it but Gould, noticing his loss quickly, was soon hot on the heels of the criminal, raised the alarm, and retrieved his precious invention. By means of mousetraps and other schemes or projects he was able to accumulate a substantial capital, some $5,000 by his own statement, at the age of twenty.[1]

New York, with its crowd of merchants and "projectors" and its seven-story buildings, allured Gould. It was here that he plunged into the speculations of the "swamp," the leather market of New York, and so made the acquaintance of the aged Zadoc Pratt, a highly esteemed and wealthy tanner who was prominent in the politics of the time. Pratt was so impressed with the acuteness of the young man that he furnished him with nearly all the capital necessary (about $120,000) to found a large tannery, which was set up in the woods outside of Lehigh, Pennsylvania, at a place ambitiously named "Gouldsboro," after the entrepreneur of twenty.

Gould remained in sole charge, while Mr. Pratt, a septuagenarian, stayed in New York. The tannery did a lively trade, but no profits ensued. Its chief owner, seized with suspicions, descended upon Gouldsboro one day and found the books of his firm in strange disorder, noting large speculative commitments by Gould through a

---

[1] What is a *projector*, is asked in the play of Ben Jonson, "The Devil Is an Ass."

> "Why, one, sir, that projects
> Ways to enrich men, or to make them great
> By suits, by marriages, by undertakings."—*Act I, Scene iii.*

The art of living by one's wits, "the art and mystery of projecting" began "to creep into the world" probably long before the year 1680, which Daniel Defoe selects as the beginning of the Projecting Age. He defines the new class harshly as men who, "being masters of more cunning than their neighbors, turn their thoughts to private methods of trick and cheat, a modern way of thieving . . . by which honest men are gulled with fair pretenses to part from their money. . . . Others, yet, urged by the same necessity, turn their thoughts to honest invention, founded upon the platform of ingenuity and integrity. . . . A mere projector is then a contemptible thing, driven by his own fortune desperate to such a strait that he must be delivered by a miracle or starve. And when he has beat his brain for some such miracle in vain, he finds no remedy but to paint up some bauble or other, as players make puppets talk big, to show like a strange thing, and then cry it up for a new invention, gets a patent for it, divides it into shares and they must be sold. Ways and means are not wanting to swell the new whim to a vast magnitude; thousands and hundreds of thousands are the least of his discourse, and sometimes millions: till the ambition of some honest coxcomb is wheedled to part with his money for it, and then *nascitur ridiculus mus.*" ("On Projectors.")

Defoe who was an excellent tradesman, and for a time a buyer of wines, shared all the prejudices of the pre-capitalist or mercantile age against the extravagant Cagliostros of the day. Yet as Werner Sombart comments, though: these fantastic, early projectors lacked a definite sphere of activity, "theirs were the ideas that were to generate capitalism."

bank in the near-by town of Stroudsburg. In alarm, believing the affairs of the company beyond repair, Pratt offered to sell his business to Gould for half of the sum he had invested. Gould, who now had wide acquaintance in New York, found a new patron, a Mr. Charles Leupp, of an old New York family and a member of the leading leather firm of Leupp & Lee.

Leupp too, after a brief season, found the Gouldsboro tannery strangely mismanaged, as if with design. Its capital was completely exhausted by the ambitious Gould during 1857 in an attempt to create a "corner" in hides. The panic of that year brought them to swift ruin, and Leupp, brooding in the parlor of his rich mansion on Madison Avenue, killed himself with a pistol-shot. For him, the involvements of the tannery had been part of a chain of misfortunes, and Jay Gould's unhappy ventures with Leupp's money were the final blow which determined him to shorten his life. A dozen years later, the mobs of Black Friday, 1869, surging through Wall Street, shouted: *"Who killed Leupp? Jay Gould!"*

In the months and years that followed, Gould's negotiations with Leupp's heirs and with his partner, Lee, for control of the defunct tannery, failed of peaceful settlement; and Lee, representing the heirs, moved to take possession of the plant in behalf of its chief owners. But Jay Gould resisted expulsion with a fiendish energy; he labored even to stir up the local population, addressing public gatherings in the streets of Lehigh, asserting to all who would hear that he was the true owner of the establishment and longed only to preserve it, while his adversaries intended to dismantle it and dismiss its workingmen. Gathering up a mixed crowd of trusting laborers and idle thugs, and stimulating them, as it is related, by liberal gifts of oysters and whiskey, to a high pitch of martial spirit, the young captain of industry marched them like a Napoleon upon Gouldsboro's tannery, which was attacked, stormed and captured in a moderately bloody clash, of a kind which was neither unusual nor alarming in those times. The *New York Herald* of March 16, 1860, noticed the episode quietly, under the heading:

TANNERY INSURRECTION IN PA.

Battle between the forces of the Swamp leather dealers—The Leupp & Lee Tannery in Gouldsboro attacked and defended—Sides of leather used for breastworks—Insurgents 200 strong—The tannery taken—Fight of the defenders—Wounded four.

Ultimately, after long delays, the forces of the law ousted Jay Gould. But he had learned much from his first armed struggle for money. He was no longer without means or weapons of offense; he had resources of deception, of speculation—and some, though it is not certain, even hold, the art of embezzlement. He was now hardened to violence as well as ruse, and his contemporaries no doubt esteemed him the more in accordance with the widely, if tacitly accepted views of such proceedings. By the law of "survival of the fittest" which an Andrew Carnegie at the very same moment was learning to respect in Pittsburgh, men like Jay Gould would go far.

4

In 1848 Andrew Carnegie, the child of poor and rebellious Scottish weavers, came with his family to Allegheny, near Pittsburgh. The upheavals of the industrial revolution had ravaged the lowlands of Scotland; and the hungry and too numerous hand-workers of Carnegie's country had migrated in a great swarm to the new continent of plenty. The newly arrived Germans, Scots and Ulstermen filled up Western Pennsylvania; here there was work for many hands, after the mass starvation of Europe; they brimmed with hope from the moment they set foot on the dock in Philadelphia or New York. If Carnegie as a child of thirteen lived here again in a misery no less disheartening than that to be seen along the Firth of Forth then it was also true that there was infinitely more opportunity here for the young and strong among the seekers of fortune, owing to the new country's earlier stage of industrial development. Though Carnegie from the age of fourteen was set to work as a bobbin-boy in a cloth mill, and spent twelve hours a day in a dank cellar, he was soon imbued with the optimism of his new country. There was no doubt in his mind, as he wrote in his first letters to relatives abroad, that the conditions of equality, universal suffrage, free land and practical invention all nurtured the "spirit of Progress," which as a boy of sixteen he saluted fervently. With delight he reported:

We will soon be surrounded by Rail Roads here [at Pittsburgh].
There are two different ones now laying tracks in the city, one from
the Far West [i.e., Ohio] and the other from Philadelphia. We will
also have another telegraph line.

The new elements, railroad and telegraph, aroused his unending
wonder. Escaping from the cloth-factory cellar, he found work as
a telegraph clerk a year later. He adjusted himself to a miraculously
new industry, a new tempo, a new world of which he writes repeatedly with rapture to his Scotch friends:

> *Our public lands of almost unlimited extent are becoming settled*
> *with an enterprising people. Our dense forests are falling under the*
> *ax of the hardy woodsman. The Wolf and the Buffalo are startled*
> *by the shrill scream of the Iron Horse where a few years ago they*
> *roamed undisturbed. Towns and cities spring up as if by magic....*
> *Our railroads extend 13,000 miles. You cannot supply iron fast*
> *enough to keep us going. This country is completely cut up with*
> *Railroad Tracks, Telegraphs, and Canals.... Pauperism is un-*
> *known. Hundreds of labor-saving devices are patented yearly....*
> *Everything around us is in motion.*

Carnegie at seventeen exuded the same quenchless optimism concerning material progress that he expounded everywhere as an old
man, fifty years later. Everything was literally in motion before
1861, and the young men were in full motion toward their chances,
their tasks, their fortunes: a whole continent to plunder, "teeming
with treasure," a vast network of railways to be built....

As a boy he was taught less piety than the native Yankees were
as a rule, but he learned much of "holy economy" in his frugal
home. And as swiftly as any other contestant in the race, he learned
to follow the line of Progress; he was consumed with the immigrant's hope and certainty of improving his lot in a society whose
resources were unplumbed, whose social compartments were ill-
defined and shifting, whose values were indeterminate and only
dimly grasped. At seventeen Andrew Carnegie, the telegraph clerk
saw himself an Agent of Progress, sending and receiving in an instant messages which only yesterday had taken weeks to communi-
cate. But quick, alert, intelligent and very "self-assertive" according
to his official biographer, the boy soon enough widened the scope

of his ambitions at every stage of the advance. He had conflicting motives; he read books avidly; hoped to be a figure in politics and journalism, but most of all he desired, as he wrote at the time, "to become independent and then enjoy the luxuries which wealth can (and should) procure." He admired intensely the large, dignified, close-fisted, silk-hatted gentlemen who passed him in the street, who loomed large already over Pittsburgh: Judge Thomas Mellon, the money-lender, J. Edgar Thomson, the railroad man, and the redoubtable Thomas Scott, with whom he sought to ingratiate himself.

Asserting that there was no "future" in telegraphy, though he earned the comparatively large wages of $800 a year, he had one day quickly accepted the offer to serve as telegraphist and secretary to Scott, who was superintendent of the Pennsylvania Railroad at Pittsburgh. Under Scott he profited from the tutelage of one of the shrewdest intriguers among the new railroad captains, a man who knew as well as anyone else how "to get something for nothing." Scott, who was soon to be president of the Pennsylvania Railroad, was impressed with the youth of eighteen, and named him his "white-haired Scotch devil." Railroading was new-fashioned and somewhat frontier in its nature, attracting "sailors from the sea, disappointed gold-seekers from the West, immigrants from the crowded cities." Carnegie advanced himself by breaking rules at opportune moments, and boldly assuming responsibility in emergencies. Small of frame, but hardy and pugnacious, he soon became a division superintendent and ruled over his rough-and-tumble crews with as firm a hand as anyone who thrived in those high-hearted days.

The great persons among whom he moved did notice the young Carnegie, and when they chose to help him on his road he traveled swiftly, without looking to right or left. From Scott he received his first lessons in finance. It was Thomas Scott who one day gave young Carnegie a tip to buy the stock of the American Express Company; and to make his first successful speculation Carnegie borrowed a small sum by mortgaging his mother's home. Some time later he fell in with a gentleman who was busy devising sleeping cars for railroads. This invention, Woodruff's Palace Car, he had helped to promote in his spare time both by force of argument and by an initial outlay of $217.50, which he borrowed—the remaining small payments being retired out of dividends. "Thus Andrew Carnegie's first considerable investment was made without the outlay of a dollar of his own," observes his biographer, Burton Hendrick; and this was "a scheme of investment that became almost the invariable rule in all subsequent enterprises." In two years the Woodruff Palace Car stock alone brought him an income of $5,000 a year! Those were flowing times.

In Western Pennsylvania, the discovery of oil in 1859 had caused a boom and a rush like that of California, and yielded even greater quantities of gold. Carnegie's "flyer" in some oil acreage netted a "gusher" which added many thousands to his expanding "reservoir." A variety of smartly placed speculations soon engrossed the young railroader's whole mind. He gained in confidence and a sense of power as he learned to purchase properties or projects for "a song," and accumulated rapidly without excessively hard work. On a vacation visit to his native town in Scotland he said, not without arrogance, to his laborious kin: "You over here are playing with toys!"

It was at this time that he exclaimed to himself with delight: "Oh, I'm rich! I'm rich!"

5

Of all these young men only one had had what might pass for a traditional education. Pierpont Morgan, of Hartford, Connecticut, was carefully reared by his father, given the opportunity of foreign travel and several years at the University of Göttingen, where he showed some proficiency in mathematics. As a young man he was morose, reserved, abrupt, and had almost no friends; his sluggish exterior suggested no talent whatsoever, and besides he was not without waywardness.

There is in his early life the account of a youthful romance. In quite sentimental fashion he had become infatuated with a young woman named Amelia Sturges, who was consumptive and declined his offer of marriage for the reason of her health. But single-minded he had pursued her, forsaking his first small business ventures to live in Paris, where he wooed Miss Sturges passionately in the face of death.

"I don't know what in the world I'm going to do with Pierpont," his father complained. Pierpont however stubbornly insisted on marrying Miss Sturges, and saw her extinguished within three months. With this tragic experience the wayward, romantic appetites in him had subsided for a long time, and he had returned to pursue the "education" which had been marked out for him by his "grim-mouthed" father.

In his apprentice years Morgan worked at the famous London banking house of George Peabody & Co., of which his father was a partner. This American banking firm had made London its base of operations so that it might take a part in directing the capital which flowed from Europe to pioneering America. Here young Morgan at nineteen was being initiated into the technical mysteries of his trade. "He was learning what bills at 60 days on Paris or Amsterdam or Hamburg were worth in francs, guilders, the marc banco..." as his biographer comments with satisfaction. He was also learning to speculate: hearing that coffee was "going up," he had borrowed a sum of money (against the advice of his mentors) and purchased a shipload of Brazilian coffee. After helping thus to make that article scarce and dear, he had sold it quickly at a handsome profit, his first considerable "deal." Pierpont Morgan at nineteen, haughty and self-assured and brief-spoken, was learning many things; and it was with his education well advanced that he arrived in the rising financial center of New York in 1857, a year later, to establish himself there upon his own, as his father's banking representative, to engage in many more lucrative "deals."

The progress of a young man like Pierpont Morgan seems painfully slow compared to that of the Jay Goulds and the John Rockefellers who were not like Morgan hampered by having received an education comparable to that of men of letters such as Motley, Emerson, and Bancroft. Much sooner than the academically instructed, without doubts or heart-burnings they directed themselves toward the one "career open to talent."

John Rockefeller who grew up in Western New York and later near Cleveland, as one of a struggling family of five children, recalls with satisfaction the excellent practical training he had received and how quickly he put it to use. His childhood seemed to have been darkened by the misdeeds of his father, a wandering vendor of quack medicine who rarely supported his family, and was sometimes a fugitive from the law; yet the son invariably spoke of his parent's instructions with gratitude. He said:

> ... *He himself trained me in practical ways. He was engaged in different enterprises; he used to tell me about these things ... and he taught me the principles and methods of business. ... I knew what a cord of good solid beech and maple wood was. My father told me to select only solid wood ... and not to put any limbs in it or any punky wood. That was a good training for me.*

But the elder Rockefeller went further than this in his sage instructions, according to John T. Flynn, who attributes to him the statement:

> *I cheat my boys every chance I get, I want to make 'em sharp. I trade with the boys and skin 'em and I just beat 'em every time I can. I want to make 'em sharp.*

If at times the young Rockefeller absorbed a certain shiftiness and trading sharpness from his restless father, it was also true that his father was absent so often and so long as to cast shame and poverty upon his home. Thus he must have been subject far more often to the stern supervision of his mother, whom he has recalled in several stories. His mother would punish him, as he related, with a birch switch to "uphold the standard of the family when it showed a tendency to deteriorate." Once when she found out that she was punishing him for a misdeed at school of which he was innocent, she said, "Never mind, we have started in on this whipping and it will do for the next time." The normal outcome of such disciplinary cruelty would be deception and stealthiness in the boy, as a defense.

But his mother, who reared her children with the rigid piety of an Evangelist, also started him in his first business enterprise. When he was seven years old she encouraged him to raise turkeys, and gave him for this purpose the family's surplus milk curds. There are legends of Rockefeller as a boy stalking a turkey with the most patient stealth in order to seize her eggs.

This harshly disciplined boy, quiet, shy, reserved, serious, received but a few years' poor schooling, and worked for neighboring farmers in all his spare time. His whole youth suggests only abstinence, prudence and the growth of parsimony in his soul. The pennies he earned he would save steadily in a blue bowl that stood on a chest in his room, and accumulated until there was a small heap of gold coins. He would work, by his own account, hoeing potatoes for a neighboring farmer from morning to night for 37 cents a day. At a time when he was still very young he had fifty dollars saved, which upon invitation he one day loaned to the farmer who employed him.

"And as I was saving those little sums," he relates, "I soon learned that I could get as much interest for $50 loaned at seven per cent—then the legal rate of interest—as I could earn by digging potatoes for ten days." Thereafter, he tells us, he resolved that it was better "to let the money be my slave than to be the slave of money."

In Cleveland whither the family removed in 1854, Rockefeller went to the Central High School and studied bookkeeping for a year. This delighted him. Most of the conquering types in the coming order were to be men trained early in life in the calculations of the bookkeeper, Cooke, Huntington, Gould, Henry Frick and especially Rockefeller of whom it was said afterward: "He had the soul of a bookkeeper."

In his first position as bookkeeper to a produce merchant at the Cleveland docks, when he was sixteen, he distinguished himself by his composed orderly habits. Very carefully he examined each item on each bill before he approved it for payment. Out of a salary which began at $15 a month and advanced ultimately to $50 a month, he saved $800 in three years, the lion's share of his total earnings! This was fantastic parsimony.

He spent little money for clothing, though he was always neat; he never went to the theater, had no amusements, and few friends. But he attended his Baptist Church in Cleveland as devoutly as he attended to his accounts. And to the cause of the church alone, to its parish fund and mission funds, he demonstrated his only generosity by gifts that were large for him then—first of ten cents, then later of twenty-five cents at a time.

In the young Rockefeller the traits which his mother had bred in him, of piety and the economic virtue—worship of the "lean goddess of Abstinence"—were of one cloth. The pale, bony, small-eyed young Baptist served the Lord and pursued his own business unremittingly. His composed manner, which had a certain languor, hid a feverish calculation, a sleepy strength, cruel, intense, terribly alert.

As a schoolboy John Rockefeller had once announced to a companion, as they walked by a rich man's ample house along their
way: "When I grow up I want to be worth $100,000. And I'm going
to be too." In almost the same words, Rockefeller in Cleveland,
Cooke in Philadelphia, Carnegie in Pittsburgh, or a James Hill in
the Northwestern frontier could be found voicing the same hope.
And Rockefeller, the bookkeeper, "not slothful in business . . .
serving the Lord," as John T. Flynn describes him, watched his
chances closely, learned every detail of the produce business which
engaged him, until finally in 1858 he made bold to open a business
of his own in partnership with a young Englishman named Clark
(who was destined to be left far behind). Rockefeller's grimly accumulated savings of $800, in addition to a loan from his father at
the usurious rate of 10 per cent, yielded the capital which launched
him, and he was soon "gathering gear" quietly. He knew the art of
using loan credit to expand his operations. His first bank loan against
warehouse receipts gave him a thrill of pleasure. He now bought
grain and produce of all kinds in carload lots rather than in small
consignments. Prosperous, he said nothing, but began to dress his
part, wearing a high silk hat, frock coat and striped trousers like
other merchants of the time. His head was handsome, his eyes small,
birdlike; on his pale bony cheeks were the proverbial side-whiskers,
reddish in color.

At night, in his room, he read the Bible, and retiring had the queer
habit of talking to his pillow about his business adventures. In his
autobiography he says that "these intimate conversations with myself had a great influence upon my life." He told himself "not to
get puffed up with any foolish notions" and never to be deceived
about actual conditions. "Look out or you will lose your head—go
steady."

He was given to secrecy; he loathed all display. When he married,
a few years afterward, he lost not a day from his business. His wife,
Laura Spelman, proved an excellent mate. She encouraged his fur-
tiveness, he relates, advising him always to be silent, to say as little
as possible. His composure, his self-possession was excessive. Those
Clevelanders to whom Miss Ida Tarbell addressed herself in her investigations of Rockefeller, told her that he was a hard man to best
in a trade, that he rarely smiled, and almost never laughed, save

when he struck a good bargain. Then he might clap his hands with delight, or he might even, if the occasion warranted, throw up his hat, kick his heels and hug his informer. One time he was so overjoyed at a favorable piece of news that he burst out: "I'm bound to be rich! *Bound to be rich!*"

CHAPTER THREE
OF EMPIRE-BUILDERS

THE people here want to hear nothing now but the fife and drum," commented Jay Cooke somewhat gloomily in the spring of 1861. He had just opened the newly established banking house of Jay Cooke & Co., on January 1, 1861, and there seemed literally no business to be done during the ominous lull before the first battle of Manassas. The tone of this man of money suggests clearly that while he might be loyal enough to the North, he did not share the martial fervor that swept through the crowd. This distaste for gunpowder was shown almost universally by the other members of the new Northern business class. Their attitude is very well typified by the colorful Judge Thomas Mellon of Pittsburgh, who in telegraphic orders at this time sternly forbade one of his elder sons residing in Wisconsin to enlist even for service behind the line. He then followed with a choleric letter:

> I had hoped my boy was going to make a smart, intelligent business man and was not such a goose as to be seduced from duty by the declamations of buncombed speeches. It is only greenhorns who enlist. You can learn nothing in the army. . . . Here there is no credit attached to going. All now stay if they can and go if they must. Those who are able to pay for substitutes, do so, and no discredit attaches. In time you will come to understand and believe that a man may be a patriot without risking his own life or sacrificing his health. There are plenty of other lives less valuable or others ready to serve for the love of serving.

The father's counsel prevailed, and the son, James Mellon, like John Rockefeller, Pierpont Morgan, Armour, Gould, and the other gifted young entrepreneurs who were of proper age, sent substitutes to the draft armies and as a rule found ways of displaying their patriotism without risking life and limb.

The rout of the first Union army spread gloom over the North, since it was now understood how heavy was the task of subduing the rebels; it was not an engagement of professional armies: a whole "nation in arms" must be conquered in its homeland, and this European experts and other observers on the scene predicted to be impossible.

But under the political gloom a great economic exuberance was spreading as if by magic. The very reverses of the Union armies, creating the need for government funds, for vast quantities of war material, clothing, uniform, shoes, munitions, transport, and for a total reorganization of the national economy, soon changed the humor of the civilians. The very collapse of the government credit, the menace of defeat, bringing debasement of the currency, was a good, since there soon developed a cycle of inflation with its pleasing picture of soaring prices for goods of all kinds; while the great mass of citizens were quickly engrossed in all the multifarious industrial activities evoked by the immense destroying and consuming of a modern war.

Behind the army lines there were lucrative tasks to be done in short order. Bankers and investors must raise a million dollars a day in money for the war government; food and produce must be multiplied; woolen cloth must be manufactured in place of cotton; rivers of pork must flow from Chicago; the new free lands of the West must be opened up quickly for productive use; the iron trade must be developed for wartime needs; railroads, which quickly proved their great usefulness in the immediate war area for troop movements, must be extended across the continent to unify the country; coal and minerals of all sorts must be dug from the earth; innumerable oil wells must be opened; farm machines must be fabricated to replace a million men in arms; in short all the demands must be satisfied for the huge national market closed off by the protective tariffs of 1862 and 1864.

In this "War Between the States," moreover, all the fullest energies of the long-retarded industrial revolution were liberated. Whether it sensed it or not, the war party headed by Lincoln hastened miraculously a transfer of power to the emergent groups of large-scale capitalism. Under Lincoln, after the Homestead Act, began the distribution of the public domain, which the federal government owned, in favor of its citizenry of free farmers and artisans: half the present area of the United States, or a billion acres of land, with all its subsoil. In a hurried partition, for nominal sums or by cession, this benevolent government handed over to its friends or to the astute first comers, the most daring undertakers, all those treasures of coal and oil, of copper and gold and iron, the land grants, the terminal sites, the perpetual rights of way—an act of largesse which is still one of the wonders of history.[1] To the new railroad enterprises in addition, great money subsidies totaling many hundreds of millions were given. The Tariff Act of 1864 was in itself a sheltering wall of subsidies; and to add further the new heavy industries and manufactures, an Immigration Act allowing contract labor to be imported freely was quickly enacted; a national banking system was perfected. And finally, to preserve the new alignment of interests, the cabalistic "due process clause" was inserted into the Fourteenth Amendment, by which the ostensible defense of Negroes' rights, as the Beards have pointed out, was made the eternal bulwark of great property rights. Having conferred these vast rights and controls, the war government would preserve them, as Conkling termed it, so as to "curb the many who would do to the few as they would not have the few do to them."

That enormous breaches were being opened in the defense walls of the old social order, breaches through which unknown adventurers and their mercenary soldiers would come raging for plunder, was perhaps not widely enough recognized at the time. Yet it did not take long for the meaning of these wonder-working changes to reach the brains of those other young men of '61 whose training and appetite led them to the marketplace rather than the battlefields. Whether engaged in money-lending, "projecting," speculating or hog-slaughtering, they sensed their chances instantly, and each in his way rushed to seize the resources, the key positions of the industrial society being hastily assembled. They would then find themselves, incredibly enough, commanders of strongholds, lords of "empires" in iron, beef, railroads or oil, to be held naturally for private gain,

[1] For had not the Republican convention at Chicago, in 1860, placed the measure for a Pacific Railroad Bill on its platform under the urgings of young men like Leland Stanford who came hurrying from California to the banner of Lincoln, though without the slightest interest in the freedom of slaves?

and once held, defended by them to the last breath of financial life against all comers. And then the triumph of the war party at the close of the rebellion would see the democratic sovereignty opening even wider the doors to treasures in lands, forests, mineral deposits, rights of way—by the only method and precedent known to a popular sovereignty: partition to those men among the people who were, as Bacon has termed it, of "violent and undertaking nature."[2] It is this process of *conquest and partition* during the "feudal period" of our industrial development that we must follow in detail, especially with reference to the small group of talented men who were to be its chief beneficiaries.

2

In the several years which had preceded the war, Jay Cooke had won respect among the business people and politicians of Philadelphia. His serene and impassive face, covered with one of the biggest and finest of contemporary beards and surmounted with a famous wide-brimmed hat, completed the aspect of dignity which he wore.

Since 1857, having separated from the bank of Clark & Dodge, he had busied himself in divers projects of his own, especially in promoting the canal works and small railroad lines which were usually in those days inspired by state subsidies and managed by private undertakers. Those companies which fell into difficulties he and a party of friends bought cheaply, "reorganized ... issued stocks and bonds, paid the state the price agreed upon and then retired with

[2]In the later transition of the Roman Empire, the "decline," which is perhaps comparable to the disintegration of our landholding and planting rulership, the government in its weakness conferred the right of local administration upon the great proprietors in the provinces, or else permitted them to usurp these rights (by seizure) which then (by usage) became "legal." In this way there arose the "dukes," "barons" and other "nobles" of the Middle Ages. By other procedures, such as the *precarium*, small landholders, who felt the need of protection in troublous times, surrendered title to the Strong, as Taine has called them, the great armed proprietors themselves hardy fighters and commanders of combative field-hands and servants. The small landholder would thenceforth occupy his land as a tenant.

The *patrocinium* was the procedure by which those who lost their land would pay a landed proprietor for shelter and support in return for their labor.

By other procedures leading to the same end, land was partitioned by force, as by the Lombards in Italy, creating "dukedoms," etc. (Cf. Thompson, J. W., "History of the Middle Ages," Ch. XIX.)

good round profits," he relates. So adept was Cooke, so "efficient in getting up parties" for new ventures, as a local capitalist wrote him, that his moneyed friends begged him to lead them in further exploits, and with such encouragement he had launched what was soon to become the greatest private banking house in America at the inauspicious beginning of 1861.

In these first dark hours of the war Cooke saw a great light. Years before, while still with the Clarks, he remembered with pleasure having overreached the Secretary of the Treasury twice by ingenious arrangements regarding interest on Mexican War loans. "So we victimized him again," he had commented in a letter on the second occasion. Why should not this great rebellion once more be "a grand time for brokers and private banking," a time for "victimizing"?

But Jay Cooke, it must be noted, had a strain of genius, he had a style, which would make him "the first modern American" in the direction of large affairs. Knowing the motives of men shrewdly, he would color all his bold transactions with the red-white-and-blue of patriotism; the "ballyhoo" of bond-selling campaigns was conducted by him with the fervor of a religious crusade. He knew the Ohio politicians well; his brother Henry, a journalist, was attached both to Governor Salmon P. Chase and to the influential Congressman, John Sherman. Through these he followed every political move at the Capitol. It was the pressing need for money by the federal and state governments which caught his eye at once; he resolved to devote himself entirely to government financing.

In June, 1861, the Pennsylvania State Legislature, which had called for 10,000 volunteers, sought a loan of $3,000,000. It was a moment when the credit of this commonwealth, owing to previous defaults, was at its lowest ebb, and Pennsylvanians a butt for the tirades of humorists such as the Englishman Sidney Smith. Now Jay Cooke, alone among the native bankers, came forward with the offer to sell the Pennsylvania 6's "at not less than par"—on the grounds of patriotism. Bestirring himself with remarkable energy, he or his agents visited every banker or every merchant in the near-by country known to have something in his stocking. Exhorted "to strike terror into the rebels," to send a flood of cash toward the front, the public oversubscribed what seemed then a large loan.

Cooke caused this news to be advertised everywhere, especially in the South, where he made it known that "the millions of the North would be forthcoming to suppress treason and rebellion." It was Cooke's début in national fame. It was considered, as he himself remarked, "an achievement as great or greater than Napoleon's crossing the Alps"; he had earned $1,000 a day during the crossing.

Like Napoleon also, Jay Cooke neither halted nor rested after victory but pushed on. Together with Anthony Drexel, he would form, he announced to Secretary Chase, on July 12, 1861, a Washington banking house which was to be closely allied to the government:

> We would wish to make our business mostly out of the Treasury operations and we feel sure that we could by having a proper understanding with yourself greatly help you in the management of your vast negotiations. . . . We could not be expected to leave our comfortable homes and positions here without some great inducement and we state frankly that we would, if we succeeded, expect a fair commission from the Treasury in some shape for our labor and talent. If you feel disposed to say to us . . . that you will give us the management of the loans to be issued by the government during the war, allowing us a fair commission on them . . . we are ready to throw ourselves, into the matter heartily. . . .

It was a bold proposition, too bold for even the pompous, vainglorious Secretary Chase to accept, since it would create a monopoly for government loan commissions. Refused, Jay Cooke pursued the harassed Secretary with his offers of disinterested assistance in the complex financial operations of which Chase, to begin with, knew almost nothing. By dining and wining the servant of the people the Philadelphia banker had occasion to win his confidence, and accompanied him unofficially to New York in his first attempts to wheedle advances out of the unsentimental money-lenders of that city. These gentlemen, named the Ciscos, Mortons, Taylors, Belmonts, were not as yet certain that they liked the war, or the way in which it was being conducted, or Mr. Lincoln, whom they did not know. Grudgingly they offered small sums at high interest. They were old-fashioned; they had neither the bubbling patriotism of Cooke nor his dazzling vision of low commissions for raising big quantities of paper money.

"... We shall go on the rocks together," said the Secretary menacingly. "I will go back to Washington and issue notes for circulation. The war must go on until the rebellion is put down, if we have to put out paper and it takes a thousand dollars to buy a breakfast."

Such threats brought at length $50,000,000 from the "shaving shops" of New York, and at 12 per cent! They were "Wall Street Copperheads"; but as always they feared the evils of "inflation."[3]

In the first great government war loans offered publicly, the "seven-thirties" of October, 1861, Jay Cooke did not have a monopoly, but his participation was so brilliant, he sold so much more than the other bankers (about one-fourth of the total), that his demands could not long be resisted. His methods had been a revelation to the banking community. He had advertised in all the press, paid all the financial reporters he could reach "with edibles and bibibles"; he had thrown agents all about the country, distributed circulars by the ton. Over his office he had hung out a flag with the legend "National Loan" emblazoned upon it; he "kept the papers fired up daily"; he dunned each war contractor and military supplyer. Thenceforth he became the sole fiscal agency of the government. A branch office in Washington was soon opened directly opposite the Treasury building, and this office became the haunt of Congressmen, government employees, lobbyists and reporters.

At forty Jay Cooke was one of the leading counselors of the war government. He had insisted that by having the sole "concession" of government loans, he could effect great savings in the handlings. His charges were actually lower than those of the older bankers who

[3]There were many acrid debates on this score in Congress. Representative Kellogg of Illinois, on February 3, 1861, in a speech on the Legal Tender bill said:

"Mr. Chairman, I am pained when I sit in my place in the House and hear members talk about the sacredness of capital; that the interests of money must not be touched. Yes, sir, they will vote six hundred thousand of the flower of American youth for the army to be sacrificed without a blush; but the great interests of capital, of currency, must not be touched. We have summoned the youth; they have come. I would summon the capital, and if it does not come voluntarily before this republic shall go down or one star be lost, I would take every cent from the treasury of the states, from the treasury of capitalists, from the treasury of individuals and press it into the use of the government."

now raged at him with envy. Moreover at great cost he built up by 1863 a far-flung organization of 2,500 subagents or "minutemen" who in that year helped him float $500,000,000 of "five-twenties" with enormous success. Before the age of the radio, the doctrine of Jay Cooke: "*A national debt a national blessing,*" was literally broadcast over the country. After the issues of legal tender, and suspension of specie payments, the dollar of course sank to from 40 to 60 cents in gold; hence it was a stream of mere greenbacks, of paper money, which the moneyed public now rushed to lend to the war government. By selling huge quantities of the bonds, at the rate of $2,000,000 a day, Cooke's commissions at .5 per cent rose to some $3,000,000 a year—though this did not include the very heavy expenses of promotion. These bonds Cooke supported in the market at par. Cooke's directing hand was now felt in the gold market and the stock exchange of Wall Street, where he curbed or prodded the speculators as he pleased. He extended his interests with amazing rapidity and with quenchless optimism; other banks came under his control; his agents were everywhere. In his onward rush he had scrambled over the heads of the older cliques of financiers. He had brought a new technique into the management of national finance, a form of mass distribution, as compared with the semiprivate disposal of government obligations to a few moneylenders in the past. Rising from obscurity, like the proverbial comet, he had come to hold the national purse-strings, and soon the expression: "As rich as Jay Cooke," became a familiar folk-saying.

A government that leaned upon the spectacular patriot-banker, that opened all its affairs to him, saw him every day in its council halls, could not long resist his further encroachments. The man who raised nearly three billions in four years to support the army at the front could not be refused the concession by Congress of a horsecar line in Washington, on which soldiers and citizens must ride. He who had "hired friends" everywhere in the press and in Congress—for he knew how to be excessively hospitable and delicately assiduous to all who lent themselves to his ends—must be heard when he clamored for the dismissal of a McLellan. If rival bankers hinted that he debauched the press, his achievements made him immune to criticism. This financier who was called the "Robert Morris of the Civil War" extended his power steadily while rendering discreet financial assistance to a Chase or direct favors to a Blaine. Was not Cooke a figure of the war machine behind the lines?[4]

His own partners in panic secretly contemplated flight with their capital. But he, with grandiose power, worked steadily to set in motion Chase's national banking legislation, which helped to unify the confused currency, taxed state banknotes out of existence while freeing capital further. The salesmen of "this banking firm, made rich by the drippings of the Treasury," as some Senators declared, promoted Chase's aspirations for the presidency. And tomorrow Cooke would labor mightily, and with the collaboration of a band of war industrialists and financiers, for the resumption of specie payment, for the complete redemption by the government of all its depreciated obligations; so that those who had invested their greenbacks, quickly won during the economic frenzy of the war, might be repaid in solid gold. After Appomattox, Cooke, scanning the plans for his million-dollar palace of "Ogontz" outside of Philadelphia, a dwelling such as the New World had not yet seen, would pine for greater projects, for new empires to seize—empires to be had once more by plunging his hands into the bottomless treasure-chest of the government.

3

For years, Oberholtzer relates, "the strong guiding hand of Mr. Cooke was felt in dominating the stock exchanges and the press." And not without reason. The markets were transformed into infernos of speculation. In New York the Goldbugs to the strains of Dixie again and again "sold the dollar short," while gold rose to a premium above 150 per cent. As the government's most patriotic banker observed often when on punitive expeditions against the bears, "no one heartily loved their country better than their pockets." What they wanted, as the press repeated often, if not gold, was "shares, shares, shares..." mining companies in Colorado, or the clouds, ministers as well as laymen, women as well as men. At times the

[4]Military historians have traced clearly the influence of tremendous political-financial pressure in Grant's disgraceful action at Cold Harbor: his hopeless frontal attack on Lee's breastworks; his refusal to acknowledge defeat or sue for permission to rescue the wounded and bury the dead during four hideout days. At this moment in 1864, the fall of the dollar, the fate of government loans which were in Cooke's hands, the approaching election campaign seemed to paralyze the soldier.

doors and windows of the exchange actually burst under the pressure of the crowd outside. The fever-pulse of this speculative passion might be taken in the Gold Room of the New York Stock Exchange, where the dealers in gold surged every day around the tinkling fountain decorated with a spouting, gilded Cupid. Here new figures joined the older wrinkled ones of Drew and Vanderbilt, swimming through the whirling treacherous tides of the market, growing strong in its lore and craft, among them the furtive little Jay Gould, with his curly black beard, his piercing dark eyes, his hooked nose, and Pierpont Morgan, the tall and stolid banker's son; and the broad-girthed Jim Fisk, who had won many an easy dollar by "running" contraband cotton through the army lines from the South. "Along with ordinary happenings, we fellows in Wall Street had the fortunes of war to speculate about," said Daniel Drew; and the Great Bear added: "It's good fishing in troubled waters."

There was speculation in goods, in produce of all sorts. In Cleveland the young merchant Rockefeller prospered under the sun of rising prices for provisions; his income early in the war increased to $17,000 in a year. In Chicago Philip Armour, who had returned from California to open a slaughtering business, sent forth salt pork and dressed beef to the Union armies and for export; in Philadelphia, the butcher Peter Widener did a rushing trade in war provisioning. Even William, the slow-witted son of Cornelius Vanderbilt, from his farm on Staten Island sold hay for the cavalry troops quartered near by; while the eldest son of Judge Thomas Mellon, the Pittsburgh banker, pleaded with his father to have money for speculation. People were making millions in wheat, he reported from Wisconsin: "They continue growing richer and don't care when the war closes."

4

After his apprentice years Pierpont Morgan in New York enjoyed, through his father's intervention, the American agency for the banking house of George Peabody & Co. Junius Morgan, like the somewhat older and better loved George Peabody, was a man of the highest business probity. This meant that he was "conservative," that in the pursuit of the most soundly profitable chances for gain he discharged his trust faithfully to those who entered into collusion with him. It meant being highly scrupulous, almost puritanical in fulfilling the letter of all contracts, so that the "good-will" of depositors and clients might be retained over a long period of years. For such qualities of conservatism and purity George Peabody & Co., the old tree out of which the House of Morgan grew, was famous. In the panic of 1857, when depreciated securities had been thrown on the market by distressed investors in America, Peabody and the elder Morgan, being in possession of cash, had purchased such bonds as possessed real value freely, and then resold them at a large advance when sanity was restored. In this way they had won the plaudits of such a statesman as Edward Everett, "for having performed the miracle by which an honest man turns paper into gold."

For the same "conservative" reasons, Peabody and Morgan, as international bankers, busied themselves during the Civil War in conducting the flight of American capital which brought great sums of money to be placed with them in London. In the *Springfield Republican*, Samuel Bowles attacked them saying:

> . . . *They gave us no faith and no help in our struggle for national existence. . . . No individuals contributed so much to flooding the money markets with evidences of our debts to Europe, and breaking down their prices and weakening financial confidence in our nationality, and none made more money by the operation.*

But such strange charges were based of course on an innocent misconception of the clear interest of the bankers, which confused their rôle with that of those common men who served because they loved to serve, as Judge Thomas Mellon would say, at Gettysburg or The Wilderness. The saner and more widely accepted view was of course that expressed by Samuel Tilden at a public banquet to Junius Morgan, some years after the war, in which the father of Pierpont Morgan was lauded for "upholding unsullied the honor of America in the tabernacles of the old world. . . . While you are scheming for your own selfish ends, there is an overruling and wise Providence directing that most of all you do should inure to the benefit of the people."

While full of probity like his father, Pierpont Morgan already under his silent, phlegmatic exterior nourished more impetuous ambitions to advance the common good. Early in 1861, when many pressed to fill war contracts, a wise Providence doubtless directed him upon a venture in war munitions, on the sensible ground that carbines were as keenly demanded as bags of coffee several years before.

A certain Simon Stevens, who had an option for 5,000 Hall carbines, through another dealer named Eastman, came to Morgan with an urgent request for a loan against this war material which he soon hoped to sell to the government at a profit. In advance, he had by telegraph arranged to sell them to General Frémont, who headed the Western Army quartered near St. Louis. Stevens, who had long been engaged in obscure transactions with customhouse officials, may or may not have divulged that he needed the sum of $17,486 from Morgan in order to purchase the carbines from the very same government at Washington whose army in the West clamored for guns. This paradoxical situation was caused by the fact that the carbines in question were found by inspection to be so defective that they would shoot off the thumbs of the soldiers using them. The quartermaster at Washington sold them for $3.50 apiece. "The government had sold one day for $17,486 arms which it had agreed the day before to purchase for $109,912," as a Congressional committee later discovered. That young Morgan knew of this situation is plain from the fact that after arrival of the consignment of guns at General Frémont's division, he bluntly presented his claim not for the money he had advanced, but for all of $58,175, half of the shipment having been already paid for in good faith

Morgan's claim for the full sum of $109,912, where he had loaned only $17,486, may have been an indication to the Congress that his part in the affair was something more than a passive money-lender's. In the ensuing investigation, March 3, 1863, a Committee on Government Contracts, amid much outcry on "pillage, fraud, extortion," had demanded that Morgan disclose the terms upon which he had entered the transaction, though without breaking his obdurate silence. The Congressmen had not been convinced that this large and sullen young man's operations "inured to the benefit of the people," and had seen fit to lecture him. Of him and his fellows their report had said:

He cannot be looked upon as a good citizen, entitled to favorable consideration of his claim, who seeks to augment the vast burdens, daily increasing, that are to weigh on the future industry of the

*country, by demands upon the treasury for which nothing entitled
to the name of an equivalent has been rendered. . . . Worse than
traitors in arms are the men who pretending loyalty to the flag, feast
and fatten on the misfortunes of the nation, while patriot blood is
crimsoning the plains of the South and bodies of their countrymen
are moldering in the dust.*[5]

Thereafter Pierpont Morgan had confined himself to the routine
dealings of the money-changer. When he wished for more bracing
sport he frequently entered the gold market and as it was very fashionable to do at the time, sold the dollar short, that is to say,
bought future options on gold at rising prices. Owing to the dark
outlook for the Union cause these were reasonably safe operations
usually attended with profit. Defeats for the Yankee armies, which
came often enough, brought a proportionate rise in gold. In these
ventures Morgan usually joined with a shifty young man named
Edward Ketchum, son of the well-known banker Morris Ketchum.
At one time in 1863 while harassed merchants bid for gold to cover
their currency needs, Morgan and Ketchum corralled a goodly part
of the immediate supply and shipped away to London $1,150,000,
driving the price up from about 130 to 171. Such speculative daring brought disapproval from official quarters. The Union League
Club, very jingoistic, called for the erection of scaffolds to hang
the gold speculators. The closing of the Gold Room in New York,
however, created only a "black market"; the only remedy for excesses which carried gold to 285 in terms of dollars being the triumphs of General Grant in 1865. Morgan's friend Ketchum was
deeply involved when the approaching fall of Richmond brought a
precipitous recovery in the dollar to almost par. To save himself,
Ketchum absconded with money and securities from his father's
bank, as well as sums belonging to Morgan, then failed, and was
sentenced to prison, branded as "the greatest defaulter of the age."

It was by normal banking operations, however, in partnership with
an experienced banker named Dabney, that Pierpont Morgan made

[5]More than half a century later, during the presidency of Woodrow
Wilson, the late Mr. George Harvey appealed to Morgan's patriotism in a
quite conventional sense by citing to him the lines from Scott: "Breathes
there the man with soul so dead, etc." The banker's eyes are said to have
filled with tears, and with emotion he offered his fullest aid to the President.
But he was then nearly eighty years of age. . . .

his steadiest gains. The banker in those early days was chiefly the servant to the merchant or manufacturer, for a safe 9 to 8 per cent, rather than the manager of the total investment. At times Morgan's business included also the sale of American railroad bonds, though they were in ill repute abroad. The bonds of the Erie Railroad were placed at 10 per cent while bonds of the ill-fated Kansas & Pacific actively sold as a "first-class investment" by Dabney & Morgan also had to be placed at usurious rates. Railroad securities were queer, new things over which Morgan pondered long and deeply. There were many strange tales of extraordinary operations by bold men such as Daniel Drew and Cornelius Vanderbilt in the securities and the treasuries of railroads, "while the directors are still wealthy—and out of prison." Although he seemed to some contemporaries dull, gruff and brusque—at certain directors' meetings he attended he was even opposed as a "dummy" director—Morgan's ambitions must have seemed solid and large enough to lay the ghost of his father's misgivings for him. Inarticulate, brief-spoken, he longed to dominate others, though he felt unable as yet to do so. Several years of further apprenticeship were to pass before he threw himself in earnest into those large railroad affairs which gave fitting scope for his ambitions and, in conflict with the strongest and most cunning adversaries, exposed his fierce will and high, truculent resolution. There is little doubt that as he grew slowly to full maturity young Morgan comprehended the future as well as anyone. In the closing weeks of the war there is record of a rare interview given by Pierpont Morgan, during a visit to London:

We are going some day to show ourselves to be the richest country in the world in natural resources. It will be necessary to go to work, and to work hard, to turn our resources into money to pay the cost of the war just as soon as it is ended.

Morgan was apparently among the few men of 1865 who sensed that the natural wealth of the country was really ample to pay for the cost of such a war.

5

The nimble Gould too was busily engaged in buying gold and selling the dollar since the opening of the Civil War. Tight-lipped, secretive, alert, he was naturally at home in the electric marketplace.

He was reputed to have set up machinery whereby informants hurried news of victories or defeats to him by telegraph almost a day ahead of his rivals. Murat Halstead, a well-known contemporary journalist, relates admiringly:

> During the war of the rebellion, Gould's firm did a large business in railway securities, and also made a great deal of money speculating in gold. Gould had private sources of information in the field, and he was able to turn almost every success or defeat of the Union army to profitable account.

This purchased information of a military or political character gave him an almost certain revenue for the duration of the war. But his real ambitions at this time lay elsewhere.

After marrying, at the outset of the war, Gould with the aid of his father-in-law, a man of some means, secured control of a small railroad in northern New York, the Rutland & Washington, a short sixty-two-mile line which was in the last stages of decay. He occupied himself by surveying and investigating this property, and became at once its president, treasurer and general superintendent. Then after a year or two he sold it out at a profit of $130,000 to an adjoining road, the Rensselaer & Saratoga, with which it was combined. Thereafter he had undertaken more and more "operations" in the little railroads which in these bustling times were being thrown up and joined together and maneuvered in every direction. An acquaintance, who was in urgent need, sold him at a low price controlling shares in a small Ohio road, which he managed to dispose of to the great Pennsylvania Railroad (then rounding out its system) at three times the original cost. Thus, when still a youth of twenty-five Jay Gould evolved a technique as a railroad operator, a technique of seizure and "conversion" which was as magical as that of the alchemist who turned dross into gold. Henry Clews, the amiable financial authority and social lion, described it as follows:

> To buy up two or more bad roads, put them together, give the united roads a new name, call it a good, prosperous line, with immense prospects . . . get a great number of people to believe all this, then make large issues of bonds, for further improving and enhancing the . . . property.

—then to sell it all at a profit to purchasers who came along. Should these be unable to run it profitably, and be obliged to go into liquidation, then Mr. Gould or his agents would very likely be found on hand at the sale and take back the road at a greatly reduced price.

Armed with this infallible recipe the young railroad captain ranged about the country, seeking out railroad properties which he could turn to use or dispose of through the brokerage house he had founded in New York, Smith, Gould and Martin. Early in 1865, saturnine and restless, Gould was busy purchasing pieces of near-by New England railroad property, which he might exploit for their nuisance value to the large Erie Railroad, when he met for the first time the remarkable chief of that corporation, Daniel Drew, and through him doubtless, the irrepressible James Fisk, Jr. Like Fisk, Gould willingly became a pupil of the Great Bear, the chief of Erie.

Jim Fisk, as he preferred to call himself, had become an agent of Drew's in the closing months of the war. He was a man who had always loved both display and tumult. As a peddler in Vermont, selling silks, shawls, silverware and tin and Yankee notions, he made all the villagers believe that the circus came into town when his wagon arrived. For that matter he had once been employed by a traveling menagerie. During the war at some physical risk he had run contraband cotton for a Boston firm; he had sold army blankets for war contractors at prodigious prices; he had engaged in a thousand and one projects and maneuvers, with the result that his partners had paid him a great prize, something like a ransom of $60,000, to go elsewhere and leave their side, a prize which he had quickly lost in the whirlpools of Wall Street. One would never have thought that the man Fisk was a born "projector." Big, stout, with blond hair, curling mustaches, wearing a velvet vest, his fat hands covered with rings, his flamboyant dress and his air of hearty good nature concealed a native shrewdness, a bluff courage, which never left him without resources.

What he offered to the crafty Drew was to negotiate the sale of a small Connecticut railroad, the Stonington, which he knew Drew controlled, to some Boston capitalists, at a goodly profit. The excellent results of this commission made Drew take a fancy to the odd young fellow, whose genial mask seemed such an excellent foil for his own stealthy and mournful aspect. (So Jay Gould too found

him a helpful colleague.) Soon Fisk headed the brokerage firm of
Fisk & Belden, which as an unknown house could execute secretly
large market orders for Drew without the knowledge of rival speculators.

Within three years of his advent to Wall Street Fisk was considered to have made himself master of the situation. It was commented that his "right bower was shrewdness, his left bower was
pluck, and his ace of trumps was good nature." In the back rooms
of his office he kept open house, a bottle of whiskey and a box of
cigars standing always ready upon his desk for his regular customers.

Gould, who had had negotiations of a like nature with Drew, soon
joined him and Fisk in elaborate Wall Street campaigns, especially
with reference to the securities of the Erie Railroad. The wizard of
speculation, under whom the two young men studied, for all his
seventy years and his doleful air, was supreme master of the affairs
of the Eastern trunk line whose stock was the speculative football
of the day. It was said in Wall Street:

> Daniel says "up"—Erie goes up. Daniel says "down"—Erie goes
> down. Daniel says "wiggle-waggle"—it bobs both ways!

Gould and Fisk too were soon "insiders" who might know in advance when the Erie shares would rise or fall, and smiling times
began for them. Only a single cloud disturbed the busy gentlemen
of the Erie ring; it was the ponderous encroachments of a berserk
force in the railroad field, the aged Cornelius Vanderbilt, whose
seemingly resistless advance menaced them all with extinction.

6

Commodore Vanderbilt in his own way played a notable part
in the national defense. With commerce-preying privateers swarming over the seas, his shipping business would have been greatly injured, or ruined, if he had not had the wisdom to withdraw in great
part, investing on the one hand in a diversity of manufacturing,
ferrying and coast-transport enterprises (now greatly stimulated),
and on the other hand, throwing himself into loyal war service,
much in the manner of Jay Cooke. Such ships as he still owned, he
like other shipowners gladly sold or leased to the war department,

though again like Cooke, not "without some great inducement." Then because of the respect in which he was held, both for his wealth and for his known aggressiveness, this formidable old gentleman was thrown into the offensive against the rebels, as shipping agent for the War Department, authorized to buy or lease for such oversea expeditions as that of General Banks to New Orleans. Now in chartering ships, Vanderbilt acted only through a sub-agent named Southard, who exacted a purchasing commission of 5 to 10 per cent, while paying what were afterward thought high rentals of $800 to $900 a day for obsolete river or lake steamers. The most serious charge leveled against Vanderbilt, afterward, was that he purchased the ancient lake steamship *Niagara* for $10,000, when he was perfectly aware that it must be used for an ocean voyage. carrying hundreds of Banks's soldiers to New Orleans. Most of the vessels used were unfit for ocean travel, or were decayed and patched up and repainted, according to Gustavus Myers. No precautions were taken for the safety of the soldiers; some vessels were inadequately provided with navigators and instruments and charts. Miraculously no storms were encountered off Cape Hatteras; the sea was smooth and the troops arrived safely at their port.

But in the ensuing Congressional investigation it was related by Senator Grimes of Iowa that

> *in perfectly smooth weather, with a calm sea, the planks were ripped out [of the S.S.* Niagara] *and exhibited to the gaze of the indignant soldiers on board, showing that her timbers were rotten. The committee have in their committee room a large sample of one of the beams of this vessel to show that it has not the slightest capacity to hold a nail.*

But it was a time of such notorious hurry and confusion, so much mischief was more or less unwittingly done, as General Grant and others complained, so many shoddy blankets, so many doctored horses and useless rifles, so many stores of sickening beef, were directed toward the front during the general excitement, that Commodore Vanderbilt's errors or shortcomings were largely overlooked. And though the severe Gustavus Myers, in his account, holds that there are sufficient signs that Vanderbilt "split" all commissions with his agent Southard, such a procedure was perhaps not unusual. In the general jubilation at the close of the war, Vanderbilt was among those who were awarded a medal by Congress in approval of their loyal services.

Though in the ripeness of his old age, sixty-eight, and in possession of a fortune of $11,000,000, Vanderbilt in 1862, far from wishing ease or retirement, determined upon new and bigger projects, whose success was to be a tribute to his amazing vitality. It was no sudden whim or inspiration that brought him into the railroad field. Ever since a painful accident, thirty years before, when on a steam-driven train destined for Perth Amboy, New Jersey, he had nearly been killed together with many others, he had abhorred steam railroads. But now there was no longer doubt as to their practical usefulness and even comparative safety. And besides, strong in his appetite for money, he must have had a "vision" of the gains won by his friend and rival, Daniel Drew, who, controlling the Erie Railroad, manipulated its stock at his will.

With his great capital, the Commodore now quietly bought control of the New York & Harlem Railroad, running from Forty-second Street to Brewster, New York, at a cost of $9 per share. Once at the controls, he kept buying Harlem stock, until it soon climbed to $50, so that he garnered millions with remarkable speed. Then by liberal payments of money or stock to the interested members of the New York Common Council—in accordance with the usual requirements of "Boss" Tweed—he obtained a franchise to operate a street-car line along Broadway, from Forty-second Street to the Battery. The acquisition of this vested right was thought to be worth so many millions more than it cost Mr. Vanderbilt that a further violent rise took place in the capital stock of the Harlem, until it was valued at more than ten times its original cost. The old shipmaster within little more than a year had won millions in personal profits without pain and proved himself a master of railroads in his own right.

An ill-timed conflict was soon stirred up by those who envied Vanderbilt his great good fortune. The politicians of the New York State Legislature, at the behest of a rival capitalist, George Law, claimed the exclusive right to grant such street-car franchises, and announced their intention of annulling Vanderbilt's privileges. He protested loudly; but the servants of the people by now had entered the game in deep fun, and meant to pluck him. They were bent on having his franchise annulled, while they sold Harlem stock short at $100 a share, a system then given greatest vogue by the operations of Daniel Drew, who was himself interested in the campaign against Vanderbilt. Scenting the plot, the shrewd Commodore had taken masses of money and bought up all the floating supply of Harlem stock, until it was cornered. Against the tactics of the Great Bear, Drew, the short sale, he had perfected the bull tactics of the corner as never before. The New York legislators were thus compelled to "stand and deliver," in greatest anguish, at the high prices to which Harlem had been driven: $179 a share! Old Vanderbilt had squeezed a million out of the politicians and their accomplices, half of it, according to general opinion, being taken from the hitherto invincible Daniel Drew. Appeals for mercy had been vain. Vanderbilt, as unrelenting as he was imperturbable, played whist while his enemies stripped themselves of their cash for him. The memorable Harlem stock corner of 1864 provided a general sensation for the public; Vanderbilt was regarded with awe, and his railroading science was considered nothing less than miraculous.

Once launched, Vanderbilt now marched vigorouslv upon a triumphant line of expansion. His overweening desire was to sweep in more adjoining railroad properties, to be combined with his profitable Harlem into a larger system. first he fixed upon the Hudson River Railroad which ran parallel to his own northward line, along the east shore of the river.[6]

Again the servants of the people barred his way; this time there were curious complaints that the new baron of railroads was bent upon creating a "monopoly." And once more the local statesmen demanded the usual inducements to soften their opposition. Vanderbilt according to his court-historians went to Albany with Mr. William Tweed, "and bent the whole force of his powerful personality to the task of obtaining authorization for the union of the roads." For a time the Hudson River Railroad stock advanced buoyantly, from $25 toward $150—then suddenly despite Vanderbilt's "induce-

---

[6]Croffut, official biographer of the Vanderbilt family, has summarized well the Commodore's railroading technique:

"1, buy your railroad; 2, stop the stealing that went on under the other man; 3, improve it in every practicable way within a reasonable expenditure; 4, consolidate it with any other road that can be run with it economically; 5, water its stock; 6, make it pay a large dividend."

ments" to the legislators, wild rumors ran about of heavy counter-
bidding by enemy interests in Albany. Soon the hand of the deep
Daniel Drew was perceived as, thirsting for vengeance, he smashed
the Vanderbilt stocks in a furious bear raid, while it was now reported that the busy lawgivers were repudiating their consent to
the railroad combination, betraying their trust and under Drew's
lead selling Vanderbilt's stocks short in a grand effort to bring
him to ruin.

"This was probably the darkest hour of the Commodore's life,"
Clews relates. "He hardly knew which way to turn. He was on the
ragged edge. He has often pathetically described his feelings at this
crisis to his intimate friends."

He stood fast, however; continued to play whist imperturbably
at 10 Washington Place while he secretly raised a $5,000,000 "pool"
among his associates to buy in all the Harlem offered. The nervous
weeks succeeded themselves, while prices held up or advanced
slowly, the Harlem stock was cornered and hidden away in strong
boxes, and the politicians and the Drew crowd grew bewildered,
"maddened."

"Don't them fellows need a dressin'?" Vanderbilt cried as he ordered his brokers to buy all stock available. His opponents had sold
more stock than actually existed. When Harlem reached 285, he
exclaimed: "Put it up to a thousand! This panel game is being tried
too often." But finally he relented and agreed to settle with his adversaries at 285, when it was indicated to him that the whole financial district would suspend operations if he continued on his course.

The lesson of it all is contained in the famous couplet attributed
to Daniel Drew:

> He who sells what isn't his'n
> Must buy it back or go to pris'n.

Vanderbilt had laid his enemies low. In his own strongly flavored
words, he had "busted the whole legislature, and scores of the
Honorable members had to go home from Albany without paying
their board bills."

In the succeeding years everything seemed to favor his bold conquests, "even the presence of desolating war," as his apologist says.
With the great capital at his command, and groups of capitalists

ready to follow him, he reached out easily for other steam highways running through the state of New York. The old New York Central, running between Albany and Buffalo, he captured by flank movements rather than by direct aggression. When its owners resisted his offer for control, he suddenly in midwinter broke connections between his own lines and the Central at the Albany bridge, refusing to handle any freight and passenger transfers. Passengers bound for New York were then compelled to walk across the frozen river from the west bank, into Albany.

At the ensuing investigation by the legislature, to which the New York Central appealed, Vanderbilt was obdurate, replying serenely that he knew nothing of what had transpired. "I was not there, gentlemen," he said. "I was at home playing a rubber of whist, and I never allow anything to interfere with me when I am playing that game. It requires as you know undivided attention."

His lawyers cited an old law which legalized his action, formerly enacted at the instance of his enemies. To those who protested at the inconvenience caused the public, the Commodore exclaimed impatiently: "*Can't I do what I want with my own?*"

Throttled, the group in control of the Central, including William Astor and Edward Cunard, surrendered to Vanderbilt, and prayed him to lead in their interests. Here was born the amalgamated New York Central trunk line, running between the seaboard and the Great Lakes.

He who had entered the fray, probably through zest for "cornering" opponents in the stock market, now expanded his railroad empire rapidly by acquiring broken-down companies, the pieces of which fell into his hands without resistance and "for a song." He added new lines, unified the whole network into one profitable machine of what seemed enormous dimensions in those days, and created a new scale, a new tempo of industrial enterprise, much as Jay Cooke had discovered new dimensions of public finance. Cornelius Vanderbilt was one of the first modern captains of industry.

He had no recognizable system for running his railroads; his books were kept in his head, or in an old cigar box, according to some reports; yet so parsimonious, so stern in management was he that he was never known to lose a day's interest on the smallest sums. He was prudent as well as bold; he would invest neither in steamships nor in steam locomotives in their pioneering stage. But once he had judged an affair to be in the fruitful stage, once entered upon it, he drove himself, men, and things with reckless energy, and with an indifference to established custom and law which stood him in good stead.

"What do I care about the law? Hain't I got the power?"

There was one sense in which Vanderbilt's prophetic "vision" has received less than its just estimate. This was in his valuation of the consolidated properties he amassed. When on May 20, 1869, he secured by the passage of one bill the right to combine all his road's with the New York Central system, as well as certain perpetual franchises, he recapitalized the new corporation at nearly twice its previous market value by ordering a stock dividend of 80 per cent, or $44,000,000. Croffut relates:

> *One night, at midnight, he carried away from the office of Horace F. Clark, his son-in-law, $6,000,000 in greenbacks as a part of his share of the profits. And he had $20,000,000, more in new stock.*

Thus Vanderbilt would appear one of the pioneers in the "watering" of stock, upon a scale also unknown before him. C. F. Adams, Jr., counted over $53,000,000 of "water" in the New York Central system by 1873, and held that "$50,000 of absolute water had been poured out for each mile of road between New York and Buffalo." But the Commodore, though he was to be abused by posterity, could pride himself upon being one of the innovators of modem corporate tactics: the capitalization according to *earnings* rather than in ratio to actual assets. Thus the Commodore was not deluded in his huge estimates; his claims for the future seem indeed modest. The so-called watered stock took account of the boundless values which adhered to his property through its completion as a supreme monopoly over common highways of trade "greater than the Appian Way."[7]

7In merging the New York & Harlem and the Hudson River railroads, there was a striking disparity in the franchises of each railroad which presented its problem. The Harlem had a franchise for 999 years; the Hudson for only 50 years; but in combining the two roads Vanderbilt's lawyers held that the longer lease of the Harlem (999 years) also applied to the franchise of the combined road. And in the course of time this view was upheld by the courts, although no legislative act sanctioned it. Questioned by a committee in after years upon this point, the Vanderbilt lawyers rested the case for their fran-

"Unconsciously to himself," as Charles Francis Adams, Jr., son of the Ambassador to England, commented at the time, "working more wisely than he knew, Vanderbilt had developed to its logical conclusion one potent element of modern civilization." He had taken the way of "imperialism" or monopoly which, in 1867, was almost a new, unseen force in the American economy. Step by step, from the manipulation of small railroad stocks, he had advanced to succeeding phases of combination, wresting profits many times the millions he originally possessed in short order, until his system of iron rails was fixed in the industrial heart of the country, all entrenched at its key positions. During the first stage of the wartime economic revolution, it was already perceptible that the railroads would have supreme power over all enterprise, provided they achieved a size consonant with the natural dominance of the vital transportation medium. And now, at the close of the great war, "bent upon fully gratifying his great instinct for developing imperialism in corporate life," he pressed in every direction along a broad front.

It was not that he saw his trunk line extending to the most distant frontiers, as John Moody, lauding his vision, believes. Indeed he at first opposed, with alarm, going west of Buffalo, saying, "If we take hold of roads running all the way to Chicago, we might as well go to San Francisco and to China." But circumstances altered his plans. The race for markets soon extended to Chicago; and his position must be made secure from all aggression. Then he could levy such tariffs as he pleased, like the medieval barons of the toll roads who taxed all who passed through their domains, all the population, all the divers industries of a broad section.[8] But to ensure this

chise for the combined system *upon the precedent of a court case.* A member of the investigating committee was Dr. Charles A. Beard, who has kindly called my attention to this incident. The Vanderbilts used the law of the land (legislative acts) as far as possible; but where this did not cover sufficiently, they used the court.

[8]To a few eyes it became perceptible shortly after the Civil War that the Vanderbilts would have a power of life and death over industry and distribution. It was known for instance that great shippers, such as the dry-goods merchant A. T. Stewart, received lower rates than small rivals, by its command of quantity service, thus permitting the great emporium to outdistance its competitors at an accelerating pace.

"What would be the result," a New York newspaper comments in 1868, "if Mr. Vanderbilt were to obtain the control of the Erie as he has of the Central control he must continue relentlessly to crush out all opposition which, by offering a competing service, or holding similar key positions or near-by strongholds, threatened the prosperity of his system of iron.

Early in his impetuous career he had come to blows with Drew, the chief of the Erie trunk line. When he had sought to raise freight rates on his own system, the Erie would counter with rates 20 per cent lower. When he had severed connections with the New York Central at Albany, the gentlemen of that road had been able to divert traffic to Drew's river steamboats, thwarting Vanderbilt's attack until the river froze over and the boats could no longer run. Now in his line of march westward, the Erie again attempted to balk him at every step. The Erie was a "guerilla," he said. He had become convinced at length that to have order he must "absorb" and control the rival trunk line himself, and in fact, began buying its shares after 1866. Pursuing his usual abrupt tactics, he commanded the purchase of Erie shares continually in the open market, hoping perhaps to "corner" Erie as he had done in the Harlem pool. But here to his rage and mortification he clashed with the wiliest, most resourceful, most ruthless of adversaries, in combination against him: the sanctimonious and treacherous Drew, the fearless Jim Fisk, the impassive, stealthy Jay Gould.

An "irrepressible conflict" between these two forces was at hand; its aspects of violence, melodrama and low comedy—as they now appear to us—were to convulse the whole care-free nation. But though the struggle was waged now in the underworld and now on an *opéra-bouffe* stage, its prize, which so few saw or comprehended at the time, was actually the rule of an economic empire. And the more he was balked by the precious trio of slippery, conscienceless Erie "guerillas," as he called them, the more furious, the more conscienceless became the onslaughts of the colossus, Vanderbilt.

road, may be judged by the policy he has adopted since the latter fell into his possession. He has so raised the price of freights from this city to the various towns along its line that it costs as much to carry goods from here to Syracuse, Rochester and other such places as is does to carry them to . . . Chicago."

CHAPTER FOUR

THE WINNING OF THE WEST

THAT a million men could return at once to the arts of peace, after Appomattox, showed clearly the immensity of the tasks to be done, the new machinery to be created—banks, mines, furnaces, shops, power houses—if the New Americans of 1865 would make their continent habitable. At the moment, as Henry Adams remembers it, they knew that they must remake a world of their own, upon a new scale of power, where figuratively they had not yet created a road or even learned to dig their own iron. "They had no time for thought," he tells us, "save for that single fraction called a railway system." This alone would require the energies of a generation. "The generation between 1865 and 1895 was already mortgaged to the railways and no one knew it better than the generation itself."

Mortgaged, but without regret. When the news of Lee's surrender was telegraphed everywhere, the numberless volunteers for the industrial revolution, as the Beards have written, "leaped forward as strong runners to the race." The returned soldiers poured into the newly opened oil fields of Pennsylvania, the mines of Nevada and California; they tilled the free land of the Mississippi Valley and of the Northwest; they manned a thousand new industries which made the iron, steam and smoke of the next decade; but in whole legions they lent their "oceanic, variegated, intense practical energies" to the building of the transcontinental railroads. (Here, as everywhere else, the forehanded young men who were to be their leaders had usually preceded them by at least four years.)

In exploiting their Great West the generation of the Civil War seemed as warlike as ever. Here in the open prairies and mountains the sweeping transition from a colonial and agrarian state of economy to an advanced phase of large-scale industry—all the swifter because so long retarded—seemed far more picturesque than its counterpart in the foot-worn marketplaces of the Eastern cities. The protagonists, armed to the teeth, flouting law, reckless of danger as of cost in gold and blood, seemed afterward both more "primitive" and more "heroic" than their circumspect contemporaries east of the Mississippi. The Western "empire-builders" were often dramatized as latter-day *Conquistadores* who had accomplished the "winning of the West"; and the poet Walt Whitman, writing at this time his "Democratic Vistas," saluted their "extreme business energy, and . . . almost maniacal appetite for wealth . . . as parts of amelioration and progress, needed to prepare the very results I demand"!

The whole symbolism of this era attached itself to the construction of the transcontinental or Pacific railroads more than to any other of its multifarious activities. By spanning the continent between the two oceans, the nation was to be physically unified at last, its natural resources thoroughly absorbed, its Manifest Destiny achieved. Hence "the winning of the West," by means of the transcontinental railroads, represented the heart and soul of the national industrial plan which engaged the whole people between 1865 and 1873. As in socialist Russia today, the vigorous progress of the railroad-builders delighted the popular imagination, was reported day by day in the newspapers of the principal cities, was attended with holiday-making, music and public orations in the towns along their line of march.

How was this plan to be carried out, how were the great railroad undertakings to be effected in the sparsely settled, virgin territories then known as "the Great American Desert," where for a long time the traffic must remain unprofitable? A generation before the visionary Thomas Benton had urged Congress to build the Pacific Railroad "as a national work, on a scale commensurate with its grandeur," the use of it to be let out to companies, who would fetch and carry on the best terms. But by 1853, Stephen Douglas had convinced everyone that the Pacific Railroad should be built by private enterprise. To encourage such construction large pieces of the public domain, all the Western territories belonging to the republic, could be detached and turned over to the railroad-builders. These resources a John Quincy Adams had wished to retain for the nourishment and profit of the citizens at large. But the view that the untaxed lands of the government should be turned over to private enterprise gained adherents in every quarter. After the enactment of Lincoln's Homestead Act, it was but a logical step to the grant of lands for the railroad systems projected during the war, and further of all the stone and timber on the lands they traversed, and of huge subsidies in cash or bonds. In this way canal-building had been encouraged earlier by the federal and state governments; and when as in Illinois, by 1850, a railroad was favored instead of a canal, the land was donated to the railroad.[1] Thus, for at least ten years before 1861 the railroads, especially in the West, were "land companies" which acquired their principal raw material through pure grants in return for their promise to build, and whose directors, combined with friendly statesmen such as Douglas, did a rushing land business in farm lands and town sites at rising prices. The technique of railroad-building was thoroughly established by 1862, when the war government with great haste passed the Pacific Railroad bill.[2]

A swarm of interested entrepreneurs buzzed about the corridors

[1] Inasmuch as the railroad lands, received without cost, could be disposed of at from $1.25 to $30 an acre by the promoters of "chains of cities," there was clearly room for private initiative and enterprise. But where the risks to capital were considered too great, the local, state or national government often underwrote the venture further by issuing bonds, which were an obligation upon the community or nation thereafter, and turning these over to the railroad captains. William Z. Ripley, an authority in this field, estimates conservatively that three-fifths of the cost of the railroads was originally borne by government, some $707,000,000 in cash, $335,000,000 in land; while recent historians, Hacker and Kendrick, in "The United States since 1865," estimate that the American railway system could scarcely have been developed "had it not been for the generosity of the federal, state and local governments."

[2] First, the railroad was organized by the "projectors" upon a blue print, and a charter obtained, involving free land grants, sometimes in alternate sections running from six to ten miles on either side of the line. Then a land company, owned by the directors of the railroad, was incorporated to develop and sell its lands. With the proceeds of the land sales, in addition to that from government subsidies, and finally from the sale of mortgage bonds in Europe, building was begun. This in turn was done by a construction company, also owned by the directors, and with a characteristic abandon, a fearlessness of high cost or error, that the early railroad-builders were famous for. Loss through extravagance by the construction company was borne with composure, since it affected nothing but the future of the railroad, whose capital stock usually represented nothing and cost the directors of the enterprise nothing.

of Congress in the early days of the war in behalf of their favorite projects. Among them were respectable Yankee manufacturers of shovels (that would be needed to dig the roadbed), such as the Ames brothers; financiers from New York, such as John J. Cisco, August Belmont and Thomas Durant; light-headed visionaries such as Josiah Perham, promoter of "Perham's People's Pacific," and George F. Train, the inveterate land and town boomer; shrewd railroad managers like Thomas Scott and J. Edgar Thomson of the Pennsylvania company; and storekeepers from the Sacramento Valley, such as Collis P. Huntington, the former watch-peddler, who represented himself as the head of the Central Pacific Railroad of California, capitalized at $8,500,000, but with nothing paid in. These men whispered in corners to the friendly and interested Congressmen, chorusing their demands for land, rights of way, and government bonds, reporting the clamor of the settlers for railroad lines, estimating the fabulous profits through land and construction work which might be won and promising much of these profits to those who entered the affair, whether they were plain citizens or Senators. . . . It was among these first comers that the railroad captains were recruited for the great cause. And the Congressmen who had the courage to help them at the start, afterward known as "Railway Congressmen," were also ready to take their part, though not too publicly, and expected their rewards.

In short order the Pacific Railroad bill was passed, and the two companies which undertook the colossal affair were given federal charters. The Union Pacific, building westward from the Missouri River, was granted 12,000,000 acres of unknown land, in alternate sections ten miles deep, and also $27,000,000 in 6 per cent, thirty-year government bonds as a first mortgage. The Central Pacific, building from the sea eastward to meet the Union Pacific, was similarly granted 9,000,000 acres of land and $24,000,000 in government bonds. Senator Henry Wilson of Massachusetts cried:

> *I give no grudging vote in giving away either money or land. I would sink $100,000,000 to build the road and do it most cheerfully, and think I had done a great thing for my country. What are $75,-000,000 or $100,000,000 in opening a railroad across regions of this continent, that shall connect the people of the Atlantic and the Pa-*

cific, and bind us together. . . . Nothing! As to the lands, I don't begrudge them.[3]

Soon afterward the enthusiastic lawgivers donated 18,000,000 acres of land to the group headed by Thomas Scott, who proposed to build the Texas & Pacific Railroad along the Mexican border; and 47,000,000 acres to another patriotic gentleman, Josiah Perham of Boston, who declared himself ready to build the Northern Pacific Railroad along the Canadian border. This and much more was freely given until 158,293,000 acres were disposed of, as much as whole kingdoms owned, and all the coal, copper, oil, gold, silver under them, all the timber and stone above them. But what was that? Nothing if only the people of the Atlantic and Pacific might be united.

Men like Collis Huntington, Durant, the Ames brothers concealed their joy as well as they could. Huntington hastened to send the triumphant but cryptic message to his partner, Leland Stanford:

We have drawn the Elephant.

Truly it was a majestic booty, an elephantine plunder that fell almost unheeded into the hands of Huntington and his associates. Certain tribunes of the people, those often styled "demagogues," protested a little, though they were soon overborne. A Senator Grimes might be heard exclaiming that "nearly all the grants of lands to railroads and wagon-roads find their way into the hands of rich capitalists." A correspondent for the *New York World* went so far as to picture the lobbyists and agents of the Northern Pacific ring, sitting in the galleries of Congress while the railroad bills were being passed, "looking down on the scene like beasts of prey."

[3]The use of public lands to promote economic development had long been advocated by the leaders of all parties. As long ago as 1828, Daniel Webster had said in a speech at Faneuil Hall:
"In most of these new States of the West, the United States are yet the proprietors of vast bodies of lands. Through some of these states and through some of these same public lands, the local authorities have prepared to carry expensive canals for the general benefit of the country. Some of these undertakings have been attended with great expense, and have subjected the States to large debts and heavy taxation. The lands of the United States being exempted from all taxation, of course, bear no part of this burden. Looking at the United States, therefore, as a great landed proprietor, essentially benefited by these improvements, I have felt no difficulty in voting for appropriation parts of these lands as a reasonable contribution by the United States to these general objects." (*"Works,"* Vol. 1, p. 169.)

President Andrew Johnson, an old commoner, warned in his speeches in 1866 that "an aristocracy based on nearly two billions and a half of national securities has arisen in the Northern States to assume that political control which the consolidation of great financial and political interests formerly gave to the slave oligarchy. The war of finance is the next war we have to fight." By such words, Lincoln's successor only added to the fury of the storm against him; for the war party, waving the bloody shirt, the triumph of its armies must be surmounted with the triumph of the Northern industrial economy.

Soon General Grant, for whose election everybody worked, as Henry Clews said, "because Wall Street business would boom," was to put an end to such animadversions as Johnson's. Smoking his favorite cigars in the palace of Jay Cooke, frequenting Jim Fisk and Jay Gould with a stolid delight, dazzled by the splendor of wealth as he was impressed by masses of artillery, Grant suffered the mounting "preëmptions" of his régime without a shadow of alarm. He knew only that the people wanted railroads; and Huntington was ready to build them at his own terms. He could hardly have seen that parallel between the Great Barbecue of his time and the upheavals of feudal ages—between the transfer of ownership, by the popular sovereignty in America, in lands, forests, mineral deposits, harbor rights, franchises, to a small group of strong men, and the ancient acts of seizure by force and collusion—an analogy which was not drawn until nearly thirty years later by the philosophic Thorstein Veblen. Here certainly began that "absentee ownership" which rested thereafter upon a form of "divine right" as certainly as did the ancient feudalistic ground of "privilege and prescriptive tenure," which is always traceable to seizure by force and collusion. Thenceforth the lords of these rich principalities or baronies, in railroads, oil, silver, copper, or iron, would own them, like the barons of old, as Veblen observed, "not by virtue of having produced or earned them . . . but because they own them."

2

In the remote California valleys news of the chartering of a Pacific railroad was received with jubilation by the Forty-niners. There, as everywhere else on the moving frontier, the settler cried for railroads; "no music was sweeter to his ears than the whistle of the locomotive," it was said. Through the state or territorial governments he pressed subsidies upon the promoters of such schemes; town and county officials vied with each other to distribute lands, terminal sites, and even cash payments, raised by assessment. In California as throughout the prairies beyond the Mississippi, the coming of the Iron Horse meant to the squatter that he could, after skimming his land, sell it for subdivision and depart westward once again.

The completion of the long-desired transcontinental railroad climaxed the heroic age of the frontier and has remained a famous affair in our history, thanks to the celebrity of the Crédit Mobilier ring after 1871. But this *cause célèbre* related only to the eastward half (Union Pacific). The adventure of Huntington and his partners in building the western half of the line, the Central Pacific, as it was then known, across the Sierras to a junction near Great Salt Lake, easily merits an equal fame.

By 1860, Collis Huntington operated with great profit a large hardware store in Sacramento, in partnership with another pioneer from the East named Mark Hopkins. At this time the pair made the acquaintance of Leland Stanford, another aggressive figure of "virile power" who had also prospered by means of a store in San Francisco. Thanks to his previous legal training, Stanford became active in politics, attended the Republican presidential convention of 1860 as a delegate, and had himself elected governor of California the following year. These three were joined by a former peddler, ironworker and gold-miner, Charles Crocker, forming the Pacific Associates, to engage in business ventures together. The "quartet," as they were often called, worked together in silence and tolerable harmony for a long period of years. Their abilities complemented each other. Huntington dominated the group, cool-headed, a tireless worker, bold and persistent, trusting no one, owning few friends; also, according to Daggett's partial account of him in his history of the Southern Pacific, he was reputed to be narrow, ruthless, untruthful, sarcastic, vindictive. Stanford, on the other hand, showed political sagacity in handling their relations with public and government. More vain and extravagant than Huntington, avid of public honors, he wielded political influence with subtlety not only at Sacramento, but also even at the National Capitol to which he came as Senator from California in 1887. It was said of him that "no she-lion defending her whelps or a bear her cubs will make a more savage fight than will Mr. Stanford in defense of his material interests." Hopkins, in contrast with the others, was quiet, methodical, close-mouthed, always busy poring over their books, worrying over detail, the "inside man" for their operations. Charles Crocker, also something of a petty politician, was most useful outside, a huge, squat figure, weighing 265 pounds, driving forward their vast construction work, "always roaring up and down like a mad bull." All of these men had made money quickly, at their trade. Huntington and Stanford had each accumulated about $100,000 after only a few years in California. If the four men ever quarreled, out of jealousy or mutual fear, their dissension was kept silent; they bore their consciences in common, kept each other's secrets and preserved an unbroken discipline against the common enemy, wherever he might be.

An engineer named Judah, enflamed with the vision of a transcontinental road, held meetings in San Francisco in 1859 and 1860, at which he described his project in detail, outlining routes and gradients across the mountains. The Pacific Associates, attending one of Judah's meetings, questioned him earnestly, heard him with excitement and from 1860 on laid their plans to have state and national subsidies turned over to them so that they might create the great iron highway to the East.

On horseback, Huntington and Crocker and Stanford, accompanied by the engineer, spied the ground, ascended the mountains of the coast range searching for the best routes leading eastward through the Nevada mining camps which they desired to link with the sea. At the top of the mountains, they halted, sat down and looked out at their wilderness of an empire. "At their feet was a precipice dropping down perpendicularly a quarter of a mile," according to a Californian's account. Never before in the memory of man had such a project been attempted. The engineer, Judah, though his actual experience was slight, assured them that it could be done—*if government aid were obtained.* For the cost would be terrible.

Was there money in it? "What should two dry-goods merchants and two dealers in hardware, who knew nothing at first hand of railroad operations," asks Daggett, "have cared about the administration of a railroad 800 miles long?"—that is to say, longer than any yet known to man. But they saw great business—with the mining communities where "the glittering piles of gold and silver were to be seen from afar," heaped up like bricks and stones at the mouth of the Bonanza mines, now connected only by mule with the seacoast. Hopefully they estimated the future traffic that would flow through their strong, close-fisted hands. They had little money, not $200,000 between them for the awful project. Yet they went on. Most of their capital the black-bearded Collis Huntington carried silently with him in his trunk, with his blue prints, on his delicate mission to Washington in 1861. In an incredibly short time he had won the prized federal charter for their Central Pacific Railroad.

A charter, and the federal government's promise to pay in bonds for work in progress, at a rate running from $16,000 plus land grants over plains, to $48,000 for construction in the mountains, this was all that the empire-builders had; for Huntington in the Capitol had exhausted their whole initial fund of $200,000 in a manner of which he left no record. The local financiers, members of the San Francisco "bank ring," among them Darius Ogden Mills, as well as the Bonanza kings of the Comstock, refused to invest in Huntington and Stanford's railroad. "Why should we," they said, "if we can get 24 per cent on our money here now in San Francisco?"

Desperately hungry for money, the four confederates now fortunately developed a variety of tactics which yielded them a continual flood. Setting aside the first mortgage they had issued to the federal government, they began selling bonds of their own; ultimately, over a long period of years some $27,000,000 was raised in this way. Then through the efforts of Stanford, who was now governor of the young state of California, they invoked the support of the state government and of the towns and counties along their route.

In May, 1863, a few weeks after building of the road had begun, elections were held in San Francisco over the question of a bond issue of $3,000,000 to be donated to the Central Pacific Railroad. Philip Stanford, brother of the Governor, drove up to the polls in a buggy. Calling on the crowd which swarmed about him to vote for the bond issue, he drew gold pieces from a bag beside him and strewed them all around. The bond issue was voted by the people.

Confronted with all the awkward delays and uncertainties inherent in democratic institutions, the Associates, who were compelled to act with promptitude and union in such a great public work, quickly developed a technique of political action such as the situation demanded and, indeed, justified in their eyes. Breaches were opened in the defenses of the law; clubs were improvised to swing over the heads of a constituency unaware of its interest and slow or doubtful in its policy. Where, in the East, Vanderbilt, then Fisk and Gould, found it most useful to work through intermediaries, such as William Tweed, who provided the expert political machinery necessary under universal suffrage, the Western empire-builders, simpler and ruder men, and by far less devious, seized upon this machinery themselves. The technique of this remarkable control, which will be discussed presently under another heading, involved a close control of the political and industrial interest of the group in order to overcome obstacles of all sorts. Soon the Pacific Associates wielded a tremendous power of "reward and punishment," now propitiating, now menacing their opposition.

"It has cost money to fix things," Huntington would say in his intramural correspondence, which he ordered burnt after being read. The passage of a bill involved "arguments" in the form of considerable sums of cash: "I believe with $200,000 we can pass our bill," he wrote in one instance from Washington. He always calculated values nicely. The rights thus acquired would then be used in the bold and lavish Huntington-Stanford manner to evoke further drafts of capital. One by one the various communities and counties along the way were lined up, and their greed and fear of each other played upon adroitly. Soon San Francisco, Stockton, Sacramento, and other towns were all compelled to give rights of way, terminal and harbor sites, and to make stock or bond subscriptions ranging from $150,000 to $1,000,000—the last sum being levied upon San Francisco. Thus Huntington wrote in 1871 to his comrades that the Central Pacific was "out to get a lot of money from interested parties along the line between the Spadra and San Gregorio pass, if it would build the railroad." His methods were clearly described by a member of the Constitutional Convention of 1878, who said:

> They start out their railway track and survey their line near a thriving village. They go to the most prominent citizens of that vil-

*lage and say, "If you will give us so many thousand dollars we will
run through here; if you do not we will run by." And in every instance where the subsidy was not granted this course was taken, and
the effect was just as they said, to kill off the little town.*

In moving accents the speaker dwelt upon the ruinous freezing-
out of "Paradise, Stanislaus County," which was overnight turned
into "Poverty Flat" through the deliberate establishment of a depot,
and hence another town, four miles further along the line, because
the railroad "did not get what they wanted." Then using the blunt-
est terms he charged: "They have blackmailed Los Angeles County
$230,000 as a condition of doing that which the law compelled them
to do." Huntington, whatever his feelings in the matter, would have
smiled inwardly at the underestimate of his work.

In 1868, the former "pueblo" of Los Angeles in Southern California, feeling its present circumstances confining and its future
career vast, gave financial assistance to the construction of the Los
Angeles & San Pedro Railroad. When shortly thereafter it was
learned that the Pacific Associates were planning a new railroad
line from San Francisco, by a southerly route, to the East, the citizens of Los Angeles clamored to have the line pass through their
town. The place was a potential seaport moreover, some said a future metropolis of 25,000 like San Francisco, though it had only
6,000 population. Collis P. Huntington, head of the proposed subsidiary, the "Southern Pacific," then announced his terms: Let the
railroad be given 5 per cent of the assessed valuation of all Los
Angeles County. To this the citizens readily agreed. They passed
over to the Southern Pacific $200,000 in stock of the Los Angeles
& San Pedro Railroad, about $377,000 in cash (through an issue of
municipal bonds), sixty acres of ground for a depot. In all these
donations amounted to more than $100 for every man, woman, child
and Indian in the town.

The levies upon the various towns and counties of California were
indispensable to the Associates, since they were operating upon a
"shoestring." In order to begin the first construction, Gustavus
Myers relates, they used the money wrested from Sacramento and
Placer County, an amount of $848,000. Then this completed, they
were able to demand the federal mileage subsidy for the first short

section. By repeating the process they were able to build the entire road without using a dollar of their own.[4]

January 8, 1863, construction was begun on the Central Pacific with the pomp and ceremony which in those days seemed to accompany every phase of development of our national industrial plan. Though it was raining hard enough over the Sacramento Valley to dampen the cheerfulest spirits, a great crowd, including hundreds of Chinese, had turned out at the levees of the river—all of them standing upon hay to keep their feet dry. Flags were waved guns were fired, a brass band made brave music; and then, at the proper moment, Governor Stanford seized a shovel and deposited the first earth for the embankment. The impetuous Crocker promptly called for nine cheers and the Central Pacific Railroad had begun building from the West Coast.

For four years, without pause, three thousand Irishmen and ten thousand Chinese coolies toiled away through desert heat and mountain cold or snow. Ever afterward, Huntington would be especially grateful to the Chinese, who worked for $1 a day, about half the wages of white men, and were ready to kill themselves for this; he was a constant advocate of unrestricted Chinese immigration, since to the muscular backs of Orientals he always attributed the successful building of a great part of the transcontinental system.

What should three dry-goods merchants and a peddler have known about building a railroad? Their engineers never found the best route for them until long years had passed. Judah's line went northward out of Sacramento, through Summit Valley and Truckee Lake in, the Central Sierras; ascending nearly 7,000 feet from water level at a steep gradient of 116 feet per mile, or 2 per cent on the average. Then it continued in a direct line to the Washoe Mountain mining region, near Carson City, across Nevada, through Humboldt

[4]"A railroad company approaches a small town as a highwayman approaches his victim. The threat, 'If you do not accede to our terms we will leave your town two or three miles to one side!' is as efficacious as the 'Stand and deliver' when backed by a cocked pistol. For the threat of the railroad company is not merely to deprive the town of the benefits which the railroad might give; it is to put it in a far worse position than if no railroad had been built.... And just as robbers unite to plunder in concert and divide the spoil, so do the trunk lines of railroads unite to raise rates and pool their earnings or the Pacific roads form a combination with the Pacific Mail Steamship Company by which toll gates are virtually established on land and ocean." Henry George, "Progress and Poverty," 1879, pp. 192–193.

Sink to the Great Salt Lake of Utah. A superior route, forty miles to the north, at Beckwourth Pass, was ignored; it rose at the maximum to a height that was 2,000 feet, lower than the other pass, and its grade averaged 1 per cent.

The work was carried on with a heedless abandon. It was sometimes found necessary to shift whole sections of the mountain line from one side of a valley to the other. In the severe winter weather of the mountain summits, tunnels had to be driven by the workers through the snow to the rock face, snow-sheds and galleries improvised to prevent settling, blasting operations had to be done over frozen ground, which must be reworked in the spring thaw. The haste of this great railroad construction—paralleled by the Union Pacific to the eastward—was afterward estimated by government experts to have caused a waste of between 70 and 75 per cent of the expenditure as against the normal rate of construction. Yet at the time there was little bewailing the cost of the American system of empire-building by private enterprise, owing to the general enthusiasm which attended its progress everywhere throughout the young and growing industrial nation. Like the enthusiastic Senator from Massachusetts, no one regretted the railroads' cost, and like the honorable Senator everyone hurried to invest if he could in the stocks of the construction companies which gave them life.

For the tremendous waste was due to no stupidity on the part of the Huntington ring, who carefully spared themselves from loss by ingenious safeguards. Before they had proceeded a hundred miles, they resorted to the clever corporate device also used by the Union Pacific ring, of creating a separate construction company, called the "Credit & Finance Corporation," which had sole right to purchase all material and carry out all building work for their road. It was to an *alter ego* of the Central Pacific, of which Huntington, Stanford, Crocker and Hopkins were the sole directors and stockholders, that approximately $79,000,000 in bonds, stock and cash received from government and investors were paid over for building work. Of this sum experts later estimated that upward of $36,000,000 was in excess of a reasonable cost of the affair, and was lost entirely, that is "lost" to the same principals. But this estimate does not include the value of water frontage, as in Oakland and other river and coast cities, which fell into the hands of the Associates.

The great losses, fixed in an enduring capitalization, would be borne by future ages of Americans, but naturally concerned the enthusiastic railroad captains little at the moment. There were instances where in their strenuous progress they encountered existing lines, such as the Sacramento Valley Railroad built for a short distance in 1859, through a rich region. Faced with the option of buying, they instead built their own line around it, over a somewhat lengthier distance in a queer and crazy course through the same valley, "because it was cheaper to build at the government expense than to buy a railroad already existing...." The fruits of the great project went to the construction company, one authority holds. "The Federal government seems . . . to have assumed the major portion of the risk and the Associates seem to have derived the profits."

Power such as they had foreseen but dimly came to the hands of the empire-builders as their railroad advanced and the Pacific Slope grew in wealth and population. The rugged topography of the state lent itself to their plans. By seizing one valley, or the passageway to it, they brought an adjacent one into their effective control, as the medieval barons had done of old by setting their castles upon the heights overlooking the rivers of Europe, or closing the mountain passes. Their network of branch lines was spread throughout the Pacific Slope, through the payment of proper ransoms by the communities which required such outlets as a matter of life and death. But more ingenious, the new barons who held the only overland route to the Pacific connected these lines with water-front facilities, which they, upon a large scale, wrested from the coast cities by the threat of extinction. Thus they would be in position to deal with the competition of the sea-carrying trade.

Traffic was sparse to begin with, but this mounted steadily, as the rich lands they held were purchased and cultivated by new immigrants, and as the people of the West Coast, "joying and sorrowing," at labor and love-making, brought forth innumerable children. The millions of acres of forest, ranch and vineyard owned by the quartet rose to incalculable value. But with the immense wealth and power they had gained, which as they now comprehended was nothing less than that of monopoly, the Huntington ring held passenger rates to 10 cents per mile, and made freight rates the highest in America. Through the most hazardous periods of their venture, as they pushed forward with prodigious energy and took undeniably great risks, their monopoly saved them from disaster.

No public opinion had opposed their strategy. Those who tended to complain of high prices, or protest against their monopoly of the vital highways of all trade, were as likely to seek positions of advantage to themselves in the new hierarchy, according to contemporary report. The complaisance of the population, their approval of the great construction, is reflected in the success of the tactics which Huntington and Stanford employed.

Nothing checked the hegemony of the quartet over the whole coast region nor limited the mounting tributes paid to them from all quarters, once they had made juncture with the eastern half of the Pacific Railroad; nothing save the approach of other barons who designed to capture their Western fastnesses themselves. Wary, sleeplessly vigilant, Collis Huntington, the leading spirit of the group, scanned all the mountain passes through which entrance might be made, with an eternal fear. By laying aside a large part of the moneys which came to them as a "war chest" to be held in readiness for all emergencies, he set an example which other giant monopolists would follow instinctively. Then he repaired to Washington during the tumultuous years under Grant, to watch over lawmakers as well as potential rivals who clamored for charters and subsidies, and who threatened to cut into the northern and southern portions of his domain.

3

Like its western half, the Union Pacific pushed forward with unexampled speed after 1865. Winter and summer, engineers heading their armies, largely made up of war veterans, proceeded from the 100th meridian westward through the Cheyenne Pass, and laid five miles of track a day, while the Central Pacific gangs labored at almost the same speed to meet them. The whole episode, source of many picturesque legends, was rightly seen as a stirring adventure in construction into which the whole nation threw itself with all its heart once its energies had been released from war. By 1867 a horde of 20,000 laborers worked with a veritable frenzy to complete the historic task.

From the hills and behind cover the red-skinned natives watched the march of the invaders through Nebraska and Wyoming. Fortunately they did not know how to tear up the heavy iron rails which cut through their prairies like bands of pain, to grip them forever. Instead they repeatedly harried and raided the building crews, who thrust them toward the Pacific Ocean. Sometimes the marauders captured a whole train, slaughtering all its crew, smashing its locomotive and burning its cars. But the workers pressed on, armed with rifles as well as picks and axes. Before their advance through the rugged Cheyenne Pass and the Laramie Hills of Wyoming picket-lines of troops extended themselves steadily. But more than the wrath of Indians, the fearful hardships of intense heat in the desert, of extreme cold in the mountains took heavy toll of the hard-driven toilers, hundreds of whom left their bones forever along the line of the Union Pacific. Yet no misadventures, obstacles or hazards, no rigors of climate were permitted to halt the furious pace of these armies of workers who were building industrial pyramids for the new age.

The camp-settlements along the transcontinental road, fleeting cities thrown up for the winter, are always remembered, always pictured in the tableaux of these later pioneers who rested and warmed themselves here. The main street, deep in sand, ran between hasty erected shanties which held either saloons or provision stores. The regular influx of sutlers, gamblers, and prostitutes, attended with the frequent shedding of blood, gave these encampments the name "Hell-on-Wheels." For they were mobile: in the spring, the land-jobbers who had been selling subdivisions, the shrewd hucksters, tapsters and harlots would be gone, leaving the "metropolis" of yesterday to bleach silently in the sun.

Again the construction armies thundered forward through the "Great American Desert," pouring out their labor, sweat and blood in that massive blundering manner with which Grant hammered through the Wilderness of Virginia. Fearful errors were made and were expiated. Through the Laramie Hills the dead-level grade built in such prodigious haste created losses estimated up to $10,000,000. Money was borrowed by the projectors in New York and Philadelphia at 18 and 19 per cent. The soft American iron rails which were solely used at a prohibitive cost must soon be replaced by the Bessemer steel, already used in England. Yet in this patriotic project of spanning the continent, who reckoned the cost? Not the friendly government inspectors who turned their eyes away; nor the stock-holders and directors of the Crédit Mobilier in New York and Washington; nor the homesteaders who cried for railroads; nor all the laborers who had been wrought up to a wild pitch; and least of all the proud onlooking nation which had news of the affair day by day, flashed along the new telegraph lines to the world's press.

By 1867 the building forces of both lines laid on some days eight miles of track. It was not clearly determined at first where the two lines were to meet. Nearing the end their rivalry ran high; a strong spirit of hostility was communicated to the crews by the masters and engineers in charge, as each side from east or west tried to con-trol a larger share of the transcontinental system, and thus obtain a larger subsidy. Near Ogden, outside of Salt Lake City, the con-struction crews paralleled each other. The Irish workers of the Union Pacific took the competition so seriously that from their lower level they exploded blasts under the Chinese workers of Huntington's Central Pacific, which the latter returned in kind, burying several Irishmen.

At last on May 10, 1869, after five years, the two lines met at Promontory Point, Utah. Spikes of gold and silver were driven into the joining tracks, and the through lines from the Missouri River (at Omaha) to the Pacific Ocean (at San Francisco) had been com-pleted. The first locomotive from the Atlantic and the first locomo-tive from the Pacific Coast stood impassively facing each other, while music blared, orators shouted, soldiers dipped their flags and fired salvos, and Indians on horseback looked on from the edges of the crowd in mystification. The whole country, from President Grant in the White House to the newsboy who sold extras, John Moody relates, celebrated this achievement. "Chicago held a parade several miles long; in New York City the chimes of Trinity were rung; and in Philadelphia the old Liberty Bell in Independence Hall was tolled again." The nation exulting over the completion of the greatest railroad in the world, an iron bridge uniting its two mighty oceans, gave itself over to holiday-making. It was the high, youthful moment of a heroic, strenuous, constructive epoch; landmark in a gigantic national industrial plan, conducted with sublime uncon-ciousness of the cost in money and human values.

The promoters of the affair too had their reasons for celebration

These elegant, silk-hatted gentlemen, in the marketplaces of Philadelphia and New York, or the corridors of Washington, had also achieved miracles of pioneering in "high finance." Through the device of the "holding company" (borrowed from French authors of a famous "bubble") they had set up the Crédit Mobilier, into whose chest the gains from contracts for the whole Union Pacific building had flowed. During the fever of post-war prosperity Durant and the Ames brothers and their associates had been able to lift the capitalization in bonds and stocks of the railroad from an estimated $50,000,000 to $111,000,000 distributed throughout the world in the fervid manner of Jay Cooke's government loans. The proceeds from government bonds, security sales, and sales of lands and town sites had all been swallowed up in the mounting costs of building or in other ways. For this work the directors of the Union Pacific had ingeniously contracted with themselves at prices which rose from $80,000 to $90,000 and $96,000 a mile, twice the maximum estimates of engineers; so that the total cost eventually was $94,000,-000. In after years no authorities or technicians, neither engineers nor accountants would ever be able to explain satisfactorily why the railroad had cost more than $44,000,000 to build, some $50,000,-000 being left forever unaccounted for.

By chance the Union Pacific in 1864 had as its chief engineer Peter A. Dey, an able and honest technician. He estimated the cost of building the first hundred miles at $30,000 per mile, and for the second hundred miles $27,000 per mile. Durant, vice-president and active head of the company, objected strenuously to such estimates, and Dey unwillingly raised his estimate to $50,000, then suddenly resigned. The contract was then given over to one Hoxie, who followed Dey's first specification carefully, but "expended" about three times as much cash as he called for! Here alone, one may account for the disappearance of $6,000,000 in two hundred miles of construction.

Hence the jubilation of the Union Pacific ring. For what profits could they have awaited, if they had confined themselves purely to trafficking in freight or passengers through the empty prairies? They regarded themselves as "empire-builders." The affair had received the political benediction of statesmen of both parties, among them a Speaker of the House and future President, Garfield, a future Vice-President, Schuyler Colfax, and an assortment of cabinet officials, Senators and Congressmen, such as Boutwell, "Pig-Iron" Kelley, Bingham, Allison and the enthusiastic Henry Wilson. These men were the stockholders of the Crédit Mobilier, or the underlying Union Pacific, purchasing for nothing or little, through Oakes Ames, himself a representative from Massachusetts, who felt that the ownership in such a vast, patriotic venture should be distributed "where it will do most good for us." He had written privately in 1867: "We want more friends in this Congress," adding with unsurpassed worldly wisdom, "There is no difficulty in getting men to look after their own property." This Crédit Mobilier stock had cost the "Railway Congressmen" nothing. But when on December 12, 1867, the Crédit Mobilier declared its first dividend—$2,500,000 in Union Pacific bonds, and the same in stock, or 100 per cent on the capital!— Crédit Mobilier stock "boomed" to $260 a share, the enriched statesmen brimmed over with their deep "friendship"; scarcely able to hide their triumph, a crowd of millionaires emerged from the Union Pacific adventure, who were to lend character to the happily turbulent period of reconstruction and industrial revolution.

4

The tall talk concerning the Pacific Railroad projects and the land rushes they opened, the gargantuan feats of town-jobbing and stockjobbing, spreading everywhere, quickly brought imitators and formidable rivals of the first transcontinental line. Charters of all kinds were applied for in Washington and the state capitols. To the alarm of Collis Huntington, the construction of the Texas & Pacific Railroad had been authorized to a group of Pennsylvanians, headed by Thomas Scott, and including Andrew Carnegie. Then, the famous Northern Pacific charter, with its 47,000,000 acres of Northwestern land, which had been hawked about for years, suddenly in 1869 fell into the hands of Jay Cooke, the "Tycoon" himself.

The financier of the Civil War, though flushed with his glorious victories, had at first cautiously resisted the railroad fever of the day. But the astute investment of his war profits in some 40,000 acres of Minnesota land, at the present site of the city of Duluth, had led him to become interested in the railroad lines of the region, especially the new Lake Superior & Mississippi Railroad, which ran from Lake Superior to St. Paul, 140 miles distant. With their usual zestful tactics Cooke & Co. had arranged to sell $4,000,000 in bonds for this road, which were secured by the land grants it had received. In the Western land operations, Cooke's field agents reported the facts, Cooke selected the lands, in Oregon and the Northwestern wilderness, and his newspaper men wrote the songs or broadcast alluring reports of the frontier. One of these lieutenants, named Sam Wilkerson, an associate of Horace Greeley and of Henry Ward Beecher, and known as a "universal journalistic genius," wrote pamphlets for Cooke which were so impassioned, that their author confessed that he himself "wanted to go right off to Minnesota." This he had done, traveling West with a party of Cooke's partners and engineers from the Great Lakes through the country which General Sherman warned was "as bad as God ever made or anybody can scare up this side of Africa," as far as Puget Sound, the "Mediterranean of the Northwest." The whole region Wilkerson wrote back was a "vast wilderness waiting like a rich heiress to be appropriated and enjoyed." From Puget Sound he reported in perfervid accents:

> There is nothing on the American continent equal to it. Such timber—such soil—such orchards—such fish—such climate—such coal—such harbors—such rivers. . . . And the whole of it is but the Western terminus of our railroad. The empire of the Pacific Coast is to be enthroned on Puget Sound. Nothing can prevent this—nothing. . . . There is no end to the possibilities of wealth here. . . . Jay, we have got the biggest thing on earth. Our enterprise is an inexhaustible gold mine.

The rumors spread that Sam Wilkerson and his party "had found orange groves and monkeys" in his route through Idaho, Montana, and the Bad Lands of Dakota. And it is as much to his enthusiasm as to anything else that the country through which he passed was soon denominated "Jay Cooke's Banana Belt."

On the map which was unfolded to potential investors there spread in the shape of a great banana the stupendous province which had been granted to the Northern Pacific Railroad, and which by the purchase of stock control at 15 cents a share in 1869 had fallen at last into the hands of the famous banker. This domain, as large as a European kingdom, Wilkerson promised, was to be "the chained slave of the Northern Pacific Railroad"—though at the same time he begged his employer "to pray for his scalp." A swarm of adventurers and land-dealers now surrounded Cooke, beseeching him to create the new Northwest Passage, to buy iron or contract labor or bridges from them. And at last one day, while his associates flung their hats to the ceiling with joy, the Tycoon announced his determination to undertake the building of the second transcontinental railroad.

His goal was to raise $100,000,000 in bonds to finance the construction, an operation which no other American would have dared. "At his bidding the American people would lay their hoards at his feet," everyone felt. The Rothschilds whom he approached withheld their aid, with a European war clearly impending. However the most distinguished statesmen, capitalists and publicists clamored to join the $5,000,000 pool which Cooke now formed. Chief Justice Chase offered himself as president of the company at a "good salary." The roster of its stockholders included, besides numerous men of money, Schuyler Colfax, Rutherford Hayes, Hugh McCulloch, as well as Horace Greeley and Henry Ward Beecher. Greeley was put down on the subscription list for $20,000 and Beecher for $15,000, in return for which both were to exert their influence on the public mind, Beecher's efforts consisting of glowing reports in his *Christian Union*. The favorable reviews of a Philadelphia and a Washington newspaper were arranged for $4,666.66; while the private secretary of President Grant, General Horace Porter, offered his friendly offices in return for a similar consideration "with alacrity."

The Northern Pacific's franchise carried with it no money subsidies from the government, in view of the enormous quantity of land granted to it. Yet early in 1870, its friends conducted a "whirlwind lobby" in Congress, for a new Northern Pacific bill, granting many extensions of the original rights. Here they were opposed by rival interests, seeking favors for a "Southern Pacific" headed ostensibly by General Frémont, the Pathfinder, and supported by the influential Speaker James G. Blaine. But Blaine was won over by kindly services such as "a not too careful scrutiny of real estate and other unrealizable collateral" against which a loan was advanced by the Washington house of Jay Cooke & Co.; and President Grant himself, into whose confidence Cooke's brother Henry had long ago wormed himself, "was firm as a rock" in support of their bill. The Congressmen were on the alert, with the richest bankers in the country concerned in the fate of the bill; though assured that they were "furthering the cause of civilization" in the territories, many of them were found to be "hungering for arguments more substantial," as Henry Cooke said, and were contented only with fractional shares in the pool.

So the Northern Pacific bill of 1870 was rushed through, and with it an extraordinary and complex agreement, by which Jay Cooke & Co. were to be its sole fiscal agents, were to receive $200 in stock for every $1,000 bond sold, and were to sell the bonds at a fee of 12 per cent. Hard terms! Not only was the enterprise gigantic, but the reward of the bankers in fees, sections of land and town sites was estimated in sums which, a short time before, had never been known to be gathered in so few hands. In Congress, a single watchdog, Senator Harlan, protested vehemently against the practices of the railroad's land companies of locating depots wherever they pleased. "Is it not enough that you give them a vast quantity of public lands to be sold for agricultural purposes? Must they be permitted to ruin the towns and enhance their own lots?" The *Philadelphia Ledger*, controlled by Cooke's envious rival, Anthony Drexel, opened fire upon the whole scheme as another "South Sea Bubble." But these warning voices were soon overborne by the clanking and thundering of Jay Cooke's juggernaut, which was fully under way in the spring of 1870.

The building work, headed by the able railroad engineer, Milnor Roberts, was pushed rapidly through the mud of Minnesota toward the Red River at the Canadian border. Soon rumors of corruption drifted back to Philadelphia, of quarrels for favor between jealous towns, of "jackals and vultures" preying upon the road through construction companies. Cooke's own partners fulminated privately against esteemed officers who were "in a ring to get rich out of the business of furnishing supplies," or complained of gambling, liquor dens and brothels opened along the route of the empire-builders.

But the bankers through their branch in New York, Philadelphia, Washington and London were selling $1,000,000 in bonds each month, sending a soothing flood of gold to the Northwest which quieted the nerves of the railroad men. In Europe Cooke's agents pressed for a great foreign loan, inviting representatives of German and Dutch banks to Philadelphia to be dined and wined at the master's palace of Ogontz, then to be sent off upon a conducted junketing party through the territories of his railroad. These parties were sometimes carefully diverted by shrewd orders from traversing the "arid, alkaline, sage brush deserts" which might have left them fatigued and disgusted "with impressions . . . utterly impossible to dispel." Thus a few millions were wrung from the wary Germans and Dutch too, despite the ill-odor into which American railroads were now falling.

A superhuman effort, however, was necessary if savings were to be gathered from the capital-hungry Americans themselves, during times which began to be disturbed by financial earthquakes in New York, war in France, devastating fires in Chicago. For this effort, Jay Cooke, who had popularized government war bonds in every hamlet and as far off as California, where the war had been only dimly glimpsed, was ready. A mighty propaganda was unloosed by the Tycoon which was designed to further immigration, land and bond sales and whose din dominated the deep uproar of the whole era.

Cooke brought pressure to bear upon the great newspapers of the country, the *New York World, Times, Herald* and *Sun*, the *Hartford Courant*, the *Chicago Post*. The writers of these journals were caressed with a hundred delicate attentions such as invitations to his home or cases of wine from his private Catawba vineyards in Ohio. In his own banking rooms he organized a perpetual exhibition of the grains, fruits and minerals of the Northwest territories. An army of his traveling agents swept the country, including clergymen, lawyers, and shopkeepers who spread his maps, pamphlets and notices, and peddled his goods as a side line. And sometimes the Tycoon himself went on selling expeditions among masters of money in person.

Cooke and his partners had the refusal of all town sites or terminus land along the Northern Pacific route. To populate their land, they engaged agents such as the German émigré Henry Villard, who brought thousands of settlers from old Europe, causing an advance of 750 per cent in the land companies' stock. Since the 1850's, Horace Greeley, who had visited California with delight, had been shouting his slogan: "Go West!" Along the route of the

Union Pacific and the Northern Pacific, his disciples, the land-boomers, staked out new streets in many a newly erected "Olympia" or "Paris" or "Athens" and wrote home countless letters calling all their friends to join them. For the Northern Pacific, men like Sam Wilkerson advertised the climate of the Northwest region as "a cross between Paris and Venice," while on behalf of the Union Pacific and its land company, the Crédit Foncier announcements were inserted in newspapers throughout the country which read as follows:

> *Prosperity, Independence, Freedom, Manhood in its highest sense, peace of mind and all the comforts and luxuries of life are awaiting you. . . . Throw down the yardstick and come out here if you would be men. Bid good-by to the theater and turn your backs on the crowd in the street!*

> *How many regret the non-purchase of that lot in Buffalo, that acre in Chicago, that quarter-section in Omaha? A $50 lot may prove a $5,000 investment.*

PARIS TO PEKIN IN THIRTY DAYS

> *Passengers for China this way! . . . The Rocky Mountain excursion of statesmen and capitalists pronounce the Pacific Railroad a great fact. . . . The Crédit Mobilier a national reality, the Crédit Foncier an American institution.*

But the noise made by Jay Cooke was greater by far. The maps, the pamphlets distributed everywhere made Jay Cooke's "Banana Belt" universally celebrated, while Duluth was immortalized as the "Zenith City of the Unsalted Seas." So filled up were the people, the historian Oberholtzer relates, with "isothermal lines, comparative latitudes and glowing facts about climates, crops and distances from New York, Liverpool and Shanghai of new cities set in concentric circles upon the American Northwest," that they were growing weary of such legends, and were ready to enjoy the satire of the Kentucky Congressman J. Proctor Knott. Rising from his seat in the House, on January 27, 1871, during debate on a land bill, Knott made a memorable speech which derived inspiration from Cooke's Man Friday, Wilkerson, and in which he referred to Duluth as the "name for which his soul had panted for years as the hart panteth for the fresh water brooks." He continued:

> *The symmetry and perfection of our planetary system would be incomplete without it. I see it represented on this map that Duluth is situated exactly half-way between the latitudes of Paris and Venice, so that gentlemen who have inhaled the exhilarating airs of the one, or basked in the golden sunlight of the other, may see at a glance that Duluth must be a place of untold delights, a terrestrial paradise fanned by the balmy zephyrs of an eternal spring, clothed in the gorgeous sheen of ever-blooming flowers and vocal with the silvery melody of nature's choicest songsters. . . .*

Then the extravagant Congressman closed by evoking a "Banana Belt" in the terms of Byron's adaptation from Goethe:

> *Know ye the land of the cedar and vine*
> *Where the flowers ever blossom, the beams ever shine,*
> *. . . Where the citron and olive are fairest of fruit*
> *And the voice of the nightingale never is mute;*
> *Where the tints of the earth and the hues of the sky*
> *In color though varied, in beauty may vie? . . .*

In the midst of its booming and clattering labors of empire-building, the country at large heard the message of Knott repeated and reprinted everywhere, and became convulsed in one nation-wide roar of laughter.

CHAPTER FIVE

TWO CAPTAINS OF INDUSTRY

THE necessities of the war, above all its high-tariff act of 1864, which had given such a strong impetus to home invention and manufacture, resulted also in a process of heightened enrichment of those aggressive individuals who came to be known as "captains of industry." Their progress toward the key positions, the fortresses of an increasingly industrial society, motivated by the revolutionizing energy of coal, iron and steam, was less spectacular, on the whole, than the swift preëmptions of the railroad barons who were inspired by regal gifts such as the seventeenth-century trading companies had received from monarchs. It was the result of much obscure, routine effort; of a constant widespread growth of technology, of a progressive division or organization of labor power into its most productive patterns.

The labors of the captains of industry in the first stage of accumulation were generally peaceful and distant from the political stage of Washington, save when they sought tariff protection. Later, when they contended with each other for commanding positions over their trades, they would be involved in high-handed and ruthless measures against each other, or opponents in adjacent industries.

A most dramatic economic event of the period was the invention of the reaper, perfected and sold in large quantities shortly before the war by Cyrus McCormick. As they quickened the handling of grains, made large farming operations possible in the prairies which were so suited to monoculture, and the Mississippi Valley the leading food-producing region in the world, the new farm machines were saluted joyfully as symbols of the "ever restless and progressive spirit of the age." They supplanted the black slaves; they pointed to triumphs "grander than the triumphs of arms, for they will develop the means of supporting millions of human beings which the implements of war only destroy." Similarly the coming of sewing machines, of leather and textile machinery, of new mining processes, of rolling mills and flour-milling and cattle-slaughtering systems represented all successive "triumphs" along the economic front, so many victories won by the industrial "shock troops" of the 1860's and 1870's.

The inventor who, sensing some current need or applying some branch of current technical knowledge, completed a new machine, seldom prospered as did Cyrus McCormick; rarely did he win the full fruits of his invention. Like the pioneers or prospectors of new minerals, the first discoverers of gold or diggers of oil wells, the inventors were soon displaced, as a rule, by captains of industry. Useful though the technologists were, they were styled by a Congressional report of 1867 as "confiding and thriftless . . . mere children in the rude conflicts which they are called on to endure with the stalwart fraud and cunning of the world." They were used and flung aside by men of ruse and audacity who had shown gifts for the accumulation of capital, who were skilled at management, that is, in "hiring and firing," and who, far from sharing the hazards of applied science, tended to enter a new affair only when its commercial character had been established beyond a doubt. In any case we have given over the "heroic" conception of the inventor as one fired by a divine spark of genius; and rather conceive that his contributions are the reflection of an increasing reservoir of knowledge which is the general property of human society—each separate invention was the compound of numerous, sometimes scores of patents—and as such, common property subject to purchase or seizure like the public domain, forests and power sites.

The war which enriched the alert in so many diverse ways often provided the quick capital necessary for the undertakers of new industrial projects. Philip Armour, who returned one day from the California gold fields to set himself up as a wholesale butcher in the thriving lake port of Chicago, supplied the Union armies with a great deal of the pork of varying quality which it consumed. Armour and the canny Jewish pork-dealer, Nelson Morris, headed two of the leading houses which, with some fifty-four others, handled 900,000 hogs a year by 1865. Their competition was keen in the early days. Each tried to get up earlier in the morning than the

others so as to search for the best carcasses in the surrounding coun-
tryside. But soon, with nine great railroads linking Chicago to the
rest of the country, their traffic in meat became more than a "winter
business"; their market was extended in every direction. And by a
process of rationalization, they began to purchase their cattle live,
concentrating all the handling and slaughtering and dressing in the
centralized Union Stock Yards of Chicago, which connected with
all the trunk lines.

It was Armour who consummated one of the most famous business "coups" of the period. In 1865, watching the progress of
Grant's armies toward Richmond with a clairvoyant eye, and being
completely persuaded of the early approach of victory and peace,
he had suddenly rushed to New York and sold quantities of pork
short at the prevailing high prices of around $40 a barrel. After
Appomattox, the crash of commodity markets, involving especially
pork, ruined hundreds of traders, made thousands of farmers the
poorer, but permitted Armour to "cover" his short contracts in
pork at about $18 a barrel, so that he gained overnight $2,000,000
in quick profits and his praises were sung in high financial circles.
With this capital he swiftly increased his meat business, buying out
weaker competitors and improving his plant until it became one
of the most ingenious and prosperous industries in all the land.

Carnegie and John Rockefeller also became preëminent as captains of industry during the war, in the realms of the iron and oil
trade respectively. Both were to figure largely in the growth of
industrial power in ways that were both similar and contrasting.
Each concentrated upon a single industry eventually, pressing his
luck or opportunity, using a conjunction of favoring circumstances
to erect an industrial pyramid, while increasing his advantage and
strengthening his position as compared with rivals in the field. The
different methods of each in creating his major opus merit special
study, as representing two examples of the type: captain of industry.

The inner circle of the Pennsylvania Railroad in which Andrew
Carnegie moved during the 1860's was an unequaled school in industry and politics. Before the doors of the Pennsylvania's offices
politicians scraped their feet respectfully. At the bidding of the
railroad, the Pennsylvania legislature passed necessary measures with
noticeable speed. When Mr. Scott, according to legend, had "no

further business" for the legislature, it would promptly adjourn. Thus all the uncertainties and hazards of democratic institutions, such as an imperialistic industrial organization could not have safely endured, were erased by strong working agreements with the mighty Simon Cameron, as later with Matthew Quay or his lieutenants. Into the hands of the group headed by Thomas Scott and J. Edgar Thomson numerous opportunities fell constantly, war industries, rights of way, terminal sites, franchises for railroad lines and street-car lines.

Watching these developments Carnegie soon sensed the future of railroad iron, which was growing to be Pittsburgh's largest business. He was a division superintendent at Pittsburgh, and the more skilled of the men who worked with him, such as the "grimy and sweaty" mechanic Piper, unfolded visions of metal bridges which were to replace the old wooden ones everywhere. In the shops of the Pennsylvania, the railroad engineer Linville showed him the first iron bridges fabricated there according to his own designs. At Pittsburgh a German named Kloman, smithy and maker of iron axles used for railroad rolling stock, exhibited his excellent wares to Carnegie and his friends, vowing that he could not turn them out fast enough. So in 1863 Carnegie, his brother Thomas, and his friends, Thomas Miller, a railroad purchasing agent, and Henry Phipps, agreed to furnish new capital to Kloman & Co., in order that more machinery might be installed. They were to receive a minority partnership in the firm; but within a few years the Carnegie brothers and Phipps acquired half, then a majority interest in the iron foundry of Kloman. At the same time Carnegie organized the Keystone Bridge Company, with the aid of the skillful artisans Piper and Linville. A year later, he turned another part of his capital to an iron-rail manufacturing company, and then to another which produced locomotives.

In 1865 he resigned from the railroad, devoting himself wholly to the arts of the salesman and the entrepreneur, on behalf of his iron companies. In master workmen like Kloman, Piper and Linville, he had gathered together, with rare luck, a technical skill which made the products he drummed for well regarded and more economical than those of others. His brother Thomas up to the day of his untimely death, was considered a first-rate ironmaster, methodical, diligent in administering his business, less "flighty" than

Andrew. Henry Phipps was a shrewd fellow worker, a perfect "inside man," parsimonious and yet also crafty in the pursuit of credit for their enterprises. It was said of him that he knew how "to keep a check in the air" as long as any man. With the aid of these men, and soon afterward that of the steel-worker Captain "Bill" Jones, men of unremitting labor and high craftsmanship whom he used with instinctive brilliance, Carnegie was to bring together, as his biographer Hendrick flatteringly writes, "the vast mineral resources of America and the new mechanisms by which they were transformed in the use of the new age."

In addition to his art of using men Carnegie also soon developed the qualities of the "commercial traveler on a heroic scale" as Hendrick says. Bubbling with enthusiasm, and full of brass, he intruded himself everywhere, buttonholed everyone, listened to everything. He cajoled and he flattered the influential men he knew, Scott and Thomson and other railroad chiefs, with telling effect. And despite early quarrels among the partners, who sometimes contended with each other bitterly for a major part of the profits, even brother against brother, the more fertile and cunning Andrew soon came to dominate the others. Even the stubborn German Kloman was subdued; at a moment of business reversal, the lion's share of his properly was surrendered to Carnegie.

For now, flourishing, the restless Carnegie no longer confined himself to the dusty and noisome foundries. He had shown marked talents, such as are nowadays frowned upon in large parts of the world, for "getting something for nothing." As a projector, a man of nimble wit, he had learned to accumulate rapidly without excessively hard work; and once he concentrated, in an attempt to excel at the booming trade in iron rails, bridge beams and rolling stock, he found himself accumulating even more smoothly.

"Carnegie was never a hard worker..." Hendrick concludes. "He spent half his time in play and let other men pile up his millions for him." He trotted about the world, established himself in New York, courted new friendships, and each fresh accession of wealth or influence augmented his self-importance. He estimated his own mental powers so highly that having become within a few years a leading factor among Pittsburgh's stovepipe-hatted ironmasters, and having the income of a millionaire in 1868, he saw no reason why he should not prosper in many other fields.

Carnegie measured other men and found them weak and slow-witted in his hands. He employed himself now at "high finance"; his office was set up near the cauldron of Wall Street. The financiers of the Pennsylvania Railroad at this time entrusted him with the delicate mission of selling bonds for them. He took $5,000,000 worth and disposed of them at a time when few would have bought American bonds "even if signed by an angel." In London, the veteran American banker Junius Morgan, with whom he negotiated, was impressed by the speed of the young Carnegie's action. To close his "deals" within a few hours he used the new transatlantic cable which Cyrus Field had recently laid. His quick commissions were large, exceeding $100,000 at a single turn, and these he turned back to the iron trade he now favored above all; the establishments of Union Iron Mills, Kloman & Phipps, Keystone Bridge, all centered in Pittsburgh.

He was thirty-three. He was more "European" than his associates; the ties with Scotland were firm in him and renewed by many visits. His plebeian Celtic forbears, common workingmen, were nevertheless of that keen, naturally endowed stock which gave the world so many philosophers, scientists, statesmen and writers. Half-cultured, agnostic, a lover of literature, with the worm of immortality in him, the successful Andrew figured to himself an ampler life in association with leading public men; he saw himself as a good squire helping the poor, owning newspapers, which spread his influence, attaching to himself men of light and learning, like Herbert Spencer whose message of "survival of the fittest" he embraced fervently. In periods of "reversion" he was gripped by a feudal notion of the rôle of wealth as one of benevolent social responsibility, something totally alien both to the methods he had used in acquiring it and to the principles in force in progressive, booming America. Hence he remained an eccentric all his life.

In December, 1868, at the St. Nicholas Hotel, he had written in his diary:

Thirty-three and an income of $50,000 per annum! By this time two years I can so arrange all my business as to secure at least $50,000 per annum. Beyond this never earn—make no effort to increase fortune, but spend the surplus each year for benevolent purposes. Cast aside business forever, except for others.

Settle in Oxford and get a thorough education, making the acquaintance of literary men—this will take three years, active work —pay especial attention to speaking in public. Settle then in London and purchase a controlling interest in some newspaper or live review and give the general management of it attention, taking a part in public matters, especially those connected with education and improvement of the poorer classes.

Man must have an idol—the amassing of wealth is one of the worst species of idolatry—no idol more debasing than the worship of money. Whatever I engage in I must push inordinately; therefore should I be careful to choose that life which will be the most elevating in its character. To continue much longer overwhelmed by business cares and with most of my thoughts wholly upon the way to make more money in the shortest time, must degrade me beyond hope of permanent recovery.

Carnegie himself in after years pondered with curiosity over his youthful resolutions. He was already too terribly involved in his business, which was an automatism impersonal and implacable. It needed that he raise more capital for it; it required that he sit all night calculating in large sums against a thousand necessities; *it* left him no peace, no room to move about in. Each of the industrialists was to learn that "one thing led to another," that once having begun here there was no escape.

Carnegie's penetrations into various cultivated circles, his literary frequentations, were in truth but "drumming trips bringing orders to the company by adding to the list of his friends." One of his literary friendships was for instance with John Garrett, the master of the Baltimore & Ohio trunk line, who was also a Scot and as great a devotee of Burns as Carnegie. One visualizes the two Celtic amateurs of literature at grips with each other: if Carnegie rode over his scruples with ease, then Garrett acquired an equal fame as a railroad president who never issued reports to his stockholders and paid dividends for long years without earnings, until his system collapsed suddenly like a gutted house. "Their mutual rhapsodizing" over their favorite poet, Hendrick tells us in his biography of the steel master, "alternated with negotiations for structural contracts." Burns and Shakespeare became practical members of the Keystone Bridge Company staff: Burns invoked to sell iron to Scottish railroad barons, and Shakespeare as a guide and mentor in board-room discussions of business plans.

Up to 1872 Andrew Carnegie's labors, though busy and fruitful enough, had lacked the singleness of direction which conquering souls are noted for. But now in his thirty-seventh year, his chief apologist writes:

> The change that came over the man resembled the religious experience known as a conversion, and like that experience it came as the exaltation of a single moment. A mind that had lived in apparent darkness was illumined by a sudden flash of light. . . . It was the dazzling brilliance of a Bessemer converter that, in the twinkling of an eye, transformed Andrew Carnegie into a new man.

During a business journey to London, the young entrepreneur made the acquaintance of the "crazy Frenchman" Bessemer, then engaged in his experiments with steel. He stood, we are told, before the blazing cauldron of the Bessemer converter, and then "jumping on the first available steamer, he rushed home" to his Pittsburgh ironworks crying: *The day of Iron has passed—Steel is King!* Thus he would appear to have had a vision of human progress by his own personal agency, as the greatest disseminator of steel, "the gleaming metal on which American settlement advanced," and at the same time of his own fabulous share in the proceeds from such gains. Carnegie is usually pictured by himself as well as others as an instrument of mighty social evolution, thanks to his perpetual self-seeking.

But there had already been a decade of practical steel-making in England. Bessemer's process for decarbonizing iron had become commercially successful toward 1856; in Kentucky, William Kelly had devised somewhat the same type of cold-air blast converter, nine years before Bessemer, but had only been derided for his pains. Then since 1865 the gifted Alexander Holley had been setting up Bessemer plants in America; soon 20,000 tons of steel rail were being rolled each year. Even the Erie Railroad was replacing some of its soft worn-out iron rails with steel, or at least issuing bonds for such a stated purpose! For six years Carnegie's own partner William Coleman had been urging him to take up steel manufacturing. It was as if he had been knocked down and dragged into his principality of steel.

It is a shy or tardy agent of progress that we see in Carnegie. "Pioneering don't pay," he would reiterate; but now his large competitors, the Cambria and the Pennsylvania Steel Company, were outstripping him. The man who was all spirit-of-enterprise had waited too long—indeed one wonders much in this connection at the significant lag between the interests of technical progress and those of business enterprise. Had not the rickety iron rails and bridges been collapsing everywhere for years with horrendous accidents as a commonplace of the time? Did not the freight cars which traveled over them remain small in tonnage capacity, keeping freight tariffs exorbitant? Did not numerous contentious factions cling to the small lines, having different track gauges, so that passengers and freight must be transferred after short hauls—a system obsolete decades before it was abandoned? One wonders if another form of society, one that was not dependent for its innovations upon the providential "blind hand" of commercial struggle, would not have moved more rapidly in matters which affected the general population so deeply.

At any rate, it was high time for Carnegie to play pioneer. "We must start the manufacture of steel rails and start at once," he said to his partners. And of course anything that Carnegie started he must "push inordinately." Once he was shown into his kingdom, given his opportunities, Carnegie rose to them with an administrative capacity for large affairs surpassed only by the socialist statesmen of modern Russia. He had the same combination of ruthlessness and optimism. Now with the aid of able lieutenants and engineers he proposed to erect the largest and the most efficient steel mills in the country, a plant that would cost the unprecedented sum of a million dollars!

Everything beckoned him to enter the new industry upon a large scale, and attempt, with a bold gambler's stroke, to seize the lion's share of its future wealth. The market for steel, the demand for it was unlimited. As a railroad worker himself he could estimate the boon it would prove to be in permitting larger tonnage movements over the more resistant and yet flexible tracks. The laying of railroad track increased at a prodigious rate after the war. The whole continent was being carved up with iron and steel tracks. While the demand was unlimited, the market had also been closed to English competition by the imposition of a protective duty of $28 per ton in 1871. The several iron companies at Pittsburgh which were his absorbing interest now were well manned and favorably located. Iron ore was adjacent in Western Pennsylvania, or could be brought down cheaply in bulk by way of the Great Lakes from Michigan. Soft coal and coke, vitally necessary to steel-making, was immediately at hand in the "Pittsburgh district." The Pennsylvania Railroad gave a quick outlet to the seaboard. And finally, to round out the conjunction of favorable circumstances, he had and could attract comparatively large amounts of capital or credit for the creation of such an elaborate plant as would bring the greatest production economies, and whose prohibitive cost would, at the same time, restrict competition to at least a limited number of firms. In an age that clamored for steel Carnegie determined at last to supply it in monstrous quantities; and under conditions of natural economy, access to raw material, facilities of transport, and markets that would give him crushing advantages over rivals in the field. Such advantages the rising barons of heavy industry pursued with as sure a scent as did the quarreling princes of olden times. It was the inexorable logic of the age of unbridled individual struggle and competition in which Andrew Carnegie grew up.

Soon at the suburb of Braddock, the ambitious building of majestic steel mills was begun by a joint-stock company for which the Carnegies, Henry Phipps and various others provided the capital. With inimitable tact Carnegie decided to name the mills after his largest prospective customer, head of the Pennsylvania Railroad, the "J. Edgar Thomson Works."

2

In Cleveland, a few hours distant from Pittsburgh, at the very same time the young merchant John D. Rockefeller, who was already noted for his sagacity and gravity, also contemplated an industrial adventure in many ways even more remarkable than Carnegie's.

The discovery of oil in the northwestern corner of Pennsylvania by Drake in 1859 was no isolated event, but part of the long overdue movement to exploit the subsoil of the country. When thousands rushed to scoop the silver and gold of Nevada, Colorado and Montana, the copper of Michigan, the iron ore of Pennsylvania and

New York, technical knowledge at last interpreted the meaning of the greasy mineral substance which lay above ground near Titusville, Pennsylvania, and which had been used as a patent medicine ("Kier's Medicine") for twenty years. The rush and boom, out of which numerous speculators such as Andrew Carnegie had drawn quick profits and sold out—while so many others lost all they possessed—did not escape the attention of Rockefeller. The merchants of Cleveland, interested either in handling the new illuminating oil or investing in the industry itself, had sent the young Rockefeller to spy out the ground.

He had come probably in the spring of 1860 to the strange, blackened valleys of the Oil Regions where a forest of crude derricks, flimsy shacks and storehouses had been raised overnight. Here he had looked at the anarchy of the pioneer drillers or diggers of oil, the first frenzy of exploitation, with a deep disfavor that all conservative merchants of the time shared. There were continual fires, disasters and miracles; an oil well brought a fortune in a week, with the market price at twenty dollars a barrel; then as more wells came in the price fell to three and even two dollars a barrel before the next season! No one could tell at what price it was safe to buy oil, or oil acreage, and none knew how long the supply would last.

Returning to Cleveland, Rockefeller had counseled his merchant friends against investments in oil. At best the refining trade might be barely profitable if one could survive the mad dance of the market and if the supply of oil held out. Repugnance was strong in the infinitely cautious young merchant against the pioneering of the Oil Creek rabble. Two years were to pass before he approached the field again, while his accumulations increased with the fruitful wartime trade in provisions.

In 1862, when small refineries were rising everywhere, when more and more oil fields were being opened, the prospects of the new trade were immensely more favorable. A Clevelander named Samuel Andrews, owner of a small still, now came to the firm of Rockefeller & Clark with a proposal that they back him in setting up a sizable oil-refinery. The man Andrews was something of a technologist: he knew how to extract a high percentage of kerosene oil from the crude; he was one of the first to use the by-products developed in the refining process. Rockefeller and his partner, who appreciated the man's worth, invested $5,000 at the start with him. The affair flourished quickly, as demand widened for the new illuminant. Soon Rockefeller missed not a day from the refinery, where Andrews manufactured a kerosene better, purer than his competitors', and Rockefeller kept the books, conducted the pulchasing of crude oil in his sharp fashion, and saved old iron, waste oils, made his own barrels, watched, spared, squirmed, for the smallest bargains.

In 1865, with uncanny judgment, Rockefeller chose between his produce business and the oil-refining trade. He sold his share in the house of Rockefeller & Clark, and purchased Clark's share in the oil-refinery, now called Rockefeller & Andrews. At this moment the values of all provisions were falling, while the oil trade was widening, spreading over all the world. Several great new wells had come in; supply was certain—10,000 barrels a day. Concentrating all his effort upon the new trade, he labored unremittingly to entrench himself in it, to be ready for all the hazards, which were great. He inaugurated ruthless economies; giving all his attention "to little details," he acquired a numerous clientele in the Western and Southern states; and opened an export selling agency in New York, headed by his brother William Rockefeller. "Low-voiced, soft-footed, humble, knowing every point in every man's business," Miss Tarbell relates, "he never tired until he got his wares at the lowest possible figures." "John always got the best of the bargain," the old men of Cleveland recall: "savy fellow he was!" For all his fierce passion for money, he was utterly impassive in his bearing, save when some surprisingly good purchase of oil had been made at the creek. Then he could no longer restrain his shouts of joy. In the oil trade, John Rockefeller grew up in a hard school of struggle; he endured the merciless and unprincipled competition of rivals; and his own unpitying logic and coldly resolute methods were doubtless the consequence of the brutal free-for-all from which he emerged with certain crushing advantages.

While the producers of crude oil contended with each other in lawless fashion to drill the largest quantities, the refiners at different industrial centers who processed and reshipped the crude oil were also engaged in unresting trade conflicts, in which all measures were fair. And behind the rivalry of the producers and the refiners in different cities lay the secret struggles of the large railroad interests moving obscurely in the background Drew's Erie, Vanderbilt's New York Central, Thomson and Scott's Pennsylvania, extending their lines to the Oil Regions, all hunted their fortune in the huge new traffic, pressing the interests of favored shipping and refining centers such as Cleveland or Pittsburgh or Buffalo to suit themselves. It would have been simplest possibly to have oil-refineries at the source of the crude material itself; but the purpose of the railroads forbade this; and there was no way of determining the outcome in this matter, as in any other phase of the organization of the country's new resources, whose manner of exploitation was determined only through pitched battles between the various gladiators, wherein the will of Providence was seen.

Rockefeller, who had no friends and no diversions, who was "all business," as John T. Flynn describes him, now gave himself to incessant planning, planning that would defeat chance itself. His company was but one of thirty oil-refiners located in Cleveland; in the Oil Regions, at Oil City and Titusville, there were numerous others, including the largest refineries of all, more favorably placed for shipping. But in 1867 Rockefeller invited into his firm as a partner, a business acquaintance of his, Henry M. Flagler, son-in-law of the rich whiskey distiller and salt-maker S. V. Harkness. Flagler, a bold and dashing fellow, was deeply attracted by the possibilities of the oil business. Thanks to Harkness, he brought $70,000 into the business, which at once opened a second refinery in Cleveland. Within a year or two the firm of Rockefeller, Flagler & Andrews was the biggest refinery in Cleveland, producing 1,500 barrels a day, having its own warehouses, its export agency in New York, its own wooden tank cars, its own staff of chemists or experts who labored to improve or economize the manufacturing processes. The company moved steadily to the front of the field, surpassing its rivals in quality, and outselling them by a small, though not certain or decisive, margin. How was this done?

In the struggle for business, Rockefeller's instinct for conspiracy is already marked. The partnership with Flagler brought an access of fresh capital and even more credit. Then in a further step of collusion, this of profound importance, Rockefeller and Flagler approached the railroad which carried so many carloads of their oil toward the seaboard, and whose tariff figured heavily in the ultimate cost. They demanded from it concessions in freight rates that would enable them to meet the advantages of other refining centers such as Pittsburgh, Philadelphia and New York. Their company was now large enough to force the hand of the railroad, in this case, a branch of Vanderbilt's New York Central system; and they were granted their demands: a secret reduction or "rebate" on all their shipments of oil. "Such was the railroad's method," Rockefeller himself afterward admitted. He relates:

A public rate was made and collected by the railroad companies, but so far as my knowledge extends, was seldom retained in full; a portion of it was repaid to the shipper as a rebate. By this method the real rate of freight which any shipper paid was not known by his competitors, nor by other railroads, the amount being a matter of bargain with the carrying companies.

Once having gained an advantage Rockefeller pressed forward relentlessly. The volume of his business increased rapidly. Thanks to the collaboration of the railroad, he had placed his rivals in other cities and in Cleveland itself under a handicap, whose weight he endeavored to increase.

The railroads, as we see, possessed the strategic power, almost of life and death, to encourage one industrial group or cause another to languish. Their policy was based on the relative costs of handling small or large volume shipments. Thus as the Rockefeller company became the largest shipper of oil, its production rising in 1870 to 3,000 barrels a day, and offered to guarantee regular daily shipments of as much as sixty carloads, the railroads were impelled to accept further proposals for rebates. It was to their interest to do so in view of savings of several hundred thousand dollars a month in handling. On crude oil brought from the Oil Regions, Rockefeller paid perhaps 15 cents a barrel less than the open rate of 40 cents; on refined oil moving from Cleveland toward New York, he paid approximately 90 cents against the open rate of $1.30. These momentous agreements were maintained in utter secrecy, perhaps because of the persisting memory of their illegality, according to the common law ever since Queen Elizabeth's time, as a form of "conspiracy" in trade.

In January, 1870, Rockefeller, Flagler & Andrews were incorporated as a joint-stock company, a form increasingly popular, under the name of the Standard Oil Company of Ohio. At this time their worth was estimated at one million dollars; they employed over a thousand workers and were the largest refiners in the world. Despite deeply disturbed conditions in their trade during 1870, profits came to them in a mounting flood, while in the same year, it is noteworthy, four of their twenty-nine competitors in Cleveland gave up the ghost. The pious young man of thirty who feared only God, and thought of nothing but his business, gave not a sign of his greatly-augmented wealth, which made him one of the leading personages of his city. His income was actually a fabulous one for the time. The Standard Oil Company from the beginning earned something like 100 per cent on its capital; and Rockefeller and his brother owned a full half-interest in it in 1870. But with an evangelistic fervor John Rockefeller was bent only upon further conquests, upon greater extensions of the power over industry which had come into the hands of the group he headed.

In the life of every conquering soul there is a "turning point," a moment when a deep understanding of the self coincides with an equally deep sense of one's immediate mission in the tangible world. For Rockefeller, brooding, secretive, uneasily scenting his fortune, this moment came but a few years after his entrance into the oil trade, and at the age of thirty. He had looked upon the disorganized conditions of the Pennsylvania oil fields, the only source then known, and found them not good: the guerilla fighting of drillers, of refining firms, of rival railroad lines, the mercurial changes in supply and market value—very alarming in 1870—offended his orderly and methodical spirit. But one could see that petroleum was to be the light of the world. From the source, from the chaotic oil fields where thousands of drillers toiled, the grimy stream of the precious commodity, petroleum, flowed along many diverse channels to narrow into the hands of several hundred refineries, then to issue once more in a continuous stream to consumers throughout the world. Owner with Flagler and Harkness of the largest refining company in the country, Rockefeller had a strongly entrenched position at the narrows of this stream. Now what if the Standard Oil Company should by further steps of organization possess itself wholly of the narrows? In this period of anarchic individual competition, the idea of such a movement of rationalization must have come to Rockefeller forcibly, as it had recently come to others.[1]

Even as early as 1868 the first plan of industrial combination in the shape of the pool had been originated in the Michigan Salt Association. Desiring to correct chaotic market conditions, declaring that "in union there is strength," the salt-producers of Saginaw Bay had sanded together to control the output and sale of nearly all the salt in their region, a large part of the vital national supply. Secret agreements had been executed for each year, allotting the sales, and fixing the price at almost twice what it had been immediately prior to the appearance of the pool. And though the inevitable greed and self-seeking of the individual salt-producers had tended to weaken the pool, the new economic invention was launched in its infantile form. Rockefeller's partners, Flagler and Harkness, had themselves participated in the historic Michigan Salt Association.

This grand idea of industrial rationalization owed its swift, ruthless, methodical execution no doubt to the firmness of character we sense in Rockefeller, who had the temper of a great, unconscionable military captain, combining audacity with thoroughness and shrewd judgment. His plan seemed to take account of no one's feelings in the matter. Indeed there was something revolutionary in it; it seemed to fly in the fact of human liberties and deep-rooted custom and common law. The notorious "South Improvement Company," with its strange charter, ingeniously instrumenting the scheme of combination, was to be unraveled amid profound secrecy. By conspiring with the railroads (which also hungered for economic order), it would be terribly armed with the power of the freight rebate which

[1]The English economist J. A. Hobson has written in this connection: "Each kind of commodity, as it passes through the many processes from the earth to the consumer, may be looked upon as a stream whose channel is broader at some points and narrow at others. Different streams of commodities narrow at different places. Some are narrowest and in fewest hands at the transport stage, others in one of the processes of manufacture, others in the hands of export merchants . . ." In the case of petroleum the logical "narrows" was at the point of refinery; and inevitably, Rockefeller and Flagler set in motion their great plan to control the stream. "Just as a number of German barons planted their castles along the banks of the Rhine, in order to tax the commerce between East and West which was obliged to make use of this highway, so it is with these economic 'narrows.' Wherever they are found, monopolies plant themselves in the shape of 'rings,' 'corners,' 'pools,' 'syndicates,' or trusts.' " ("The Evolution of Modern Capitalism," p. 142.)

garrotted all opposition systematically. This plan of combination, this unifying conception Rockefeller took as his ruling idea; he breathed life into it, clung to it grimly in the face of the most menacing attacks of legislatures, courts, rival captains, and, at moments, even of rebellious mobs. His view of men and events justified him, and despite many official and innocent denials, he is believed to have said once in confidence, as Flynn relates:

> *I had our plan clearly in mind. It was right. I knew it as a matter of conscience. It was right between me and my God. If I had to do it tomorrow I would do it again in the same way—do it a hundred times.*[2]

The broad purpose was to control and direct the flow of crude petroleum into the hands of a narrowed group of refiners. The refiners would be supported by the combined railroad trunk lines which shipped the oil; while the producers' phase of the stream would be left unorganized—*but with power over their outlet to market* henceforth to be concentrated into the few hands of the refiners.

Saying nothing to others, bending over their maps of the industry, Rockefeller and Flagler first drew up a short list of the principal refining companies who were to be asked to combine with them. Then having banded together a sufficient number, they would persuade the railroads to give them special freight rates—on the ground of "evening" the traffic—guaranteeing equitable distribution of freight business; and this in turn would be a club to force other elements needed into union with them. They could control output, drive out competitors, and force all foreign countries throughout the world to buy their product from them at their own terms. They could finally dictate market prices on crude oil, stabilize the margin of profit at their own process, and do away at last with the dangerously speculative character of their business.

Their plans moved forward rapidly all through 1871. For a small sum of money the "conspirators" obtained the Pennsylvania charter of a defunct corporation, which had been authorized to engage in

[2]By hearsay the legend has come to me of a private conversation between Mr. Rockefeller and some old friends at dinner long ago in which the oil baron said with emotion: "*I discovered something that made a new world and I did not know it at the time.*"

almost any kind of business under the sun. Those who were approached by the promoters, those whom they determined to use in their grand scheme, were compelled in a manner typical of all Rockefeller's projects to sign a written pledge of secrecy:

I,—— ——, do solemnly promise upon my honor and faith as a gentleman that I will keep secret all transactions which I may have with the corporation known as the South Improvement Company; that should I fail to complete any bargains with the said company, all the preliminary conversations shall be kept strictly private; and finally that I will not disclose the price for which I dispose of any products or any other facts which may in any way bring to light the internal workings or organization of the company. All this I do freely promise.

At the same time, in confidential pourparlers with the officials of the Erie, the Pennsylvania and the New York Central Railroads, the men of the Standard Oil represented themselves as possessing secret control of the bulk of the refining interest. Thus they obtained conditions more advantageous than anything which had gone before; and this weapon in turn of course ensured the triumph of their pool.[3]

The refiners to be combined under the aegis of the South Improvement Company were to have a rebate of from 40 to 50 percent on the crude oil they ordered shipped to them and from 25 to 50 per cent on the refined oil they shipped out. The refiners in the Oil Regions were to pay *twice as much* by the new code (though nearer to New York) as the Standard Oil Company at Cleveland. But besides the rebate the members of the pool were to be given also a "drawback" consisting of part of the increased tariff rate which "outsiders" were forced to pay. Half of the freight payments of a

[3]With unbridled competition in the Oil Regions the different refiners could not know from day to day what their raw materials would cost, as new wells came in or gave out. A refiner in Cleveland might buy his petroleum at $5 a barrel for future use; then on the following day, his competitors might cover their needs for half, or vice versa. Similarly the railroads would experience a heavy demand for cars at one period, succeeded by periods of slackness when prices were low and production was discouraged. New inventions, such as that for pumping oil through pipes (Van Syckel's pipe line of 1865) added further to the confusion of the trade, upsetting the elements of cost and supply anew. In the two processes of refining and carrying the petroleum, the dominant interests were resolved therefore upon rationalization, come what may.

rival refiner would in many cases be paid over to the Rockefeller group. They competitors were simply to be decimated; and to make certain of this the railroads agreed—all being set down in writing, in minutest detail—"to make manifests or way-bills of all petroleum or its product transported over any portion of its lines . . . which manifests shall state the name of the consignee, the place of shipment and the place of destination," this information to be furnished faithfully to the officers of the South Improvement Company.

The railroad systems, supposedly public-spirited and impartial, were to open all their knowledge of rival private business to the pool, thus helping to concentrate all the oil trade into the few hands chosen. In return for so much assistance, they were to have their freight "evened," and were enabled at last to enter into a momentous peace pact with each other by which the oil traffic (over which they had quarreled bitterly) was to be fairly allotted among themselves.

By January, 1872, after the first decade of the oil business, John Rockefeller, with the aid of the railroad captains, was busily carrying out a most "elaborate national plan" of his own for the control of his industry—such planned control as the spokesman of the business system asserted ever afterward was impossible. The first pooling of 1872, beautiful as was its economic architecture and laudable its motive, had defects which were soon plainly noticeable. All the political institutions, the whole spirit of American law still favored the amiable, wasteful individualism of business, which in Rockefeller's mind had already become obsolete and must be supplanted by a centralized, one might say almost *collectivist*—certainly cooperative rather than competitive—form of operation. Moreover, these "revolutionists" took little account of the social dislocations their juggernaut would bring. Like the railroad baron, Vanderbilt, working better than they knew, their eyes fixed solely upon the immediate task rather than upon some millennium of the future, they desired simply, as they often said, to be "the biggest refiners in the world. . . ."

To the principal oil firms in Cleveland Rockefeller went one by one, explaining the plan of the South Improvement Company patiently, pointing out how important it was to oppose the creek refiners and save the Cleveland oil trade. He would say:

"You see, this scheme is bound to work. There is no chance for anyone outside. But we are going to give everybody a chance to come in. You are to turn over your refinery to my appraisers, and I will give you Standard Oil Company stock or cash, as you prefer, for the value we put upon it. I advise you to take the stock. It will be for your good."

Then if the men demurred, according to much of the testimony at the Senate Investigation of 1876, he would point out suavely that it was useless to resist; opposition would certainly be crushed. The offers of purchase usually made were for from a third to a half the actual cost of the property.

Now a sort of terror swept silently over the oil trade. In a vague panic, competitors saw the Standard Oil officers come to them and say (as Rockefeller's own brother and rival, Frank, testified in 1876): "If you don't sell your property to us it will be valueless, because we have got the advantage with the railroads."

The railroad rates indeed were suddenly doubled to the outsiders, and those refiners who resisted the pool came and expostulated; then they became frightened and disposed of their property. One of the largest competitors in Cleveland, the firm of Alexander, Scofield & Co., held out for a time, protesting before the railroad officials at the monstrous unfairness of the deal. But these officials when consulted said mysteriously: *Better sell—better get clear—better sell out—no help for it.*" Another powerful refiner, Robert Hanna, uncle of the famous Mark Alonzo, found that the railroads would give him no relief, and also was glad to sell out at 40 or 50 cents on the dollar for his property value. To one of these refiners, Isaac L. Hewitt, who had been his employer in boyhood, Rockefeller himself spoke with intense emotion. He urged Hewitt to take stock. Hewitt related: "He told me that it would be sufficient to take care of my family for all time ... and asking for reasons, he made this expression, I remember: *I have ways of making money that you know nothing of.*' "

All this transpired in secret. For "silence is golden," the rising king of oil believed. Though many were embittered by their loss, others joined gladly. The strongest capitalists in Cleveland, such as the wealthy Colonel Oliver H. Payne, were amazed at the swift progress Rockefeller had made, at the enormous profits he showed them in confidence to invite their cooperation. Payne, among others, as a man of wealth and influence, was taken into the board of directors and made treasurer of the Standard Oil Company. (The officers of the South Improvement Company itself were "dummies.") Within three months by an economic *coup d'état* the youthful Rockefeller had captured all of Cleveland's oil-refining trade, all twenty-five competitors surrendered to him and yielded him command of one-fifth of America's output of refined oil.

Tomorrow all the population of the Oil Regions, its dismayed refiners, drillers, and workers of oil, might rise against the South Improvement Company ring in a grotesque uproar. The secret, outwardly peaceful campaigns would assume here as elsewhere the character of violence and lawlessness which accompanied the whole program of the industrial revolution. But Rockefeller and his comrades had stolen a long march on their opponents; their tactics shaped themselves already as those of the giant industrialists of the future conquering the pigmies. Entrenched at the "narrows" of the mighty river of petroleum they could no more be dislodged than those other barons who had formerly planted their strong castles along the banks of the Rhine could be dislodged by unarmed peasants and burghers.

CHAPTER SIX
THE FIGHT FOR ERIE

WHILE millions of tamers and workers were bringing forth bumper crops of grain, hordes of cattle and mountainous heaps of iron ore, coal, oil and other minerals which moved in a continuous stream from the earth, through the factories, elevators, and yards of the industrialists to the markets, a momentous struggle developed among certain soldiers of fortune for the rule of the iron highways over which the greater part of this stream of commodities flowed. Late in 1869, Charles F. Adams, Jr., who was becoming a specialist in railroad affairs, came upon evidence of a "vast conspiracy" which began in an attempted seizure of one of the principal trunk lines in the East; then in wide ramifications enveloped the national currency system, the political leaders of several of the state legislatures, the federal government, members of the presidential cabinet itself. The machinations of the "conspirators" seemed at the time of historic significance to both the Adams brothers, who believed that successive crises had been precipitated by them, culminating finally in the nation-wide panic of 1873. Sensing the new powers at work in the situation, the deep alterations in American society, they had tried to expose the principals of the plot; they wrote "Chapters of Erie," unfolding the whole sensational story in a form still substantially correct. They were beating drums, setting up signal-fires; yet no one had been alarmed, or had the time to be alarmed.

The contests which were waged unremittingly, and by no means bloodlessly, for more than five years, involved rule of the lines between New York and Chicago, the most fruitful traffic in the country, which would have enabled those who controlled it to extend their empire over the weaker systems which ran farther west even to the Pacific. In these memorable contests, which we record in some detail, the principal villains and heroes were Drew, Gould and Fisk of the Erie faction, and Commodore Vanderbilt, and later, J. Pierpont Morgan, for the New York Central party. There were various minor characters as well, "soldiers and villagers," statesmen and justices, and there was the public which looked on now with enjoyment, or now in angry bewilderment.

By 1866 Commodore Vanderbilt in pursuance of his plans of consolidation had bought enough stock in the Erie Railroad to announce confidently that he intended to add this line to his growing system.

The group of railroads thrown together as the Vanderbilt system complemented each other nicely: the Harlem gave a terminus and franchise in New York; the Hudson River Railroad continued from its juncture with the Harlem tracks up the east shore of the river to Albany; and thence the New York Central ran up the Mohawk Valley to Buffalo, and connected with the Lake Shore (in which the Commodore had also invested) as far as Toledo. His eye was fixed upon the Michigan Southern and its Chicago terminal, when he perceived that the Erie Railroad was moving in the same direction. In apprehension, he made overtures of friendship to Uncle Daniel Drew, purchased about 20,000 shares of Erie stock and had himself elected a director of the road. He now owned a prominent share of its capital, had the secret collaboration of Drew as he believed, and might subdue the Erie's opposition to his triumphant westward march.

But soon sufficient signs appeared that all was not well. There was no trusting the deep Uncle Daniel; for shares of Erie stock were pressed steadily upon a declining market, as if flowing from a concealed underground stream, while Vanderbilt continued buying. In 1866 Drew had loaned his railroad, of which he was treasurer and chief stockholder, $3,480,000 on the security of 28,000 unissued shares of its stock, and 3,000,000 of its convertible bonds. Now Drew bought and sold Erie stock in Wall Street, using the collateral he possessed—whether lawfully or unlawfully it is not known—to cover his operations. This was one source of supply; but there were more.

In the same year, at the proposal of Jay Gould, who roamed

about trading in little railroads, Drew together with his agents Fisk and Gould had bought a small company, the Buffalo, Bradford & Pittsburgh Railroad, as a private transaction of their own, for $250,000. Against this sum of assets the new owners had with splendid imagination issued $2,000,000 in bonds. They then proceeded to lease their road to the expanding Erie system for 499 years, the ransom being assumption of the smaller company's bonded indebtedness by the larger one. Thus $2,000,000 of Erie convertible bonds (convertible into shares of capital stock) passed into the hands of the three confederates in exchange for their Buffalo, Bradford & Pittsburgh, which had cost them one-eighth of the sum. Through the right of bond conversion Drew, Gould and Fisk now had a large reserve supply of Erie stock, which they continued to sell steadily through 1866, as far as they dared, while agents of the great "bull" Vanderbilt purchased them almost as soon as they were offered.

"Buy Erie," Vanderbilt ordered his brokers. "Buy it at the lowest figure you can, but buy it!" His holdings increased visibly, and knowing nothing of the secret acquisitions of the Erie ring he assumed that the market would soon be bare of offerings. He possessed more shares than were known to exist. Erie's stock climbed to 95. The shorts, he told himself gloatingly, would be soon trapped as in the famous Harlem corner. But suddenly a wave of crisp, newly printed Erie shares struck Wall Street, 50,000 of them, and smashed the market, so that the price broke to 50 a share, and Vanderbilt in the calamitous process was loser by some millions of dollars to the party headed by Daniel Drew.

The rage and mortification of the Commodore now passed all bounds. Determined upon defeating his treacherous adversary, and also seizing control of the opposing railroad in order finally to form a combination or pool for fixing traffic and freight rates, he now took elaborate measures to assure himself of ownership. A group of Boston financiers headed by John S. Eldridge, in charge of the small Boston, Hartford & Erie Railroad, had been building westward—largely under Massachusetts subsidy—and had planned to connect with the Erie to bring Erie coal to Boston. This railroad too had been overladen with debt by its builders, and was without funds for further construction. Its directors had previously purchased a sizable block of Erie shares as a means of bringing about a consolidation. The Boston financiers were a new factor in the control of Eric, and courting Vanderbilt's favor they now entered into a secret agreement with him to vote their shares at the approaching election of directors so that Drew would be ousted. In return, Vanderbilt would have the Erie absorb their New England railroad, by advancing them four millions in bonds, thus furnishing them with funds for the construction they so loved to carry on.

Daniel Drew was now given notice that his days at the head of the Erie were numbered; moreover an injunction issued at the Commodore's complaint overhung him, and restrained him from voting his illegally obtained stock.

Hat in hand, and with tears flowing from his old eyes, Drew came to beg his ancient rival for mercy. Was it by a whim, a moment of sentimental weakness that Vanderbilt forgave the old drover—something that he was rarely known to do? More likely Drew had convinced his adversary that in happy accord, they, as two mercenary captains, might win many fruitful victories at the cost of common enemies, the "outsiders." Thus a successful pool formed with the purpose of advancing Erie stock might easily erase Vanderbilt's recent losses, and Vanderbilt had to admit that no one knew better how to manage such forays nimbly than did the Speculative Director of Erie. Finally, Vanderbilt undoubtedly admired the wily old man and was the last one to be shocked by his ruthless proceedings.

The bargain was struck. It was agreed that in response to the clamor of the outside public Drew was to be officially ousted, and a "dummy" director put in his place, while he remained in actual charge of their mutual affairs. This was done at the stockholders' meeting of October 18, 1867, and the new interests, including the Boston financiers, elected their directors. The two young, almost unknown, allies of Drew, James Fisk, Jr., and Jay Gould, who appeared to have intruded themselves in the Boston faction, were among the new members of the executive board of a great railroad for the first time in their lives, with the approval of Vanderbilt. Then, soon afterward, to Wall Street's surprise, Drew reassumed his former position. Peace, and subservience to Vanderbilt control, was the order of the day; and Erie's mercurial stock rose rapidly under the bidding of the new pool which Vanderbilt interests backed.

But soon all did not appear well to the Commodore; he found mysterious selling of Erie in the market, readily offered shares. When he called a meeting of the New York Central and Erie directors together to pool traffic and equalize rates, he found to his surprise that Drew, Gould and even his recent allies from Boston had grown disaffected and were ranged against him. And to his great anxiety, he learned that the Erie Railroad proposed to make large new issues of bonds for purposes of construction and expansion. Its rails were six feet apart; and it was now planned to spend many millions to lay a third rail, inside, at the standard gauge, so that trains from the Michigan railroads could connect with its lines. And, with unsurpassed boldness, in defiance of Vanderbilt, the Executive Committee of Drew, Fisk and Gould, the "Erie ring," now secretly authorized the issuance of a mass of new convertible bonds, ten millions more!

Once more the impetuous Vanderbilt saw that he had been outwitted and deceived; that he must at once buy an absolute majority of the much augmented supply of Erie's stock in the open market if he would control the situation. And with a great oath he ordered his brokers again to "buy every damn share that's offered."

But what if the Erie ring simply printed infinite quantities of stock, issued unlawfully against "convertible" bonds which had not even been publicly sold, against which no funds had been paid to the railroad? How could he shore up the flood of paper pouring from their printing presses? He must have the law upon the conspirators.

Early in 1868, the highly, obliging Judge George C. Barnard of the New York State Supreme Court (and of the Tweed ring) enjoined the Erie directors from further issues of securities, and ordered them to return to the treasury one-fourth of the shares recently issued, as well as the $3,000,000 of convertible bonds dated 1866. Jove-like, Judge Barnard fired injunctions like bolts of lightning, while the cohorts of Vanderbilt took heart, and Erie's stock rose 30 points to 84. Vanderbilt and his party had some 200,000 shares accumulated; and it looked as if the Erie bears, thanks to the majestic intrusion of the Law, were badly cornered at last.

Out of their midst, however, Jay Gould now emerged as the effective leader, displaying craftiness, promptitude and boldness in action which showed him a worthy foe of the craggy Vanderbilt,

Hurrying to the town of Binghamton, New York, he uncovered a judge of the state's Supreme Court who heeded fully his own substantial reasoning, and sent forth counter-injunctions. But better still, before the hour of Judge Barnard's injunctions, Drew, Gould and Fisk, with forethought of what was coming, had taken the whole $10,000,000 of recently issued bonds, and assigning them to a broker unaffected by the court orders, had them converted into 100,000 shares of stock. Then, always pretending to obey the court's orders, a messenger boy was ordered to carry the stock-book containing these new and forbidden shares to a place of deposit assigned by the court. But by prearrangement the burly Fisk, lurking outside the door, intercepted the boy, wrenched the stock-book from his hands, and disappeared!

In the financial markets there spread the most terrible uncertainty as to what was coming, not only for the contestants but for business in general, as a consequence of so much deviltry. Drew and Fisk suddenly flung a great mass of the disputed Erie shares (whose fate none had known) upon the market, causing a riot in Wall Street, "as though a mine had been exploded." Upon the stock exchange trading was suspended in Erie; brokers poured out into the street shouting and gesticulating like madmen; and above their tumult sounded the mad roars of the Cyclopean Vanderbilt who, it appears, had been cheated once more out of an enormous sum of money reckoned at between five millions and seven millions of dollars.

Again and again the Commodore had grasped hungrily for the Erie Railroad and each time by a deft move his opponents had wrested the prize from his reaching arms. The more shares he bought with his good money the more they printed, in order to reduce his portion of the ownership. Jim Fisk had said publicly: "If this printing press don't break down, I'll be damned if I don't give the old hog all he wants of Erie!"

There was no more time for temporizing. Calling upon Judge Barnard again, Vanderbilt had him order the arrest of Drew, Gould and Fisk for contempt of court. Then for the unhappy railroad a receiver friendly to Vanderbilt was appointed.

But once more the rulers of Erie had been forewarned of the enemy's strokes. At the railroad headquarters on West Street, amid great excitement, they gathered quickly all the funds received from their stock-market transactions, all cash in banks or in the company's treasury, all securities, documents and incriminating evidence, and made ready to flee.

Notices, warrants and writs were known to be on their way at ten o'clock of the morning of March 11, 1868, when Daniel Drew, Jim Fisk and Jay Gould, after emptying the safes in West Street, and cramming a great bundle of six millions in greenbacks into a valise, threw themselves into a hack and rode at top speed toward the Eludson River. At the Jersey City ferry, a formidable body-guard of Erie porters and detectives already waited to escort them on their westward journey into the free and open spaces of New Jersey. It was a close call; the deputies, hard on their heels, had managed to arrest two directors and clap them into Ludlow Street Jail. Some others had escaped in rowboats across the river.

Arrived in Jersey City the men of Erie established their main offices in the hotel known as Taylor's Castle, hard by the Erie depot. They threw armed guards about the place and renamed it "Fort Taylor." To the newspapers which followed the *cause célèbre* day by day, the breezy and irrepressible Fisk made the following state-ment:

> *The Commodore owns New York, the Stock Exchange, the streets, the railroads and most of the steamships there belong to him. As ambitious young men, we saw there was no chance for us there to expand, and so we came over here to grow up with the country. . . . Yes, tell Mr. Greeley from us that we're sorry now that we didn't take his advice sooner—about going West.*

2

To the huge entertainment of the general public, the War of Erie continued to rage all through the year 1868, with mounting effects of the burlesque and the sinister. Daniel Drew now seemed the much subdued prisoner of Gould and Fisk, who held him bound to them in a manner that showed their complete grip over his darkest affairs. Intensely aroused by the prize of millions of greenbacks in their grasp, the two young men surpassed themselves in brilliant strata-gems directed against the Vanderbilt party. On the one hand they undertook a famous division of spoils with the local statesmen and judges, which the parsimonious Commodore, though goaded to extremities, felt too poor to attempt on such a scale. In the next breath, before the press and the people, in raillery or in earnestness, they denounced their famous enemy as one who lusted for monopoly at all costs, "of all the railroads that tie up with the West," and presented themselves to popular opinion as friends of the masses. And to lend color to such claims, Jay Gould reduced passenger rates to Buffalo from seven dollars to five, a strong blow at the hard-pressed Vanderbilt. Finally, having high respect for the Commodore's prowess, and not trusting the foregoing measures, they also had recourse to arms. Jersey City's Chief of Police furnished at their request a squad of police to augment the force of railroad detectives who patrolled the streets and wharves near "Fort Taylor"; three twelve-pound cannon were mounted on the piers; and Jim Fisk, at the head of a squad of four dozen men, equipped with Springfield rifles and lifeboats, strutted about, bursting with pride: he was now "Admiral" Jim Fisk.

In the financial center of New York, a period of stringency followed the flight of the Erie ring. The removal of between six and seven millions in currency, at a time when Vanderbilt and the bankers who financed him were reported to be embarrassed, caused a decline in securities, and even a fall in the dollar. But with iron nerve the Commodore held on, no one knew how. He had a mass of Erie shares, upon which the banks refused to lend him further sums of money, as a fraudulent security; they would accept only his New York Central stocks as collateral.

"Very well, gentlemen," his broker said, as if by authority, "if you don't lend the Commodore half a million on Erie at 50, and do it at once, he will put Central on the market tomorrow and break half the houses on the street! You know whether you will be among them."

Vanderbilt was ready to bring the whole financial structure down in his ruin. With pistol pointed at their head, the bankers and the disheartened speculators continued to follow their leader, willy-nilly, in his dark hours.

As exiles in Jersey City, the rulers of Erie—with the exception of Drew who shut himself up in a room and prayed most of the day— had arranged their lives tolerably well among the unfamiliar scenes. The undersized, almost effeminate Jay Gould showed at this juncture his heroic qualities. The management of the great railroad system was in his hands and all its departments were brought together in the Jersey City hotel. Silent, humorless, and under a habitual nervous tension, the little man with piercing black eyes labored tirelessly or calculated all the day upon their involved affairs. Even Drew, grown senile, could no longer fathom the limitless ambitions of this deep young man, who spoke little, stroked his black beard continually, or nervously tore up pieces of paper into thousands of little bits for hours at a time, at his desk.

Jim Fisk, though he got on famously with his strange confederate, offered a remarkable contrast to him. Where Gould was abstemious, Fisk was open-handed and spent his money freely; where Gould, who kept his mouth shut and his money hidden, was cautious or diffident, Fisk was loud and self-confident. Yet his braggadocio concealed his real shrewdness, and with his verve, his ready jests, his strewings of charity—like a Robin Hood—he diverted attention from his monumental unscrupulousness. And though Gould's life was a torment, showing too plainly the cross of his overweening money-lust, Fisk rejoiced, brangled and drank while engaged with unequaled zest in the multitudinous details of his office. At the railroad headquarters of Taylor's Castle, he installed his buxom mistress, Josie Mansfield, whose dazzling white skin, whose thick black hair and gray eyes enthralled him so long and fatally, for whom he had forsaken his lawful spouse, and upon whom he lavished vast sums of money in his mad infatuation. Though Gould was himself puritanical in his private life, and disapproved of his partner's lavish style, he would say nothing. Though his was the directing brain, he knew how much he owed his success at the outset to the brimming energies, the audacity, and the unfailing good spirits of Fisk, whose cunning cynicism he understood better than anyone else.

Cut off from the financial capital, their situation was by no means comfortable, and the aging Drew complained bitterly. They held Erie, but the enemy held New York. It was rumored that Vanderbilt had offered a prize of twenty-five thousand dollars for the kidnaping of the trio; and one day a band of forty evil-looking New York toughs had crossed the river, and laid siege to the Erie offices. They retired to the Empire State only upon the appearance of superior forces.

After but a few weeks of enforced exile, Jay Gould suddenly departed for Albany upon a secret mission of tremendous importance. He bore with him a big valise containing $500,000 in greenbacks. At the state capitol, as Charles F. Adams explains, "he assiduously cultivated a thorough understanding between himself and the legislature," an understanding which later figured in the books of Erie as "legal expenses," eventually costing $1,000,000.

Gould, convinced that he had not heeded the letter of the law sufficiently, lobbied for a measure which would legalize the new issues of Erie convertible bonds for the sake of "construction and improvements." On behalf of Vanderbilt a formidable body of legal counselors, headed by the young, silver-tongued Chauncey Depew, descended upon Albany to advocate the condemnation of the Erie ring and all its lawless proceedings. Faced with such moneyed contestants, the excitement of the tribunes of the people passed all bounds. Never had such bounties been offered for good-will of state Senators. Riotous scenes were succeeded by more secret and muffled ones behind closed doors in hotel rooms or in saloons with the agents of both forces. On the whole, led by the astute Senator William Tweed, the statesmen conducted themselves with remarkable poise, and led the Erie and the New York Central men to bid against each other until the maximum levies were gathered from both.

Gould, arrested by order of the Supreme Court, remained in the custody of a sheriff's deputy, but continued his elaborate negotiations from his hotel suite. He admitted afterward having overpaid one man "in whom he did not take much stock" by $5,000. What did he pay then to those in whom he did take stock? Others were said to have received as much as $100,000, while, according to Charles F. Adams's account, still others received $70,000. Above all Senator Mattoon, chairman of the committee reporting the Erie Bill, appears to have been marvelously enriched after confidential interviews with both sides, and aroused the bitterest envy among his colleagues.

> *Fabulous stories were told of the amounts which the contending parties were willing to expend [reports Adams]; never before had the market quotations of votes and influence stood so high.*

An "investigation" ordered by the Senate thereafter (April 10, 1873) showed that more than a million dollars had been expended by Drew, Gould and their associates in the one year 1868 "for extra and legal services." But in the final stage Gould's extravagant generosity—perhaps owing to inexperience—was justified when the tide of battle swung to him. It had become known that Vanderbilt, with whom Tweed pretended to side because of an earlier pledge, would pay no more to have the bill defeated. In a rage the legislature had turned against him and passed the measure substantially as Gould desired it, and Governor Fenton, also believed to have been "assiduously cultivated," signed the bill. The indefatigable, unsleeping Gould in his first great political campaign, moving soft-footed everywhere, pressing money upon each lawgiver or menacing him through many quarters with defeat in his home district, triumphed at last by bold, hard work. His actions were made legal; his rule of the 800-mile trunk line was unchallenged—save in the city of New York, where a trivial charge of contempt of court overhung him.

In the following year his enemies made a serious effort to have the act of 1868 repealed, but Gould, testifying before the New York Senate Railroad Commission, spoke with impassioned eloquence in his own behalf. These continual hearings and investigations by the representatives of the people were the great public comedies of the times. His judges included members such as Mattoon, to whom he had previously justified his great designs behind the closed doors of hotel rooms or saloons by proofs valued as high as $20,000 at a time. And now before the same judges, turned sanctimonious and impartial, he must appear to justify in the eyes of the world what he had already proved in private. This shadowplay was part of the period's moral customs and social traditions, and Gould showed himself equal to his part. Though his heart might be full of contempt for the vultures who preyed upon his business, he would proceed to justify his ways to God and man, by pleading pathetically or impetuously in his own defense, and by playing upon their fears.

It was he, Jay Gould, who had saved the Erie Railroad:

And as long as that law (of convertible bonds) is unrepealed, I should do what I did again; I should save the road. . . . If that was repealed, I think Mr. Vanderbilt would have the road, but as long as it is not repealed it is held in terrorem over him.

Gould invoked, perhaps for the first time—here is immortal comedy—the specter of the arch-monopolist of railroads devouring the common people. The only way by which Mr. Vanderbilt's New York Central could continue to make exorbitant profits upon its watered stock would be through the control of the Erie and the end of its competition:

> *They would then control clear through to the Pacific shore; they could make the price of flour every day in New York or New England a dollar less or five dollars more; they could make the price all winter long.* . . .

He, Jay Gould, was for "competition," first, last and always. Warning, cajoling and appealing, Gould won his case and continued on his triumphant way.

The public, on the whole, seemed tolerably satisfied that the omnipotent Vanderbilt had been dislodged by new elements. Gould moreover had shown the highest abilities. He had shown himself equal to Vanderbilt in direct combat; he won acclaim through having seized a great railroad system in the teeth of the most ruthless adversary, who possessed the largest fortune in the country. He had shown himself master of Drew in both cunning and imagination, manipulating the markets with surpassing brilliance and working the printing press with even more reckless abandon. When the going was roughest, when the plot lay thickest, Gould had seemed only more dispassionate, his voice softer, only his eyes glowing more black. And from the whole campaign which so enriched him, he also absorbed rich lessons in statesmanship which he was never to forget.

In a statement made under oath before an investigating committee of the New York State Legislature, in 1873, he explained the principles of his successful political tactics, saying:

> *In a Republican district, I was a Republican; in a Democratic district I was a Democrat; in a doubtful district I was doubtful; but I was always for Erie!*

He had learned, moreover, that it was not enough to conquer a whole legislature; but one must buy the judges as well. In this direction his jovial and florid comrade, Fisk, operated with great sagacity after the spring of 1868; he made overtures to Tammany Hall and was soon well regarded there. As a means to ensure undisturbed rule over Erie's domain, William Tweed and his colleague, Peter Sweeney, had both been elected to the board of directors of the Erie Railroad. And though officially pledged to Vanderbilt, their secret influence, it was widely believed, had been thrown to the side of Gould.

Finally it was still necessary to make peace with Vanderbilt, a mighty power who must somehow be mollified. In the summer of 1868 overtures were made by both sides. Vanderbilt himself had written to Uncle Daniel a secret message:

> Drew: I'm sick of the whole damned business. Come and see me.
> Van Derbilt.

When the two met at Vanderbilt's house, the Commodore is believed to have said with his usual forthrightness: "This Erie war has taught me that it never pays to kick a skunk." He proposed terms which were severe, but appealed to the exiles more than perpetual isolation and attack from such powerful quarters. Drew, Gould and Fisk were to make restitution, repaying the Commodore $2,500,000 in ready money, another $1,000,000 subsidy in return for an option on fifty thousand shares of his stock, and $1,250,000 in bonds—in all a total of some $4,550,000 which he asserted had been stolen from him by way of the printing press. Drew accepted the terms meekly; and at a further conference early one morning in September, 1868, at which Gould and Fisk appeared in the Washington Place residence, a lasting accord was established, which brought immunity on old charges against them. It would appear that the Erie men assented to Vanderbilt's hard terms, somewhat reluctantly according to Fisk's account:

> The Commodore was sitting on the side of the bed with one shoe off and one shoe on. He got up, and I saw him putting on the other shoe. I remember that shoe from its peculiarity: it had four buckles on it. I had never seen shoes with buckles in that manner before, and I thought if these sort of men always wear that sort of shoe I might want a pair.
>
> He said I must take my position as I found it; that there I was, and he would keep his bloodhounds (the lawyers) on our track; that he would be damned if he didn't keep them after us if we didn't

take the stock off his hands. I told him that if I had my way I'd be damned if I would take a share of it; that he brought the punishment on himself and he deserved it. This mellowed him down. . . . I told him that he was a robber. He said the suits would never be withdrawn until he was settled with. I said (after settling with him) that it was an almighty robbery; that we had sold ourselves to the devil, and that Gould felt just the same as I did.

Vanderbilt had lost in any case about a million and a half in his jousts with Gould, and gave the new rulers of Erie a wide berth after this. He swore that he would "never have nothing more to do with them blowers," and he never did. But the transactions which brought peace were probably unique, as Fisk judged, in all the annals of "high" capitalism.

3

The Erie ring had returned to New York in triumph. Jay Gould was president and treasurer of the company, but Jim Fisk, its vice-president, was better known as the Prince of Erie. Desiring to set himself up in a style befitting the feudal power he disposed of, Fisk caused the offices of the railroad to be moved, upon their return from New Jersey, to the marble halls of Pike's Grand Opera Palace, at Twenty-third Street and Eighth Avenue, which was then grown to be one of the widest and most fashionable thoroughfares in the city.

From the marble-paved theater lobby at the street level, with its frescoed walls, illuminated by great gas chandeliers with a thousand pendants of cut glass, and ornate with gilded balustrades, a grand staircase ascended to the railroad offices on the second floor. The officers' suite was also decorated in Oriental splendor of silken hangings, mirrors, rich rugs, marble statuary and carved oaken furniture. Close by was a massive strong-box or vault that ran through several stories of the building; and in the cellar was kept the famous printing press which was so important a weapon of offense and defense. The executive offices were surrounded also by a heavy iron grill and guarded night and day against ever present dangers of attack or process-servers.

Here the former circus laborer and notion-peddler, Fisk, with his

pard Gould, who had run barefoot over the thistles to tend his
father's cows, throned over their lordly domain. For his own amusement Fisk launched operettas or musical revues such as New York
doted upon in the Opera House below, which became often the
scene of "glittering assemblies of fashion"! He loved the crush of
crowds, loved to move among the admiring glances drawn to him,
dressed in a scarlet-lined cape, a frilled shirt over his expansive
bosom, in the center of which sat the immense flashing diamond
sparkler of wide fame. Behind the Opera House Palace on West
Twenty-fourth Street were Fisk's home and stables, joined to it by
a secret passageway. Close by on the same street was the home he had
given to Josie Mansfield. And with her, or with a pair of his theater
queens, all laces and flounces, on either arm, he would go driving
to Central Park on fair days, the attraction of all eyes, in his swift,
gleaming coach of bright blue with its red running gear.

There was an aura about him, compounded of his gaudy costumes
(as a colonel of a militia regiment), his sensational frauds, his scan-
dalous private life, and his charities to poor old women or news-
boys who approached him. In song and story, "Fisk never went back
on the poor." Florid chronicles of his time likened his life to

> the sweep of a fiery meteor, or a great comet . . . plunging with
> terrific velocity and dazzling brilliance across the horizon, whirling
> into its blazing train broken fortunes, raving financiers, corporations,
> magnates and public officers, civil and military, judges, priests and
> Presidents.

Much of this legend, especially of Fisk's generosity, was over-
colored; yet it all had value to this Barnumlike railroad president
and goes far to explain the power and prestige he enjoyed.

Behind the ponderous silhouette of Fisk the terribly sober Gould
worked unceasingly to exploit his opportunities, which now seemed
boundless. During prosperous seasons, the Erie rulers levied toll as
they pleased, much like the Commodore himself, over their own
broad territory. There were trade wars for Gould's attention at
other seasons, armed conflicts with rivals, delicate negotiations with
Tammany, forays into the stock market, new consolidations and
expansions toward the west; and finally there were the many horrendous disasters on the line of the Erie, such as lent the road its

picturesque reputation lasting almost down to the present day.[1] But from season to season the young railroad master marched upon his road to fortune, almost unswervingly, exciting the wonder and also the terror of those few contemporaries who had occasion to see him from close by.

Like the great military vassals of other times who might legitimately waylay merchants and pilgrims, unarmed bishops and abbots, or all who passed through their toll roads, so Gould and Fisk took tribute large and small along their right of way. The case of the Pennsylvania Blue Stone Company, a famous example, showed also their necessary alliance with a statesman such as Tweed. From the quarries of this flourishing company, the Erie had refused to carry building material into New York unless it received a ransom in the shape of a partnership in the business. What was the quarrying company worth without the railroad? Cut off from its market the company was compelled after a short struggle to accept Gould, Fisk and William Tweed as its partners—these directors of Erie seeing to it thereafter that no other stone was carried over their lines, while Tweed as the head of Tammany arranged that the city government should buy all of the company's stone at extremely favorable prices.

[1]In an appeal to the Railroad Committee of the New York State Legislature (Proceedings of January 14, 1869), Gould himself submitted a confidential letter from his superintendent, in order to show that new issues of bonds and stocks must be authorized.

The condition of Erie's rolling stock and tracks was most alarming. "The iron rails have broken and laminated and worn out beyond all precedent," warned the official, "until there is scarcely a mile of your road, except that laid with steel rails, between Jersey City and Salamanca or Buffalo where it is safe to run a train at the ordinary passenger or train speed, and many portions of the road can only be traversed safely by reducing the speed of all trains to 10 or 15 miles per hour.... We cannot and do not attempt to make the schedule time with our trains; nearly all lose from two to four hours ... and it has been only by the exercise of extreme caution that we have been able thus far to escape serious accident."

Such evidence, produced on the pretense that the officers wished funds in order to buy steel rails, aroused the protests of certain "watchdogs" of the public interest, which in turn brought from a vice-president of the road, a certain Diven, the rejoinder: *The public can take care of itself. It is as much as I can do to take care of the railroad.*

Questioned as to the actual value of Erie stock Gould answered candidly: "There is no intrinsic value to it probably; it is speculated in here and in London and it has that value."

Other notable adventures of Gould's involved the preëmption, in similar fashion, of coal mines, ferries and harbor rights; of strategic railroad links to the west, for whose ownership the New York Central and the Pennsylvania could be made to "pay through the nose." By swift, secret operations he added the weak Atlantic & Great Western Railroad, running between Cincinnati and St. Louis, to his system; then the Pittsburgh, Fort Wayne & Chicago, which the Pennsylvania Railroad only wrested from him by hurriedly calling a special session of the state legislature to outlaw his marauding intrusions. Those who faced Gould with weak arms received short shrift from him. Even Daniel Drew, ousted in 1868, had tried to raid the stock of Erie in one of his famous bear operations. Gould, pretending at first to be in connivance with his old mentor, for the sake of financial sport, had suddenly turned and ambushed him, in a brilliantly executed "corner." Frantic and weeping, the aged Drew saw himself ruined beyond repair; he found the screws turned upon him as mercilessly as he had been wont to turn them upon others; he was driven from Wall Street forever after this last disastrous adventure.

The victorious road of a Gould was strewn, according to gloomy report, with the financially lifeless bodies of so many victims destroyed by ruse that he soon came by the name of "the Mephistopheles of Wall Street." One distracted victim of his deceiving counsel rushed upon Gould in his private office one day with a loaded pistol, crying out with frenzy that he and his family had been deliberately betrayed and ruined. Upon the instant Gould, in fear of his life, had given the man a check for the full $25,000 which had been entrusted to him. It came in time that he must be wary for his own person; like one of the nobles of feudal Italy he moved about, defended from physical assault by his bravos.

The post-war period became thoroughly hardened to the repeated collisions between the railroad barons which might burst forth at any moment anywhere in the coal fields of the East or the wild gorges of the Rockies. The scope of these conflicts varied in accordance with the magnitude of the prize at stake, from mere street clashes to summer campaigns which were not lacking in bloodshed, and were waged fiercely enough with a couple of dozen soldiers, peasants and field hands on either side.

The Erie ring, from Gould and Fisk at the head, to the merest legal and political henchmen who ran its errands, all understood the importance of controlling the new coal fields being opened up in Pennsylvania, and the freight highways which connected them with the markets. In January, 1869, when a new railroad had been constructed by private promoters for 100 miles between Albany and Binghamton, called the Albany & Susquehanna—at the cost of state and county subsidies—a bitter struggle developed suddenly for the control of this link between the hard-coal regions and New England—a struggle in which the Erie ring met with a signal defeat.

Opposition to the president of the road, one Ramsey, who had worked hard to build it and profit from it, arose from an obscure coal-mining corporation chartered as the Delaware & Hudson Canal Company, which had its own reasons for coöperating with Erie. They strove to seize the road as a spur for their own system. The agents of Erie, carrying bundles of cash, were quickly thrown out into the country to buy up stock held by the townships along the way which had underwritten part of the building cost. Fisk, taking the field himself, paid bounties for the interest of town councilors, with his usual high-handedness and resolution. But in the opposing camp he met with uncommonly stout resistance. To the support of Ramsey came a rival coal company, the Delaware, Lackawanna & Western, out of whose shadows there emerged a new and most vigorous personality, almost as crafty as Gould, and more pugnacious than Fisk himself: it was the thirty-two-year-old New York banker J. Pierpont Morgan.

With the share-holdings deadlocked, a duel of legal strokes and counterstrokes began and continued through the spring and summer of 1869. The board of directors being evenly divided between the two forces, there were sometimes wrestling bouts for control of the stock-books. Finally, believing that he had sufficient law on his side, Jim Fisk at the head of a dozen Erie porters marched to Albany to take over the headquarters of the little railroad; there he encountered the enemy and called on him to stand and surrender. "Rush in, boys, and take possession—throw that gang out!" he cried. But some twenty thugs stepped through a door, and hurled Fisk and his men down the stairs of the Susquehanna office. The Ramsey

Morgan party met force with force, bribe with bribe and duplicity with duplicity. The outcome of the first phase of battle was that Ramsey and Morgan had possession of the Albany end of the road, while Fisk retired to its western or Binghamton terminus, where with the aid of local authorities he fortified himself strongly.

All traffic on the Albany & Susquehanna stopped; its affairs were in lamentable confusion, and the natives along its route, who with high hope of ensuing benefits had invested their savings and taxed themselves for its completion, were not only bereft of transportation but bewildered and frightened at the terrorism of the opposing captains.

The combat took ever new and fantastic turns. Feeling ran high. To end the deadlock, the Ramsey-Morgan party finally despatched a force of armed men, estimated by the press to be between 150 and 450 in number, who boarding a train one morning at Albany, rode down toward Binghamton to possess themselves of all the stations on the route and storm the Fisk entrenchments at Binghamton. At the same time, an equally formidable mixed body of Erie's Bowery toughs and sheriff's deputies departed for battle from Binghamton behind their own engine. Outside of a long tunnel, fifteen miles beyond Binghamton, the enemy locomotives, whistling and tooting their bells wildly, breathing fire and fury, met in head-on collision. "There was a crash and a smash," according to the accounts which have come down to us, "and the Albany locomotive rolled off the track, leaving the other without cowcatcher, headlight or smokestack."

The warriors of both armies had all jumped off as the two steam chariots collided, and yelling defiance had fallen upon each other with clubs, spades, axes and firearms. But the Ramsey-Morgan thugs were the better armed, and the Erie soldiers soon had the worst of it. Retreating as fast as they could, tearing up tracks and destroying trestles, they went back toward Binghamton, where they barricaded themselves anew and called regiments of the National Guard to their rescue.

The scene of battle shifted to various courts, under the dispensation of more or less collusive tribunes. The Albany faction made new issues of stock, after the fashion of Jay Gould; and the Erie ring countered with injunctions on the ground of fraudulent stock-watering. The quarrels of the armed railroad workers, of opposing station-masters at every depot, were exceeded by the contests of separate and rival boards of directors who passed resolutions accusing each other of "fraud, violence, criminal and morally reprehensible practices" in a romantic rhetoric which neither party blushed to use. More vociferous, the original owners of the Albany & Susquehanna trumpeted their charge that Gould's party were but "unscrupulous usurpers who, by a sort of legerdemain," seized control of the stockholders' property, stole Erie's money, and so demoralized its service as to bring "calamities of unusual horror, damage and death."

At last public opinion shifted from high amusement or fascination to anger; Governor Hoffman of New York finally moved to take over the railroad at the petition of both factions and operate it until the dispute was ended by the state Attorney-General. Weary of the stubborn struggle, Gould, who was already absorbed in far greater adventures on another front, was willing to retreat discreetly when Ramsey was once more elected president, on September 6, 1869, and he allowed the Albanians to sell out control at an inflated price to neutral interests.

Pierpont Morgan, who had directed much of the campaign with a ruthlessness which now for the first time called attention to himself, had emerged with much credit. The balked Erie ring in its turn had acquired some of the unpopularity of Vanderbilt, and the "victory" of the newcomer Morgan was greeted with applause. He had demonstrated himself a force to be reckoned with, as truculent, as relentless in the fight, as crafty in legal subterfuge as the Erie men themselves; and his official biographer relates with pardonable pride that

> *Mr. Morgan made himself universally respected as an able financier in 1869, when he came out victorious in a memorable struggle for the control of the Albany & Susquehanna Railroad, which had fallen into the clutches of Messrs. Fisk and Gould. The contest was waged not only by litigation, but also by force of arms. . . .*

The *New York Times* reflected the general pleasure at the outcome of the weird struggle, concluding: "Justice, though tardy, is on the right track at last." Gould and Fisk had won little glory in the affray, but were apparently paid off well in the end. With his usual aplomb and philosophic detachment, the Prince of Erie rallied his comrades at Pike's Opera House over their reverses. *"Nothing is lost save honor!"* he exclaimed.

4

But all through the summer of 1869, the unfathomable Jay, moving about with soft tread and grave mien, was in pursuit of far greater game than a small Eastern coal road. It was the mark of his genius that nearly every defeat he suffered was turned into a victory: in the Albany & Susquehanna affair, after long litigation he was to end by liquidating his hard-won shares at a large profit in the final settlement. And with each fresh conquest he hastened without rest to undertakings more hazardous and difficult, and of a greater magnitude. He had a true gift for large affairs, and a kind of virile power to conduct many of them at the same time. His decisive conquest of Vanderbilt had stamped him as a master of railroad "operations." Though in its physical character as a machine of transportation, as a part of the American social-economic order, the Erie steadily augmented its ill-fame; although, as the historian Gustavus Myers had estimated, Gould may have added not a locomotive, a train or a station while increasing its fixed capital by about sixty-five millions in the few years of his reign, he might have explained if he wished that such criticisms touched matters of little consequence. The grand objectives from which his eyes never wavered lay in a totally different direction from any conceivable form of social duty, which in any case no authority was so senseless as to urge upon the great freebooters of his age.

The reservoir of money which lay in the Erie treasury under the nervous hands of Gould was in itself an engine useful for mighty "operations." Through its alliance with "Boss" Tweed the Erie ring also had some voice in the management of the New York City funds, amounting to between six and ten millions of dollars, deposited in New York banks. During seasons when markets were cheerful and money was "easy," the wizard of Erie could manipulate some twenty millions in currency, in conjunction with the Tammany men. Now as Gould's far-flung plans matured he applied with masterly skill the technique of stock speculation which he had learned from Uncle Daniel Drew.

After having sold Erie short at a good moment, Gould would

cause his associates to make sudden large withdrawals of cash from the banks under their control, so that money became "tight," loan rates shot upward (sometimes to over 100 per cent per annum), while stocks and grains and cotton collapsed in time with the planned raids, which were executed from season to season, without warning and with unfailing success. It was widely known that on certain occasions Henry N. Smith of the brokerage firm of Smith, Gould and Martin, together with Tweed, "drove up to the Tenth National Bank, the Black Friday institution, in a cab, and drew their balances out, Smith alone taking $4,000,000 with him, which he kept several days at home under lock and key."

Emboldened by his success in corralling a great part of New York's supply of ready money, Gould's mind was soon possessed by a scheme which envisaged nothing less than cornering the whole nation's currency. With the resources at his command, he could easily manage the floating supply of gold traded in every day in the Gold Room of the New York Stock Exchange. It remained only to take care of the federal Treasury's holdings of some seventy-five to eighty millions in some manner. If he could but lay his hands on this hoard, or *neutralize* it, the price of gold, metal basis for the national currency, could be manipulated at will and driven up to a tremendously inflated figure.

At the very time of the Erie wars on various fronts, Gould had begun to encircle government officials at Washington. In May, 1869, Abel R. Corbin, lawyer, speculator and lobbyist, wedded to President Grant's sister and considered very close to the White House, was tactfully approached by the Mephistopheles of Wall Street, and persuaded to contract for the purchase of $1,500,000 of gold at 133, though without payment on his part. Corbin, an old man, was very excited at the prospects which Gould unfolded for him, and apparently showed a lively sense of gratitude for the favors extended to him. To him and to other politicians high in the President's confidence, Gould also stressed the noble political motives underlying his campaign: the cheapening of greenbacks, renewed inflation, would cause the Western grain crops to move rapidly, and to be sold in Europe, stimulating all trade, and incidentally enriching the railroads. For never had farmers and merchants prospered so much as when it had taken, during the war, some $2.80 to buy a dollar's worth of gold, he argued. The dollar was too close nowadays to its gold parity; gold must be raised again; the dollar must fall.

In the gold market, where brokers traded every day against the legitimate currency needs of importers and commercial houses, rumors were stealthily introduced of Gould's coming campaigns, and in view of the general respect entertained for him as a free-roving economic power, created a vigorous following movement. But opposed to the bulls in gold were massive vested interests; the great banking houses, such as Jay Cooke & Co., which had bought and sold over two thousand millions in government bonds and "legal tender" and reinvested and multiplied their profits in inflated money. Now they exhorted the government to complete the process of deflation and make all obligations redeemable once more in "hard money" valued at the traditional gold standard. Upon a rising trend, the tide swayed backward and forward, in response to the masterly touches of Mephistopheles' golden baton.

In June President Grant, passing through New York on his way to a great Peace Jubilee in Boston, stopped at Corbin's. There the confederates besieged him with their entreaties; and on board the *Providence*, the following day, luxurious floating "palace" of the Narragansett Line, belonging to Fisk, Grant had become the guest of the Prince of Erie himself, who paraded in the uniform of an admiral after his own fancy among the glittering mirrors, the carved gilt furniture and the stirring airs of a brass band. While Fisk, bursting with vanity and flashing with all his sparklers, blocked the view of the assembled journalists and the brilliant crowd, Gould always hovering at the President's ear pressed his views upon him anew, but got no reply from the stolid little man, who puffed at his black cigar without uttering a word of his opinions. Disappointment at the President's evasiveness or uncertainty leaked out; gold dropped several points toward 125.

Unresting worker, Gould tried at least to keep himself intimately informed of the government's immediate fiscal policy. Through his and Corbin's direct influence, General Daniel Butterfield, prominent Union League politician and a friend to the Goldbugs (as they were popularly called), was appointed federal subtreasurer at New York. Propaganda for inflation was now actively disseminated in the press; hired lobbyists besieged all the doors of the statesmen.

In New York, for effect, a great banquet was given to Secretary of the Treasury Boutwell, at which the Erie ring played their part; and Boutwell, "with a superficial parade of purity and superior virtue, as well as genius," according to the *New York Herald*, "declared that he would not heed the gold gamblers, and that what was done in Wall Street was 'none of his business.' " Gold resumed its rise, and was quoted at 133.

The President's brother-in-law Corbin was then paid a check for $25,000 against his part of the profits, perhaps to show him how it felt, or to inspire him further. When next the President passed through New York on September 2, 1869, and visited Gould's accomplice, Corbin seemed to have exerted himself in earnest. Word went forth like wild fire that Grant had given orders to Secretary Boutwell not to sell any of the government's gold, advising him to continue "without change until the present struggle between bulls and bears is over." In a swift flurry, gold was marked up to 137.

The pool, which had been proceeding cautiously up to now, began its drive in earnest. A purchase of $1,500,000 in gold was opened in the name of subtreasurer Butterfield, without payment on his part; an attempt to confer a similar service was apparently made for General Horace Porter, private secretary to the President. And then Gould, the inscrutable, toward September 15 disclosed his plans to Jim Fisk (who had by his own relation known them only vaguely and remained skeptical), telling him in a guarded manner probably that Mrs. Grant and thereby her heroic spouse as well were involved in their net. Fisk now entered the affair with his combined gusto and slyness. In the marketplace he spread the amazing rumors by queer winks and nods; while Gould brought to bear his heaviest artillery with the mathematical precision he was noted for in such engagements. During the general buying wave which drove the price of gold above 141, the Tenth National Bank, Tammany-controlled, placed all its resources at the service of the ring. Its certified checks were issued in unlimited amounts against purchases of gold which were used as collateral. Up to the night of Thursday, September 23, when gold closed at 144¾, Gould and his confederates were believed to have accumulated forty millions in gold, or twice the available floating supply, thanks to the boundless credits opened by his banks. The man who in youth had busied himself inventing mousetraps was at the end of September, 1869, in a strategic position to engineer a gigantic "squeeze" in the national money market—unless the government entered the situation in determined fashion.

But here, at this fruitful stage, the alarm was suddenly given. That perennial friend and watchdog for the people, Horace Greeley, began thundering against the Goldbugs in the *Tribune*, after September 15, denouncing a vast gold conspiracy and calling upon the Treasury to sell gold and purchase bonds so as to relieve the growing currency tension. In Washington the Tycoon himself, Jay Cooke, made urgent representations to Boutwell and Grant, while the volatile Wall Street mob with rising excitement swung back and forth from one side to the other.

In their extremity the Goldbugs now applied the screws to the old siminist Corbin, who upon the spot wrote an importunate letter to President Grant, confessing his predicament and beseeching him not to ruin his own kin by unloading the government's gold. The slow-moving or wavering military hero, now thoroughly apprized of the situation, was deeply agitated and determined at last to move upon them with the force he usually showed when aroused. At his order a letter was written by his wife to Mrs. Corbin, urging that Mr. Corbin should sell his gold at once, and stating that the President disavowed all connection with him. Corbin, paralyzed with fear, must have communicated this alarming turn of affairs to Jay Gould in the night of September 23, or early the following morning. It needed but little more to convince Mephisto that the game was up.

What Jay Gould's final dispositions were for the business day that followed will always remain an obscure page of our history. Fisk always vowed that he was misled, the innocent tool of that "singular man" Gould. It was strange if no one smiled or coughed at Fisk's assertions. He was neither impoverished by his misadventures, nor were his intimate ties with Gould weakened in the least thereafter. . . .

Friday, September 24, 1869, was plainly marked to be the climax of the gold ring's campaign. Jim Fisk in person was to unloose an avalanche of buying orders, which would close the great trap, tightening the gold corner unbearably, so that the price might soar toward 200! But his buying was to be done in the name and at the sole responsibility of his brokers, Belden and Speyer, according to signed agreements made ready for that fateful day. The buying drive was to be continued unremittingly with rising pressure until word came by telegraph from Washington during the day that the federal government was in motion.

The market of "Black Friday" opened in pandemonium, after successive days of increasing tension. Above the uproar could be heard always the bellowing of the stout Fisk to his brokers to bid for all the gold that was offered; while reports were circulated publicly that Gould had prepared a list of names of 200 firms which had sold him gold futures, and would demand settlement without mercy. Starting from 150 gold climbed spectacularly amid frenzied trading to 160 and 165, while concerns of all sorts hysterically directed their agents to buy gold at any price. The riotous scenes that developed in exchanges all over the country were like to engulf the whole nation in ruins. During the mad gyrations of the day, from Boston to San Francisco banks and brokerage houses closed their doors, while the streets of the financial centers were thronged by a milling mob. In Philadelphia, the clocklike indicator of the gold market could no longer keep up with the lightning fluctuations, and finally a black flag with a skull and crossbones was thrown over its face by some distracted humorist, and trading continued under the funereal emblem. But in the temple of the New York moneychangers the scene, almost surpassing all powers of description, has been painted by Gustavus Myers in a purple passage of his "History of the Great American Fortunes":

> Here could be seen many of the money masters shrieking and roaring, anon rushing about with whitened faces, indescribably contorted, and again bellowing forth this order or that curse with savage energy and wildest gesture. . . . The little fountain in the Gold Room serenely spouted and bubbled as usual, its cadence lost in the awful uproar; over to it rushed man after man, splashing its cooling water on his throbbing head. Over all rose a sickening exhalation, the dripping, malodorous sweat of an assemblage worked up to the very limit of endurance.

What deepened the calamity was not merely the rise, but the catastrophic fall of gold which began with dramatic suddenness at midday as the government swung into action, when Boutwell ordered millions flung upon the market "as publicly as possible." Within fifteen minutes the whole structure toppled and the price broke at once to 138. While brokers swooned in the crush and stampede, "the agony depicted on the faces of men who crowded the streets," as the newspaper accounts affirm, "made one feel as if Gettysburg had been lost and the rebels were marching down Broadway." In the morning men who had been unable to buy gold announced themselves ruined with wild laments; and after the noon hour, great numbers who had paid too much in turn announced themselves insolvent with equally unrestrained expressions of grief, and menaces of death to the crazed brokers of the gold ring.

At the height of the frenzy, two of Fisk's "queens," by common report, had driven merrily through the financial section to witness their hilarious patron's triumph. But they had seen to their horror only a mob of ruined speculators besieging the offices Fisk and Gould were wont to frequent, crying for the heads of the conspirators. Fisk, perhaps feigning not to have heard of last-minute developments, made his way to the house of the abject Corbin to abuse him for a treacherous scoundrel; while Gould had fled from the lynchers by a back door.

Like an inspired fiend, Jay Gould had ridden out the storm to safety. He, "the guilty plotter of all these criminal proceedings," as the Congressional Committee of 1870 held, "determined to betray his own associates, and silent and imperturbable by nods and whispers directed all." He had miraculously saved himself in the face of disaster on the morning of September 24, selling all the gold he possessed upon the crest of the buying wave evoked by his agents. The cyclone of calamity had given favoring winds to his escape. Opinion differed afterward as to whether he had gained nothing, lost all he possessed, or garnered eleven millions of dollars at one coup.

In the aftermath, Jay Gould obtained twelve sweeping injunctions and court orders from his complaisant judges, prohibiting the Stock Exchange and the Gold Board from enforcing contracts or rules of settlement which he broke. The Erie ring's brokers, Belden and Speyer—the latter of whom had gone temporarily insane—defaulted completely and none of the bids they made were ever honored. Their bankruptcy did not affect Fisk in any way, since all the buying they had done to drive up the market was "in their own name and at their sole risk" according to signed documents found in his possession. Everything had been foreseen! No written order signed by Fisk was ever found. It was said that he and Gould had agreed to settle a large annuity for life upon each of the bankrupt brokers, and that Fisk's payment was through a perfectly satisfactory division of the prize with Gould.

President Grant was compromised by "indiscreet acceptance of courtesies," for the trail of the investigation, as Garfield wrote confidentially, "led into the parlor of the President." Though it did not touch him, it touched a member of his family; and so the conventional hearings by legislators ordered in 1870, and directed by men who held stock in the notorious Crédit Mobilier, took evidence which, as Henry Adams has said, "it dared not probe and refused to analyze." Executives, judiciary, banks, professions and people were all smirched, Adams concluded, "in one dirty cesspool of vulgar corruption."

How could Gould as a private individual have been punished for his perfectly legal whim to buy whatever quantities of gold he could obtain? There was not a law in the country that struck at the actions of the prodigious "self-made man" and no one understood this better than the unhappy "Railway Congressmen," Garfield and Blaine. Moreover, his motives, as he insisted at the ensuing investigation without once losing his self-possession, were blameless; he labored only in the interests of the people and especially the Western farmers. But Fisk had proved to be a bull in the china shop. He had turned the solemn hearings into low farce.

In a vein of injured innocence he dwelt on the "treachery" of the President's brother-in-law Corbin. With his own hands he had tried to punish the old man for his "infamy." Then, beside himself with more or less feigned excitement, Fisk called Heaven to witness that he had been wronged. He desired only to make a clean breast of everything. Let Mrs. Corbin, and finally Mrs. Grant, he clamored, be brought to the bar of justice. Alternately frightened and amused, the tribunes in Washington chose to pay him off with immunity, as a respectable merchant placates a loud-mouthed fishwife so that she may leave his respectable premises the sooner.

"Let everyone carry out his own corpse!" Fisk bellowed. And his inquisitors of the Congressional committee, understanding him perfectly, asked no further questions. They reported only what everyone knew: that "for many weeks the business of the whole country was paralyzed" and that the "foundations of business morality were rudely shaken."

CHAPTER SEVEN

GRANDEURS AND MISERIES OF EMPIRE-BUILDING

THE decade after the Civil War was on the whole an ingenuous and light-hearted one. Certain of its aspects made it appeal to later historians as a "Gilded Age"; and its closing years (of depression) alone suggested a Tragic Era. The Americans largely worked hard, drank hard, boasted often and loudly, and contended fiercely with each other for the same objects, while thinking the same thoughts and wondering at the same miracles of mechanical progress, or of Manifest Destiny in its ascending march, "uniform, majestic as the laws of being, sure of itself as the decrees of eternity." Everywhere was observed the same banging and hammering of "empire-" or mere town-building; the tumult of gold rush or land boom; everywhere the towns are "live," the streets of all the cities "are filled with brilliantly garbed shoppers and theaters, hotels and railways are crowded with jubilant throngs laden with inexhaustible sums of money."

To our great fortune, Mark Twain, the true child of the Gilded Age, swam at the vortex of the rush of gold-seekers, in the region of the Comstock Lode. Here at Virginia City he describes in "Roughing It" the sidewalks swarming with people, the streets themselves crowded with freight teams and other vehicles:

> Joy sat on every countenance, and there was a glad, almost fierce intensity in every eye that told of the money-getting schemes that were seething in every brain and the high hope that held sway in every heart. Money was as plenty as dust. . . . There were military companies, fire companies, brass bands, banks, hotels, theaters, "hurdy-gurdy houses," fights, murders, inquests, riots, a whiskey mill every fifteen steps, a dozen breweries, and half a dozen jail and

station-houses in full operation, and some talk of building a church.
The "flush times" were in magnificent flower!

If the Americans thought of themselves at all, it was as a restless, pushing, energetic, ingenious race, Henry Adams reflected—adding that this was perhaps not universally correct. Uncritically they accepted the same standards of merit to which Charles Dickens and so many other visiting moralists alluded so often.

"Well, sir, he is a smart man," was the repeated defense made of the famous persons who had so quickly preëmpted railroads, ore fields and harbor rights. Jay Gould was universally envied for his smartness and so was Jim Fisk smart; and though Beecher thundered at him as "the glaring meteor, abominable in his lusts, and flagrant in his violation of public decency," the age admired him without stint; at his worst "he had only done what others would have done in his place."

In the fall of 1870, following a dispute over wages, there was a strike of the brakemen on the Erie Railroad, and Fisk, vowing that he would never "submit to dictation," gathered together a thousand armed men, whom he sent up from New York under orders to shoot any workers who offered resistance. In this way he put down the "revolt" with great promptitude, and the press brimmed over with plaudits for the Prince of Erie. But if titles (Prince or Colonel) and honors were showered upon Fisk, statues were erected to the equally formidable Vanderbilt, who had managed to pour some $53,000,000 of "absolute water" into his railroads and turn this into gold! After the final consolidation of the New York Central system, extraordinary public honors were paid to the new owner and master, in May, 1869—though to be sure some of these festivals were bluntly ordered and paid for by himself. A statue was unveiled with much ceremony in a station at St. John's Park; and upon the pediment of the new railroad warehouse in Hudson Street memorial bronzes in *alto relievo* represented the Commodore himself, larger than life, standing in a central niche "rather stiff and dressed in the fur-lined coat he was fond of wearing." On either side he was flanked with an immense field of bronze devoted to the story of his life; marine affairs were represented on the right, sailing vessels, war vessels and Pacific Mail steamboats; while on the left were his railroad bridges, steam locomotives, and passenger cars. A popular and elegant orator of the day, Mayor Oakey Hall of Tweed Ring fame, likened Vanderbilt to Franklin, Jackson and Lincoln, as "a remarkable prototype of that rough-hewn American character which can carve the way of every humbly-born boy to national eminence...."; while a Bishop prayed that "as riches and honors had been heaped on Vanderbilt, he might devote all his ability to the cause of humanity and seek to lay up treasures in Heaven."[1]

For in truth a people who gave themselves as in a crusade, as Mr. Van Wyck Brooks has called it, to the exploiting and the organizing of the material resources of their continent, saw the grand social result achieved only in measure with the vigorous self-seeking of individual appetites. Hence the age adored a Vanderbilt or a Fisk, as models or roughness and strength, of shrewdness rather than of taste or moral refinement; and it tolerated the adulteries of Henry Ward Beecher no less for his silver tongue of a demagogue than for the reason that his religious newspapers and lecture business were projects of national scope. But then also, because of the very uniformity and poverty of private lives in the average, it may have enjoyed all the more freely, as Paxton Hibben suggested, "the atmosphere of profligacy" which surrounded Dr. Beecher no less than "Colonel" Fisk.

The ceremonies at this time in honor of the Iron Horses and of the Vanderbilts, Huntingtons and Fisks who bestrode it, reflected faithfully how the railroad developments of the time symbolized the nation's Manifest Destiny. "Surveying the whole field ... I fixed on the railroad system as the most developing force and largest field of the day and determined to attach myself to it"—so wrote a young New Englander whose family line boasted two Presidents, and who in another time might have carried on the family traditions of public service. Yet now groping for a "career open to talent" the younger Charles Francis Adams struck for the railroad field

[1]On all the bonds of the New York Central Vanderbilt caused his portrait, one of the finest physiognomies in America according to Greeley, to be engraved. A bondholder appeared before him one day and said: "Commodore, glad to see your face on them bonds. It's worth 10 per cent. It gives everybody confidence." The Commodore smiled grimly, the only recognition he ever made of a compliment. "'Cause," explained the visitor, "when we see that fine noble brow, it reminds us that you never'll let anybody else steal anything!"—C. K. Croffut, "The Vanderbilts."

though he knew the hazards, knew how dark and double were the ways here.

But those who could not become railroaders might at least invest in their stocks and bonds. Everybody was a speculator; everybody made "ventures," as an observer of 1870, Medberry, reported. Railway bonds sold like "hot cakes" abroad and at home; speculators in all kinds of schemes sought bonanzas for their greed. Medberry, in his "Men and Mysteries of Wall Street," relates:

> *Gold was the favorite with the ladies. Clergymen affected mining stock and petroleum. Lawyers had a penchant for Erie. Solid merchants preferring their customary staples, sold cotton or corn for future delivery or bought copper or salt on margin.*

The one fact that seemed to make prosperity perennial was the vast expansion of the railroads and all the resultant activities: the heightened demand for coal, iron, engines and materials, the kindled excitement in the factories, the call for laborers on every side, the rising wages, the swollen profits, the luxurious spending. Between 1865 and 1873, 35,000 miles of railway track were laid—as much as was built in the two generations preceding, and in itself a tenth of the whole world's railway mileage. With towns, such as Chicago, Duluth or St. Paul, doubling or quintupling in the decade, credit easy and optimism cheaper still, land- and town-site booming more and more frenzied, immense sums of money, saved or borrowed, were being invested with a beautiful abandon in heavy industrial goods, in the machinery not only of present transportation but of future growth. . . . With prices high, with bumper crops flowing over the new railways to Europe from the swiftly opened West, and their mortgage debts redeemable in "legal tender," even the most hard-bitten farmers became enthusiastic, enjoying great gains by inflated prices of wheat (at $2.50 a bushel), and buying stock in railway and banking enterprises. States and communities were vying with each other to promote the building of roads "that could not do anything but a paper business for years to come," as J. G. Pyle writes, "and the reckless discounting of these securities for the benefit of promoters and construction companies . . . the hypothecation the future proceeded rapidly, built a towering pyramid of hope." For the sake of railways most of which had only a future usefulness, the people turned over the proceeds of fifteen hundred million dollars, "not of money, but of grain, clothing, coal, iron and other substances," as an English economist, Professor Bonamy Price, remarked after 1877; goods which they actually possessed or expected to produce in the future. In return for these sums, they had the securities or promises of the railroads (and allied enterprises) to pay them interest and dividends, promises well rated and respectfully regarded and having a high market value so long as the course of empire-building remained as uninterrupted, "uniform, majestic ... sure of itself" as ever.

What rude awakenings the young nation must suffer repeatedly! After the moods of despair or disgust aroused by the report of the Gold Conspiracy, in 1870, it had gone back to its exacting tasks only to be startled anew by the scandals of the Tweed Ring in 1871. Here were episodes which could no longer be dismissed with the shrug or wink of indifference. "What are you going to do about it?" Tweed had been wont to say. But the predations of the political engine erected in Tammany Hall had gone too far. When the City of New York's debt was being doubled every two years, it was high time for the business men's Committee of Citizens to expel the marauders.

The trail had led once more to the Opera House of the Erie ring; for, as one of Fisk's earliest biographers observed in 1871, "Tammany Hall and the Erie Ring were fused together and ... contrived to serve each other faithfully."[2] Tweed was disgraced, and he and Peter Sweeney were hastily dropped by Gould from the railroad's board of directors. And now Jim Fisk could no longer, at his pleasure, imprison in the Ludlow Street Jail journalists who libeled him—as in the case of the intrepid Bowles of the *Springfield Republican*.

Enemies crept around more and more boldly as the disrepute of

[2]Judge Barnard, who had discharged injunctions like thunderbolts on behalf of Vanderbilt yesterday, was today at the complete service of the Erie ring; his person and office were part of the spoils involved in the alliance with the Tweed organization. Thus, at the time of the Albany & Susquehanna affair, Judge Barnard would issue whatever court orders were necessary to the lords of Erie, sometimes holding himself in readiness for their call at the apartment of Josie Mansfield, where he was not averse to the charms of cards, champagne and vivacious feminine company.

the Erie, called "Scarlet Woman" among railroads, increased. The vast sums of money raised by watering its capital continually were being poured into "the laps of wantons" by Fisk, according to common rumor. The princely suite of offices above the opera, barricaded and guarded, was the scene of nightly carousing and gambling. The scandals now rapidly multiplying concerning Tweed, Sweeney, Fisk, Josie Mansfield and their circle began to injure the credit standing of the company, at a time when financial conditions abroad were already shaken by war in France. The foreign, especially the British, holders of its bonds and stocks could liquidate their investments only at severe sacrifice. And each accident or wreck which caused the newspapers to scream in headlines *"Erie Massacre!"* only increased the trouble. The conviction spread among the weightiest persons, such as Junius Morgan, the Rothschilds, and August Belmont, that the Erie money machine had "gone too far," and like the Tweed Ring, in its drunkenness of power no longer observed the least of the proprieties.

Jay Gould and Fisk had fortified their position remarkably, a short time before, by causing the New York State Legislature to pass the Erie Classification Act. By this extraordinary measure, only one-fifth of the board of directors could be voted for or changed in any single year's election. Hence, without even possessing a dominant stock-ownership, the Gould-Fisk management could perpetuate itself for years to come, and easily prevent outside interests from entering the control. When English investors had complained of Gould's policies—especially of all the printing of bonds which debased their investments—Gould had easily aroused the native lawgivers to defend him against resentful attacks of the hated Britishers. Catch an Albany statesman helping John Bull! The long-swindled faction of Englishmen, who had many millions of pounds at stake, were then forced to abandon all legal attempts to obtain justice. With growing alarm the English saw that when they sent over newly purchased Erie stock to be transferred to their names, and to be voted as they desired, President Gould seized upon it and used their proxies himself, while the courts (Judge Barnard) and the state legislature upheld his actions. This was too much for human flesh to bear: it was not mere skullduggery; it was theft.

"Impatient of the Law's delay," as the New York Assembly's investigating committee of 1873 related, the foreign faction had begun, toward 1871, an elaborate political campaign against the "pirates" Gould and Fisk. American leaders, high in public esteem, including General Daniel Sickles, William Evarts and General Samuel Barlow, were employed as counsels to direct a "defense fund" which began at $300,000 and mounted afterward to $750,000, according to some estimates. These quantities of gold were employed in Albany to lay "substantial reasons" before the legislators on behalf of the un-happy British money-lenders. This was of course the one practical remedy for their trouble. To Gould's dismay, it began to take effect.

In a recent stock-market foray—the Chicago & Northwestern corner—Henry N. Smith, a member of the Erie ring, saw himself knifed in the back by his chief; the cornered stock had gone down, instead of up, as he had been led to expect. Ruined, he had turned upon Gould in vengeance, stolen the books of the Erie and given them over, together with other damaging evidence he pos-sessed, to the counsel for the protesting faction, General Barlow. Gould's enemies gaped at the documents in their hands; they had enough, plainly, to place the crafty Jay behind prison bars.[3] It was at precisely this dangerous moment in the affairs of the Erie ring (November–December, 1871), with Tweed on the verge of destruc-tion, Judge Barnard helpless to aid them, and incriminating evidence fallen into the hands of their financial enemies, that Jim Fisk too was involved in dark private scandals.

His fair yet unfaithful mistress Josie had for some seasons formed her fatal attachment to the gilded youth Ned Stokes, upon whom in turn she lavished much of the money which the Prince of Erie paid her. Stokes, though of good family originally, had turned blackmailer because of his chronic need for money. Through collu-sion with Miss Mansfield, he had armed himself with the most com-promising letters which Fisk had written her, wherein the railroad baron was shown to be not merely a transgressor of the Ten Com-mandments, but also—and what could be worse!—a cuckold. The unhappy Fisk had paid and paid, to avoid publicity, sums ranging between $5,000 and $25,000 at a time. Then, unable still to redeem

[3]According to indications in the recently published "Letters of Henry Adams" (Boston, 1931), General Barlow told Henry's brother Charles of his discoveries, and by these the two brothers were led to issue their "Chapters of Erie" in October, 1871, which, appearing at the tune of Tom Nast's power-ful caricatures, played its own part in the drama.

his letters, and harassed beyond endurance, he had stopped paying the shameless pair, and suffered that his once adored Josie should enter suit against him. The country at large now licked its chops as the scandal of this suit burst forth in the preliminary hearings of November 25, 1871. The public was promised by the metropolitan press that at the ensuing trial there would be "complete and damaging exposure of the crimes of said Fisk, Jay Gould and their confederates, and their division of the Erie Railroad spoils with the Tammany Ring." The affair ranked almost as high in the public favor as the melodramatic trial of Henry Ward Beecher and Libby Tilton.

Late in December, a few days before hearings in the case of Mansfield vs. Fisk were to be resumed, Jay Gould in deep alarm at so many ominous developments decided that Fisk must go. With little sentiment he asked his brother-in-arms to resign from the board of directors of Erie. He was now working in desperate haste upon a plan for the "reformation" of the Erie board under respectable leadership, including such leading figures as John Jacob Astor, August Belmont, Levi P. Morton; it was a plan, to be sure, which considered not for a moment the relinquishment of absolute power over the money machine in his hands. But the problem of Fisk soon solved itself adequately.

Renewed hearings in the case of Mansfield vs. Fisk on January 6, 1872, had proved sensational enough to please the strong appetites of the press. The cast was excellent: Miss Mansfield testifying against Jim Fisk was a fascinating Phryne, in a robe of "heaviest black silk, cut à l'Impératrice, while the "exquisite Ned Stokes...an Apollo, all glorious in a new Alexis overcoat of a dull cream color" was Gilded Youth itself, and Jim Fisk, jeweled, corpulent, with full mustachios, made a first-rate villain, equal to dishonoring a good woman and, for the sake of money, calumniating a youth of family as the "fancy man" of a demimondaine.

After the day's calamitous mischances, Fisk, bewildered and wretched in all his bulk, returned to Pike's Opera House (in the afternoon) where he busied himself in the arrangements for his departure from the Erie management. Then at four o'clock he walked to the Grand Central Hotel at Broadway and Fourth Street, on some obscure mission of his own. He was ascending the grand staircase of the hotel when the maddened Stokes, waiting for him pistol in hand, appeared at the landing above and fired point-blank at him. Fisk cried out in terror and pain, fell and rolled down several steps. He struggled to rise. Once more Stokes fired into his body, and fled, only to be seized in the street a few minutes later.

Late that night the Prince of Erie breathed his last. His body lay in state at the Opera House, while the grief-stricken Erie and Tammany men wept freely over his bier. The funeral was splendid; the Ninth Regiment, followed by a great crowd, paraded in honor of the dead Robin Hood. A meteor of the financial skies had passed off into the darkness beyond. Nast's bitter cartoon on that day showed Tweed, Gould and David Dudley Field mourning over the grave of Fisk, and was entitled: *"Dead Men Tell No Tales!"*

2

In these days there were strange lights and sounds everywhere, many signs of ill-omen to be read. Above the wreckage of reputations and hopes scandal would be floating like a pall over the blessed land. In the early weeks of 1872, Jay Gould was barricaded in his Erie citadel, while a line of sentinels defended him against the insurgent stockholders who were vigorously leading the "Erie Revolution."

Under renewed pressure the "reform" legislature at Albany repealed the Erie Classification Act. A new board of directors was now elected, and a new president in Gould's place. Yet Gould not only continued to hold the fort by force of arms, but tenaciously fought, at many a litigious turret and battlement, each step in the advance of the scaling party.

In this opéra-bouffe siege of Pike's Opera House, the fickle public and press applauded each gain of the brave revolutionists, as yesterday they had cheered on Gould and Fisk against Vanderbilt. When the "revolutionists" made exposures, and opened suit against Gould for $12,800,000, Erie's stock crashed in the market, everything looked dark for Gould, and the public cheered wildly. Finally, on March 11, 1872, in a virtual *coup de main*, the soldiers of the party of dissenting stockholders headed by their "other" president, one Archer, succeeded in storming the Erie offices, overpowering the Erie thugs, and possessing themselves of the company's books and papers. The triumph of the Erie Revolution was attended with general jubilation throughout the country and a break in Wall Street. Bearding Gould in his den, the insurgents waved in his face the evidence they had, which was incriminating enough to send him to jail. But instead of the implacable foe they knew, they found a man of lowered resistance who made gracious gestures of conciliation. Let there be peace, he said, like the victor of Appomattox. He offered upon the spot to lay the whole case for arbitration before Horace Greeley, the sage of New York. This being refused by the conquerors, Jay Gould not only bowed to the inevitable and abdicated, but in the complex, protracted negotiations in which both parties must be presently involved he generously offered to coöperate with his erstwhile opponents!

At bay, he himself offered to make restitution, though it would ruin him. He would restore as much as he could of the "plunder"— alleged to be twelve or thirteen millions of dollars—if they would leave him his financial life. And more, he whispered into their ears, the railroad property they had captured at last had nothing left in it. There were no visible assets, as they perceived, against the $64,-000,000 of securities which he and his associates had printed during the past five years. But if they would only be his friends, enter into an alliance with him quietly, and follow him—for who knew the labyrinthine way better than the wily Gould—he would not only restore, but would lead them into the promised land. There would be gold enough for all.

A Molière, a Balzac alone could paint the strong passion, the glittering eyes of greed, which Gould, Circe-like, aroused in the swine, jackals and wolves who pursued him: the Dixes, Belmonts, Astors, Morgans, Goldschmidts, and others who figured in the dissenting stockholders' faction. What he asked of them was that they cease combat, join arms with him, as soldiers of fortune, against the common enemy outside. He would conduct great pool operations in the Erie stock in whose profits they would all rejoice with each turn of the wheel.

Now the situation was changed; the insurgent stockholders and their lawyer-generals were no crusaders for religious virtue, but practical, upstanding business men, seeking to recover lost moneys. Gould's offer was to replace some six millions in securities and money, while in return he was to receive from them an option on 200,000 shares of Erie stock at 30, the low price to which it had fallen. By engineering a bull movement, raising Erie stock to 60 or 75, he would further revive their depreciated holdings.

The bargain was struck in secret; all pending suits were withdrawn by the "revolutionists" and the slippery Gould began his uncanny prestidigitation. On one day, as a recent biographer of his relates, "it was reported that Gould intended to restore the plunder he had taken, and Erie advanced violently. Then a denial would follow, and the stock declined." But with each change in the market Gould and his mates were forehanded, buying at the bottom and selling at the top. Then with a flourish, "as publicly as possible," according to the plan, the agreement of restitution was announced: Gould was to turn over the Opera House and adjoining buildings held in his name, and in addition stocks to the par value of $6,000,-000. At this favorable news Erie bounded forward sensationally, and Gould unloaded all his 200,000 shares through his many brokers, "reimbursing me for the money I have paid Erie," as the *New York Times* reported him to have said on January 24, 1873. This was Jay Gould's last bow to the Scarlet Woman of railroads. The securities he had surrendered proved to be worth only $200,000. The road was looted. Once more this craftiest of Americans had outmaneuvered his enemies and out of defeat snatched new millions.

3

Gould was still at large, traveling for his health in the Far West and studying with interest divers railroad properties there; but the evil he did lived after him. The subsequent collapse of the Erie Railroad, and the distribution among so many investors of its worthless paper (in lieu of their savings) were the pre-conditions, as Charles F. Adams, Jr., noted, "intimately connected with the sharp stringency then existing in the money market."

Nor was he the only destroying power now moving through the land. At the very moment of the scandals concerning Fisk, and the Erie Revolution, tumultuous uprisings in the Oil Regions of Pennsylvania were following John D. Rockefeller's masterly campaigns of expropriation.

Early in 1872, by a leak of information, word appeared in the press of the Oil Regions "of a gigantic combination among certain railroads and refiners to control the purchase and shipment of crude and refined oil from this region." Then, shortly afterward, by a premature release, a subordinate official announced the proposed new schedule of freight rates doubling the old ones on February 26, 1872. The meaning of this was at once plain to the men along Oil Creek. These turbulent, easy-going oil-diggers realized that their margin of profit would be wiped out, that the oil combination, already called the "Anaconda," would seize the whole refining industry and have the producers at their mercy. The Oil War of 1872 was on.

On February 27, the streets of Titusville, Pennsylvania, were black with demonstrating oil-diggers. The *Oil City Derrick* had made known the names of the South Improvement ringleaders in a blacklist. Mass meetings, parades, speeches exhorting to burn the enemy refiners' oil, to tap the enemy tanks, to lynch the "conspirators." A secret association of the independent oil men was formed at once and bound its members by fiery oaths and ritual to "unite against the common enemy," to stop all oil production, to sell no more to the refiners who were members of the Combination or Anaconda. Petitions were addressed to the Pennsylvania legislature and to Washington. Among the practical measures urged by the marchers and demonstrators was the building, of an independent railroad freight line, since from the existing railroads the oil men "expected only robbery." It was further advocated that an independent pipe line be built by government subsidy.

The stoppage of oil began. For a time no one would sell the buyers of the Rockefeller combination oil at any price offered. The men of the South Improvement Company could wait, though their refineries must be shut down for lack of crude oil. They could wait patiently until famine and greed broke the ranks of the fighting oil-diggers, marching in holy union today, but hungry for money tomorrow, and torn with dissension or suspicion. These men were known to be long on protest, but short on money for the fight.

Yet the oil war continued with unexampled bitterness. The produces knew only that a fiendish, an unheard-of conspiracy was directed against them; they moved not a drop of oil, and their clamor steadily filled the press, alarmed the statesmen. Though Rockefeller, Flagler and their partners kept quiet, hoping the storm would blow over, the railroad barons leagued with them were the first to give way.

The historic American experiment in large-scale combination had met with a fanatical resistance on the part of the individualists of the Oil Regions, which caused losses to the railroads. The aged Commodore of the New York Central, who had some years before placed his son William Vanderbilt in the management of his property, ordered the freight tariff reduced. He said ingenuously: "I told Billy not to have anything to do with that scheme...." The railroad barons, who had shown little honor in the first place, were also the first to show the white feather and make public expiation. The oil of "outside" refiners moved again over their lines.

At a secret meeting of the independent oil men with the railroad chiefs, Scott and William Vanderbilt, Rockefeller and his agent P. H. Watson (who was actually president of the South Improvement Company) intruded themselves boldly and, denying their part in the combination, made efforts to placate their opponents and participate in the new agreements promulgated. They were ejected with quite violent language, and Rockefeller went away "seeming very blue indeed." The uprising, then, was no mere sound and fury this time. In response to the popular agitation, the Pennsylvania legislature soon revoked the charter of the South Improvement Company. The Anaconda was slain; the individualists of oil were jubilant at their victory, and sold their oil now freely to the broken parts of the combination at momentarily high prices. John D. Rockefeller, in wary retreat, brooded thoughtfully over the lessons of his first great industrial battle.

Time would prove if he were right. Would not the chaos of "oversupply" and falling prices reappear tomorrow to harass the heedless diggers of oil? Then he would cling to his plan, which was the thing of destiny; the cleverest, and now the most vociferous of his adversaries, men like John Archbold and Henry Rogers, would comprehend this and join forces with him. There was to be little peace for him; and in the ceaseless conflicts of his age, he would be tempered into a great war lord.

During forty years the Standard Oil men marched from trial to trial like habitual felons, before the public was convinced that it was not dealing with the archcriminals of the age, but with destiny.[4]

---

[4]The Common Law, since the time of Elizabeth, had condemned Monopoly or Conspiracy in trade, such as tended "to the impoverishment of divers artificers and others who before by the labor of their hands In their art or trade

The opposition was always on behalf of a laissez-faire individualism. Miss Tarbell, in her crusading days, before she turned official apologist for famous capitalists, was but championing (and in the name of her expropriated father) the wastefulness, the competitive anarchy of the independent Pennsylvania oil-producers. Rockefeller, on the other hand, was literally the instrument of economic determinism; he was the more or less conscious guiding genius of a process of concentration which held in view the national (and even international) rather than the local organization of oil exploiting. Under his example American capitalism advanced swiftly toward a new phase, transforming, as the most profound social prophet of the century was saying at this very time, "the pigmy property of the many into the titan property of the few, transforming the individual and scattered means of production into socially concentrated forms." This is the true character of the historic process which passes before our eyes in the American scene of the '70's and '80's.

It was an age which seemed "gilded" or "tarnished" or "dreadful" or "tragic" by turns; yet an immensely fruitful age, under whose surface movements of strife and confusion, of repulsion and attraction, one capitalist expropriated others, the strong steadily went on destroying the individual independence of the weak, and in systematic fashion "the large capitals got the better of the smaller ones." Thus all the scattered individual means of production were being brought together, as Marx wrote, into the "new centralization," hastening the development of society, breeding the new technical means for "those tremendous industrial undertakings which can only arise as the outcome of the centralization of capital." And the birth-throes of a new social order, but added to the turbulence of the age, with its sounds of ringing arms, its shouts of the conquerors, groans of the fallen. Under Rockefeller, a giant industrial machine was raising itself over the land.

Thenceforth, though persecuted and pilloried, himself the most hated man of the age, he would retain his lead, hang on like death

have maintained themselves and their families, who will now of necessity be constrained to live in idleness and beggary." Such statutes reflected the responsibility of the Tudor régime for the survival of its peasants and laborers at a stipulated level of existence, a responsibility which was completely rejected as a feudal relic by the new barons of eighteenth- and nineteenth-century industrialism.

to his great unifying idea, advancing anew after each momentary retreat, evading all attempts at regulation, until the Standard Oil, with its refineries, pipe lines, tank wagons, ships and foreign terminals, had become an industrial empire as far-spreading as the British Empire, until Babylon and Nineveh and Peiping were illuminated by Standard kerosene. Rockefeller's organizing genius would create the "mother of Trusts," soon to spawn a score of other great "Trusts" in whiskey, cattle, beef, sugar, coal, iron and copper. The Standard Oil "Trust," as a corporate device, as a capitalist construction, had the beauty of one of the new steel suspension bridges. A bridge between the past and the future.

4

While Jay Gould kept the marketplaces of the Eastern cities in turmoil, his railroading exploits surpassed by only little a hundred other such "operations" carried on simultaneously in all parts of the country. Thus the long-established Baltimore & Ohio Railroad had been expanding its capital debt continually, by selling its securities to foreign investors. "Notwithstanding these great increases in liabilities," writes John Moody, "the company continued to report large surpluses and to pay large dividends—generally ten percent annually"—and this right through the battles of the Civil War when much of its trackage was destroyed. In the same way, Carnegie's friend Thomas Scott had floated many millions in bonds against the charter he had obtained for the Texas & Pacific Railroad, which was to run from the Mexican Gulf ports to Southern California, although but a few miles of the road had been actually constructed. The sagebrush deserts of the Far West, like the rich prairies of the Northwestern territories, were carved up with brief, inglorious "streaks of rust," running under grand names such as "St. Paul & Pacific," or "Kansas Pacific," endowed with subsidies in cash or millions of acres of land grants, but all equally impoverished and often boasting of nothing more than one or two worn-out locomotives and ten miles of track. Scandal and heavy misfortune followed these hopeful ventures, of which the notorious Union Pacific affair was the outstanding example at the time.

All through 1872, in the Crédit Mobilier, the construction company which had built the first transcontinental road, "thieves' quar-

rels" had been brewing, but were kept muffled up to the hour of
Grant's election. Ever since the railroad had been completed three
years before, the brothers Ames, as one faction, and the group
headed by Durant had been at loggerheads over their shares of the
rich building contracts. The litigation between the factions revealed
how Oakes Ames, Representative from Massachusetts, had been distributing a quantity of stock among the most influential members of
Congress ever since 1867. The investigations he had sought to fore-
stall by such artful measures burst forth like a bombshell in January,
1873. Jay Cooke, using all his mighty influence in Washington, had
been unable to stop the exposures, which he declared were "nonsense" and would damage our credit abroad, but which everyone
clamored for.

"The House seethed like a cauldron," the watching lobbyist
Henry Cooke wrote to his brother. "You cannot imagine the de-
moralization in Congress." Called to testify to his part before the
House, and believing his case desperate, Oakes Ames called the roll
of corruption himself from a memorandum he drew from his pocket.
In the gifts of the Crédit Mobilier (in its *preferred list* one might
say nowadays) were implicated Republicans and Democrats alike:
James Garfield, a future President; the Democratic floor leader,
James Brooks (who had got $15,000 so that the other side would
be "taken care of"); the Vice-President, the Vice-President elect,
and numerous Senators and Representatives. Colfax, Garfield, Wilson and others lied or brazened their way out of the scrape. In
scenes of soaring passion, witnessed by galleries packed with the
throng of Washington society, bitter recriminations flew back and
forth. It came out that the direct profit of the group in the Crédit
Mobilier must have exceeded $33,000,000, as shown in the House
Report of February 20, 1873; other estimates ran as high as $50,000,-
000 (forever unaccounted for). By fraudulent procedure the first
mortgage securing the government's loan of $27,000,000 had been
set aside, and a new first mortgage executed and sold, the proceeds
of which were also diverted to the holding company.

In a fury the "radical" Republican machine had turned upon
Ames and impeached him, Claude Bowers holds, "as a warning to
corrupt Congressmen against turning State's evidence." The Democrat Brooks was similarly expelled "for being a Democrat"; while
the rest whose names were smirched by the inquiry, and who ex-

postulated bravely à la James G. Blaine, were exonerated and survived. Yet the tale of appalling waste, of crime and turpitude shook the whole country like a mighty quake and set many a weak structure to rocking. In the bourses panic seethed; thousands lost their savings in Union Pacific's fall, while distress spread quickly to the grain-growing regions. From the rostrum the tribunes of the people, those who had not frequented the railroad barons, began to speak out, in tones soon to become familiar whenever such provocation arose, against the giant corporations which overran the country, "wielding and controlling immense sums of money and thereby the greatest influence and power ... so that in effect, in many State Legislatures, they became the ruling power of the State." The era of Tarnished Reputations unrolled itself, and the lingering humiliation it brought is commemorated in one of the eloquent speeches of Senator George Hoar, some time afterward:

> *When the greatest railroad of the world, binding together the continent and uniting the two great seas which wash our shores, was finished, I have seen our national triumph and exaltation turned to bitterness and shame by the unanimous reports of three committees of Congress that every step of that mighty enterprise had been taken in fraud.*

5

These days even the Indians were restive. In the summer of 1873 raids by the embittered Sioux along the extending line of the Northern Pacific in the Yellowstone Valley caused the death of five or six white railroad workers. At the instance of Cooke troops were called to cover the advance of the engineers. The bearded cavalrymen in blue crossed the Missouri River in large force, with the audacious ill-starred Custer at their head. As the soldiers cleared the Black Hills of their red-skinned proprietors, the pioneers crept behind them, grubbing the earth for gold and silver.

Jay Cooke, the heroic financier of the war, who now carried forward the country's second transcontinental railroad, had attained after the war a style of grandeur scarcely known in all the Western world. His mansion outside of Philadelphia, "Cooke's Castle," as Justice Chase called it, had fifty-two rooms; its walls were decorated with frescoes, and further ornamented with three hundred paintings and statuary and glass paintings of Indians all about. It contained a theater, fountains, conservatories, and finally an Italian garden, "facing a wall built to resemble the ruined castle of some ancient nobleman." But like Robert Morris before him, Jay Cooke too lived in agony among his marble halls and palace walls.

Among the many burdens which weighed down the great banker in 1872, had been the election of Grant, most costly and yet necessary to him. Again and again he had had to help "save a state"—this at a time when but a fifth of the railroad loans he needed could be sold in London or anywhere, while drafts upon his office for "construction" continued regularly at the rate of $1,000,000 a month. His methods of business harked back to an older, simpler period, when the alliance with press and political cliques was an open and direct affair. He would groan at the importunities of a Blaine, a Chase; to him the politicians were so many Oliver Twists. To add to his woe a section of the Northern Pacific tracks, hastily engineered, suddenly sank into a northern lake and had to be resurrected with great pains. The titular president of the company, one Smith, had to be ousted suddenly for excessive corruption. By the beginning of 1872, the railroad had overdrawn $1,600,000; a year later, its overdrafts stood at $5,500,000, its bonds were selling at a heavy discount, and all of this must be carried by one man.

It is the tragedy of the banker that he must exude confidence among all who surround him, come what may. Gigantic successes ever since 1861 had made the Tycoon seemingly invincible. To his partners who bombarded him with warnings nowadays as the Crédit Mobilier scandals spread mistrust of such projects as his, this eternal optimist, calm, white-bearded, ruddy-complexioned, with the eyes of a young man, gave no sign of fear. In his great pride he gave repeated assurances of his ability "to make good." Money loaned at times at 160 per cent a year; it was so scarce that laborers on the Northern Pacific were paid it vouchers or scrip after October, 1872. Yet Cooke determined to launch a great pool, creating a bull movement in his securities and distributing added quantities of them among the public. To win quick profits and tide him over his difficulties, he prepared also for the new government the refunding operations of 1873, by which $300,000,000 must be financed. But to, here in a field where he had been supreme for a decade and held a complete monopoly, a cabal was suddenly directed against him by his rivals.

In June, 1871, Pierpont Morgan, who had won respect by force of arms as well as business acumen, joined forces with Anthony Drexel, the largest banker, after Cooke, in Philadelphia. Drexel, Morgan & Co. was a powerful combination, aided by the prestige of the Drexels in Philadelphia and linked with the bank of J. S. Morgan in London. Joining with other envious spirits "young Morgan," as Cooke called him, moved to wrest the monopoly of government financing from the Tycoon in the year following.

Drexel "owned" Childs, the head of the *Philadelphia Ledger*, which had never ceased attacking the Northern Pacific as a "South Sea Bubble." Now they caused the rumor to be circulated that Cooke needed the new government funding operation "to bolster up their credit, which had been impaired by the connection with the Northern Pacific." So the contest between the jealous bankers led to a resounding failure for the $300,000,000 government loan of February, 1873. The Cooke party was disgusted by the sabotage of the Morgan and Drexel group; but though news of the failure caused the price of gold to rise in London, and money to become "tight," with dangerous consequences everywhere, Morgan might exult now at having conquered a measure of financial equality with Cooke.[5]

The seven years of plenty after the war must now make way for seven years of dearth in a land literally "flowing with milk and honey." The excesses of the "golden age" caused forebodings even after 1871 and 1872, though they were but the natural, characteristic movements of the appetites of greed which consumed all who marched in the great procession toward fortune. In those who led the procession dishonesty, chicane, vulgarity and a fierce passion for lucre were curiously united, as the Beards have observed in their history, "with an intelligence capable of constructing immense agencies for economic services to the public...." A mere handful of contemporaries, such as Charles Francis Adams, Jr., shook their heads because the stock exchanges seemed the haunt of

[5]Though widespreading disaster flowed from the jealous contentions of the bankers behind closed doors in Washington, Drexel and his friends boasted of having downed Jay Cooke, according to the private reminiscences of a Philadelphia financier noted in Barron's diary long afterward.

gamblers and thieves; the offices of our great corporations appeared as secret chambers in which trustees plotted the spoliation of their wards . . . the halls of legislation were transformed into a mart where the price of votes was haggled over, and laws, made to order, were bought and sold.

Alarming incidents succeeded themselves. In November, 1871, the Chicago fire and the simultaneous failure of Charles Yerkes, the embezzling stockbroker of Philadelphia, sent their distressing vibrations not only through North America but through Europe. With one movement Europe now sought to throw back the American securities she had purchased with such abandon yesterday, into the limbo of crudeness and insecurity which the American society now seemed to her. It was a picture that was only too true.

The settlers who had so swiftly opened the new lands could no longer sell the mountainous stores of grain which they brought forth. Nor could they buy the wares of merchants and manufacturers. The war in France, a crash in the bourse of far-off Vienna in 1872, timed with the frauds of the Union Pacific, had slackened the pace of railroad-building, and this in turn spread idleness to the factories, shops and mines who gave the materials for empire-building. Soon the till was bare. It was as if a landowner in possession of a rich estate had determined to spend twice the increment from his estate in drainage construction. The drainage was an excellent operation which would benefit the land when it was done; but in mid-career he must pause. His savings and his income were gone; a part of his land must now be sold to pay for the drainage system which, left incomplete, helped as yet in no way, and burdened him the more. So with America and its railway madness.

The whole country had strained its nerves to the utmost to build up, to double its transportation machinery within eight years, exceeding by far its needs for a long time to come. Technicians pointed out afterward that in 1860 there had been 1,026 inhabitants for each mile of railroad; but by 1873 there were only 590 for each mile of track. The railways earned, as a rule, little or no return; in the future they would stand us in good stead, and it was a splendid "saving" on the part of the community. But government, investors and foreign bankers had provided some three billions of dollars, Europe roughly half of this. The Americans besides borrowing to the limit had plunged all their savings in "long term capital goods," in land, railroads and factories—they had no ready money, only title to "frozen assets." Now what if all at once optimism should be replaced by fear, at home and abroad, while the foreign banker or the widow on the farm clamored for ready money, for gold, in lieu of the promises on paper they possessed? Would the skyscraper of hopes come tumbling down?

Early in September, 1873, "that consummate master of speculation," as the press habitually named Mr. Jay Gould, sniffed the gathering storm. In the marketplace there was mounting excitement; borrowers were called by banks; bears hammered all the list; more borrowers were called. On September 8 one large firm of money-handlers, known to be connected with crippled railroads, closed its doors; on September 13, another. Rumors besieged the stoutest reputations, and a newspaper editor implored the Mephistopheles of Wall Street to do his fellow citizens the favor of quitting the country for "a third of a century." In Philadelphia, the façade of Cooke & Co. remained imposing, calm; behind its doors the partners whispered in low voices, or fumbled in strong boxes with masses of Northern Pacific bonds, notes upon railway iron and land companies.

"I feel an unfailing confidence in the God in whom we put our trust," wrote Jay Cooke to his brother. "I do not believe He will desert us."

On the night of September 17th, President Grant arrived at "Ogontz," the palace of Cooke, ate, drank with him and smoked the private brand of cigars which the Tycoon always kept in readiness for him. In this peaceful magnificence, sitting for long hours, speaking almost not at all with his dignified friend, the little General was shyly happy. In the morning the two men lingered over their breakfast, while Cooke, impassive as usual, read alarming telegrams from his partner Fahnestock in New York. At once Cooke proceeded to his Philadelphia office by carriage, revealing nothing to the President. There he learned that at eleven o'clock Fahnestock, having drawn a number of prominent bank presidents into his office, had at last with their advice closed the doors of the branch in New York. The great doors of Jay Cooke & Co. in Third Street, Philadelphia, creaked and were swung shut a few minutes later,

while Jay Cooke, turning his face away from the men who surrounded him, wept freely.

"The news spread like a fire in one of the Northern Pacific's own
prairies," writes Oberholtzer. The largest and most pious bank in
the Western world had fallen with the effect of a thunderclap.
Soon allied brokers and national banks and 5,000 commercial houses
followed it into the abyss of bankruptcy. All day long, in Wall
Street, one suspension after another was announced; railroads failed;
leading stocks lost 30 to 40 points, or half their value, within the
hour; immeasurable waves of fear altered the movement of greed;
the exchanges were closed; the stampede, the "greatest" crisis in
American history, was on.

"All about the failure of Jay Cooke!" newsboys hawked throughout the country.

For ten days the mad rout continued. The stronger railroad chiefs,
bankers and industrial captains fought each other mercilessly amid
the wreckage of their broken hopes and enterprises. It was a *sauve
qui peut* of rats. A Jay Gould flies about preying upon the rich
débris; and in the vast confusion, hulking figures such as that of
Cornelius Vanderbilt stand out, moving vigorously in their own
defense. To the appeals of his fellows Vanderbilt is adamant. "He
had no intention of being caught up in the whirlpool himself and
engulfed with the rest of the ruined," writes his biographer. So a
Morgan, a Rockefeller, a Carnegie rode out the storm with damage
more or less, while in the jettison of great enterprises and invaluable
assets younger adventurers, hitherto unknown, a Harriman, a Frick,
plunged in to wrest many a prize from the financially dead and
dying.

In the recoil of the forward movement all the services administered by the existing economic institutions, all circulation of things,
is halted while the "flight of capital" continues and money passes
out of circulation into hoarding. Where yesterday credit flowed
liberally to finance stores of goods, to move commodities of all
sorts, to aid the various projects of empire-builders, now no celebrated name, no merchandise commands any money value in the
marketplace but gold itself. The wealth of mountains of ore, of
iron foundries, of machines and factories, of rich farm lands, of
ships and railroad tracks, is called nothing but illusion. From 1873
to 1879, according to important personages in the iron trade who

were associated with Carnegie, "you could not give away a rolling mill"; nor could a 2,000-mile-long transcontinental railroad be sold even for a bagatelle. Now the constructive effort of those who yesterday were advancing the public good by seeking their own selfish ends is seen but as the dance of pursuers and possessors.6

No "act of God," no crop failure, no swarm of locusts over the land had brought great change over the smiling order of things. Indeed the stores of flour and cotton were bigger than ever; there were the identical subterranean riches of iron, coal and copper and oil, and an ever pressing need for food, clothing, machinery. And finally there were the same formulae of equality, the same rights safeguarding both property and personal liberty, although the settlers' farms continued to fall under the hammer and hundreds of thousands of muscular, industrious laborers wandered the streets begging for bread. Yet under the surface, to one who looked searchingly it appeared that the community no longer depended in any inclusive measure upon "the skill, dexterity and judgment with which its labor was applied," but in an increasing sense upon the groups of men who had placed themselves in a strategic position to organize and negotiate for the community's skill and labor. The laborious crowds in the cities were *free* to endure idleness or lowered wages; the digger of coal or of oil, the planter of corn and cotton, was *free* to accept such sums as were offered for his produce. Yet many who had before neither learned nor had occasion to practice a "holy thrift" had now no schooling to enjoy the leisure and liberty which was their privilege. A contemporary's account, cited by Gustavus Myers, recalls to us the disordered readjustments which followed the panic:

6Repeatedly Marx in his analysis of capitalism dwells upon the indignity of the money system which gave humans the air of crawling upon all fours. In a panic, owing to the general disturbance of the pecuniary mechanism, he demonstrates in "Capital," Volume I, "money suddenly quits this ideal form of money of account and materializes as hard cash. Profane commodities can no longer replace it. The use value of commodities becomes valueless, and their value is replaced by their own form of value. A moment earlier, the bourgeois, drunk with the arrogance of prosperity, was ready to declare that money was a pure illusion, and to say that commodities were the only money. Now when the crisis comes the universal cry is that money is the only commodity. As pants the hart for cooling streams, so does his spirit pant for money, the only wealth."

The winter of 1873–1874 was one of extreme suffering. Midwinter found tens of thousands of people on the verge of starvation, suffering for food, for the need of proper clothing, and for medical attendance. Meetings of the unemployed were held in many places, and public attention called to the need of the poor. The men asked for work and found it not, and children cried for bread. . . . The unemployed and suffering poor of New York City determined to hold a meeting and appeal to the public by bringing to their attention the spectacle of their poverty. They gained permission from the Board of Police to parade the streets and hold a meeting in Tompkins Square on January 13, 1874, but on January 12 the Board of Police and Board of Parks revoked the order and prohibited the meeting. It was impossible to notify the scattered army of this order, and at the time of the meeting the people marched through the gates of Tompkins Square. . . . When the square was completely filled with men, women and children, without a moment's warning the police closed in upon them on all sides.

One of the daily papers of the city confessed that the scene could not be described. People rushed from the gates and through the streets followed by mounted officers at full speed, charging upon them without provocation. Screams of women and children rent the air, and the blood of many stained the streets, and to the further shame of this outrage it is to be added that when [the attention of] the General Assembly of New York State was called to this matter they took testimony, but made no sign.

Soon the famished workers made haste to offer their labor for anything that might be paid them, where they had formerly enjoyed relatively high wages. Here was one of the "goods" of the immense débâcle coming out. In the annals of the great industrial barons it is told in one instance after another how each grasped at the uncommonly favorable opportunities offered to him. Thus Rockefeller after manly expiation had come to terms with the diggers of oil and entered a contract to buy a great part of their crude petroleum at the high price of $3.25 a barrel—a contract which depended upon an unfeasible pledge on their side to limit output. When as foreseen they could not control their flushing wells, he turned upon them saying: "You have not kept your part of the contract—you have not limited the supply of oil—" and cut his price to $2.50; then as the depression deepened, to $2, and later to 82 cents a barrel, while his own refined product was lowered in more moderate stages and the profit margin remained high. Carnegie on the other hand, who also possessed, as it was said of Rockefeller, the sense of "the critical moment for action," now pushed rapidly the construction of his huge steel mills. It was his genius to realize "that the real time to extend your operations was when nobody else was doing it," an associate said. By using cheap labor freely during the depression he would be fortified against competitors when the flush period returned. So at the same time Jay Gould roved through the West eyeing the ruined hulks of transcontinental railroads; while newcomers armed with capital lustfully appraised the value of mighty fragments cast off, the *disjecta membra* of an industrial system's agony. It was a profound truth that Carnegie uttered afterward: "The man who has money during a panic is the wise and valuable citizen."

PART TWO

PART TWO

CHAPTER EIGHT

RISING FROM THE RUINS

DURING the downward run of the markets, the great fortunes shrink, the masters of money retreat to strong positions. While the economic storm continues, while prices fall, the proper tactics for the possessors of capital are those of flight and self-defense. It is a cautionary experience; there are many casualties, cruel transfers of individual fortunes. Yet he who possesses even a modicum of unimpaired capital is as one who watches the sand run down in an hourglass, while fully aware that he may, at the given moment, turn the glass over and begin the process anew.

It is no time for sentiment. No one comes to the rescue of the open-handed Jay Cooke. If Thomas Scott's notes go to protest, Andrew Carnegie does not answer his calls for help. Refusal to aid his first benefactor, the man who had launched him into money-making, Carnegie himself admitted gave him "more pain than all the financial trials which I had been subjected to up to that time." It was the tune to keep close to one's own books, and meet one's own notes. If there was any liquid capital left it could be used, best of all, to purchase the properties sacrificed by the needy after shrewd estimates of their distress value. Carnegie had no thought for Scott's bankrupt railroad ventures, the pieces of which fell quickly into the hands of men with reserves, Gould and Huntington. In his own iron business, his partner Kloman, upon whose mechanical skill their reputation was founded, fell into difficulties; and Carnegie in 1873 acquired the craftsman's share of the business, eliminating him for good and all.

During the troubled years, as between 1873 and 1875, those who are already strongly entrenched extend their position with ease. The Vanderbilts, father and son, add new railroads in Ohio, Indiana and Illinois to their New York Central system, so that they are

enabled at last to enter Chicago upon their own tracks. The Vanderbilts also reach out for coal lands to unite with their railroads.
In their need for cash they must go to Russell Sage, the hoarder,
"somber, crafty, reclusive," who has cash when no one else has it,
and demands 12 to 14 per cent for its use. While the Vanderbilts enter Chicago, Gould captures a transcontinental railroad,
fulfillment of a boyhood dream; Collis Huntington, with the Pacific
Coast unaffected by the world depression, proceeds to build a second one; and unknowns like James Hill or Henry Villard take possession of other railroad principalities. Outside of Pittsburgh thousands of acres of coal lands fall into the hands of Henry Frick, a
youth barely past twenty, who is building himself a kingdom of
coke. Almost as young a newcomer is Edward H. Harriman, all
expert stock-exchange speculator since early boyhood, who turns
the sudden ruin of others to his own great gain. In the meantime,
during the general deflation of values, and thanks to the promised
resumption of specie payment, the banker, as creditor, strengthens
his position measurably. The capital of Morgan, boldly used, gives
him a wider sway than before; he steps easily into the place once
occupied by Cooke.

   The twenty years after 1873 formed a period of unequaled material progress in the United States. At the Centennial Exhibition
soon organized in Philadelphia, the infinite resources and the technical culture of the nation were now bravely displayed to all the
world. There was George Westinghouse's air brake and Dr. Sellers's
kinematoscope; there were gas stoves and high-wheeled bicycles;
Corliss's 1,400 horse-power engine, and Bell's miraculous little telephone. Machinery of all kinds had grown larger and more ingenious,
in keeping with fifty-ton locomotives. There came new methods of
tilling the land, of mining and smelting the ores of the earth, of
preparing food, of making shoes, cloth, buttonholes, and to these
thousand and one "improvements" was added soon the broad application of electric power.
   Truly, wrote Henry George in 1879, the wisest men of the foregoing century, had they foreseen these engines, workshops, factories, steam hammers and threshing machines, would have been
thrilled "as one who from a height beholds just ahead of the thirst-

stricken caravan the living gleam of rustling woods and the glint of laughing waters." They would have seen the new forces elevating society, lifting the poorest above the possibility of want; they would have seen "these muscles of iron and sinews of steel making the laborer's life a holiday . . . realizing the golden age of which mankind have always dreamed. . . . For how could there be greed where all had enough?"

Instead, neither discovery nor invention lessened the toil of the people. "All the dull, deadening pain, all the keen maddening anguish . . . involved in the words 'hard times,'" concluded Henry George, afflicted the American society, as much as the old world. And where the conditions of material progress seemed most fully realized, where population was densest, wealth greatest, the machinery of production and commerce most highly developed, *there* were to be seen "the deepest poverty, the sharpest struggle for existence, and the most of enforced idleness."

The period, free of foreign or civil war, was nevertheless extremely warlike and fiercely contentious in its very day-to-day existence. In the accounts of the economic historians it is always seen as an age of "intense competition." The process of preëmption, suggested in foregoing pages as beginning upon a large scale during the Civil War, now declared itself more openly. Its objectives were clearly exposed, the prize at stake was ever larger, the race swifter, the collisions angrier. Moreover it was not only the wealth of the land—augmented by human increase and toil—that was preëmpted, but also the great highways of industrial traffic, the means of production, and finally the strategic "narrows" through which the stream of commodities must pass from the earth to the consumer.

The seizure of the railway system, attended with unprincipled conflicts, was the phase which was most clearly noticed by the public at the time. Henry Adams has commented of the Erie ring:

> *It was something new to see a knot of adventurers, men of broken fortune, without character and without credit, possess themselves of an artery of commerce more important than was ever the Appian Way, and make levies, not only upon it for their own emolument, but, through it, upon the whole business of a nation.*

Yet at the same time the whole business of the nation was also being seized upon and organized into larger units by "knots of adventurers." These adventurers expropriated or retired competitors in their territories; then as industrial barons, grouped in pools and combinations, they set to preying upon adjacent industries less organized than their own. So railroads would get the best of coal-mine operators, then having conquered them, would exploit the industries which depended upon supplies of coal. Or syndicates owning grain elevators or slaughterhouses would enter into collusion with the railroads to exploit the producers of grain and of cattle; oil-refiners would exploit those who drilled for petroleum, then would conquer or combine with their erstwhile opponents to exploit the underlying consumers altogether.

In all these cases the disposition of power, the division of "spoils," was settled no more peacefully than were the rivalries of the old feudal barons; sometimes they were not unaccompanied by bloodshed and by tremendous waste and destruction. Nor was the continually raging warfare in the economic society softened by any recognizable code of chivalry such as the Middle Ages boasted. A just and impartial government saw to it that there was never any interference in the contest, whose rules were derived from those by which man had conquered the animal world, according to certain academic observers. One such observer, L. F. Ward, writing upon the "Psychological Basis of Social Economics," maintained that the "principle of deception" or "superior cunning" was the chief element of success in such a struggle.[1] The shocks and derangements of the social system, the conflicts, assumed enormous size at certain times when whole sections of the population found the lords of railroads, the barons of industries, ranged against them in coalitions. Farmers, seized with despair at discovering their helplessness to control or even reach their markets, would band together in great numbers for a show of resistance. Laborers found their employers ranged in combinations against them, and saw themselves forced either to accept the terms offered or abandon their special skill and join a "standing army" of the unskilled. They, the em-

[1] "The method was that of the ambush and the snare. Its ruling principle was cunning. Its object was to deceive, circumvent, ensnare, capture. Low animal cunning was succeeded by more refined kinds of cunning. The more important of these go by the names of business shrewdness, strategy and diplomacy, none of which differ from ordinary cunning in anything but the degree of adroitness by which the victim is outwitted." Cited by T. Veblen, "Theory of Business Enterprise," pp. 56–57.

ployees of a thoroughly unified industry (like the Standard Oil Company or certain railroads), were as much owned by its masters as were the machines. Though their labor was subject to a more intense division and was infinitely more fruitful than before, they had no more power than the machines to make bargains for the use of their muscles. In their extremity they would sometimes combine in their own behalf and challenge their employers, now to endurance contests and now to the bloodiest industrial conflicts which this republic of freemen had ever known.

So shaken was the period—though there was no foreign enemy at the border, no rebel within—so tumultuous with earthquakes and shocks, business triumphs and reprisals, boom and panic, profit and waste, that many have questioned whether the returns compensated for the ultimate losses. Only in this primitive manner of struggle could human industry have become "socialized," the small scattered producers expropriated, and society organized upon a gigantic scale, all equipped with its present huge machinery. Else, as Marx said, "the world would still lack for railways." Assuredly the Goulds and Vanderbilts, the Rockefellers and Carnegies, moved upon the crest of a historic wave of "centralization." Yet often their profit-seeking seemed to be served best by resisting or restraining the historic process, by combating the very constant advance of the "state of the industrial arts" wrought by innumerable technicians and workers.

In examining the careers of our barons in detail we observe them not only combining and organizing but often using a technique of disturbance and derangement for "blocking the business system" at some point, as Veblen has surmised. We feel antithetical tendencies in them; their mutual repulsions, their "thieves' quarrels," seem to impede for a long time the overwhelming force of attraction which drives them toward a foreshadowed "community of interest," a culminating system of Monopoly.

2

In the highly developed Eastern states, the continued advance of the Vanderbilt dynasty illustrated the phase of consolidation that the railroad-builders generally entered upon after 1873. The New York Central system was still a strictly family enterprise, though it was capitalized at $90,000,000, and extended its main lines and branches through the most industrious zone of the country, between New York and Chicago.

Cornelius Vanderbilt, a grand old octogenarian, attended to the development of his railroad in his own canny and mysterious way. We know that in later life he grew increasingly eccentric, attended the séances of mesmerists and clairvoyants, communing now with a dead son, now with the shade of the departed Jim Fisk, who from the other world sometimes advised him on his knottiest business problems. Further counsel he may have received also from those sensational feminists, Victoria Woodhull and Tennessee Claflin, who much diverted New York in the '70's, and whom Vanderbilt was known to patronize. Other signs, in these later years, of something resembling distraction in the old Commodore were his bequests to public charities, to churches, and even to educational institutions such as he had openly despised all his life long. He, who had dispensed with book-learning for eighty years, relented, and under the urgence of his second wife's pastor, a Dr. Deems, turned over a million to the founding of Vanderbilt University in Nashville. (He had wished to build a towering monument to General Washington, idol of his childhood, but was convinced at length that there were enough of such things, and that a new university would be a monument to his own enduring glory.)

In the meantime, there was no relenting in the vigor with which he fought opponents in the railroad field. Constant rate-wars were waged between 1873 and 1875, and again toward 1877, in the service between New York and Chicago. In turn pressing for advantage, the New York Central, the Pennsylvania, the Erie, the Baltimore & Ohio, forced down passenger fares from $22 to $12, and grain rates from a level of 36 to 42 cents a bushel to as low as 12 cents; then in an interval of peace, their tariffs would be rushed up again to the earlier levels, while rebates were given secretly to favored groups of shippers. Yet however confusing all these maneuvers may have been to the public, the old Vanderbilt remained as instinctively forehanded as any of the railroad captains who directed them. Moreover he made alliances with "middle lines" in the West, continued his campaign of "improvements and extensions," though much of this, to be sure, at the public cost. Thus in laying underground the

Fourth Avenue tracks of the Harlem Railroad, on which his lines entered the city, he caused the erection of the massive tube and elevated roadbed which was greatly admired in the '70's as a marvel of engineering. The cost of this was $6,500,000; and the Board of Aldermen of New York were persuaded to pass a bill by which the city shared half the expense of making permanent and safe the New York Central's roadbed.

When the Commodore fell sick in 1876, excited speculation raged as to the size and disposition of his fortune. Newspaper reporters watched day and night from vantage points overlooking the red-brick house on Washington Place; and on at least one occasion premature reports of the railroad baron's decease were hawked under his windows by news-boys:

VANDERBILT DYING!

Hearing these the irascible old man crawled out of bed and shouted down the stairs to visiting journalists: "I am not dying! The slight local disorder is now almost entirely gone, and the doctor says I will be well in a few days. Even if I was dying I should have vigor enough to knock this abuse down your lying throats and give the undertaker a job!" (This, at any rate, is a translation by a Victorian biographer of the Commodore's expressive language.)

He fought prodigiously with death, as he had with life, but on the fourth of January, 1877, he passed away at last, at the age of eighty-three, surrounded by a mob of hymn-singing children, grandchildren and great-grandchildren who heartily sped him on his road.

With but slight family bequests, the Commodore left in the hands of his once despised heir William the geometrical sum of $94,000,-000 in the shape of railroad and other securities. This fortune was generally reckoned as the first industrial fortune of the world; and by the will of the deceased it was to be held intact, constantly increasing in size, an economic monolith in which a dynastic family fortified itself. The event aroused the liveliest amazement everywhere; and even in England Mr. Gladstone commented upon the dangers such a fortune held for the people at large, especially when it carried with it no "obligations to society" as in the case of the great English properties. To Chauncey Depew he said:

I understand you have a man in your country who is worth $100,000,000, and it is all in property which he can convert at will into cash. The government ought to take it away from him, as it is too dangerous a power for any one man to have. Suppose he should convert his property into money and lock it up, it would make a panic in America which would extend to this country and every other part of the world, and be a great injury to a large number of innocent people.

The character of the son who now took command of the giant railroad system offered strong contrasts to the father. He was homely and stout, while his parent had been handsome and erect; he believed in routine rather than in inspiration; finally, he was timid where the other had been pugnacious. Until he was forty-five he had been relegated to living upon a farm in Staten Island, some said because of his health, others because his father thought him sluggish and stupid. Patient and submissive in the face of torrents of paternal abuse, he evidently preferred to play the part of the "mistrusted prince" the better part of his life, rather than miss a fortune of a hundred millions. Yet he seems to have managed well as a gentleman farmer. His hired men were said to be hard-driven; and the master either sat upon a rail fence to watch them all day or practiced the habit of appearing suddenly amongst them in the fields to harry them from idleness.

How William Vanderbilt eventually won the confidence of his father is described by the family historian, Croffut. As he tells it, William used to get his fertilizer from the city, and one day he got some from his father's Fourth Avenue stables and took it home on a scow. When he saw his father the next day he asked him how much he would charge for ten loads. "What'll you give?" asked the Commodore. "It's worth $4 a load to me," said Billy. His father agreed to this, having the impression that this was twice what it was worth. Next day he saw his son with another scow all loaded and ready to start for Staten Island. "How many loads have you got on that scow, Billy?" he asked. "How many?" asked his son, pretending surprise. "One, of course." "One! Why, there's at least thirty!" said Vanderbilt. "No, father, I never put but one load on a scow— *one scowload! Cast off the lines, Pat!"*

The senior Vanderbilt, comments Crofutt, was struck dumb with a mixture of chagrin and gratification. He was probably sizing up Billy anew, and wondering whether he might not make a railroad man like himself, after all. So Billy was at last given a small bankrupt railroad in Staten Island to manage, and then when nearly fifty, taken into the family business: the New York Central.

Here he showed himself a laborious, methodical fellow. In the repair shops he spied upon the workmen by sudden stealthy intrusions, as he had done on his farm; he watched over all details, inspected every engine, all petty expenses, overseeing all the books, scrutinizing every bill, check and voucher passing through the offices of the great road, and even answering all letters in his own hand. In conversation he was often "abrupt, brusque, . . . rude"; he was a pessimist of a cheerful sort, thinking men and women as a rule "a pretty bad lot," and suspecting everyone around him to be in a league to get the advantage of him.[2] In the midst of a whirl of giant affairs he always found time to complain of petty impositions. In an age of terrific struggle, such as his father would have reveled in, including contests with new adventurers of industry, with the Standard Oil party, or with labor unions, William Vanderbilt was easily frightened and prone to compromise rather than fight to the bitter end.

The upshot, the significant lesson to be drawn from William Vanderbilt's character and situation, was that he prospered. The Central earned from 16 to 20 per cent on its real capital, even during the lean years after 1873; and in some eight years, despite certain notorious blunders, he succeeded in doubling the grand fortune which his father had taken ten times as long to accumulate.

[2]The reader must not be surprised at the fantastic parsimony of a Vanderbilt who while enjoying an income of roundly twenty millions per annum, nevertheless haggled over pennies in the bills submitted to his company, or upbraided the restaurateur who sent his lunch to his office for including the charge for coffee that was not ordered. The man of giant undertakings is fully aware, as no person of small means is, that pennies and mills multiplied many thousandfold make a momentous difference in results. This principle Billy Vanderbilt had learned from his notoriously stingy father, who on his deathbed had refused the bottle of champagne prescribed by his doctor, saying: "Won't sody-water do instead?" Such economy, perfectly logical in industrial affairs, is projected gratuitously into private life—often in strange contrast with the magnificent station and lavish scale of living of the nabob. . . . It is like the punctuality of the retired fire-engine horse who rushes out needlessly at the sound of the fire-bell.

Upon all sides, during the brief reign of the younger Vanderbilt he was harassed by pirates and freebooters of the railroad world. No sooner had he in 1878 acquired the valuable Lake Shore Railroad, leading toward Chicago, than a ring of shifty undertakers began to construct the "Nickel Plate Railroad" paralleling his line to Chicago. The syndicate which built this road, according to Henry Clews, "had solely for their object to land it upon either Gould or Vanderbilt." They overcapitalized and padded the construction costs in the traditional way of railroad barons, and were on their last financial legs when Vanderbilt in fear and trembling bought them out at a king's ransom. Had he waited another month, Clews estimates, the younger Vanderbilt could have had the pirate property at his own terms. Once he assumed its obligations he saw his error at once, and mourned for years afterward over his premature surrender.

In 1883, a similar blackmailing expedition brought another ring of rakish promoters to the west bank of the Hudson River itself, where in the heart of the Vanderbilt territory a new line, the West Shore, began building operations. The financiering of the West Shore was as notorious as that of the "Nickel Plate" several years earlier, and was instigated by opposing capitalists connected with the Pennsylvania Railroad. Freight and passenger rates were now lowered in a rate war, while Vanderbilt made but feeble efforts to raid the Pennsylvania's hard-coal fields with his own companies. In the end, he capitulated again, and arranged to buy the ramshackle West Shore, in order to have peace. The cost of these defeats was borne in an increase of capital debt as new shares of stock were issued to pay for the added properties—items which were figured forever in the cost of upkeep which the public paid for. "The Nickel Plate and the West Shore," according to Clews, "brought 1,000 miles of needless road to divide traffic with the Vanderbilts."

To add to Vanderbilt's woes, Jay Gould between 1873 and 1879 kept up a steady attack. Rounding out, during these years, a nationwide railroad system, the Union Pacific in the West and the Wabash east of the Mississippi, Gould threatened to divert all of his western traffic from the New York Central unless he were given an interest in the Vanderbilt lines. Such a step was of course unthinkable.

At the same time the exposures of the "Hepburn Committee" of the New York State Legislature, in 1879, made known the secret agreements between the railroad heads and the oil-refiners. There were complaints of "tyranny" over the cost of milk in New York, half of which, it was alleged, paid tribute to Mr. Vanderbilt. There were complaints of the freight service he gave, which was deliberately held to a snail's pace so that the extra-fare "Merchants' Express" would be forced upon shippers. The tremendous enrichment of the Vanderbilt system particularly, the knowledge that Vanderbilt himself held 87 per cent of its capital stock, aroused fear and envy. On top of many public plaints there now came threats of special taxation by the state, which to Vanderbilt meant only the blackmail of politicians.

Harassed, wretched in all his being, for the very possession of vast wealth, Billy Vanderbilt burst forth one day before a newspaper reporter with his famous apophthegm: *"The public be damned!"* The actual circumstances have been misunderstood. Billy Vanderbilt, a man of much softer mold than his father, has been represented as the paragon of capitalist despotism. In reality he had simply been explaining why the fast extra-fare mail train between New York and Chicago was being eliminated. It wasn't paying, he asserted. But the public found it both useful and convenient; should he not accommodate them?

"The public be damned. I am working for my stockholders," he had answered his interlocutor. "If the public want the train why don't they pay for it?"

However, Vanderbilt by his famous outburst had thrown a harsh light upon the divine power enjoyed by the railroad barons. The free Americans, and especially petty tradesmen among them, were hurt in a tender spot and roared with indignation. Bowing to the popular clamor, Vanderbilt took steps to dispose of part of his great holdings in the New York Central. His suave counselor, Chauncey Depew, has explained his actions as follows:

Mr. Vanderbilt, because of assaults made upon him in the Legislature and in the newspapers, came to the conclusion that it was a mistake for one individual to own a controlling interest in a great corporation like the New York Central, and also a mistake to have so many eggs in one basket, and he thought it would be better for himself and for the company if the ownership were distributed as widely as possible.

Through a syndicate headed by Pierpont Morgan, of Drexel Morgan & Co., 250,000 shares were sold to British and American investors at $130 each. All this was done in profound secrecy. Announced by Morgan after the deal was completed, the sale netted his group a quick profit of $3,000,000, while Vanderbilt acquired $30,000,000 in cash. Moreover Morgan gained in financial prestige by having skillfully executed "one of the most remarkable railroad transactions" of the day, one which had silenced the public, and also allayed the fear or hostility felt by railroad barons in adjacent territories. Gould was conciliated at the same time, and a competitive war with his Wabash, St. Louis & Pacific Railroad was averted, although this did not remove the materials of conflict elsewhere. Furthermore, Pierpont Morgan, now entering the board of directors of the New York Central, and acting as its fiscal agent, became a power among the railroad men.

3

After the "recovery" or 1879, the Vanderbilt system, like its neighbor in Pennsylvania, reinvested its great profits in extending its lines to more distant points and in effecting working agreements with "feeder" railroads. In general, the construction labors of the post–Civil War period, after a comparative lull, were resumed on a far greater scale between 1880 and 1890. Five trunk lines now plied between the Atlantic and the Great Lakes at Chicago. Numerous "middle railroads" radiated out of Chicago through Indiana, Illinois, Iowa, Nebraska, Missouri, Kansas and the West in general. For control of certain of these, such as the Chicago & Northwestern, Vanderbilt, Gould and the Pennsylvania ring competed incessantly. And across the Rocky Mountains, four additional transcontinental lines were virtually completed to the Pacific Coast in the same decade, which saw the laying of over 70,000 miles of track.

In the "granary of a nation" lying between Chicago and Omaha, the contentions of the railroad barons led to the first efforts at combination between the different hosts. In 1870, the "Omaha Pool," a form of "gentlemen's agreement," was quietly set up to establish coöperation between the competing lines, so that rates were stabilized, traffic was divided evenly, and profits and operating expenses equally shared. A few years later the same form of agreement was effected among the Southwestern lines. These were the first attempts at combination among the large carriers which had sprung up in the new territories.

By the 1880's all railroads in a competitive field had their pooling arrangements or gentlemen's agreements with rivals. But the controls upon them were weak; it was not yet clearly established among their ambitious leaders whether they could trust each other and whether it was more profitable to coöperate with or to blackmail, undermine and wreck their opponents. Hence north, south, east and west these vast public enterprises, headed by fiercely aggressive individualists sitting in their offices in New York, fought each other tooth and nail for the available trade, or now, in exhaustion, entered into colluson with one another.

The old stockbroker Henry Clews has given us a clear picture of the national industrial plan which was being pursued by the more "rugged individualists" of his time. He tells us:

> *Speculators were quick to perceive that they could build new lines on the same routes for much less cost than the old ones [especially after '73] and that, with a lower capitalization, they could easily compel the pool to admit them to membership, with all the privileges of a ready-made traffic, and ... guarantees of ... exemption from competition. ...*
>
> *New roads were built, or sets of old detached ones were connected, so as to afford additional parallels to the existing trunk lines, with no other object than to compel the latter to support them by dividing with them a portion of their traffic, or to accept the alternative of a reckless cutting down of rates.*

The effect upon the underlying consumers of alternate peace and war in transportation was bewildering, to say the least. Under the reign of competition freight rates would fall. But then the bursting of a corner in wheat, with the resultant rush of demand for cars, would bring a suddenly doubled or trebled tariff from the flinty railway officials. Grain would be moved at 15 cents a hundredweight; then this rate would be changed to 10 cents; then as suddenly, in the same season, lifted to 40 cents. The promulgation of a new railroad pool would mean further changes. A very real "censorship" over every aspect of the business of shippers grew up, certain large ones, like the Standard Oil, being nourished with secret rebates, while others were stamped out. There was finally the power for "making and ruining cities" or whole regions. A farmer appeared one day to complain before a New York legislative committee that the Vanderbilt railroad "would move his farm in Herkimer County out to the banks of the Mississippi River, in effect, allowing the man who lived on the banks of the Mississippi River to send his products at lower rates than he can." Likewise protests were made over the long-haul and short-haul differentials, by which it was made to cost $1.50 more per ton to ship coal to a point mid way between the Pennsylvania's anthracite mines—to York, Pennsylvania, for instance—than all the way to the seaboard. But for all these economic disturbances and derangements, which came and went in the most inexplicable manner, there seemed no rational motives to those who were ravaged by them.

In a speech in Congress, on April 27, 1886, Senator Spooner disclosed a notorious case "where a single remark from a railway president over a glass of wine at a hotel table brought a war of rates which cost $5,000,000 of revenues before it was ended." Their accord broken, the giant adversaries fell upon each other in an endurance test of financial punishment. They engaged in physical combats at bridgeheads; they refused to transfer merchandise from each other's freight cars; and as far west as St. Joseph, they slashed rates against each other, bringing a short-lived joy to one region, or economic desolation to another.

There was no social police to end this intermittent internecine conflict. Legislators seeking to intervene could establish no balance between the shifting interests. Neither a fair division of the spoils nor rational service could be enforced by the best efforts of the lawgivers over long periods. And the efforts of state legislatures before 1887 to intervene and to regulate traffic rates precipitated confused and truly anarchic conditions. The transportation problem (so simple in itself on the basis of social service) became a "Gordian knot" as the railway chiefs evaded or laughed at attempts to control them. They put absurd obstacles in the way of regulations, stopped or slowed up their trains, threatened to remove their service entirely, even to boycott whole regions or commonwealths, unless the objectionable laws were removed from the statute books! For such an era, a man like William Vanderbilt, who loved to ride behind fast trotting horses or to dream among the mediocre paintings in his art gallery, seemed little fitted. His monopoly over a section of the country sustained him well; and his immense fortune bore its own impetus. But more aggressive monopolists pressed to supersede him. And when this somewhat tormented nabob pitched forward suddenly at his desk and died of a burst blood-vessel, in 1885, his affairs were undergoing a significant change. In the interests of a great brood of hungry little Vanderbilts of all sorts, a powerful investment banker now administered his estate of $200,000,000, diversified in hundreds of enterprises.

During a generation, the natural impulses of the railroad barons, as of the captains of industry, led them to set upon each other, with sandbag or in ambush. With the levers of giant machines in their hands they would effect destruction, dispersion and anarchy, engulfing the millions of citizens over whom they had power of life and death. It is the opinion of Thorstein Veblen, supported by much precise evidence of experts, as by Riegel's in his "History of the Western Railroads," that the predestined consolidation of the whole American transportation system was retarded at least forty years after it had become a logical necessity. Although the efforts of the monopolists such as Gould, Huntington, Hill and Morgan were in the long run directed toward sweeping rivals from their field, any detailed account of their tactics shows them as often inclined to "blocking the social system" at strategic points, as to "rationalizing" it. Such a view is most clearly borne out by the career of Jay Gould, the "purest" of the mercenary adventurers of his time.

CHAPTER NINE

MEPHISTOPHELES

WHILE the productive labors of a society, the functioning of its ships and railroads, its mills and factories, give the effect of a beautiful order and discipline, of the rhythmic regularity of the days and seasons, its markets, by a strange contrast, seem to be in a continual state of anarchy. Here the same services and commodities, produced every day with perfect routine, go through a mad dance. The market, as Marx has pointed out in a striking passage, is like a "city without a plan." Yet only in the market can the capitalist take his reward. Here he must move without a faltering step under pain of instant destruction. He must tell none what his plans are; he must smile or remain impassive when he is in torment or danger. For his business is difficult, laborious and risky. He must show infinite resourcefulness, efficiency, sagacity. He must, as Marx states it,

> have fine hearing and a thick skin; must be simultaneously cautious and venturesome, a swashbuckler and a calculator, careless and prudent. He must, in fine, develop all the qualities of an experienced man of business.

By this definition of the man of the market, Jay Gould seems the capitalist par excellence. During all the heroic, turbulent period we review he seems the very soul of the movement of industrial revolution; he shows the "purest" traits, if one may call them so, of the great entrepreneur.

Where certain of his rivals, intoxicated with power, learned to crave glory too, Jay Gould seemed to place himself above such human vanities. Nor did any social interest, or any sentimental consideration, as of the size or beauty of an enterprise, deflect him for a moment from his marvelously logical line of movement. No human instinct of justice or patriotism or pity caused him to deceive himself, or to waver in any perceptible degree from the steadfast pursuit of strategic power and liquid assets. Others, such as Rockefeller and Morgan, had their friendships, personal loyalties to colleagues or members of their class. Gould, who had only *agents* rather than confidants or allies, seemed to enjoy most the rôle of "the one against all"; self-contained, impassive to all pleas or reproaches, he seemed content with his loneliness. For most of his days he lived, as it has been said of Harriman, who resembled him so much, "in the necessary isolation of a ship's commander when on sea duty." At times he seemed to soar above the others like a destroying angel.

What would he have done, or rather what great works would he have *undone*, if his health had not failed him? He lived in the agony of a consumptive, not daring to admit his infirmities for fear of the enemies always ranged against him. While plunged in his large designs, he would pass nights without sleeping, coughing blood in terrible spasms, walking the street outside his home until dawn. He died prematurely, in the midst of life, and his vast unknown plans foundered with him.

In all the things he did, he seemed pervaded with a demoniac pessimism, which in sober retrospect does him much honor. There were certain developments which must have filled him with an enduring mistrust of the very system which he exploited so brilliantly. At the height of his career, after the Civil War, the commodity markets of the world seemed to resume their prolonged downward trend, which they had shown ever since the Napoleonic wars. The earth, in these years, from its civilized states and wildest colonies seemed to belch forth a torrent of goods; the armies of labor were constantly multiplied, and new inventions, new machines appearing with bewildering rapidity added to abundance and cheapness incessantly, while making obsolete existing machinery and destroying fixed capital. Hence what appears to others a wanton destructiveness in Gould, his intermittent raids or attacks, were but testing operations carried on against a system he may have believed foredoomed. Thus possessed of terrible doubts, he was constantly turning his supposed advantages in securities, or goods, into ready money; assumed gains, surplus value, in perpetually renewed campaigns must be turned into cash. He never deceived himself.

He was a small man, weak in physique, and he loved power—the realities of power rather than its vestments. "I did not care at that time about the mere making of money," he said with reference to his sensational exploits in the Missouri Pacific Railroad. *"It was more to show that I could make a combination and make it a success."*

The giant size of a project, the dangers it offered, the speed and skillful precision with which it must be carried out—all this stirred his strange imagination. Since his boyhood he had dreamed of making a transcontinental railroad; and now in 1873, free of the Erie, he had begun to buy shares of the celebrated Union Pacific. Its stock of $100 par value had sunk to $30 after the Crédit Mobilier scandal; then even to $14. He continued buying.

"I found myself a very large owner in that property," he admitted to a committee of United States Senators some years later. "Then ... I found that there was ten millions of bonds that came due in a month or two.... It was rather a blue condition of things."

When Daniel Drew had parted company with him in 1868, he had jeered: "There ain't nothing more in Erie." But Gould and Fisk had shown him a trick or two. So with Union Pacific. Though looted, the tremendous line which took days to traverse suited perfectly the bold plans being formed by the Mephistopheles of Wall Street.

In accordance with his large designs, one broken railroad after another was quickly taken over by Gould throughout the Middle West and the Southwest. From Thomas Scott, whom he found "very much broken up, financially, physically and mentally," he acquired a working interest in the Texas & Pacific, which had been chartered in 1871 to run between Galveston and San Diego, but was virtually unbuilt. From Scott also he purchased an important newspaper, the *New York World*. Then he reached for fragments of defunct railroads, franchises, land grants about to be forfeited. These included the ill-fated Kansas Pacific (which had gained great subsidies in land and money), now fallen into receivership; the Denver Pacific, the Wabash, the Missouri Pacific, all of which, together with connecting and feeding lines, gridironed the West. Then, by effecting favorable transfer agreement with Collis Huntington, he would gain an outlet to the sea via California. In the meantime, the Pacific Mail Steamship Company was acquired by him in conjunction with Huntington to keep ocean carrying-rates by way of Panama from competing with the land crossing. To these properties he was to add, by systematic raids, the rich telegraph monopoly of the Western Union Company; then the new rapid-transit lines being built in New York to carry her millions back and forth to their unremitting labor; finally a series of coal mines; and toward the end, railroads running to the Eastern seaboard, to round out an industrial empire which spread its crazy network from one shore of the continent to the other.

The railroads, the telegraph lines, the ships, the newspapers, all were part of an imperial plan to capture strategic sections of the country's industrial system, and, by blocking it first at one point, then at another, to levy infinite toll upon it.

To understand the scope of the man's tactics one must note that his domination was carried on by strategic "working controls" rather than by ponderous outright investments. He was an "absolute master," as a shrewd investigator for President Cleveland reported, "of the art of creating coördinate boards of directors that had complete control of adverse interests." Thus the ruin of certain properties which he controlled at slight expense might be turned to his own pecuniary gain. All his tactics, therefore, hinged upon what Thorstein Veblen has defined as "disturbance of the industrial system." He would pursue a deliberate policy of mismanagement "as a matter of principle," deriving his gains from the discrepancies between the real value of the affair and its supposed or transient value in the security markets. In good times he would give an appearance of gauntness and misery to his enterprise; in bad times he would pretend affluence. Sin and weakness were simulated when he was buying control; "prosperity," when he longed to sell out. At all times, from his position of vantage, he would be as one who deals out marked cards in the game of buying and selling capital, since he would be fully able to foresee the "nature, magnitude and incidence" of all the risks he created. His system could no more fail than loaded dice.

Moreover, his analysis of the railroad prospects of the Great West was an uncommonly penetrating one. With his unsentimental eye he saw at once that it was useless to engage in a legitimate shipping and passenger business while waiting for the thinly settled prairies to fill up. Nothing justified the present building and operation of

large railroad systems save that other entrepreneurs would do so if
he did not. And though there would be no adequate volume of
freights to support such ventures, one must be beforehand in seizing
the strategic positions essential to a future monopoly. Thereafter,
there were only two ways of making the operation pay: by owning
an unchallenged monopoly of a given territory and "charging all
the traffic would bear" (though this was not certainly profitable);
or by manipulation of its capital in the markets—and none knew how
to do this better than Jay Gould. When the structure collapsed,
Jay would be somewhere else. Then it must be set up again. . . .

Students of these affairs have sometimes questioned the social
value of Gould's labors. Disappointed investors, the hard-pressed
public which perforce patronized his lines, often cursed his name
as that of an evil genius. But he would have answered: "We are not
in business for our health!" Every tactical advantage must be translated quickly into cash, to be used again in new ventures. Those
who did not imitate Jay Gould, or did not go as far as he did, probably learned to regret their error.

One becomes impersonal when at the head of mighty corporate
enterprises; one does not feel at close hand the disillusionment or
ill-will of the customers, as one might in the days of guilds and
mercantile capitalism; one is even less sensitive when one regards the
customers as an inferior class.

2

The failure of the European harvest in 1879 and the movement
of bumper crops brought prosperity to the Western farmers and
large profits to the Union Pacific Railroad. Once more, despite the
staggering debts saddled upon it, the road was a "financial success,"
Gould reported. Then at the time of the Granger agitation, there
arose a clamor against Gould's management—"as though," he comments softly, "it was a dangerous thing to have one man control a
road."

In this vein, before the Senators of the Pacific Railroad Commission on May 19, 1887, he related his exploits of 1875 to 1879:

> *I thought it was better to bow to public opinion, so I took an op-
> portunity, when I could, to place the stock in the hands of investors.*

In the course of a very few months instead of owning the road I was entirely out of it. . . . Instead of being thirty or forty stockholders there were between 6,000 and 7,000, representing the savings of widows and orphans . . . also a great many lady stockholders.

The magnanimous Jay! Always innocent-minded gentle comments from him! Let us watch, then, what really took place.

No sooner was he in command of the transcontinental road than Gould realized with his inside knowledge the potential threat of two connecting but dilapidated lines which had grown up out of the railway madness of the Southwest. These were the Kansas Pacific and the Denver Pacific, both endowed with land grants and both emptied of the state subsidies and local and foreign capital they had been able to command. Yet though their tracks were now mere "streaks of rust," ending in the desert, they made a line toward the seacoast parallel to the Union Pacific. The knowledge of this possible source of mischief Gould kept to himself. He saw that if he bought the almost worthless stock of the Kansas Pacific, selling at between 10 cents and $3 a share toward 1874, and of the equally worthless Denver road, he could threaten the business of the Union Pacific—that is to say of his own railroad. Now if by means of such threats he could force the Union Pacific to purchase and consolidate with itself the Kansas and Denver roads, at favorable terms, this would have the effect of raising the price of the smaller roads far beyond the original cost to him.[1]

Soon Gould "suggested" to his fellow directors of the Union Pacific that it might be advisable to purchase the paralleling Kansas Pacific and Denver Pacific roads, the terms for these bankrupt lines being an even exchange of shares with the comparatively prosper-

[1] Q. Why should Gould wish to injure his own property?
A. Because in general he stood to gain more profit through being the agency which did the injury than he lost as part owner of the Union Pacific's property.
Q. But he was selling his own Union Pacific a "gold brick"? And to that extent lessened the value of the Union Pacific?
A. True. But he had invested in only 10 per cent of the capital stock of the Union Pacific, costing him $1,000,000, let us say. Thus by forcing worthless railroad iron upon it, he would with his left hand cause its capital to shrink by 10 per cent; this would represent in the property which he held in his right hand, a loss of $100,000. But with his left hand he gained $10,000,000 by the sale of the said "gold brick," leaving him a net profit of $9,900,000.

ous Union Pacific. This proposal was at first not taken very seriously, the Union Pacific feeling that "it had the situation under control," and need not burden itself with two profitless lines. Gould then found himself for a time with two nearly worthless properties on his hands and little prospect of improvement for them in the future. But when Gould meant war, his contemporaries who knew him used to say, "He made a suggestion; and if it was presented with special gentleness there was in it the greater scope for warfare."

Several of the directors of the Union Pacific, Russell Sage, Sidney Dillon, and Cyrus Field, were the henchmen of Gould; the others actually stood in awe of him. Artfully he played upon their hopes and fears, and as a rule, they hesitated to cross the uncanny man.

In a certain sense it was true that he had "improved the finances" of the Union Pacific. Timed with a very slight improvement in the rate of business between 1875 and 1879, the cash position had been built up, first, by withholding interest payments due on the mortgage debt to the federal government; second, by *charging a large portion of operating expenses to the construction account*, thus capitalizing current disbursements as increased assets! While the properties deteriorated, as Riegel in his painstaking history of the affair states with admirable underemphasis, Gould ordered high dividends, almost $12,000,000 being paid out in several years to the directors and stockholders. (Shortly afterward, when Charles F. Adams, Jr., became president of the Union Pacific, he found a mysterious floating debt of ten millions, the consequence of Jay's little tricks.)

Yet in February, 1879, Gould had a pool in Wall Street, directed by the experts James Keene and Addison Cammack, drive the stock up toward 70. With exuberant reports of the company's financial progress being circulated, widows and orphans and lady stockholders rushed to buy the stock. Then Gould, "bowing to public opinion," as he termed it, quietly unloaded upon them some 200,000 shares at a profit of ten millions. Nevertheless, though he was out of the stock, he would still have a determining voice in the management of the Union Pacific during the interval before the election of new directors.[2]

But with certain of the larger stockholders refusing to comply

[2] To the surprisingly ill-informed Senators who questioned him in 1887, Gould related "with face perfectly controlled, his words chosen with great gentleness," according to the *New York Times* of May 19, 1887, that, on

with his plans for merging the Kansas and Denver systems into the
Union Pacific, Gould had concluded that the trouble with his plan
was that it did not carry a sufficient threat. He had then departed
upon a swift tour of the West; from an observation car his dark eye
rolled about taking in everything, while his fertile brain shaped a
beautiful conspiracy.

In a series of lightning-like transactions he bought the Wabash,
the partly completed Missouri Pacific, the St. Joseph & Denver,
the Missouri, Kansas & Texas, and certain other little lines. Thrown
together with his previous holdings, they made a huge potential
system, stretching across the continent in a somewhat longer line
than the Union Pacific, but competing with it all the way to
Cheyenne.

It was by no means easy to arrange this railroad system *à la fan-
taisie.* Throughout the campaign, corsairs or freebooters as unfeel-
ing as Gould himself hung upon his flanks, lay in ambush, or threw
up barricades in his way. Henry Clews in his "Fifty Years of Wall
Street" gives the details of some of these affrays.

Presiding over the Missouri Pacific was a certain "Commodore"
Garrison, formerly in the employ of the old Vanderbilt, himself a
sea-dog of the Panama steamship lines in Gold Rush days. When
Gould sent word to Garrison that he would pay $1,500,000 for
control of his road, Garrison answered that the offer was $500,000
too low. Then Gould had rushed to confront him in person, gently
smiling in his beard, and raising his offer, but Garrison only laughed
uproariously, rubbed his hands, and said that his price was $2,800,-
000.

> *Gould observed that he could have bought the road on the pre-
> vious day for $2,000,000. And the Commodore explained that the
> difference between yesterday and today was $800,000. Gould said*

moral grounds, he had resolved to liquidate his Union Pacific stock and withdraw from its management. It was high time!

"*Senators:* According to the ethics of Wall Street, do you consider it within
the limits of your duty while a director of the Union Pacific to purchase
another property and to design an extension of the road which would
perhaps ruin the Union Pacific?

"*Gould:* I don't think it would have been proper. That's the reason I let it go.

"*Senators:* Did you consider your duty to the government? How would the
government claim ($27,000,000) have been affected by building a parallel
line?

"*Gould:* It would have been wiped out."

nothing and retired. He made another effort on the following day. The Commodore too had been thinking. His thoughts cost Mr. Gould one million dollars, for his price on the third day of the negotiations was $3,800,000. Gould did not express his thoughts, but his speech demonstrated that he appreciated the danger of delay. He said: "I'll take it."

In the case of the Denver Pacific, adjunct to the bankrupt Kansas Pacific, there had been similar vicious obstructions to Gould's marching orders. Minority interests contested claims of ownership; some of these counterclaims were in behalf of German bondholders who were represented here by Henry Villard. This also held up the bargain for the great consolidation with the Union Pacific. But by secret arrangement between Gould's agents and a friendly receiver, a favoring decree from a complaisant judge was obtained in the nick of time, seven days before the final deal was made. When at last all this patchwork railroad system, embracing some 5,000 miles of broken-down or incompleted trunk and feeder lines, was rounded up, Gould delivered his ultimatum to those directors of the Union Pacific who held out against his demands. He intended, he said, "to build immediately to the Pacific Coast by way of Salt Lake City." Where the Union Pacific had enjoyed a thorough monopoly of interocean traffic up to that time it was now encircled by the inscrutable Mephistopheles of Wall Street. The pistol at their throats, there was plainly little for the Union Pacific men to do but surrender. A member of the opposing faction, consisting of Boston financial interests, has described the terror that gripped them.

The Union Pacific people were startled at the prospect of a parallel road and hurried to New York. A meeting was held at Jay Gould's house. On half a sheet of note paper, which I saw, were written the terms of consolidation of the Kansas Pacific and the Union. By these terms not only, as was first proposed by Gould, was Kansas Pacific and Denver Pacific exchanged dollar for dollar for Union stock, but we agreed to take from Gould's hands at the price he paid for them, the Kansas Central and other securities he had secured as his weapons.

Within a week, as rumors of the "merger" were cunningly spread among the public, Kansas Pacific and Denver Pacific stock rose from $3 toward par. In return for his stock in these enterprises Jay Gould was given some 200,000 shares of Union Pacific which he disposed of quickly—if he had not sold them short in anticipation. A crash was inevitable and when that came, "he wanted to be somewhere else."

Henry Villard, the German émigré who had worked during the war as a Washington newspaper correspondent and as an immigration agent for Jay Cooke, looked on admiringly, commenting in his memoirs:

> Gould having purposely let his intention to consolidate the Kansas Pacific with the Union Pacific be known, the stock of the former, which had sold as low as 3 less than four years before, was quickly quoted as high as the latter and followed it far above par. Gould, not long after the consolidation, sold all his stock. He was understood to have cleared more than ten millions of dollars by the operation, which was one of the principal episodes in that speculative time.

The ill-starred Union Pacific Railroad had been looted when Jay Gould arrived to take over its control. Yet in a few years, as in the case of the Erie, he had been able to set it up nicely and extract from it altogether some twenty millions.

"His touch is death," Daniel Drew had truly said of Gould long before.

3

Years of furious activity succeeded themselves; though his hands were upon a thousand affairs at once, the unsleeping Gould devoted himself chiefly to the "upbuilding" of the Great West, in his usual manner. His manipulation of the chain of railroads broken up, resold, or joined to his principal systems, usually the Wabash and the Missouri Pacific, kept the Western states in a continual turmoil. There were destructive rate wars, which brought low tariffs to the populace, but were succeeded immediately after by pools, such as that of Omaha in 1870, into which Gould forced his way. Then, unwilling to limit his movements, or unable to hold peaceful agreements, or seeing glittering chances before him, Gould would break forth, fighting again with the other railroad barons.

Over the division of business between Nebraska and Denver, Colorado, Gould's Wabash engaged in a cut-throat rate war with the rich Chicago, Burlington & Quincy, long established in the "middle" territory. The Burlington fought back aggressively. There resulted an extension of parallel lines by each company, strenuous and wasteful duplication of the railway service, and finally compromise or combination against the "common enemy," those who traveled or shipped goods over the railways.

At one moment the citizens of Denver, hearing that Gould was approaching them with one of his roads, were thrown into terror, and set about building a branch line of their own to connect with another trunk system.

To the north, Gould had met with determined opposition, and found the field well occupied, especially by the Burlington. Therefore shifting his plans, as was his wont when he met with too stout defense in one quarter, he dismembered most of the Wabash line, sold parts of it to his rivals, and converged with all his energy and attention upon the unexploited Southwestern territory. Here he met with success in "building up" the Missouri Pacific and the allied Texas Pacific (which he had acquired from Scott) to a condition of monopoly over Kansas, Texas, and a vast empire which stretched from the Mississippi to the Sierra Nevadas.

The Missouri Pacific, upon which the State of Missouri once lavished $25,000,000 in subsidies, had fallen into the railroad baron's hands for $3,800,000, as we have seen. This line he kept for himself. By diverting traffic to it, adding small connecting roads, building extensions, and "growing up with the country," he soon erected a system that ran over 5,000 miles of track from St. Louis west to Omaha, and southwest to El Paso.

He was ever afterward proud of his "constructive labor" in the Missouri Pacific's territory. The railroad's receipts had risen twentyfold during his management, he was apt to boast. "We," he added passionately, boastfully, "have made the country rich, we have developed the country, coal mines and cattle raising, as well as cotton.... We have created this earning power by developing the system." He believed this, as Harriman and other railroad monarchs after him believed that they built the country and its wealth, they had "made the Great West!"

Gould clung to the Missouri Pacific as to no other property, with a certain sentiment; it was to remain as a family heirloom down to quite recent years. But loving this railroad he could not help raping it occasionally, as he did the Wabash, and so many others. Under favorable reports, made by extraordinary accounting devices which none else might control, he would raise the value of his stocks, sell, depreciate, and repurchase them. So the Wabash, which had but little traffic or reason for existence at the time, and which was mismanaged with "trained incompetence," as Thorstein Veblen would say, its treasury empty, its stock maintained by secret loans at a high price—the poor Wabash was to crash in a sensational débâcle, in which it appeared afterward that Jay Gould was in no way involved. He was simply not there when it happened.

The Missouri Pacific too paid dividends "by curtailment of necessary repairs and replacements," its stock price remaining high in the face of a mounting deficit. Wherever Gould moved or struck upon the map of the country, "the effects of his management never wore off entirely," observes Riegel in his "History of the Western Railroads":

> There was never any effort to build up a strong, soundly managed group of roads . . . the one dominant note was speculation. Both in prosperity and depression he pursued his aim shrewdly and relentlessly. . . . The roads that he touched never quite recovered from his lack of knowledge and interest in sound railroading.

To the west, as he saw in his march to monopolistic power, his growing railroad system needed egress across the Sierra passes to the sea. Here, for a long time, only one railroad hurdled California, the Central Pacific, which, meeting the Union Pacific at Ogden, Utah, constituted the only land route to the sea. And at this point Jay Gould came into collision with the celebrated Huntington-Stanford ring which "owned" California, a group in every way as resourceful, as pitiless and treacherous as he.

Since 1873, we note that Gould had held a large interest, bought from the weakened Tom Scott, in the Texas & Pacific. Little of it had been built, though it was to have a right of way to the sea, forming with the Northern and the Union Pacific a third transcontinental line, along the 32nd parallel. This largely unbuilt line Gould intended to use as the western outlet of his Missouri Pacific system. It had a vast land grant—28,000,000 acres—part of it ultimately to be forfeited owing to non-construction. Gould and Scott promptly created a construction company, controlled by himself, with which alone the railroad could make building contracts—this modeled of course after the Crédit Mobilier.

In the name of Gould, Scott pushed forward the oceanward march of the little Texas & Pacific. Facing him the implacable Huntington, occupying the only two passes across the Colorado River canyon, barred the way to the sea. Thus during the late '70's, amid the whirl of countless undertakings, we find Gould and his revived ally, Tom Scott, belaboring the government at Washington for help, for subsidies, for relief from the enemy interests. We read in the Huntington-Colton letters how on December 17, 1877:

> *Jay Gould went to Washington about two weeks since, and I know, saw Mitchell, Senator from Oregon. Since which time money has been used very freely in Washington. . . . Gould has large amounts of cash and he pays it without stint to carry his points.*

A few months later, May 3, 1878, Huntington writes privately that the Gould faction "offered one member of Congress $1,000 cash down, $5,000 when the bill was passed, and $10,000 of the bonds." "The greatest mistake was in Gould coming to Washington," Huntington said, for prices rose in measure with the competition in bribery. But wary after recent trials, the Congressmen accepted favors from both sides and granted nothing to either. This curious conflict, to which we shall revert later in reviewing the further activities of Huntington, was soon amicably settled between the two masterful financiers who had so many points in common, and who were subject to common dangers from without. The contestants—presumably competing with each other for "the life of trade"—were like mercenary feudal captains who fought only for hire, and after a season's campaign easily came to terms with each other. While pretending before Congress and all the world to be hurling defiance at each other forever, the two were agreeing that Huntington's Southern Pacific system should become Gould's railroad link with the sea. Then, for a yearly subsidy, Gould's Pacific Mail Steamship Line raised its tariff sufficiently to leave the California railroad monopolists undisturbed and supreme in their possessions.

Thus Gould and Huntington had arrived secretly at an amazing pact for their mutual interest and self-defense, giving virtual monopoly over the traffic of nearly half the United States. But the little, soft-spoken railroad chieftain had many other large under-takings to absorb all his attention. For elsewhere, in the East, he was pushing invincibly into new industrial domains.

4

The magnetic telegraph after the Civil War captured everyone's imagination by its magic and speed. In this field one of the earliest and richest monopolies had been created through the amalgamation of various small companies during the 1850's into the Western Union Telegraph Company. On its board were such dignitaries as John Jacob Astor and William H. Vanderbilt. In Wall Street Jay Gould for some time had been eyeing the stock of this company covetously. His motives, he himself explains:

> The telegraph and the railroad systems go hand in hand, as it were, integral parts of a great civilization. I naturally became acquainted with the telegraph business and gradually became interested in it. I thought well of it as an investment, and I kept increasing my interests.

But when Gould adored some object, he must, like the gods, "render it mad." The Western Union directors would have nothing of Gould on their board, just as the New York Yacht Club would not admit him as a member of their exclusive society, and just as Mrs. William B. Astor never invited the Goulds to her quadrilles.

Forming an alliance with the stock-market "wizard," James Keene, and other speculators, Gould began "shorting" Western Union; and soon the bears won a million apiece at this destructive operation, while the owners grew consternated. But as if this were not enough, the wily little man, with the advice of a technician, a certain General Eckert, set about building a telegraph line of his own along the tracks of his railroads, which he named the "Atlantic and Pacific Company." Once more in his campaign for power Gould set up the cry of "monopoly" at his antagonists, declaring that he alone would restore "competition"; and this time the *New York World*, which he had owned since 1873, aided him powerfully in molding public opinion. Soon he had cut heavily into his opponents' business, which declined $2,000,000 in one year. Blackmailed, the

Western Union had either to buy or to sell; it capitulated at length and bought Gould's company for a large sum, reputed to be ten millions.

But no sooner had he sold, and all were heaving a sigh of relief, than Jay Gould struck again, tirelessly. He complained that his friend General Eckert had not been given a job in the consolidated telegraph system, and that his own interest was not represented; and so like a prestidigitator he soon evoked another telegraph company, "as good a company as I had taken him from." Once more, his biographer relates, he competed bitterly with the two other telegraph companies. After confusing rate wars, which baffled the public, came renewed capitulation. The newly born "American Union" was also bought in; Gould's man was given a place in it; and in return Gould pledged himself to create no more telegraph companies; and his adversaries breathed more easily at the thought that they were at least well rid of him.

But no! they were to have only brief respite. Calling Jim Keene, Addison Cammack, and Sage, shrewdest of stock traders, Gould organized a third and final campaign to "break" the Western Union stock and take possession of the whole enterprise. His newspaper attacked the credit of the company; "by every trick and art of Stock Exchange manipulation, Gould forced down the price of Western Union stock," taking millions of profits on the short side. Then as the plunging bear, Keene, went mad over his gains, it soon appeared "that the stock was absorbed by some party or parties as fast as it was thrown out." The bears were trapped on the recovery, when it was realized that quantities of the stock disappeared from the market rapidly at low prices. But worse, to Vanderbilt's complete surprise and extreme mortification, the unfathomable Gould turned up in 1881 with control not only of Western Union, but also of the American Union Telegraph Company, which he had sold to Vanderbilt a short time previously.[3]

[3] In a legislative investigation, one of Gould's allies in the "telegraphic war" related:

"... In the continued depression of our stock [Western Union], a number of speculators confidently expecting a further decline sold large blocks of borrowed stock, anticipating an opportunity to buy back very low. They imagined themselves following an experienced leader; but who instead of selling was buying, and who was, perhaps, not unwilling that these gentlemen should make it easy for him. He had proposed to himself to end telegraphic war by

Making his peace with the distinguished confraternity of Astor, Morgan, Huntington, and Vanderbilt the younger, he now brought his work to its flowery and watery culmination—the others complaisantly sharing the spoils with him. And soon one could see his hand at the helm of the great telegraph monopoly, by the process of "watering" capital that followed in 1881; a huge stock dividend of 38¼ per cent was declared, the capitalization was raised to $80,000,000, and all the three companies amalgamated into Western Union.

Gould's private offices were now removed to the fifth floor of the massive, bomb-proof citadel of the Western Union Company, a gloomy pile, six stories high, costing $2,200,000 and considered by Clews one of the wonders of the time, for its greatness, height, width, breadth, and modern elevators. Here Gould's person at least was safe. For the pitiless tactics he pursued were not such as to make him immune from physical danger.

In the Western Union affair, a certain Major Selover who had joined with Gould in the supposed short-selling operations, had found himself deceived and trapped, like the others. Major Selover brooded over the matter so long that his suspicions began to take tangible form and to body themselves forth in violence, according to Henry Clews's relation:

> The Major and Keene met one morning at the rear entrance of the Stock Exchange in New Street and interchanged intelligent glances on the subject, after the fashion of those passed between Bill Bye and his companion at the card table with the Heathen Chinee. Selover walked down the street with blood in his eye, and meeting Mr. Gould on the corner of New Street and Exchange Place, caught him up by the collar of the coat and a part of his pants and dropped him in the areaway at a barber shop.
>
> The little man promptly picked himself up, went quietly to his office, and made a transaction by which Selover lost $15,000 more. This was his method of retaliation.

purchasing control. When he had purchased ten millions or more of the stock thus thrown on the market, he agreed to terms of peace. The stock at once rose with great rapidity. Then was heard a howl great and long. These speculators had to buy in their stock, and at every bid for it the market bounded up. Take the matter of speculation out of the case, and what is left? Absolutely nothing."

Jay Gould could scarcely venture safely into the street these days. Like the *condottieri* of the old Italian cities, he must be followed by bravos at his heels. A detail of plain-clothes policemen headed by a Captain Byrnes guarded his movements night and day.

Alone in his citadel in the Western Union building, while managing the great telegraph combination and also extending his network of railroads through the heart of the United States, Jay Gould, for his own restless soul's comfort, took part in many minor forays. His fine hand was always at the pulse of the market; he was aware of its slightest vibrations. He exercised a remarkable control over the press in general through the Associated Press; the *New York World* he owned, and it published news and opinions as he wished.[4] He scanned the telegraph, or manipulated it, as an open book to the secrets of all the marts; he was a director of scores of corporations. He had spies and agents everywhere. Thus, he could turn from his larger campaigns to bag small game too. One day the broker Addison Cammack came to him, and hinted that James Keene (who was now his enemy) must be far overextended. Keene, who had won his first stake in the mining stock market of San Francisco, gambled in everything, Bonanza mines, railroad stocks, lard, opium, and fast horses. At the moment he was engaged in an attempt to corner the whole national wheat supply. Now, in a sudden devastating bear raid, Cammack and Gould fell upon Keene when his guard was down, and began selling everything he held. Bankers became timid, brokers began demanding more margin, loans were called, prices crashed. In the jungle of the stock market one beast of prey was tearing another to pieces. Keene, who had grown to believe himself infallible, was shorn, like the veriest lamb, of seven millions and turned adrift, a bankrupt. It was a grievous lesson.

At the time of his failure [Clews relates] he was chief of a syndicate which had purchased 25,000,000 bushels of wheat, which would soon have netted many millions of profit. . . . The syndicate went to pieces, and both profits and capital vanished.

[4]"And just as Buckingham's creatures, under authority of the gold thread patent (in the time of King James II) searched private houses, and seized papers and persons for purposes of lust and extortion, so does the great telegraph company which, by the power of associated capital, deprives the people of the United States of the full benefits of a beneficent invention, tamper with correspondence and crush out newspapers which offend it." Henry George, "Progress and Poverty," p. 193.

Yet Keene, the Silver Fox, was to return again and again from the no man's land of bankruptcy, so miraculous was his gambling sense, and do battle with all corners anew.

In the immediate vicinage the roving dark eyes of Gould soon distinguished toward 1881 a new and golden opportunity, a new prize to contest for. The City of New York was having its first rapid-transit system developed, in the shape of the steam-driven elevated railways; and two companies, the Manhattan Elevated and the New York Elevated Railway Company, were in the field. He saw the future of this property and in 1881, after he had seized the telegraph combination, determined to have possession of it. Here is one of his most famous financial exploits, one that may be regarded as the most brilliant of his last period.

After studying the problem for some time he concluded that in order to buy the properties cheaply for himself, as in the Western Union case, he must harass and block the present management at every turn, he must make them wretched in mind and body, he must convince the owners that their investment was a ruinous one.

At first he attacked the Manhattan Elevated through the courts, and his procedure may be followed day by day in the newspaper he controlled. On May 18, 1881, Attorney General Ward, acting upon information he possessed, appeared before a justice of the New York State Supreme Court and asked leave to begin suit on behalf of the people to annul the charter granted to the Manhattan Elevated Railway. At the same time, the *New York World*, in its editorial and financial columns, carried on a tirade against the existing owners, suggesting that the company was insolvent and that its directors were guilty of conspiracy. In the meantime, over the telegraph wires which Gould owned, garbled despatches and strange rumors were circulated in all directions.

From a level of 57 the stock of Manhattan Elevated soon fell to 29, although the condition of the company appeared actually most promising. Now Gould and Sage began buying the stock while the attacks of the *World* and a battle of writs and injunctions kept the price at weak or "reasonable" levels. In Gould's office at the Western Union Building, Judge Westbrook of the Supreme Court (formerly Gould's legal counsel) prepared a petition in bankruptcy for the unhappy traction company.

But once Gould's party had taken over a major share of the stock,

the price of Manhattan Elevated advanced, smiles spread everywhere and, miracle of miracles, the company was found to be
sound and solvent. The *New York World,* after a five months'
campaign, seemed appeased. It reported on October 18, 1881:

> *Manhattan Elevated opened today at 45, sold down to 37, and
> closed at 43, the recovery following the announcement of an agree-
> ment between the elevated companies . . . [we have] never be-
> lieved but that Manhattan would be rescued by men who have the
> brains and the means to make the most of it.*

Jay Gould was now in charge of the company which owned the
first two elevated railways in New York. Among those who helped
him reach this point was Cyrus Field, one of the original stockholders, who had conspired with him ever since the Erie days,
1871. But Field was a distinguished man, originator of the sub-
marine cables; he was socially prominent and known as a powerful,
enthusiastic leader in speculations and investments. He thought at
first that it would be well to work closely with Gould, rather than
otherwise; he made a good front, and became titular head of the
Manhattan Elevated Railways.

Once in command of the city's elevated railroads, Gould, Sage and
Field issued more capital, manipulated their shares upward, raised
the passenger fares, and harvested rich profits. However, all was not
as well as it seemed. In portions of the press, especially in the then
crusading *New York Times,* Gould was subjected to heavy bom-
bardment; he was a "scourge," a "pirate," a "corrupter of public
servants," the Devil in human guise. The *Times* declared:

> *There is no more disgraceful chapter in the history of stock job-
> bing than that which records the operations of Jay Gould, Russell
> Sage, Cyrus W. Field and their associates in securing control of the
> system of elevated railroads in New York City.*

Such animadversions would have mattered little to the deep little
man, as accustomed to the malice of his rivals as to the envy of those
whom he defeated in the race. Mr. Field, however, the tall, white-
bearded social lion among the trio, who had been the willing instrument of Gould, was nettled by the attacks. He showed curious
symptoms of a public conscience; he sought to defend himself or
make amends in some form. To the great vexation and disgust of

Gould, Field, as the titular head of the Manhattan Elevated, determined to lower the passenger fares from ten to five cents, announced that he considered his company an institution for the public service and the development of his city—not to speak of his own large landholdings—and carried a faction among the stockholders over to his side.

To Gould's mind—as a pure tactician of capitalism—nothing could have been more insane and wasteful than such a policy, which conflicted seriously with his own ingenious plans for the treatment of New York's transportation system. It ran counter to all his usual schemes for planned mismanagement or derangement, such as opened the way to the pecuniary results he desired. And when Field used his resources to buy large blocks of stock in his railroad and reënforce his control, Gould determined to be rid of the "reformer" in their midst.

Together with Sage, he laid his snares stealthily. They waited for the good moment to strike—as the bravo with his stiletto waits for his victim to turn his back. They encouraged Field to buy, while they sold him their stock. When, by all their vehicles of information, they knew that Field was "overloaded," they fell upon the market in one of their catastrophic raids. Field's credit collapsed and the price of Manhattan Elevated broke almost in half. He was ruined but Gould "rescued" him, by consenting to take over his encumbered securities at a sacrifice to Field of many millions, "a state of things which Gould was generally accused of having produced."

The circumstances of this affray were unusually pathetic and lingered long in the public mind through rumor and report. Mr. Field, previous to his association with Gould, had been of high moral repute, a popular citizen engaged apparently in some public-spirited enterprises which happened to be useful to land and building developments. He was, moreover, the father of several beautiful and gifted daughters, one of whom, in her memoirs, described the sad chute of their gorgeous household, which came at a time when Mr. Field's health was sinking. So destitute did he become in the end that money was raised for him by sympathetic friends such as J. P. Morgan, and his last years seem to have been passed in long mental and physical anguish.

The successful outcome of this business with Manhattan Elevated and Field enhanced for Gould a reputation which in certain aspects was awkward. He was at the height of his temporal power; buying and selling, building and tearing down great railway systems, over a territory between the Mississippi, Missouri and Colorado rivers. He operated in a country which exceeded in dimensions Germany, Italy, France and Spain combined; he employed directly every day more than one hundred thousand men; while as an early biographer admiringly reports, "his word was law throughout the vast interest in his control established in many states and territories—almost from ocean to ocean." No man in the United States possessed more power than Mr. Gould, it was said; and none enjoyed more luxury than he, whether upon his yacht, the *Atalanta*, with its carved furniture and rare tapestries, or in his queer gingerbread Gothic castle outside of the city, at Irvington-on-Hudson.

Among the masses themselves, awe and terror spread of his power. What could be done with a man who controlled the press service and the telegraph system as well as railroads, a man who could read all minds, scan all secrets, form opinion and rumor, hasten or delay events? In 1884, during the stormy contest for the presidency between Blaine and Cleveland, it was charged that Gould was holding back the election returns which passed over Western Union wires, either in the interests of Blaine, or to secure himself from loss in the market in the event of Cleveland's success. A mad crowd filled the streets, threatened to sack the Tribune Building, and then urged before the massive Western Union Building, singing:

Hang Jay Gould to a sour-apple tree!

It was strange music. Imperturbable as ever, Gould reported the next day, on being questioned, that he had been at his country home nursing a cold and consoling himself in his greenhouse among the thousands of the largest orchids in the world, which he cultivated as his chief hobby.

The workers themselves combined against him in 1884 and 1885 under the belligerent and somewhat ritualistic banner of the Knights of Labor; their strikes, attended with unprecedented destruction and bloodshed, were heavy blows. Yet even such assembled might, such collective force, was vain to overcome him.

On the whole he retained his extraordinary composure through these trying events. His face was a mask, his eyes, "glowing like coals" but even and calm of glance, seldom revealed the fearful tension under which he labored, the agonized nights, the fatigue, the racking illness and pain borne successfully by his supremely vigorous spirit, which in another time would have been equal to the most heroic exploits. Always he must remain unhurried, soft-spoken. None must know and none knew his ways and movements. Only one instance was generally heard of when his guard was lowered. He was ill, but appeared with his doctor at a directors' meeting. Here the unexpected opposition of his old partner Russell Sage caused his nerves suddenly to snap, and precipitated a scene of hysteria, from which his doctor led him raving to his bed.

It was at this time that the hosts of enemies he had gained began to gather together to plot his downfall, modeling their tactics and general procedure after the methods of the great money master himself. In the ceaselessly troubled precincts of Wall Street, these mercenary soldiers, who could seldom trust each other with their backs turned, were all united against him. Their repeated conspiracies against Gould formed some of the most romantic legends of the Street. In 1881 a great storm blew down the wires of his telegraph companies. Gould was at this time compelled to use a messenger-boy service and the brokers, Cammack and Travers, kidnaped his boy and replaced him with a spy who resembled him. For days the spy brought Gould's most secret communications to the enemy headquarters at the Windsor Hotel, where they were opened and then sent on to their proper destinations. Grievous losses came to Gould in this manner before he discovered the ruse.

In 1882, at the time of the spectacular collapse of his Southwestern railroads, his credit was attacked; rumors were spread that he was heavily in debt to banks and must soon unload masses of securities he held upon a declining market. Calling witnesses to his office, he had his private secretary bring bundles of bonds and stock from his vault and displayed them. There were $53,000,000 of securities which he possessed outright, and much more elsewhere, he declared. Thus it was seen that he had been mysteriously forewarned and had completely escaped the ruin of his own railroad enterprises.

Two years later renewed attacks, timed with the general financial depression, undoubtedly brought him to the edge of danger. Men whose financial life he had apparently taken years before revived to fill the ranks of his enemies, James Keene, his former partner,

Henry N. Smith, Charles Woerishoffer, a celebrated plunger who died young, and many other Wall Street leaders united to "break" Gould at the time of the Grant and Ward panic in 1884, when his railroads were falling in ruins and he was thought to be heavily laden. He attempted to support the market against heavy onslaughts. But day by day he was brought lower; his Missouri Pacific, his Western Union, everything he owned was hammered down to bankruptcy levels. The unbelievable thing happened. Jay Gould was beaten. Halstead relates:

> *One morning he had his lawyer execute an assignment of his property, and on the following day—a beautiful Sunday morning—his yacht went down to Long Branch where the bear operators were summering. Gould's emissaries landed and held a conference with his foes. They bore his ultimatum—a copy of the assignment and a statement that unless the bears made terms with him he would on the following morning . . . give public notice that he was unable to meet his engagements.*

According to the obscure allusions of his biographer, he had assigned a portion of his unencumbered holdings so that it would remain to his heirs. Officially he, in person, would descend into bankruptcy to the extent of millions. And his failure would create a far greater panic than that which was now raging, one in which the very concerns with which the bears had contracts would founder in the universal crash, making them, too, heavy losers. Thus, like Samson, he stood ready to tear down the house in which they all lived. The bears after long conference agreed to "let up" on terms of receiving 50,000 shares of Western Union at 50, which they had sold much higher. They expected him to fail in any event soon after.

But Gould now used the very money they released in order to turn upon them and smite them hip and thigh. He cornered his Missouri Pacific and other stocks in which his adversaries were short, trapped them and forced them to stand and deliver. Once more he had miraculously escaped from the fate he prepared for so many others.

Nevertheless he was deeply alarmed by the near-catastrophes of 1884-85. More prudent in his last years, he husbanded his reserves until his war chest was ample once more. Then after several years of comparative armistice, he would assume the offensive again. At the very hour of his death in 1892 he would be bent upon new campaigns of conquest, as vast, as impenetrable as ever.

CHAPTER TEN

CAESAR BORGIA IN CALIFORNIA

THE development of the Great West during the '70's and '80's continued unabated. Its outward effect was one of extraordinary material progress, whose wonders were perpetually recited by the pioneers; while obstacles or deficiencies in the total plan were dismissed with that brimming optimism which was not only native in Americans, but particularly prominent in the Westerner.

The Westerner had come from the East partly because he chafed under the restrictions of a well-organized society and partly because he had faith that, with an equal chance in a new country, he would be able to amass the wealth he had failed to win in the East. By the testimony of one historian of the region's economy, R. E. Riegel,

> *each individual Westerner expected to become wealthy and famous; each city expected to become the metropolis of the West; and each state expected to become the industrial and artistic center of the nation. Before this spirit obstacles disappeared as if by magic. Some of them later reappeared with increased force and potency, but others were gone forever.*

The rapid growth of the whole region, the swift industrialization by the use of large machines, enmeshed even the most hard-headed business men in the dream of future cities, farms and railroads, even of trade with the Far East.

Yet rapidity of development was but the result of the higher technical knowledge attained slowly in the East and in Europe. Hence the plan of exploitation which soon stamped its character upon the West was that of great machines quickly introduced where only yesterday the native Mexicans or Indians had been expropriated from the virgin land. The new railroad line of the

Central Pacific across the Sierra Nevada, in 1865, represented the highest engineering knowledge of the period; the tremendous tunneling of Sutro and Mackay in the Comstock Lode, in 1872, reflected the growing mechanization of deep mining for silver and gold. In Montana, Marcus Daly and. William A. Clark sank their great copper mines, only a few years after the Indian campaigns of Custer and Miles had cleared the country. Thus, in the wild fastnesses of the Rockies, amid sheer barrenness, industries of giant size sprang up overnight.

The industrial plan of the Great West, in its tempo and dimensions, can only be likened to the operations of contemporary Russian engineers who build Manchesters and Pittsburghs overnight in their steppes. But in the absence of any social formulae other than that of individualism, the leaders who carried forward the exploitation of the last American frontier were chosen simply by themselves: at first as the survivors in a struggle of ruse and violence; then by virtue of a stronger equipment in capital. Faced with such mighty arms in the hands of a few self-chosen leaders—who soon wielded machine technology and political influence in measure with their great capital—the crowd of pioneers who had flocked to the West quickly found themselves reduced to the condition of helpless subjects.

The adventures of the exploiters who seized the principal mineral deposits, forest lands, mountain passes and valley roads in the West seem far more magical than that of their fellows in the Eastern cities. Here were contests fought by strong men in the open rather than intrigues in stuffy board-rooms. There were well-nigh insuperable hazards to overcome, calamities of nature, the menace of rival expropriators. And here as elsewhere the railroad barons, Collis Huntington, Henry Villard and James Hill, who were busy organizing the regional traffic into giant systems, held the key to the whole economic situation and did reverence to no one.

Huntington and his partners, Stanford, Crocker and Hopkins, controlled by possession of the Central Pacific; they were in the post of the king in the castle, the baron on the crag. Though their project should normally not have "paid," their autocratic powers permitted them to charge as their toll the highest passenger and freight rates in the country. Moreover the opening of the Bonanza mines of Western Nevada gave them nourishment in traffic and helped to carry the heavy debts they had saddled on their railroad, such debts as similar enterprises collapsed under.

But once having begun such an adventure one dare not stand still. Huntington, the leader of the group, who carried the chief responsibilities of their affairs on his broad shoulders, knew a thousand cares and dangers. Repeatedly in his letters he gives way to doleful complaints: "This business . . . will kill me yet!" There were moments when he would have liked to sell out and decamp; but none would then undertake his hazards, despite the great prize in sight. And when certain interests did come with offers, he instinctively, greedily raised his price.

The problems before the ring known as the Pacific Associates were manifold. They must hold and fortify their monopoly of the Pacific states. This meant seizing the water front at the ocean and river ports, as well as certain other existing railroad projects such as the California Central (which ran lengthwise through the state), and the badly constructed short line which plied between Sacramento and San Francisco. But though they had control of 85 per cent of the California roads, as Daggett relates in his history of the Southern Pacific, this was not enough. All possible rival encroachments must be forestalled by prompt if stealthy measures. The federal government, for instance, had made generous grants to the rival Western roads in order to stimulate the competition between them, as between dry-goods merchants in a village. For this purpose several charters had been issued to other interests which boded no good to the California quartet: a "Texas Pacific" along the 32nd parallel, an "Atlantic Pacific" along the 35th, and a "Southern Pacific," which had been in the hands of the ill-starred Frémont for a time—all these mere projects on paper, yet likely to reduce the monopoly of the Huntington ring over their domain.

As early as 1868, with their main line almost completed, the group secretly acquired the California charter of the Southern Pacific, then began large building operations in the region of Los Angeles, and actually transferred their main interests to the new company. All records of their earlier construction company, the "Contract & Finance Company," were burned, and the offices were moved from San Francisco to Sacramento. A new holding company, the "Western Development Company," was set up to conduct their business in the promising southern territory.

There were rumors afloat of these intricate proceedings, and of what they portended; yet Stanford denied them publicly. But six months later, in September, 1868, the annual report of the Southern Pacific was sent to the Secretary of the Interior with a letter signed in Huntington's own hand. This brazen falsification was continued; all relations between the various corporate units controlled were kept obscure. Twenty years later, Stanford would admit before the Pacific Railway Commission:

Well, the necessity of obtaining control of the Southern Pacific Railroad was based really upon the act of Congress providing for its construction. It became apparent that if that last was constructed entirely independent of the Central Pacific, it would become a dangerous rival, not only for the through business from the Atlantic, but . . . for the local business of California. It was of paramount importance that the road should be controlled by the friends of the Central Pacific.

It was necessary, in short, that the quartet defend all California from invaders, cover the rest of the state with their network of branch lines and feeders, and block all the transcontinental entrances to their territory with their own lines. With the Southern Pacific in their hands, they still had two other rivals to block; on the one hand Thomas Scott, who held the Texas Pacific charter, and on the other the interests who acquired the right of way of the somewhat mythical "Atlantic & Pacific." These contests would keep them busy enough later on; but for the time being they occupied themselves with exploiting the southern part of their state.

Here, their agents in the field had given dazzling reports of the soil richness; but population was almost nil. Huntington, Stanford and Crocker traveled the beautiful southern country in person, studying the ground. The few communities, Los Angeles, San Diego and Santa Anna, were mere villages, with a saloon to every fifty-five inhabitants.

Crocker later declared that "when the Southern Pacific was built through the southern San Joaquin Valley, the company could have started with a railroad train at Sumner, at the south of the valley, and come to Stockton, and with one engine and one train of card

hauled every living soul that lived in the valley out at one haul."
This was as late as 1876.

No traffic here yet, but there was need for haste, if only to fore-
stall future opponents in the field. Quickly they laid down their
tracks, levying upon communities as they went and acquiring huge
sections of land as grants along the right of way. Against these acquisitions they issued $40,000 in bonds and an indiscriminate amount of
stock for every mile of road they built, and passed these over as
usual to themselves, that is, to the construction company of which
they were the sole owners.[1]

But from Southern California, the quartet now sought egress
toward the populous East as well as the ports of the Gulf of
Mexico. Besides the pass in the northern part of the state used by
their Central Pacific through Summit Valley, there were only two
other routes known to them: at Yuma, Arizona, near the mouth
of the Colorado River, and at The Needles, midway between Yuma
and Summit Valley. But toward Yuma, that irrepressible railroader
Thomas Scott was building his Texas Pacific as fast as he could
make it go without tangible funds.

A collision between the two forces was inevitable. But the conflict between the hosts of Huntington and those of Scott (behind
whom Gould maneuvered) was staged not only in the deserts and
canyons of the Southwest, but also in the halls of Congress, where
for years the statesmen tried their best to judge between the quarreling barons. While these two enemies remained locked in mortal
combat, the fortunes of war were to be deeply affected by the intrusion of a third party in the shape of Boston financiers, who
sought to drive a track of their own, the Atchison, Topeka & Santa
Fe, between them. And when the Southern Pacific turned to beat off
the flank attack of the Santa Fe, the Santa Fe would find itself
suddenly engaged with still other intruders from other quarters.
The railroad wars of the Southwest were an extraordinary mêlée,
one of the strangest and most noisome since the days of Frederick
Barbarossa in the twelfth century.

So throughout the known ages of history the strong captains
have led their bands of followers to the seizure of the mountain

[1]Several years later when the Southern Pacific was first offered to Jay
Gould, at its reputed cost, he declared the price high at half the capitalization
they had fixed per mile of track.

passes, to be guarded for toll ever after, so long as force could hold them. Thus, in an Alpine pass—now traversed by a beautiful auto- mobile road—between Italy and Germany, I have seen upon a height naturally controlling a narrow gorge, first the ruins of a Roman stronghold; then, built many centuries later, a section of Gothic or feudal construction, dating perhaps a thousand years later; and finally, surmounting it all, a Renaissance building of the fifteenth or sixteenth century with its toll gate. The barons had never let go their grip over this trade route.

In the field, the gargantuan Crocker directed the soldiers of the Pacific Associates, while the many-handed Huntington hied him to Washington, there before the tribunes of the people to defend his Western empire.

2

Huntington, with his large, deeply lined face, his long nose and black beard, might have sat for Holbein as a great vassal of the Renaissance period, or some militant prince of the Church. Passion- ate, vindictive and yet supremely forehanded, he pursued his ends now with bluntness and now with infinite guile, and by many paths. His mission was elaborate and delicate, required several years' time, but was discharged on the whole with fair success.

The capital was full of railroad barons, who having allowed a decent time to elapse since the Crédit Mobilier scandals, fully two years, belabored the President and the Congress for federal bounties of all sorts. Failing of this—they could never understand why such friendly policy should be gradually abandoned—they lay in watch to see that no bones were thrown to the other dogs.

In the miraculously preserved private correspondence of Hun- tington for the four years between 1874 and 1878, we have an inti- mate record of the ebb and flow of the railroad war. There was Scott, who possessed a charter and a right of way, wanting badly government cash, and a guarantee of bonds, such as the Union Pacific had won, in order to continue his own march to the sea. Huntington, now fairly strong in funds, wanted the charter or the right of way across the territories and Indian Reservations in his path of 1,000 miles—the things in which Scott was rich. One would think they might have clasped hands and united to exploit the great region together. Was there not room for both of them to "grow up with the country"? But Huntington, stubborn and unforgiving, believed he controlled all the approaches; while Scott felt absolutely certain of a strategic advantage in the sympathy of the federal government at Washington. In other words, as Huntington wrote it down in private, *"Scott has about the same advantage over us in Washington as we would have over him in Sacramento."*

On the whole neither Huntington nor Scott were helped by Congress at this time, in spite of a great program of "junketing parties," donations of railroad passes, and cash payments by both sides, as well as promises of all sorts to lawmakers, whom Huntington characterized simply as *"the hungriest set of men that ever got together."* During a long harassing sojourn in Washington, Huntington, at any rate, prevented "harm" from being done. In a negative sense, he succeeded in stopping or postponing indefinitely the "investigations" for which some embittered factions—styled by him "communists"—clamored; and second, in the matter of interest due on the government's first mortgage of $21,000,000, Huntington won a long respite of twenty years and never returned the full sum.

The Huntington letters, which are not lacking in incisive literary qualities, speak of "fixing" committees, "convincing" public servants, "switching Senators" or "persuading" the most exalted cabinet members. They tell how he manipulated the mind of the Secretary of War; or how he caused a President to cease "being cross" and "to laugh heartily." Profound documents these, yielding us the richest instruction in the diplomacy and statecraft of the time.

The duelists strike at the weak places in each other's armor. Scott points to the connection between the "new" Southern Pacific and the Central Pacific monopoly. To aid Huntington would be to aid monopoly. Huntington on the other hand, in hearings before the "Railway Congressmen," promises that, given a charter, he will actually build the road, whereas Scott, he intimates, is insolvent. California, he says, wants a connection with New Orleans in a hurry. As to his affiliations with existing parallel roads, he protests that he has severed all such interests—which he did legally. (In a secret message to his comrades he urges now that "the S. P. should be disconnected from the Central Pacific as much as it well can be.") But at Scott's instance (a retaliating stroke) Congress resolves in

1876 to investigate the Southern Pacific's rights to certain lands in California, its route having been unlawfully changed from that designated on the original blue-prints. Yet nothing comes of this. Huntington reports in June, 1876:

> There is a terrible fight kept up on us in Washington. But while they may bite us, they will not eat us up.

But the "T & P folks" are always "working hard at their bill." It was of Scott, veteran trafficker in franchises and corrupter of public officers, that Wendell Phillips said: "The members of twenty legislatures rustled like dry leaves in a winter's wind, as he trailed his garments across the country." The wily Scott returns to the attack ever and anon. Now Huntington reports him offering the blue sky—"all the money—say $40,000,000—that the Act would give him!"

Huntington works hard at his lobbying, not only in Washington, but in Virginia, New York, Kentucky, as well as in the Western commonwealths of California, Nevada and Arizona. Sometimes he complains that he and his agents must work twenty-four hours a day. He cries out under the great tension: "I am fearful this damnation Congress will kill me." It costs so much money "to fix things," he wails. $200,000 to $500,000 each session, and there is no end!

But at the height of his labors, Senator Hoar (Massachusetts) sounds the alarm of another Crédit Mobilier before the Senate and the public. Persons in the employ of a Pacific railway, he declares, were in Washington during the passage of a bill favorable to the railway's interests, and at an ensuing meeting of the directors, authority was given to expend $167,000 for "special legal expenses." A government director, present at the board meeting, testifies that he left the room when this matter came up because he did not want to know what these expenses were for. By this exposure, the Congress is stampeded; the buyers of franchises and statesmen make sullen retreat. But Huntington turns to new tactics.

In the interim the engineering gangs of the Southern Pacific had proceeded as far as the California state line to Yuma, Arizona, blocking one of the two available entrances to California. For the further progress of the line they decided to abandon temporarily the issue of a federal franchise and obtain separate charters from the states or territories they traversed, Arizona, Nevada and New Mexico.

Huntington had urged this course some time before, in 1875, to his lieutenant, David Colton:

> If we had a franchise to build a road or two roads through Arizona (we controlling, but having it in the name of another party) . . . it could be used against Scott. Cannot you have Stafford [governor of Arizona] call the legislature together and grant such charters as we want at a cost of say $25,000? If we could get such a charter as I spoke to you of, it would be worth much money to us.

These state charters were easily obtained. But now the remaining obstacle was the existence of a government Indian reservation at Yuma. Authority from the War Department must be had for building a bridge across the Colorado, and tracks. The Texas Pacific saw the advantage of the possession of this strategic point, Riegel recounts, and in 1876, though the end of its main line was still 1,200 miles distant in Texas, it applied for permission to break ground at Yuma. General McDowell, in authority on the ground, granted his permission at first, then in an afterthought revoked it, to wait for War Department orders. Huntington bestirred himself, as he related, to get the Secretary of War "out of an ugly idea"—of authorizing Scott's passage—"in about twenty minutes." Then while the Secretary of War hesitated, the California quartet had the brilliant notion of taking the law into their own hands and rushing tracks across the Indian reservation that barred their way through Arizona. This was done with a great burst of speed, Crocker throwing a permanent bridge across the Colorado River under the noses of the federal soldiers, whose commanders by some means were led unofficially to ignore the restraining order they had received. Thus the California ring at one blow had a *fait accompli* to display. The people of the region, intensely excited by the prospects of land-booming and town-site jobbing in the wake of the longed-for train service, were up in arms, and ready to fire at the government troops if they intervened. It was probably at this moment, when nobody knew what precedent to follow, that Huntington by putting the President "in a good humor" obtained an executive order authorizing his construction, on October 9, 1877.

The Southern Pacific now laid its tracks at great speed across the southern tier of Arizona and New Mexico, toward Texas. Scott was beaten. Gould, now a dominant voice in the Texas & Pacific, came forward with terms of peace. The two roads made a juncture at El Paso in 1882, establishing the country's second transcontinental trade route.

At this very moment there was turmoil, comic, fierce and incessant, elsewhere in the Rocky Mountain states. Two smaller railroads fought for the middle passage through Colorado and New Mexico to the Pacific. One, the Denver & Rio Grande, had been started by the citizens of Denver as an act of self-defense, to head off Jay Gould. The other was the Atchison, Topeka & Santa Fe led by the Bostonians Nickerson and T. Jefferson Coolidge. Both aimed for Santa Fe, a rich trading area ever since the seventeenth century under Spanish rule. The one good entry into New Mexico was the Raton Pass, and because of the mining boom at the time (1878) both lines rushed engineering crews to take possession and start work. The Santa Fe got there first; then fought off the Rio Grande to the West, in the engagement known as the "Canon War" which took place at a wild pass near Canon City, the only entrance to Leadville, Colorado. The local citizens armed themselves and fought on both sides; most of them aiding the Santa Fe.

Here were new and terrible anxieties for Huntington and for Gould. The Santa Fe now occupying a very good line of approach to the sea was a menace to the Southern Pacific and the Union Pacific both. In the fury and confusion of railroad war, construction on all these roads was done with incredible carelessness; a great part of the Santa Fe trackage and roadbed, for instance, had to be completely remade within fifteen years.

At the advance of the terrible Yankees heading the Santa Fe Huntington and his comrades rushed to bar the way. The one remaining breach in the natural barrier of California was at The Needles, midway in the Sierras, where a passage across the Colorado Canyon could be made. Once more the Southern Pacific rushed its line to occupy the pass, crossing the Mojave Desert. A third branch of the Huntington lines now traversed the Colorado River at The Needles and successfully blocked the approach of the Santa Fe to California, for the time being.

The new adversaries had the authority of an old federal charter for the "Atlantic & Pacific," and Huntington, in alliance with Gould, who was equally alarmed by the intruders, used clever means to acquire a holding company which was known to have shares in the so-called Atlantic & Pacific. Soon they turned up with control of the enemy's charter! The Southern Pacific, in which all the interests of the California quartet had been centered, now held a complete monopoly of every route across California. The only existing rival was far to the North, where Villard completed the building of the Northern Pacific to Puget Sound.

While enjoying a complete land monopoly, the Pacific Associates were never free from the fear of competition by the sea. Therefore Huntington bought steamships after 1873 and organized the Occidental & Oriental S.S. Co. in order to continue their carrying business to the Far East over their own line and to "knock out" the Pacific Mail. But other railroad chiefs resented the capture of the ocean-carrying trade by Huntington. War in this field was threatened until Huntington, on behalf of the Associates, and Gould, on behalf of the Pacific Mail, reached an accord by which the latter long-established steamship line agreed to make Panama the terminus of its transpacific route and to make of San Francisco merely a port of call. As a result of this pact, reached shortly before 1880, for which both the Union Pacific and the Huntington railroads paid Pacific Mail an annual blackmail fee mounting into millions, the railroads gained from the elimination of the steamships, and carried goods across the continent at such terms as they saw fit.

"For more than forty years," concludes Stuart Daggett, "the Southern Pacific interests sought with varying success to modify the intensity of water competition by agreements with or purchase of competing lines." Communities in their general territory which had some access to competing railways or ships—and they were few —were tolerably well off. But the rest were left to the mercies of the California quartet, who in general charged average tariffs of 2.04 cents per ton mile as late as 1885; who raised or lowered individual items on their tariff at will; who favored or discouraged certain towns in accordance with their interest in the situation; or gave rebates to certain industries, such as the Standard Oil's distributing agency, or their own Rocky Mountain Coal & Iron Company of Colorado. Daggett, in his very temperate history of the Southern Pacific, concludes after long study that their rates on long- as well as short-haul business were always higher than in the East, because of the completeness of their monopoly. Thus, he holds, the very development of the state, of its resources, its circulation of goods and services, was *retarded.*

Repeatedly the distressed burghers of San Francisco and other Pacific communities tried to break through the economic bands that held them down. On one occasion a group of hardware merchants calculated that it would be cheaper to have a cargo of nails shipped from New York to Antwerp, across the Atlantic, discharged and reshipped on a British vessel around Cape Horn to Redondo, California, than to use the direct rail connections of the "Octopus." But this was a desperate measure, involving the equivalent of a complete circumference of the earth's surface and taking almost half a year. Wherever they turned the pioneers found themselves encircled by a Huntington, a Gould, a Villard, a Hill. In the early '90's the Californians attempted a new sally, building a new railway down the San Joaquin Valley from San Francisco across the Mojave Desert, to join with an "outside" road. The local patriots were stirred up to generous stock subscriptions. But of course among them were quietly introduced the friends of Huntington and Stanford, especially the rich Western sugar refiner, Spreckels. When the road was completed, it was surrendered, after curious negotiations, as the California terminus of that other giant railroad monopoly, the Santa Fe, which was now acting in perfect collusion with the Southern Pacific.

Economically encircled, the people of the Pacific Coast were also ruled through a political dictatorship directed with brilliant technique. Huntington bought the newspapers to "control or burn" them, as he said. About the offices of the Southern Pacific in Sacramento a horde of political heelers hovered. Huntington once complained pathetically in a newspaper interview in 1890:

> *I have seen the ante-rooms down here in this building full of men trying to learn or get something out of politics. Why should they come here? This is no place for them. But then they were not to blame. The tip went forth that political work was being done at Fourth and Townsend Streets and they merely followed the tip. ... Things have got to such a state that if a man wants to be a constable he thinks he has first got to come to Fourth and Townsend Streets to get permission.*

The petty political job-seekers in their naïveté had gone to the rail-road headquarters, believing simply that the state capitol was really located there.

In many polemics and pamphlets of the '80's and '90's, certain of the pioneers who were less reconciled to their station described publicly the form of control exercised by the "Octopus" of California. Up to 1895 no governor of the state was nominated except at the wish of the Southern Pacific. The police commissioners of San Francisco, the harbor police, and the judges of two federal courts in San Francisco were appointed at the instance of Leland Stanford; while Congressmen and Senators from the region were sometimes members of the railroad group directly, Stanford himself going to Washington as a California Senator in 1887.

When California had, in accordance with a custom growing up at the time, established a Railroad Commission of three members in 1881, Stanford and Huntington saw to it that at least two of the members were appointed by themselves. In the committee of 1881, Stoneman, the independent one among the three, reported that when the commissioners were elected, he, "it was understood, repre-sented the popular interest; another gentleman [S. J. Cone] ... the feeling of the corporations, and a third was a 'sandlot' man." With the sand-lot man (one who joined in the current mob demon-strations against Chinese or Japanese immigrants), he thought he had a majority for the people. "But in a short time the sand-lot man sold out and did not amount to anything."

Using to the full their immense power over the whole Pacific Slope, the Associates rounded out an "empire" with its steamships, its affiliated railroads, its coal and iron mines, its great landholdings, and its army of political retainers, over all of which they ruled unchallenged. In 1884 Huntington, who had completed the Chesa-peake & Ohio Railroad in the East, actually proposed that the whole Southern Pacific system be "consolidated," from San Francisco to Newport News, though it would have been impolitic to do so. To a friend he boasted that he could travel over his own lines from Yokohama to New York. His alliances with the mighty industrial groups of the East were firmly cemented after 1890, with Gould, with Carnegie, from whom he bought his steel, and with the Stand-ard Oil, whose petroleum he carried westward at favoring rates.

Working together with remarkably little dissension (save toward the end of their association) the quartet directed their affairs with firmness and unsurpassed craftiness. Such opposition as they met with in various quarters from time to time, the importunities of outsiders who sought to learn their secrets or blackmail them, brought them together in a close working union, an effect which we see repeated elsewhere in the other great industrial rings of the time. Their henchmen too were filled with this intense *esprit de corps*. And one, General David Colton, who became a minor partner in the '70's, entrusted with extremely confidential work, wrote in 1878 to Huntington:

> *I have learned one thing, we have got no true friends outside of us five. We cannot depend on a human soul outside of ourselves, and hence we must all be good-natured, stick together and keep our own counsels.*[2]

There were great trials and great risks in such huge undertakings. The Associates were often overextended; and Huntington must often besiege the "German" bankers in New York for cash. But year by year as millions of people of the Great West paid toll to the quartet who controlled the price of their lands, who raised tariffs upon their crops with deadly effect in good season, the crushing debts of the system were fully redeemed; Hopkins and Crocker who died earlier left some twenty millions to their heirs; Stanford bequeathed thirty millions to found Stanford University in memory of his

[2]The terms of General David Colton's participations in the Pacific Associates' enterprises were hard. He signed, as a bond, a demand note for $1,000,000 and received securities having a very restricted market at the time. He could also be put out entirely at the order of his partners, after two years' notice, and of course made bankrupt. Finally in managing the Western Development Company for them, Colton found his chance to get relief from his obligations by a little financiering. He suddenly declared a "melon" or dividend distribution of $13,500,000 surplus profits in railroad stocks and bonds, which would give him a large share. Huntington and Crocker were furious when they learned of these proceedings and threatened to ruin Colton, who then repudiated his actions.

At his death, soon afterward, they discovered manipulations (of this "true friend") scarcely distinguishable from embezzlement, and a long and bitterly fought suit against his heirs in connection with the promissory note of $1,000,-000 followed.

Providentially Mrs. Colton had kept the letters of Huntington—which were supposed to be destroyed as received—and these were revealed at the trial, and were also used in the evidence taken by the Pacific Railway Commission in 1887.

son; while Huntington's fortune was variously estimated at between fifty and ninety millions. Huntington and Stanford owned enormous vineyards in California—100,000 acres—and in the East constructed palaces after their own fancy; Huntington's home being the vast and melancholy pile which long stood at Fifth Avenue and Fifty-seventh Street, New York, as a Gothic monument to the new peerage of America. So extensive were Huntington's interests that at his death in 1900 only the Standard Oil family, acting through the ambitious Harriman, possessed the resources to buy them over from his widow.

CHAPTER ELEVEN
GIANTS OF THE NORTHWEST

WHILE Huntington was overrunning California and the Southwest, James J. Hill and Henry Villard, two prodigious captains of fortune, arose to contest with each other the rule of the Northwestern territory lying between the Great Lakes and the Oregon coast. Whoever seized the existing and future routes of trade here would have the control of an area embracing eight huge and barely populated states which held incalculable resources. The panic of 1873 had been severely felt in the trans-Mississippi section; in its wake there lay scattered all the débris, broken rolling-stock and dissevered members of bankrupt railroad and steamship lines, tracks, terminals, lands, all waiting for the hand ready and willing to grasp them.

This Hill and Villard saw. Both men had little means at the start; but both spied out the ground thoroughly, calculated the prize at stake and then strained every nerve to capture the river and seaports, the valley routes and mountain passes. Hill proceeded westward from the Mississippi River as his point of departure, building upon a defunct railroad as the foundation for his future Great Northern system. Villard centered upon the coast and rivers of Oregon and moved eastward over the incompleted line of Jay Cooke's old Northern Pacific. Each pressed for the crushing advantages of monopoly; and each sought by every means possible to clear the other from his path.

Nearly twenty years before this time Jim Hill, a boy of eighteen, had come from southern Ontario to Minnesota Territory to try his luck in the trading post of St. Paul (called "Pig's Eye"). Hill was methodical, abstemious, and laconic in speech, though now and then he was given to towering passions. He also possessed a rugged constitution, a tremendous physical endurance, which was fortunate in a place where you might literally have to fight for your life at any moment with drunken Indians or wild pioneers. Working at the river's edge as a shipping agent and a trader, Hill grew up with the frontier community, married, saved money steadily until he had accumulated $100,000 by the age of forty, and was highly respected.

During his sojourn the experience of St. Paul accurately mirrored the revolution of the frontier everywhere. Like the other outpost towns St. Paul quadrupled in size between 1856 and 1873. Here one was at the head of navigation on the Mississippi. Now in 1857 the first shipments of Minnesota grain, and soon after the famous Minnesota flour, passed through Hill's hands, bringing presentiments of economic triumphs to come. During the second year of the Civil War a torrent of grain, cereal and flour issued from the deep black soil of the Northwest, to be reshipped at St. Paul. Hill, as a shipping agent for the new railroad branch that soon reached the frontier town, then as a warehouse owner and commission merchant on his own, found himself stationed at one of the natural crossroads of Western trade. He had his hand at the pulse of the region's industry; he knew the soil richness of Minnesota and the Dakotas beyond; he knew the mounting size of the crops from year to year; he knew the rate at which immigrants were coming into the territory and the pressing need for transportation. As a part owner after the war of a small line of freight boats which ran up the Red River (of the North) to Winnipeg, he knew the development being carried on beyond the border over which he himself had come as a Canadian emigrant. So Jim Hill knew the lay of the land; and when one of the two small railroads which had been chartered by Minnesota Territory in 1862 collapsed before his eyes in the panic of '73, he became possessed with a dream. He went perfectly "romantic." He had the pioneer's vision of mountains of gold before him and it never left him.

The so-called St. Paul & Pacific which ran northward out of St. Paul had been blessed with a federal as well as a state charter, and with a grant 5,000,000 acres of Minnesota lands; but it was cursed with a capitalization of some $28,000,000 in bonds of various classes, more than half of this sum being a first mortgage advanced by trusting Dutch investors. Every species of up-to-date financiering had been tried on this little railroad: part of its capital had been spent for promotion; its bonds had been watered; money had been diverted to construction companies, and tracks which were laid at such enormous cost could now scarcely be negotiated by any trains. Moreover the purpose of the big Northern Pacific Railroad, which also ran through Minnesota from Duluth westward, had been to hold the little road down because its charter promised competition. In 1874 for the second time in its brief history the St. Paul & Pacific was being operated by a receiver, this time by a Mr. Farley, an acquaintance of Hill's. Its bondholders were in despair, ready to sell out at any price. Soon its valuable land-grant would be forfeited for want of construction according to the provisions of its charter; and it would dwindle away into the proverbial "streak of rust," as ghostly as the abandoned mining towns in the Sierras.

Only Hill saw any future in this road. He made his own investigations, scanned the reports of the receiver, and sought to arouse the interest of certain of his associates in the section. Among these was a man named Kittson, his partner in the shipping business along the Red River. Through two Canadians he met, Donald A. Smith (the future Lord Strathcona) and George Stephen (Lord Mount Stephen), he learned that the western provinces of Canada sought a connection between Winnipeg and St. Paul on the Mississippi. To these three he confided his calculations concerning the St. Paul & Pacific Railroad. In its franchise and acreage alone he saw tremendous future values. Hill seemed to have "a perfect knowledge of the whole thing." After long conferences, the four men concluded that the railway would be a good thing for them to get possession of, if it could be had for nothing. The country was terribly in need of railroad service. Perhaps the Dutch bondholders would sell their claim cheaply? The would-be purchasers, at any rate, possessed almost no cash and could give little more than their promises to pay whatever was agreed upon.

In 1875 Hill and his Scotch friends began their campaign. With seeming innocence they picked up whatever bonds could be had in the market at 6½ to 8 cents on the dollar. Then they began to put out feelers to the foreign bondholders.

An agent who had been sent over from Holland to look over the property was met by Hill as well as by the receiver. The Dutch visitor saw the thing darkly; it would take millions in money to place the road on its feet; and such further sums the bondholders would never contribute after the way in which they had been duped. Moreover Hill and the receiver "knocked" the road pretty hard, as Pyle, Hill's official biographer, relates. The Americans were certainly combined in a sort of conspiracy of silence about the prospects of the enterprise as they saw it. It has also been charged (and as stoutly denied) that Hill had the receiver of the railroad, Farley, as his confederate.

While speaking in the most doleful tones of the bad risks the business presented, Hill lay awake nights figuring out its actual value, and the best offer he could dare to make upon the fore-closed mortgage bonds. In his own hand—the papers were published by his biographer—Hill estimated the value of the road as it existed to be $12,216,718; he then added the value of the land and town sites at $6,500,000. "How the eyes of the Dutch Committee would have bulged if they could have seen the prospective estimate of what he was going to get," Pyle comments, as if he himself naturally would have entered into the scheme with the "most honest," "most constructive" of American railroad-builders. Hill would offer five millions. "A total property value of twenty millions to be had at a little more than twenty-five cents on the dollar." Hill's apologist fairly gloats over his hero's shrewdness in overreaching the far-off Europeans.

Besides, there was more that Hill and his confederates knew, thanks to the complaisant receiver. Hill had no means of paying five millions, nor any such intention; his group could muster up not a tenth that sum. The negotiations extended themselves for one year, then a second year, while the plotters quietly hatched their affair. Everything grew more promising, although no word leaked out. In 1877 the accounts of the receiver were curiously juggled so that improved earnings were not revealed, except to Hill. There was expended "on additions, improvements and equipment," Pyle tells us, "$188,250, which had been charged to operating expenses instead of to construction." This item of false accounting, when properly understood, nearly doubled the reported earnings of the road, a point of great significance to Hill. Besides, there was more that he saw; a continued influx of immigrants and town developments in the lonely and nearly empty territories near by indicated to

Hill that there would be more crops raised in Minnesota and more traffic, by 50 to 60 per cent, the following year. Of all this Hill said nothing and finally closed his deal with the distressed foreigners. He and his friends assumed the bonded obligations of the road at one-fifth their value and gave their mere promissory note for $1,000,000 as a pledge of good faith. Everything was at last "neatly corralled" by way of a friendly foreclosure suit on March 13, 1878.[1]

Now during a strenuous period the partners labored to salvage the enterprise which they held at the start only by a thin shoestring. With the receiver still officially in charge, and Hill directing, construction was rushed through to the Canadian border at Pembina, where junction was had with a branch of the advancing Canadian Pacific. Thus a line was opened from Winnipeg to the Mississippi River. To raise money Hill held rousing land sales before the immigrants at $2.50 to $5.00 an acre; the partners pledged every scrap of property they possessed; and Stephen found valuable credit resources in the Bank of Montreal, of which he was an agent. By the added construction, their land grants had been saved, and by taking title to additional acreage more money could be raised. Finally a boom year came in 1879.

"You can have no idea of the rush of immigrants to Minnesota this year," Hill writes to his partners. "We are laying a mile and a half of iron a day."

The masses of Norwegian and Swedish peasants who flocked to Minnesota and produced by their labor a bumper crop of 32,000,000 bushels of wheat—though the state was only partly settled as yet—saved Hill and caused the earnings of the road to be tripled. Soon the partners, as Pyle tells it in his colorful account, "were gloating over the statistics of operation of the St. Paul & Pacific." They reorganized the railroad under the name of the "St. Paul, Minneapolis & Manitoba" in October, 1879, and capitalizing it at $16,000,000 in bonds and $16,000,000 in stock, were able to distribute five million of the capital outright to each partner. A pretty year or two of

[1]The receiver Farley, several years afterward, sued Hill for $5,000,000 alleging that he had conspired to get the property for Hill and had afterward been "left in the cold." The testimony of the receiver, by evidence of his own character, was considered untrustworthy by the Court and besides, no documents incriminating Hill were produced.

business. ". . . The time was ripe," Hill said afterward. "The growth of the country just at that time helped us."

Jim Hill was a short, thick-set man of about forty, with a massive head, large wrinkled features, long black hair, and a blind eye. His unique exterior—like a "grim old lion"—reënforced by a naturally stern manner, gave him in time a formidable reputation in his territory. He was known always to be "a very hard man in business," among railroad men "the hardest man to work for." He carried everything in his head, worried, systematized, labored himself or drove on the others around him with unflagging energy. He had no small scruples; rough-hewn throughout, "intolerant of opposition, despotic, largely ruling by fear," his contemporaries said, "he was also given to personal violence in the department offices of his road."

This aggressive figure, who seemed to have roused himself in middle age, saw things in a large way. In his conquering march through the Northern territories, he developed new methods of business, departing widely from the petty mercantilism of the age which preceded his. He wrote to his partner Lord Mount Stephen his plain view: "It is our best interest to give low rates and do all we can to develop the country and create business." This was no mere philanthropic intention; he labored for large volume rather than for small orders at high rates. He was "sounder" and by far more "efficient" than his confreres in this business; and he ended by becoming something of an engineer himself. It is characteristic of him that although when he came into the railroad business the locomotives, like resplendent pet animals, bore names, Hill gave them numbers, doubled their tractive power until his road had the most powerful engines, the longest trains. In the same way he laid his roadbeds only after the most exhaustive surveys of grades and curves. The bridge he threw over the Mississippi between St. Paul and the present Minneapolis was one of the most massive granite structures ever made at the time. So his own headquarters in St. Paul were made as "solid and bare as a prison"; his house too, "grimly strong as a feudal fortress," rendered burglar- and cyclone-proof through the use of huge beams of steel. This efficient groundwork by an undoubtedly able administrator, surmounted by shrewd buying and selling and ruthless "hiring and firing," brought fundamental economies year after year, and cleared the way for tremendous expansion.

Steadily, the "Manitoba" advanced its lines and branches over the prairies of Dakota and Montana, while Hill seemed to ride before it in many expeditions, spying out the unknown country at his personal risk, camping in the open, studying soil, water, climate, resources. "Before the other lines got a foothold," Pyle relates, Hill threw his railroad into the Red River country, and was soon trafficking in the greatest part of its huge wheat crops. His chief adversary, the slowly reviving Northern Pacific, he blocked off or undermined by rate competition. Westward into the foothills and mountains of Montana he proceeded, tapping the new mines of Daly and Clark, whose enormous copper tonnage he wrested from rival railroads in 1882. Then like Cooke, Hill sent agents into every corner of Europe, armed with stereopticon slides, to bring immigrants by the hundred thousand at low fares into his domain. For these he founded schools, churches and communities, encouraged cattle raising and tree planting. For would they not be his subjects, sending out and calling in a flood of goods forever?

The Manitoba soon became a power; in its rear were accumulated a defense system of grain elevators and lake steamers which rounded out its shipping business; in its van lay the West Coast. Hill could not go backward. Pyle tells us how, on a camping expedition in 1884, over an open fire, Hill burst out expansively to his companions:

With a prophetic look he pointed to the Rocky Mountains then growing golden, and said: "The Manitoba will even cross those great piles of rock and earth and press on to the Pacific Ocean, until Seattle, Tacoma and Portland are connected with the East by the best constructed transcontinental road in America."

But there was already a railroad chartered to traverse all this region: the Northern Pacific, of such unhappy fame, which Hill's line paralleled just under the Canadian border. The new interests connected with Cooke's old enterprise looked with bitterness at the encroachments of Hill. With his low costs, his economical planning, he was equipped to compete as mercilessly as Rockefeller in his large-scale oil-refining. And like Rockefeller, Hill meant to "rule or ruin."

He played his hand warily while laying future plans. He sought to propitiate certain of his powerful rivals such as the Union Pacific lying to the south of him. But with Villard, who, having taken the place of Jay Cooke, managed the Northern Pacific in spectacular fashion. Hill would have no peace; nor would he permit himself to be bought off. He would tear the Northern Pacific, its tracks and land grants, from Villard's hands, and thus double-track his own system. The Northwestern states between the Great Lakes and Puget Sound were soon as loud with the alarm of railroad war as any other region.

2

A man of wide culture (compared to our indigenous economic leaders), of varied adventure and high imagination, Henry Villard (né Heinrich Hilgard) had come from Bavaria to the United States in 1853 at the age of nineteen, and soon proceeded as far west as Colorado. After working as a traveling journalist for German newspapers, then as a war correspondent for Greeley's *Tribune*, Villard had made himself useful in the immigration service of Jay Cooke. Quick-witted, magnetic and eloquent, Villard seemed to win successes with but the least exertion; he attracted friends and followers everywhere. In 1871 he revisited his native country. The knowledge of railroad affairs he had gathered brought him eventually an appointment as financial agent for the groups of defrauded German bondholders. Thus, having returned to the United States, in 1874 he toured Oregon to examine the affairs of the Oregon steamship lines and railways in the interests of the foreign investors.

Introduced to the transportation business on the Pacific Coast, all he learned determined Villard to acquire and unite these various properties, part of which had fallen from the hands of Cooke and as to whose value the foreign creditors were permanently disillusioned.

He was dazzled by the discovery of a beautiful frontier province, giant forests, mineral deposits, rich farm lands in the broad Oregon valleys. His memoirs, written in the Victorian manner in the third person, say:

> *What he saw of the scenery of Oregon on the way to Portland in the California, Yoncalla and Willamette valleys filled him with enthusiasm. . . . His lengthy printed report to the committee contained favorable accounts of his impressions of western Oregon,*

and expressed his belief in the promising future of the country and consequently in the certain improvement in the prospects of the bondholders. The greatest assurance of this lay in increase of population. . . .

He saw that "the vast region drained by the Columbia and its tributaries formed a very empire in its extent." Deep into this inland empire the ships proceeded up the long Columbia and Snake rivers. Its material development was absolutely dependent, he felt, "upon the present and future transportation facilities within its limits." At this time the western limit of the Northern Pacific Railroad lay only at Bismarck, on the Missouri River.

According to one account given in Barron's diary by W. H. Starbuck, a colleague of Villard's, an account graphic enough though perhaps faulty in its recollection of details, Villard, while studying and occupying himself with the shipping business on the Northwest Coast, made inquiries concerning the Columbia River Line ships. These were owned by the Oregon Steam Navigation Company, and Villard "unexpectedly found that they were earning handsomely, but could be bought for three million dollars." Thereupon he acquired from the owners a four months' option for $100,000, which he and his associates bestirred themselves to raise, and which permitted the purchase of a majority stock control in these shipping properties.

Villard went to New York, *incorporated his option* under the name of the "Oregon Railway and Navigation Company" with 60,-000 shares of capital stock, not paid. He then went to the Farmers' Loan & Trust Company of New York, and by a wonderful piece of legerdemain executed a mortgage against the properties to be acquired. He was able to use the proceeds, as well as the funds from further bond sales, to purchase in accordance with the terms of his option control of the steamship companies of Oregon. Thus with a single stroke (like so many of his brilliant contemporaries) he had actual possession of a property which was soon valued at $10,000,000. "Then came the boom of 1879 and soon Villard and I were rolling in money," concludes Starbuck's account.

Shortly afterward, Villard took steps to unite certain other shipping companies of the Pacific Coast and river trade with his own holding company. To these were added various allied short railroads, already constructed in the region, including a line running up the Columbia Valley, and soon the daring Villard was issuing glowing statements to the speculative public of Wall Street, according to Henry Clews's account—"a carefully prepared report showing immense and unprecedented earnings." The stock of Oregon Railway & Navigation which Villard confesses "five months before had been given as a bonus" to certain Wall Street leaders, rose to a price of 95. This was simply due, as his autobiography tells us, to the fact that

> net earnings of the two constituent . . . companies were sufficiently large to warrant the payment of bond interest and eight per cent dividends on the stock, payment at which rate had already been commenced. This astonishing increase naturally raised Mr. Villard to a still more commanding position in Wall Street.

We see here a style of campaign which has become familiar to a modern generation. Stock issues flowed rapidly, and dividends seemed to be paid almost as soon as the capital was raised, without the least delay for use of the capital. Soon, against visible assets estimated at $3,500,000 (fully mortgaged) some $18,000,000 in stock was issued and placed on the market. With the aid of the Wall Street pool leader, Woerishoffer, Villard, as Henry Clews relates, "had the stock bulled to 200." Here the old broker in his own memoirs comments, with unkindness or with envy—it is hard to tell—"as a stock waterer Villard had probably no superior in that important department of railway management."

Having "glory and cash" aplenty and standing high in Wall Street, Villard now for two years pursued a brilliantly conceived campaign to consolidate his gains and fix his grip on the "narrows" of the Northwestern arteries of trade. First, he and his group began preëmpting a route along the Columbia River, by "laying down a cheap narrow gauge road." It was an expensive process; the line would be useless in a few years and would have to be torn up; but thereafter, at least, no other adventuring knight of railroads could move down the south bank of the Columbia River, the only side on which railroad tracks could be laid.

He and his men then secretly scoured the huge region, spying out the valleys and mountain passes and river banks that must be possessed. Villard, with imagination aflame, had a tremendous plan afoot which envisaged nothing less than seizure of all the possible routes and approaches to the Pacific Ocean in the Oregon and Washington country, thus blocking the line of march of the second transcontinental railroad, the Northern Pacific.

One stroke follows another, as Villard moves among the rival railroad groups, mysteriously skirmishing for vital positions, as in a game with pawns and mock artillery. Now he seizes the confluence of the Columbia and the Snake River, destined, as his engineers showed him, to be the gateway to the Pacific Northwest; now he occupies the northern approaches to the Columbia River Valley in Washington, "the most strategic positions and richest agricultural areas." It was, as his agent in the field reported to him, "a country well worth fighting for," since it prevented the forging of a link of some 200 miles by the Northern Pacific between Lake Pend Oreille and the head of navigation on the Columbia.

In the meantime he conducted campaigns to hamper the enemy's construction, setting the rival towns against each other, lobbying in the state capitols, or now shifting his movements with almost comic haste when he learned that the opponent was circumventing him by moving up another valley.

"Let me drop everything else," his lieutenant Thielsen reports, "and let me get our road up Union Flat... and some distance over into the Clearwater country located, with right of way secured, and even commence work on it before the other party can make preparations or is aware of what we are doing."

Huntington understood the process quite clearly. He himself had railway interests in Oregon, and he set up a cry of alarm, "threatened and remonstrated with the Union Pacific people," so strongly that Gould and Dillon, who had been conniving passively with Villard, were detached as allies. But the progress of Villard could no longer be stopped.

Having seized the mountain passes and valleys, Villard relates how he also gathered valuable coal deposits to unite with his transportation business. Thus fortified, having the Northern Pacific well bottled and clashing with it at every point, he tried to negotiate an accord for dividing the traffic. After some resistance the hostile Northern Pacific men in October, 1880, signed a presumably friendly prorating agreement with the Villard roads and ships, allowing passage of freight and travelers from one line to the other. But by this means the enemy was only treacherously biding his time. His intention was to raise great sums of money in order to crush Villard in Washington and also Jim Hill, whose Manitoba in the Dakotas paralleled his line.

But in November, 1880, Villard learned of the secret sale by Northern Pacific of $40,000,000 of its first mortgage bonds to a powerful banking syndicate headed by Drexel, Morgan & Co., August Belmont and others. Villard relates: "The transaction, then unparalleled in its magnitude, assured to the company $36,000,000 of money, which was then generally assumed to be sufficient for the completion and equipment of the entire main line." Thus within a month the Northern Pacific was in a position to advance against him and his "entire defensive position was entirely changed."

The case was desperate. Should the Northern Pacific, crossing Idaho, reach the Columbia River, then certainly the market value of Villard's whole pyramid of sprawling little rail and ship lines would crumble away overnight. Villard therefore resolved upon measures as desperate as his circumstances warranted. He hurried to New York and formed the famous "blind pool" of 1881 which for its Napoleonic boldness of conception long represented a peak in the high finance of the epoch.

All through 1880 Villard had been making secret purchases of Northern Pacific stock. But now he called together all the moneyed persons who had been following him in his exploits and who heartily admired him because wherever he went almost instantly securities bloomed and flowered with rich dividends. Ernestly and confidentially he addressed a gathering of about fifty persons in his office asking them to subscribe to a "syndicate" in the sum of $8,000,000. The purpose of the syndicate, or pool, he did not divulge in his confidential circulars save to a very few trusted associates such as George Pullman and the German plunger, Woerishoffer. Beside himself with emotion, with the strange eloquence he possessed in such emergencies, he indicated to his followers that the undertaking had such tremendous potentialities for profit and power that one dared not speak of it. The very mystery of the affair caused a rush of subscriptions. Villard's office in New York was crowded with speculators, and the subscriptions soon commanded a premium of from 25 to 40 per cent.

In the summer of 1881 Villard called another meeting of the subscribers to reveal his plans for buying the Northern Pacific, and they now agreed to subscribe $12,000,000 more to the formation of a new corporation, the "Oregon & Transcontinental Company," a holding company which at once issued $30,000,000 of stock among the subscribers for the $20,000,000 of cash paid in. Finally in September, 1881, after sensational maneuvers in the market, control of the long railroad passed to Villard. He then joined it with his Pacific Coast properties under the new holding company, which had the widest powers to "construct for the others" as usual, to merge the others, to engage in mining, shipping, land-jobbing, town-building, or to seize every possible natural site or position of advantage. Nothing seemed to have been overlooked in the charter.

Thousands of men now labored in the mountains to finish the main line of the Northern Pacific. No sooner was he in full charge of the system than Villard, in 1881, declared a dividend of 11 $\frac{5}{10}$ per cent to its stockholders "against improvements made from earnings," a gesture typical of him. At the same time the new president made a tremendous effort to populate his railroad barony. He filled the entire world with his pictures, stereopticon slides and "literature" illustrating the Eden-like Northwestern territories. Hundreds of his immigration agents spread their dragnet throughout Europe and England, hauling the peasants from Germany and Sweden in by the thousands to Oregon and the Columbia Basin; depopulating sometimes whole villages in Russia. These vast migrations, which brought, in one instance a train of 6,000 wagons across the Rockies, were inspired of course by an excessive enthusiasm. In the case of the Scandinavians especially, agents were reported to have deceived the peasant "by painting too bright a picture of the future awaiting him in the new land."

When the road was completed Villard, who had a passion for publicity and for eye-filling gestures, advertised the business to the whole world by making a record-breaking passage across the continent "on business." Through the courtesy of other railroad officials he was able to arrange for a special train running through without stopping except for a change of locomotives every 200 miles. The whole Western public watched his progress and cheered him on, he recalls with pride, as he descended at Portland in less than half the regular time, the fastest trip ever made.

The completion of the main line to the Pacific in 1883 was attended with a series of celebrations through which Henry Villard moved like a great prince occupying the whole stage. His private train passed in a triumphal procession through the newly made towns along the way. In his car his guests of honor were President Arthur, General Grant, Secretary Evarts and other cabinet members, ambassadors such as Viscount James Bryce, Congressmen, governors; newspaper reporters, soldiers and Indians filled four special trains. In the incidental entertainments, exhibitions of track-laying were held, followed by artillery salutes, speech-making and the music of brass bands. Sitting Bull was brought from captivity for one occasion. And for the final festival of the Golden Spike, on September 8, 1883, the Crow Head tribe and their chief appeared and in a symbolic gesture formally ceded their hunting grounds to the big chief of the Northern Pacific, who described the historic affair of the Golden Spike in his memoirs:

A thousand feet of track had been left unfinished in order to give the guests a demonstration of the rapidity with which the rails were put down. This having been done, amidst the roar of artillery, the strains of military music, and wild cheering Mr. Villard hammered down the "last spike."

The affair left an unforgettable impression upon Bryce who, pondering upon the character of the American institutions, wrote shortly afterward in his "American Commonwealth":

... These railway kings are among the greatest men, perhaps I may say the greatest men, in America.... They have power, more power—that is, more opportunity of making their will prevail—than perhaps anyone in political life, except the President and the Speaker who, after all hold theirs only for four years and two years, while the railroad monarch may keep his for life.

Yet in this case the king was not fated to rule for long. At the very time that Henry Villard stood sunning himself in glory, doffing his hat and bowing to the madly cheering throng, at this moment when six houses were being torn down in Madison Avenue, New York, to make way for the palace of the railroad "magnate," his spirits were heavy and he felt himself in utmost danger. Like a deadly disease the secret deficit of his whole enterprise was increasing, eating into the core of the thing.

In demeanor and in word he dared not show his great trouble, standing as before an abyss and with a mask of composure. But three months before the festive completion of the road private report from his officers had showed the cost of construction through grievous miscalculation to have exceeded the original estimates by $14,000,000, which, added to an existing deficit of $5,500,000, made it impossible even for such a magician as he to escape disaster. Magician though he was and elected by himself to develop a Northwestern empire, Henry Villard apparently knew little enough about railroad-building. For the ceremony of the Golden Spike he had to borrow a good locomotive from Jim Hill, according to gossip retold long afterward in Barron's journals. In all his work there had been a woeful haste and waste, a costly series of errors and lootings by the inside "construction company," typical of much of the hurly-burly empire-building of the day.

Here is the testimony of an able railroad chief at the time. James Hill, in intramural correspondence with his old fellow conspirator, Lord Mount Stephen, spoke of the "long stretch of entirely worthless country on the other Pacific roads" (Union and Northern Pacific); of their bad grades and high interest charges, winding up: "I feel . . . that they are not really competitors," that is, with an honestly capitalized well-constructed road. He added also in a letter to Charles Elliott Perkins, head of the friendly Burlington, what he thought particularly of Villard's "developments":

> *The lines are located in a good country, some of it rich, and producing a large tonnage; but the capitalization is far ahead of what it should be for what there is to show, and the selection of the routes and grades is abominable.* Practically it would have to be built over.

Villard now realized that all his confident statements to his associates and followers would be discredited. His securities would decline. Moreover, blows seemed to fall upon him every day from unexpected quarters. Small privateers who pounced upon franchises or built short rail lines in his territory practiced blackmail upon him. In Washington his mighty adversaries, Gould and Huntington, lobbied to bring about the forfeiture of the Northern Pacific's land grant, causing him to reply in outbursts of indignation—though he himself had used the same tactics yesterday when trying to capture the road from its previous owners. Finally, at this evil hour the pressure of Hill's competitive strokes was too much. The Manitoba, the future Great Northern, crept steadily through Villard's domain, preëmpting the business at lower rates, while Hill boasted privately that he meant for the moment to keep his tariffs down in certain regions so that "opposition enterprises must be bankrupt." Hill could show on a piece of paper what it cost exactly to haul a loaded car over the grades of the Northern Pacific and what it would cost over his own line. According to Pyle, his intensely admiring biographer:

> *Mr. Hill let Mr. Villard have his fill of glory; did not sulk or protest when he became the talk of two continents; took care not to offend his amour propre, and thus succeeded very well in maintaining a working understanding by which the Manitoba Company was permitted to go its way in peace. . . .*
>
> *The Northern Pacific . . . most powerful concern in the Pacific Northwest [its steamships having eliminated river competition] . . . had no terrors for Mr. Hill. He knew its financial condition, notwithstanding the . . . apparent plethora of cash. Better yet he knew its operating condition. . . . He was in no hurry or fret, because he knew that every day reduced the power of the Northern Pacific to carry its own burdens. . . .*

Now in his extremity began the grim pursuit of credit for Villard, over whom a shadow hung. He issued $20,000,000 more in mortgage bonds with ill success. His securities continued to sink. As his grip weakened his former associates stabbed at him from behind with the stiletto, according to the traditional ethics of their trade in Wall Street. As he tottered they pushed hard. His recollections are painful here:

> *Mr. Villard learned then the lesson taught him so often in Wall Street, that the throng of people which follows with alacrity the man who leads them to profits, will desert him just as quickly when he ceases to be a money-maker for them. He soon found that many of his most trusted friends, who formerly visited his offices regularly, had sold out their holdings and stayed away. He even discovered downright treachery among his confidenial advisers, two of*

the Oregon and Transcontinental directors using their private knowl-
edge of the condition of the company for enormous "short," sales of
its shares.

Collapse came swiftly on the heels of his triumph. In January, 1884, owning that "neither he nor the Oregon & Transcontinental could be saved," Villard resigned from all his united enterprises, which sank toward the gulf of bankruptcy together amid the tre-mendous clamor of investors who had been brought to ruin, a scandal as sensational as anything which Jay Gould had ever evoked. Among promoters of "large railway combination," Villard was long the butt of public anger and the popular press pointed bitterly to the luxurious mansion on Madison Avenue in which he still con-tinued to live after his reverses. Here Villard dwelt amid so much costly and empty splendor because he had "no other city home" and "for reasons of economy," while pondering new magic for the future. Though his memory was hated in the Northwest country, where "the specter of monopoly haunted the settlers," he had more or less knowingly, and after his own happy-go-lucky fashion, hastened the process of centralization taking place in the industrial life of America.

With Villard ousted, his holding company ruined, the weak-ened Northern Pacific Railroad itself was to be pushed to the wall, according to the plan of empire in Mr. Jim Hill's mind. During the 1880's, the disposition of power upon a large or small scale must still be decided by the individual prowess, or the lust for combat, of the gladiators—whatever the effect upon the underlying population. And though it was widely believed that Hill's development of the Manitoba into the Great Northern Railway was for a long time the gratuitous fulfillment of his private ambition, causing great economic disturbance in the region, he proceeded unchecked toward the Pacific. By 1887 his line extended 1,500 miles from St. Paul; and from the peaks of Montana which he had reached he could see the Pacific Coast. This "greatest railroad autocrat of his time" could no more stand still or retreat than the others. He too carried on great colonizing operations. By pressing a button at his heaquarters streams of "stereopticon slides, photographs and data concerning the advantage of settling on the Great Northern came forth," as Hill's son recalled. He built more solidly, more painstakingly than Villard, but like Villard pressed always through traffic agreements, joint leases or rate wars with his adversaries toward the crushing advantages of monopoly.

In cementing what was finally to be the most perfect railroad monopoly in the country, Hill extended his sphere also through the Middle West. He saw that the extensive network of the Burlington system would act as a "feeder" for his highway to Asia, while in the North he designed to add the Northern Pacific to his own transcontinental trunk line as a "double track."

As the rival railroad under new hands found itself fighting for existence, it provided trouble for Hill, which he reflects in his correspondence of 1890 with Lord Mount Stephen:

> *You may think I am going pretty fast in the Northern Pacific matters. . . . It is pursuing a very aggressive course almost regardless of permanent cost and business judgment . . . doing both the "Manitoba" and the Canadian Pacific Railroad great damage and in such a way as to compel both to spend large sums of money to no good end. . . .*
>
> *But I am very sure that if we get what we want there the results will be more than ever considered in another place. . . . The entire property controlled by the new company would have an earning capacity of about $3,000,000 a month. And this, with the advantage of removing all expensive rivalry and competition, would alone save 5 per cent., which is $1,000,000 per annum. . . .*
>
> *The more I think it over, the more I am convinced that the thing for us to do is to "take the bull by the horns" and get control of the Northern Pacific, and by one stroke settle all questions at once.*

The first phase was to be financial war to the bitter end, union being long delayed, owing to the chaotic industrial upheavals of the '90's. Only after appalling waste and delay would the quarreling barons finally make common cause at the call of the leading banker of the age.

But in the meantime the victories or defeats of Hill, of Villard, of Huntington and Gould brought in either case little rejoicing to the settlers of the West. It was a saying among the farmers of Minnesota and the Red River Valley: "After the grasshoppers we had Jim Hill. . . ." Their grain and cattle could move only over his highway to his huge lake steamers, and into his elevators and storehouses—from beginning to end at such terms as he fixed. It passed not unnoticed that in 1883 the earnings of his Manitoba were tenfold that of his first year, and that he suddenly ordered a "melon" of $10,000,000 to the stockholders "against improvements and acquisitions."

Nor did the population of the Columbia Basin love their conqueror, Villard, during his brief reign. Since his ships controlled water competition, freight rates in Oregon and Washington had an arbitrary character; here as in California a shipment of fire bricks, let us say, from Liverpool to Walla Walla (by way of Cape Horn!) could be made as cheaply as over the direct route of the Northern Pacific. Moreover Villard held his hand over the towns that grew up, determining their development, economic growth or decay according to his pleasure. Thus at times Seattle and Tacoma would feel strangled or "downcast," while Portland rejoiced because Villard centered operations at the mouth of the Columbia; or later Portland would howl while he built a connection to Seattle.

Turn where they would, the free pioneers of the West found their case equally desperate. Jay Gould held the Union Pacific; Huntington, the Southern Pacific. In California, for instance, as the historian H. H. Bancroft relates, there was hardly a county which had not burdened itself by incurring tremendous debts as ransom to the railroad systems; for they had been urged on by their local statesmen, and "all the newspapers paraded the benefits to be received from every railroad scheme . . . Thus urged by the legislatures and the press, the people had passed under the rod with the greatest equanimity." But soon afterward in many a pamphlet or small-town gazette one could perceive the altered temper of the settlers as they sensed dimly the fact that while the great machines of steam and iron had opened larger opportunities to them, these opportunities were no longer under their control. A threshing machine could be brought in short time from Chicago to the San Joaquin Valley, but as Frank Norris related in his tendentious novel, the article might have to travel several hundred miles beyond its destination to the "main reshipping point," then be sent back to its purchaser and delivered at the pleasure of and the price fixed by "The

Octopus." Or, when the market bespoke a pleasant profit to the farmer for his season's toil, then "The Octopus," with supreme cunning and omniscience, would remember to raise the freight rates high enough to dash all such hopes of profit.

The settlers who had welcomed the railroads as a blessing now perceived that in accordance with the "American system" they were operated as much with a view to hindering the industrial community as to serving it. Their spokesmen, who came sometimes to Washington now, denounced the "railroad kings" in strange language, as "blood-sucking vampires" who practiced "licensed larceny." A bushel of wheat, they protested, worth fifty cents in Minnesota was put down in New York at from $1.20 to $1.25. "Submit to our extortionate rates," the railway officials said to them in effect, "or your wheat, corn and oats may rot in your granaries without a market!"

In the magnificent spaces of the West especially were the settlers helpless against the common carriers. Thousands of them had undergone great hardships in order to arrive at the frontier, where as it is pictured to us they were presumably to live as automatons exporting and importing freight endlessly. Boarding trains from New York or Chicago the immigrant had often been obliged, as Congressional records show,

> to take his chances, living upon the hard benches of springless cars for many days at his own expense, very often without fire or water, owing to neglect of employees, who care nothing for the comforts or necessities of foreigners.

As early as 1873 a measure was actually placed before the United States Senate for the prevention of cruelty to travelers upon railroads, much like the humanitarian statutes afterward introduced for the protection of horses and other animals.

Once arrived, the settler in the new country sometimes found that the railroad kept him away from the best lands, which at the same time were not patented in order to avoid taxation. Over the use of the land there would be many angry collisions, during which "homesteaders" would be expropriated by force of arms.

But while the tillers of the soil felt themselves subject to extortion, they saw also that certain interests among those who handled the grains or cattle they produced, the elevators, millers and stock yards, or those from whom they purchased their necessities, the refiners of oil, the great merchant-houses, were encouraged by the railroads to combine against the consumer. In the hearings before the Hepburn Committee in 1879 it was revealed that the New York Central, like railways all over the country, had some 6,000 secret rebate agreements, such as it had made with the South Improvement Company. The dry-goods house of A. T. Stewart, the New York merchant, had been especially helped by the Vanderbilts to "build up and develop their business."

The counsel for the legislative committee asked:

"They were languishing and suffering?"
"To a great extent."
"This is deliberately making the rich richer and the poor poorer
... *through the instrumentality of the freight charge."*

In the meantime the political representatives whom the disabused settlers sent forth to Washington or to the state legislatures to bring redress seemed not only helpless to aid them, but were seen after a time riding about the country wherever they listed by virtue of free passes generously distributed to them. That the farmers should be bound to their acres and have literally no way of moving about or seeing the world while their betrayers and tormentors went lording it over them in palace cars—this was simply too much. Their envy and fury were roused particularly by the "free-pass evil," as is shown by the frequent visits of farmers' delegations to Washington on this ground alone.

Since formal opposition worked little good, the Western agrarians ended by banding themselves together in a vast organization called the Grange, which after several years of development during the '70's accumulated a membership of a million and a half American peasants hailing from 15,000 different communities. This secret society of the Patrons of Husbandry, by which the Americans sought to resist the railroads, had (like the Masonic Orders) its signs, grips, passwords, oaths, degrees and other impressive paraphernalia. Its officers were called Master, Lecturer and Treasurer and Secretary; its subordinate degrees for men were Laborer, Cultivator, Harvester and Husbandman; for women, who took an important part in the whole ritualistic organization, there were titles such as Maid, Shepherd, Gleaner and Matron; and still higher orders entitled Pomona

(Hope), Demeter (Faith), and Flora (Charity). Soon in eleven Western states the Grange, though it was ostensibly fraternal and social in character, became a power in politics, packed the legislatures with its members and established railroad commissions which were to end railroad abuses of all sorts.

The railroad barons were in turn rendered furious by such intervention. Huntington vituperated against his opponents in 1877, calling them alternately "agrarians" and "communists." He and the others devoted themselves to capturing the various railroad commissions in each state. Those that were not so captured were in most cases utterly bewildered by the complexity of a problem which it was in the interest of the railroad owners to render still more complex. The inept Granger laws were disobeyed and resisted. In some cases a kind of *cordon sanitaire* was drawn about the disaffected regions, which were faced with a total loss of transportation; so that, after one or two years, commonwealths like Iowa, Minnesota and Wisconsin were forced to remove their regulative laws from the statute books, as at the point of a pistol.

Thereafter the agitation of the hard-pressed "agrarians" took other turns; for years after the "crime of '73" there were crusades toward inflation or "free silver," measures which were designed to cheapen or even pardon the debts of the farmers while raising the value of their product. Yet little came of all these poorly directed efforts—save that the "pass evil" was certainly checked in great measure. At any rate the famous optimism of the pioneers tended to subside slowly and heavily, while it was reported in the Western press everywhere along the lines of Huntington, Gould or Villard that "nothing is heard but one continuous murmur of complaint."

CHAPTER TWELVE

CERTAIN INDUSTRIALISTS AROSE

THE very outcries of the underlying population during the late 1870's and the 1880's, of workers who found their wages being reduced, of farmers in much greater number who found the value of crops deflated, while freight tariffs and other services or goods they must obtain remained relatively high—all this testified to the strategic power held by the railroads over their regions and over broad sections of the nation's commerce.

Both by example and by the facilities they offered (of opening a nation-wide market) the combined trunk-line systems suggested plainly to the industrialists in other fields that they organize themselves in similar fashion. But in addition to broader markets and swifter, cheaper circulation of goods in larger cars, drawn by heavier locomotives, the secret tactics of the rebate gave certain producing groups (as in petroleum, beef, steel) those advantages which permitted them to outstrip competitors and soon to conduct their business upon as large a scale as the railways themselves.

The method of combination once established, it communicated itself with remarkable speed throughout the industrial system. In rapid succession, joint-stock companies of much larger capital than ever used before began to exploit natural resources, such as copper and soft coal, or new industries such as steel, barbed wire, bicycles, telephones, electric power. These big units of enterprise seemed to, spring up to full size almost overnight. The period of large-scale production, of rings, syndicates and pools, was at hand; the golden age of small industries was virtually ended. Although the number of business enterprises continued to increase slowly, an overwhelming share of the production was carried on in the few "million-dollar plants" in each field. This new scale and new technique brought the great increase in American manufactures, always pointed to by historians, by which in the ten years after 1880 manufactures rose in value from five billion dollars to more than nine billions, making the United States in very short order the premier industrial nation of the world. But more, the very process of enrichment (by the industrialist) was made comparatively quick, a fact which was remarked by many observers. In a public address in Chicago, in 1883, a United States Senator exclaimed:

> *Never in human history was the creation of material wealth so easy and so marvelously abundant, its consolidation under the forms of . . . vast units of power . . . monopolies which absorb and withdraw individual and independent rivalries. Herein are dangers it will behoove us to gravely contemplate and consider what forces shall be summoned to counteract them.*

But for the very reason that forces leading to combination were at work in the society, the general effect of the period was one of strenuous contest for the market, of anarchic, individual appetite and money-lust, of ruinous competition conducted with more terrible instruments than before, out of which a few giant industrialists arose. . . . These had possession of what Adam Smith would call "secrets of manufacture," and J. A. Hobson, "private economies," for producing or distributing their goods, which enabled them to overtake all their rivals and virtually to expropriate them.

At Braddock, on the Monongahela River, the new "million-dollar" steel works of Carnegie modeled after the great Bessemer plants of England were ready for production in 1875. It was a troubled period when the new mill began to roll forth its steel. But the output of the new metal in America was destined to increase almost fiftyfold by 1890; and within three years of its beginning the Carnegie steel company was to have a larger share of its field than any rivals. "Whatever I engage in I must push inordinately," Carnegie had written in his diary.

In greatest measure the large-scale production of the Carnegie mills seems due to the genius of Captain "Bill" Jones, craftsman of steel-making, whom Carnegie had fortunately hired to superintend his plant. Though he was possessed of little formal education this burly war veteran had made himself a brilliant technician of the new craft. He perfected both process and machinery; in time, his papers were to be read before the Royal Society of London, and his technical patents were to be the prized possession of a steel Trust. But in addition this lovable giant, whom Carnegie called "the most remarkable character I ever met," infected the hundreds of men who worked under him with his own intensity and herculean energy. Carnegie, as he himself said, "had no shadow of a claim to rank as inventor, chemist, investigator or mechanician." Therefore he felt all the more keenly the value of Jones's service, and on one occasion even offered him, by way of encouragement or to bind him, a partnership, that is, a fractional share in the mounting profits of the corporation. But in the realm of high finance and stock-juggling, Jones the sooty demigod of steel became only a humble and frightened workingman. He begged only to be allowed his salary, a large one to be sure, "like the President of the United States," but with neither the risks nor the fabulous rewards of the partners.

Demand for steel grew insatiable toward 1880 as railroad construction passed all bounds; and since a mounting share of this increased tonnage came to the Carnegies, it rested upon Jones to carry a heavier load year by year. With unfailing ingenuity, Jones improved his furnaces, raised his tonnage output and speeded up his labor force until the amount of pig iron smelted per week in his mills exceeded anything known at the time. Then the spiral of rising production would go around again, ever higher while Carnegie lashed his men to greater efforts. In 1889 Captain Bill Jones was working to repair a faulty furnace with his own hands when an explosion of molten metal struck him and he died horribly. Steelmaking was not safe then, nor is it wholly safe today. In place of Jones, the martyr of steel, younger men whom he had trained entered the business, such as Charles Schwab, who rose swiftly from the ranks of common labor. Thomas Carnegie too was carried away in mid-career by illness. Yet the heartbreaking drive continued; out of Pittsburgh mountains of steel ingots and rails rolled, "the gleaming metal" upon which civilization advanced.

Thinking no more of early retirement to a life of literature and public service, Andrew Carnegie continued steadfastly at the helm of his steel company, to the exclusion of all other enterprises. His, hard blue eyes were sunken in that "worst species of idolatry," as he himself had called the endless amassing of money. According to

Schwab, who came to work for him in 1879, Carnegie seldom came near his plant and had but the scantiest knowledge of its technique. But from an office building in New York or Pittsburgh, or a castle in Scotland, he managed the "hiring and firing" with uncanny skill. Within four years, Carnegie Brothers & Company, running day and night, were rolling 10,000 tons of steel a month, their profits reaching $1,625,000 in a year. And every increase of production with the same or reduced man-hours augmented profits.

"When was there ever such a business!" Carnegie exclaimed. Henceforth he "put all his eggs in one basket and watched the basket." Relieved of the routine of detail and the endless care of management, as Bridge describes him in his "Inside History of the Carnegie Steel Company," the little Scot roamed freely over the whole field of industry, as an advertiser and ambassador at large for his business. He spied everywhere upon the construction needs of railroads, or the plans of statesmen in two continents for armored battleships; and brought in many a big contract. "Supplied with a daily report of the product of every department of each of the works," writes Bridge, "he had the leisure to make comparisons and prod with a sarcastic note any partner or superintendent whose work did not rank with the best." With a few scathing words on a postcard or telegram he would spur on the best of his men by a system of "unfriendly competition" for which he became celebrated and dreaded.

"We broke all records for making steel last week," his managers would telegraph him. And he would answer at once: "Congratulations! *Why not do it every week?*" Or one manager would report a huge order received and filled, and his reply would be: "Good boy—Next!" Or they signaled to him: "Lucy Furnace No. 8 broke all records today," giving the figures. And Carnegie returned: "What were the other ten furnaces doing?"

There was no satisfying the man. Nor was there any peace for his workers and partners, driven alternately by generous money rewards or tongue-lashings. Some of them, as Bridge explains, whose jealousies and rivalries were played upon incessantly by the domineering master, did not speak to each other for years. Others would rebel at Carnegie. Jones would send in his resignation with almost "rhythmic periodicity" only to be tempted back by handsome gifts and apologies. But most of them turned their anger at the Carnegie taunts into renewed and fiercer efforts to surpass each other's labor, while Andy, as one of them said, "drove the whole bandwagon."

He was one of the chief "boosters" of his age. He talked in public or wrote or permitted himself to be interviewed upon every subject under the sun, and always managed to advertise his great steel company. Moreover he was as bold as he was canny in the negotiations for pools among the various steel producers, or in breaking these pools and underselling the field. The price of steel rails, supported by a tariff of $28 per ton, had declined steadily from $110 to $70. But Carnegie, popping in everywhere, buttonholing every railroad president, "shaded" the market habitually. "We went out to the various railroads and persuaded them to give us orders at $65 a ton. . . ." he relates. He worked closely with the heads of the trunk lines, East and West, Gould, Vanderbilt, Dillon and Huntington. To Huntington, who was "very hard up often," he gave credit shrewdly. Yet he followed no policy of unthinking generosity. When demand ran high, and markets were scarce, he showed little mercy, broke his contracts for delivery and raised prices.

An incident mentioned in Barron's diary is illuminating. Carnegie had made a contract at a low price with Gould for the structural steel of the St. Louis Terminal Bridge. Delivery of steel was suddenly halted, although the Carnegie people were supplying steel to other people. Jay Gould sent an emissary of his, General Fitzgerald, to Carnegie to discover the reason.

> Carnegie said, "Why, General, you know the price of steel has advanced and it is more profitable for us to sell it to others."
> Of course General Fitzgerald puffed and blew and stormed and threatened the courts.
> Mr. Carnegie quietly replied: "There's just what the courts are for—to settle all differences. I am astonished that you, General, should be so warm over such a little matter that can so easily be settled by the courts."

In the end Gould's company had to pay $365,000 more for their steel, because they had to have the steel immediately and Carnegie knew it.

Another device of Carnegie Brothers, which brought much business, was to ingratiate the railroad purchasing agents by allowing them a commission of as much as $2 per ton on rails—which, as a "reform" president of the Santa Fe declared one day, was "simply stealing." His continued close relations with the railroad men also enabled Carnegie to win secret rebates for his steel shipments over their lines, which helped him further to get the advantage of competitors. But in using all these shifts, some of which Carnegie himself admitted to, he was simply neutralizing rivals who moved with equal stealth and freedom from scruples through the jungle of the market.

Though it was a new country, being built up with great ringing and hammering everywhere, as terribly in need of machines and railroads as Russia today, a condition of "overproduction," of cut-throat competition arose again and again to demoralize various industries, especially the new steel. Carnegie, who possessed the largest steel works and enjoyed various conjunctions of circumstances, such as cheap ore shipments over the Great Lakes and immediate access to the coke fields outside of Pittsburgh, soon had his hand over the market. He could "shade rails" to $65 a ton when others asked $70, because Captain Jones could make them at $36, and a few years later would be producing them at under $20!

In their great perplexity as to how the volume of production should be allotted and the disordered price structure sustained, the steel masters began to come together in secret peace-conclaves. These first moves toward ending "ruinous" competition, that is, toward inaugurating monopoly prices, were made in the late '70's. Carnegie for the first time in the councils of the gentlemen of the steel trade, all Quakers or Pennsylvania Dutch, with black stovepipes and flowing side-whiskers, who "fought and shook hands" but never trusted each other's word for an instant. An attempt would be made to allocate orders in a pool of rail- and steel-billet makers. With difficulty agreements would be reached as to the share each one would enjoy. Carnegie would vociferate over the too small part allowed to his company and menace his contemporaries with destruction: "I will then undersell you in the market and make good money doing it!" The pool would hold together for a time, as a form of loose, secret government of industry, which abolished competition. But in these "middle ages" of American industry, individual members would impatiently break from their agreements, and would soon go poaching upon each other's preserves. Most often it was the "piratical" Carnegie who would break from the bonds, and who was said by his rivals to be "always on the alert to gather in business at lower prices than the others could afford."

Then after much distress in the steel trade, chronically subject to feast and famine, the rivals would come together again. But with each resumption of the steel pool, the sharp-trading Carnegie would fight for a larger and larger share of the trade. He alone could supply the whole country with its steel beams and girders; and as for rails, "Remember, gentlemen," he would warn, "I can roll steel rails at a ton!" This was at least half boast.

The repute of a "pirate" grew for Carnegie. He himself confesses that submission to the pools irked him. He was for "individualism" ad infinitum; especially since he possessed deadly advantages in the race, and saw the future of complete domination written large for him. He would "break the bonds at the first opportunity." He for his part believed thoroughly in competition, as he wrote in "Triumphant Democracy," since he knew himself equipped to do away with all the others and remain alone ruling over the empire he had conquered.

The expansion of the Carnegie steel company during a quarter-century was equaled only by the Rockefeller group in petroleum. When, by 1880, the J. Edgar Thomson steel works earned profits at the rate of 130 per cent per annum, or more than its original investment, Andrew Carnegie had almost 60 per cent of its stock, which was closely held among the partners. In 1881, "Carnegie Brothers & Company, Ltd." was incorporated at $5,000,000 capital, with Carnegie still holding the lion's share, but indebted to the company for $1,750,000 of stock. This debt he retired quickly out of profits, which soon mounted to between two and four millions per annum, continuing the same process indefinitely. Thus his slightly more than half-share of an initial capital of $1,250,000 increased to a majority share in a capital of several hundred millions created simply by reinvestment of tremendous winnings. And along the road, he acquired other companies and properties vitally needed for his growth, whose cost, by his usual method, was retired out of their own profits.

In 1883, a great new steel plant, which had been built by Pittsburgh rivals according to the most modern manufacturing design at Homestead, close by the Carnegie works, fell into difficulties, chiefly owing to violent labor disputes. At this moment, with the steel market considerably lower, Carnegie came forward with an offer to buy out his competitor at the cost of construction, which was $350,000. In a few years Homestead paid for itself many times over. At the same time Carnegie determined to make an alliance with the coke industry which supplied him with the fuel needed for the Bessemer process, and purchased in 1883, as we have seen, an 80 per cent interest in the H. C. Frick Coke Company, the largest producers in the Connellsville region. The absorption of Frick Coke showed the tendency of big industrialists to extend their control over connected industries, or earlier processes of their own business, such as fuel or iron ore. But for Carnegie the move was a fateful one, in another sense. In Henry Frick he acquired one of the younger geniuses of big business who would in a few years direct all the Carnegie producing interests during their most prosperous and most dramatic period.

2

Henry Clay Frick, who was born in 1849, the descendant of German-Swiss immigrants to western Pennsylvania, was, like Edward Harriman, one of the aggressive newcomers who fought their way to power during the disasters of 1873. His own parents were of modest circumstances; but his grandfather, Abraham Overholt, the famous whiskey distiller, was passing rich. Although there would seem to be no need for haste, Frick, after brief schooling, was early given the usual American business apprenticeship in the general store of a relative; in this education, he was watched over and counseled by the whole strong, sanctimonious, grasping Pennsylvania-Dutch family. Having some skill for bookkeeping since the age of thirteen, the silent, methodical boy three years later won enough approval to be given a post at the Overholt distillery at a thousand dollars a year.

Henry Frick was small and slight of frame; his face was pale, his features somewhat delicate and regular, his jaw unusually strong and prominent. Somewhat ailing in health, he engaged in no active sports as a boy, and had almost no friends. He arose early, worked hard, and retired early to bed or to a game of solitaire. George Harvey, who was to be his official bard, accorded him the sole desire to emulate his grandfather, to "become a millionaire" some day in his own right. While having such views for himself, Henry Frick remained rather lonely, communicated few of his feelings even to his family, held his own counsel and lived within himself. He seemed cold, firm, inflexible. This quiet exterior he would retain all his life, even when under great stress. Underneath this mask was a smoldering passion which vented itself only upon a few occasions in terrific outbursts of temper, in "volcanic rage."

But the Overholt distillery in the Connellsville region was situated almost directly over the great seam of bituminous coal, which with its low phosphorous content after the "coking" process would be found indispensable for the smelting of iron ore into steel by the Bessemer method. The family of Frick, with the rise of the iron and subsequently of the steel trade toward 1870, were among the active purchasers of Connellsville coal acreage. These days, everyone talked of the "cinders" and the ugly little coke ovens that were beginning to dot the black landscape. While watching over the scattered investments of one of his Overholt uncles, Frick himself became keenly absorbed in the future of the industry. And soon, March 3, 1871, with the aid of his relatives—and by anticipating a legacy of $10,000—he was able to make his first purchase (in partnership) of one hundred and twenty-three acres of coke lands. Then he bought more coal lands, hundreds upon hundreds of acres, staking his father's credit, borrowing money at banks against every possible form of pledge or security. Out of these properties came "Frick and Company," in which he held a one-fifth interest.

The solitary young fellow of twenty-one now fanatically pursued his objective. What he saw with every month that passed was the chance to seize power over a vital link in the new industrial system. It was a particularly brutal business: the exhausting, laborious mining of coal, with its giant laborers, stripped to the waist, toiling, sweating before the fiery coke ovens whose ruddy flames lighting the sky at all hours have made the Connellsville coke region memorable. A terrific explosion because of a faulty excavation, burying thirty miners alive, frightened one of his uncles. Nothing deterred by such misfortunes to his laborers, Frick used early profits or promissory notes to buy out the other partners, and increase his own share.

Late in 1871, he appeared before the bank of Judge Thomas Mellon in Pittsburgh, and besought this dignified and widely esteemed money-lender for large credits—$10,000 at 10 per cent, to build fifty more coke ovens. What he did was to show, with something approaching eloquence, and "in the most painstaking detail" that the coking process was an essential factor in the fabrication of steel. The shrewd and strong founder of the House of Mellon saw with the boy of twenty-one, and furthered the plans of Overholt's grandson—at 10 per cent.

The Mellon investigator on the ground reported confidentially: "Lands good, ovens well built, manager on job all day, knows his business down to the ground." The loans were repaid out of earnings, then increased. . . .

When the raging panic caught Pittsburgh in its tide, "it was an awful time," Frick relates. But while business grew paralyzed, and most mines were shut down, Frick showed unflagging energy and resourcefulness in managing and selling. He kept on selling Connellsville coke at any price rather than close up. He rode out the storm, and when it had passed he was one of the few left standing.

As a youth in trade, we are told that Frick had early become "a master of all the honorable tricks." The panic brought him fortune, as it did Carnegie. He used credit as an instrument for infinite accumulation and increase; borrowing money where he saw clearly a substantial profit, he would soon repay, then borrow again upon an ascending scale. He was one of the first to open up the profitable miners, or company store. When money became scarce in 1874 he issued his own "scrip" for goods at his store. Harvey tells us that from the House of Mellon—the father, and also the young son Andrew keeping very close to his movements—Frick received credits of $100,000 during the depression, though there were bad enough moments, in one of which the Mellon bank was compelled to close its doors. In the pursuit of credit, it would not be too much to say that he was as devious, as persistent, is Henry Phipps of Carnegie Brothers. This is the man of whom the legend persists that he had so trained his carriage horse that the bourgeois nag would proceed automatically from banker to banker in Pittsburgh, with no order from the driver.

"Only one subject interested Frick: coke." As he had expropriated the acreage of farmers who were in need and who were told nothing of the future value of coke, so Frick proceeded to expel from the field his largest competitors. One of these, A. S. Morgan & Co., while in difficulties proposed joining forces with him. But Frick, who secretly hungered for their lands, remained coy and distant, and in due time acquired the property at foreclosure. During the years of depression coke had fallen to 90 cents a ton. But after four years of arduous existence, Frick found demand rising. Reopening the Morgan mines in 1878, he held in his hands the production of two thousand additional acres of coal land. He alone now accounted for 80 per cent of the Connellsville coke. With the resumption of steel-making at full blast, demand for coke swelled, and Frick pitilessly raised the price of coke. The steel masters might bluster and groan, but Henry Frick stood in undisputed command of the sources of their fuel, and challenged them to proceed further without him. The price of coke was now fixed by him at $3.60, eventually at $5 a ton. Henry Frick at the age of thirty was a millionaire, a baron of coke.

Frick's largest customer, Andrew Carnegie, had been struck with admiration at the manner in which the screws had been turned on him. Nor could he sleep easily while the other possessed such a formidable advantage over him. They might have fought to the finish. But Frick attracted Carnegie strangely. In coke- as in steel-making, rivals fell before the advance of both men, year by year. Carnegie recollects in his autobiography:

> We found that we could not get on without a supply of the fuel essential to the smelting of pig iron. . . . The Frick Coke Company had not only the best coal and coke property, but . . . in Mr. Frick himself a man with a positive genius for its management.

After the proper overtures, the two joined forces, Carnegie Brothers buying at first a half-control of the coke company.

It was true that Frick, in the spirit of John D. Rockefeller, had shown an extraordinary capacity for management; organizing his means of production for a large scale, weeding out waste minutely, unifying all his mining operations, all shipping and selling into a compact machine. Efficiency was his idol, and all that was weakly human was to be stripped and flung aside. Those who came in contact with this imperious young man felt the steel in his nature. Some admired him, especially his fellows, or bankers such as the Mellons for whom he was "good as gold," though "self-confident, impetuous, and inclined to be daring in his affairs," according to the elder Mellon. His workers on the other hand were moved by a unanimous, passionate hatred of him. They were hard-driven at their heavy tasks; and when they rebelled and struck they met with an implacable resistance. The fields of Connellsville might literally run red with blood, as they sometimes did, but in the end the miners must yield to the law of Frick.

The union of the Carnegie and Frick companies in 1883 had given an overwhelming impetus to the industrial machine which the two men now assembled in the form of a "vertical" combination. Several years later, in 1889, Frick became general manager of the whole combination, rationalizing, coordinating its activities in a swift, smooth-flowing circulation from raw materials to finished product. At the head of this great machine which reared itself in a blackened, roaring Pittsburgh, the partners, Carnegie, Phipps, Frick and others, formed a compact, close-mouthed, loyal brotherhood, which was called "Carnegie Associates." There was no group in their own field which could withstand their pressure. There was nothing like it anywhere, save the economic juggernaut which Rockefeller and his friends were building in the oil trade.

3

In John D. Rockefeller, economists and historians have often seen the classic example of the modern monopolist of industry. It is true that he worked with an indomitable will, and a faith in his star à la Napoleon, to organize his industry under his own dictatorship. He was moreover a great innovator. Though not the first to attempt the plan of the pool—there were pools even in the time of Cicero—his South Improvement Company was the most impressive instance in history of such an organism. But when others had reached the stage of the pool, he was building the solid framework of a monopoly.

Rockefeller's problems were far more difficult than those for instance of Carnegie, who quickly won special economies through constructing a very costly, well-integrated, technically superior plant upon a favored site. In the oil-refining business, a small still could be thrown up in the '70's for manufacturing kerosene or lubricating oil at a tenth the cost of the Edgar Thomson steel works. The petroleum market was mercurial compared to iron, steel and even coal; there were thousands of petty capitalists competing for advantage in it. Hence the tactics of Rockefeller, the bold architecture of the industrial edifice he reared, have always aroused the liveliest interest, and he himself appeals to us for many reasons as the greatest of the American industrialists. In no small degree this interest is owing to the legend of "Machiavellian" guile and relentlessness which has always clung to this prince of oil.

After the dissolution of the South Improvement Company, Rockefeller and Flagler had come to a conference of the irate diggers of petroleum with mild proposals of peaceful cooperation, under the heading of the "Pittsburgh Plan." The two elements in the trade, those who produced the raw material from the earth and those who refined it, were to combine forces harmoniously. "You misunderstand us," Rockefeller and Flagler said. "Let us see what combination will do."

There was much suspicion. One of Titusville's independent refiners (one of those whom Standard Oil tried to erase from the scene) made a rather warlike speech against the plan, and he recalls that Rockefeller, who had been softly swinging back and forth in a rocking chair, his hands over his face, through the conference, suddenly stopped rocking, lowered his hands and looked straight at his enemy. His glance was fairly terrifying.

You never saw such eyes. He took me all in, saw just how much fight he could expect from me, and then up went his hands And back and forth went his chair.

At this very moment, Rockefeller was arranging anew the secret rebate with the leading railroads of the country, which had been so loudly decried in 1872. Upon the refined oil he shipped from Cleveland he received a rebate of 50 cents a barrel, giving him an advantage of 25 per cent over his competitors. Once more the railroads continued a form of espionage for his company. But all arrangements were now effected in a more complete secrecy.

Equally secret was the campaign Rockefeller pursued to amalgamate with his own company the strongest refineries in the country. According to Miss Tarbell's "History," he now constantly "bent over a map of the refining interests of the country," or hurried from one secret conference to another, at Cleveland, New York, or at Saratoga, "the Mecca of schemers," where long hours of nocturnal debate in a certain pavilion brought into his plan the refineries of Pittsburgh and Philadelphia. Look at what combination has done in one city, Cleveland, he would say. The plan now was for all the chosen ones to become the nucleus of a private company which should gradually acquire control of all the refineries everywhere, become the only shippers, and have the mastery of the railroads in the matter of freight rates. Those who came in were promised wealth beyond thir dreams. The remarkable economies and profits of the Standard were exposed to their eyes. "We mean to secure the entire refining business of the world," they were told. They were urged to dissemble their actions. Contracts were entered into with the peculiar secret rites which Mr. Rockefeller habitually preferred. They were signed late at night at his Euclid Avenue home in Cleveland. The participants were besought not to tell even their wives about the new arrangements, to conceal the gains they made, not to drive fast horses or put on style, or buy new bonnets, or do anything to let people suspect there were unusual profits in oil-refining, since that might invite competition.

In this campaign perhaps fifteen of the strongest firms in the country, embracing four-fifths of the refining trade, were brought into alliance with the Standard Oil Company by 1875–78. Among them were individuals who had opposed Rockefeller most strenuously a season before: the ablest of these, J. J. Vandergrift and John Archbold of the Pennsylvania oil regions, Charles Pratt and Henry Rogers of New York, entering the family of Standard Oil as partners by exchange of stock. They continued under their own corporate identity as "Acme Oil Company," or "Pratt & Rogers," but shared the same freight advantages as Standard Oil, used the same sources of information and surveillance, the common organization of agents and dealers in the distributing field.

"I wanted able men with me," Rockefeller said later. "I tried to make friends with these men. I admitted their ability and the value of their enterprise. I worked to convince them that it would be better for both to coöperate."

In the meantime a campaign no less elaborate and bold was pursued to eliminate from the field those firms whose existence was considered superfluous. Rockefeller did not "confiscate" his opponents outright. In the interests of his great consolidation he measured the value of their properties without sentiment, and gave his terms. Thus a plant which had cost $40,000 might in the future, after his own plans had matured, be worth little more than $15,000, or 37 cents on the dollar. Such an offer he would make and this only. The victim, as the case might be, would surrender if timid, or attempt resistance in trade, or practice blackmail upon him, or fight him to the finish and have resort to the highest courts.

Where a "deal" across the table could not be effected, Rockefeller might try a variety of methods of expropriation. With his measured spirit, with his organized might, he tested men and things. There were men and women of all sorts who passed under his implacable rod, and their tale, gathered together reverently by Miss Tarbell, has contributed to the legend of the "white devil" who came to rule over American industry.

A certain widow, a Mrs. Backus of Cleveland, who had inherited an oil-refinery, had appealed to Mr. Rockefeller to preserve her, "the mother of fatherless children." And he had promised "with tears in his eyes that he would stand by her." But in the end he offered her only $79,000 for a property which had cost $200,000. The whole story of the defenseless widow and her orphans, the stern command, the confiscation of two-thirds of her property, when it came out made a deep stir and moved many hearts.

In another instance a manufacturer of improved lubricating oils set himself up innocently in Cleveland, and became a client of the Standard Oil for his whole supply of residuum oils. The Rockefeller company encouraged him at first, and sold him 85 barrels a day according to a contract. He prospered for three years, then suddenly when the monopoly was well launched in 1874, his supply was cut down to 12 barrels a day, the price was increased on some pretense, and the shipping cost over the railroads similarly increased. It became impossible to supply his trade. He offered to buy of Rockefeller 5,000 barrels and store it so that he might assure himself of a future supply. This was refused.

"I saw readily what that meant," the man Morehouse related to the Hepburn Committee in 1879. *"That meant squeeze you out— Buy out your works. . . . They paid $15,000 for what cost me $41,000. He [Rockefeller] said that he had facilities for freighting*

and that the coal-oil business belonged to them; and any concern that would start in that business, they had sufficient money to lay aside a fund and wipe them out—these are the words."

In the field of retail distribution, Rockefeller sought to create a great marketing machine delivering directly from the Standard Oil's tank wagons to stores in towns and villages throughout the United States. But in the laudable endeavor to wipe out wasteful wholesalers or middlemen, he would meet with resistance again, as in the producing fields. Where unexpectedly stout resistance from competing marketing agencies was met, the Standard Oil would simply apply harsher weapons. To cut off the supplies of the rebel dealer, the secret aid of the railroads and the espionage of their freight agents would be invoked again and again. A message such as the following would pass between Standard Oil officials:

We are glad to know you are on such good terms with the railroad people that Mr. Clem [handling independent oil] gains nothing by marking his shipments by numbers instead of by names.

Or again:

Wilkerson and Company received car of oil Monday 13th—70 barrels which we suspect slipped through at the usual fifth class rate— in fact we might say we know it did—paying only $41.50 freight from here. Charges $57.40. Please turn another screw.

The process of "Turning the Screw" has been well described by Henry D. Lloyd. One example is that of a merchant in Nashville, Tennessee, who refused to come to terms and buy from Standard Oil; he first found that all his shipments were reported secretly to the enemy; then by a mysterious coincidence his freight rates on shipments of all kinds were raised 50 per cent, then doubled, even tripled, and he felt himself under fire from all parts of the field. He attempted to move his merchandise by a great roundabout route, using the Baltimore & Ohio and several other connecting roads, but was soon "tracked down," his shipments lost, spoiled. The documents show that the independent oil-dealers' clients were menaced in every way by the Standard Oil marking agency; it threatened to open competing grocery stores, to sell oats, meat, sugar, coffee at lower prices. "If you do not buy our oil we will start a grocery store and sell goods at cost and put you out of business."

By this means, opponents in the country at large were soon "mopped up; small refiners and small wholesalers who attempted to exploit a given district were routed at the appearance of the familiar red-and-green tank wagons, which were equal to charging drastically reduced rates for oil in one town, and twice as much in an adjacent town where the nuisance of competition no longer existed. There were, to be sure, embittered protests from the victims, but the marketing methods of Standard Oil were magnificently efficient and centralized; waste and delay were overcome; immense savings were brought directly to the refining monopoly.

But where the Standard Oil could not carry on its expansion by peaceful means, it was ready with violence; its faithful servants knew even how to apply the modern weapon of dynamite.

In Buffalo, the Vacuum Oil Company, one of the "dummy" creatures of the Standard Oil system, became disturbed one day by the advent of a vigorous competitor who built a sizable refinery and located it favorably upon the water front. The offices of Vacuum conducted at first a furtive campaign of intimidation. Then emboldened or more desperate, they approached the chief mechanic of the enemy refinery, holding whispered conferences with him in a rowboat on Lake Erie. He was asked to "do something." He was urged to "go back to Buffalo and construct the machinery so it would bust up . . . or smash up," to fix the pipes and stills "so they cannot make a good oil. . . . And then if you would give them a little scare, they not knowing anything about the business. You know how . . ." In return the foreman would have a life annuity which he might enjoy in another part of the country.

So in due time a small explosion took place in the independent plant, as Lloyd and Miss Tarbell tell the tale, from the records of the trial held several years later, in 1887. The mechanic, though on the payrolls of the Vacuum Oil Company, led a cursed existence. forever wandering without home or country, until in complete hysteria he returned to make a clean breast of the whole affair. The criminal suit against high officials of the Standard Oil monopoly included Henry Rogers and John Archbold, but the evil was laid by them to the "overenthusiasm" of underlings. Evidence of conspiracy was not found by the court, but heavy damages were awarded to the plaintiff, who thereafter plainly dreaded to reënter the dangerous business.

These and many other anecdotes, multiplied, varied or even distorted, spread through the Oil Regions of Pennsylvania and elsewhere through the country (as ogre-tales are fed to children), and were accumulated to make a strange picture of Mr. Rockefeller, the baron of oil. Miss Tarbell in her "History," written in her "muckraking" days, has dwelt upon them with love. She has recorded them in rending tones with a heart bleeding for the petty capitalists for whom alone "life ran swift and ruddy and joyous" before the "great villain" arrived, and with his "big hand reached out from nobody knew where to steal their conquest and throttle their future."

But if truth must be told, the smaller capitalists, in the producing field especially, were themselves not lacking in predatory or greedy qualities; as Miss Tarbell herself admits, they were capable of hurrying away from church on Sundays to tap enemy tanks or set fire to their stores of oil. What they lacked, as the Beards have commented, was the discipline to maintain a producers' combination equal in strength to that of the refiners. The other factors in the industry engaged in individualistic marketing or refining ventures were very possibly "mossbacks," as one of the Standard Oil chieftains growled, "left in the lurch by progress."

4

The campaigns for consolidation, once launched, permitted Rockefeller little rest, and engaged his generalship on many fronts at once. In a curious interview given while he was in Europe, cited by Flynn, he himself exclaimed:

> How often I had not an unbroken night's sleep, worrying about how it was all coming out. . . . Work by day and worry by night, week in and week out, month after month. If I had foreseen the future I doubt whether I would have had the courage to go on.

With unblinking vigilance he conducted throughout his company an eternal war against waste. We have spoken of his unequaled efficiency and power of organization. There is a famous note to his barrel factory in his careful bookkeeper's hand which has been cited with amused contempt by his critics, to show how attention to small details absorbed his soul. It reads:

Last month you reported on hand, 1,119 bungs. 10,000 were sent you beginning this month. You have used 9,527 this month. You report 1,092 on hand. What has become of the other 500?

It is not a laughing matter, this affair of 500 barrel bungs, worth at the most a dollar or two in all. Rockefeller's hatred of waste told him that in a large-scale industry the rescued pennies multiplied a million times or more represented enormous potential gains. This was to be true of all the great industrial leaders after Rockefeller's time; the spirit regarded as parsimony is a large-visioned conception of technical efficiency in handling big machines. Thus the feeding of horses, the making of his own glue, hoops, barrels, all was carefully supervised and constantly reduced in cost. Barrels were cut $1.25 apiece, saving $4,000,000 a year, cans were reduced 15 cents, saving $5,000,000 a year, and so forth. In absorbing the services of J. J. Vandergrift, in 1872, Rockefeller had acquired as an ally to his enterprise a combination of small pipe lines called the United Pipe Lines. His lieutenants then constructed more pipes; and by 1876 he controlled almost half the existing pipe lines, some running 80 to 100 miles, to the railroad terminals and shipping points. At this time the largest pipe-line interest in competition with Standard Oil's was the Empire Transportation Company, headed by Colonel Joseph Potts, but dominated by the officers of the Pennsylvania Railroad, which held an option over the entire property.

Himself an aggressive entrepreneur, Potts soon found that he must expand or suffer extinction. To the alarm of the Rockefeller organization, he purchased several big refineries in New York and proceeded to pipe crude oil from the oil fields and over the railroad to seaboard. Rockefeller vehemently petitioned the railroad to withdraw from his domain. Refused at an interview, he promised that he would take his own measures, and left his adversaries with expressions of sanctimonious regret, the form in which his most deadly threats were usually offered.

It was war, a war of rates. He moved with lightning speed. At once the other railroads, Erie and New York Central, were ordered to stand by, lowering their freight rates for him while he slashed the price of refined oil in every market which Potts reached.

But Potts, a stubborn Presbyterian, fought back harder than anyone Rockefeller had ever encountered. He replied in kind by further price cuts; he then began to build larger refineries at the coast ports, lined up independent oil-producers behind him, and reserves in quantities of tank cars, in barges, ships, dock facilities. During the bitter conflict, with which, as Flynn relates, the hills and fields of Pennsylvania resounded, both sides, and the railroads supporting them as well, suffered heavy wounds. Yet Rockefeller would not desist, since Standard Oil's whole system of organization was endangered.

In the midst of this furious engagement a great blow fell upon the enemies of John D. Rockefeller, as if given by the hand of the God to whom he constantly prayed. During the summer of 1877 the workers of the Baltimore & Ohio Railroad struck against wage cuts and their strike spread quickly to adjacent railroads, raging with especial violence in the Pennsylvania system. The most destructive labor war the nation had ever known was now seen in Baltimore and Pittsburgh, with militant mobs fighting armed troops and setting in flames property of great value in revenge for the many deaths they suffered. During this storm which the railroad barons had sown by cutting wages 20 per cent and doubling the length of freight trains, the Pennsylvania interests quickly came to terms with Standard Oil, so that they might be free to turn and crush the rebellious workers. The entire business of Empire Transportation was sold out to the oil combination at their own terms, while Potts was called off. In Philadelphia, Rockefeller and his partners, quietly jubilant, received the sword of the weeping Potts.

The oil industry as a whole was impressed with the victory of Standard Oil over a railroad ring which had seemed invincible in the past. In a movement of fear many other interests hastened to make terms with Rockefeller. By the end of 1878 he controlled all the existing pipe-line systems; through a new freight pool he directed traffic or quantities of supplies to the various regions or cities as he pleased.

By 1876 this industry had assumed tremendous proportions. Of the annual output of nearly 10,000,000 barrels, the Standard Oil Company controlled approximately 80 per cent, while exports of petroleum products to the value of $32,000,000 passed through their hands. But in 1877 the great Bradford oil field was opened with a wild boom, the uproarious coal-oil scenes of '59 were enacted anew, crowds rushed to the new fields, acreage values boomed, oil gushed out in an uncontrollable flood—half again as much oil as existed before came forth almost overnight. The markets grew demoralized again, just when Rockefeller seemed to have completed his conquest of the old Oil Regions.

What was he to do? In the two years that followed he directed his organization at the high tension of an ordnance department in wartime, so that piping, refining and marketing capacity might be expanded in time, and the almost untenable supply handled without faltering. With utmost energy a huge building program was carried on and further millions were staked on the hazardous business. Then, holding down the unruly producers, he imposed harsh terms through his pipe lines, refusing storage, forcing them to sell the oil they drilled "for immediate shipment" at the depressed prices of 64 to 69 cents a barrel, or have it run into the ground.

The overproduction could not be stopped. The oil men raged at the great machine which held them in bonds. Once more the independents gathered all their forces together to form a protective combination of their own. They founded the Parliament of Petroleum. They raised funds to construct an immense "free" pipe line running over the mountains to the seaboard, and ridding them at last of the railroads which hemmed them in. The new Tidewater Pipe Line would break Standard's control over railroad rates and bring crude oil to the sea.

Rockefeller's agents now lobbied in the state legislature of Pennsylvania to have the proposed pipe line banned. Failing of this his emissaries were thrown out over the state to buy up right of way in the path of the enemy's advance. But the Tidewater's engineers moved with equal speed and secrecy, eluded the defenses which Rockefeller threw in their way and by April, 1879, completed their difficult project.

From successive stations, the great pumps were to drive oil over the very top of the Alleghenies, and down to Williamsport, touching the Reading Railroad, which had joined forces with the independents. Amid picturesque celebration—while the spies of the Standard Oil looked on incredulously—the valves were opened, the oil ran over the mountain and down toward the sea! Rockefeller was checkmated—but to whom would the producers and their free pipe line sell the crude oil at the seaboard? They had no inkling, though they berated him, of the extent of his control at the outlet.

The opposition to the Rockefeller "conspiracy" now rose to its climax of enthusiasm. The hundreds of petty oil men who fought to remain "independent" and keep their sacred right to flood the market or "hold up" consumers at their own pleasure, won sympathy everywhere; and with the aid of local politicians in New York and Pennsylvania they also had their day in court. Their tumult had grown so violent that at long last the lawmakers of Pennsylvania moved to prosecute the monopolists for "conspiracy in restraint of trade." Writs were served and on April 29, 1879, a local Grand Jury indicted John D. Rockefeller, William Rockefeller, J. A. Bostwick, Henry Flagler, Daniel O'Day, J. J. Vandergrift and other chieftains of Standard Oil for criminal conspiracy, to "secure a monopoly of the oil industry, to oppress other refiners, to injure the carrying trade, to extort unreasonable railroad rates, to fraudulently control prices," etc. Simultaneously in New York State, the legislature appointed a committee of investigation of railroads, headed by the young lawyer A. Barton Hepburn. Forced to look at all the facts which were brought out by the Hepburn Committee, the nation was shocked. The railroad interests, as archconspirators, were at once under heavy fire. But no one understood the scope and meaning of the new phase reached in industrial life at this stage, save perhaps Mr. Chauncey Depew, who in a moment of illumination exclaimed on behalf of the railroad interests he so gallantly championed: "Every manufacturer in the state of New York existed by violence and lived by discrimination. . . . By secret rates and by deceiving their competitors as to what their rates were and by evading all laws of trade these manufacturers exist." This was God's truth and certainly true of all the other states in the Union. And of course under the prevailing circumstances there was nothing to be done, save recommend certain "regulative" laws.

With Rockefeller, there had arisen the great industrial combination in colossal and "sinister" form; he was the mighty bourgeois who was to expropriate all the petty bourgeois and his name was to be the rallying cry of parties and uprisings. The outlook for monopoly seemed dark, yet the trial, in the name of a democratic sovereignty which held "sacred" the property of the "conspirators," whatever the means by which they may have preëmpted or confiscated such property—was to be simply a comedy, and was to be enacted again and again. Before the bar of justice, Rockefeller and his brilliant lieutenants would appear, saying, "I refuse to answer on the advice of counsel." A Henry Rogers, a Flagler, would use every shift which such philosophers of the law as Joseph Choate or Samuel C. T. Dodd might counsel. They would "refuse to incriminate themselves" or evade reply on a point of technicality, or lie pointblank. Or, as in the case of the terribly cynical Archbold, they would simply jest, they would make mock of their bewildered prosecutors.

It was Rockefeller who made the most profound impression upon the public. He seemed distinguished in person; with his tall stooping figure, his long well-shaped head, his even jaw. His long, fine nose, his small birdlike eyes set wide apart, with the narrowed lids drooping a little, and the innumerable tiny wrinkles, made up a remarkable physiognomy. But his mouth was a slit, like a shark's. Rockefeller, impeccably dressed and groomed, thoroughly composed, pretendedly anxious to please, foiled his accusers with ease. Every legal subterfuge was used by him with supreme skill. Certain of his denials were legally truthful, as Flynn points out, since stockownership concerning which he was questioned was often entrusted temporarily (in time for such trials) to mere clerks or bookkeepers in his employ.

But the moment came when he was asked specifically about his connection with the notorious refiners' pool of 1872.

"Was there a Southern Improvement Company?"

"I have heard of such a company."

"Were you not in it?"

"I was not."

His hearers were amazed at the apparent perjury he made pointblank with even voice and an inscrutable movement of the eyes. But no! He had been only a director of the *South Improvement Company*, and not of the "Southern Improvement Company," as the prosecutor had named it by mistake.

If Rockefeller was embittered by the cruel fame he won, he never showed it. The silence he preserved toward all reproaches or questions may have been a matter of clever policy; yet it suggested at bottom a supreme contempt for his critics and accusers alike.

"We do not talk much—we saw wood!"

There were times when his movements were hampered, times when he dared not enter the State of Pennsylvania though the authorities there called for him impatiently; times when it was equally convenient to remain almost in hiding at his New York headquarters in Pearl Street, while the world at large howled against him. Yet he moved with unequaled agility and force against all serious attacks upon his industrial barony.

The menace of the Tidewater Pipe Line which cut through his network of railroads and refineries he must crush at all costs. This was far more important than any impeachment of his character. Fertile in expedients at a crisis, he could also be infinitely patient. It used to be said: "To Mr. Rockefeller a day is as a year, and a year as a day. He can wait, but he never gives up." Now when he perceived that the Tidewater's line to the sea was a reality, he besieged it from all sides. On the one hand he offered to buy all the oil it ran, a tempting offer which would have made the affair most profitable to the stockholders. Rebuffed here he proceeded to use the inventions of his rivals and build a long pipe line of his own to the sea. Night and day his engineers and gangs labored in the mountains, to connect the Bradford fields with the Standard Oil terminal at Bayonne. Then before the walls of Bayonne, where lay his great coastal refineries and storage tanks, his pipe line was stopped by an interested railroad from which he would have removed his freight business. The Town Council of Bayonne was induced to be friendly and grant a franchise; the Mayor who resisted for a time was suddenly won over; and in all secrecy, because of the need of haste to prevent a blocking franchise by the railroad, his gangs assembled. There were 300 men ready in the night of September 22, 1879, with all materials, tools, wagons gathered, waiting for the signal—the swift passage of an ordinance by the Town Council and its signing by the Mayor. Then with mad speed the trench across the city was dug, the pipes laid, jointed and covered, before the dawn. The National Transit Company was completed as the largest pipe-line system in the field.

His own line of communications was now secured against the enemy. But he also pursued a campaign of secret stock purchased for control, gaining a minority interest in the Tidewater company, creating dissensions within, damaging its credit, detaching its officials, instigating suits for receivership, serving writs, injunctions, and more writs, until the managers seemed to struggle for their very sanity. Day by day these blows fell mysteriously, until in 1882 the adversary surrendered and effected the best agreement possible under the circumstances. By this a minor part of the oil-transporting business was apportioned to itself and it yielded up its independence after four years of fighting an unresting, infinitely armed master. All the pipe lines were now amalgamated under Standard Oil control; the great railroads, notably the Pennsylvania, were forced by agreement and in return for a stipulated yearly ransom to retire from the business of oil transportation forever. John D. Rockefeller at the age of forty-four had accomplished his ambition—he was supreme in the oil industry, "the symbol of the American monopolist."

5

Up to 1881 the forty-odd companies controlled by Rockefeller and his partners formed a kind of *entente cordiale* bound by interchange of stock. This form of union being found inadequate or impermanent, the counsel of the Standard Oil Company, Samuel C. T. Dodd, came forward with his idea of the Trust. By a secret agreement of 1882, all the existing thirty-seven stockholders in the divers enterprises of refining, piping, buying or selling oil conveyed their shares "in trust" to nine Trustees: John and William Rockefeller, O. H. Payne, Charles Pratt, Henry Flagler, John Archbold, W. G. Warden, Jabez Bostwick and Benjamin Brewster. The various stockholders then received "trust certificates" in denominations of $100 in return for the shares they had deposited; while the Trustees, controlling two-thirds of all the shares, became the direct stockholders of all the companies in the system, empowered to serve as directors thereof, holding in their hands final control of all the properties. The Trustees could dissolve any corporations within the system and organize new ones in each state, such as the Standard Oil of New Jersey, or the Standard Oil of New York. Nor could any outsiders or newly arrived stockholders have any voice in the affairs of the various companies. The Trustees formed a kind of

supreme council giving a centralized direction to their industry;
Such was the first great Trust; thus was evolved the harmonious
management of huge aggregations of capital, and the technique
for large-scale industry.

Dodd, the resourceful philosopher of monopoly, defended his
beautiful legal structure of the "Standard Oil Trust" both in a
pamphlet of 1888 and in an argument before a Congressional committee of that year. It was but the outcome of a crying need for
centralized control of the oil business, he argued. Out of disastrous
conditions had come "coöperation and association among the refiners, resulting eventually in the Standard Oil Trust [which] enabled the refiners so coöperating to reduce the price of petroleum
products, and thus benefit the public to a very marked degree." In
these arguments, learned economists of the time, such as Professor
Hadley, supported Dodd. The Trust, as perfected monopoly,
pointed the way to the future organization of all industry, and
abolished "ruinous competition."[1]

From their headquarters in the small old-fashioned building at
140 Pearl Street the supreme council of an economic empire sat
together in conference like princes of the Roman Church. Here
in utmost privacy confidential news brought by agents or informers
throughout the world was discussed, and business policies determined. The management and responsibility was skillfully divided
among committees: there was a committee on Crude Oil, a committee on Marketing, on Transportation, and numerous other departments. By these new processes markets or developments everywhere in everybody's business were followed or acted upon.

Every day the astute leaders rounded together by Rockefeller
lunched together in Pearl Street, and later in a large and famous
office building known as 26 Broadway. No one questioned the pre-
ëminence of John D. Rockefeller, though Charles Pratt usually
sat at the head of the table. The aggressive Archbold was closest
to John D. Rockefeller. His brother William Rockefeller, an ami-

[1]Dodd explains (in "Combinations," 1888) its origin: "It was a union not
of corporations, but of stockholders.... From time to time now persons and
capital were taken into this association. As the business increased new corporations were formed in various States, some as trading companies, others as
manufacturing companies. In some cases the stocks of these companies were
placed in the hands of Trustees instead of being distributed to the owners.
Out of this grew what is known as the Standard Oil Trust."

able mediocrity, but immensely rich as well, and long trained in the use of money, depended most upon Henry H. Rogers. Rogers took a more dominant place in the management with the passing years. He is described by Thomas Lawson as "one of the most distinguished-looking men of the time, a great actor, a great fighter, an intriguer, an implacable foe."

These, together with Brewster, Barstow, J. H. Alexander and Bostwick, were the leaders who carried on their industrial operations throughout the world like a band of conspiratorial revolutionists. But "there was not a lazy bone nor a stupid head" in the whole organization, as Miss Tarbell has said. Behind them were the active captains, lieutenants, followers and workers, all laboring with the pride, the loyalty, the discipline and the enthusiasm born of the knowledge that "they can do no better for themselves" anywhere than under the "collar" of the Standard Oil. Freed of all moral scruples, curiously informed of everything, they were prompted by a sense of the world's realities which differed strongly from that of the man in the street. They were a major staff engaged in an eternal fight; now they scrapped unprofitable plants, acquiring and locating others; or now they gathered themselves for tremendous mobilizing feats during emergencies in trade. They found ways of effecting enormous economies; and always their profits mounted to grotesque figures: in 1879, on an invested capital of $3,500,000, dividends of $3,150,000 were paid; the value of the congeries of oil companies was then estimated at $55,000,000. Profits were overwhelmingly reinvested in new "capital goods" and with the formation of the Trust capitalization was set at $70,-000,000. By 1886 net earnings had risen to $15,000,000 per annum.

"Hide the profits and say nothing!" was the slogan here. To the public prices had been reduced, it was claimed. But after 1875, and more notably after 1881, despite the fluctuations of crude oil a firm tendency set in for the markets of refined oil products. Upon the charts of prices the rugged hills and valleys of oil markets turn into a nearly level plain between 1881 and 1891. Though raw materials declined greatly in value, and volume increased, the margin of profit was consistently controlled by the monopoly; for the services of gathering and transporting oil, the price was not lowered in twenty years, despite the superb technology possessed by the Standard Oil. Questioned on this, that "frank pirate" Rogers replied, laughing: *"We are not in business for our health, but are our for the dollar."*

While the policy of the monopoly, as economists have shown, might be for many reasons to avoid *maximum* price levels—such as invited the entrance of competition in the field—it was clearly directed toward keeping the profit margin stable during a rising trend in consumption and falling "curve" in production cost. Similarly in perfecting its technology the Trust was guided by purely pecuniary motives, as Veblen points out, and it remains always a matter of doubt if the mightier industrial combinations improved their service to society at large in the highest possible degree. As often as not it happened that technical improvements were actually long delayed until, after a decade or more, as in the case of Van Syckel's pipe line of 1865, their commercial value was proved beyond a doubt. It was only after rivals, in desperation, contrived the pumping of oil in a two-hundred-mile-long pipe line that Rockefeller followed suit. So it was with the development of various by-products, the introduction of tank cars, etc.

The end in sight was always, as Veblen said, increase of ownership, and of course pecuniary gain rather than technical progress in the shape of improved workmanship or increased service to the community. These latter effects were also obtained. But to a surprising degree they seem accidental by-products of the long-drawn-out struggles, the revolutionary upheavals whence the great industrial coalitions sprang.

The greatest service of the industrial baron to business enterprise seemed to lie elsewhere, as Veblen contended. "The heroic rôle of the captain of industry is that of a deliverer from an excess of business management." It is a "sweeping retirement of business men as a class from service . . . a casting out of business men by the chief of business men."

John D. Rockefeller said that he wanted in his organization "only the big ones, those who have already proved they can do a big business. As for the others, unfortunately they will have to die."

6

The obscure tumult in the Oil Regions in 1872, the subsequent exposures of the railroad rebate and the oil monopoly in 1879, made a lively though unclear impression upon the public mind. Now the more imaginative among the mass of consumers felt fear course through them at the thought of secret combinations ranged against them, the loud demagogue was roused from his slumbers, the reformer set off upon his querulous and futile searches. But among the alert entrepreneurs of all the money marts an entirely different response must have been perceptible. With envious lust the progress of the larger, more compact industrial organizations, like that of Carnegie Brothers & Company, or the associations formed by a Rockefeller, was now studied. Ah-ha! there was the way to profits in these confused and parlous times. How quickly and abundantly those fellows accumulated cash and power! "I was surprised," confessed William Vanderbilt before a committee of New York legislators in 1878, "at the amount of ready cash they were able to provide." He referred to the oil-refiners' combination. In the twinkling of an eye they had put down $3,000,000 to buy out Colonel Potts's pipe-line company. And in the following year Vanderbilt, commenting to the Hepburn Committee at Albany on the shrewdness of the Standard Oil ring, said:

> There is no question about it but these men are smarter than I am a great deal.... I never came in contact with any class of men as smart and alert as they are in their business. They would never have got into the position they now are. And one man could hardly have been able to do it; it is a combination of men.

The storms of public indignation, as we have seen, vented themselves chiefly upon the railroad heads who "discriminated against the little fellow" by the rebate and freight pool. But far from being frightened at such protests the money-changers hastened to throw their gold at the feet of him who promised them crushing, monopolistic advantages. So Villard, in 1881, by whispering his plans to conquer all the Northwest overnight, attracted instantly a powerful following of capitalists to his "blind pool." So the lawyers or undertakers who came forward with plans for secret trade, associations or pools in salt, beef, sugar or whiskey, were now heard with intense excitement by men who yesterday were busy ambushing or waylaying each other in the daily routine of their business.

They would say to each other, as in the Salt Association, formed earliest of all, "In union there is strength..." Or, "*Organized we have prospered; unorganized not.*" "Our combination has not been strong enough; the market is demoralized." And others would murmur fearsomely: "But we will be prosecuted for 'restraint of trade.' There are state laws in Maryland, Tennessee and elsewhere which hold that 'monopolies are odious.' There is the common law against trade conspiracy. . . ."

Then a bolder voice among the plotters would say: "How much did you make last year? Not a cent? Are you making anything now? Well, what do you propose to do? Sit here and lose what capital you have got in the business? There is only one way to make any money in a business like the —— business and that is to have a pool."

Thus the trail would be blazed. The industrialists, like the railroad barons before them, came together in furtive conferences, much mistrusting each other, but lamenting together the bad times and owning to the folly of competition among themselves; while those who made pools, as they heard by rumor, in oil or salt flourished. After much bickering and jockeying, the lawyers would draw up binding agreements by which the amount of output would be fixed, quotas and territories would be assigned to each member, and business orders proportionally allotted, with fines levied upon those who broke the rules. These planning agreements the members of the pool would promise faithfully to live by.

The first pools, crude experiments in a "federalism" of industry, were as inept as the first weak devices for union among laborers. Their tactics and results differed widely. By 1880, certain pools such as the salt pool had got the margin of profit much higher by "pegging" the market price of a barrel of salt at about double what it was formerly, and holding steadily to this level. Their procedure usually avoided raising the market price too high. This would beget fresh competition. However, they kept prices "moderately" firm, although supply might actually be abundant. The essential object in view was "to increase the margins between the cost of materials and the price of the finished product," and this was effected, according to Ripley, "in almost every case."

A variety of economies were gained by pooling, depending upon the firmness of the association. Railroads were forced to give rebates; inefficient or badly located plants were closed down; excess sales forces and labor were reduced, a "war chest" was accumulated and competitors were driven out. To intruders the cost of necessary machinery might be made more burdensome. Thus in connection with the Wire Nail Pool, independents declared to government investigators:

> We found the market in which we could buy machines [to manufacture nails] was very limited, most of the machine manufacturers having entered into an agreement with the combination to stop making them for outside parties.

In some cases the pool might, as in the case of salt in 1881, decide to "slaughter the market" for a season, giving the *coup de grace* to overstocked competitors in some areas, then resume the even tenor of their ways. Or they would sell low in one section which was pestered by competition, and recoup off the general market. The pools, in short, claimed to represent the party of "modernity," of progress by specializing machinery, buying raw materials cheaper, utilizing more by-products, research units, export development, advertising and selling in common. While "not wishing to take the position of posing before the public as benefactors to any extent," yet they claimed that industry was more stabilized, prices were seldom raised inordinately, and labor was paid higher wages—though here one famous manufacturer, John Gates, admitted that this was done on demand, in periods of affluence, when it was seen they had high profits and desired to avoid labor troubles. Generally they assumed a marvelous command over the labor situation—here was one of their surest gains. The workman became truly their commodity; for in time of a strike, orders could be shifted to other factories in a different section of the country and these kept running full blast.

In other cases, it was also notable that a technique of central control, extremely rigid and absolute, was developed. Immediately upon formation of the Distilling & Cattle Feeding Association, as Ripley relates, prices were cut sharply to force competitors into the pool, rivals were bought up or forced out, sometimes by negotiation and sometimes by intimidation or violence. Then by 1889, from twelve to twenty whiskey distilleries were operated on behalf of eighty-three plants previously existing, great savings were effected, and profits were steady and high enough to "accumulate a surplus for purpose of contest with outsiders." Thus the "whiskey ring," as Henry Lloyd wrote at the time, regulated the liquor traffic as no government could up to then or ever since effectively do, decreeing where and how much liquor should be made, and enforcing their decree, controlling alcohol, hence the sciences, medicine, even the arts and poetry. By February, 1888, only two large independents out of eighty distilleries resisted the combination. These were in Chicago, and one of them in April of that year published in the *Chicago Tribune* the fact that they had caught a spy of the combination in their works; later, tampering with the valves of their vats was discovered; then offers of large bribes if they would sell out their plants. In December, according to Lloyd's account, this distillery became the scene of an awful explosion:

> *All the buildings in the neighborhood were shaken and many panes of glass were broken.... There were 15,000 barrels of whiskey stored under the roof that was torn open, and if these had been ignited a terrible fire would have been added to the effect of the explosion. A package of dynamite which had failed to explode, though the fuse had been lighted, was found on the premises by the Chicago police.*

7

The most successful of the early industrial pools was formed toward 1880 by the slaughterhouses of Chicago. Here at the natural transshipment center where numerous great railroad trunk lines converged, the grain, produce, cattle and swine of the West seemed to flow toward the world markets as through a bottle-neck held in the hands of packing-houses, elevators and millers.

"I like to turn bristles, blood, and the inside and outside of pigs and bullocks into revenue..." said the astute Philip D. Armour. This puritanical and grasping dealer in pigs was among the first to note the enormous waste of labor and material in his trade. Both he and Nelson Morris had soon ceased to sell cattle "on the hoof," and had begun to systematize the work of despatching, dressing, smoking and canning steers in their stockyards by large-scale methods. After the Civil War, Morris had begun shipping frozen beef during the winter to points as far distant as Boston; and in 1874, the Cape Cod Yankee Gustavus Swift had revolutionized the industry by introducing the refrigerator car, under the Tiffany patents, with its bunkers and tanks for ice, and its heat-proof doors. So instead of shipping merely smoked or frozen meat in winter, it became possible suddenly to sell at all seasons of the year to every corner of the globe. By dint of further technical advance contributed as well by the firms of Cudahy Hammond (later Wilson & Company) and others, the stockyards of Chicago became the home of a gigantic and rhythmically functioning industry, which was soon famous throughout the world for the "mass production" of animal food. By an ingenious arrangement of the yards, and division of the labor, the droves of cattle which poured into Chicago were disassembled with amazing rapidity. Passing swiftly through winding viaducts into pens they would be suddenly stunned, dropped through trap-doors into slaughtering rooms, then killed. Thereafter laborers hung the carcasses by wire around the legs to a moving trolley-line, cut up, bled, dressed, and classified them. The operations of the laborers, chiefly Negroes and Slav immigrants, gathered in mighty armies, was thoroughly and shrewdly regimented and driven at top speed throughout the process. Finally every by-product, every species of animal raw material, was put to use, so that tremendous economies were gained on every hand in a hundred different ways.

The opportunity for large-scale management of the slaughtering trade, after the coming of the refrigerator car, had brought quickly a movement of consolidation among the numerous firms. The little houses were bought up by bigger ones; distributing agencies or large packing-houses were set up in strategic centers such as Omaha, St. Louis and Kansas City, and fleets of refrigerator cars were formed to carry the dressed-meat and vegetable traffic which now proceeded to boom magnificently.

Armour, Morris and the other packers who used to give each other "a wallop with a smile," at length arrived at a complete "gentlemen's agreement" which ended all competition between them. Thus unified, the Big Four of meat, as distributors, faced the consumers with their compact organization and fixed price system. On the other hand, as refiners (or "processors") of raw material, they confronted the disorganized producers, that is, the farmers, with the same concealed unanimity. At the stockyards, ever since 1880, according to Charles Edward Russell's lively account in his

"The Greatest Trust in the World," only four buyers would come to bid on the cattle offered each morning:

> The first offers a low price, the second is not interested, the third is not interested, nor is the fourth in a hurry to make a purchase. The next day the buyer for another one of the Big Four sets a price, and the other three refuse to buy.

The price is low, but there is no other buyer. No "conspiracy" is perceptible; there is only an accidental harmony of minds.

These overlords of beef now had their hands over the market in live cattle. Cooperating with each other firmly and using the utmost secrecy, they were also able to fight with remarkable effect against the rulership which the great railroads held over them in turn. During the '80's the beef pool soon forced down rates on their shipments, obtained rebates like the oil-refiners, and set up refrigerator car companies through which all perishable food and vegetables must be handled solely, receiving indirect toll from farms of the South, the Middle West and the Pacific Coast. Moreover their combination was able to force the railroads to pay them a "mileage" fee of three-fourths of a cent per mile for the use of their refrigerator cars. Where a railroad seemed tardy in complying with such orders, as in the case of the New York Central, it was punished almost at once, according to Russell, by the diversion of as much as 150 cars of freight per week. Thus, empty or laden, the refrigerator cars brought a perpetual ransom from the railroads to the barons of the packing-houses, who ruled unchallenged over a mighty national traffic in food.

Neither from adjacent industries, such as railroads, nor from would-be invaders of their field, nor farmers nor middlemen nor consumers, would the packers brook interference. Resistance in every direction was met with an implacable force, now operating through financial and now through political "influences." Widespread and violent strikes of the workers were broken in 1886, in 1894 and again in 1904 by the united front of the stockyard firms and a system of uniform blacklisting carried out by them with perfect discipline. This aroused the admiration of captains of industry in all other fields, and gave Chicago long ago its atmosphere of violence.

The power of the kings of animal food was supreme, grandiose and feudal; and sad to relate, like many earlier dynasts they abused it. There was none to say nay if they used diseased swine, goats, or cows in making their famous sausages or hams or tinned beef. For thirty years, although millions of persons patronized them, the four or five overlords in Chicago alone decided what sanitary measures of inspection or approval should be taken. They themselves did not eat this dressed food which they disseminated so widely to an invisible public, toward whom their moral attitude was strictly detached and impersonal. Overwhelmingly bent on pecuniary gains to be derived from the handling of the animal carcasses, and also prone to utilize with ingenious technology a steadily inferior product, they were universally believed guilty of many lapses which did small honor to the American table. Yet none oversaw their activities, and few protested even when frequent cases of sickness or even death were traced directly to their merchandise. It remained for Mr. Upton Sinclair to arouse all the country and galvanize a President, a quarter of a century ago, by his pathetic account of the stockyard laborer who fell into a vat and involuntarily became preserved calf's foot jelly or potted beef. This was undoubtedly one of those splendid poetic exaggerations which become immortal and stir men's minds forever. Such things did not happen often, of course—yet the tale, told in Sinclair's novel "The Jungle," published in 1904, seemed to be the first blow which actually shook the thrones of the monarchs of meat.

The appearance of the early, crude combinations in industry aroused from time to time no little fear, indignation and oratory in certain sections of the public. Even in 1872 an excited Congressman rose from his seat to vituperate the conspirators of brine, urging that the government take over the manufacture of salt, like the kingdoms of olden times, rather than tolerate the daily oppression of every housewife in the land. And after salt, he continued prophetically, why not sugar and fish and eggs and pork and flour? Was the "square meal" in free America to be put forever out of reach of the "square eater" by the predatory combinations grasping at the American breakfast table? In the same year, even President Grant had had occasion to denounce the combination of the oil-refiners as a "monstrous conspiracy," causing the Rockefeller associates to enter upon their long career of innocent denials; while the other capitalists who combined in pools were prompted by popular suspicion to move about their business as with rubber-soled shoes.

But, besides the resistance of tradition and the common law, the pools were weakened by dissensions among their members, by their greed, private ambitions and long-rooted habits of hoodwinking each other. There were many instances where control was lamentably weak. A conference of wire-nail manufacturers was held in the late '80's, at which prices were to be fixed for the coming season. At lunch time one of the leading members slipped away to send a telephonic message by a boy, in which he offered at once to "shade" the rates just fixed by the combination. By chance the message fell into the hands of the chairman of the pool, who, convening the members after lunch, displayed on the spot the evidence of their colleague's treachery.

A corporation lawyer who helped to draw up many agreements between copper-mine operators is cited by Barron as saying:

> *It is a large order . . . that always breaks a pool. The manufacturer will figure that he can pay his fine to the pool, take a big order, and with the profit on this be in a stronger position than any of his competitors who may then try to break the pool. Suppose there is a ten-per-cent profit in his business, and he can get a $1,000,000 order by cutting to five-per-cent profit. He does not regard it as dishonorable, if it is a "fine" pool to pay the $5,000 fine, and then say to his competitors: "I have paid my fine."*

Now if they wish to fight and use up cash, he has $45,000 more than they. Thus, according to this ostensible authority, Mr. Edwin Jackson, the pools would usually run several years, beget competition by the prosperity they enjoyed, break up into a fight for the survival of the fittest, then come together again, shamefaced, recalling how happy had been the days of restricted competition, to try the strength of union once more.

Plainly the pool was a transitory form, and nothing showed it more clearly than the quarrels and rate wars of the different railroads, which, though having attempted to pool their resources for many years since 1870, continued for a generation thereafter to verge between struggle without quarter and hypocritical agreement.

The chief difficulty resided in the fact that though everyone agreed upon the sweets of combination and understood the prize of monopoly, there was conflict eternal over who should have the most of the prize. The formation of pools called forth economic war, and their dissolution, usually a short time later, or the entrance of a powerful invader brought renewed war. In the meantime there were no rules, no arbiters, no courts to appeal to, since the government of the time recognized only the principle of keeping hands off these vital economic matters, and continued to hold sacred life, liberty and property. For a long time the ranks of the baronial class remained torn between the contradictory impulses toward combination and individual competition, between the tendencies to rational unity and dispersion. Only against the rebellions of workers, seen from below, did they seem to act with unison; seen from above they were bitterly and treacherously divided. The period between 1873 and 1893 was marked as deeply by its belligerency as by its significant combinations.

However, certain leaders, such as John D. Rockefeller, whose conceptions are far in advance of his contemporaries, seem to give direction to the continuous social revolution. The inertia of the crowd may oppose him for a time, but he is confident of the correctness of his judgment. He ignores the bitterness of petty capitalists crushed out under his feet. When other industrialists attempt the weak union of the pool, he forges already the Trust. He is as one who feels the turn of the current before others; at first he seems to be navigating against it; then it shifts as foreseen, and he moves forward with an overwhelming force behind him.

CHAPTER THIRTEEN
MORGAN AND THE RAILWAYS

D URING the post-war years of misery and exaltation the communities of bankers established in the great American cities had been flourishing. The national banking act of 1863 and the banking law of 1865 had done away with the confusion of local currency, and permitted the bankers to buy government bonds which were interest-bearing, and then on the security of these bonds to issue their own banknotes to borrowers at the current loan rates. But though national and private bankers alike were mightily enriched during the war, they were further benefited by the establishment of "sound money" in 1873, when the government stopped silver coinage. By "resumption" the tremendously inflated debts which creditors had contracted with the money-lenders in paper were thenceforth to be honored in gold. There were, to be sure, hungry and hazardous years during the '70's; but by 1879, when crop failure in Europe brought a great influx of gold to the United States, full "recovery" was enjoyed.

The traditional character of the banks, private or national, was but little altered from that given by the elder mercantilists of the 1830's and 1840's, such as Moses Taylor, founder of the City Bank, and George Peabody, who laid the foundation for the present J. P. Morgan & Co. The money-lenders, as they had been since the Middle Ages, were but the agents of government and industry; as intermediaries, they received deposits, sold or bought bills of exchange and made loans against dry goods and other merchandise but with the view to earning interest and security of principal. Yet the increased wealth and size of the banks and the momentous economic shiftings of the period were to bring at last deep changes as well in banking practice. Here too a tremendous and revolutionary process of centralization was to take place by which the rule of

money-lender or "financier" was to supplant that of the "manufacturer" or the undertaker of business projects. In this significant
transition, the forty-year-old banker, J. Pierpont Morgan, who had
steadily kept himself abreast of his fellows, the Taylors, Rothschilds,
Belmonts, Seligmans and Mortons, was to be a famous innovator.
The contradictions of the business period in which he lived, the
quarrels of rival barons, their disasters, led him more and more to
abandon the passive role of the intermediary, receiving and lending
moneys, and to attempt more and more often direct intervention in
national industrial affairs. The times, the advanced stage of the industrial revolution, bringing catastrophes in measure with the augmented size of all operations, called for such intervention, such
centralized control as he offered; the boldness of Morgan's character,
moreover, fitted him for the rôle he would assume.

Quitting the underworld of Civil War profiteers and the equally
shady political henchmen of the Erie affair, Morgan in his middle
years frequented decidedly better company. In 1873 he competed
successfully with Jay Cooke for the distribution of government
bonds; and then, with a syndicate of leading New York and Philadelphia bankers, successfully carried out the great refunding operations of 1877. Thus the wartime "6 per cents" were replaced with
"4 per cents" to the extent of $235,000,000; and additional quan-
tities of government loans were floated for the purpose of buying
gold abroad and effecting specie resumption. In these divers operations of a season or two, the associated banks had earned commissions
of $25,000,000, and of this Drexel, Morgan & Co. had garnered
a large share. With sound money reëstablished and business reviving
slowly, it was high time that the bankers resume the work of raising long-term credits for the heavy construction so sorely needed.
To this work the broodingly silent, brusque-mannered Morgan who
was then, as later, a "bull on America," now gave himself *con amore*.

In 1879, William Vanderbilt had entrusted the sale of 250,000
shares of New York Central stock to Morgan, whereby the latter
with his colleagues had taken a quick profit of $3,000,000 as his
commission; in addition, Morgan became a director of the New
York Central. A year later we find Drexel, Morgan & Co. par-
ticipating in the banker's syndicate which raised $40,000,000 in
bonds for the badly battered Northern Pacific Railroad, again at a
charge of 10 per cent; These were only two of a number of re-

markable operations, remarkable for their size at the time, which Morgan carried out with much technical skill.

The chief object of the investment banker in his flotations of securities was to capture the differential between the price he arranged to pay for capital and the price which he could induce a broad public of savers or investors to pay him for it when he distributed it piecemeal. With funds of his own which he had accumulated, let us say five or ten millions, Morgan could obtain options on railroad or industrial capital, giving advances to the needy borrowers, and then in a campaign of some days or weeks in the security exchanges or money centers, land the capital upon the public at home and abroad. By working with a syndicate of investment bankers who shared his commissions and provided more customers of their own, he could indefinitely extend the scope of his operations. Furthermore part of the money realized for the railroad or other enterprise being kept on deposit either in his own or in associated banks could be used again and again for the buying and selling of capital, while the commissions from the turnover grew like a snowball. It is little wonder then that Morgan's enthusiasm for big projects mounted; he became a recognized leader in railroad ventures and each success augmented his prestige among a following of capitalists. He would probably have thrown himself into investment promotions without restraint or fear of the future if it were not for his hard-bitten banking partner, Drexel. For Morgan was a "plunger," according to the financial gossip of his contemporaries, and Drexel, who always clung grimly to his gold, had occasion to bail him out when he exceeded himself.

But no matter how much Morgan's appetite was whetted for large-scale investment banking, the condition of the railroads after 1873 gave him pause. "By the 1880's," writes John Moody, "about twice as many railroad lines had been built as the country could profitably employ." In 1876 two-fifths of all railroad bonds were in default; in 1879 sixty-five roads, capitalized at $234,000,000, were foreclosed, and between 1873 and 1879 it was estimated that European investors had lost $600,000,000 through bankruptcies and frauds. In 1884, after a brief whirl of "prosperity," conditions were little better. Poor's Manual stated that the entire capital stock of the railroads, then about four billions of dollars, represented water; all of the share capital, and a large portion of the bonded debt issued in the preceding three years, was "in excess of construction" —pure hopes, sold to the public. Yet unremitting competition in the railway field continued. By 1884, five trunk lines ran between New York and Chicago, and two more were building, though three would have been ample, and most of these roads were on the verge of bankruptcy. The Empire-Builders had continued their building only so long as stocks and bonds could be landed on the public. But thereafter in the contest for the existing business they fought and destroyed each other without quarter. In the East, the Pennsylvania contested the entrance of the B. & O. into New York; in the West, Hill relentlessly carved into the Northern Pacific's freight territory and pressed Villard toward bankruptcy; in the canyons of the Rockies railroad gangs waged hand-to-hand fights for the capture of the new mining centers. Charles Francis Adams, who had become president of the Union Pacific in 1882, complained bitterly of the condition of his business some time later, before a Senate Committee. "Everywhere," he said, "there is an utter disregard of fundamental ideals of truth, fair play and fair dealing." Cut-throat competition, secret rebates, blackmail had brought conditions which were intolerable even to the primordial individualists of the 1880's. Stockholders complained, directors were bewildered, bankers were frightened; the railroad system as a whole seemed headed for financial disaster.

The sudden panic of 1884 which was precipitated by the machinations of the broker Ferdinand Ward, a Pied Piper of Wall Street who with his magic tunes led hundreds of investors, including his partner, the son of Ulysses Grant, to their ruin, deepened the anarchy of the money markets. Despite the wealth of the republic and its pressing needs prospects were now so gloomy for the holders of American securities that commentators in the English press were advocating "some heroic remedy." At this moment Cyrus Field, the distinguished New York capitalist of ocean cables and elevated railway lines, sent a despatch over his own wires to Junius Morgan in London, a week after the Grant & Ward failure:

> *Many of our business men seem to have lost their heads. What we want is some cool-headed strong man to lead. If you should form a syndicate in London to buy through Drexel, Morgan & Co. good securities in this market, I believe you would make a*

great deal of money and at the same time entirely change the feelings here.

Thus, as Corey comments in his study of the House of Morgan, the anarchic market clamored for leadership, and had began already to turn to one house for such strong leadership.

Neither the elder Morgan nor the already formidable "young Morgan" hastened to the rescue of their confreres. Pierpont bided his time; whatever his plans were, he spoke his mind to no man. His character as it now formed itself showed a kind of stubborn courage, tremendous arrogance and cynicism. To Owen Wister he said: "A man always has two reasons for the things he does—a good one and the real one." He nowadays seldom gave more than the "good" reasons for the things he did. He longed to "consolidate" things, to impose the stabilizing order of high finance on "competitive skullduggery." Self-confident, solid, owning high credit, Pierpont Morgan extended his power slowly over men and groups. By his conception of financial statesmanship he would struggle for a central control of the economic machine. For now between 1877 and 1885, there came the catastrophe of labor war, augmenting the effects of the destructive duels between railroad barons. Morgan approached his problem in detail through the business before him. As Lewis Corey relates:

> *The immediate task, seldom the far-flung objective, absorbed Morgan, at once the strength and weakness of the man. Concentrating upon immediate tasks, determined by the dynamic problems and changes of American enterprise, Morgan moved unimaginatively, massively, but irresistibly, with the irresistibility of economic compulsion, to the "Morganization" of industry by means of new financial procedure and institutions, imposing the control of the financier over industry and integrating industry and finance.*

In October, 1884, the aging William Vanderbilt made a confidential statement to the Board of Directors of the New York Central:

> *I can tell you one thing: our old road will not be behind any of its rivals, whether they are young or old. The rates to the West may be any figure that the other lines may choose to make them. ...The fact is that there has got to be a further liquidation. Some*

companies among the trunk lines have confessed that they were not making much money. . . . I feel the depreciation.

Thus, in somber vein, Vanderbilt dwelt upon the intermittent rate wars on west-bound freight to Chicago, which made the seasons that followed memorable.

The Pennsylvania Railroad, most powerful of the Central's competitors, held a far more complete monopoly over the traffic, the industry, and even the laws of its state. Over the adjacent region as well, the oligarchic band which headed the Pennsylvania extended their sway rapidly by the construction of numerous branch lines. With Thomas Scott now retired, the younger men in command, G. B. Roberts, Frank Thomson, and A. J. Cassatt, managed the system so aggressively that its traffic greatly exceeded that of any other railroad. From the most intensely industrialized part of the country, between the seaboard and the tier of big cities, Chicago, Cleveland, St. Louis, Cincinnati and Pittsburgh, all the grains, coal, oil, iron and machinery were forced through the arteries of their road. But the astonishing prosperity of the Pennsylvania system gave joy neither to its public nor to its neighboring railroads. South of the Pennsylvania's traffic belt the Baltimore & Ohio's trunk-line business was eaten away; northward, the New York Central too saw that the vigorous growth of its competitor promised to be achieved at its own expense. The building of the West Shore line along the Hudson River, directly parallel to Vanderbilt's road, was believed by Vanderbilt to be instigated by the Pennsylvania ring. The West Shore enterprise, mentioned earlier, in which men like George Pullman, Astor and General Horace Porter were involved, penetrated the heart of the Central's territory. More than mere "blackmail," as Vanderbilt had called it, it was a prelude to the entrance of Pennsylvania into New York, which Cassatt ultimately accomplished many years later by his great tunnel under the Hudson.

Peaceful though he was, Vanderbilt had been goaded at last into a war of extermination. He had cleared the decks for action, cut labor costs and freight rates heavily. In addition he searched for a means of striking a deadly blow at his rival. Toward 1883 his chance had come.

In the anthracite-coal region of Pennsylvania, the small Philadelphia & Reading Railroad had been accumulating a coal monopoly;

grown quickly rich, it almost alone offered a lively threat to the Pennsylvania Railroad. The Reading, as it was called, sought access to the sea on the one hand, and connections with the Western markets on the other. Taking this strong young road as the nucleus for a parallel system, Vanderbilt had come forward with the project of the South Pennsylvania Railroad, which as a continuing line from the Reading in the East would free western Pennsylvania, and especially the industrious city of Pittsburgh, from the "thraldom" of the Pennsylvania. Carnegie, for instance, who must send three-fourths of his heavy steel wares over the Pennsylvania tracks at "noncompetitive" rates, had for years been groaning at the exactions of the great railroad to which he owed his schooling and his early success. Some time before he had subscribed funds to build the Pittsburgh & Lake Erie, then he had seen this gobbled up by the Vanderbilts, who immediately came to terms with the Pennsylvania. But by 1883 Vanderbilt had turned to Carnegie with his own maturing plan; a line to connect with the Reading and to extend across Pennsylvania to Pittsburgh—a bold thrust at the Pennsylvania "sphere of influence."

"What do you think of it, Carnegie?" asked Vanderbilt.

"I think so well of it," replied Carnegie, "that I and my friends will raise $5,000,000 as our subscription."

"All right," said the head of the New York Central, "I'll put in $5,000,000."

With Vanderbilt and Carnegie there were associated certain financiers of oil, William Rockefeller and the brilliant newcomer William C. Whitney (allied with O. H. Payne recently by marriage). These were also eager to weaken the hold of the Pennsylvania over the Oil Regions.

As the West Shore Railroad had proceeded up the Hudson River to prey upon the New York Central, so Vanderbilt and his associates menaced with their own campaign of spoliation the length and breadth of Pennsylvania. Work was started at furious speed; men blasted their way through the mountains, leveled roadways, and built bridges (one of which still stands uselessly across the Susquehanna). And with equal despatch an "inside" construction company was set up, which began using the proceeds of some $40,000,000 in stocks and bonds issued to the public. The economic duel which now raged, though it meant a war of rates for a time, no longer served the public interest in any way, and was generally "viewed with alarm." Wages would be forced down, and losses would be borne by both adversaries, a condition which would soon reflect itself in the bankruptcy of one or the other, as well as in declining markets and business activity. "*Competition between railroads is well-nigh impossible,*" as John Moody points out. Building two lines over the same route simply means enormous waste of capital which impoverishes society in general. And in the aftermath of the struggle, all charges, freight and passenger, would be raised excessively to the bewilderment of the population.

All this grotesque wastefulness of the "American system"—especially in the light of its destructive effects upon the securities, the railroad paper which lay in the strong boxes of the banks—was as fully seen by Pierpont Morgan as by anyone on the spot. In England whence he returned in June, 1885, he had heard most unpleasant views of American financiering and "railroad-wrecking." The New York Central stock which he had sold abroad had suffered a dividend reduction of from 8 to 4 per cent. His own future as an investment banker was now closely linked with the fate of the great railways and heavy industries; and as he himself testified in the following year, he "became satisfied that something should be done to bring more harmony among the trunk lines." He was resolved to do his part; and soon, as he tells us, he conceived a way by which "sufficient pressure could be brought on Mr. Vanderbilt to induce him to sell out." What this pressure was is not clear; but even the richest railroad barons when engaged in war need the ammunition which the banker keeps in his till.

It is the theory of Gustavus Myers, historian of many of our men of great fortune, that most of them, like Vanderbilt and even Carnegie, lacked the attributes of physical courage, whatever other ferocity they might possess. The massive Morgan, on the other hand, with his bold and measured address, his meaningful silences, whose whole truculent person suggested dogged courage, seemed to cow the others like some old Viking captain. His handling of the sale of New York Central stock, several years earlier, had already gained for him the confidence of Mr. Vanderbilt; and the latter entrusted to him finally the task of "adjusting the difficulties between the Central and West Shore roads."

Morgan's plan, set forth with much firmness upon his return

from Europe, was to end hostilities and competition all along the line. He proposed that Vanderbilt sell out his piratical South Pennsylvania construction to the Pennsylvania at a low price; in return the Pennsylvania group would sell out the "blackmailing" West Shore line (now operating under receivership and cutting rates all the way to Buffalo) to Vanderbilt. As a final measure Morgan invited the quarreling barons on an afternoon of July, 1885, to come on board his yacht, which, by a happy notion, he had tastefully named the *corsair*; and there make their peace.

A memorable peace conference, as it was a memorable conflict, no longer of individuals engaged in a race for accumulation, but of grouped monopolistic interests: an oligarchy of oil, steel, and railroad overlords in conflict with the power of another railroad monopoly. Here were profound symptoms of a new phase of the industrial or capitalist revolution: the great monopoly or Trust can make unlimited profits when confronted with unorganized, divided sections of consumers and vassals; on such ground it is irresistible. But confronting other organized, powerful groups, its gains are checked; and in the ensuing struggle for advantage, the fate of the whole economic society seems at stake.

The opponents were inconceivably bitter. Vanderbilt, having recently been blackmailed in the "Nickel Plate" road, was stubbornly set against buying in the West Shore. The Pennsylvania men on the other hand refused to buy the South Pennsylvania construction, Roberts having exclaimed impatiently to Morgan's partner, Drexel: "I am not anxious to buy a hole in the ground." But Morgan insisted that Pennsylvania take over Vanderbilt's pirate project in return for 3 per cent debenture bonds to be assumed by them. "I decided that something should be done," concluded the rising dictator.

The *Corsair* steamed idly to and fro, in the outer New York harbor and along the Hudson, carrying its strange crew of latter-day pirates. "Roberts and Chauncey Depew of the Central did the talking; Morgan, six feet and two hundred pounds of him, sprawled in a chair, smoking his eternal black cigar, intervening in the discussion now and then in his sharp, brusque fashion." The *Corsair* steamed idly on until nightfall, Morgan apparently bent on holding his guests till they came to terms with each other. Roberts continued most obdurate. If the Pennsylvania bought the "South Pennsylvania" it would simply be pulling the other faction out of a scrape.

"Oh, no!" growled Morgan. "They'll not get out whole." The New York Central too would have heavy costs in acquiring the West Shore. At last Roberts came around. "We then went to work with Vanderbilt..." Morgan's testimony proceeds. He must have exercised an almost hypnotic influence over both Depew and Vanderbilt. At sunset the pipe of peace was smoked. Morgan, as Roberts related, had brought about a general understanding "with a view to securing remunerative rates of traffic and ...harmony along the lines."

But a provision of the Pennsylvania state constitution forbade the railways of that state to purchase a competing line. Morgan, on the witness stand afterward, explained candidly how he evaded this law:

> Roberts said it was necessary for someone to be the purchaser of the South Pennsylvania other than the Pennsylvania Railroad. As a firm we [Drexel, Morgan & Co.] could not do it, but as an individual feeling the importance of what was at stake, I was prepared to do what I could and to give the use of my name and signature to act as purchaser of one for the other.

It was an evasion of the law. But what of that? Ten years later, as Ida Tarbell tells it, the barrister Elbert Gary, speaking of some daring proposal of Morgan's, remarked with cautious formality: "I don't think you can legally do that." And Morgan replied stormily: "Well, I don't know as I want a lawyer to tell me what I cannot do. I hire him to tell me how to do what I want to do."

As a consequence of these vast negotiations, Morgan was entrusted with the business of "reorganizing," the two pirate properties which were exchanged. The South Pennsylvania had its capital written down to $3,500,000 in 3 per cent bonds guaranteed by the Pennsylvania, which covered more or less the actual cost of the thing; and at the same time the West Shore had its bonded indebtedness cut in half, approximately, while the stock was assessed. Despite the "wry faces" often made by passive investors who lost heavily in the process, Morgan generally put through his capital reorganizations in high-handed fashion and with "unusual success," since the securities, once the "water" had been squeezed out of them, gained a better standing in the market. For this surgery, the "Doctor of Wall Street" exacted high fees; his official historian Hovey tells us: "From $1,000,000 to $3,000,000 is generally put down as the commission going to the House of Morgan . . . *for knowing how to do it and doing it.*" Part of this might be paid in bonds or new stock, and brought Morgan representation on the board of directors of the new company, which he usually demanded in order to oversee the management. Out of the tremendous conflict of the railroad barons, Pierpont Morgan's were the only gains. He had an extraordinary way of bludgeoning the contestants into accepting his terms under pain of bringing down the whole structure upon their heads.

One element of discontent showed itself after the Pennsylvania-Central treaty. The interests in charge of the Philadelphia & Reading road protested that they had been betrayed. Encouraged to expand yesterday, and brimming with natural ambition to rival the great trunk lines, they now saw that Vanderbilt had "let them down" after committing himself to a "gentlemen's agreement" to aid them and causing them to incur larger expenditures. He was no gentleman, they cried loudly. But they too were in a condition of bankruptcy, and Pierpont Morgan set upon them at once to reorganize them as drastically as ever, by reducing existing bonds and assessing the stockholders. Taking command of the weakened coal road, Morgan pledged himself "to bring about satisfactory agreements with all the anthracite roads and also the trunk lines which shall secure to the Philadelphia & Reading, when reorganized, its *just share of the business at remunerative rates.*" This harmony, this complete collusion with large confreres in the field, they could not have reached themselves, apparently, without Morgan's intercession. Here one saw the power and the transcendent value of this man of "heroic remedies," this domineering "man of destiny" who became the decisive voice in the economic order.

In the Reading settlement there was much bitterness at Morgan, and a prolonged legal suit followed in which the facts set forth above were freely aired. But it availed little to combat the Corsair, who largely carried his points everywhere and though already a director of numerous roads East and West, forced himself upon the board of the coal railroad. Then—having gained the utter, crestfallen respect of the lords of the railroads, the Vanderbilts

Robertses, Huntingtons, Garetts—he proceeded to link one coal mine and coal road with the other in a strong monopoly, along the lines of his own plan.

2

The task which Pierpont Morgan had set himself was no easy one. Peace and "community of interest" might be enforced upon the Eastern front, but in many sectors in the West, from the Mississippi River to the Pacific Ocean, in the mountains and over the plains conflict still raged. Along the Canadian border, the weakened Northern Pacific carried on without Henry Villard; but Jim Hill continued his raiding tactics. It is evident from the guarded correspondence of Hill and Mount Stephen that certain powerful banking interests in New York—most likely Morgan—attempted to call a halt to the rate war between the two "Granger" roads in the Northwest. But Hill, while concealing his design of building to Puget Sound, continued his attacks. In the Southwest Gould held the region in an uproar by his conduct of the Missouri Pacific system; while Huntington, suddenly extending his line along the 36th parallel to Norfolk, Virginia, fell into difficulties, the new Chesapeake & Ohio Railway needing the services of a financial rescue-party headed by Morgan. But most alarming of all to Morgan were the predations of a bold new gladiator, Edward H. Harriman, a New York stockbroker who became the active head of the Illinois Central Railroad in 1887, and immediately showed himself a man of elemental force, formed by the times.

The figure of the dynamic Harriman, much younger than the others, and arriving therefore late on the scene, is worth studying. Born in Hempstead, Long Island, in 1848, the son of a disappointed, far-wandered minister, Edward Harriman received almost no schooling. At the tender age of fourteen, in wartime, he went to work as a "pad-shover" or quotation-boy in Wall Street. Here in the quicksands and jungles of the market he gathered with precocious talent a thorough education in capitalism during seven years of close observance. Watching the shrewd and jovial "Commodore" Vanderbilt, the tigerish Gould, the solemn "Deacon" White, the lonely "Wizard" Jim Keene, he soon learned how "corners" and "pools" were devised, how financial ambuscades were laid and pits were dug, and how all the thousand and one disasters and joyless triumphs of the stock market came about. By disposition Edward Harriman was a bear; and in September, 1869, while still a head clerk in a broker's office, he used all his small means to sell the market short on the occasion of Jay Gould's Black Friday conspiracy. So at the age of twenty-one he possessed the $3,000 needed to equip himself with a seat in the Stock Exchange, acquiring clients and gambling in his own name as well.

At the outset a skillfully executed raid on Deacon White's cornered coal stocks had brought Harriman overnight a booty of $150,000 and achieved for him a reputation as a floor broker. There were reverses too. A few years later, in selling short the stock of Delaware & Hudson, he met with an unexpected and crushing defeat, at the hands of powerful interests like the Astors, and saw his till emptied bare of cash. Thenceforth he proceeded with more wariness; he would need ammunition; he must accumulate a war chest patiently. At any rate, his clients numbered August Belmont, members of the Vanderbilt family and its lieutenants, and even occasionally Jay Gould. Brilliantly deceptive in his day-to-day operations, impassive, laconic, quick-thinking and far-calculating, this young man came to be known as a gifted technician of Wall Street offenses and sieges. This he would have remained, in view of his native capacity for turning defeats into victories, escaping again and again from pitfalls and whirlpools, and lurking beasts of prey. He would have continued so—always relentless in his business, religious in after hours—had he not married in 1879 a Miss Averill, the daughter of a small railroad-owner, William J. Averill of Ogdensburg, New York. Thereafter he had grown interested in all the particular problems of his father-in-law's little Ogdensburg & Lake Champlain Railroad which was located in the northeastern part of New York State. In time, sensing the financial advantage of the situation, he determined to press the majority stockholders of the road to sell out to him. This done, he repaired and reorganized the property and then jockeyed the New York Central (Vanderbilt) group into bidding against the Pennsylvania gang, while developing his little line's "nuisance value" to the highest pitch.

In this first *coup d'état* of Harriman's, we are innocently told by his official biographer, George Kennan, nearly all the principal stockholders of the Ogdensburg & Lake Champlain Railroad had become "discouraged by President Macy's last report" of their business condition. It is a curious coincidence that Harriman was not so "discouraged," but instead, "at a meeting of the board of directors in October 1883, named a price at which he would either sell his own stock [knowing it would not be bought] or buy the stock of the other owners. . . ." So the others "decided to sell" and "Mr. Harriman thus became practically the sole owner of the property." This he ultimately landed on the Pennsylvania Railroad, who hastened to buy it, merely in order that Vanderbilt might not have it.

During the "railroad-mad" period of the 1880's, Harriman, like many others, bought and sold the pieces of paper which represented railway constructions, on an ever increasing scale. In a season of panic, due to the assassination of President Garfield in 1881, he had entered the market boldly and "held up" the shorts in one sizable Western railroad, the Illinois Central. When he was done he had squeezed enough profit to become, after some opposition, one of the directors of this respectable company, whose president was a distinguished member of the New York aristocracy, Mr. Stuyvesant Fish.

Edward Harriman's reputation at this time was somewhat unpleasant. Like Jay Gould he was thought to be a pretty cold-blooded gambler in the securities which make up Wall Street's stock in trade, rather than a "sound" or "responsible" leader of shipping and transportation affairs. His reputation would cling to him all his life, though thanks to his great mental agility he did learn much about managing railroad systems, and especially "financiering" them, a game at which he soon surpassed nearly everyone ranged in the field. It was rumored that Harriman, in the classical way of Gould, would soon "break" his railroad. But instead, the Illinois Central under his guidance flourished sensibly and advanced itself in its territory. Thus came the first clash with J. P. Morgan, who in 1886 was now directing the expansion of the New York Central lines into Iowa, on behalf of the heirs of William Vanderbilt.

The trouble between the two railroad systems came from their simultaneous desire to invade Iowa and wrest from each other the Dubuque & Sioux City Railway which traversed that state. The Illinois Central had leased the smaller line, and in 1886 its directors authorized Harriman to get control of the road by negotiation or purchase. Through bold market operations, Harriman outmaneuvered Morgan and gained a large ownership though not quite a majority in Dubuque & Sioux City. The remaining stockholders, led by Morgan, were determined to block the Illinois Central at the approaching stockholders' meeting by demanding an extortionate price for their retirement. Morgan intended to "squeeze" Harriman or hurl him out of his path.

The meeting, however, proved to be a deadlock. Though the Morgan faction held a scant majority of the shares, Harriman cleverly seized upon a legal formality, the failure of the banker to have the "assignment" of the stock authenticated in the State of Iowa. By sharp legal practice, despite uproarious protests, Harriman as chairman of the meeting proceeded to reject all the Morgan proxies and vote the remaining shares, as he desired, into the control of his own railroad. Morgan fumed over this defeat, and would never forget nor forgive "that little fellow" Harriman. These men were to cross each other's path again and again as unyielding antagonists; one was as arrogant and as overweeningly ambitious as the other. Harriman, according to James Stillman, liked most of all to "plan something that everyone says is impossible, then to jump in with both feet and do it." His acts of hostility did not lessen the confusion, the "anarchy" which J. P. Morgan fought against in the railroad world. Besides, it was apparent after a few years had passed that the successes of Harriman had brought to his following the most powerful of money lords, the men of the Standard Oil.

3

Since 1879, when the Hepburn Committee in New York State had made its exposures and its quite moderate recommendations, the hue and cry after the railways had known no abatement. Universally the evils of powerful combinations in industry and trade were traced to the conspiratorial action of the railroad masters. Moreover the scandals of stockjobbing and railroad-wrecking multiplied in the early '80's. Tales of the quick fortunes seized by the men who possessed themselves of the common carriers, and of the purses they maintained for political corruption, aroused hot resentment in the breasts of honest middle-class Americans of almost every section Even Henry Clews commented toward 1884 in his memoirs:

If any facts could be supposed to justify the doctrines of socialism and communism it would be the sudden creation of such fortunes as these which within a very few years have come into the hands of our railway magnates.

What then must have been the feeling of the politician, his nose scenting nervously each change in the voters' temper? The "Millionaires, and Monopolists' Banquet" to Blaine at Delmonico's, in the summer of this year, did not help that colorful statesman in his contest with the "reformer" Cleveland. That he should dine with Jay Gould, "one of the most sinister figures that have ever flitted bat-like across the vision of the American people," and with H. H. Rogers, Cyrus Field, Russell Sage and Armour, and at Delmonico's to boot "where champagne frothed and brandy sparkled in glasses like jewels," to the members of the popular press was but a sign of Blaine's desperate drive for a "corruption fund." Nor did it escape the eye of politicians that farmers and tradespeople throughout the Southwest, where a great strike raged along Gould's Missouri Pacific, aided the workers heartily in their struggle. In these years, whenever business flagged in the state legislatures or in the halls of Congress the statesmen rose from their seats and denounced the railway "robbers" in furious rodomontades. That railroads like the Union and Southern Pacific, which owed their inception to federal subsidies of cash as well as land, refused to repay the government mortgage added fuel to the flame of the statesmen's rhetoric. Their proposals varied from divers plans of regulation to the construction of a People's Railroad by the government, upon a narrow gauge, for the cheap transport of freight; from a nation-wide People's Canal System to legislative acts compelling the humane treatment of immigrant and native passengers—propositions which were always speedily voted down, thanks to the watchful lobbies maintained by the Collis Huntingtons, Goulds and Vanderbilts.

Resistance to government measures came not only from men like Huntington but also from enlightened publicists such as Lawrence Godkin, editor of *The Nation*, who fought as in a sacred cause against the "confiscation of private property," giving warning that the holdings of owners and investors would soon be transformed into, "eleemosynary or charitable institutions" once the government intervened. Hitherto the state legislatures had passed many acts designed to control the roads—though to be sure many of them, as in New York or Pennsylvania, were conceived at the instance of the railroad chieftains themselves in order to hold down rivals. Yet the constitutional right of the state legislatures to intervene had often been sharply questioned; and upon this issue the Supreme Court finally ruled in the celebrated Wabash *vs.* Illinois decision of 1886. According to the highest court of the land, the different states had no right to regulate *interstate commerce* or interfere in any way with traffic moving across their border.

In railroad circles there was now high jubilation at this judicial victory; but popular opinion, expressed by farmers, labor unions, and, significantly, large shippers, was whipped up to rage, and demanded federal action as a last resort. With eminent good sense the Congress now decided that something must be done, that the appeal of the people must be heeded, if we would not make ready, as John Sherman said, "for the socialist, the communist, the nihilist."

For a year the Interstate Commerce Act was debated; the Representatives and Senators persisted in long disagreements upon their respective measures. Nearly all of them seemed honestly bewildered by the problem. Many of them wished not to harm the existing railway system; others wished honestly to do the least that was expected of them. Before such technical and economic problems, the "modesty, meekness and confessions of ignorance" of most seemed amazing to some of the members. Finally, with dead hearts, both chambers passed the Interstate Commerce Act, and the great "revolution" of 1887 was effected—"a bill that no one wants ... and everybody will vote for," as one Representative shrewdly remarked. By this measure, "competition" in general was to be fostered, rebates were forbidden, as was pooling, or exacting higher freight tariffs for short hauls than for long hauls, or discriminations between persons, places and commodities; further, reports and accounts were required of the railroads, shippers were permitted to sue them for as much as $5,000, and a Commission to carry out these measures was set up.

Soon it appeared that these orders were instrumented in practically no way. And then the old guardsmen of the Supreme Court harried the Act on every flank for nearly twenty years, limiting the powers of the Commission, defending private property by their own decrees, preventing the Commission from fixing rates—thus turning the momentous act into little more than a "scarecrow," as the Beards have said. As to the demand for accountings of their affairs, the railroad officials soon found that they could refuse these with impunity; and protestant shippers forced to bear costs of prosecution soon learned that complaint was useless.

This happy turn of events by which it was arranged that the "agrarians" and "communists," as Huntington called them, had their law, and the barons had their railways, was not clearly understood at the start. The railroad people passed through a season or two of terror, as shown by many a private letter of the time. Gloomily they announced their official abandonment of pools and resumption of uncontrolled competition, while in actual practice all their movements were now conducted with profound secrecy. A certain uneasiness and even panic spread over the markets. In 1888 railway rates fell, and despite a general increase in gross revenue, a dangerous decline in the net earnings of the great systems was reported everywhere.

The intrusion of the popular sovereignty had produced a veritable emergency. No sooner had the government attempted to impose its control on behalf of the mass of consumers, and outlawed all collusive practice such as pooling and rebates, than it became clear to the railroad leaders that a real control, fashioned for totally different ends, must be laid down. The vital error of the bill was its failure to control rates. "Competition was well-nigh impossible" for these giant machines with their tens of thousands of workers, as Moody has said; their large scale, their profoundly cooperative, economic character called for a true control from within if, under the existing scheme of capitalism which the government and nation still sanctioned, complete breakdown were to be avoided. The moment called for action and Pierpont Morgan, who had watched these developments with deep anxiety, now came forward with his further plans for "community of interest." In the face of the confusing laws of the land he would set up his own machinery of control through concentrated financial power. In December, 1888, Drexel, Morgan & Co., Brown Brothers & Co., and Kidder, Peabody & Co., as a combination of investment-bankers, at the instance of Morgan issued a "Private and Confidential Circular" to all the heads of the large American railway systems, calling them to conference on matters of state. Under the stress of the emergency the "nation within" and its leaders swung into action.

The first conference began in the richly furnished library of Morgan's house on Madison Avenue. Here amid the paintings, the ancient manuscripts, the objects of antiquity, the glowing tapestries, which this man of "gorgeous tastes" had assembled, the barons of the railroads came together on January 8, 1889. Present were the saturnine Jay Gould and his son George for the Missouri Pacific, Charles Francis Adams for the Union Pacific, Frank Bond of the Chicago, Milwaukee & St. Paul, A. B. Stickney of the Chicago, St. Paul & Kansas City, George Roberts of the Pennsylvania, and Chauncey Depew of the Vanderbilt-owned New York Central, as well as half a dozen other magnates. The meeting was secret, though rumors of its occurrence, and afterward statements by participants, were spread in the press and corroborated the existing impression that it was one of the grandest, most solemn and momentous events in American high finance, bearing on nothing less than the disposition of supreme industrial power in the country.

Morgan's private circular had stated as the ostensible object of the meeting: to enforce provisions of the Interstate Commerce Act and "maintain public, reasonable, uniform and stable rates."

Here were stubborn railroad presidents, the peers of the age, accustomed to brook no one's command and habitually mistrustful of each other, given in Machiavellian fashion to spying out the other's secrets and falling upon each other from ambuscade. Now they were brought together at the instance of the pontifex of banking to compose a Magna Carta of Railroad Barons! Some of them had refused to come; one even declaring publicly that "no combination of bankers can set up to whip the country's railway managers into line like so many senseless cattle." The Chicago & Alton president, for instance, had denied having any "responsibility" to "Wall Street" whatsoever. But the rest represented perhaps two-thirds of the nation's carrier mileage.

Morgan, as chairman, in his "usual direct fashion," as brusque and forthright and frowning as ever, read an ultimatum:

"The purpose of this meeting is to cause the members of this association to no longer take the law into their own hands when they suspect they have been wronged, as has been too much the practice heretofore. This is not elsewhere customary in civilized communi-

ties, and no good reason exists why such a practice should continue among railroads."

As Hovey, official biographer of Morgan, relates, "The men who ran the railroads and the men who furnished the money to construct them were face to face for the first time at a formal meeting. . . . To put it simply, the representatives of capital intended to show the railroad men the whip. They intended to convey to them . . . that further misbehavior would be punished by cutting off the supplies."

Morgan talked sharply of lawless conditions in the railroad trade, and of the evils they bred for the financial community. Indignantly then President Roberts of the Pennsylvania oligarchy retorted:

> *"Speaking in behalf of the railway people of this country, I object to this very strong language, which indicates that we, the railroad people, are a set of anarchists, and this is an attempt to substitute law and arbitration for anarchy and might."*

A Western railroad president, Stickney, spoke up warningly. "The public," he said, "are sure to think we are conspiring to do something that we ought not to do."

And Charles Francis Adams, who had for seven lean and tempestuous years now been president of the Union Pacific, and who a year later was to be ambushed and discarded by Jay Gould, spoke with remarkable bitterness of the common situation in which they found themselves. The great difficulty in railroad affairs, in his mind, lay "in the covetousness, want of good faith, and low moral tone of railway managers, in the complete absence of any high standard of commercial honor." There was the Interstate Commerce Act, which he himself had helped to frame. It must be enforced, he insisted, "both among yourselves and all others—it is a law, and as such it should bear with equal weight upon all." The great question was whether "any gentleman representing a railroad company is prepared to stand up and say before the public and before us that he is opposed to obeying the law, and further, that in matters of controversy he prefers to take the law into his own hands rather than submit to arbitration."

There was the rub. Could a railroad president be a "gentleman" and adhere to a "gentlemen's agreement"? None could forsake his own covetousness and the hope of fulfilling it by force of arms whenever necessary, nor trust the wisdom and justice of a council or a chosen arbiter from among his fellows. It was too hard. Yet Morgan pressed his proposal—evidently a permanent (and secret) rate-making organization, that which government had not dared to accomplish. A committee of three was elected by the conference, after high wrangling, to devise a governing organization among the "anarchist" railroad presidents, in effect a nation-wide pool; it would have established fines, regulated and settled all disagreements over rates or service.

At the resumption of the conference two days later, January 10, there was a renewal of acrimonious discussion and plain speaking. As Hovey says: "At times the meeting resembled a meeting of the chiefs of the fighting clans of Scotland." Roberts of the Pennsylvania made great murmur at Morgan's severity, concluding "but I can stand it I suppose if the others can"; then turning upon Morgan, he mocked at those bankers "who, with all their horror of railroad wars and rate-cutting, are usually ready to help along disturbing factors by *selling the securities of any parallel railroad originated.*"

To this charge Morgan made a reply which was an important, a solemn pledge, backed by the associated bankers, Kidder, Peabody, Brown Brothers, the Barings, all in a massed union on his side:

> *In regard to the remarks made by Mr. Roberts in regard to the bankers and the construction of parallel lines, I am authorized to say, I think, on behalf of the [banking] houses represented here, that if an organization can be formed . . . [practically upon the basis submitted by the committee], and with an Executive Committee able to enforce its provisions, upon which the bankers shall be represented, they are prepared to say that they will not negotiate, and will do everything in their power to prevent the negotiation of, any securities for the construction of parallel lines or the extension of lines not approved by the Executive Committee. I wish that distinctly understood.*

With a show of satisfaction and confidence, Morgan announced after the conclusion of the first stormy meetings: "I consider the Western rate wars as practically at an end." Had not the magnates present pledged their "personal word of honor" to abide with each other peacefully? The Gentlemen's Agreement of 1889 represented a "revolution" in the country's industrial affairs, as the *Commercial & Financial Chronicle* of New York commented at the moment. But at heart, Morgan found its results disappointing to his vision of a supreme economic control. Factions among the railroad barons hail-from the Chicago region had simply sneaked around the corner and made a pool of their own, resolving to "separate the discussion from the banking interests." As one of them related afterward: "We did not swallow the whole arrangement evidently prepared for us."

The glaring weakness of this first effort of Morgan's at nation-wide government of the American railway system was seen in the very season that followed. In the Northwest, Jim Hill, who had refused to attend the conferences of 1889, brought his Great North-ern line at last to the sea in 1890, and thus helped fling the rival Northern Pacific into bankruptcy. At the same time the Union Pa-cific, under the leadership of Charles Francis Adams, underwent sore trials; its secret floating debt had never been erased since the management of Gould, a decade before; the government mortgage and all the accrued interest still unpaid overhung the company like a sword. And in the meantime, Adams in revelations published in the posthumous notes of Barron tells us how the transcontinental railroad was being undermined, how its credit was cut off, and how a "mysterious increase in operating expenses in 1890" brought it again to the verge of failure. In the background there hovered the evil genius of the Union Pacific who up to the hour of his death, in 1891, schemed to possess himself of the road once more. Adams relates:

> In the meanwhile I was receiving assaults from all quarters of the West, from a hand which I could not see, and could not understand. There would be something published in Chicago, and then copied in the East, attacking our credit, and then there would be an attack upon us in some Salt Lake City paper, or at Portland, Oregon, and the ball would move around the country to hit us in the back. I thought it was some attack from our rivals in the railroad business. I even suspected the Vanderbilts, and the lines to Chicago that were opposing the Northwest Alliance. . . . It was none other than the hand of Jay Gould. Of that I am satisfied. He would throw a ball against the wall in the West, and see it bound back in the East. Having me in this position with money tight, and a large floating

debt, my resources failing, the western management crippled, the earnings showing poorly, where they should have shown handsomely, the Gould trap came into play.

Finally Mr. Gould threw off the mask, and came out openly in an interview in the New York Evening Post, *in which he attacked me, and the credit of the company, and said that as a large stockholder he was going to turn me out of office, and take the management of the company himself.*

For two years Morgan, who had brought a certain measure of peaceful confederation to the Eastern front, saw only intestinal struggle and "anarchy" among the Western trunk lines. He could wait. But as his official biographer observes, it was only too clear "what the future aim of a man of Mr. Morgan's type was bound to be." If he could not influence men by talking to them, he was bound to seek to control them by force. *"Everything taught him the need of getting control himself in order to accomplish his ends."*

Morgan by reputation was now a "national figure"; his reputation was of power, of success. He called a second general conference for December, 1890; and the railroad magnates came again, sheepish and somewhat chastened by events during two hard years which had made them needier of credit than ever before. Collis Huntington, Jim Hill and Russell Sage were new additions to the meetings; there were casualties to be noted, such as the missing Adams who had been made to "walk the plank" by Gould. These men now seemed almost ready to accept their fate at Morgan's hand. They attempted to relieve the gloom by a little jesting at their own expense.

"I have the utmost respect for you, gentlemen, individually," says President A. B. Stickney, "but as railroad presidents I wouldn't trust you with my watch out of sight."

And to this Jay Gould, grown mellow, in a rare moment of levity, adds a story about Daniel Drew which is cited by Lewis Corey:

> *At one time Drew went into a Methodist Church while a revival was in progress, and listened to a convert telling how sinful he had been, lying, cheating and robbing men of their money in Wall Street. Greatly interested Drew nudged a neighbor and asked:*
> *"Who is he, anyhow?"*
> *"That's Daniel Drew," was the reply.*

Morgan had recently effected an agreement between the Vander-bilt family and the Pennsylvania Railroad, for cooperation between them "with power to decide all questions of common interest, to avoid wasteful rivalry and to establish uniformity of rates between competitive points," by means of an advisory council which he himself dominated. He now proposed the same plan for the group of Western trunk lines. An advisory board was set up, though with-out stipulated absolute powers. No fines or penalties were provided for. However, in Wall Street the triumph of Morgan was now sensed. A total change in "the animus of management" had been effected by him, according to the *Commercial & Financial Chronicle.* The freebooter was no longer to be tolerated either by the "parties that furnished all new money needed" or "the party that owns the old money invested." And Morgan himself exulted: "Think of it— all the competitive traffic of the roads west of Chicago and St. Louis in the control of about thirty men. It is the most important agreement made by the railroads in a long time, and it is as strong as could be desired."

In the protracted campaign against self-seeking railway barons, against money-lenders who financed parallel construction, against the political system of government, Morgan was spreading his own direct, secret authority by the tactics, destined to become famous, of interlocking directorates. He acted moreover as fiscal agent for numerous great systems, in which he held a share of the stock-ownership, and saw to it that one or more directors represented him. Within a decade of campaigning which now began, he would have more than a voice, he would have virtually absolute control in twelve great systems: The Great Northern (Hill), the Northern Pacific, the Chicago, Burlington & Quincy, the Southern Railway, Central of Georgia, Louisville & Nashville, Reading (Jersey Central, and Reading Coal & Iron), Erie, Hocking Valley, Lehigh Valley, Santa Fe (in part), St. Louis & San Francisco (in part)—some 55,555 miles of track, over $3,000,000,000 in capital.

The inevitable drift to concentration was completing itself. Soci-ety had called forth a Morgan, political government having abdi-cated or deliberately refused to accept its functions; and Morgan was perfecting an organization which was ready to account for the supreme economic control of the country. Under him were the brilliant financial lieutenants who carried the burden of detail in the

House of Morgan toward 1890, such as Egisto Fabbri, Charles
Coster, J. Hood Wright and the others who were once known as
the "Apostles" of "Pierpontifex Maximus." In the railroad field itself
he soon had the direct alliance not only of the Vanderbilt and the
Pennsylvania rings, but also of the remarkable Jim Hill, whom he
had met for the first time in 1890, and who had won his unstinted
confidence. With such massed force and wealth as his system of
alliances, his "money Trust," represented, he could push on rapidly
toward the subjugation of those few remaining adversaries who,
themselves in possession of associated monopolies, were in a position
to dispute his authority. The contests of the future were to be not
between men, but between economic dinosaurs of elemental power.

CHAPTER FOURTEEN

THE ROBBER BARONS

THE newly rich who had so quickly won to supreme power in the economic order enjoyed an almost universal esteem for at least twenty years after the Civil War. Their glory was at its zenith; during this whole period they literally sunned themselves in the affection of popular opinion. The degree in which they had won a general public consent is reflected in many a candid and even naïvely ecstatic chronicle in the press, a press with which they of course maintained the warmest and most inspiring relations.

The type of the successful baron of industry now presented itself as the high human product of the American climate, the flower of its own order of chivalry, much wondered at, envied or feared in foreign lands whose peers had arrived somewhat earlier at coronets, garlands and garters. Though the American parvenu was "rough-hewn," he was certainly "nature's nobleman," as the sage of Wall Street, Henry Clews, exclaimed; and what a splendid showing he made when compared with the "English parchment nobility" or any other! "The modern nobility springs from success in business," Clews solemnly avowed, and a thousand native philosophers shouted assent to him.

The historian of the house of Vanderbilt wrote:

America is the land of the self-made man—the empire of the parvenu. Here it is felt that the accident of birth is of trifling consequence; here there is no "blood'" that is to be coveted save the red blood which every masterful man distills in his own arteries; and here the name of parvenu is the only and all-sufficient title of nobility.

Was it not self-evident that these "owners and managers of colossal capitals," as Tilden said in a public address, worked better than they knew for the benefit of the people? And who had disputed with Jay Gould when he, bristling before the Senators who inquired 5into his private affairs, had cried: "*We* have made the country rich, *we* have developed the country. . . ."?

But to tell only how the captains of industry "made themselves and the country rich" would be to leave out much of the story. We must turn aside from their purely mercenary operations to picture to ourselves for a moment how these barons of coal, iron, or pork, by a natural and concomitant effort to which many interests led them and many voices called them, extended their sway throughout the social order; how like earlier invading hosts arriving from the hills, the steppes or the sea, they overran all the existing institutions which buttress society; how they took possession of the political government (with its police, army, navy), of the School, the Press, the Church; and finally how they laid hands upon the world of fashionable or polite society, which in all times seems to persist as a "kept class" attached to the ruling power yet holding a subtle sway over this power as well as over the manners and opinions of the people.

These virile parvenus who had become the "controllers of enormous industrial wealth" in their mature years, wrote Murat Halstead, a reputable Middle Western editor, were not the representatives of money bags merely, but

> the types of that American pluck and enterprise and those traits of industry that have built up the greatness of the nation. As such he would indeed be bold who would challenge their right to sit in the highest assembly of the country as representatives of the American people.

Although he plainly required neither defense nor urging, the claim was constantly made for the baron that he might rightfully take command of the popular institutions; or, as another spokesman termed it, "without hesitation or apology assume the place to which he is entitled in commerce or the industrial arts, in professional life or society." So like the landed gentry, the military chieftains, or the priestly class of old, Veblen tells us, the new captain of industry in his turn now received "the deference of the common people," became the "keeper of the National Integrity," and with a becoming gravity offered himself as philosopher and friend to mankind, as "guide to literature and art, church and state, science and education, law, and morals—the standard container of the civic virtue."

In short order the railroad presidents, the copper barons, the big dry-goods merchants and the steel masters became Senators, ruling in the highest councils of the national government, and sometimes scattered twenty-dollar gold pieces to newsboys of Washington. But they also became in even greater number lay leaders of churches, trustees of universities, partners or owners of newspapers or press services and figures of fashionable, cultured society. And through all these channels they labored to advance their policies and principles, sometimes directly, more often with skillful indirection.

The spirit of our barons led them by many paths to worship in the House of God. It would be false to deny or overlook the strong religious impulse shared by most of the great possessors of money, who were nearly all apparently true believers, godly men and generous champions of the Church.

The unconscionable Daniel Drew, for instance, would always repair to his home or his church in his hours of trouble and pray vociferously to the Lord. In his mystic faith he possessed a seeming affinity with those predatory warriors of other centuries who turned so easily from the field of slaughter to kneel in prayer before the altar of God. "Call upon me in thy day of trouble: I will deliver thee, and thou shalt glorify me." The others, who were no less aggressive, seemed to attribute freely to their predominantly Puritan or Protestant faith the strength in themselves which had borne them through all the trials of long competitive struggle. Not only did they have, as Veblen has said, Old Testament traits of ferocity, jealousy, clannishness and disingenuousness, but also the "economic virtues" which are associated with Christian sobriety and self-denial.

In all his days, Jay Cooke, the lordly financier of the Civil War days, had never lost an opportunity to do service to God. He had always kept the Sabbath strictly, prayed much and scrupulously, while he "also served" in war by selling government bonds at a commission. With the same calm, deacon-like air, he bought church-bells for neighboring churches of Philadelphia, distributed pensions for needy ministers of the gospel, as he bought newspapers, or gave cases of wine or valises of greenbacks to needy politicians. And at the same time he would caution his personnel to be virtuous, God-fearing and without pride, as he had always been. When in the midst of great affairs of war and money he saw a young assistant of his riding about the streets of Philadelphia in a "four-in-hand," he paused to write a message of wrathful warning, as some years later Rockefeller would warn his associates to refrain from driving fast horses or buying costly bonnets for their wives.

In his needy youth, John Rockefeller had saved dimes and collected the dimes of others to aid his church; he had continued most faithfully to do glory to God in many ways, with touching and humble gifts: five cents for the Sabbath school, twelve cents for a mission, ten cents for a religious paper—all noted in his diary since the age of sixteen. Then as he prospered he gave himself over more and more to a pious evangelism: in the Bible classes he taught at the age of twenty-eight in Cleveland he urged his pupils, as Flynn relates, to arm themselves with the Puritan virtues. He took as his text: "Seest thou a man diligent in his business he shall stand before kings." He warned his hearers, further, to be "moderate," not to be "good fellows," to take no drink nor to gamble. Through the years, the faith of the evangelists, with its deep emphasis upon the liberty of the individual conscience, grew stronger in Rockefeller, while his brothers-in-arms, members of the Standard Oil family, all seemed imbued with a similar spirit; Archbold, Pratt, Stillman and Vandergrift were all men of strong will, of self-discipline, and prudent, rational life; and God's reward for so much diligence, so much self-denial, so much humiliation of the flesh, so much parsimony, was to be that great multiplication of worldly goods which would permit them to "stand before kings." They sought the Lord and they invoked the Lord during the adventure of great undertakings and combats, or at the end of the day's labors, and the Lord made them to prosper. Hence when upon one occasion of a princely gift to the Church the bitter cry of "tainted money" was set up against Rockefeller, he said simply and feelingly: *"God gave me my money."*

The booty of so many providentially profitable engagements was, then, "God's Gold," as John T. Flynn has said in his biography of Rockefeller; and in part, at least, the barons carried it back to do glory to God, and to pay Him His due. Some of them surpassed each other in presenting Him with gifts of barbarous magnificence;

others, whose evangelical faith forbade such archaic displays, expended even greater sums to build sacred edifices of noteworthy plainness and severity. In either case they hastened to confer substantial parts of the booty taken in successful raids, as if fearing that God would be angry unless much money were paid. The mighty churches of New York and Chicago were filled to bursting with the Astors, the (younger) Vanderbilts, the Rockefellers, the Wanamakers, the Morgans, the Armours, the Pullmans and all their kin, who paid for these churches.

In certain of the more aggressive of the money lords, as the penetrating Thorstein Veblen notes, the system of devout observances, the faith in an "animistic propensity of things" reflected very clearly a survival of predatory traits, like those of the raiders and plunderers of earlier ages of Christendom. This view is certainly borne out in the case of men like Henry Frick and Pierpont Morgan, who both tended toward those patterns of worship which were more glamorous and archaic than that of the Calvinists. Frick, who was the child of Pennsylvania Dutch ancestors, as his friend George Harvey tells us, ended by departing from the plain Lutheran faith of his fathers and "later in life, attending the Protestant Episcopal Church, whose form of service appealed more strongly to his sense of dignity, harmony and beauty." Here all that "régime of status," as Veblen so aptly interprets it, the hierarchic system of master and slave, dominant and subservient, drawn from an early, predatory scheme of society, might well please a Frick or a Morgan.

Morgan was known to be "imperiously proud," rude and lonely, intensely undemocratic toward his fellows, and was equal to throwing articles of food or clothing at his servants when they nodded and forgot his wants. Endowed with "gorgeous, Renaissance tastes," the master of the yacht *Corsair* loved to surround himself as much with men and women of physical beauty as with the plunder of ages of culture. Flouting opinion, he appeared in public before newspaper reporters with one of his favorites, and lived openly with another, according to one of his recent biographers, Mr. John Winkler. Yet this man who brooked no interference with his private pleasures or financial undertakings, and who sinned much by his own lights, derived a genuine satisfaction from religious devotion of the most ritualistic category. Leaving his office at 23 Wall Street upon afternoons, he would go to kneel in St. George's Church, and sing hour upon hour his favorite hymns played by his favorite organist. And when he brought trophies to propitiate the Lord they were gifts of barbaric extravagance, such as that of $500,000 for the erection of St. John the Divine, vastest of all the contemporary religious monuments at the time.

Pierpont Morgan soon became the great lay figure of the Episcopal Church of his day; when conventions were held, he appeared as a deputy from New York, bearing all the important visiting prelates, divines and lay guests, in a private "palace car" on one of his railroads to the convention city, and entertaining them upon the most lavish scale in a private house which he rented. But most of all was Pierpont Morgan thrilled by the splendors of Rome during his foreign tours; the pomp, the marble spaces, the gilt and tapestry of the Vatican and of St. Peter's awed him. He would have bought the Sistine Chapel if it were for sale; he wished that he might have a bed to sleep there and gaze at the frescoes. He felt most at home in the Eternal City, visited it more and more frequently, and there he died. His last will and testament would be headed with a profession of his faith. Like all men he had been born in sin, and the only hope of salvation lay in the doctrine of the Atonement. "His beliefs were to him precious heirlooms. He bowed before them as the Russian bows to the Ikon . . . " the rector of Morgan's church has told us of this most devout of the money masters.

Still others, however, among the great parvenus approached the institution of organized religion in the more rational spirit of lowchurchmen or even of skeptics. To James Hill, the Western railroad leader, there resided in the church a miraculous controlling force for the masses of people, whose value could scarcely be measured. Himself a Protestant, and somewhat negligent in his observance, he suddenly donated a million dollars for the establishment of a Roman Catholic theological seminary in St. Paul. To those who wondered why he should make such offerings to a church of which he was not a member, he said:

No nation can exist without a true religious spirit behind it. Laws that forbid teaching Christianity are the weakest things in our government. . . . I do not care what the denomination may be.

And further:

Look at the millions of foreigners pouring into this country to whom the Roman Catholic Church represents the only authority that they either fear or respect. What will be their social view, their political action, their moral status if that single controlling force should be removed?

This "undigested mass of foreign material" for whose migration to the prairies of the Northwest Hill, mighty colonizer that he was, was more responsible than anyone else, should be dealt with, adds his biographer, by those who alone have the power to mold it; in short, by the anointed agents of the only authority it understands or obeys. "This," concludes Hill's official apologist, "is as much a matter of business as is the improvement of farm stock or the construction of a faultless railroad bed."

More candidly than any of his contemporaries Hill has suggested to us the immense and varied services which the religious institution was expected to perform. The Church was to buttress the new régime of status, it was to control, to pacify, to console, to "render unto Caesar the things which are Caesar's." Was it not imperative, then, that the new rulers come generously to the support of the Church? And while the barons of lard or oil or coke invoked the beneficence of the churchly power, the officers of the Church in their turn now gave themselves over to a free and excited pursuit of the barons.

A new species of pastor flourished in the church of Luther and Calvin, the church of "holy poverty." In Minneapolis, toward 1888, the young preacher Frederick T. Gates had met with much success in raising huge sums of money among certain flour magnates for churches and universities. At a meeting with Rockefeller, Gates's mixture of fanatical zeal and business sense had cast its spell over the oil baron, who at this time was beginning to suffer the embarrassment of his grotesque wealth: his earnings could scarcely be spent or even reinvested adequately, and at the same time they brought upon him the universal reproaches, the ignominy of a long succession of public trials, castigations and prosecution. Now Gates showed himself a counselor able to guide Rockefeller both in this world and the next; as his confidential business agent he negotiated for him several remarkable transactions, such as the purchase of the limitless iron ore fields of the Merritt brothers ("the seven iron men") in Minnesota, which were bought during an emergency for a bagatelle; at the same time Gates, as the mentor of Rockefeller's soul, directed his prodigious investments in public charities which, begun in 1890, were conducted upon a scale befitting the man's princely power, and most certainly fitted him to scale Heaven's walls. For the support of the college in Chicago, which had been languishing since 1856, Rockefeller was induced to subscribe $600,000 alone, on condition that the pork-packers and dry-goods merchants of the Western metropolis contribute together an equal sum.[1]

At the time of Rockefeller's fabulous gift, a convention of the American Baptist Educational Society was being held in Boston. Henry D. Lloyd, watching these events with the eye of a profound skeptic, recalls the wild thrill of joy which swept over all Baptist Christendom. There was a "perfect bedlam of applause, shouts and waving of handkerchiefs. One of the godly men present sprang to his feet exclaiming, 'God has kept Chicago for us! I wonder at His patience!' " The audience rose spontaneously and sang the Doxology. And soon afterward everywhere from the pulpit and the religious press it was said or written: "The oil trust was begun and carried on by Christian men. They were Baptists. . . . " The president of the oil combination was worth twenty-five millions, "but he neither drinks nor smokes tobacco. . . . Few men lead plainer lives than he. . . ." Moreover the "four most prominent men in the oil trust are eminent Baptists, who honor their religious obligations and contribute without stint to the noblest Christian and philanthropic objects. . . . All of them illustrate in their daily lives their reverence for living Christianity." The monarch of oil had won ardent defenders at a time when they were sorely needed. "People charge Mr. Rockefeller with stealing the money he gave to the church," said the pastor of the Euclid Avenue Baptist Church,

[1] To Thorstein Veblen, writing "The Theory of the Leisure Class" during the years of McKinley and Hanna, such an action as Rockefeller's, such "conspicuous consumption" was unconsciously intended to call attention to his "successful predatory aggressions or warlike exploits." The distribution of immense charities, no less than sumptuary extravagance showed "ability to sustain large pecuniary damage without impairing his superior opulence." At the same time, in a most direct manner, the school and the Church were naturally passing under the sway of Rockefeller, Morgan, Hill and the others who had newly conquered the social system. The agreements in force were not evinced by direct pledges or legal contracts, but were tacit and maintained with a sensitive indirection.

Cleveland, "but he has laid it on the altar and thus sanctified it." These words fell like music upon the ears of the harried John Rockefeller. He was convinced that he had taken the right course; this cautious, calculating man began to give with a generosity the world had never seen before to all the religious and missionary and educational institutions which caught his eye. The excited pastors now swarmed about, hat in hand, emulating Frederick Gates. Clergymen of other sects raced to surpass the Baptists; one such of a competing denomination approached one of the Baptist chieftains of the Standard Oil with a call for a subscription.

"But I am not of your church," said the great man.

"That does not matter," said the minister; "*your money is orthodox.*"

The religious institutions, especially the evangelistic churches and foundations centered in the large American cities, now by dint of "revivals" or "drives" accumulated extensive reservoirs of money running in some instances to between ten and fifteen millions. Their directors, men of the stamp of the Reverend Dr. Frederick Gates, became great investment bankers in their own right, buying and selling securities, lands, properties. The "consumption of devout observances," an industry which had been lagging, was now visibly revived in America. Filled with gratitude, the soldiers of the Church needed no direct marching orders from their chief benefactors, the captains of industry. In their thousandfold activities throughout the world, as missionaries, as therapeutic agents, as healers of the sick and the poor, they contributed to the defense of the established order. To the "heathen Chinee" they brought the Western way of life, with its cotton breeches and kerosene oil; in the slums of the cities they sought to "save the souls" of the strayed, and return them to sober and diligent toil.

But one of the most favored departments of all this labor of conservation was to be the establishment of the Young Men's Christian Association, first sponsored by that great layman John Wanamaker. Here (as in the universities) a popularization of salutary physical sports was rapidly furthered, sports in which Veblen has seen embodied those traits of force and ruse which were most pleasing to the new barons. Thus the aggressive Harriman, founder of the Boys'

Club in New York's East Side, could be found at regular intervals directing the young, chiefly in the "manly art" of boxing.

In the universities and colleges, the older of which originally had mainly been theological seminaries, the spirit of conservatism had been notably strong; the trustees who endowed or directed the universities were of course, from the beginning, the most opulent and also the most "respectable" members of the community. Now as the overlords of beef, department stores, banks and especially of railroads began to assume leadership in educational affairs—though almost none of them, except Pierpont Morgan, ever boasted a university education—a revolution in policy was effected which is generally pictured as the triumph of technology and applied science over the classical humanities. Willingly, the Armours, McCormicks, Pullmans and many other industrialists gave their moneys to the establishment of the new "institutes of technology" or to scientific schools and various polytechnic institutes which augmented year by year the economic resources of the nation. Although much could be said under this head upon the social usefulness of this policy, here it is more pertinent to trace the increasing sphere of influence of the barons.

In the world of learning, the janissaries of oil or lard potentates, with a proper sense of taste and fitness, sought consistently to sustain the social structure, to resist change, to combat all current notions which might thereafter "reduce society to chaos" or "confound the order of nature." As a class, they shared with their patrons the belief that there was more to lose than to gain by drastic alterations of the existing institutions, and that it was wisest to "let well enough alone." While ministers of the Baptist Church defended the Trusts as "sound Christian institutions" against "all these communistic attacks," the managers of Rockefeller's Chicago University also championed the combinations year by year. One professor of economics, Dr. Gunton, especially distinguished himself on this score; and another, a teacher of literature ostensibly, declared Mr. Rockefeller and Mr. Pullman "superior in creative genius to Shakespeare, Homer and Dante," a declaration which made a lively impression at the time. In the meanwhile, a third teacher, a Professor Bemis, who happened to criticize the action of the railroads during the Pullman strike in 1894 was after several warnings expelled from the university for "incompetence."

At Syracuse University in western New York, to mention only one instance, a gifted young instructor in economics, John Commons, was similarly dismissed by the Chancellor. His strongest interests were discovered to lie in the rising labor movement, and the university, endowed by Mr. John Archbold of the Standard Oil Family, frowned upon such learning. Here the students sang, according to John T. Flynn:

We have a Standard Oil pipe running up to John Crouse hall,
And a gusher in the stadium will be flowing full next fall.
We need the money, Mr. Archbold,
We need it right away.

And in Chicago, upon news of further gifts of three millions they sang:

John D. Rockefeller
Wonderful man is he.
Gives all his spare change
To the U. of C.
He keeps the ball a-rolling
In our great varsity.

But in his philanthropies, Rockefeller gave money in many ways strange and wonderful, often known only to himself. Some of the largest of his bequests to "sociological foundations" in later years, it was noted, were directed to the mitigation of "crimes against property." At times it was difficult to understand the guiding principle which fostered extensive missionary work in China at a moment when the workers of his Colorado Fuel & Iron Company were being shot down or burnt alive in industrial war. But in such cases, especially among the great Protestant donors, the distributions were made with that full "liberty of conscience" which had been used in the process of accumulation. Rockefeller himself once stated with complete candor:

I believe the power to make money is a gift of God . . . to be developed and used to the best of our ability for the good of mankind. Having been endowed with the gift I possess, I believe it is my duty to make money and still more money, and to use the money I make for the good of my fellow man according to the dictates of my conscience.

All accounts speak to us of the new "gold rush" of the '80's and
'90's, in which the men and women who had gathered incalculable
wealth from the mines of California, the forges of Pittsburgh, the
mountains of Montana, moved upon the old cities of the East as a
conquering army which laid siege to its most inaccessible social fastnesses. "With no qualifications other than the fortunes they had
obtained," as a society matron commented invidiously, but better
armed and provisioned than ever any besieging force had been, the
New Rich now marched upon the "social capitals" of the nation.
From the West and from the South and from everywhere, the "sil-
ver-gilts," the "climbers," the nouveaux riches, came to assault the
citadels of society, and were soon thronging the heights so carefully
guarded. This latter-day invasion is described with tremulous emotion in the memoirs of a woman of the New York aristocracy, Mrs.
J. Van Rensselaer King:

> The West was yielding tremendous riches. . . . Steel barons, coal
> lords, dukes of wheat and beet, of mines and railways, had sprung
> up from obscurity. Absolute in their territory, they looked for new
> worlds to conquer. The newspaper accounts of New York society
> thrilled the newly rich. In a great glittering caravan the multimil-
> lionaires of the midlands moved up against the city and by sheer
> weight of numbers broke through the archaic barriers.

Why did they come to the East as in a returning wave? Why
did the barons, fortunate in their own baronies, and the wives of
the barons clamor for the "social capitals," for the "more advanced
civilization of the East," for New York, and her near-by summering
or watering places such as Newport, or the "far-famed spa" of Saratoga? After the unremitting labor and vigilance of their own or
their parents' lives, after the prosaic, flat surroundings of home, as
Clews tells us, they came to take their ease, to live if possible a regal
and courtly life, replete with delicate luxuries and extravagances
and charmingly artificial or archaic customs. New York, Saratoga,
Newport or Long Branch opened for the first time unknown vistas
to these minen and railroad-owners' families. They were thrilled
with the "rustle and perfume, the glitter and show, the pomp and

circumstance," of a world of costly refinement. Everywhere they beheld splendid mansions, great emporiums of dry goods and fancy articles of all sorts, jewels and plate and flowers and embroidery. Soon they must discard their two-button gloves, their ginghams and calicos, as they did the airs of the provincial midlands, donning the French silks, the genuine laces, the arm-length gloves as well as the regards and poses of their Eastern sisters. And above all New York, drawing them as a great magnet, soon formed their spirit, as Henry Clews relates,

> by its restless activity, its feverish enterprise and opportunities . . . but more particularly by its imperial wealth, its Parisian, indeed almost Sybaritic luxury and social splendor . . . the roll of splendid equipages in the "Bois de Boulogne of America," the Central Park; the constant round of brilliant banquets, afternoon teas and receptions . . . beautiful women and brave men threading the mazes of the dance; scenes of revelry by night in an atmosphere loaded with the perfumes of rare exotics, in the swell of sensuous music. . . . Soon nothing remains for the wives of the Western millionaires but to purchase a brownstone mansion, and swing into the tide of fashion with receptions, balls and kettledrums, elegant equipages with coachmen in bright-buttoned livery, footmen in top-boots, maid-servants and man-servants, including a butler, and all the other adjuncts of fashionable life in a great metropolis.

Here they might stay and equal or surpass the foremost of the predecessor aristocrats in "conspicuous waste," demonstrating to all those who did not know them in person the enormous wealth possessed in their own right, the ability to pay, the ability to "sustain large pecuniary damage" without discomfiture.

What is "society," the final charmed circle of the "polite world" or "court," if not a survival of a feudal institution? In ancient times the bravest and most faithful of a ruling prince's vassals lived with him in his castle to defend him with their arms and to serve him with their hands. Later, in the age of the Renaissance, at the palace of the Italian or French prince the functions of the courtiers were but relics of those necessary rôles they filled in earlier centuries. Instead, elegance, wit, fashion flourished in the salon of the all-powerful monarch, and set the tone for the superior caste, the "aristocracy" of the society at large. A Louis XIV at Versailles was preëminent in courtly manners; but under his dullard heirs the charm of the court faded swiftly, and the "tone" was set for society in the brilliant salons of Paris by the great landowners, the receivers-general, the holders of royal and monopolistic business concessions. . . .

So Washington's failure to become the court or social capital for America toward the end of the nineteenth century was symptomatic of the profound shift of power from the political leader to the industrial chieftain. Almost never elegant or aristocratic before the Civil War, society at the political capital was found even more disappointing after the war by visiting foreigners. They mourned the absence of theaters and opera, and remarked at presidential receptions not only their lamentable informality, but their real crudeness. Even in the years of Grant, an Englishman describing a "crush" at the White House complains of the manner in which the hundreds of guests maul and shove each other to consume "six dozen chickens," and "green seal whiskey by the gallon and dozens of gallons."

But then there had been no veritable *monde* in the young republic, whose traditional splendor and authority outshone the rest. For all that was said, the world of Boston and Philadelphia and New York merchants or landowners had represented only a staid, provincial society. New York and its old Dutch "Knickerbockers" had been given to pretensions of "exclusiveness, refinement, courtesy and public dignity." Yet its social life was as ingenuous as that of the other cities before 1870; the gatherings for picnics and rustic festivals were as much a characteristic form of entertainment as the gatherings in parlors.

But the strategic economic advantage of the Erie Canal, as it had made New York the largest commercial center, had made it eventually the social metropolis of the nation. Among its "old families," the descendants of butchers, fur-dealers and land-jobbers, who possessed no aristocratic tradition of social customs and intercourse with each other, the dominant pecuniary standard had finally established its own mold; nowadays their wives confronted each other wearing diamond tiaras, "dog-collars" and "sunbursts," and the waltz (earlier considered "indecent") had become the mode even in the stuffy circles of the Knickerbockers toward 1876. And finally after strenuous competition Mrs. William B. Astor, "gifted with

marvelous social talent," as Ward McAllister said, had "by the ac-
clamation of society itself" risen above her competitors to the position of queen at a "supreme court of social appeals" and polite
fashion.

Always a "silent power," recognized even by the "solid, old quiet
element," McAllister relates, possessing good judgment and great
administrative capacity for her rôle, Mrs. Astor had sought to unify
society, to blend together the "solid respectable element of the community," so as to prevent anybody else from forming a dictatorship
over social events. In this work, Mr. Ward McAllister, a dandy of
mellowest Southern and Yankee race, had become grand-vizier and
arbiter elegantiarum, ruling on precedence, limiting the number of
guests or players in the aristocratic stage to "Four Hundred," a
mystical and significant number fixed at the famous Centennial ball
of 1876. Society in New York became concentrated and centralized
like the railroads or the slaughterhouse system; and New York's
social court overshadowed all others. "Not to have received an invitation to an Astor ball; not to have dined at Mrs. Astor's," as the
minister of a fashionable church reported, was in the polite world
equal to a sentence of banishment for life.

"We wanted the money power," Ward McAllister, inventor of
the Four Hundred relates; then adds wistfully, "but not to be
controlled by it." The terms of admission were not exacting. For
how could they be, in a nation of roturiers? A Jay Gould, widely
feared, might be excluded from a fashionable yacht club, but his
son George was easily admitted. The profane and scornful old parvenu Cornelius *Van der Bilt* was unthinkable in a parlor; but his
grandson William K. *Vanderbilt* would see all doors open to him
in time.

It was not hard to make up the roll of the "400"—actually six
hundred by most accounts—who were to be *en évidence* the whole
year round, until, as Mrs. John Drexel said, "we society women
simply drop down in harness." There were few pork-packers' or
ironmongers' wives who could not, after employing a suitable
genealogist, prove connection with King John or King William
the Conqueror, or at least one of the early Huguenots, or "First
Families of Virginia." "Four generations of gentlemen" were declared adequate by New York's Autocrat of Drawing Rooms, Mc-
Allister. And in some meritorious cases the process was visibly

hastened; for the gold standard and pecuniary tastes of the time were imposing themselves with implacable force everywhere. Once somewhat circumspect in their manner, the leaders of the mercenary society now gave themselves over to a frenzied race of display and consumption; so that, as the irrepressible dandy McAllister said: "A fortune of a million was now nothing. One needed a fortune of ten, fifty, one hundred millions to be counted rich."

Franklin's apophthegm, "Time is money," was nowadays applied in a thousand ways not only by the millionaire materialists, but by their votaries and retainers. In the press a man's income at various stages of his life would be reckoned by the month, day and hour— "in the impressive method of calculating revenues which has of late come so much in vogue," as Croffut writes in 1885. Thus of a certain railroad president it would be said that in his youth he earned "$12,000 a year, or $1,000 a month, or $34 a day, or $1.42 an hour" counting the hours during which he slept! And with a further effect of literary conceit these precise numerical valuations were used as the most effective adjectives by which bridges, houses, dogs, parties, yachts, horses might be qualified and described. We are told now that Mr. Gould's "$500,000 yacht" has entered a certain harbor, or that Mr. Morgan has set off upon a journey in his "$100,000 palace car," or that Mr. Vanderbilt's "$2,000,000 home" is nearing completion, with its "$50,000 paintings" and its "$20,000 bronze doors."

Mr. W. H. Vanderbilt's palace and the adjoining one of his daughter on Fifth Avenue, extending the full block from Fifty-first to Fifty-second Street, like the mansions of the Astors was the visible trophy, the monument of a triumphant dynasty. Constructed in the style known as "Greek Renaissance," the building of the William H. Vanderbilts' home was prolonged for nearly two years before the eyes of the wondering New Yorkers. It would have taken longer; but with a premonition of approaching death Vanderbilt ordered that native brownstone be used instead of imported marble. And so it had been completed, and furnished with Italian tapestries, marble balustrades, Japanese lanterns, medieval armor, and bric-a-brac and art treasures to suit every fancy, in time for his declining years. After 1880 the two great houses, and the French château of William Kissam Vanderbilt close by, filled the surrounding streets of the city with their brilliant illumination; they gave warning that the owners of two hundred millions would soon make a drive toward "the top of the social heap." Yesterday, the peasantlike William Vanderbilt had been haggling with his father over the price of scows of dung from the Vanderbilt horsecar stables; today his son's wife prepared festivals which were to "surpass in splendor, in beauty . . . in luxurious and lavish expense any scenes before witnessed in the New World."

The preparations for Mrs. William K. Vanderbilt's fancy-dress ball of March 26, 1883, had been so stunning, so formidable that the highest circles of the "solid old" society were filled with alarm. For many weeks, histories, novels and illustrated books had been ransacked for authentic details, while costumers and milliners in the larger Eastern cities toiled away at their tasks.

Up to this moment, we must recall, Mrs. William Astor had never called upon any of the Vanderbilts, and none of the Astors were invited to the coming ball. The court of society's queen was therefore convulsed in a great social crisis. No one knew what should be done. Then at last, the queen saw that there was no escape from the dilemma. Amid a general sensation throughout the plutocratic world, as the historians of the affair report, "Mrs. Astor unbent her stateliness," went to call upon Mrs. Vanderbilt, "and in a very ladylike manner made the *amende honorable!*"

The fancy-dress ball of 1883 signalizes a historic peace and "combination" between the Astors and Vanderbilts. For this memorable evening, fulsomely described in the press of two continents, Mrs. William K. Vanderbilt was costumed as a Venetian princess, Mr. Cornelius Vanderbilt as Louis XVI, and his spouse as "The Electric Light," in white satin trimmed with diamonds, and with a superb diamond headdress. In the drawing-rooms of the Vanderbilt palace, with its cluttered interiors in Japanese or in French style, hung with flowing masses of pale red velvet, drapery which was embroidered with foliage and jeweled butterflies, the noble throng ate, drank, and danced through the night. For the six quadrilles which represented the high moments of the ball, the dancers formed in the gymnasium on the third floor, moved down the grand staircase of Caën stone (fifty feet high), and swept through the great hall (sixty-five by twenty feet) into a drawing-room (forty by twenty feet whose whole wainscoting of carved French walnut had been torn from a French château and hauled across the ocean. A memorable evening which, as it broke the last barriers between the Astors and Vanderbilts, also broke all bounds for "conspicuous consumption."

3

In New York, "nature's noblemen" all joined in the frenzied contest of display and consumption. Mansions and châteaux of French, Gothic, Italian, barocco and Oriental style lined both sides of upper Fifth Avenue, while shingle and jigsaw villas of huge dimensions rose above the harbor of Newport. Railroad barons and mine-owners and oil magnates vied with each other in making town houses and country villas which were imitations of everything under the sun, and were filled with what-nots, old drapery, old armor, old Tudor chests and chairs, statuettes, bronzes, shells and porcelains. One would have a bedstead of carved oak and ebony, inlaid with gold, costing $200,000. Another would decorate his walls with enamel and gold at a cost of $65,000. And nearly all ransacked the art treasures of Europe, stripped medieval castles of their carvings and tapestries, ripped whole staircases and ceilings from their place of repose through the centuries to lay them anew amid settings of a synthetic age and a simulated feudal grandeur. Such demands made the fortune of decorators, furniture-dealers and art-dealers, who sold trainloads of second-hand furniture and shiploads of "old" paintings.

George Gould, the son of Jay (who had successfully eluded imprisonment in days gone by), was another of those who slept in a bed priced at $25,000. In the country, outside of New York, he had built himself amid sunken Italian gardens and fountains a villa called Georgian Court, the main section of which was 250 feet long, ornate with marble staircases and columns, vast mural paintings, glittering chandeliers, and Louis XIV furniture.

A Mr. Darius Ogden Mills, former storekeeper and mine-owner, arrived in New York one day with his gold from the Sierras, and paid the highest price ever paid for land in New York, at Fifth Avenue opposite St. Patrick's Cathedral.

After purchasing it [Clews relates] Mr. Mills gave carte blanche orders to a noted decorator of New York and during a trip to Cali-

fornia the work of decoration was done. On his return he at once took possession of a mansion of which a Shah of Persia might have been proud. He was delighted with all that had been wrought ... the richly carved woodwork, the gorgeously picturesque ceilings, the inlaid walls and floors and the tout ensemble of Oriental magnificence. His contentment was complete. But a surprise awaited him. It was the decorator's bill for $400,000. This, it is said, slightly disturbed his serenity. It caused him to look with a critical eye on the splendid decorations which constituted a study of the fine arts at such high rates of tuition.

But Mr. Mills, who at least lived and flourished in his new home, was more fortunate than his saturnine fellow Californian, Collis Huntington. In New York, the master of the Southern Pacific system built, at an expense of two millions, the impressive grey stone pile which stood long at Fifty-seventh and Fifth, a monument to the new feudalism and the great baronage. "But after it was completed he could never be persuaded to live in it," Gustavus Myers relates. "His reason was a belief in the superstition that men build houses only to die in them." (This had been the fate of William H. Vanderbilt a few years earlier.)

The newcomers, arriving in New York, one by one fell under the spell of the marble grandeur they saw. Riding in Fifth Avenue in 1880 with his young friend Andrew Mellon, the coke master, Henry Frick, pointed out one of the best residences of the city (that of a Vanderbilt), and mused: "I wonder what the upkeep of the one on that corner would be ..." Three hundred thousand dollars a year? It was all he had ever hoped to possess. Yet the nouveau-riche Frick was already accustomed only to having "always the best," his biographer tells us. The day came when the home of George Vanderbilt slipped from his hands to those of the Pittsburgh millionaire.[2]

Yet it was not enough for the barons to reside in marble halls

[2]After each boom, in a wave of money madness new peers arose who sought to outdo their predecessors. They cruised in glittering trains, they ordered a dozen portraits of themselves painted at once. One, a young banker, Otto Kahn, was reported to have established his home in Long Island under extraordinary circumstances. Finding the landscape flat, he had hundreds of tons of stone and sand hauled by train to make a hill or artificial bluff, from which his country house might have a vista over the sea!

of a splendor suitable to their station. In such surroundings it was requisite to consume in a manner that Lucullus would have understood and approved. Of themselves the Vanderbilts, Mills, Mackays and Goulds could have despatched but small quantities of edibles, beverages, tobaccos and perfumes and favors. It was requisite that they call in whole companies of servants to man their houses and aid in the general consumption of superfluities. And as the problem of expenditure of so much quickly gotten wealth pressed upon them, new ways of consumption must be devised from season to season; a never-ending game of invention and excitement must be pursued in which the aid of great crowds of one's friends and competitors and their wives must be invoked as witnesses and participants in the ceremonials. These might behold how the man of force and ruse had become finally, as Veblen terms it, a discriminating connoisseur "in creditable viands . . . manly beverages, and trinkets, in seemly apparel and architecture, in weapons, games, dances and narcotics." To bring them together it was necessary to resort to the giving of rich presents, high banquets and prolonged entertainments. Thus there arose the unique sumptuary organization of the American multimillionaire home, where stupendous feats of prodigality were carried off with the utmost case and dash. The home of a Mr. D. O. Mills, for instance, was directed by his commissaries like a vast hotel. At an hour's notice his retainers were ready to serve one hundred guests for lunch or dinner.

The number of servants, of course, was the most direct measure of the refinement and superfluity of one's art of life. McAllister, the Reverend Dr. Nichols and other social arbiters show us that in the mansion of the genteel captain of industry there must be five or six servants to receive you, as well as a butler. The butler and three servants in livery served the dinner. Orchids, "being the most costly of flowers, were introduced in profusion." To serve a cup of tea two servants were necessary. A stable of from six to ten horses was considered proper for a variety of carriages, ranging from the opera bus and the four-in-hand to the one-horse cabriolet and the basket phaëton for young ladies.[3]

---

[3]It was a legend that one financier of persistently humble tastes who loved horses had pictures placed in his stables, and in general had them so handsomely decorated that he really preferred to spend most of his time there alone among his animals.

During Dinner, McAllister says:

Soft strains of music were introduced between the courses, and in some houses gold replaced silver plate and everything that skill and art could suggest was added to make the dinners not a vulgar display but a great gastronomic effort, evidencing the possession by the host of both money and taste.

The truth is that once arrived in the metropolis of fastidious luxury, installed at last in the palace of Dives, the nobility of American business seemed bored, bewildered, lost. The excitement of empire building and destroying had gripped them like a powerful drug, so long as it had lasted; but it had not prepared them in any sense for an art of leisure, or for cultivated intercourse with each other, such as was practiced successfully in the courts of sixteenth-century Italy or the salons of eighteenth-century France. Few of them knew how to talk, or knew what to do with themselves. Perhaps one or two individuals in all the crowd, a Henry Villard or a William C. Whitney, possessed education or were innately cultured.

Whitney, a young lawyer-politician who had married the daughter of a Standard Oil magnate, had known surpassing triumphs both in politics, as Secretary of the Navy to Cleveland, and in high finance as a member of the Yerkes-Ryan-Widener traction ring. His great palace on Fifth Avenue at Fifty-seventh Street was immediately one of the landmarks of New York, and his fantastically lavish entertainments were the private sensation of the Four Hundred, to which he had been admitted at once by grace of his old Yankee pedigree. Tall, slender, distinguished-looking, magnetic in his talk as he was mysterious in his financial operations, Whitney, as Henry Adams recollects, "after having gratified every ambition and swung the country almost at his will . . . had thrown away the usual objects of political ambition like the ashes of smoked cigarettes; had turned to other amusements, satiated every taste, gorged every appetite, won every object that New York afforded, and not yet satisfied, had carried his field of activity abroad, until New York no longer knew what most to envy, his horses or his houses. . . ." Adams held Whitney to have been one of the few educated men of his own generation who had gained a signal social success. The day came when, after long-repeated trials, he had won the English Derby, to cap all his triumphs. There was then truly nothing left to live for.

But against the instance of Whitney or the diverting H. H. Rogers, who was the friend of Mark Twain, the masters of money and industry such as Morgan, Vanderbilt, Harriman, Stillman, William Rockefeller, were all of them typically "great silent men" with little enough to say in polite conversation, save on the score of their business operations. James Stillman, the narrow-eyed "sphinx" of the banking world, rigid in manner, and wearing always the "cold smile of a Japanese statesman," confessed in his last years, when he had gone into retirement, that he knew not how to enjoy himself. *"I have never in all my life done anything I wanted,"* he said, *"and cannot now."* Stillman relates that his friend William Rockefeller, who was almost as rich as John, would sit in perfect silence at home with him, for fifteen minutes on end, and assured the banker that he loved him because he did not have to speak to him at all. Harriman too wore a mask of silence perpetually. One night he asked Stillman to leave the opera with him between the acts and return to his "den." Stillman thought that Harriman was going to unfold some great affair to him. But the railroad nabob merely sat smoking silently for long minutes. Fatigued, evidently craving company or consolation of some sort, he nevertheless had nothing to say, and his colleague parted from him with scarcely a word. But the most laconic of all these men was J. P. Morgan, who carried his manner to a systematic rudeness.

There were subjects of course upon which they could talk freely either in private or in general society. Carnegie playing golf with the publisher of books, Frank Doubleday, asked him: "How much did you make last month, Frank?" It was impossible to tell but once a year, the publisher replied. "I'd get out of it!" said Carnegie firmly. The immortal donor of free libraries who was the most articulate of the industrialists had no further thoughts upon the making of books than the cash profit to be derived from them.

These men were scarcely fit to bring up their own children. They, who expended all their energy in the exploiting of a railroad system, of machinery, of a power plant for the new continent, had "had no time for thought," as Henry Adams said. Henry Lloyd recalls having heard one of the greatest business geniuses of the country say to his son: "I will be perfectly satisfied with you if you will only always go to bed at night worth more than when you got up this morning." Yet unlike Roman fathers they reared their sons in most cases as indolent princelings. Jay Gould, for instance, brought up his eldest son George "in the lap of luxury," as befitted the heir of a railroad and telegraph monarch; in a manner which caused even the denizens of Wall Street to raise their eyebrows. . . .

The lives of the colossally rich were generally "no more worth living than those of their cooks," said Henry Adams, who respected both money and social position. His friend Cabot Lodge, the scion of New England "Brahmins," professed himself shocked by the emptiness and the vulgarity of the talk he heard everywhere in society. It was no longer taboo to speak of one's own money or one's neighbors', of the cost of Mrs. Belmont's "rope of pearls" or Mrs. Drexel's "Sunburst" or Mr. Morgan's notorious Raphael—was it genuine?—or Mr. So-and-So's disease. Even the beauty of land and sea, as at a Florida beach, or the thought of unprospected Heaven itself, as Frederick Townsend Martin tells us in his "Passing of the Idle Rich," brought up suggestions of railway projects still to be carried out! Theodore Roosevelt, a vivacious and imaginative descendant of New York Knickerbockers, admitted to feelings of intense boredom in the presence of the giants of trade:

I am simply unable to make myself take the attitude of respect toward the very wealthy men which such an enormous multitude of people evidently really feel. I am delighted to show any courtesy to Pierpont Morgan or Andrew Carnegie or James J. Hill, but as for regarding any one of them as, for instance, I regard Prof. Bury, or Peary, the Arctic explorer, or Rhodes, the historian—why, I could not force myself to do it even if I wanted to, which I don't.

But Charles Francis Adams, the brother of the brooding philosopher and dandy Henry, who had struck out for a railroad career long ago, speaks even more bitterly. Swallowing his compunctions he had proceeded to make and lose much money for twenty-five years. Better than Theodore Roosevelt he had known Jay Gould, Russell Sage, Sidney Dillon, Tom Scott, Pierpont Morgan and James Hill, as friends and enemies; and in his autobiography he speaks of them in retrospect with remarkable forthrightness:

Indeed, as I approach the end, I am more than a little puzzled to account for the instances I have seen of business success—money-getting. It comes from rather a low instinct. Certainly so far as my observation goes, it is scarcely met with in combination with the finer or more interesting traits of character. I have known and known tolerably well, a great many "successful" men—"big" financially—men famous during the last half century, and a less interesting crowd I do not care to encounter. Not one that I have ever known would I care to meet again either in this world or the next; nor is one associated in my mind with the idea of humor, thought or refinement. A set of mere money-getters and traders, they were essentially unattractive. The fact is that money-getting like everything else calls for a special aptitude and great concentration, and for it I did not have the first in any marked degree, while to it I never gave the last. So, in now summing up, I may account myself fortunate in having got out of my ventures as well as I did.

Limited in their capacity of enjoyment and bored, yet prompted to outdo each other in prodigality, the New Rich experimented with ever new patterns or devices of consumption. In the late '70's, the practice of hiring hotel rooms or public restaurants for social functions had become fashionable. At Delmonico's the Silver, Gold and Diamond dinners of the socially prominent succeeded each other unfailingly. At one, each lady present, opening her napkin, found a gold bracelet with the monogram of the host. At another, cigarettes rolled in hundred-dollar-bills were passed around after the coffee and consumed with an authentic thrill. . . . One man gave a dinner to his dog, and presented him with a diamond collar worth $15,000. At another dinner, costing $20,000, each guest discovered in one of his oysters a magnificent black pearl. Another distracted individual longing for diversion had little holes bored into his teeth, into which a tooth expert inserted twin rows of diamonds; when he walked abroad his smile flashed and sparkled in the sunlight. . . .

As the years pass new heights of fantasy and extravagance are touched. One season, it is a ball on horseback which is the chief sensation. To a great hotel the guests all come in riding habit; each of the handsomely groomed horses, equipped with rubber-padded

shoes, prances about bearing besides its millionaire rider a minia-
ture table holding truffles and champagne. Finally a costume ball
given by Bradley Martin, a New York aristocrat, in 1897, reached
the very climax of lavish expenditure and "dazed the entire Western
world." "The interior of the Waldorf-Astoria Hotel was transformed into a replica of Versailles, and rare tapestries, beautiful
flowers and countless lights made an effective background for the
wonderful gowns and their wearers. . . ." One lady, impersonat-
ing Mary Stuart, wore a gold-embroidered gown, trimmed with
pearls and precious stones. "The suit of gold inlaid armor worn by
Mr. Belmont was valued at ten thousand dollars." The affair, reported in the new "yellow" press of Pulitzer and Hearst, caused a
general storm among the citizens of New York, and its sponsors
felt obliged to take sudden refuge in England.

The press now followed the festivals of the "plutocrats" with a
persistent fascination as rumors of shadier ceremonies were spread
about, at which shapely theater queens burst forth from pies carried
to the table upon the shoulders of servants; or, clad only in spangles
and scales, swam in a huge glass tank of elaborate construction.

But in the search for novelty the holiday-makers ended by arriving at effects of allegory more significant still, which dramatized
their own humble beginnings. Thus a coal baron would hold a great
party one day in a simulated coal mine. Or a gold king would alter
his banquet hall to resemble the interior of a gold mine. Food was
brought by waiters clad like miners, picks and shovels decorated all
the walls.

Finally, against the outcries of moral blue-noses in times of hardship, the modern Sybarites declared that their carnivals were designed to create employment, and that the proceeds were to be devoted to charities. Such a view was plausible enough. In a sense the
pressure upon the New Rich to gormandizing and jollification but
reflected the need for "draining away" the surplus wealth which
was concentrated in their hands by the existing system of industrial
organization. Thus in later years the "Poverty Social" came strongly
into vogue. At one such reunion held at the home of a Western millionaire, the thirty guests came attired in rags and tatters. At a cost
of $14,000, as F. T. Martin relates,

scraps of food were served on wooden plates. The diners sat about on broken soap boxes, buckets and coalhods. Newspapers, dust cloths and old skirts were used as napkins, and beer served in a rusty tin can . . . !

The organization of "conspicuous waste" by the owners of masses of money may be said in fact to have had a clear economic justification. Yet to effect a redistribution of wealth in this fashion was a stupendous and well-nigh impossible task which was never to be completed.

4

One of the most prominent forms of consumption resorted to in time came to be the "grand tour" of Europe, which in itself gave birth to many further mediums of consumption. It was the American woman of the '80's and '90's, and not the often dour, brusque, fatigued captain of industry, who stormed the fastnesses of culture beyond the sea. It was the wife and daughter of the lord of bathtubs or sausages who went rushing about the palaces and museums of the mother continent, while the industrialist himself, "bored, patient, helpless," pathetically dependent upon his women, as Henry James and Henry Adams have pictured him, wondered "what all these things must have cost" a Lucullus or a Francis I.

In the grand tour, the women promptly absorbed antiquity and culture with highest speed; they imported European tutors, dancing masters and painters who flattered them. They ended by importing the last, lingering descendants of Europe's noblest houses, and so mingling their plain American blood with the blue blood of Italian, Hungarian and Balkan princes, not to speak of English peers. Out of the grand tours came the famous transatlantic marriages which made such sensation in the era after the Civil War. The high point in this wave of international weddings was the union of Mrs. William K. Vanderbilt's daughter Consuelo with the Duke of Marlborough in 1895, whereby Blenheim House with its two hundred servants became one of the "frozen assets" of the New York Central. By 1909, Gustavus Myers calculates that more than 500 American women had married titled foreigners, and that the draining away of surplus of some $220,000,000 became possible as a consequence.

It is perhaps a significant coincidence that during the heyday of the international marriage, the leisure activities of the American baronial cast—more closely affiliated with the leisure class of Europe—now reached a higher stage of perfection. Hitherto the new multimillionaires had known the pressing need of covering broad wall spaces or vast floors, and had purchased at reasonable cost Europe or even native oil-paintings by the yard. Sir Joseph Duveen, for instance, who was formerly a dealer in second-hand furniture and objets d'art, had been wont to send down from New York truckloads of Louis XV chairs, Reniassance chests, Houdon busts, Oriental rugs and European tapestries for the home for the street-car magnate, Peter Widener, in Philadelphia. Long ago, the clamor for antiques, for "old things," for all sorts of broken-down furniture, murky paintings and worm-eaten volumes, had arisen from the quickly enriched, who thereby simulated a long-existent status of apparently hoary old age. Yet necessary though these decrepid articles might be, almost as necessary as the coat-of-arms or heraldic bearings which were everywhere produced for the families of industrial barons, they would long have balked at paying a king's ransom for worn pieces of painting or sculpture by Old Masters which were no larger nor heavier than similar products freely offered in commerce. But at length the suggestions of noble kin may have introduced an element of refinement and self-consciousness to the fashions in decoration; while the unremittingly emulative race may have further spurred the Americans to new efforts

Soon each owner of a trunk line or chain of coal mines must have his private art collection and his art gallery attached to his home. Like the successful military chieftains of old times, whose progeny were being united to their own in these days, the captains of industry began to fill their own castles with the loot and plunder of the ages; the paintings, the tapestry, the china, the ancient illuminated manuscripts began to flow as in a torrent to the western shores of the Atlantic as William Vanderbilt, Pierpont Morgan, Henry Frick, Whitney, Stillman, Havemeyer, Widener and many others began to bid against each other. The physical seizure of the "spoils" of civilization, as Henry James called them—trophies, as Veblen, his contemporary, said—assumed proportions both huge and grotesque.

One of the first in the race for accumulation of paintings toward 1870 had been William H. Vanderbilt, the sluggish, unhappy and fabulously wealthy heir of Cornelius. His apologists assure us of the sound taste and judgment with which Vanderbilt the Younger bought paintings and equipped his art gallery. He insisted, Croffut tells us, that he would not buy pictures against his will. "He liked pictures," as Croffut relates, "which told a story, with either strong or cheerful subjects." "Other things might be very fine," he would say, "but until I can appreciate its beauty I shall not buy it."

Undoubtedly the pictures and the business of gathering them in amused and distracted the hard-driven capitalist. He would stare at them for long hours in solitude. There is an infantile pleasure always to be derived from the play of story and color in paintings of a certain type, such as Vanderbilt usually purchased. These, according to a critic in the *Nineteenth Century Magazine* for October, 1898, were by Millet, Detaille, Meissonier, Rosa Bonheur, Bouguereau, Jules Breton, Daubigny, Fromentin and others of their caliber—all military and battle scenes and rustic subjects. There were also besides the rubbish of a now forgotten style of French art, works by American and English painters, such as Samuel Coleman, James Hart, Tait, Beard, and Guy, and also divers Germans of the nineteenth century. Vanderbilt paid fat prices, especially for the Bonheurs and for the huge pictures by Meissonier which treated of the Napoleonic period: "Arrival at the Château" cost the unprecedented sum of $40,000; a war painting by Meissonier brought $50,-000, and a group of portraits, including that of the railroad magnate himself, netted $188,000. In the judgment of posterity Vanderbilt's whole collection contained only one good painting, a Delacroix. Yet he came to reckon himself a connoisseur of art in his own right.

Asked by a famous artist which of his pictures he enjoyed most, he gave the astonishing reply: "I enjoy them all." Nudes and all representations of the partly undraped human figure he eschewed and banned from his collection, while enjoying thoroughly the naked beasts of toil drawn by Rosa Bonheur. Standing one day before a painting of oxen at the plow, this peasant of Staten Island said: "I don't know whether it is art. But those oxen are right." Just so he himself had seen and worked with them many a time.

He had never fancied the work of Corot, who was highly favored in the Gilded Age. But at length he purchased two small examples by the Barbizon painter, "because he was tired of having people tell him he must." For all this doubtful collection which overflowed the "floridly grandiose" Vanderbilt home the railroad baron paid up to the time of his death in 1885 the colossal sum of $1,500,000. The pictures were not purchased "as a speculation," we are told by his official biographer; but then it is remarked with satisfaction that the money was "well invested," as paintings "increase in value with age and especially after the death of the artists."

Drawn by the gold of America, the works of art continued to pile up and to be measured exactly like barrels of pork, bales of cotton, or railroad stocks and bonds. Colonel George Harvey in his "Henry Frick the Man" cites a most illuminating phrase of the coke baron: *"Railroads are the Rembrandts of investment."* For railroads would always go up! Likewise the paintings for which Gould competed with Vanderbilt, or Stillman with Havemeyer or Morgan. Were not Rembrandts, by the same token, the railroads of artistic merchandise, the invaluable jewels among all commodities? Even during possession some paintings were seen to increase sometimes a hundred, a thousand fold more rapidly than the certificates of the best-managed joint-stock companies.

With the highest optimism, William Vanderbilt and his rivals purchased tons of the bright, strident canvases of the French romantic school, which had been bought *en masse* by dealers from the Paris studios, garnished with expensive frames, and sold dear. "I have seen pictures," writes a contemporary art critic, "hanging on the walls of private buyers in the United States so similar (all being in the French style) and so mannered, though by different artists, that one would think they were all by one man who had entered into a contract to furnish the walls."

The art galleries, the auction rooms which exploited the new market in oil paintings teemed with frauds and fabrications. According to accounts of the period hundreds of nondescript or spurious canvases were imported and sold as "Old Masters." To those who felt alarm at the passage of art from Europe, it was often said, "Europe is being relieved of works of art which are hearty good riddance." At one time an American railroad magnate in Rome bought out a whole family collection of paintings, known as the "Massarenti collection"; and of this it was said by museum authorities at Berlin: "It would be difficult to name a second [collection] that is so void of good things and contains so many mediocre pictures and forgeries of great names..." In one case the owner was reported

THE ROBBER BARONS

to have paid $1,000,000 for a property assessed at 200,000 francs, and so taxed, that is, valued at $40,000. Some paintings proved after brief examination through a lens to have three signatures, one on top of the other, and by American painters of the "Hudson River School" at that!

Into this new game or distraction no one plunged with more zest than Pierpont Morgan, and no one was, to begin with, gulled more often and thoroughly than he. In his New York and in his London mansions he had placed "art treasures" from every corner of Europe, "every sort of beautiful and artistic work," as Hovey writes, from tiny miniatures set in little jeweled frames to great paintings by Old Masters, church ornaments, tapestries, porcelains, books and manuscripts.

One day a noted art-dealer showed the financier a small but exquisite Vermeer.

"Who is Vermeer?" asked Morgan. Vermeer's importance was explained to him, also there was added "the commercially speaking, important information that Vermeers were almost unobtainable by private collectors . . ." Whereupon Mr. Morgan asked the price, which was $100,000.

"I'll take it," he said, and he transferred a fortune to possess a painter of whose existence he had never heard, though he was one of the most illustrious names in European art, passed over in the hue and cry after Rembrandt.

It was in this way that Morgan also purchased his first, notorious "Raphael" which we are told was offered to all the great European galleries at a fraction of the price he paid for it, and refused as spurious. He was sometimes reproached for having been "indiscriminate," and the "water" in his art collection was at one time compared favorably with that of his own masterly artistic creations: the steel and the shipping Trusts. There was at least one occasion in Morgan's experience when he felt obliged to return a sacred object he had acquired to the Italian government from whose possession it had been stolen, and pocket the loss. Others acted according to the dictates of their conscience. But as an outcome of much dealing in spurious, falsified or stolen goods, there arose the "art expert" or professional agent, to prompt the tyros of culture in their first toddling steps. Men like Bernard Berenson of Boston were employed at high wages to scrutinize the pictures offered to our industrialists;

and Morgan in time, as Hovey reports, had his "agents in Antwerp, Vienna, Paris, Brussels, Rome—in fact, in almost every Continental city, whose business it is to buy for Mr. Morgan whatever they judge is a masterpiece." By such measures much useful work was done at last in the transportation of the European treasures to the undecorated American continent.

By degrees not only Morgan, but his competitors, Widener, the former butcher and political ward-heeler, Frick the coke king, Altman the dry-goods colossus, Havemeyer the sultan of sugar, and others were tutored and instructed until they might each be hailed as "the most enlightened Maecenas of our time." The process of costly education may be observed in the career of Henry Frick as an art patron. He, as Harvey admits, often bought paintings of "varying merits ... many of which he subsequently disposed of." The chronological list of his acquisitions shows him taking during the late '80's and the '90's chiefly the product of Nattier, Hoppner, Greuze, Bouguereau, Daubigny and the other Barbizon painters. Then after a dozen years have passed, toward 1899, under professional counsel, sounder works begin to fill out his growing collection, those of Velasquez, Van Dyck, Hals, Vermeer, Holbein, Rubens and even the rare El Greco.

In the history of human civilization there had been no such sweeping displacement of works of art, at any rate since the days when the successful military captain, Napoleon, had plundered the Italian cities. It was shown now that this great good work could be done by men without taste. With the ultimate transfer of these priceless collections to museums or permanent galleries open to the public there would be important consequences for American civilization itself. But one wonders if the native barons foresaw such effects on our painting and sculpture. In any case, contiguity with so many noble monuments of art, one would expect, should have worked toward the improvement or refinement of the patrons, tastes and sensibilities, This however was rarely the happy outcome.

Morgan, who professed a love of literature, indulged this by expending many millions of dollars for the faded manuscripts of the sad Keats, the prolific Scott, and above all of the romantic Byron, after whose poem "The Corsair" he named his own yacht, and whose "Don Juan" was possibly not without effect upon his own private life. To round out his treasure store of sacred objects, ancient manuscripts, religious relics, miniatures, and objets d'art of every sort, he must have not only the Gutenberg Bible but the original manuscript of "Leaves of Grass." During these years, Walt Whitman moldered and pined away in Camden, and a group of English writers, modest enough in means, such as Symonds and the Rossettis, collected a fund to keep body and soul together for the good gray poet. When he was buried, the manuscript of "Leaves of Grass" went naturally to repose in the Morgan library, the white marble Italian mausoleum of culture on the grounds of Morgan's Madison Avenue home.

For these latter-day patrons culture was nothing organic, filling their own lives or the life about them with beauty, but something steeped in the dust of old palaces or museums, something touched with death. The presence of the noblest paintings left unchanged their aggressive and acquisitive appetites; sleeping in priceless Renaissance beds once occupied by kings and their concubines, and in boudoirs decorated with Fragonard murals, softened them in no way, apparently. Sometimes they had the droll aspect of the aborigine who decorates his person with the *disjecta membra* of Western civilization, with pieces of tin can for his earrings, or a rubber tire for a belt. Such is the suggestion given to us by the unforgettable picture of the hard little Henry Frick, "in his palace, seated on a Renaissance throne under a Baldachino and holding in his little hand a copy of the *Saturday Evening Post.*"

CHAPTER FIFTEEN

AGAIN THE ROBBER BARONS

WHILE busy carving up the country into baronies, over-running the social capitals, penetrating the schools and the churches, the captains of industry worked also with unremitting vigilance in the field of political action. Here public opinion, as it accepted the pecuniary doctrines of the railway or industrial magnate, seemed also to welcome his penetration, through the government, into the highest assemblies of the country: the Congress, the Senate, and even sometimes the President's cabinet.

The masters of business who sat in the upper chamber of Congress (or "Millionaires' Club," as it was humorously called), or their close associates who became Representatives or governors of states, make up a long and distinguished roll which, to mention only a few, includes Leland Stanford of the Southern Pacific monopoly, George Hearst, the gold-mine owner; Chauncey Depew, president of the New York Central, and Henry B. Payne of the Standard Oil family; William Sharon and James G. Fair, the Nevada Bonanza kings; Stephen B. Elkins, mine-owner and railroad operator; and William A. Clark, the Montana copper baron. Further, among the professional politicians there were also shrewd former tradesmen or lawyers, such as James G. Blaine, Nelson Aldrich, bankers and ironmasters, such as Marcus Alonzo Hanna, James Cameron, and after them Penrose, Platt and Foraker. Furthermore the opposing party, the "outs," were like the Republicans, who were usually the "ins," also led by masters of business or corporation lawyers. August Belmont and Samuel Tilden stood high in the leadership of the Democratic party at an earlier period, as did W. C. Whitney, Henry B. Payne, and James Hill in the time of Grover Cleveland.

It would seem that every industrial group and every great monopoly was almost directly represented in the political councils of the nation. the better to "enrich themselves and the country." On the whole, the practical policies they advocated were carried out with much persistence and loyalty; and though the general program they pursued seemed paradoxical, it was crowned with success.

Paradox arose from the existence of democratic institutions, universal suffrage, equality before the law and equality of privileges. The masters of industry, though imperialists in their daily business, were confronted with democratic and individualistic lawmaking bodies and their judiciary and police departments. They quickly developed a technique for dealing with the democracy. Having virtually completed the conquest of the nation's resources and possessed themselves of lordly properties or seized the "narrows" of trade, the barons were thereafter most happy to advocate complete laissez faire within the nation. They were uncommonly eager to have existing private-property rights sanctified and protected by all the authority of the country. Having won extraordinary economic privileges in the conduct of their business, they saw no objection to leaving to the people at large the residue of individual liberties and rights; they would keep the whole charter of so-called popular liberties intact. Finally, as a fiscal policy for the nation they advocated a "sound currency"; to "raise the standard of living" they successfully urged the protective tariff; and to keep marauders of other races or colors away, to safeguard both here and abroad their growing investments, they generally insisted upon a big navy.

In nearly all sections of the country the masters of capital or their lawyers showed at first an obvious enthusiasm to become the doges of the republic. In California the campaigns of the Pacific quartet, for measures useful to the Southern Pacific, for the election of Stanford as governor or Senator, were all carried on in the open, with gold coins flung among the crowd at the polls. In Ohio the campaign for the elevation of Henry B. Payne to the Senate in 1884 was conducted in the back rooms of saloons, whence an "inundation" of greenbacks spread over the state, gold being less common east of the Rockies. In the mountains of Montana, several years later, a deadly duel raged between two copper barons, Marcus Daly and William A. Clark, each of whom aspired to the Senate, both purchasing newspapers and poisoning the public mind against each other, until at last after a decade of exhausting combat Clark went to Washington and all was tranquil again.

Yet, as Mr. Andrew Mellon observed one day to Colonel George Harvey: "It is always a mistake for a good business man to take public office." Direct intrusion of the masters of big business, while it seemed logical in measure with their stake in the society, often proved unfortunate. Thus Henry B. Payne by his ingenuous procedure in the Senate called down upon himself the anger of his fellow tribunes. Again and again when bills were introduced aiming at railroads or monopolies—though without serious chance of being enacted—Mr. Payne would stand up and cry monotonously: "I object!" On one occasion he even read into the records his own public eulogy of the Standard Oil; so that the other Senators were beside themselves with vexation at his crude tactics, and one of the worthiest of their body arose in anger, saying:

> *A Senator who, when the governor of his state, when both branches of the legislature complained to us that a seat in the United States Senate had been bought; when the other Senator from the state arose and told us that was the belief of a large majority of the people of Ohio ... failed to rise in his place and ask for the investigation which would have put an end to the charges, sheltering himself behind the technicalities which were found by gentlemen on both sides of the chamber ... I should think forever after would hold his peace.*

Among the Pacific Associates a quarrel arose toward 1885 between Huntington the generalissimo and Stanford the political "front," when Stanford had himself elected Senator in place of Huntington's friend A. A. Sargent. In 1890 Huntington forced Stanford to resign the presidency of the Southern Pacific in favor of himself. Then in a statement to stockholders Huntington declared:

> *In no case will I use this great corporation to advance my personal ambitions at the expense of its owners, or put my hands into the treasury to defeat the people's choice. ... if a man wants to make a business of politics, all well and good; if he wants to manage a railroad, all well and good; but he can't do both at the same time.*

All these were heavy darts aimed at Stanford. Huntington did not object to the defense of the Southern Pacific's political interests. On the contrary no one labored so unremittingly and brilliantly as he in this very field. The point at issue, as Stuart Daggett has said, was whether the occasion for defending the railroad politically should be used to advance the personal interest of an individual, or his own public glory. General politics in itself was stuff and nonsense to Huntington; and he felt that Stanford by growing absorbed, even in a moderate degree, had neglected his duties to the Southern Pacific.

For the long run, to effect the great ends which all the barons clearly held in common there were much better ways than that of having themselves elected to public office: there was a method, a technique of political action, comprehensive though devious, "Machiavellian" or "jesuitical"; and its secret principles may be pieced together from the less guarded scraps or fragments of expression of the barons. Or, as in the case of Collis Huntington and John Archbold of the Standard Oil, the grand design for a manual or lexicon of political art in a capitalist democracy can be composed from their voluminous private correspondence, which has been so fortunately preserved in each case.

Though the representative institutions of the republic had developed the political tradition of a two-party alignment with presumed differences of principle between the two, the barons as a class actually showed no sentimental allegiance to one as against the other over a long period of time. In its early days the "radical" Republican war machine, flushed with its triumphs, had seemed to attach to itself the strongest personages in the country. In 1872, Clews tells us that he rallied all his fellow brokers to the support of General Grant because "Wall Street business would boom." In 1880 the ineffable Henry Ward Beecher was for "God and Garfield!" But in the case of Grant's election Clews holds that even "the leading Democrat merchants and bankers in different parts of the country are anxious that the Republican Party may completely triumph." The words of Gould, that in every election or district he was "for Erie," right or wrong, had become universally known. In almost identical words, a generation later H. O. Havemeyer, the head of the sugar Trust, had said under oath that his American Sugar Refining Company had no local party predilections, "no politics of any kind ... only the politics of business." Huntington especially shows such impartiality, making shifts from one party to the other. His private instructions to his partners read:

. . . Piper [pseudonym] is a wild hog; don't let him come back to Washington, but as the House is to be largely Democratic, and if he was to be defeated, likely it would be charged to us, hence I think it would be well to beat him with a Democrat.

In another communication to Colton, Huntington says:

I hope . . . [X] is elected and . . . [Y] defeated, as it was generally understood that our hand was over the one and under the other . . .

In Congress, among the paid agents of Archbold is the Democrat Sibley, who as freely recommends certain of his Republican colleagues to the "good offices" of the Standard Oil leader as he does Democrats. In 1884 the "reformer" Cleveland runs against Blaine, amid high political excitement throughout the land. "What about this man Cleveland?" wires Jim Hill to Tilden. *"He is all right,"* is the reply, and Hill spreads this good word among his friends and retainers in the Northwest.

When Cleveland the knight of free trade was elected, Carnegie the steel master wired Frick from Europe:

Cleveland's landslide! Well, we have nothing to fear and perhaps it is all for the best. People will now think that the Protected Manufacturers will be attended to and quit agitating. Cleveland is a pretty good fellow. Off for Venice tomorrow.

And Frick, who as president of the Carnegie company gave the Republican campaign fund $25,000 (a comparative minimum), answered:

I am very sorry for President Harrison, but I cannot see that our interests are going to be affected one way or the other by the change.

For Cleveland too, as we have recently learned from newly published documents, was "enveloped" by groups of the industrial barons. On May 28, 1894, the financial journalist Clarence Barron notes the secret gossip which associates Cleveland at some recent period (probably between 1889 and 1892) with the stock-market pool working in Distilling & Cattle Feeding shares; the speculation is directed by none other than Jim Keene, Wall Street's "Silver

Fox," in the interests of Oliver H. Payne, William C. Whitney, Senator Calvin Brice of Ohio and Nelson Morris. But Nelson Morris and one Greenhut make $1,500,000 suddenly by "selling out on their associates." And so the informant comments: "I hear that Cleveland had a loss at one time of $75,000 on this account."

That "party," finally, "amounts to little" is also the theme of another chronicle of the time, written a good many years afterward, by Frederick Townsend Martin, in his book, "The Passing of the Idle Rich":

> *Among my own people I seldom hear purely political discussions. When we are discussing pro and con the relative merits of candidates or the relative importance of political policies, the discussion almost invariably comes down to a question of business efficiency. We care absolutely nothing about statehood bills, pension agitation, waterway appropriations, "pork barrels," state rights, or any other political question, save inasmuch as it threatens or fortifies existing conditions. Touch the question of the tariff, touch the issue of the income tax, touch the problem of railroad regulation, or touch the most vital of all business matters, the question of general federal regulation of industrial corporations, and the people amongst whom I live my life become immediately rabid partisans. It matters not one iota what political party is in power, or what President holds the reins of office. We are not politicians or public thinkers; we are the rich; we our America; we got it, God knows how; but we intend to keep it if we can by throwing all the tremendous weight of our support, our influence, our money, our political connection, our purchased senators, our hungry congressmen, our public-speaking demagogues into the scale against any legislation, any political platform, any Presidential campaign, that threatens the integrity of our estate. . . .*

Under the democratic system long established in the United States a proper view of the professional politician (in the unwritten manual of the barons) held him as a sort of "honest broker," as the Beards have said, between the contending economic forces in the society or between competing undertakers. The function of the machine politician was to carry out his commissions faithfully. For this reason a man like Huntington was always ready to "pay much money" in order to effect practical working agreements in politics and have the seal of the sovereignty placed upon his transactions. Whenever these working agreements broke down, there usually followed a comedy of errors which illustrated all the better the underlying principles in play.

May 8, 1890, a young Republican prosecuting attorney in Ohio, with the enthusiasm of an amateur, began a suit to annul the charter of the Standard Oil Company. At once Mark Hanna wrote him the letter which contained the famous lines: *"You have been in politics long enough to know that no man in public office owes the public anything";* and which concluded: "I understand that Senator Sherman inspired this suit. . . . If this is the case I will take occasion to talk to him sharply when I see him."

In the same realistic vein Collis Huntington wrote to his henchman Colton the many letters which allude to public officeholders simply as field agents entrusted with management of the lawmaking institutions on behalf of railroad monopolies. On April 3, 1877, he wrote:

> *We should be very careful to get a U.S. Senator from California that* will be disposed to use us fairly, *and then* have the power to help us. . . . *[X], I think, will be friendly, and there is no man in the Senate that can push a measure further than he can.*

At almost the same time he wrote to his partner, Charles Crocker:

> *I fully appreciate your position and need of . . . [X, a United States Senator]. I fear when he gets there* he will not be earnest in our interest as formerly. *Stanford thinks I am mistaken, and I hope I am.*

And further, he wrote from Washington:

> *If you could get the right man on that line in Arizona to work . . . there, to agitate the question in the territory . . . offer the S. P. a charter that would free the road from taxation, and one that would not allow interference with the rates until ten percent was declared on the common stock, I believe the legislature could be called together* by the people *for $5,000 and such a charter granted.*

On a trio of Congressmen who are evidently "developing" in promising fashion Huntington commented:

> *I hope . . . [X] will be sent back to Congress. I think it would*
> *be a misfortune if he was not. . . . [Y] has not always been right,*
> *but he is a good fellow and is growing every day. . . . [Z] is al-*
> *ways right and it would be a misfortune to California [sic] not to*
> *have him in Congress.*

Here it is as if we are overhearing the secret conferences of the
Western railroad magnates, Huntington, Stanford and Crocker. The
phrases which have been emphasized point to the political principles
which animate Huntington and his mates. The interests of California, of the United States are to his mind completely identified
with those of the Pacific Associates. A Senator is to be judged
"right" or "growing" only when he "uses us fairly" or "helps us" or
is unfailingly "earnest in our interest" or is a "good fellow"; a state
or territorial legislature exists to grant railroad charters to such
groups as his own and "not allow interference with the rates"; and
finally all these public servants, having been chosen in democratic
fashion by popular election, bring the effective support of "the
people" (whose representatives are thus "called together" at a reasonable cost), to place their sanction upon the undertakings of the
great barons. These are but a few of the guiding principles which
enable us to pursue our examination of the political tactics of these
forceful leaders.

Huntington himself has left us the frank and forthright justification for his adventures in bribery in a letter of 1877 (year of the
Southern Pacific's great Congressional fight), which deserves its
measure of immortality:

> *If you have to pay money to have the right thing done, it is only*
> *just and fair to do it. . . . If a man has the power to do great evil*
> *and won't do right unless he is bribed to do it, I think the time spent*
> *will be gained when it is a man's duty to go up and bribe the judge.*
> *A man that will cry out against them himself will also do these*
> *things himself. If there was none for it, I would not hesitate.*

By his own lights, Huntington did nothing that was not in the line
of "duty," one perceives; and his judgment that those who "cried
out" against such "duties" would willingly do these things themselves under altered circumstances was only too often corroborated.
John Archbold, who conducted most of the secret contact work for

the Standard Oil over a period of many years, also took the same view of public officers. The best of the politicians were those who were most potent and those who did their "duty" most faithfully: men like Senators Quay, Foraker, Penrose and Congressman Joseph Sibley, an ardent patriot, a demagogic waver of the "bloody shirt." Pious man though Archbold was, politicians who stubbornly refused to see the light, and especially "reformers" such as Henry Lloyd, who launched his books against the "Anaconda of Oil," were enough to throw him into a towering and profane rage. To Lloyd, Archbold accorded only the meanest and most mercenary motive: that of sharing in the proceeds of damages which enemies of the Standard Oil Trust hoped to collect. Men like Lloyd did no good to anyone and simply served to raise the final cost of political privilege.

To control the officeholder's power for evil, and to gain time, Huntington and his fellows felt it "a man's duty to go up and bribe...." At first, as we have seen in the case of Cornelius Vanderbilt, Gould and of the Crédit Mobilier ring, the methods were exceedingly transparent; the railroad chieftain went to the state or national capital with a valise full of greenbacks; or he sat directly in Congress, like Oakes Ames, giving out stock to other Congressmen that they might be prompted to look after their own property. Collis Huntington, to be sure, was a subtle master, who whenever possible secured signed evidence, such as canceled checks given in payment, so that the men involved were "ever afterward my slaves." Yet even by such careful measures there was tremendous waste. Congressmen or state legislators could not be trusted to control their appetites when a fabulously rich railroad magnate or banker appeared on the scene. The professional politicians became obstructive or "played honest" until prices were raised to fearful figures by forced bidding.

As time passed, we find Huntington groaning over the disbursements, which were always listed in the books under the headings of "General Expense" or "Legal Expense" or "Extra Legal Expense." He exclaimed in one letter in a mood of discouragement: "They might as well take the road and be done with it." He inveighed against Gould for appearing in person at Washington during the discussion of an important railroad measure. Representatives in state legislatures were often especially hard to control, and Huntington himself said: "Buying votes of a legislature was a bad policy." Indeed it was much more effective and economical if one dealt directly with the head of a political machine, be he the Senator or the governor of a state, or someone strategically placed in a committee on railways, Trusts or interstate commerce. On October 29, 1877, we find Huntington writing to Colton:

> I saw Axtell [Governor of New Mexico] and he said he thought that if we would send him such a bill as we wanted to have passed into a law, he could get it passed with very little money; when, if we sent a man there, they would stick him for large amounts.

Direct appearance in a body of lawmakers or direct bribery was then clumsy, wasteful, difficult to conceal, connected with dangerous company, and its costs susceptible of infinite increase automatically from year to year, like blackmail. For instance, a Senator or Congressman who was a member of an important committee might "switch" his position on a bill, then ask for solid inducements to "switch back." Besides even Huntington, Gould or Rockefeller had moments when the state of public opinion, aroused to fury against them by incautious or inept "deals" or errors, set them on their guard.

Instead of outright bribery, highly subtle methods of distributing rewards to political friends came into play. In California, for instance, one of the three members of the State Railroad Commission, the lawyer S. J. Cone, had occasion to purchase as an investment a large ranch of about 100,000 acres. This he did through a subsidiary land company controlled by the Southern Pacific, at a price which was perhaps half that paid by other citizens. The agent of the all-powerful railroad would appear to have been amazingly weak or stupid in the transaction, for the buyer resold his land within six months at double its cost to him. After a few years as railroad commissioner this lawyer of modest practice emerged a millionaire; yet no overt actions were ever laid to him.

Warily, Huntington, notes that his adversary Scott offers too much money and too openly. It is sheer folly; the other is but victimizing himself. "I keep on *high ground*," he reports, "so that we cannot be hurt by any investigation." It was also well to "keep on high ground" in order to leave no evidence in the hands of potential blackmailers. In fact they must be kept "under the gun" perpetually:

I am glad to know that you have Luttrell under your charge, but you must be careful and not let him get anything to strike back with. . . . He must have solid reasons *or he will go back on you.*

In the Pacific Railway Investigation of 1887, Huntington stated candidly that he was opposed to giving politicians or voters free liquor and cigars too open-handedly. On the other hand, he and his fellows had no objection to "looking after" Senator X, by letting him "borrow" some money. Similarly, John Archbold might now and then make a "loan of $1,000" to a Senator, as an "investment" suggested by the friendly Congressman Sibley. And where Scott or Gould gave free passes on all the roads touching Washington, Huntington organized huge "junketing parties" on private trains at a cost of tens of thousands of dollars, by which politicians, their families and journalists might go on exhilarating excursions through his broad territories.

In time, all of the captains of industry found it greatly to their advantage to use the system of the hired "lobbyist," a type of professional public agent who had flourished from the earliest days of the republic, but who came to assume a tremendously important and confidential role in the last quarter of the nineteenth century. In this manner Jay Cooke and his brother Henry had been able to do heroic deeds with Congress immediately after the Civil War. All the "interests," banks, railways, mines, steel, munitions and war materials, ended by having their specialized go-betweens or lobbies. The working of one lobby is described most vividly by Huntington in a letter of January 14, 1876:

I received your telegram that William B. Carr has had for his services $60,000 S. P. bonds, then asking how much more I think his services are worth for the future. . . . In view of the many things we have now before Congress . . . it is very important that his friends in Washington should be with us, and if that could be brought about by paying Carr $10,000 to $20,000 per year, I think we could afford to do it, but of course, not until he had controlled his friends. I would like to have you get a written proposition from Carr, in which he would agree to control his friends for a fixed sum, then send it to me.

In this manner, the railway chief or oil magnate or sugar-refiner was able to simplify his operations by obtaining the "friendship" of a whole group of public officials en masse for an outright payment annually to a wholesale broker in political privilege.

The highest development of political technique came to flower in the heyday of "Uncle" Mark Hanna, who as "boss" of the Republican party rendered its tactics so attractive to the industrial captains that a clear majority of them rallied to its banner and paid rich tribute to its treasury.

It was at this time, as we have learned from the pilfered "Foraker Letters" that the pervasive methods of the lobby were augmented by a system of controls of *strategic committees* and their chairmen. Thus an industrial commission is appointed in 1898, ostensibly to strike a blow at the Trusts. But among its members are machine politicians such as Senator Boies Penrose of Pennsylvania, who keep in close touch with the secret political bureau of Standard Oil, and show Archbold *in advance* the report being prepared by the committee. Archbold objects to parts of the report, and Penrose and his committeemen "tone it down"; then it is submitted anew to the Standard Oil chieftain and he replies finally: "We think the report is so fair that we will not undertake to suggest any changes."

No less devoted was Senator Joseph Foraker, Republican, of Ohio, who while occupying strategic positions in Senate committees received considerations from the Standard Oil Company running as high as $44,000 in a single period of six months—this coming at the very time when he was busily engaged in preparing the anti-Trust planks of the Republican platform.

By 1890, a truly formidable tide of popular unrest was running through the country, and much of that popular consent which the barons had gained during the preceding twenty-five years seemed forfeited. During the debates over the tariff bill in Harrison's administration, the Republican party seemed to share the obloquy of its richest champions. The general outcry arose that the tariff "held the people down while the Trusts went through their pockets." Henry Lloyd by his vigorous pamphleteering pictured an America in which the citizen was born to drink the milk furnished by the milk Trust, eat the beef of the beef Trust, illuminate his home by grace of the oil Trust, and die and be carried off by the coffin

Trust. The Repulicans were hard-pressed, but were more sagaciously led than ever. In Washington a bargain was apparently struck among the professional politicians to enact the new and higher protective-tariff measures, while passing at the same time certain measures of supposed anti-Trust legislation.

"Though the Republican leaders were much averse to providing such control of Trusts," writes H. J. Ford, in the "Cleveland Era," "they found inaction so dangerous that on January 14, 1890, Senator John Sherman reported from the finance committee a vague but peremptory statute to make trade competition compulsory. . . ." Its first section declared that every "contract, combination or conspiracy in restraint of trade, or commerce among the several states or foreign nations is hereby declared to be illegal." This bill, however, with its "impenetrable language" made no attempt to define the offenses it penalized, and created no machinery for enforcing its provisions. At the same time, jurisdiction over alleged violation was given over to the courts, "a favorite congressional mode of getting rid of troublesome responsibilities," as Ford observes. Once more, as in the case of the Interstate Commerce Act of 1887, a Senator remarked that no one knew what the bill would do to the Trusts, but nearly everyone agreed that "something must be flung out to appease the restive masses." Thereafter, two presidents, Cleveland; and McKinley, expressed their complete skepticism as to the efficacy of the Sherman Law, and made almost no move to enforce it; while the Supreme Court especially, and the Constitution itself, stood like a rock of salvation opposed to the "so fearful . . . assaults upon capital," as Justice Stephen J. Field, brother of Cyrus and David Dudley Field, termed it.

Yet there were seasons of danger which gave pause to the triumphant nabobs. A long series of hostile demonstrations and ominous conflicts broke forth; after the strikes and riots of 1885 and 1887, which touched only part of the country, there came episodes more fateful still: the Homestead uprising against the Carnegie steel works in 1892, the Pullman strike led by Eugene Debs in 1894, and then the march of "General" Coxey's impoverished rabble of unemployed upon Washington. The historic cry for inflation arose anew from the farmers and small merchants who were bowed down under their debts. And at last from the "safe and sane" leadership of a

Tilden or a Cleveland, the old Democratic party finally passed into the hands of the fiery young Western orator who would have rescued suffering people from "the cross of gold."

Before this "wave of the socialist revolution," this onslaught upon the "rights of property" on behalf of more or less ruined laborers, merchants, farmers, miners and country lawyers, at "this league of hell," a great shudder swept the ranks of the barons. 1896 is a red year in all the chronicles, memoirs, biographies of the period. There is a tumult among them, now loud, now secret; frantic preparations are made as for a death struggle, while the wheels of industry are virtually halted.

Now Mark Hanna, chairman of the Republican party, showed an energy, a cool nerve for the great emergency, that was akin to genius. He moved in the highest places, levying staggering assessments, such as $400,000 from the beef group, and $250,000 from the Standard Oil. Hysteria spread in these purlieus: "You make me think of a lot of scared hens," said Hanna to a meeting of great industrialists. Men like James Hill, who had been having his troubles with labor, surreptitiously changed their political allegiance from the Democratic to the Republican banner. "There is an epidemic craze among the farmers and . . . those who receive wages or salaries," he wrote to J. P. Morgan, July 15, 1896. He urged that the managers of the McKinley campaign "should get to work *at once*," adding that "I will do anything or everything in my power to further the end we all have in view."

Everyone labored in the sacred cause. Mr. Hill bought a newspaper in St. Paul, *The Daily Globe*, "to keep it from falling into the hands of the free-silver interests"; and Mr. Archbold sent Foraker money for another newspaper in the East. The *New York Sun*, the *New York Tribune* joined in the hue and cry. Workmen were assured that all employment would be forfeited should Mr. Bryan be elected. Tons of literature, pamphlets by the million were circulated everywhere by Hanna. In New York on the eve of the election, the city was decked with flags and a monstrous Republican parade took place, with 80,000 marchers demonstrating against Bryan, one section consisting of 5,000 bankers and brokers, who cheered for Pierpont Morgan. Before such an irresistible combination of defensive force, led so brilliantly by Hanna, Bryan's hosts were rolled back in decisive defeat—the moment of "class struggle" passed by "God's in his Heaven—all's right with the world," Hanna telegraphed McKinley.

2

God was in his Heaven, but in one section of society, that of the masses of labor, opposition to the conquerors of industry had developed in most menacing form by 1885. Where the landed aristocrats, the associations of farmers or other groups among the consumers had failed to check for a moment the sweep of the captains of business, labor steadily organized itself into combinations, the better to deal with the concentrated force of its employers. Against the threat of labor's growing might, and its demands which they held intolerable, the barons exerted themselves with promptitude, with tremendous energy and with an unflinching ruthlessness. In the United States, as in almost no other industrial nation, the encroachments of organized labor were halted or neutralized or completely nullified.

Here we need regard only certain aspects of the American labor movement—whose picturesque special history, in any case, has been well told by others—and particularly those aspects which illuminate the principles and the tactics of the industrial barons in their "heroic age."

The owners of land, capital and the means of production sought to give as little as possible to labor, as they did everywhere in the world after the handicraft régime had disappeared and factory labor had taken its place. Where the pre-capitalist hand worker, as his own master, had been wont to take the full proceeds of his labor and to produce only "for his needs," all the "surplus value" arising from the division of labor in the eighteenth century and the introduction of machinery thereafter went to the commander of capital; indeed all the value derived from the process which was not needed to keep body and soul together for the hired workman was so disposed of. This order of things was no more questioned by the earliest American owners of land, goods and machines than by any others. Yet in the new continent the wages of labor were relatively high; and many a small capitalist in the period before the Civil War complained bitterly of this condition, as of the scarcity of laborers and their transiency. The hordes of poor immigrants who poured into the country soon turned from regular toil in mills for twelve or thirteen hours a day to possess themselves of the free lands of the frontier, where they could labor as masters of themselves.

But wherever possible and as long as possible the owners of factories and industries, spurred by competition, sought to hold their laborers to the lowest possible wages and the longest hours; and toward the middle of the nineteenth century to render the motions of labor as simple, as mechanical as possible, so that great numbers of women, children and unskilled Negroes could be pressed into service. From the beginning the managers of industrial enterprise favored the free immigration of subjects of every race and land under the sun to this asylum of freedom—even if they had to be brought here in contract labor gangs.

Since the 1870's the Carnegie steel company in Pittsburgh, for instance, had begun the systematic hiring of immigrants. The report of social workers for the Pittsburgh Survey, issued by a foundation established by Mrs. Russell Sage, relates:

> It is a common opinion in the district that some employers of labor give the Slavs and Italians preference because of their docility, their habit of silent submission . . . and their willingness to work long hours and overtime without a murmur. Foreigners as a rule earn the lowest wages and work the full stint of hours. . . .
>
> Many work in intense heat, the din of machinery and the noise of escaping steam. The congested condition of most of the plants in Pittsburgh adds to the physical discomforts . . . while their ignorance of the language and of modern machinery increases the risk. How many of the Slavs, Lithuanians and Italians are injured in Pittsburgh in one year is unknown. No reliable statistics are compiled. . . . When I mentioned a plant that had a bad reputation to a priest he said: "Oh, that is the slaughter-house; they kill them there every day." . . . It is undoubtedly true, that exaggerated though the reports may be, the waste in life and limb is great, and if it all fell upon the native born a cry would long since have gone up which would have stayed the slaughter.

In hard times, the manufacturers were not responsible for the souls of their hired hands, like the manorial lords of the Middle Ages; few measures of safety were provided in mines and mills, where hundreds and even thousands were killed and maimed annually. Little heed was paid to the quarters in which workers and their families resided, the food they ate or the water they drank, With the passing of time, toward 1890, 10 per cent of the population of our great cities were housed in slums as terrible as those of the wretchedest places in the Old World. And in the neighborhood of the big manufacturing works, stockyards, and mines, the unlovely shacks of laborers, communities clustered, like the cottages of servants and hired hands in feudal times.

A great steel manufacturer noted for his lavish philanthropies would acquire an additional mill in Pittsburgh, and in taking this over would also take possession of the row of company houses in which the workers resided. Thus Carnegie, buying Painter's Mill in Pittsburgh, renovated its producing plant thoroughly; but the notorious "Painter's Row" on the south side of the town was left untouched—with its five hundred people living in back-to-back houses, without ventilation, having cellar kitchens, dark, overcrowded sleeping quarters, no drinking water whatsoever, and no sanitary accommodations worth the name.

In Pittsburgh, in the coal fields of Pennsylvania, in the New England textile cities and in the neighborhood of the Chicago stockyards laborers lived huddled together in company "patches" varying from the quality of shambles to "model towns" such as that of Pullman, outside of Chicago. But unlike the baron of the feudal castle, the owner of the latter-day mill or mine used his servants with no lordly spirit, but instead with that dispassionate logic, with that "holy parsimony" which marked all his undertakings, large and small. This was to be seen in every contract with or usage of the laborer. If the very enterprising Pullman Company expended some $5,000,000 per annum in wages, at an average rate of $600 a year, it contrived through the model town in which its subjects were housed to win back a great part of this sum, renting them houses, selling them food, gas, water and a variety of compulsory services or conveniences at what were afterward proved to be enormously profitable rates. Thus not only from the employees' labor were famous profits taken, but even from their hours of rest and refreshment.

But in a period of adversity and idleness, the workman was in no way assured of food or lodging, as even the medieval serf had been. His wages might be sharply reduced, or might wholly disappear, as in 1893 at Pullman: the exactions of his landlord continued; so that here as in the mining communities with their "company stores" he might receive almost nothing in his pay envelope, after "deductions," or might labor on in debt until evicted.

In this rich, spacious country, the laborer who was "worthy of his hire" might move on toward the receding Frontier, where new demand for his labor was incessant, where homestead farms were open to those willing or able to wander far enough, or possessing the capital needed to till them. So that the lot of the worker, especially the native worker, was almost never as cruel as in the densely populated regions of Europe. But between 1885 and 1893, the margin of free soil had dwindled finally to a negligible residue; while at the same time the effects of thoroughgoing combination and mechanical standardization in the industrial system seemed to remove the last vestiges of "natural rights." Now in desperation the workers banded themselves together more and more often in secret orders or in craft unions, or simply in crusades to wage industrial war on their masters.

From earliest times the commanders of industries had shown the sternest resistance to such combination of the workers against themselves as they formed on their own behalf. The most notable labor disputes before 1860 had arisen in the first great textile mills of the country, located in New England; and the resolution of the masters in opposing the "unlawful" demands of labor is shown by the famous words of Colonel Borden, cotton-maker of Fall River, whose men, women and children struck in 1850 against the thirteen-hour day:

I saw that mill built stone by stone; I saw the pickers, the carding engines, the spinning mules and the looms put into it, one after the other, and I would see every machine and stone crumble to the floor and fall again before I would accede to your wishes.

So a generation later Jim Fisk, in a strike of the Erie brakemen, "sent a gang of toughs from New York under orders to shoot down any man who offered resistance," arousing widespread admiration for his sterling courage. This opposition of men like Fisk to labor's claim of a special "interest" in its situation was largely typical of American sentiment. And that grand oracle Henry Ward Beecher sounded the feeling of the majority of citizens who were not urban laborers, in 1877, when he cried out that "laborers' unions are the worst form of despotism and tyranny in the history of Christendom!"

The barons of industry continued to set aside all softer considerations for those of progress in the economy and technology of their business. Mine-owners found ways of altering the weight of a ton of coal which the worker must dig, from 2,340 pounds to 2,700 or even 4,000 pounds. In his telegraph monopoly, Jay Gould supplanted old employees with inexperienced persons at much lower salaries, which in the view of his apologists was "both just and politic"; the stockyards houses trained their personnel in the art of a first, simplified mass-production; while railroad men such as Jim Hill boasted: "I will make one engine do the work of three and dispose of two crews."

In the railroad field, where workers felt themselves particularly indispensable owing to the need of experience and the close coördination of all movements, they tended to unite most effectively in their own interest. In 1877, the actions of the Baltimore & Ohio and the Pennsylvania railroads in twice reducing wages by 10 per cent, and then running "double-headers," that is, thirty-four freight cars in place of seventeen cars, behind a single engine and manned by a single crew of men, were passionately resented, and provoked a determined strike which soon swept into other railways, and assumed a "national" character. The armies of trainmen, in their desperation, developed a violence surpassing that of the English "machine-wreckers" in earlier days. In Pittsburgh, more than $5,000,000 of property was destroyed by the rioting and looting workers, and the railroad chiefs were only saved by calling out militia and finally detachments of federal troops, who succeeded in putting down the strike with no little bloodshed. From this time, John Commons points out, the industrial barons made a habit of calling soldiers to their assistance; and armories were erected in the principal cities as measures of convenience.

Though the railway strike was broken, remarkable enthusiasm was now engendered among the workers, and there resulted a great expansion of the recently organized Knights of Labor, the secret and fraternal organization which carried on throughout the country a kind of crusade against capitalism.

By 1885 the Noble Order of Knights of Labor held a certain terror for the rulers of great industries. A victorious strike against Jay

Gould's Missouri Pacific Railroad in this year brought numerous recruits to the banners of the Order, which aroused immense hope among the workers through having conquered the man who was reckoned both the strongest and the wiliest of capitalists. The might of this curious labor union was much exaggerated in the press, one widely reprinted article in the *New York Sun* in 1885 asserting that five men exerted autocratic powers over 500,000 workmen:

> *They can stay the nimble touch of almost every telegraph operator, can shut up most of the mills and factories, and can disable the railroads. They can issue an edict against any manufactured goods so as to make their subjects cease buying them, and the tradesman stop selling them. They can array labor against capital, putting labor on the offensive or defensive, for quiet and stubborn self-protection or for angry, organized assault, as they will.*

Gould, however, with his usual shiftiness, did not abide by the terms of settlement he had accepted; he discriminated against union members, directed shop-work to other plants where it could be done at lower cost, and precipitated in the following year, 1886, a second and more violent strike. Here were involved 9,000 men directly, under the leadership of the flaming Martill Irons; the uprising spread to adjoining railway systems, railway properties were besieged and captured by workmen, and business was paralyzed in a broad zone of the country.

Terence V. Powderly, Grand Master of the Knights of Labor, wrote his challenge to Gould, saying:

> *The system, which reaches out on all sides, gathering in the millions of dollars of treasure and keeping them out of the legitimate channels of trade and commerce must die. . . . I play no game of bluff or chance. I speak for 500,000 organized men . . .*

And Gould in the accents of a Self-made Man replied:

> *In answer to these personal threats, I beg to say that I am yet a free American citizen. I am past forty-nine years of age . . . I began life in a lowly way, and by industry, temperance, and attention to my own business have been successful, perhaps beyond the measure of my deserts. If, as you say, I am now to be destroyed by the Knights of Labor unless I sink my manhood, so be it.*

Gould's letter was widely publicized and brought many flattering encomiums, which had up to now been withheld from him. He won this strike, after long struggle and deprivation for the inhabitants of the whole Southwest, as he had won the Western Union strike of 1883.

But henceforth, after 1886, even greater force and sovereign authority was marshaled on behalf of the alarmed industrial chieftains. Pinkerton detectives and industrial spies were used to weed out union men. The lockout, especially used by Carnegie, and the "blacklist" or "iron-clad oath" (not to participate in a union) were enforced by monopolists acting in concert. Finally, after the Haymarket riot in Chicago, where the explosion of a deadly bomb stirred public opinion to boiling pitch, all the forces of law and order, from local magistrates and militia to the President and the Supreme Court, united to crush the "conspiracy" of labor.

In 1886 and 1887 the courts began to interfere actively with the movement to organize labor; and in 1888, the first celebrated "injunction" was issued by a federal court in connection with a Western railway strike, and was justified on the ground of the Interstate Commerce Act, which forbade "conspiracy in restraint of trade." Soon arrests and trials without jury were ordered, as in the Pullman strike of 1894. Here President Cleveland sternly intervened, by sending armed troops to run the mail trains, saying to those who pleaded on behalf of the workers: "You may as well ask me to dissolve the government of the United States!"

Thus the very laws which for long years it was found impossible to enforce against collusive combination or conspiracy among the industrialists were invoked with remarkable promptness and effectiveness against the associations of laborers. These judicial decisions were rendered in the name of sacred rights of property; and as the Beards have noted, they were rendered on the same grounds and at the very same time that the new direct income-tax law was being declared unconstitutional by the Supreme Court, following the appeals of Mr. Rockefeller's lawyer, Joseph Choate.[1]

[1] The metaphysics of "natural liberty," pecuniary or otherwise, as Veblen continents in his "Theory of Business Enterprise," was firmly founded in the Constitution of the land. The owner retained all freedom of contract, and was ever to be deprived of "life, liberty and property" without due process of law.

On the other hand, the workman under the standardized, concentrated

There is a beautiful instance of the resourcefulness with which the courts rose to the emergency at this time, cited by Henry Pringle in his "Theodore Roosevelt." In 1884, a bill of the New York State Legislature championed by the young Assemblyman Roosevelt, and designed to halt the manufacture of cigars in filthy city tenements, became law, but was promptly nullified by the state Court of Appeals. This high court gave the following decision upon the natural liberties of cigar manufacturing:

> *It cannot be perceived how a cigar maker is to be improved in his health or his morals by forcing him from his home and its hallowed associations and beneficent influences.*

This decision to Roosevelt represented legalism in its worst guise, blocking reform legislation such as he sought; it was used with endless fertility in the labor struggle. Before such assembled authorities and powers, courts, police, legislators, President, the Knights of Labor as a militant "industrial union" was baffled, and collapsed. Happily for the captains of industry, the ranks of the labor army were torn with dissension; Utopians, "anarchists," Marxian socialists and "craft unionists" contended with each other long and bitterly, until the faction headed by Samuel Gompers, with its narrow and tempered craft-union program, arose from the ruins of the Knights of Labor.

The most spectacular conflict in all this period of industrial war was undoubtedly that which took place in 1892 at the big Carnegie steel works known as Homestead. This strike illustrates at once the insurrectionary spirit to which the workers were roused at this time, and the well-nigh invincible defense furnished by the giant corporations in America led by such resolute captains of industry as Henry Frick, then president of the Carnegie company. Homestead was a strategic engagement, as we shall see, which the great steel monopoly was determined to fight to a finish.

Frick, for the decade before his arrival as head of the Carnegie

form of economic life which machine industry imposed might have no choice left him in the acceptance of a contract for his labor. He might starve. But, the necessities of a group of workmen are, under the law "not competent to set aside. . . . the natural freedom of the owners of the processes to let work go on or not, as the outlook for profits may decide. Profits is a business proposition, livelihood is not."

company, had been, as a baron of coke, foremost among those who utilized labor with pitiless "efficiency," and strongly resisted "collective bargaining." He had wished to introduce as rapidly as possible the successful methods of his coke company into the steel works, which in the view of the workers involved the destruction of such labor associations as had already established themselves in the field.

In the brief depression of 1884–85 Carnegie, who professed to oppose the use of "scabs" and said: "Thou shalt not take thy neighbor's job," suddenly shut down his Edgar Thomson works in Pittsburgh. Here the triple eight-hour shift had ruled for a time; but he had found that Chicago steel mills using the twelve-hour shift were paying 6 per cent less than he for crews of laborers. Hence he introduced new equipment and machinery throughout his plant, prepared to return to the "double-turn" or twelve-hour shift, and publicly blamed the workers' organization (Amalgamated Association of Iron and Steel Workers) for "allowing other Bessemer mills to work at less wages than we pay." After a prolonged, though peaceful lockout—Carnegie's favorite method of fighting labor— he had forced his men to come back on a nonunion basis, to accept certain cuts in wages and in man power, and was soon ready to face his Western competitors with economies estimated at 19 per cent against their previous advantage of 6 per cent.

The continual pressure upon labor always present at the Carnegie mills was further intensified with the coming of Frick as executive manager in 1889. Frick at heart felt that there was no place for labor unions under the mass-production system he envisaged. His proposals for sweeping reductions of wages and for nonunion contracts brought a strike by the Amalgamated Association of Iron and Steel Workers. Agreements favorable to the workers were reached, after a brief and spirited but orderly strike, and these were to hold good for three years, to July, 1892. But in the spring of 1892, Frick, though knowing his company was earning $4,000,000 per annum, made the official pronouncement that it was "headed for bankruptcy" unless "industrial control" were wrested from the union. Yet, before presenting his new labor contracts to the men (with Carnegie's more than tacit approval), he made elaborate preparations for the life-and-death struggle which such sharply lowered wages would inevitably provoke. On the one hand he made arrangements to shift orders for goods to the Braddock and Duquesne mills of his firm; on the other hand, he brought in Pinkerton detectives to study the ground of the steel works, threw up ramparts with loopholes all around Homestead, and ordered 300 Pinkerton guards held in readiness for its defense.

To the unionists all these war preparations meant only one thing: that the man who had long been the storm center of bloody labor strife in the Connellsville coke fields was moving to crush out their union once and for all, even before they had the chance to pass on his demands. The strike began on July 1, 1892, as the plant shut down; and Frick moved at once to bring in nonunion men or "scabs," in order to reopen, as he announced, on July 6. He based his actions upon "the inviolability of 'property,' no less than on 'life and liberty' guaranteed by the Constitution." By the testimony of a Congressional committee, he was "stern, brusque and autocratic" in his negotiations. Moreover the high-handed Frick did not wait for the Governor, the police or the militia of Pennsylvania to support him, but engaged himself to bring a battalion of armed industrial guards up the Monongahela River in tugs, at midnight of July 6. What followed was to be one of the famous "dramas of capital and labor," from which Andrew Carnegie so often sought to exculpate himself.

The Homestead men had been working in the mill at that place, many of them since it was first built. They had seen it grow from a small beginning to one of the finest and best equipped plants in the world. They were proud of that plant and proud of the part that they had had in its progress.

So writes John Fitch, in his "The Steel Workers," and perhaps he exaggerates little in indicating this "pride of workmanship" felt by the laborers. According to Veblen's theories, the laborers were eternally concerned with "industry," with their work and their product; while the owners were nowadays chiefly occupied with the "administration" and profits.

Over the hills rising from the river were their cottages, many of them owned by the workingmen . . . and now these homes were in jeopardy [continues Fitch]. They could have gone back to work. . . . But that means giving up their union . . . self-disenfranchise-

ment. So when the Pinkerton men came, the Homestead steel work-
ers saw in their approach an attempt at subjugation at the hands of
an armed force of unauthorized individuals. A mob of men with
guns coming to take their jobs ... to take away the chance to
work, to break up their homes—that is what passed through the
minds of the Homestead men that morning.

The brawny men of the Bessemer furnaces, the whole population of
Homestead, transformed into raging demons, were waiting for the
Pinkertons when they arrived at dawn of July 6. What followed—the
rioting, the killing of guards and workers, the capture and torture of
the Pinkerton guards—the possession of the Homestead plant by the
workers, the five months' long struggle—none of this may have been
foreseen by Henry Frick, but it was certainly in key with the instigating measures he had taken. The steel works were soon besieged
and captured by government soldiers. Although at first throughout
the world popular sympathy supported the beleaguered laborers,
their front was broken finally, as a result of the New York anarchist
Berkman's misguided attempt to assassinate Frick. In the end the
light wounds of Frick, "intrepid" and "lion-like," brought him glory
and hardened the resistance of the steel masters until they had won
the day. He despatched an exultant cablegram to Carnegie, far off in
Europe as usual:

Nov. 21: Strike officially declared off yesterday. Our victory is
now complete and most gratifying. Do not think we will ever have
any serious labor trouble again.

By letter at the same time Frick wrote that though the losses
from the strike had been great, $2,000,000, they "had been charged
up so that we swallowed the dose as we went along. . . ." The
company showed profits of $4,000,000, or 16 per cent on its declared
capital, after losses counted. And he summed it all up by adding:

We could never have profited much by any of our competitors
making and winning the fight we have made. We had to teach our
employees a lesson, and we have taught them one that they will
never forget.

This was accurate, and Frick alone deserved the glory which fell to
him for having freed the steel industry forever from the "tyranny"
of labor.

"Congratulations all around—life worth living again—how pretty Italia," Carnegie wired him. And John D. Rockefeller (taking heart from Frick's heroic stand against "anarchy") wrote to Frick "approving his course and expressing sympathy." In his own factories Rockefeller would permit no collective bargaining, but only "company unions" in the time-honored relationship of "obedient servants and good masters."

The kind of labor union which the American industrialists everywhere preferred and established was described by Charles M. Schwab, who succeeded Frick as president of the Carnegie Steel Company, in a confidential talk with Barron:

> Since that day [of the Homestead strike] I have never had labor unions in any of my concerns. We make our own labor unions. We organize our labor into units of 300 and then the representatives of these 300 meet together every week. Then every fortnight they meet with the head men. Although we are only twenty or thirty and they three hundred representatives . . . we never allow dictation. We discuss matters but we never vote. I will not permit myself to be in the position of having the labor dictate to the management.

The great industrial trusts which were formed in the 1890's plainly feared the intercession of organized labor in their process of production and in the heavy industries checked its advance thoroughly. To combat labor troubles they possessed many advantages. This was readily admitted by John W. Gates, head of the steel and wire Trust, which employed 36,000 men. Although resisting unions and collective bargaining, Gates and his colleagues protested that as they installed labor-saving machinery they tended to increase wages in accordance with the rising output per workman, though they distinctly confessed that "these increases in wages had not been given excepting as the result of demands on the part of the workingmen themselves; that the Combinations made no pretenses toward generosity."

In introducing technical economies, in adjusting wages, in the hiring or firing of their workers, the barons exercised their sacred rights over colossal properties in a manner which closely paralleled the "Divine Right" of feudal princes. As an example of such absolutism, there was the instance of John "Bet-a-Million" Gates, startling the country by suddenly shutting up his big Chicago plant and, in a time of plenty, throwing many thousands of men out of work. "The steel and wire business is in bad shape," Mr. Gates announced to the press, though none had noticed this as yet. His real motive was rumored in financial circles to be something else. Having previously sold his own stock short in the Wall Street market, it was reported he now desired to create a bear market. A very short time later without any further ado he reopened his factories and ran them full tilt!

In the coal fields, however, labor war often raged as the miners in dismal regions of Pennsylvania, Ohio and Illinois struggled against their lot, most of them at a "subsistence wage" of $358 to $450 a year up to 1900. In the great Pennsylvania coal fields, those resplendent magnates, the Vanderbilts, J. Pierpont Morgan, and Cassatt of the Pennsylvania Railroad had after a process of "squeezing" smaller capitalists added most of the anthracite mines to their railroad domains. Anthracite mining was "a business . . . not a religious, sentimental or academic proposition," as George F. Baer, the mine-operator, asserted. The coal mines were consolidated upon a grand scale around the Philadelphia & Reading Coal & Iron Company, of which Baer was president, and prices of anthracite were sharply advanced $1.25 to $1.35 a ton in 1900.

In the meantime the grievances of the miners cried out to Heaven. Their children, as Samuel Gompers related, were "brought into the world by the company doctor, lived in a company house or hut, were nurtured by the company store . . . laid away in a company graveyard." Under John Mitchell, leader of the United Mine Workers, they rose in May, 1902, in a great strike of 140,000 miners, which menaced the country with an acute coal shortage for the coming winter.

As months passed, appeals were made to Pierpont Morgan to bring about a settlement; but he refused to "interfere" and ordered the strikers to go back to work. "Then, and not till then, will we agree to talk about concessions."

Hard pressed, the groups of business men in the coal regions, after six months of coal shortage and suffering, made petition at last to President Roosevelt, saying, as Lewis Corey relates in his "The House of Morgan":

> *Is J. Piermont Morgan greater than the people? Is he mightier than the government? . . . Morgan has placed a ban upon us which means universal ruin, destitution, riot and bloodshed. . . . We appeal from the king of the trusts to the President of the people.*

The President, aroused to the utmost, was resolved to intervene and force arbitration between the two camps. He threatened to man the mines with federal troops. Morgan and most of the coal-operators yielded; but to effect arbitration it was necessary to hold conferences with a representative of labor. This, at the last moment, men like George Baer obdurately refused to do, holding that they could not "meet a criminal. . . . " To the President they used "insolent and abusive language," insisting that no union-labor man must appear among the arbitrators. It dawned on the President then, as Henry Cabot Lodge relates, "that the mighty brains of these captains of industry would rather have anarchy than tweedledum, but that if I used the word tweedledee they would hail it as meaning peace." Roosevelt therefore humorously agreed to appoint his labor man as "an eminent sociologist," whereupon there was tremendous and instant relief, according to his own account. Morgan eagerly ratified the truce. Although the mine-operators had vowed there was no need for intervention, the impartial committee appointed by the President to investigate the coal fields found appalling conditions, and awarded the demands of the strikers for a 10 per cent wage increase, meanwhile denying recognition of their union.

The long strike ended in a compromise; but it is remembered for other reasons. In the midst of the contest George F. Baer, the president of the Philadelphia & Reading company, had given utterance to an immortal declaration which epitomized forever the concept of a "divine right" over labor held by the coal barons. In answer to pleas by a devout person for Christian mercy to the miners he wrote in a letter:

> *The rights and interests of the laboring man will be protected and cared for by the Christian men to whom God has given control of the property rights of the country. Pray earnestly that right may triumph, always remembering that the Lord God Omnipotent still reigns.*

CHAPTER SIXTEEN

CONCENTRATION: THE GREAT TRUSTS

1893: panic! Like the tropical hurricane or the earth tremor, it breaks always with fearful suddenness for the great masses of men. Business men who yesterday were affluent tear up the day's newspaper and fall sobbing at the feet of their wives, crying, "We are ruined!" So the reminiscences and engravings of the time picture the ravages of these regularly recurring economic storms. Behind the heavy red or green velours curtained windows of the thousands of middle-class American parlors, the national melodrama is re-enacted in its familiar, classical form. A warm glow of gas lamps floods the rich interior with its bric-a-brac, its gilt and burled walnut furniture, its lacy doilies and what-nots. There is an ornate marble fireplace, and over it the legend: *In God We Trust*. Here sits the master of the house, with his plump cheeks, his full, curling mustaches, his fine Prince Albert, facing his wife, long-corseted, elegantly dressed in her gorgeous velvet robe. On her face there is a look of composed alarm; upon his one of rending anguish. For ruin has fallen upon their house. Tomorrow their hopes, all their worldly possessions, their home with its Oriental bric-a-brac, gas lamps, what-nots, must disappear all together in the gulf of bankruptcy.

In reality the wreck of the small undertaker, pathetic though it seems, is of little moment compared with the mass effects of depression upon the general populace. Chiefly it signifies that transfer of individual fortunes, that expropriation of pygmy capitals by giant capitals which is so greatly hastened with each renewed phase of the economic cycle. Sometimes his individual folly or greed leads a man to the graveyard of business; but more often nowadays it is the consequence of a "deliberate mismanagement," skillfully applied under the system of absentee ownership. Large railroads and other enterprises, plunged in reckless expansions, are now seen by the disillusioned to have "officially overstated" their income, to have paid dividends out of capital, and to have given a semblance of extraordinary value to securities which were in fact worthless. At the beginning of 1893, the National Cordage Trust declares a 100 per cent stock dividend, in addition to its usual payments at the rate of 10 per cent in cash per annum. The investors who had entrusted their savings to this corporation are filled with joy. But a few weeks later, in May, the insolvency of the company is announced, a receiver is appointed, and the treasury is found to be empty. The mishaps of the Santa Fe and Baltimore & Ohio railroads, to mention only a few of the great enterprises that collapsed with incredible suddenness, showed a mismanagement and waste of capital no less grievous than that of National Cordage. Yet these alarming and cruel "deflations" do not seem to afflict giant fortunes, whose owners, forewarned and forearmed (as may be judged), pass calmly through the crisis to emerge relatively enhanced in strength.

Sore losses are met by the middle class of savers and investors; but for the hosts of workers in cities and mills, or tillers of farms, the excesses of individual heads of overcapitalized enterprises result in more drastic and extensive derangements. As grains and stocks crash, factories and commercial houses to the number of 15,000 shut their doors, and 500 banks are plunged in bankruptcy, the "flight of capital" and the hoarding of gold mounts in pace with stark fear and hysteria. Through the whole economic organism, now more close-knit and interdependent than ever before, the general dislocation and paralysis is quickly transmitted. Uncomprehending the farmer stares at his cotton which is nearly worthless, his corn which he must use for fuel. And with even less comprehension the laborer feels his thinning pay envelope, or in extreme penury leaves the bitter hovel which he and his family may no longer occupy, to join in those mass uprisings which color the time: the great strikes in the industrial cities or the coal fields, the burning of railroad cars, the combats with soldiers. And before the year is out while William Bryan thunders against the "Goldbugs in Washington," "General" Jacob Coxey's "Industrial Army," uniformed in rags, but with flags and banners flying, begins its long march across the country to offer the President a "petition in boots."

Disaster now literally seems visited upon the whole nation; but it comes no longer through an Act of God, evil season, war or flood, or through weakening energy and skill of the people. It comes, though the whole continent still cries out for productive enterprise, because those who lead in such enterprise have no further wish to produce or to construct. They, the barons of industry, are now in the grip of the "rich men's panic" (as the panic of 1893 and others were vaguely but truthfully called). No longer captains of industry "enriching others while they enrich themselves," they wish only to see to their pecuniary interest, to vie with each other in converting all their capital investments into ready money or gold—so far as possible. Yesterday, they had been engaged in "over-saving" as J. A. Hobson interprets it. They had been setting aside more and more capital with which to pay for long-term improvements, drains, railroads, ponderous new machinery; they had been preparing themselves ever for the day when they must bring forth still greater quantities of cotton cloth or steel, while making no provision that the buying power of the community increase enough to consume such quantities. The decline of such buying power, the stage when all prices and wages seemed to them "too high" had brought a sudden cessation of such capital investment or "saving," and in its train "glut" and stagnation. Now, as J. A. Hobson interprets it:

> *The true excess shows itself in the shape of idle machinery, closed factories, unworked mines, unused ships and railway trucks. It is the auxiliary capital that represents the bulk of over-supply, and whose idleness signifies the enforced unemployment of large masses of labor. It is machinery, made and designed to increase the flow of production of goods, that has multiplied too fast for the growth of consumption.*

Evidencec of uncontrolled capital investment were the doubling of railroad indebtedness, in many cases, between 1880 and 1890, the tremendous increase in the size and range of industrial combinations of all sorts. But what else could be done under a scheme of distribution which brought to a few men incomes of from ten to twenty millions per annum, while even the skilled among the underlying population enjoyed a purchasing power of no more than $500 a year —and this by no means stable? And even this mass purchasing power would be undermined by the masters. "The workmen now earns the equivalent of a barrel of flour each day," William Vanderbilt had complained to the stockholders of the New York Central Railroad in advocating wage reductions. Yet at the same time preparations of all sorts were made to produce and market more flour, more goods, more railroad services than the people could afford to use.

The intimate statements, the authorized documents of the time show us that the income of the captain of industry is often so great that he literally cannot consume it himself or cause it to be consumed. Thus Murat Halstead tells us that toward 1890, a year before he died, Jay Gould's income was approximately ten millions of dollars a year. "Mr. Gould cannot begin to use even a small portion for his own personal use—even a small part of the interest which his dividend money alone would yield. He must reinvest it, and he does reinvest it. It is safe to say that he takes this money... and buys other securities." In other words, he makes new capital investments.

In the case of the Vanderbilts, we are also told that they applied their immense income from two hundred millions of securities to capital investments in new railroads lines, in opening more coal mines, and in introducing new machinery which diminished hand labor. We see Rockefeller also prompted by the same irresistible impulse—extending new pipe lines, erecting new terminals, building tank ships, acquiring new factories. "The more the business grew," Rockefeller states, "the more capital we put into it, the object being always the same: to extend our business by furnishing the best and cheapest product." Another industrialist states that "the first wedge calls as a rule for the second, and so the great railway I was building made further and further demands upon me. To satisfy these, I extended my activities...." And Andrew Carnegie, who said that he hoped that the time would come when he would no longer have to expand his business, remarks that he always found that "to put off expanding would mean retrogression." We find him in 1885 reconstructing and altering his Pittsburgh works radically, so that steel may be produced more swiftly, with fewer hands. We find him later investing more capital in changing from the Bessemer converter to the improved open-hearth furnace—and always he, like Gould and Vanderbilt and others of their rank, seeks to resist the tendency of wages to rise and keep pace with the increasing prosperity and productivity of industry.

"They extended their activities." During the whole period the race between overcapitalized industries continued; railroads in addition to those already existing tried to reach Chicago or the Pacific through undeveloped territory. Industrialists, coming upon new machinery which gave them an advantage, tried to despatch rivals whose methods were obsolete, always adding to the output and the improvement of their plants far beyond the needs of the existing population or its current purchasing power. From beginning to end their whole policy of management, as Hobson has commented, served to spread "underconsumption," to make depressions "deeper and more lasting."

The approach of "hard times" was pretty largely foreseen by the more important captains of business enterprise, not because they possessed supernatural sight, but because they were posted at the very nerve-centers of the industrial system. Not only were they generally able to escape the heaviest blows of adversity and stand "like a rock against the wave," but the end of the storm would see these powerful figures more solidly entrenched, the field swept clear of opposition.

In the Northwest we see Hill accumulating cash in the treasury of his railway, while watching uneasily the federal government's fiscal policies. As fear of suspension of specie payments spread, we find Jim Hill hoarding, "always quietly on the watch." In the notes of Clarence Barron, Samuel Hill, son of the railroad magnate, recalls the time of the Baring failure:

In May, 1890, James J. Hlll told me: "We are going to have a panic next September. It will take five years to get over it." He had advices daily from every capital of Europe. At that time he predicted within four days the exact date of the panic. Then he had nothing in his box. As he said, "Not a pound of meal." He had only cash. He had sold everything in Great Northern and Northern Pacific. Perhaps he had $50,000,000.

These are no doubt boastful statements and should not be swallowed entire; yet they indicate the tactics clearly. Hill, according to letters in Pyle's biography, had also foreseen the failure of the rival Northern Pacific line which he longed to control, saying to his partners, "That company has run its length." The depression, he judged accurately, would be more massive, more prolonged than ever before, because everything was "built-up," we were "no longer a frontier country. . . ."

January 24, 1890, the brilliant Harriman wrote to the directors of his railroad, the Illinois Central, urging severe retrenchments. "It would be unwise at this time to pass any resolution adopting a policy for a large expenditure of money. . . . Our whole force should be devoted to *making* and *saving* money." Thus while the Erie, the Baltimore & Ohio, Northern Pacific, Union Pacific, Reading, Sante Fe, and a hundred and forty-nine other roads capitalized at $2,500,000,000 collapsed, Harriman's road went through the panic with no lack of resources. Then as the crisis deepened and passed its climax, we note also how Harriman was in position to use the chances it offered. Taking command of the huge but bankrupt Union Pacific, he would, according to the statement of Otto Kahn, levy great sums from his associates for equipment and improvements because "labor and materials were then extremely cheap."

During the crisis those barons who had the largest war material, the heaviest reserves, the strongest positions at the "narrows" of trade, pressed their advantages without stint. The collapse of the ambitious Reading Railroad in the Pennsylvania coal regions would be the occasion for the Morgan-Vanderbilt combination to sweep together into one monopoly the mines and carriers of this field. The loss of gold from the federal Treasury in 1894 would furnish the chance for the pool of money-lenders which Morgan headed to make loans to the government at its own terms. In the year of the panic, finding opponents gathering in force to share his profits, Carnegie would break suddenly from the steel pool and cut prices sharply, saying to his rivals: "I can make steel cheaper than any of you. The market is mine whenever I want to take it." In short, the more powerful the monopoly, such as that of Carnegie in steel, or of Rockefeller in oil, or of Havemeyer in sugar, the more they extended their domain over the industry they exploited, holding their margin of profit firm, while using to the full the demoralization of the raw-materials industries which fed into their own.

Carnegie, for instance, not only expanded the capacity of his mills several times in the five years after 1893, but also made provisions for enormously increased sources of raw iron ore at low prices. The powerful alliance of the Carnegie and Rockefeller interests in the Lake Superior ore business, John Moody holds, "caused a great fall in the price of iron ore and forced many small producers to the wall. Their holdings were thereupon bought in by the Carnegie and Rockefeller combination."

During all this period of economic misery, the great Trusts, as Montague concludes in his painstaking study of their activities, "were scarcely inconvenienced." Their steadfast growth, their large-scale economies and their stability, revealed how much they were on the side of destiny.

2

The '80's had witnessed the emergence of industrial pools and loose or secret combinations of all sorts, until by 1890 there were, according to Ripley, approximately 100 such associations, in whiskey, sugar, tobacco, cattle feed, beef, wire nails and even bicycles and electric appliances. The Sherman Anti-Trust Act of 1890, designed to check such "conspiracies," had caused, in truth, no more than a momentary consternation. The owners of large business enterprises were not interested in statutes. "Forces greater than any man or group of men could cope with," as Miss Tarbell writes, were leading them to combination.

Through the hard times, the sugar Trust no less than the Standard Oil was an instance of how successfully such things could be managed. By the Havemeyers' consolidation of seventeen refineries into the American Sugar Refining Company in 1887, on the principle of Standard Oil, the firmest grip had been won over the field. The margin of profit at approximately 1.10 cents per pound had been constantly held in all weathers, and the American Sugar Refining Company had thus been able to pay on its magnified capital dividends of 9 per cent in 1892, 22 per cent in 1893, and 12 per cent in 1894–99. With opposition conquered, H. O. Havemeyer would quietly raise the price of the American breakfast: "Who cares for a quarter of a cent a pound" he would say blandly. Not only was the sugar monopoly sheltered by the protective tariff, which Havemeyer once called "the mother of Trusts," but it prospered also during a long period of years from a collusive arrangement with customs officials for "short weights." Some 2,500,000 (at a moderate estimate) had been diverted from the Internal Revenue department of the government in this manner. This was the sum, at any rate, which had to be disgorged one day upon public exposure of the affair.

Challenged in the State of New York as a monopoly, the American Sugar Refining Company had appealed to the Supreme Court in Washington, and ultimately received the sanction of the highest court in the land, which declared:

> *There was nothing in the proofs to indicate any intention to put a restraint on trade or commerce, and the fact that trade or commerce might be indirectly affected was not enough to entitle the complainants to a decree.*

The celebrated Knight Decision of the Supreme Court in January, 1894, had shown once for all that the government of the United States had no intention of prosecuting the Trusts. This memorable decision, nullifying for the time the Interstate Commerce Act and the Anti-Trust Law, brought into being a great crowd of Trusts, combinations or "holding companies." In the next five years, there were three hundred such monopolies formed, many of which sprang almost at birth to giant size.

The economic inventions of the Rockefeller associates were adopted in old and new industries with revolutionary effect. Corporation lawyers who could wriggle through the laws, or who were skilled in negotiating among irreconcilables and fashioning agreements between them, were now in demand. Elbert Gary, the Chicago lawyer, or George Perkins, the Morgan partner, or the firm of Sullivan & Cromwell who operated under the benevolent New Jersey corporation laws, were leaders in this work of legal reconstruction. They would bring together the suspicious and hostile individuals, placing them in different rooms, while the corporation lawyer or, as was often the case, a Morgan partner "kept them apart... and himself went from one to the other arranging terms."

Between dawn and dark Trusts were thrown up. So a lawyer talking to Barron relates how in 1892

> *Sullivan and Cromwell transferred the Southern Cotton Oil Trust into a New Jersey Corporation in a single night. They locked their doors at six o'clock, drew one hundred and seventy-five agreements, and landed the Cotton Oil Trust under a New Jersey charter before daylight. They must have got at least $50,000 for this night's work.*

Sometimes, Barron tells us, the lawyer creating the combinations felt the laws of the states so strongly against him that he would have to "take his gripsack and papers and get out of the way over in New Jersey. . . ."

Thus Gary and John W. Gates, in short order, out of an industry in which "every man's hand was against his neighbor's" formed the wire-nail Trust. The Moore brothers, conquerors of Wall Street, and owners of a match monopoly, formed in quick succession the National Biscuit Trust, the tin-plate Trust and the steel-hoop Trust. In Chicago, large steel interests were grouped together by Gary to form the Federal Steel Company, second only to Carnegie's group in size. At the same time, under the active stimulus of the House of Morgan, which now entered the steel trade with zest, there came tumbling forth—to Carnegie's intense vexation—the National Tube, the American Bridge, the American Sheet Steel corporations; while in another field there arose, with Morgan's aid, the General Electric, a huge monopoly of a newborn industry. Moreover in the virgin field of public utilities, the forceful group of William C. Whitney, Thomas Fortune Ryan, Charles T. Yerkes, Peter A. B. Widener, H. H. Rogers, William Rockefeller, moved with "precaution and deviltry" to round up gas and electric companies and urban railroads. Still another group of aggressive Yankees led by Theodore Vail hastily swept together most of the new telephone companies into a nation-wide monopoly, which was to grow into the American Telephone & Telegraph Company; while other interests, pouncing upon new industries created by technologists such as Edison, Westinghouse, Thomson and Houston, gathered in their own hands the production of all electric appliances and machinery required by the public utilities.

So in a greatly shortened period of time the new resources, gas and hydro-electric power, passed through such a process of centralization as had taken place in the railroads or the oil trade, nearly a generation before. The same principles and tactics were seen at work, though at a swifter tempo. The dominant men in each industry emerged after ruthless destruction of their adversaries. In the process of consolidation, there were the usual movements of treachery and ambuscade, of attraction and repulsion, and the usual effects—enforced delays by interests who held out for tremendous ransoms before they would retire from the field.

Backed by the House of Morgan, Charles Coffin, a rising entrepreneur of electrical machinery, erected a great enterprise on the basis of the patents of two English inventors, Thomson and Houston. The company which bore the name of the inventors was reorganized as the General Electric Company and the English partners, Thomson and Houston, "squeezed out" by financial sleight-of-hand. In a moment of confidence, Coffin, president of the General Electric Company, confessed to George Westinghouse (as Barron's notes record) how he had done this trick:

> He told me how he ran his stock down [says Westinghouse] and deprived both Thomson and Houston of the benefits of an increased stock issue. He was enabled by the decline in stock which he had forced, to make a new contract with both Thomson and Houston, by which they waived their rights to take new stock in proportion to their holdings under their agreement with the Company.
>
> I said to Coffin, "You tell me how you treated Thomson and Houston, why should I trust you after what you tell me?"

For the General Electric was now engaged alternately in waging price wars against its adversaries, Westinghouse and Insull, and in coaxing them to enter into combination with itself. Coffin admits that he "had been cutting prices fearfully," in order to "knock out" other electric companies. Then once having established his street-car motors or dynamos in a given district, though rivals might offer their own products at lower rates, Coffin could charge what he wished: "The users willingly pay our price as they cannot afford to change the system."

Westinghouse stubbornly held to his own way: "I said most emphatically that I would not go into any electrical combination of which . . . I was to be the head. I had done work enough. . . ." In vengeance the General Electric and the House of Morgan bombarded him on many fronts, not only in trade, but in the money markets where his credit was at stake.

> From all the stock-market sub-cellars and rat-holes of State, Broad and Wall Streets crept those wriggling, slimy snakes of bastard rumors. . . . "George Westinghouse has mismanaged his companies. . . . George Westinghouse . . . is involved beyond extrication unless by consolidation with the General Electric. . . ." There came a crash in the Westinghouse stocks.

So Thomas Lawson, the florid historian of "Frenzied Finance," pictures the contest which was successfully terminated only when he, like a "broker-general," "as an expert in stock market affairs, was called in for assistance" to Westinghouse and drove a heroic bargain.

Like Huntington, Gould and Archbold before him, Coffin perfected Machiavellian tactics for negotiating with the governments of the cities or regions to which he brought electrical illumination. Coffin at one time came to Westinghouse

> *and asked him to raise with him the price of lighting from $6 per [street] lamp to $8 per lamp. Westinghouse said that $6 gave fair manufacturing profit, but Coffin said that the Thomson-Houston policy was "boodle" and that it cost in payments to officials about $2 per light, and if they made the price $8 they could spend $2 with the aldermen, etc., and still get their manufacturing profit.*

Thus in the new electrical industry the cost of political privilege came to be calculated with exact science. But in the field of public utilities, in the organizing of street-car lines, lighting and gas companies for the industrial cities of the country, the pace of exploitation was even more frenzied, while the barter of political patronage so necessary for the disposal of eternal franchises owned by the people was carried on with gargantuan cozenage and fraudulence.

In New York, William C. Whitney, who had helped Tilden and Choate to bring down the House of Tweed, used his own knowledge of local politics as well as his prestige as a former presidential cabinet member to obtain for a time virtual control of Tammany Hall. The new technology sometimes bestowed on aldermen or city government officials means to astonishing wealth. Thus a certain Jacob Sharp had bought a franchise for the Metropolitan Traction Company by payments of as much as $500,000. Denounced by Roscoe Conkling in a sensational prosecution, Sharp had been imprisoned, and died raving in delirium. But before his death, in 1887, he had sold his holdings to William Whitney and Thomas Fortune Ryan. These and other properties, such as the Brooklyn Railroad, were later combined under the head of a great "holding company" by Whitney and Ryan; and by feats of stock-market legerdemain, and "trained mismanagement," à la Jay Gould, the pair multiplied their original, trifling capital a thousandfold, emerging with two of the quickest and largest fortunes of the whole era of Frenzied Finance.

In Chicago the electric railroads were preëmpted by the former embezzler Charles T. Yerkes. Under his domination, writes Burton J. Hendrick, in "The Age of Big Business," the Chicago aldermen "attained a depravity which made them notorious all over the world. They openly sold Yerkes the use of the streets for cash. . . ." Yerkes bought the old street-car lines, made contracts with his own construction companies for their rebuilding, "issued large flotations of watered stock, heaped securities upon securities and reorganizations upon reorganizations." The maxims of the man whom Theodore Dreiser has dramatized in "The Financier" were in themselves fascinating. He would say: "It's the straphanger who pays the dividends." And further: "The secret of success in my business is to buy old junk, fix it up a little and unload it upon other fellows."

This he did. After reducing the railway system of Chicago to chaos, he unloaded everything upon his old New York friends, Ryan and Whitney, and then decamped forever to London.

In Philadelphia, there was the former butcher Peter Widener, who stepped into Yerkes's place after the latter had fled. He was suave, jovial and firm, successful in local politics, and in harmonious agreement with Senators Quay and Penrose, who controlled the political favors of the region. With the coming of the trolley car in 1887 and the incandescent lamp of Edison, Widener, grasping his opportunities, became a master of immense public utilities, ultimately of giant holdings which would have made old Vanderbilt and Gould turn over in their graves. No less than Yerkes was Widener credited with picturesque character and explosive sayings. One day a group of minority stockholders in one of the companies which he, together with Whitney and Ryan, dominated somewhat vigorously objected to a proposed change in their articles of incorporation. Whereupon Widener as chairman said to them firmly: *"You can vote first and discuss afterward."*

In this wise the new reserves of natural power and the new machines devised by technicians during the decade that followed 1893 were seized and exploited with extraordinary despatch. The momentous grant of invaluable franchises—to provide cooking-fuel, electric lighting for streets and homes, to transport the masses of city dwellers back and forth to their tasks in the great urban conglomerations which dotted America—this, as well as the donation of invaluable hydro-electric power-sites to men of the caliber of Yerkes, Whitney, Ryan and Widener, was effected almost in the twinkling of an eye, and without a cry of protest. These possessions in turn were combined and pressed through the process of "trustification," under which virtually all the industries of the country were being organized. It was these great promotions, not only in public utilities, but in steel, tobacco, cottonseed oil and a hundred other products which engaged the attention of the country, as examples of "Frenzied Finance" rather than the underlying process of consolidation that was going on. For though consolidation had come at first as a technical advance over unbridled competition, it ended by becoming a fantastically profitable occupation to the undertakers and bankers, wherein technical or economic gains from combination were secondary to the prospective profits from promotions.

Under existing corporation laws, the promoter would first set up a brand-new corporation of a stated capital in which, as a Trust, he intended to combine all his purchases. Then he would go out and form a syndicate of bankers or "underwriters" to furnish cash or credit with which to buy in the scattered properties. And once the properties were combined, the undertaker usually found ways of multiplying their market value ad infinitum, by the instrument of the stock market.

Rarely were two and two put together without footing up to five or seven or sometimes fifty in the terms of the new Trust capitalization. Thus in setting up the American Tobacco Company the artful allies Whitney and Ryan had begun by issuing to the public an initial capital of $10,000,000, which was increased in 1898 to $70,-000,000; then finally, when they changed the company into a New Jersey corporation in 1904, they celebrated with a rousing recapitalization of $180,000,000! According to one of the fantastic legends of Wall Street, Whitney and Ryan together had used little more than $50,000 in promoting the tobacco Trust, and capturing its stock.

Other promoters and investment bankers, in the halcyon days of McKinley and Hanna, did no less. For promoting the American steel and wire Trust Gates got himself most of its $15,000,000 in stock, which he then sold up and down in the market. For promoting the tin-plate and steel-hoop Trusts, the Moores paid themselves $5,000,000 and $10,000,000 respectively. According to Montague, the National Steel Company, valued at $27,000,000, was capitalized at $59,000,000; the American Steel Hoop Company, with a money investment of $14,000,000, issued $33,000,000 in securities. The American Steel and Wire, with $80,000,000 capital, was later valued by Mr. Morgan himself at $40,000,000. But greater by far than all of these would be the "water" in the mammoth steel Trust which certain interests were now dreaming of.

A typical story of the madness of those times for industrial promotions, for the making and selling of pieces of capital, is told by Moody. When one of the smaller steel and iron Trusts was being formed, a party of steel men were on their way to Chicago one night after a buying tour. The men had been drinking and were in a jovial mood.

"There's a steel mill at the next station," one of them suddenly remembered; "let's get out and buy it."

It was past midnight when they reached the station but, thundering at his door, they pulled the owner out of his bed and demanded that he sell his plant.

"My plant is worth $200,000—but it is not for sale," he said irritably.

"Never you mind about the price," answered the hilarious purchasers. "We will give you $300,000—$500,000."

Yet even at these terms, fat profits were reaped from the amalgamations crazily patched together; and hosts of new multimillionaires soon went cruising about the country in their "glittering trains" ordering new portraits of themselves and their wives and palaces in Newport or Florida.

Nevertheless a power which overshadowed all the rest remained in the hands of the earlier organizations created by the three foremost exponents of business enterprise: Morgan, Carnegie and Rockefeller. The first because he had created a virtual monopoly in banking, a "money Trust"; the second because of his death-grip on the key industry of the country; the third, Rockefeller, because his amassing of industrial profits continued at such a high rate that an immense reservoir of cash was accumulated, which sought outlet through investment-banking operations of a size exceeding even those of Pierpont Morgan.

Let us glance at these three organizations, in their final stage of development, studying their tactics, scale of operations, and relations with each other.

3

The last decade of Carnegie's career as steel master, after the Homestead battle, witnessed an unparalleled expansion to the very limits of his field. It was under the aggressive management of Henry Frick that the Carnegie Steel Company completed its organization as a vertical Trust, spreading its operations in a continuous thousand-mile-long chain from its own iron mines over its own ships and railroads to its furnaces and rolling mills.

In 1892 Frick had told Carnegie it was "hard to estimate what blessings will flow from our recent complete victory." The cost of labor thereafter had been lowered by about 20 per cent, ultimately by far more, as technical economies were constantly attempted. In the lean years between 1893 and 1898 Carnegie, in accordance with his familiar maxims, proceeded to use cheap labor and cheap material in order to double the size of his plant. Some years before, S. G. Thomas's open-hearth furnace process for the smelting of iron had been introduced to replace ultimately the less efficient Bessemer converters. Then, in 1890, one additional steel mill had been purchased; and after 1892 the young superintendent Schwab had directed the building of another mill at Braddock. Finally, to keep pace with all these gains and with the swifter rhythm of production, the partners Frick and Carnegie had resolved to reach out for vaster reserves of iron ore.

> *Very early in his management Mr. Frick [writes Harvey] had realized that control of sources of supply of raw material was essential to full independence of the manufacturing unit in which he was welding the segregated and competing plants. Its own coke that company had; its own ore it must have.*

A Pittsburgher, H. W. Oliver, of the farm machine company bearing that name, had been among the first Eastern capitalists to "plunge" into the Minnesota ore fields, opening a mine in the Mesabi in 1802. During the Homestead strike he had begun to negotiate with Frick and Carnegie.

"Oliver's ore bargain—nothing in it—just like him," Carnegie said at first. But Rockefeller—to whom Carnegie referred in his private correspondence as "Reckafellow"—was now known to be acquiring large sections of the Mesabi Range, which in 1892 easily seemed as promising as the Pennsylvania oil lands in 1859. Soon "Reckafellow" would own all the railroads out there "and that's like owning the pipe lines," Carnegie commented with alarm. There would be a "squeeze," he concluded.

"I was astonished," says Rockefeller in his reminiscences, "that the steelmakers had not seen the necessity of controlling their ore supply." If he could but "slip in," he would, dominating petroleum already, truly become lord of the American underground. He might even begin to make steel at Lake Superior ports.

In the face of such a threat Carnegie moved swiftly. For $500,000, advanced as a mortgage loan, he obtained a dominant interest in the mining companies gathered in by Oliver. Then he began to "trade" with "my dear fellow-millionaire"—as he addressed "Reckafellow" directly—whom he considered a "hard bargainer" but always sought to mollify. By consenting to purchase no further ore lands in Minnesota, and pledging payments "in gold of standard weight and fineness," Carnegie was able to obtain from Rockefeller a fifty-year lease, at extremely favorable terms, which brought ore in quantity to Erie ports at a net cost of $1.45 per ton. No other steel-producer in the world now had such a strategic grip on such abundant supplies. By lease or ownership Carnegie held two-thirds of the Mesabi deposits, the highest-grade Bessemer ore in existence. In two years the Oliver mining investments—purchased, as usual, "for nothing"—had paid for themselves, as annual output rose from 29,000 to nearly 2,000,000 tons of ore. As for the deal with Rockefeller, Carnegie always chuckled over it, saying long afterward, in 1912: "It does my heart good to think I got ahead of John D. Rockefeller." He was now equipped to undersell the world.

"Last year was really fine, under the circumstances," Carnegie wrote to Frick, as he pondered the reports for 1894, which showed him $4,000,000 in net profits. "Next year may not be better. But a year comes when I think double." His prophecies, couched in his own curious language, are sure. He watched the books like a hawk, he scanned the tonnage figures for the individual mills, the costs, the profits, and in person or over the cable always clamored for more! more! more! When he came to Pittsburgh he wanted reports:

"Figures, my friend, figures!" he would say to Schwab. His visits were dreaded by his force; none but the late Captain "Billy" Jones and Henry Frick dared to brook his cold will. At his lashing the clouds over Pittsburgh lay in an ever thicker pall, the smoke and flame by night grew more lurid still. It was a "continuous fire festival," as a contemporary of the time noted; and out of the "work and murk," out of the rivers of black smoke and dirt and the weariness of legions of muscular men, the stream of steel ingots swelled always, the millions in gold piled higher and higher.

In all directions throughout the world, the great steel master extended his market. To Russia Carnegie sold armor plate for her navy; and although a crusader for world peace he exerted himself also to build most of the big navy here too, sometimes attempting to "trim" the federal government itself in the process. In September, 1893, informants, former employees at the Homestead plant, brought to the Secretary of the Navy, H. A. Herbert, evidence that the Carnegie company had failed to temper armor plate "evenly and properly," that they

> had plugged and concealed blow-holes, which would probably have caused a rejection of plates by the government inspectors, and had re-treated, without the knowledge of the inspectors, plates which had been selected for the ballistic test, so as to make these plates better and tougher than the group of plates represented by them.

The informants stated that some of the plates, after having been selected and set aside for testing, "had been secretly and without the knowledge of the government inspector, re-treated at night—that is, reannealed and retempered." Now the statements of Messrs. Schwab and Corey, the plant superintendents, sworn statements of precise time of treatment and heating of plates, were therefore alleged to be false. The investigations which ensued, directed by Captain Sampson in 1894, sustained all the charges, and recommended penalties of 15 per cent upon all the amount of armor. Schwab, Frick and Carnegie came to Washington, upon invitation, and expostulated, testified, in vain. Frick disclaimed all knowledge of the deception; he attributed the surreptitious removal and "re-treatment" of plates by night to "over-enthusiasm" on the part of workers. Finally, Frick, who was now an art patron, wound up by saying that uniformity in steel was unattainable. Each beam or plate was like a poem. "You might as well say that a painter could execute an equally good picture every time. Millet painted but one 'Angelus.'" Yet Mr. Cleveland had been unaffected by learning thus—of the artistic temper of armor plate and, with a mild rebuke to the great steel company, imposed a fine of $140,484.94, or 10 per cent of the value of the steel.

Periodically the loyal, secretive band of Carnegie Associates met in grave conference of which the minutes were carefully kept. It needed unremitting vigilance, sleepless labor to carry on the Carnegie steel operations at the pace at which they were expanding. For by 1899 they had made stupendous gains: profits of $20,000,000 were garnered and 70 per cent of the country's steel exports were made by them.

At such meetings all reports of the aggressions of new competitors or combinations in steel, of political problems connected chiefly with the protective tariff, or labor questions, were thoroughly aired and stratagems devised. A secret agent, for instance, would bring the alarming news that steel-makers in Chicago were obtaining from the Pennsylvania Railroad preferential shipping rates of $1 a ton less than those paid by the Carnegie company. At once Carnegie resolved to break the strong grip of the railroad monopoly over Pittsburgh. Secretly he bought control of a dilapidated railroad line, the Pittsburgh, Chenango & Lake Erie, extending from Conneaut Harbor, at the lake, to within thirty miles of his steel works. He then proceeded to complete a freight line serving his own properties solely and connecting with the ore vessels of the lakes.

In alarm the Pennsylvania officials hastened to offer concessions; but Carnegie remained coy, evaded them. In the meantime, as they begged for interviews, he summoned a young man who was in charge of traffic matters.

"I must have the exact rebates that are being paid our competitors. How you are to get them I don't know and don't care. But I must have them."

In short order, the young amateur of espionage—but why should one think espionage rare in heavy industry?—placed the desired information in Carnegie's hands, according to Hendrick's account: "From that day to this no one has ever learned how he obtained these, the closest of all railroad secrets." And, the biographer of

Carnegie adds with remarkable naïveté, the service was considered so great that the young man was "in due course" admitted to partnership in the Carnegie Steel Company.

Facing the lords of the Pennsylvania Railroad with precise evidence of their secret rebates to competitors, Carnegie was now able to beat down their huge overcharges of one million and a half per year. Peace was made at last, but Carnegie did not abandon the spur freight line to the lake, afterward renamed the Pittsburgh, Bessemer & Lake Erie. For all his promises and bargains he soon returned to complete this as one of the vital links in the chain of industrial units which composed his "vertical" Trust, and which was almost completely rounded out by the season of 1896–97. Such expansion was now imperative: a matter of immediate self-preservation.

Between 1896 and 1898, the large steel amalgamation in the West "framed" by that patient negotiator Elbert Gary in collaboration with Pierpont Morgan gave much concern to the Pittsburgh steel masters. But whereas the Federal Steel Company was vastly over-capitalized (at $200,000,000 against a book value of only $56,000,000), the Carnegie organization remained without "watered stock" or bonds on which payments must be met, with little debt to bankers, and possessed its own "war chest," almost unlimited in size. The Carnegie Associates formed a "close" partnership of the old style rather than such a monopolistic bureaucracy as investment bankers these days were instituting in one trade after another. All of the combinations in raw steel, or pipe, or sheets, could soon be made to feel Carnegie competition painfully. He urged a policy of "armed neutrality":

> We should look with favor upon every combination of every kind upon the part of our competitors; the bigger they grow the more vulnerable they become. It is with firms as with nations; "scattered possessions" are not in it with a solid, compact, concentrated force.

Then when the National Tube Company (Morgan-inspired) was announced, he said:

> I note pipe combine, which I hope is to go through. We want to play independent producer there, but should keep the matter very quiet.

To meet the maneuvers of the Carnegie Associates, wily and fierce, equipped to "rule or ruin" their field, was indeed a formidable task; and Gary, who longed with Morgan's aid to develop the steel mills he headed upon a grander design for the conquest of world markets, found it impossible to gain a foothold in the export trade.

In 1898, with the Spanish-American War looming, he had taken a dinner of canvas-back duck with Carnegie; and between them, the two men had once more pooled half the rail tonnage of the country. While the people warred with a foreign power, the steel masters found it wise to make peace with each other. Prices were held high and enormous profits were taken for the season. But what if to-morrow Carnegie broke from the pool—then the future of the Morgan steel fictions trembled in the balance. Panic might be unchained.

In anxiety Gary would say to Morgan: "Now if we could buy the Carnegie company..."

And Morgan would answer: "I would not think of it! I don't believe I could raise the money."

4

In the meantime, the years of depression after 1893 had wrought no less signal changes in the nature of the Standard Oil Company. This industrial empire, which continued to conquer markets and sources of supply in Russia and China as well as at the frontiers of the two Americas, was in no way checked by the period of general hardship. Nor had prohibitive laws, or condemnation of the company in certain regions such as the State of Ohio, hampered its progress in any degree. The order of dissolution in Ohio had simply been resisted by every legal subterfuge conceivable to its counsels; and then after seven years the Standard Oil had simply sloughed off its skin, and appeared as a New Jersey holding corporation.

But after 1893 the Standard Oil Company had a dual character. It was no longer simply an industrial monopoly, composed of men who simply owned and managed their oil business; it became, in great part, a reservoir of money, a house of investment bankers or absentee owners. So rapid had been the increase in annual profits, from $15,000,000 per annum in 1886 to $45,000,000 on 1899, that there was always more cash than could be used as capital in the oil and kindred trades. It became inevitable that the Standard Oil men make reinvestments regularly and extensively in new enterprises which were to be carried on under their absentee ownership. By a coincidence these developments came at a time when John D. Rockefeller announced his "retirement" from active business.

Moody in his "Masters of Capital" relates:

> The Rockefellers were not the type of investors who were satisfied with five or six per cent. . . . They meant to make, if possible, as large profits in the investment of their surplus cash as they had been accustomed to make in their own line of business. But to make money at so rapid a pace called for the same shrewd, superior business methods. . . . To discerning men it was clear that ultimately these other enterprises into which the Standard Oil put its funds must be controlled or dominated by Standard Oil. William Rockefeller had anticipated this development to some extent years before when he had become active in the financial management of the Chicago, Milwaukee and St. Paul Railroad. But it was not until after the panic of 1893 that he and his associates began to reach out aggressively to control the destinies of many corporations.

John D. Rockefeller at this time possessed a fortune that has been estimated at two hundred millions; his brother William owned probably half as much, while his associates who usually moved in conjunction with him or his brother, Rogers, Flagler, Harkness, Payne, and various others combined now to form a capital of a size probably unprecedented in history. Soon the money markets felt the entrance of the Standard Oil "gang" in strange ways, as they began buying and selling pieces of capital, industries, men and material. This omnipotent group had brought a "new order of things" into the world of high finance. They had introduced into Wall Street operations, according to Henry Clews, "the same quiet, unostentatious, but resistless measures that they have always employed heretofore in their corporate affairs." Where a Gould might sometimes face the chance of failure, or a Commodore Vanderbilt have to fight for his life, Clews continued wonderingly, these men seemed to have removed the element of chance:

*Their resources are so vast that they need only to concentrate on
any given property in order to do with it what they please . . .
that they have thus concentrated . . . is a fact well known. . . .
They are the greatest operators the world has ever seen, and the
beauty of their method is the quiet and lack of ostentation . . . no
gallery plays . . . no scare heads in the newspapers . . . no wild
scramble or excitement. With them the process is gradual, thorough,
and steady, with never a waver or break.*

In the conduct of these far-flung undertakings the Standard Oil
family had always the loyal coöperation of the captains and lieutenants who wore their "collar" so contentedly, and who sent confidential news every day from all parts of the world. The "master
mind" in these investment operations nowadays would seem to have
been Henry Rogers; while important alliances, as we have seen,
were effected with Stillman, the astute commander of the National
City Bank, and Harriman, the rising giant of railroads.

After the headquarters of Standard Oil had been removed from
Pearl Street to the high building at 26 Broadway, the active leaders
of The System, as Thomas W. Lawson termed it, would go upstairs
every day at eleven o'clock, to the fifteenth floor, and gather together around a large table. It was the high council of a dynasty of
money, and men everywhere now spoke with bated breath of the
commands which went forth from this council, and of the power
and relentlessness of The System. In his romantic history, "Frenzied
Finance," the stock-market plunger Lawson seems to blubber at
the stupendous holdings of the Standard Oil "gang" toward 1900—
"its countless miles of railroads . . . in every state and city in
America, and its never-ended twistings of snaky pipe lines . . . its
manufactories in the East, its colleges in the South, and its churches
in the North." The guarded headquarters of Standard Oil aroused
and have always aroused an awe which Lawson accurately reflects:

*At the lower end of the greatest thoroughfare in the greatest city
of the New World is a huge structure of plain gray-stone. Solid as
a prison, towering as a steeple, its cold and forbidding façade. . . .
Men point to its stern portals, glance quickly up at the rows of un-
winking windows, nudge each other, and hurry onward, as the
Spaniards used to do when going by the offices of the Inquisition.
The building is No. 26 Broadway.*

John D. Rockefeller, with the aid of Stillman, had been making strategic investments in many banks, insurance companies, railroads, and public utilities; but most of all his tastes led him to accumulate underground wealth in iron and coal mines as well as oil.

Far to the North in Minnesota, the Merritt brothers toward 1890 had stumbled upon the Mesabi iron range, gambled all the money they possessed to exploit it and connect it with civilization by a short railroad. Through Rockefeller's clerical adviser, the Reverend F. T. Gates, a small loan was at first extended them and the bonds of the Merritts' railroad spur passed into his hands. (His agents were early on the scene—even before those of Carnegie and the steel barons.) In the panic of 1893, the adventurers who had discovered the iron ore fields appealed to Rockefeller for further aid; but with each negotiation, the grip of the oil baron upon the Mesabi deposits tightened, until the Merritts, ruined, must relinquish their hold and sink out of sight. Thus for a sum that the Merritts claim to have been only $420,000 Rockefeller acquired the largest iron deposits in the world, forming thereof the Lake Superior Consolidated Ore Mines, which he sold in 1902 to the United States Steel Corporation.

While the oil monopoly functioned automatically under the command of technicians and experts and smoothly extended its gains, all of the Standard Oil captains now practiced the arts of large-scale investment. Henry Rogers, often with the collaboration of one or the other Rockefeller, acquired possession of the new gas companies which offered such serious competition to the Standard's kerosene business. Here he worked by preference with reputedly shady characters of the stamp of Addicks, a Boston gas-company promoter and debaucher of town councils, Lawson the manipulator of stock markets, and a shifty agent or spy named Burrage.[1]

Under Rogers the "money machine" of The System reached its highest perfection. Many feats of Wall Street magic were performed

---

[1]An element of the underworld of finance colors the operations of Rogers, by several accounts. The man Burrage, according to Barron's notes, attempted several times to betray the confidence of Rogers, yet Rogers continued for a time to invite him to his house, for reasons of his own.

Once when Rogers had A. C. Burrage at the foot of his table with four other guests, one of the guests said to Rogers: "How can you tolerate that Mr. Burrage opposite you at the table?" Rogers said: "I am enjoying it immensely. I was thinking all the time how he would look after I had plucked him."

by him and his aides, in order to "have a little fun," as he would say. The most notable example of all these ventures in investment banking was that of Amalgamated Copper, in which the Standard Oil men and the National City Bank collaborated. Through Thomas Lawson acting as broker, Rogers brought together several copper properties owned by the old prospector Marcus Daly. They included the Anaconda Copper Company costing $24,000,000 and certain others purchased for $15,000,000. Of this famous deal, John T. Flynn gives an excellent résumé of the initial transactions:

> *First he [Rogers] and William Rockefeller took title to the mine properties, giving to Marcus Daly a check on the National City Bank for $39,000,000, with the understanding that the check was to be deposited in the bank and remain there for a definite time.*
>
> *At the same time Rogers organized the Amalgamated Copper Company with a lot of clerks as dummy directors. Next he transferred all the mines to this Amalgamated for $75,000,000. The Amalgamated gave him not cash, but all of its capital stock. Then he took this $75,000,000 of stock to the National City Bank and borrowed $39,000,000 on it. This took care of the check to Daly and his friends.*

Rogers and his party have the copper trust in their possession; but they owe the friendly National City Bank $39,000,000; and besides nothing is further from their thoughts than to mine copper. That may be well enough for "captains of industry" of yesterday who like to own and oversee their business. But Rogers now engages the flamboyant Lawson and the shifty A. C. Burrage to stir up a market for Amalgamated shares at 100 to 125, and the whole $75,000,000 of stock is landed upon a public, largely in Boston, which is now frenzied for "coppers." The bank is repaid its $39,-000,000 and Rogers and company pocket $36,000,000 profit, without having used a dollar of their own. This was "The System" Rogers used, according to Lawson's impassioned confessions, which tumbled ministers, doctors, lawyers and shopkeepers throughout the country to ruin, and sent "their innocent daughters out to walk the streets."[2]

[2]Lawson's highly colored account in his book "Frenzied Finance" is borne out by the secret notes of Barron, and reports of the time. One of the oldest and best-known Wall Street brokers, who witnessed these events from close at

Such a "money machine" was unbelievably good. It is Flynn's supposition that John D. Rockefeller himself refrained in great measure from the more audacious expeditions of his brother William, and of Rogers. But Barron's journal refers frequently to the same procedure on John's part. The broker F. H. Prince tells him:

> *John D. Rockefeller is worth a billion. He makes his money by simply tipping out $500,000,000 of securities, then the market goes down and he takes them back at his leisure. Of course the market cannot stand the weight of his selling. He is the one man who knows what everybody else is doing, and nobody knows what he is doing.*

As a member of the board of directors of the Chicago, Milwaukee & St. Paul Railroad, William Rockefeller had long ago struck up a warm friendship with James Stillman, the president of the National City Bank. The latter, stirred at all he learned of the efficiency of the Standard Oil management, and of its hierarchic and centralized government, so much like that of the Roman Catholic Church, modeled his own bank after it. He bought Standard Oil stock and became one of the family. Sphinxlike, autocratic, silent, he came closer always to the Rockefellers whom he so much resembled. The Standard Oil Company, which had been up to now acting largely as its own banker, found an astute and discreet counselor in Stillman. Through him their money flowed to the new gas, copper and steel companies; through him, finally, into the spectacular railroad operations of Harriman, whose rising star Stillman also perceived from the start. At any rate "the City Bank . . . from now on, in certain circles, became known as the 'Standard Oil bank.'" It was the machine through which their greatest exploits were carried out.

Soon, John Moody relates, "the fifteen directors of the Standard Oil Company of New Jersey held directorships in innumerable banks, insurance companies, traction companies, electric light, gas and industrial concerns of every sort." Through Stillman they domi-

---

hand, assured the writer: "Lawson's book is exaggerated but quite true."

Later, as Rogers "plucked" Burrage, so he plucked Lawson, when the latter disappointed him as "a leader of the market." On a further foray in Amalgamated—the process described above could be repeated of course as often as profitable—Lawson was left stranded when dividends were suddenly passed by "insiders," causing him a ruinous loss. "I cannot be responsible for the cupidity of a Boston speculator," Rogers is reputed to have said, and nothing more.

nated a constellation of banks: the National City, Hanover, Farmers
Loan and Trust, Second National, United States Trust; they were
involved in the new American Smelting and Refining combination,
in the copper mines of Montana and the iron deposits of Minnesota;
in United Gas Improvement, Interborough Rapid Transit (with
Belmont), Brooklyn Rapid Transit, and Metropolitan Securities
(with Whitney and Ryan). Finally, according to John Moody,
Rockefeller even approached Carnegie, and "tried to buy him out."
It was Rockefeller's desire to solidify his interests in his ore lands, his
ore railway in Minnesota, as well as his fleet of freight vessels on the
Great Lakes. But Carnegie, who had been offered $157,950,000 for
his business by the Moore brothers in 1898, now demanded nearly
twice as much. John D. retired, and bided his chance.

The banker Stillman had "gone right after Harriman, regarding
him as the next great promoter after the Standard Oil group," by
his own account. After 1896, the flow of Standard Oil gold and
credits into the little stockbroker's railroad projects became a Niagara. For Harriman, as Stillman convinced the others, was a man
after their own heart. The boldness of his schemes for combination, his ingenious devices for reciprocal purchases of stock in related railroads, and for interlocking directorates through "working
majorities" (which were actually aggressive minorities dominating
passive investors) and the quick, ripe fruits gathered from his undertakings—all this appealed to the Rockefellers strongly. Armed with
such credits, Harriman now climbed swiftly over the heads of other
railroad captains during the closing years of the century, to reign
as a "Napoleon" of the national railway system during a brief, dazzling career which was ended suddenly by the complete exhaustion
of his health and his early death.

This "human dynamo," as his associates began to call him, had
supreme confidence in himself. "When he started on a course, nobody could swerve him from it. He would go right through despite
all opposition and carry the situation alone," says a Union Pacific
man. "He would not understand public sentiment or why he had
public opposition in many cases." With his gift for swift and elaborate calculation, he was instinctively impatient or scornful of the
criticism of slower-witted folk surrounding him; he feared neither

God nor Morgan nor the pangs and scruples of conscience. An obituary notice of him declared that the secret of his victorious career was his utter lack of moral scruples. Had he not cast these overboard, he would have stumbled at the very first step he took. One of his last steps was that of breaking the man who had opened the gates of the railway paradise for him—Stuyvesant Fish. Fish himself was a fellow of smaller knavery; and when Harriman found that his old friend could not be trusted with railroad treasury funds, he flung him aside without mercy or gratitude.

As he had once clashed with Morgan in 1887 over a small Middle Western feeder railroad, so he opposed him again in the "reorganization" of the Erie which Morgan initiated after its renewed failure in 1893. Acquiring some of the Erie bonds, he led a protective committee in vigorous opposition to the Morgan plan, and within six months he had been able to balk the great banker and force a change of capitalization. At the outset Harriman had distinguished himself among men by practicing a form of economic terrorism; but soon he made bolder strokes.

Among the 156 railroads which collapsed in the depression of 1893–96 was the Union Pacific, whose history was as malodorous as that of Erie and which had also never completely recovered from the ministrations of Jay Gould. When it fell finally in 1895, its limbs and branches—the Oregon ship and rail lines united with it after Villard's crash—were torn away, and its condition was so woeful that Pierpont Morgan, being appealed to, refused to assume charge of its affairs.

This would seem to be the great banker's chief tactical error. With Morgan's tacit consent, Jacob Schiff of the esteemed banking house of Kuhn, Loeb & Co. attempted the reorganization of the Western trunk line and induced the Vanderbilts to take part in his plan.

"But in the latter part of 1896, Mr. Schiff and his associates became conscious that some secret but powerful influence was working against them." Schiff assumed that it was concealed sniping from the house at 23 Wall Street; but at Morgan's he heard: "It's that little fellow Harriman, and you want to look out for him."

"I am the man," Harriman admitted when Schiff confronted him. What did he propose? To issue $100,000,000 in bonds at 3 per cent, against the credit of Illinois Central which he controlled. Schiff could not get money under 4½ per cent. "I am stronger than you are," Harriman wound up.

Schiff asked: "What is your price?"

Harriman replied: "There is no price. I am determined to get possession of the road."

After long delays, skirmishes and masked thrusts, Schiff returned finally to yield to Harriman, on behalf of his faction, chairmanship of the Union Pacific's directors "if you prove the strongest man. ..." The bargain was struck. Within a year, the defunct railroad was sold to the new interests according to the Harriman-Schiff plan; $81,000,000 were easily raised to meet immediate government loans and other obligations. Then, under Harriman's leadership, in anticipation of a boom which he forecast, $25,000,000 more capital was raised for the road. Schiff "walked the floor at night" in these days, while Harriman captured the old Oregon rail and ship lines of Villard, pushed new construction, built tunnels and great cut-offs with furious speed, with an amazing expenditure of energy. Thus, this new dictator of railroads saw his and the Rockefeller investments, according to his official biographer, increase in value 1,400 per cent within eight years! In 1901, five years after the entrance of Harriman, John W. Gates commented that the Union Pacific was indeed "the most magnificent railroad property in the world."

Harriman was not merely a bold and gifted administrator; he had, to a degree which Morgan might keenly envy, skill in carrying out "reorganization parties" such as the notorious Chicago & Alton affair. According to Professor Ripley, the "reorganization" of this bankrupt road by the Harriman-Rockefeller-Stillman group was attended with the injection of $23,000,000 of water into its bonds and stocks. Then the new managers had paid themselves liberally, and sold their Alton stocks and bonds. Harriman was also not above selling railroad and other properties which he and his associates personally acquired to be merged into the larger Union Pacific system at a fine price, in the classic manner of Jay Gould. In the seven years following 1893, he accumulated one of the first fortunes in the country.

Yet these feats alone would not have offered so much menace to the system of "community of interest" which Morgan and his associates laboriously erected day by day over the economic life of the country. It was the spreading network of the Harriman-

Rockefeller railway and industrial investments that caused alarm. The Union Pacific itself had now become a mighty money-chest, its interlocking controls reached the middle roads, such as the Illinois Central Railroad of which Harriman still remained a director, and great Eastern systems such as the Baltimore & Ohio. But in 1900, when Collis P. Huntington died, Harriman and his band of multi-millionaires were able to buy from Huntington's widow the whole railroad empire he had built up: the Southern Pacific, with its direct line to San Francisco. For this transaction Harriman promptly raised over $50,000,000, which brought a majority stock control.

Harriman and the Standard Oil "gang" in alliance were now taking over the key railroads, as well as the chief underground resources of the nation in oil, iron and copper, while Morgan won over the banking system of the country, and at the same time Carnegie fastened his grip on the major industry of the country, steel. Such simultaneous concentration of force among the opposing dynasts furnished the materials for "irrepressible conflict."

In the steel trade Carnegie must break forth to combat the encroachments of the new Morgan Trusts; but having fought to a finish, the survivor would have to negotiate or fight for his life against the arrayed might of the Harriman-Rockefeller dynasty. And who could safely foretell a happy issue from such a contest?

"How can you beat the Standard Oil party, with their sixty millions of income per annum?" exclaims James Keene, the wizard stock-market leader who now acts as one of Morgan's lieutenants. "They have control of all the industries, are getting all the railroads and the street railways, and will in a few years own the whole country. I can see no stopping them."

CHAPTER SEVENTEEN

THE EMPIRE OF MORGAN

O F the three dominant financial groups which contended with each other for supreme power over the country, the banking organization known as J. P. Morgan & Co., by its close-knit, compact nature, by the solidness of its plan and its firm yet far-spreading fingers of control, suggested itself as the most formidable engine for economic rulership. The Morgan power by no means rested solely upon the gold possessed by Pierpont Morgan himself or by his partners -though that was considerable. The intricate and diversified manner in which this power was expressed is in itself astonishing and demands precise explanation. At the same time no other of the great money-lords confronted the turbulent age with so purposeful a mind and so resolute a program as Morgan.

The banker occupies the pilot-room of the capitalist system. By his intimate connection with his clients the banker is easily in a position to "know all, see all, hear all." As safekeeper for the public, and with his own money chest, he guards a reservoir of gold or credit, susceptible of usage in a thousand ways for the contraction or the infinite expansion of loan capital in the form of short- or long-term credits. The merchant, the industrialist, the railroad manager come running to him with their negotiable paper, their collateral good and bad, their pledges or promises to pay; they come in fat or lean days, to seize opportunities for enrichment or to save themselves from embarrassment or even extinction. And always the banker, "lynx-natured, thin-lipped, keen-eyed, hard-favored ... with lowered head," as Balzac paints him in the "*Comédie Humaine*," gazes calmly into the secrets of men with his devouring stare. His mind is always plunged into the future which holds the secret of whether the gold he lends will be repaid in full and with interest; or now it measures the chance of sharing the proceeds of a promising speculation; or calculates how far he may go in levying toll, because of the desperateness of an exigency, while still preserving "business honor" intact.

But the private banker, especially the private banker engaged in investment promotions, stands in a more strategic position still than the general money-lender. In the work of originating issues of stocks and bonds (that is to say, long-term capital), his field is boundless, especially in a country whose population doubles in two decades, whose industrial construction must be extended almost incessantly, whose underground resources demand ever larger exploitation. This was the work which Morgan carried on as he bought and sold and created issues of capital; carried on with supreme confidence—"a bull on America." Of the moneys he raised for railroads like the Northern Pacific or the New York Central, by means of vigorous public flotations in the market of savers and investors, a mounting share in the form of promoter's commissions adhered to him; large parts of the total sums also remained with him for deposit and could be set to work in further projects. Beyond this, he would open to himself still further resources of the public's capital, as will be presently shown.

It was in the "reorganization" of bankrupt railroad properties, however, that the largest and most glittering opportunities for power came first to Morgan. With the prostrate client, whether it be an Erie Railroad or a Northern Pacific, in desperate need of fresh working capital, Morgan with his reserves of ready money could appear and impose hard terms. His work consisted first in the scaling down or reduction of old debts to a size which could be safely carried before new debts were contracted; this he would do, no matter how bitterly the ruined bondholders cried out. Second, he demanded a dominant voice in the management of those enterprises which he helped salvage, by acquiring payments in the form of stock, or appointing himself or his agents directors, members of a "voting trust."

The field of operations for marketing securities enlarged itself sensibly in the boom of the later '90's. "Thus it was," writes Mr. Justice Brandeis, "that they [the investment bankers] became promoters, or allied themselves with promoters," the manufacturers of securities. And the Justice continues with humor, "Adding the duties of undertaker to those of midwife, the investment bankers became in times of corporate disaster, members of security holders' 'Protective Committees'; then they participated as 'Reorganization Managers' in the reincarnation of the unsuccessful corporations, and ultimately became directors."

But often the mere need for new money brought from the banker a counterdemand for a seat in the management, membership in the board of directors. Or he asked that the stockholders' proxies be deposited with him. "When once a banker has entered the Board— whatever may have been the occasion—" Mr. Brandeis concludes, "his group proves tenacious and his influence usually supreme; for he controls the supply of new money."

What shapes itself now in the mind of the great banker, as he verges from long, brooding calculations to negotiation or action, is the tremendously difficult plan for centralized control in which the warring railroad captains and even conflicting industries may be brought to labor peacefully and submissively together under his dictatorship. The times demanded such a control; one saw this clearly enough in 1893 and in the years that followed; and the Industrial Commission not long afterward appointed by Congress to study these very questions declared, on the subject of railways alone: "At no time in the history of American railroads has the need of efficient, wise and firm supervision by public authority of the terms and conditions of transportation been more imperatively demanded than at the present time." But by then, 1900, it would seem too late to have spoken, for Morgan would have assumed for himself this "public authority," this role of dictator which no one else seemed equal to, and no other man or group—up to the emergence of the Rockefeller clan—was in so strategic a position to seize.

As in 1889 Morgan had called together the leading railroad men in another conspiracy to create a monopoly of trunk lines, so now in the decade that followed he pursued the same object, stubborn, silent, unswerving as ever. In his mind, control of the country's transportation machinery held the key to centralization of power everywhere else. To be sure there were other famous individuals, each in his way formidable enough, who worked more or less consciously to further industrial unification—Vanderbilt, Carnegie, Frick, Rockefeller, Huntington, Hill—yet none but Morgan, his official apologist Hovey declares, "stood so steadfast for combination." None was to carry so far the purposive process of concentration, whose accomplishment lends to Morgan's career its chief glory.

Hovey tells us candidly that as soon as he became an influential factor in the financial world, he exerted a constant pressure in this direction, and as a result of his solid and simple stand, fate threw larger opportunities in his hands than in those of any other man of his generation. In the period from 1893 to 1900 the railway systems of the country, gigantic, sprawling, and weakened to the point of helpless impoverishment by competitive battles, were forced with very few exceptions, to undergo complete reorganization. Mr. Morgan proved himself the most successful reorganizer, and *he used the power and prestige thus gained to eliminate competition from the railroad business.* The next ten years brought forth numbers of industrial combinations; Mr. Morgan bested everyone at this sort of work; *and every corporation he formed or influenced did away with real competition.*

It was with this "solid and simple" heroism, though with ingenuous phrases, that Morgan would say: "We do not want financial convulsions and have one thing one day and another thing another day."

The process of conquest over so great a region is exciting to watch in its decisive stages between 1893 and 1901. It was at first gradual, like the almost invisible advance of a thin line of skirmishers; then it grew into full and furious conflict for all the points of advantage, before the eyes of all the astonished, ignorant citizenry.

During the latest depression, the House of Morgan[1] as a fighting organization was complete in all its parts, equipped much as it is today. In 1889, as forty years later in 1929, the house possessed a great amount of that "good-will" which is so vital to the investment banker in dealing confidentially with his clients. It was known to hold literally to its contracts or "deals" with colleagues or accomplices; it impressed the legion of small investors, speculators and dealers with its "responsibility," and "integrity." Only the venerable though much smaller firms of Lee, Higginson and Kidder, Peabody in Boston, and the German-Jewish group of Kuhn, Loeb in

---

[1]Drexel, Morgan & Co. became J. P. Morgan & Co. in 1895, at the death of Anthony Drexel.

New York, approached Morgan's in these qualities of venerable probity toward its collaborators.

To be armed at all points, to see around corners, to have eyes peering everywhere, Pierpont Morgan had surrounded himself with a group of lieutenants who were able, energetic and often, as it happened, handsome as well. The standard of looks among his loyal younger men was so high as to cause the remark that "when the angels of God took unto themselves wives among the daughters of men, the result was the Morgan partners!" In Wall Street, they spoke of "Jesus Christ and his Twelve Apostles"—though Morgan was an ugly, lowering figure, charged with vitality, curt, decisive, with rare moments of tears and passion, which only a few saw. The ablest of his partners were Charles H. Coster, the railroad expert, Egisto Fabbri, the Italian economist and mathematician, George W. Perkins, who came from the First National Bank, George S. Bowdoin, J. Hood Wright, and Robert Bacon, future ambassador to England, of impeccable appearance but of lower tactical ability than the others. Coster especially was remarkable as a sort of "financial chemist." He had joined forces with Drexel and Morgan in 1884, and ever since then carried on all their elaborate railroad reorganizations; he is remembered as "a white-faced, nervous man, hurrying from meeting to meeting [of the fifty-nine corporations of which he was a member of the board of directors!] and at evening carrying home his portfolios. . . ." A great master of detail, but of frail health; he was suddenly carried away by a slight cold which quickly developed into pneumonia. Like the other Morgan partners he had given all of himself to the immense tasks of economic organization with a courage and energy that might have been fruitful to the government or the society at large under another dispensation. All of the Morgan partners were rewarded with liberal shares in profits, toiled madly, and died young. By 1900, as Lewis Corey remarks, the first generation of them were all dead. Only "Jupiter" Morgan "had come through that soul-crushing mill of business retaining his vigor, health and energy."

There was a division of labor by which their work was departmentalized; one specialized in government finance; another in railroads; another in steel companies. They wove together a broad network of relationships, and all reported back continually to the supreme commander for important decisions, wherever he might be.

But the most impressive thing that could be perceived, if one looked deeply enough at all this mysterious labor, this heaving and shaking of worlds, was the progress of Morgan's ruling idea: an *imperium in imperio* of banking under his supreme command. Inalterably he continued to weld the numerous banks, trust and insurance companies into whose control he penetrated into a single concentrated financial structure, a solid pyramid at whose apex he sat. In this campaign of secret alliances he acquired direct control of the National Bank of Commerce; then a part ownership in the First National Bank, allying to himself the very strong and conservative financier, George F. Baker, who headed it; then by means of stock-ownership and interlocking directorates he linked to the first-named banks other leading banks, the Hanover, the Liberty, Chase. Soon he had spread his control to the great insurance companies. In the largest of these, the New York Life, George W. Perkins was vice-president, and at the same time a partner in the House of Morgan; in the case of the great Equitable Life Assurance Society, Morgan was to pay $5,882 a share for control.

The three great life insurance companies which Morgan dominated, the New York, the Equitable and the Mutual, together owned approximately a billion dollars of assets toward 1900. They must invest from $50,000,000 to $55,000,000 each year. Their management (Morgan or Perkins or Baker) would, as officials for trust and life insurance companies, buy securities from themselves as investment bankers, that is, as partners or lieutenants of the House of Morgan! What could be more perfect? Morgan and his general staff had not only got the ownership of the goose that lays the golden eggs, Mr. Brandeis concludes, but also of the golden eggs laid by somebody else's goose. "They control the people through the people's own money." As the Armstrong investigation in New York, which was directed by Charles Evans Hughes, and the later Pujo Committee investigation disclosed, Morgan directed a great pool of banks and insurance companies toward the purchase of securities which he floated; but then the proceeds of these securities must be deposited either directly in the House of Morgan, or in his controlled banks, the First National, the Bank of Commerce, etc., which soon were to represent public deposits of $1,300,000,000. Thus the power of the Morgan Associates was "dynamic" as opposed to the static wealth of landowners or merchants who possessed goods.

"The power and the growth of power of our financial oligarchs comes from wielding the savings and quick capital of others," Brandeis said. It bred a concentrated control over a vast portion of the nation's savings, which extended itself with amazing speed.

2

From his power to allot securities at will to the various institutions under his influence, it will be seen how much greater Morgan's domination was than his own personal wealth. He was in an admirable position, far more so than even men like Rockefeller and Carnegie for all their huge direct incomes from industry, to bring order—to end a condition he referred to contemptuously as "one thing one day, another thing another day."

The unremitting vigilance and activity of his banking house reflected the anxieties that went with imperial power. The lights at 23 Wall Street, where the major staff and personnel seemed never to sleep, would be shining far into the night when all else was dark over New York. And Pierpont Morgan himself, though he traveled frequently to distract mind and body at doctors' orders, was burdened intolerably by the superhuman tasks he had undertaken. The hard living, the drain upon his energy seemed to burn him up. He appeared poorly, to those who observed him intimately, living in pain for long periods, turning away food brought to him and puffing only at his eternal black cigar. Traveling through Egypt in a resplendent private car, a companion of his noted how, at the receipt of cablegrams from New York, he would be plunged in long glowering calculations, hours upon end, while the incredible, half-ruined pyramids of other emperors and other ages which he had come to gaze at drifted by his window unnoticed.

In 1893-94, with nearly half the railroad mileage of the country in receivership, there were unheard-of difficulties in the path of centralization. The rigidly capitalized railroads as a rule could not withstand a long depression and falling receipts.

No single financial problem in the previous history of the world [writes John Moody] equaled in difficulty or magnitude this reorganization of the railroads of the United States. These crazy financial structures had been patched together by any possible method of co-

*hesion. They were leased, interleased, subleased; bought in whole or
in part; and securities of every degree of inflation represented ques-
tionable claims upon them.*

Through a maze of financial detail, opposing claims, debts, spurious loans of broken or plundered enterprises, the Corsair and his
lieutenants moved irresistibly to impose order "upon conditions of
his own," as his apologist writes. Then having "financiered away
the discrepancies between earnings and outgo," he would retain always his controlling voice in order "to prevent further mishaps or
the use of bad judgment"; and afterward, there would always be
"the necessity of extending that control to still other lines which
might become competitors and start the old difficulties afresh. . . ."

Morgan's immediate interest at an early date had been attracted
to the group of Eastern coal railroads, which to his mind dominated most vital parts of the industrial organism. In Pennsylvania the
Reading Railroad, headed by a certain McLeod, had shown ambitions
to expand. Occupying a strategic position near the seaboard, it had
been used in the struggle against the Pennsylvania Railroad in 1885,
by Vanderbilt, Carnegie and others. Its president, after 1887, cam-
paigned vigorously to build up a 5,000-mile system, acquiring control of other coal roads, and designing to penetrate the New England market by the Poughkeepsie freight bridge.

When Morgan had frowned upon this plan, McLeod had said:
"I'd rather run a peanut stand than be dictated to by J. P. Morgan,"
and he had gone to the Speyers for credits—at 9 per cent, or more.
Whereupon the coal regions rang with war. In his most imperious
manner, Morgan had notified men of capital that "they must not
expect to maintain friendship with him if they continued to help
McLeod finance his projects in New England." And that, as Hovey
said, "was a hint sufficient," closing off sources of fresh credit to
the Reading. Furthermore, Morgan used his complete control of
the New York, New Haven & Hartford Railroad to cut off New
England; he attacked the Reading's securities in Wall Street, until
the collateral offered for loans by the enemy capitalist had so shrunk
that their position was untenable and the railroad was plunged into
receivership.

The resultant "reorganization" was of course conducted by
Morgan, who placed one of his tools, George F. ("Divine Right")

Baer in direct charge. With the aid of the Lord and of Morgan, order was imposed. The instrument of the "voting trust" absolutely controlling the property for a certain period of time was introduced in the process soon called "Morganization." Thus bondholders took heavy losses as the obligations they held were "scaled down" to sums considered supportable under the distressing circumstances—a ruthless wiping out of debt, from which the property emerged greatly relieved, naturally, and for which the Morgan Associates grew notorious. To all protests, he would say gruffly: "Your railroad? Your railroad belongs to my clients!"

Another typical exploit of the depression was the seizure of a chain of ruined railroad systems in the South, 9,000 miles of track were grouped around the old Richmond Terminal Company, capital debt slashed away, former owners and claimants banished, and the whole conglomeration revived as the Southern Railway. So Morgan carried on the fatal process of centralization, the expropriation of the "lesser capitals by giant capitals," ending disastrous rate wars, and effecting great territorial consolidations.

But if the process of Morganization had its great social usefulness in welding together the productive forces of society as an integrated whole, so did it involve new and onerous costs in the shape of fees to the managers of the general reorganization, and the excessive capital debt which was ultimately saddled upon these means of production and whose burdens were borne thereafter by the great public. For the investment banker was forever under the dual temptation to sell "gold bricks" to the corporations he controlled or amalgamated, and to sell out to the public securities en masse against the Trusts which he combined—no matter what the ultimate social costs might be.

Thus, down East Morgan obtained control of the New Haven, which ran through the country of his boyhood and unified the scattered New England systems, so that one no longer needed to transfer at Springfield in order to ride from Boston to New York. In the process he merged with the New Haven all the divers local systems he had acquired: the Old Colony line of steamships and rails, the New York & New England, the Shore Line and 128 other properties —leaving the amalgamated company in complete monopoly of the New England states. But in effect, he had saddled a tremendous charge of debt upon the New Haven Railroad; the properties purchased by him as a promoter were sold to himself as a director of New Haven, at prices which he alone determined and which the world never heard of until long afterward when the once rich railroad reached the end of its rope. By 1894, a few years after his "fatal entrance" into New Haven affairs, according to Barron's diary, the consolidated company had assumed $100,000,000 of indebtedness, a burden which eventually proved too heavy.

In Pennsylvania the same process of Morganization was carried out with little regard to the final costs for the community. The hard-coal mines were nearly all indirectly owned by Eastern railroads over whom Morgan held influence or a decisive voice: these were the New York Central, the Pennsylvania, the Lehigh Valley, the Lackawanna, Erie, and New Jersey Central. When an independent group known as the Pennsylvania Coal Company arose to offer competition to the anthracite monopoly, Morgan at once hastened to buy control of the newcomer in the open market, paying an average price of $552 per share for its stock, in order to eliminate opposition entirely. Then he turned over this purchase to the Erie Railroad at a price which was termed by the Industrial Commission of 1900 the highest ever paid for such properties. Yet it was not high if it brought command of all the Eastern seaboard's fuel. Similarly in the soft-coal regions, the Hocking Valley Railroad, the Baltimore & Ohio and Chesapeake & Ohio were soon swept into the unified control of the unified system which held through "the purchase or interchange of stock," at once the coal mines, the roads that carried their coal to market and the banks which financed them all.

Every year, according to the Industrial Commission's report of 1900, traffic in coal was now allotted evenly, output was restricted to a fixed amount—33 per cent under capacity, so experts estimated. Prices were steady and high; railroad rates were extremely high: 6 to 10 mills per mile per ton for anthracite, and 3 mills for soft coal, when at this very moment Carnegie was hauling iron ore from Lake Erie to his works at Pittsburgh at 1/3 mill per ton mile. At the same time the condition of the coal-miners, for long years "comparable to that of slavery in the South" as the government commission reported, was kept unchanged; and the insurgent move-

ments of the miners up to 1901 were resisted, as we have seen,
with that peculiar ruthlessness which fervent Christians such as
George Baer and Pierpont Morgan, no less than the Spanish Conquerors, sometimes invoked.

In his march to power the imperious banker knew how to make
governments as well as small capitalists and armies of rebellious
laborers bend to his will. At the time of the Treasury crisis in 1894
and 1895, great fears spread everywhere as to the solidity of the
national currency. With a universal cry rising from the hard-pressed
people for inflation and for the "unlimited coinage of silver"—at
a moment when the government's gold reserve was dwindling—it
was presumed that specie payments would be suspended at any
moment by the federal Treasury.

In 1894 the Secretary of the Treasury, with Cleveland's consent,
had been compelled to go to Morgan to borrow $50,000,000 for
the purchase of foreign gold. Morgan had thundered "Impossible!"
—that is, save at his own terms, which he ultimately forced the government in its extremities to accept; terms which were afterward
furiously attacked in Congress as extortionate and unpatriotic. By
mobilizing a powerful coterie of banks, life insurance and trust companies the Corsair had succeeded in financing the government's needs
and "saving his country" at usurious rates.

According to James Stillman's account, Morgan had been hard
put to it to raise the needed funds; he came to Stillman, "greatly upset and over-charged, nearly wept." Stillman had thereupon cabled
to Europe for ten millions of Standard Oil gold, and gathering
ten more from other sources, had brought this to Morgan, saying:
"I have twenty millions."

"'Where did you get them,' cried Morgan. And ... *il bondit
de l'abîme de désespoir au pinacle de bonheur,* and became perfectly
bombastic and triumphant as the Saviour of his country. He took
all the credit. But then you see Morgan was a poet—Morgan was
a poet!"

But "saving the country" once had been insufficient; the gold
had been drained away rapidly again by the great hoarders, the
gold reserve had vanished anew. Cleveland, under fire for his deal-

ings with the banking consortium, had been forced nevertheless to come, hat in hand, for a further issue of gold bonds in 1895, at terms imposed by the Morgan syndicate, and called by the financial historian A. D. Noyes "extremely harsh" and "unpitying toward the emergency of the government."

Once more there was sharp trading to be done with Washington. Fearful of popular opinion, the President had resisted paying the "pound of flesh" exacted. The story has often been told of how Morgan, rebuffed by the President, waited alone and played solitaire at his hotel in Washington, massively silent, stubborn in his certainty—as the government's gold reserve sank to only a day's supply—that Cleveland, having no other refuge, must in the end submit once more to him, the master of Wall Street.

Under the previous plan, the bankers had loaned the government money to purchase gold, then used the conversion privilege to draw off government gold anew! Now the high interest rate fixed by Morgan was the price paid, according to Hovey, for his promise to see to it that the flight of gold was stopped.

Getting the new 4 per cent gold bonds from the government at 104, the syndicate offered them at 112, and on news of the powerful Morgan support, the open market price soon rose to 118 and even to 123. It was not merely the huge immediate profits reaped by the Morgan syndicate which enflamed public opinion—(at a Congressional investigation, the Corsair refused to divulge these, saying, "*I decline to answer*"); it was the effect of secret negotiations between the President and the all-powerful banking syndicate composed of Morgan, Stillman and Belmont (acting for the Rothschilds) that roused the storm and fed the furious "yellow" journals of Pulitzer and Hearst. The charges of a "sinister complot" to control the national destiny, the thunderings of the young demagogue from Nebraska against "bondage" and "bribery" left Pierpont Morgan outwardly unaffected. Impassive and solitary as Rockefeller—he had not fifty acquaintances in all his own purlieus of Wall Street who knew him personally—Morgan "never thought of meeting the public half-way with an explanation," his historian records. He continued intrepidly with the main business at hand: to sweep together railroads into a few giant, regional systems, to consolidate numberless industrial enterprises into great Trusts after his own watery fashion.

3

In the golden age of McKinley when the government itself, as
Henry Adams observed, seemed to be encouraging finance capital
"to pool interests in a general Trust," there were gathered under
the dominion of the House of Morgan between 45 and 50 per cent
of the national railroad mileage according to various estimates.
Hovey counts 55,555 miles owned or dominated by J. P. Morgan &
Co.; but Corey's estimate, of 30,446 miles directly and 37,700 indirectly controlled, seems more accurate. Adding to this mileage the
Pennsylvania system, for which Morgan was fiscal agent, the Gould
Southwestern lines, closely affiliated with him at various times, and
finally the railroad empire of James Hill in the Northwest, we have
a grand mileage of almost 100,000 toward 1900, virtually half of
the country's railway tracks. The largest single group of roads now
lying outside of Morgan's sphere were those of the Rockefeller-
Harriman combination. From Maine to New Orleans in the deep
South, from the Atlantic seaboard to the Mississippi the Morgan
network extended itself; and by a last step linked with Hill's Northern roads it formed a completed transportation system carrying
goods from the Atlantic seacoast to the Far East.

In reorganizing the repeatedly bankrupt Northern Pacific after
1893, Morgan had measured lances with Jim Hill; he had found
that without that railroad captain's collaboration he could not re-
establish the Northern Pacific at all. There had been interviews
and trading conferences in London and New York. Finally the
management of the two competing Northern lines had been entrusted altogether to Hill, who had won the banker's regard and
become his firm ally. Thus no sooner did the people of the Northwest obtain their two completed parallel trunk-lines than these
were seen to pass quietly into the unified control of Hill and
Morgan. As Hill wrote in confidence:

> The sole object ... was to bring together as nearly as possible
> the general policies of the Northern Pacific and Great Northern, so
> that both companies ... would avoid unnecessary expenditures in
> building new lines, or in the operation of existing lines. We believe
> this could only be done by the holding of a large and practically a
> controlling interest in both companies by the same parties.

Then in further elaboration of their plans, it was decided in 1896 to purchase jointly the Chicago, Burlington & Quincy Railroad, a great feeder line running from Chicago through the richest grain regions of the Middle West. Morgan bluntly related his plan of unification to a committee of Congress afterward:

> I think it was in 1898 or in 1899 that I made up my mind that it was essential that the Northern Pacific should have its eastern terminus in Chicago, in the same way as the New York Central, of which I am a director, has its western terminus there. . . .

So at his command, there reigned an effective "community of interest" in the railroad world, which only that "little fellow Harriman" menaced.

In the meantime other realms of industrial wealth waited to be conquered and enjoyed, Morganized, watered and distributed as investment securities to the public on the crest of financial "booms." In the banking house at Wall and Broad streets Morgan's legal and mathematical experts developed a perfect technique for the swift framing of industrial Trusts such as the International Harvester Company, and the General Electric Company. Trade wars, as between the two biggest electric-machinery manufacturers, General Electric and Westinghouse, were usually terminated by a financial statesmanship which brought a Morgan partner to the board of directors in each. Finally, the colossal steel industry which grew with fantastic haste from year to year in the United States, yet suffered from "feast and famine" and ferocious price wars, invited Morgan's unifying genius.

The combination of the Western steel-producers in 1898 under the head of Federal Steel figured as the mightiest industrial corporation, in size of its capital, known up to that time, and the profits from its promotion gave Morgan much cause for satisfaction. At Morgan's insistence the sanctimonious Gary was appointed to its command.

"Judge Gary, you have put this thing together in very good shape," said Morgan. "We are all very well pleased. Now you must be president." And this naturally was done.

The amalgamation of the great mills in the Chicago region, the framing by Morgan of other Trusts in the related business of pipes, bridges, sheet and hoop steel (which then ceased to buy their raw ingots from Carnegie), all this gave the country's leading steel master more and more concern. During the brief war boom of 1898-99 there had been room for all; there had been peace and collusion. But the outlook was now dark with the promise of future hostilities as powerful Trusts ranged themselves against him. The new times irked Carnegie, who felt himself getting on in years. He had never collaborated with other interests easily, except on terms of mastery. The head of a "close corporation," he had no wish to become hereafter a great investment banker with multitudinous outside interests and allied with thousands of stockholders and petty absentee owners. He was now at odds with Frick, who, according to Harvey, "foresaw the trend of the times," and who wanted the Carnegie Steel Company to become part of the consolidation movement. After January, 1899, it was noised abroad that the world's steel king was ready to sell out and become the world's leader of philanthropy.

Carnegie nowadays leaned more and more upon his lieutenants, Frick, Phipps, Schwab and others; yet, since 1896, there was estrangement between him and Frick growing from a dispute over the contract price paid for coke to the underlying H. C. Frick Coke Company. In mournful tones, Carnegie wrote to his friend Lord Morley that though he was more tired than ever, he must give a closer eye to his business and could trust no one.

In May, 1899, Frick had come to Carnegie with the offer of the Moore brothers to buy the entire steel works. The offer was accepted, an option payment of $1,170,000 was made—partly furnished by Frick—and then the deal had fallen through to Frick's deep chagrin, and the option had been forfeited to Carnegie. Among the causes of the failure the secret opposition of Morgan has sometimes been mentioned. The Moores had counted on George F. Baker of the First National Bank to finance them, and on ex-Governor Roswell Flower, a famous market leader, to sell the Carnegie stock in Wall Street. But Flower had died, and Baker, probably at Morgan's instance, had refused credit. In any case the war profits gathered in 1899 happily showed Carnegie that he had placed his ransom too low. According to Moody's theory, Carnegie now bided his time, "until the Morgan interests had plunged so deeply into the steel business, in connection with Federal Steel Company, the National Tube, the American Bridge, that they could not possibly back out..." He, Carnegie, would then show them how shaky their footing was, at the brink of an economic abyss. But in the meantime Frick must be eliminated, Frick with his far-flung affiliations in high finance, his intimate connections with Wall Street, with the great bankers whom Carnegie hated and feared. In October, 1899, Carnegie had his grounds for an open break.

Returning from Scotland in this month, Carnegie noticed that Frick had purchased some land adjoining the steel company's mills, the Wiley farm, above Peter's Creek, presumably to prevent construction of a rival plant or to hold in reserve for possible contingencies. This land Frick sold to the Carnegie company at $3,500 an acre. The story of the conflict has been told in many ways, but never so well as in the more recent chronicles of Barron:

> When Carnegie came back from Scotland he always had the records of the meetings read to him.... Now Carnegie never allowed a man to get away with a dollar from him or his properties and he never forgave a man if he lost money. So when he came to this item of $1,500,000 paid to Frick for the Wiley farm, he said to Frick, "What did it cost you?" and Frick intimated that that was his personal affair. Carnegie said that he would show Frick quickly that it was not.... The vote to purchase was rescinded and Frick forced to take back the property for which he had paid only $500,000.

It was open war, Frick denouncing Carnegie's "high-handed" tactics and demanding apologies. Each took hostile measures against the other. Finally Carnegie pressed Frick to surrender his share of partnership in the Carnegie Steel Company at terms fixed previously, years before, in a so-called "iron-clad agreement" whereby the stock was valued by its paid-in "book-value" rather than its current market-value in the light of recent earnings. Thus in vengeance, Carnegie would have deprived Frick of some $10,000,000—ultimately as it proved of far more—this being the difference between the stated and real value of Frick's hard-earned minority interest.

At one stage of the quarrel, Carnegie visited Frick at his private office, insisting stubbornly upon the carrying out of the "iron-clad agreement," and threatening also to strike at Frick's interest in his coke company too. In turn Frick may have threatened to cut off the supply of coke at once. Carnegie, sitting on the edge of a chair close to Frick's desk, had been nervous and impatient, while Frick had spoken in low tones. Then the autocrat of the Homestead struggle, always cool and self-possessed up to a certain point, suddenly "burst into flame." The mad fiend in him raged wildly, and he must have flung himself upon the older man; for in the next moment, Carnegie was seen by those outside the room in full flight down the hall, with Frick close upon his heels.

In the muffled duel that followed Frick was ousted from the chairmanship, but retained his share of stock in the teeth of Carnegie's fiercest efforts to break him. All respectable interests, friends of both, begged them to spare the country such a scene, in which "secrets of the steel trust's" fabulous profits would leak out.[2] At this Carnegie had been induced to give up the fight. Besides, great events were preparing themselves before which the significance of their quarrel dwindled, and from which both parties reaped loot enough to satisfy "business honor."

4

For good reason Gary, head of the Morganized Federal Steel Company, had been begging his chief to buy out Carnegie's mills. There had been a lull in which the leading interests acted peaceably toward each other. But at the end of 1899—while President Charles Schwab of the Carnegie Steel Company discreetly appeared here and there offering to sell out the company—Carnegie suddenly broke the steel-rail pool and began underselling the market. The phase of conciliation had passed.

In the summer of 1900, we find Carnegie sending Schwab war orders from Skibo Castle in Scotland: "A struggle is inevitable and it is a question of the survival of the fittest." "This is a crisis which can be used to enhance the value of the property, or which not

[2]If there had been a legal suit in public, the embittered Frick would have published a boastful letter of Schwab's in 1899, showing that the Carnegie Steel Company was already grown so strong it did not need tariff protection. "You know we can make rails for less than twelve dollars a ton" it ran. "I know positively that England cannot produce pig iron for less than eleven dollars fifty cents per ton. . . . This would make rails at net cost to them of nineteen dollars. What is true of rails is equally true of other steel products. As a *result of this, we are going to control the steel business of the world.*"

being properly used will depreciate it." "You have only to meet the occasion, but no half way measures." Then further: "We will observe an *'armed neutrality'* as long as it is made to our interest to do so. . . . If they decline to give us what we want, then there must be no bluff. . . . If it is a fight they want, here we are 'always ready.' Here is a historic situation for the managers to study—Richelieu's advice: *'First, all means to conciliate; failing that, all means to crush.'* "

In full tide of prosperity a profound crisis shaped itself. The scattered makers of nails, wire, tubes, pipes, boiler plate and a thousand other steel products who had formerly bought their raw materials from Carnegie were now "integrated" into Trusts, thanks to Morgan and his allies. Controlling from 75 to 100 per cent of their market for finished steel, they obtained their own raw material, ingots and steel billets; they held up the selling price two and three times higher than before. Gates in the wire-nail Trust, the Moore brothers in tin plate, the new tube interests, had all notified Schwab that they would no longer need Carnegie steel; the American Bridge, which had been a mere assembling plant for Carnegie structural shapes, rails, and beams, now set up its own blast furnaces and steel-converting plants.

Now in retaliation Carnegie plans to make finished articles himself in competition with all the world; he says to Schwab, of one company after another which Morgan has organized, "we should go into making their products at once. . . . Lose not a day . . . crisis has arrived, start at once, hoop, rod, wire, nails mills. . . . Spend freely for finishing mills, railroads, boatlines. . . . Our safety lies in being independent and running our business in our own way. Whenever we do so we have the big trusts at our mercy." "We have no Union in our works. . . . The sales department is not responsible for market prices, but it is for keeping the works full. . . ."

The cablegrams fly thick and fast to the battle front at Pittsburgh. July 11, 1900, Carnegie writes:

Briefly if I were Czar, I would make no dividends upon common stock; save all surplus and spend it for a hoop and cotton tie-mill, for wire and nail mills, for lines of boats upon the Lakes for our manufactured articles and to bring back scrap. . . .

His rivals Carnegie despised. Was not the National Tube Company, as afterward proved in the Stanley Committee hearings, and by the admission of Morgan's expert, composed of $19,000,000 assets in scattered plants, while capitalized at $80,000,000? This was typical. It earned now 17 per cent on this inflated capital with a 90 per cent monopoly in all pipe. But Carnegie had a new process for making pipe, with the use of reduced labor and cheap steel. What would happen when he began to compete?

He set on foot a series of operations designed to create havoc among all the steel companies of the country. To fight Morgan he announced that he would go into the tube business in direct competition with the National Tube Company. His agents purchased 5,000 acres of water front at Conneaut, on Lake Erie, and let contracts for the construction of a $12,000,000 tube plant, of the most modern design. To fight Gates, of the American Steel & Wire Company, he announced a gigantic rod mill to be erected at Pittsburgh. To ward off Rockefeller he ordered the construction of a large fleet of ore-carrying vessels. He thus became "an incorporated threat and menace to the steel trade of the United States," as contemporaries observed.

Attacks upon Carnegie now came from the other side. Was it by Morgan's order? The Pennsylvania Railroad, which had made peace with Carnegie in 1890, by offering special rebates, was in 1899 headed by Cassatt, under the system of "community of interest." In unison with the Baltimore & Ohio, with which it was linked by stock purchase, the Pennsylvania now doubled freight rates from Pittsburgh to the seaboard. "With a stroke of his pen" Cassatt, as the furious Andrew exclaimed, had decreed that "Pittsburgh is stricken out as a manufacturing center...." The steel master threatened mass conventions of the people and was restrained with difficulty. He seethed with anger: "We will teach Mr. Cassatt and Mr. Vanderbilt a lesson.... A life and death struggle!... The Deliverance of Pittsburgh is my next great work."(!) Uniting with George Gould, who had delusions of grandeur, and at the moment schemed rebellion against the Morgan "collar," Carnegie drew plans to connect his short Bessemer line, Lake Erie to Pittsburgh, with the Western Maryland, 150 miles from Pittsburgh, thus to open a way eastward to the seaboard, by new construction over the Allegheny Mountains. He would use the millions in his war chest to cut his way to the sea! Gould in the meantime professed to be building a new independent transcontinental railroad which had San Francisco as its western terminus.

At the start of the steel war, the entire steel trade of the country was thrown into confusion. There was actual panic among the railroad-owners and millionaires of Wall Street; there was panic in the offices of Morgan, where to a great extent the bag was held for the vast paper amalgamations of the past four years, some $500,-000,000 in steel securities. All rushed to Morgan, crying in effect: "Save us! We must get rid of Carnegie; he will wreck both himself and us; he is a business pirate." Years afterward, Gary said, "It is not at all certain that . . . the Carnegie Company would not have driven entirely out of business every steel company in the United States," especially the eight great metal trusts which had recently arisen. Was it a bluff? The railroads too were in a panic to head off the new piratical combination which struck at Morgan's network of trunk lines. What would become of the plan of "community of interest"?

"Carnegie is going to demoralize railroads just as he has demoralized steel," Morgan said to Schwab at this time.

It was very hard. The master of bankers had moved mountains to unify the railroads; he had cunningly devised the system of reciprocal investments in stocks, of interlocking directorates—violating the law, facing prosecution continually—yet seen the great Union Pacific trunk line slip from his hands, revived, headed by the immitigable Harriman and enjoyed by the Standard Oil party. He had never acknowledged his bitterness at this error which measurably impaired his railway domain. Now for several years his whole attention had been directed to the new steel monopolies; and in turn, he found them at the mercy of the implacable Carnegie. Tomorrow the Federal Steel, National Tube, and the others—in a great trade conflict—might tumble into bankruptcy, all the fiction of their bonds and stocks destroyed. The railroads too would be involved in the general ruin prepared for them all. By the autumn of 1900, where he had stubbornly resisted Morgan was beaten down. He was now amenable to pleas that the Carnegie interest—and with it the Rockefeller ore companies—be bought in if it were at all possible.

CHAPTER EIGHTEEN

BATTLE OF GIANTS

O PEN war in the steel trade, as the more temperate money-masters realized, would have proved "disastrous to the weaker combatants and costly and wearing to the strongest." It would have exposed both ironmongers and investment bankers to the censure and attack of the public, which was instinctively felt nowadays to be the "common enemy" offering a "common danger."

Instead, a great dinner party to young Mr. Schwab, the president of the Carnegie Steel Company, was arranged for the evening of December 12, 1900. It was one of those informal parliaments to which "all the biggest men in New York" would be invited, seventy-five of the ungartered peers of American industry, including Mr. Morgan. Here without the interference of police or Senators the issues of heavy industry could be faced peacefully and a balance of power effected.

Was it a comedy, prearranged and managed from the wings by the crafty Andrew? Mr. Morgan, Gates, the Moores, and behind them the great bankers and dealers in securities present at the dinner were now deeply enough involved in the new steel Trusts. They all suffered vertigo at the thought of forthcoming events, when "Smiling Charlie" Schwab arose to address them in his excellent tenor. A born actor, an emotional and imaginative after-dinner speaker, using a plain, hearty, workaday charm with real disingenuousness, Schwab played his part to perfection.

He began as usual by saying that there was only one subject upon which he could speak—steel. But he could sing siren-songs of steel. He took his hearers—and especially the great banker who had been tactfully placed at his side, and whom he must have kept always in the corner of his eye—"up to the mountain tops" to view

the future millennium of metal. The steel requirements of the country, this perennial optimist told his hearers, would be twenty million,
nay, thirty million tons a year within a decade. Carnegie had made
$21,000,000 last year; 1900 was yielding profits at the annual rate
of $40,000,000 net, and it was only a beginning! It was a picture of
eternal prosperity at which his boldest hearers gasped; and to this
was added a vision of the future steel Trust which the Carnegie men
were building, having perhaps a hundred specialized plants, placed
at the most rational sites possible, rather than a few mills turning
out two dozen different steel products each. This was of course the
plan of "integration" and expansion for its mines, ore, ships, railway,
and mills which the Carnegie company had already announced.
And so in finishing, Schwab gave not only his dream of future prosperity and unity, but also in the same breath a menace of ruin for
the smaller steel works. To his auditors Schwab had painted both a
scientific millennium and a financial hell of clashing interests.

Thenceforth everything worked like a charm. Morgan took
Schwab aside and asked him a hundred rapid questions. He could
no longer rest. Some weeks later, another meeting took place between Schwab and Morgan, and there was an "all-night sympo-
sium," at which Schwab set forth statistics on the values and
on the character of the companies which should be brought into
the amalgamation. The plan roughly indicated that to the Carnegie
and Federal Steel combinations as the two largest groups there were
also to be added the wire-nail, tin-plate, hoop, and bridge Trusts. It
was to be a combination of Trusts, of a size which only the charla-
tan "Bet-a-Million" Gates had hitherto conceived: "the billion-
dollar corporation." Now would the "old man" of steel sell? It was
dawn, according to Burton Hendrick, when at last Morgan said:
"Go and find his price."

There was little hesitation now in Carnegie. The great anxiety
for him was now whether he would ask enough. After putting their
heads together for a long time, Carnegie and Schwab scribbled a
sum upon a piece of paper: in bonds and stock the price on the
Carnegie Steel Company was placed at $492,000,000!

In accepting, with a brusque decision, this stupendous ransom, of
which Carnegie was to receive over $300,000,000 in bonds and pre-
ferred stock, Morgan did not see Carnegie. Only several weeks
afterward in January, 1901, did they meet coolly for fifteen minutes'

brief interview, which according to Morgan's statement "made Carnegie the richest man in the world."[1]

The machinery of the House of Morgan now swung into action for its "biggest deal." Day and night the two partners, Bacon and Percival Roberts, labored together with Judge Gary and all the warring clansmen of the other steel companies. In the long and acrid debates, during which the Morgan partners kept the various steel barons caged in separate rooms, while Pierpont Morgan himself usually waited impatiently outside, it was finally arranged among other things to retire the swashbuckler Gates wholly from the steel trade. (At the moment the latest scandal raging over Gates had reference to his loss of a million dollars at a single throw of cards in a Pullman car to the son of Levi Leiter.) But to be rid of the old freebooter, the American Steel & Wire Company which he controlled must be bought in at a whacking big price. There was much growling, brow-beating and fist-pounding by Pierpont Morgan, and much patient pleading by Gary, nothing of which budged the king of barbed wire from his determination to have his price. Morgan was kept waiting outside in another room, as Miss Tarbell relates, while Gary "traded." Finally, after hours had passed, beside himself with rage, Morgan came in, "big and fierce, his eyes like coals of fire. 'Gentlemen,' he said, pounding the desk, 'I am going to leave this building in ten minutes. If by that time you have not accepted our offer, the matter will be closed. We will build our own wire plant.' And he turned and left the room."

John W. Gates scratched the top of his head, wondering aloud whether "the old man" meant what he said, finally concluding:

"I guess we will have to give up."

Gary relates that he had never seen Mr. Morgan more elated in all his life, "like a boy going home from a football game."

And Gates had gone off, hugely enriched, but unforgiving; swearing to "have fun in the market," to work mischief and set ambuscades at every possible moment for the masters of Trusts. The retirement of this gargantuan gambler was in itself a sign of the

[1] They met again a year or two afterward, on the deck of an ocean steamship. Carnegie said: "I made one mistake, Pierpont, when I sold out to you. I should have asked you $100,000,000 more than I did."

And Morgan, red-faced, glowering, said: "If you had, I should have paid it to you," adding, according to the legend, "—if only to be rid of you."

supplanting of captains of industry with investment bankers under the new dispensation.

But after several weeks of organization Gary and the other architects of the steel Trust called to Morgan's attention that the affair must be still further enlarged.

"We ought to have the Rockefeller ores," Gary said.

"We have got all we can attend to," Morgan growled. Gary urged him nevertheless to see John D. Rockefeller.

"I would not think of it."

"Why?"

"I don't like him."

It was remarkable how little love there existed between the greatest of the overlords of money. The stronger they were the more they hated each other. Even Pierpont Morgan could never browbeat Rockefeller and his associates, or force them to collaborate with him at his own terms. Nevertheless, Morgan reluctantly went to Rockefeller in person, and asked him point-blank for a "proposition" on the ore lands. According to Henry Frick's account (as related by George Harvey) the oil baron, now in "retirement," had refused to talk business, expressed regret that Mr. Morgan had put himself to unnecessary trouble . . . and suggested that he talk with his son, who had charge of such matters and would undoubtedly be pleased to wait on him.

After further calculation, Gary gave an "outside figure" as the bid for the great reservoir of underground iron; and Morgan invited John D., Jr.—then twenty-seven years of age—to call upon him. Harvey relates:

"I understand," said Mr. Morgan brusquely, "that your father wants to sell his Minnesota ore properties and has authorized you to act for him. How much do you want for them?"

Young Mr. Rockefeller rose from his chair and, with an evenness of tone suggestive of his father's, replied:

"It is true that I am authorized to speak for my father in such matters, Mr. Morgan, but I have no information to the effect that he wishes to dispose of his ore properties: in point of fact, I am confident that he has no such desire."

"And what did Mr. Morgan say?" quietly asked Mr. Rockefeller when his son repeated his remarks.

"Mr. Morgan said nothing; he sat quite silent."

"And what did you do?"

"I picked up my hat and, bowing as courteously as I know how, I said, 'If that is all, Mr. Morgan, I bid you good afternoon,' and walked out. Did I do right, sir?"

Mr. Rockefeller meditated for an instant and replied thoughtfully:

"Whether what you said was right or wise, I would not venture to judge; time alone can answer that question; but I may say to you, my son, that if I had been in your place, I should have done precisely what you did."

Impossible to go on with the steel Trust. Without Rockefeller's ore they were subject to an indeterminate extortion in the future. At this crisis, Henry Frick, whom Rockefeller had admired ever since the bloody victory of Homestead, was called in to act as go-between and lead through the impasse. The best he could do was to effect a settlement that was $5,000,000 above Gary's "outside figure," a price which Morgan sanctioned with some misgivings. The sum involved has remained a mystery, one authority fixing it at $32,000,000, and another at slightly less than $80,000,000. Rockefeller would never divulge his gains from the "squeezing" of the Merritt brothers; on the other hand, he may have been chagrined at having sold too *cheap*. At the time, the most sanguine of engineers had been unable to calculate the limitless extent of the Lake Superior deposits, whose mere surface scoopings by steam shovel supplied more than half the Bessemer ore of the country.

The Super-Trust was a reality; the long-awaited "billion-dollar corporation" with all its congeries of industries, its medley of mills and properties of all sorts, its 168,000 workers, and its vast tonnage production, was at last put together at Morgan's bidding, and was formally introduced to the world on April 1, 1901, as an investment proposition. For though the economic purpose of "integrating" and stabilizing the steel trade upon a nation-wide plan was implicit in this "greatest of commercial transactions" the real motive of the investment banker now showed itself as overweighing all other possible social or technical considerations. The real business at hand was, through a species of inflation, to extract from the mass of middle-class investors a price in payment for stocks and bonds exceeding even the fabulous prices which Morgan had paid for the capital of the divers steel works.

Against tangible assets of $682,000,000 possessed by the "United States Steel Corporation," Morgan underwrote and offered for sale whole masses of new securities: $303,000,000 in mortgage bonds, $510,000,000 in preferred stock; and $508,000,000 in common stock, making a grand total of $1,321,000,000 to be taken from the community's savings, as the economist would say, and poured into "long-term capital investment." But of this capital approximately half represented purely "water"; two-thirds of the preferred stock, and all of the common could be accounted for only by "good-will." Now this "good-will," though, it might have held some value—as for instance the "Carnegie" name or brand in a competitive situation—actually disappeared in a monopolized market. Whatever Morgan had paid under compulsion for his collection of "good-wills"— to men like Carnegie and Gates—was now worthless; multiplied they were worthless still. In addition, the repeated fees to promoters of the underlying Trusts (such as Federal Steel and American Steel & Wire), when added to Morgan's syndicate fee of $12,500,000 and subscription profits of $50,000,000, footed up to a grand total of $150,000,000 as the cost for launching the completed steel Trust. Promotion costs plus "good-will" would be imbedded forever in the capital structure of the steel industry, exacting immense fixed charges annually upon the whole community in the shape of interest payments and dividends. To support this inflated capital, to carry these charges, a levy would be made and resolutely maintained by keeping a profit margin as high as possible; the price system must carry the load of fictive debt. One of the ways in which this was done is suggested by the manner in which steel-rail quotations were held stationary for thirteen years after the formation of the steel Trust, at $28 per ton. The wonder of it was that the toil of nearly 200,000 nonunion laborers working twelve hours a day would support this burden; the wonder of it was that the country, growing by leaps and bounds, needing steel in a thousand forms, would willingly pay toll to the bankers who commanded this key industry without owning it.

The amalgamation of the steel companies represented "progress," was a predestined step toward a more centralized and coöperative economic system. But under the leadership of finance-capitalism inherent contradictions developed by which much of the gains were forfeited. The flotation of the steel Trust was characteristic of the recklessness with which capital was poured into heavy industry during years of frenzied finance with no thought of maintaining the buying power of the masses of consumers. Thus the tremendous *overproduction* of "future goods," plant, machinery, raw material in their several processes, would set the stage for chronic depressions. There would be a few Trusts, making mountains of pig iron and cotton cloth, harvester machines and biscuits, which only Mr. Morgan or Mr. Rockefeller could pay for but could not use, while millions of potential consumers were held workless and penniless. And then to augment profits the great Trust would introduce new labor-saving machinery, a more intense division of labor, year after year, thus demobilizing additional masses of consumers.

Under the command of the investment banker, the industrial monopoly reached its final stage of large-scale production; yet in the face of such great technical advantages, ways were found of nullifying much of the social gain to the community at large. How superior was the United States Steel Corporation to the preceding competitive system in a social sense we shall never know. Certainly this question which would be asked in a society ruled by workers and their engineers never entered the minds of the Morgans, Garys, Schwabs. We do know, for instance, that Schwab (in his private correspondence with Frick) actually indicated a cost to the Carnegie works of $12 per ton for steel rails, then selling at $23.75. The new Trust, which domestically found it necessary to bring about a "moderate" increase in the price of steel rails to $28 per ton, became in a great degree more "inefficient," judging by the yardstick of price, than the old Carnegie company.

Nevertheless there were halcyon days at Wall and Broad streets in the spring of 1901. There had been a "favorable" balance of trade in the three preceding years; the country was prosperous, and the bankers' syndicate easily gathered together a (pledged) fund of $200,000,000 with which to float the new steel stock. As the Morgan circular announcing the sale of the securities went forth, salesmen were thrown out over the country, a buzz of excitement and anticipation was created, so that the first days of trading in U.S. Steel resulted in huge turnovers. The old master, Jim Keene, at the head of a battalion of stockbrokers, created a "churning" activity for steel, under cover of which quantities of the common stock might be landed upon the public. One of the leading floor-brokers who carried on this exhilarating work has recalled that the stock pool would each day "sell 100,000 shares to the public and buy back only 10,000."

All was well, and Mr. Morgan departed for European watering resorts to refresh his health. The world's press was loud with stories of the "Economic Emperor"; in music halls in America the song was chanted:

> It's Morgan's, it's Morgan's,
> The great financial Gorgon's . . .

In the meantime a huge bubble was being blown in Wall Street, as a host of new steel millionaires, from Pittsburgh and elsewhere, descended upon New York and tossed their quickly won fortunes overnight into the market. After them followed a wild crowd, such as Wall Street had never seen—clerks, servants, waiters thronging the streets about the Stock Exchange, buying into the new Morgan Trust, one after another.

But the older, cooler heads among the steel masters, men like Henry Frick and Phipps of the old Carnegie Steel Company, quietly, cunningly sold out their holdings, contemplating with fear the Niagaras of "water" flowing into Wall Street, the stupendous bureaucracy of the Super-Trust in steel, the impending dangers for the national savings. For instance, Harvey says:

> Mr. Frick was unquiet. He . . . appreciated the danger of the company's heavy over-capitalization. . . . Careful study . . . convinced him that declines in earnings were inevitable, and he began to liquidate his holdings.

Carnegie, according to gossip, jested, half in earnest, that he would recapture his steel company by foreclosure, since he had been paid chiefly with its first mortgage bonds. . . . But soon the whole house of cards was to be rudely shaken from top to bottom by a cataclysm of epic proportions which engulfed the House of Morgan only four weeks after its triumph in steel.

2

In the Northwestern tier of states, Jim Hill, who, like Gary, acted nowadays as one of Morgan's 'field marshals," rounded out an industrial and agrarian empire. Hill's grain- and lumber-carrying lines ran through Wisconsin, Minnesota, North and South Dakota, Montana, Wyoming, Oregon and Washington, with no competition worth the name. They tapped also rich natural resources; in Minnesota a fabulous ore acreage had been picked up with the purchase of a logging railroad which possessed an old land grant, and this, valued eventually at $450,000,000, was added to the United States Steel holdings. The Hill lines connected also with big lake steamers, chains of elevators and storehouses at St. Paul, Chicago and even Buffalo. All the network of this great modern trading company, spreading even across the Pacific, to Japan and China, was well built, financially solid to the weather.

The collapse of the paralleling Northern Pacific line had brought it into Hill's hands in 1896, as we have seen, by Morgan's reorganization. In defiance of state and federal laws, the Great Northern group held half of the common stock of Northern Pacific, providing, as Hill said, "dual control by the same interest"; there was, furthermore, an amount of Northern Pacific preferred stock outstanding. Here it is important to note that in the common stock of Northern Pacific (a large minority of which was held by Morgan and Hill) *was vested the privilege of retiring all the Northern Pacific's preferred stock at any of the annual meetings regularly held on January 1 of each year.*

Through Hill's roads Morgan's railway system, industries and banks dominated the northern half of the Great West. But against this grouping there was always the growing shape of Harriman's gigantic combination. He too was financially solid. Like Hill, he had the air, as Otto Kahn said, "of bending men and events to his will." But the various invasions of Harriman would have been impossible without tremendous draughts upon the reservoir of money at 26 Broadway. Else he could not have seized and rebuilt so quickly the Union Pacific; nor added to this Collis Huntington's huge Southern Pacific, which was "an empire, not a railroad," as Harriman said. This company, besides its rich freight territories, dominated ocean shipping from the Gulf of Mexico to the Japan Sea. To carry these enterprises, Harriman's biographer tells us, the men of the Standard Oil family "gave Harriman financial support when he needed tens of millions of dollars, in credit or cash."

A terrific conflict prepared itself between these two giants of railroads, the one allied with Morgan and holding the northern half of the Great West, the other allied with the Rockefellers and dominating the southern territories west of the Mississippi. There were points of conflict at several points, as at the Oregon coast, where both systems competed, Harriman having captured for the Union Pacific Henry Villard's old Oregon ship and railroad lines. To the south, Harriman feared that Morgan and Hill would occupy another transcontinental route, and he therefore took his own defense measures of seizing the ground himself. But in its expansion plans, the Morgan-Hill combination was actually moving in another direction; it had concentrated upon the Middle West.

Hill planned long in advance and secretly to buy the rich Chicago, Burlington & Quincy Railroad, as a means of entrance to Chicago, and also as a great feeder network in the "garden of Paradise" of the Mississippi plain. He labored to this end in the face of Harriman's anxious efforts to seize the same road. The Burlington would parallel the Union Pacific's trunk line from Omaha westward to Cheyenne, the Burlington would form, as Hill vividly expressed it, in relation to the twin transcontinental lines of Great Northern and Northern Pacific, "the point and moldboard of a plow, the beams and handle of which are constituted by the former system," that is, Great Northern and Northern Pacific. Thus with the addition of this third large railroad, built long ago "on honor" by the early New England railroad captain Forbes, the Western transportation machine of Morgan and Hill would be rounded out, and the whole country mapped in huge "regional systems" and "territorial combinations."

"A big mosaic was being put together," writes the enthusiastic Pyle, concerning Hill, "by forces so great, so far above any permanent individual contradiction or interference, that he [Hill] looked upon himself as their servitor. . . ." This spirit of serving destiny, of obeying "the constant drift of combination" did not at any time prevent Jim Hill and the Morgan Associates from "lining their own pockets," in the vernacular of the time; that is to say, purchasing long in advance at from $100 up to $175 large blocks of Burlington's $110,000,000 of common stock, which were later to be disposed of at $200 a share to the Great Northern–Northern Pacific system.

"It was the only price at which it could be bought and we had great difficulty in getting it at that," Mr. Morgan would say afterward in explanation; "and in the next place . . . it was worth a great deal more than that. . . ." Had it then been difficult to get the Burlington shares at less than 200 from the group of its stockholders, among whom were investors such as Jim Hill, long forewarned that the road was to be absorbed by the larger adjacent systems? The price was paid; the bargain struck.

Now Hill exulted in the giant combination he had devised, which balanced the westward movement of cotton, provisions and immigrants with the eastward returning movement of timber, and ore in bulk—making full cars both ways, the passion of any railroad man. But there were further great advantages. Hill writes to Lord Mount Stephen, early in 1901:

> We could not build a great permanent business, extending across the continent and even across the ocean, on the basis that tomorrow the rate might be changed, or the party with whom we were working to reach the different points of production had some other interests or some greater interests elsewhere. It was necessary that we should have some reasonable expectation that we could control the permanency of the rate and be able to reach the markets. . . .
>
> Now we know that we are able, not to compete alone with railways, but to compete in rates with ships going from New Orleans, or any other system of transportation. Now we are able to make a rate that will take that business [meaning Southern Pacific's].

He had needed the power to make a low, stable rate for a long haul across the prairies of the United States, over the Rockies, and then by ship to the Orient. Thus he began, like some great merchant of Renaissance times, "to reverse the needle of trade," to send a flood of cotton to the Orient via his cars and lines and to bring back silks to Seattle.

This notion of controlling or easily competing with any service which could be given to the Orient by a parallel ship-and-rail system, that is, the Southern Pacific–Union Pacific, shows us how desperate was the emergency for the other railroad party whose head-quarters were really 26 Broadway. Henry Flagler and William Rockefeller, as owners of the Chicago, Milwaukee & St. Paul, had previously refused to sell their road to Morgan at any price, not wishing to provide the enemy Morgan-Hill lines with an entrance to Chicago. Harriman too had hoped to capture the Burlington, in order to ward off danger, buying a small stock interest here as well, late in 1900. But when it was learned that after swift, secret ma-neuvers, Morgan and Hill had captured the Burlington, there was high tumult at the rival headquarters; the head of the Union Pacific saw himself outflanked in his own Middle Western territory.[2]

As soon as he learned of this stroke Harriman in a towering rage went to meet Hill in the home of George F. Baker. To the end, he and Schiff, banker for the Union Pacific, maintained that Hill had made his transaction secretly rather than "openly" as claimed; and now Harriman on behalf of the Union Pacific asked to be given a one-third interest in the Burlington and offered to furnish one-third of the purchase money. This demand and offer Hill declined even to consider.

"Very well," Harriman is reported to have said, "it is a hostile act and you must take the consequences."

3

Thus as an accident of the particular, it was the Burlington that chanced to be the bone of contention. The opposing forces dis-pute the ownership of a Middle Western trunk line, described, to be sure, as the "finest railroad property" in its region; it is a gate-way to Chicago, and its main line is susceptible of development into

[2]Hill's motives are explained in another letter to Lord Mount Stephen: "The best traffic of the Great Northern and Northern Pacific is cotton and provisions west- and lumber and timber east-bound. The [Union Pacific] lines run through the cotton country, from New Orleans through Texas, and, Arkansas. The great provision centers are Kansas City, St. Joseph, Omaha, Chicago and St. Louis, none of which are reached directly by the Great Northern and Northern Pacific. Both companies have to divide the through rate with some other line to reach those important points. Now as to lumber from the Coast, we have to divide our rate with lines south to reach Chicago, Illinois, St. Louis, Iowa, Nebraska, Kansas, etc. The Burlington lets us into all these districts and commercial centers, over better lines and with better terminals than any other road."

a new transcontinental route to the coast which would neutralize the power of the Union Pacific. But in reality the causes of the conflict are long smoldering ones; with two such adversaries, either of whom is ready to strike for a complete economic hegemony, confronting each other, there is continual tension all along the line; and any border incident is enough to light the explosive fuse.[3]

Pierpont Morgan, assured by Jim Hill that affairs were progressing satisfactorily, reposes in Aix-les-Bains after April 20, 1901, "enjoying the baths and basking under the bland, blond skies" of Alpine France. According to John Winkler's account, he takes his ease after arduous campaigning, and in full view of the foreign colony diverts himself with the companionship of "a Frenchwoman of title and quality."

In the meantime Harriman swiftly forms his plan to strike against the mighty machine of transportation raised by Hill and Morgan. The Burlington can no longer be bought; its stock is locked up jointly in the treasuries of the Great Northern and Northern Pacific companies, and the gates are shut. But he had noted that the back door lay open. To be possessed of the Burlington, he would purchase the Northern Pacific, to which half of the Burlington stock had been allotted. He "would buy the mare to get the filly." Through the jungles of the marketplace he knew his way; he or his informants knew where stock was to be had, knew even that the Morgan people, who held with Hill some $35,000,000 of the $155,000,000 common and preferred capital stock of Northern Pacific, had been selling here and there to take advantage of the prevailing high prices, following the profitable Burlington acquisition. But where Villard twenty years before had needed $8,000,000

[3]An example of the tension under which both parties now labored was a collision early in 1901 at another outpost of the Harriman-Rockefeller system, in Utah. Harriman had been greatly aroused by the mysterious activities of Senator William A. Clark, the copper king, who was building a line from his Utah mines to Los Angeles and San Pedro on the Pacific, along a gorge called the Meadow Wash. The suspicion came to Harriman that Hill, with his southerly branches of the Burlington line reaching to Denver, would unite with Clark to seize the Union Pacific's traffic across the Sierras. Rapidly preparing for the fray, he utilized an old right of way along this same Meadow Wash gorge in Utah, and threw gangs of armed men into conflict with Clark's workers, the two construction companies now fighting each other in hand-to-hand combat, now crossing each other's tracks during prolonged hostilities, until peace was effected all along the railroad front.

for his "blind pool," Harriman in his secret raid would need $78,-000,000. He would then control two-thirds of the railroad territory of the country from New Orleans to Seattle, from Winnipeg to San Pedro, California, and would have the Morgan-Hill system bottled up.

From the Union Pacific treasury, from the Standard Oil "gang," from Kuhn, Loeb & Co., and the Rockefeller-controlled National City Bank, Harriman levied over $60,000,000, to which he added also all the credit he himself owned.

> The boldness of the plan [writes J. G. Pyle] . . . allied it to a work of genius. From those two grim old lions [Morgan and Hill] who guarded the way, the quarry was to be matched before they sensed the presence of an enemy. The implications of the project were tremendous. Suppose the Union Pacific interests gained control of Northern Pacific. At once the Great Northern would have had to make terms with its new owners, or bear the brunt of incessant hostile attack along two thousand miles of battle front. It would have been shut into the narrow strip between its line and the Canadian border. As the Union Pacific would succeed also to a half interest in the Burlington, the situation there would be a permanent deadlock. All the system of relations and the scheme of traffic worked out so carefully by Mr. Hill would have been either suspended or destroyed. There could be but one issue from a position so intolerable. He would have had to make the best terms he could. .

Moreover the whole continuous traffic chain from New England and New York to Puget Sound, so patiently linked together by Morgan, would have been sundered. Hill afterward declared that in this event he would have recommended that his stockholders sell their line at once at the best terms they could get.

Domination of a railroad or industrial corporation is often feasible with only a minority interest of 10 or 12 per cent of capital stock held by an aggressive group. But in Northern Pacific Morgan and Hill owned almost 30 per cent control out of $75,000,000 preferred stock (then possessing voting rights) and $80,000,000 common stock, "larger than is usually held," Hill said. It had never occurred to them that they would need more. "I did not think at the time that it was at all likely," Hill afterward confessed, "that anybody would undertake to buy in the market the control of

$155,000,000 of stock"—as a counterstroke to the acquisition of Burlington.

But the moves were well guarded. At a moment when the House of Morgan was heavily burdened with its involvements in the steel Trust, it chose to liquidate a block of 10,000 shares of Northern Pacific, which dropped into Harriman's hands; then another of 13,000, as the market steadily rose; then from quarters friendly to Morgan, another block of 35,000 shares was dislodged. Then, after a last lightning-like assault on the market, Harriman saw that he had in his hands $42,000,000 of the preferred shares of Northern Pacific, or a clear majority of that issue, and somewhat over $37,000,000 of the common shares, "which lacked being a majority of the common by about 40,000 shares."

The quiet, continuous rise of Northern Pacific stock (of about 20 per cent) had made Jim Hill in his office at Seattle increasingly uneasy; it was to him "like a steady fall of the barometer." Mr. Morgan was in Europe, leaving only the erratic Robert Bacon in charge at 23 Wall Street. Hill did not understand what was happening; he thought that it would be better if he were in New York. Calling upon the officials of the Great Northern to give him a "special" to St. Paul, "with unlimited right of way over everything," he made the quickest run to the Mississippi River that had been made up to that time and arrived in New York on the afternoon of May 3. He proceeded at once to the offices of Kuhn, Loeb & Co., to see Mr. Jacob Schiff. They were old personal friends who had formerly been directors together on the Great Northern.

Schiff now freely admitted that Kuhn, Loeb & Co. were buying Northern Pacific on orders from Harriman.

"But you can't get control," cried Hill. "The Great Northern, Morgan, and myself were recently holding $35,000,000 to $40,000,-000 of Northern Pacific stock, and so far as I know none of it has been sold."

"That may be, but we've got a lot of it. You secretly bought the Burlington . . . now we're going to see if we can't get a share by purchasing a controlling interest in the Northern Pacific."

Hill left the office of Schiff in bewilderment; then he immediately had Bacon cable to J. P. Morgan in Aix-les-Bains for authority to buy at least 150,000 shares of Northern Pacific, preferably the common stock, which was more valuable for purpose of control. Schiff had claimed that the Union Pacific party had on May 3 an overwhelming majority of the desired stock. But in reality, Harriman, stricken ill and confined to his home on May 4, was extremely worried, because, as he said, the common-stock control was still unsettled, and "the Northern Pacific could, on the 1st of January following, retire the preferred shares, of which we had a majority." He therefore telephoned Kuhn, Loeb & Co. and advised that 40,000 more common of Northern Pacific be purchased on the morning of Saturday, May 4, 1901. But Schiff, as pious a man as J. P. Morgan or John D. Rockefeller, was at the synagogue, and was reached only after much delay. He counseled buying no further, so that the order of Harriman, sick abed, was ignored.

Morgan was fully apprised of all the dangers of this new crisis. He said, as quoted by Hovey:

... *"When that news came to me, I hadn't any doubt about the fact of the matter. And at the same time the news came so strong— whoever had acquired it—I felt something must have happened. Somebody must have sold. ...*

"I feel bound in honour when I reorganize a property and am morally responsible for its management, to protect it—and I generally do protect it. So I made up my mind that it would be desirable to buy 150,000 shares of stock, and with that I knew we had a majority of the common stock; and I knew that actually gave us control, and they couldn't take the minority and have it sacrificed to Union Pacific interests."

During the night of Sunday, May 5, came the cable of authorization from Morgan to his lieutenants in New York. And on Monday, Northern Pacific "came strong from London, and opened with a burst of activity in the Street," according to Harriman's relation. The Hill-Morgan forces took the field; their brokers led by Jim Keene swarmed over the floor bidding eagerly for Northern Pacific common and taking all that could be had at prices that advanced steadily from 110 to 131. Harriman now knew that all was not well, and stormed at Kuhn, Loeb. Tuesday, May 7, the Morgan brokers continued their aggressive buying, and ran the price of the common up to 149¾—an advance of nearly 40 points in two business days.

The spectacular contest, which no outsiders then understood, but which filled the mobs in the marketplace with money lust, was quickly concluded—both parties claimed—on the afternoon of Tuesday, May 7, when the Morgan crowd had snatched away their full 150,000 shares, giving them more than half the common stock of Northern Pacific. From France Morgan had ordered that the stock be bought at any price; the cost of control was immaterial, so that he had it. It was by no means a "question of prestige," as Hill afterward testified hypocritically; but veritably "a life-and-death struggle" between the two moneyed hosts, in which, according to Barron's gossip, John D. Rockefeller *"expected Morgan to go at any moment..."*

But then as a by-product of these agonies of high finance there was produced a general catastrophe in the form of a sudden panic unforeseen, peculiarly atrocious and wanton.

Holding the price of "N. P." far too high and ignorant of the serious cause, the crowds of speculators had begun to sell the stock short with the expectation of buying it back later at lower prices; so that very quickly a large short interest was accumulated. But every share of Northern Pacific bought by the two adversaries was taken out of the market and was "going into the box" for control. Hence there developed, according to authorities on the subject, a frightful corner, in the sense that no stock was available for repurchase to those who had sold it short. Speculators on May 9 made frantic efforts to cover as rumors of the corner spread, and wildly bid up the price to 300, to 500 a share. Finally in one hour, while all the financial world seemed to turn completely insane, Northern Pacific soared to $1,000 a share—while all the securities, stocks and bonds of the whole country simultaneously fell in a grand smash from 15 to 40 per cent. For money was now fearfully scarce, loaning at 40 to 60 per cent; the shorts and the houses they dealt in were believed to be ruined, and were forced to throw overboard everything else they possessed to repurchase Northern Pacific stock. It was, as Hovey relates,

a curious and terrible state of affairs on the Stock Exchange; the extraordinary need for cash, for four or five days, had steadily forced the sale of all kinds of stock except "N. P.," and now the selling movement suddenly became a deluge which swept all values madly downward. So many shares were sold that it was impossible to keep track of them all, while above this ghastly confusion and wreckage, balloon high, hung the perfidious cause of it all—the stock which no one could buy.

it was the lurid, melodramatic climax of a speculative mania which had gripped the country ever since McKinley's inauguration in March, 1897, and the subsequent boom in Trusts.

The cataclysmic disturbance was felt in all the financial capitals of the world. In Europe Morgan rushed to Paris upon news of the Wall Street panic. From the offices of Morgan, Harjes & Cie., he issued emergency orders, swore at "idiots" and "rascals" who sought to interview him; and, according to Corey, threatened one reporter with "murder." To another, who asked him if "some statement were not due the public," since Morgan was being blamed for a panic "that has ruined thousands of people and disturbed a whole nation . . ." he replied in memorable words:

"I owe the public nothing."

A money pool was formed in New York to lend to needy houses; —a syndicate in which it is noteworthy the Rockefeller-controlled National City Bank, largest in New York, did not participate—and the two adversaries agreed to delay demands for delivery of Northern Pacific stock and to fix the market price at no more than $150. As the smoke cleared away, and the financially dead and dying were borne off, the press headlines screamed:

"J. PIERPONT MORGAN CONTROLS NORTHERN PACIFIC"

Which was only partly true; Harriman showed fight, insisted that the preferred stock could not be retired legally and secured legal opinions that he had formal control—but the Standard Oil family called off their dogs of war and Jacob Schiff especially sued for peace. For, as Mrs. Burr, writing on behalf of Stillman, said: "Both sides were . . . threatened from without," by the enflaming of public opinion over the wanton conflict. In great haste and shame for their destructive mischief, they signed terms for an immediate armistice: on the new board of the Northern Pacific, Harriman and William Rockefeller at last were admitted as directors, while Morgan retained dominant control. Yet from the abyss of disastrous struggle, a final step toward lasting community of interest had been made.

THE ROBBER BARONS

4

One may imagine the temper in which Pierpont Morgan returned to New York. Only he and his closest associates knew how near the end the "system" which he had been so long building was brought by the onslaughts of those who, after the elimination of Carnegie, figured as his greatest adversaries. That this had been done, moreover, in his hour of fullest triumph, after the launching of the steel Trust, made the affair all the more bitter. It was his favorite Robert Bacon who probably bore the brunt of "Jupiter's" rage and profanity, since all indications lead us to believe that upon Bacon lay responsibility in the emergency.[4] But for many reasons, including especially the state of the public mind, the purpose that now dominated virtually all the participants in the historic market conflict of May 3–9, 1901, was to seek peace, to base their actions at last upon the principle of "community of interest" so that "such things could not happen again."

The preferred stock of Northern Pacific, held by Harriman and the Standard Oil party, could have been retired at par at the approaching stockholders meeting, over which Morgan and Hill ruled by a slender majority. Due to have ejected the enemy would have meant such a long contest of litigation, in full view of the public, as the hounds of the press thirsted for. In their egomania, the leaders of both sides "might have continued to tear up Wall Street and injure large property interests including their own," comments Hill's biographer. But every calm reasoning voice in their midst urged them to desist in their "thieves' quarrel" over the spoils. Better to enjoy these peacefully in union with those intruders who had proved the power of their arms, while defending themselves against "the common enemy," the public, who, though menacing now in angry uproar, was truly the source of all enrichment.

The scheme for transpacific exploitation, writes Pyle, "was part of a commercial expansion greater than had been seen since Venice was in her prime." It was for this prize that both railroad captains,

---

[4]From the Harriman camp came the logical contention that since they had already gained effective control, it must have been "Robert Bacon, not Kuhn, Loeb & Co., who bid the stock up from 112 to 149 in the attempt to get control of it."

Harriman and Hill, had so jealously competed as to cause a conflagration which "swept through Wall Street and threatened commercial solvency in many capitals of the world." Was it not possible, Hill asked himself, "to build a strong fortress where, in peace or war, those who had seen the work of their hands grow great might establish it against all assaults and for all time to come?"

The antagonists of yesterday meeting at a conference at the Metropolitan club, May 31, now turned to Hill's idea of a holding company, in which their peace pact might be perpetuated. Thus, instead of taking the perilous course of ejecting the Harriman-Rockefeller interest, as he would have liked to, Morgan launched the project of the Northern Securities Corporation. He himself said like the others that they "wanted peace in their time." "My idea was, I can't live forever, and J. P. Morgan & Co. may be dissolved." He said further, concerning his investment in the Northwestern carriers, "I wanted to put it in a company with a capital large enough so that nobody could ever buy it."

The device of the "holding company," as proposed by Hill, was somewhat novel at the time, especially upon the scale (capitalization of $400,000,000 and with the purpose intended: to unite the warring financial interests in holy union. As a gigantic work of financial architecture, it was in many senses more remarkable, more significant even than the huge steel Trust, and merited fully the immense excitement it aroused throughout the nation.

Hill himself described the project clearly in a letter of May, 1901:

> The cost of administering the affairs of the holding company would be practically nil, as it would only draw dividends on the shares held by it and divide the money so received, by check, to its own shareholders. You will see how strong the holding company would be. It would control the Great Northern and Northern Pacific, and those two roads would control by ownership the Chicago, Burlington & Quincy . . . it could also . . . hold the shares of coal or other companies which, while of value in themselves and of value to the railway company for the traffic they would afford, the charters of the railroad companies are not broad enough to enable them to hold with safety. [My emphasis.] . . . For myself I feel that the future would be secure, and we would have certainty in the situation, and the control of these properties safe. Unless we do some-

thing of this kind, we will always be subject to attacks, like the recent one to secure control of one or other of our properties.

These were the terms in which Hill and Morgan spoke of the Northern Securities Corporation in private; such were the objects freely and openly discussed in the gossip of the financial press as well. Yet when the new corporation was announced in the autumn of 1901, it stipulated openly no other corporate purpose than that of investment in "valuable papers."

The Hill-Morgan group now exchanged its shares of Great Northern and Northern Pacific stock for that of Northern Securities Company of New Jersey. The Union Pacific people did likewise with their hard-won Northern Pacific stock, for which they received $82,500,000 of the new holding company's capital. Among the fifteen directors, Harriman and William Rockefeller figured, and Hill was elected chairman. The lieutenants of Morgan numbered ten out of the fifteen. But the Harriman-Rockefeller party were now admitted to the highest places in the Morgan hierarchy, being also directors of the Northern Pacific itself; thus cabals behind closed doors of directors' rooms were impossible. The peace conference at the Metropolitan Club was the conclusion of a "pyrrhic victory" in which Morgan made concessions which were pleasing enough to the implacable enemy of yesterday.

It was with visible relief that announcements were sent forth from the offices of Kuhn, Loeb & Co. and also from J. P. Morgan & Co. that "an understanding has been reached." Both parties, especially Hill and Harriman, publicly denied any part in "the supposed contest" of May 3–9. Jacob Schiff, the head of Kuhn, Loeb & Co., always full of "prudence" and "conservatism" and rendered sick by recent affairs, wrote unctuous letters to Morgan. Hill called Harriman "Ed," and Harriman called Hill "Jim." And all of them referred to the Northern Pacific panic as an "Indian dance," an affair of ghosts with which they had nothing to do!

There was good reason, it was high time, for such explosions of fraternal love in the quarters of the oligarchs. On September 6, 1901, while these plans for the disposition of one-half the transportation system of the continent were reaching fruition, the anarchist youth

Czolgosz assassinated the benign McKinley. Eight days later the well-loved President "of the chocolate éclair backbone," to quote a famous phrase of his successor in office, passed away, while Mark Hanna looked on dazed with grief, and tremor after tremor shot through Wall Street. The panic of May was resumed. Morgan himself, hearing the news on the wings of wild rumors that fled through the financial district, "had wheeled like a man stricken"; had "cursed and staggered to his desk while his face flamed red and then turned ashen."

The new President, vigorous and familiar figure, known the past twenty years and considered to be happily "shelved" in the vice-presidency, was that peculiar composition least understood by the barons, indeed less than the bearded anarchist or the red-shined socialist: he was a "reformer." There was no mitigating the alarm, the cold shudderings that passed through the steel masters, the oil barons and the railroad captains. All possible pressure was brought to bear upon the White House from quarters near and far, by friends and enemies, as Henry Pringle shows; he was exhorted to be "close-mouthed and conservative," to "go slow," as Hanna said, and do nothing "to upset confidence"—tears were shed for "confidence"—by the very interests who were the most generous patrons of the Republican party chest.

Mr. Roosevelt did in truth proceed at the outset with a becoming prudence. But at last the greatly feared, the awaited and the inevitable happened. The reformist "Rough Rider" soon placed himself at the head of the extraordinary mass movement of protest, which after 1901 swept the country in a great wave, a wave that had swept it before, like the cyclones of Kansas, the grasshopper pests of the Northwest or the droughts, quite native to the climate, but leaving it afterward fundamentally unchanged and as much like itself as before.

Imperceptibly the atmosphere had been changing. Of late years the "yellow" press of Pulitzer and Hearst had been giving undue attention to the doings of the multimillionaires of industry and the Idle Rich: the construction of kingly palaces, the divorces, the costume balls of a stunning extravagance at the Waldorf-Astoria—of all these things there were gloating and lurid accounts, while the occasion was not lost to paint at the same time the naked wretchedness of miners and unemployed workers. To these "exposures," the bombardments of comic weeklies such as *Life* as well as the caustic sayings of "Mr. Dooley" were added; and also the harangues of "radicals" and "muck-rakers" who arose on all sides. The followers of the young governor of Wisconsin, Robert La Follette, as of William J. Bryan, or of Eugene Debs, seemed to be swarming over the land. In vocal adherence and color they ranged from the deep socialist red of disillusioned immigrants and brawny Pennsylvania miners to the pink of humanitarian ministers of the gospel such as Washington Gladden or crusading college professors—of whom there were many more than are easily recollected—and of the ineffable, silk-hatted "Goo-Goos" whom Lincoln Steffens in his memoirs has pictured for us unforgettably. But by many signs they gave warning that the wind had veered, and the tide was swollen to groaning volume, ready to break upon the heads of the "Plutocracy."

There had been incidents provocative enough during the millennial administration of McKinley; the barbarities of John Gates and other heroes of Frenzied Finance, the violent strikes, the successive announcements of monopolies and Trusts evoked by the magicians of the House of Morgan or of Standard Oil; and finally the futile and baseless devastations of the Northern Pacific Panic of May 9—all this and more had been agitating the great crowd of respectable middle-class freemen. The ominous sense of a shrinking margin of practical liberties pervaded men, as each successive step in the nation-wide consolidation of the country's resources and means of production brought no tangible gains to the population at large. The great coalitions of the barons seemed to be made with no eye to the needs of workers in the cities or of farmers and little tradespeople in the broad rural regions. Certain of the Trusts, such as the Standard Oil or the American Tobacco and the meat-packers' association, had spread undying hatred among the petty capitalists who had been ruthlessly expropriated. The cry had been rising always for the "regulation" of the Trusts who were "eating like a canker into the very vitals of society." But when the young professor William Z. Ripley published his alarming analysis of the character and scope of Northern Securities, the vague fears of the populace focused themselves upon the newest corporate Frankenstein created by Morgan. The popular leader from the White House glimpsed with horror all the monstrous complot of the "subjects without a sovereign."

The Northern Securities Corporation was smaller in size than the Standard Oil or the United States Steel monopoly; but, as Ripley held, it was just such a Wooden Horse as the Greeks had reared to conquer the Trojans. Its two lines, comprising 9,000 miles of track which paralleled each other and were engaged in active competition for freight and passengers, "by making the stockholders of each system jointly interested in both systems, and by practically pooling the earnings . . . by vesting the selection of the directors and the officers of each system in a common body, to wit, the holding corporation . . . would promote the interests not of one system at the expense of the other, but of both at the expense of the public. . . ."

This was the ruling idea in all of the advancing, encircling chain of Trusts. But in the case of the Northern Securities the belief was voiced that by owning properties of all kinds, by exchanging its shares with those of existing capital securities—there was really nothing to prevent a corporation from eventually owning the whole of the United States, all up and down its whole length and breadth. The future of Abraham Lincoln's "plain people" was by now seen as dark and almost hopeless, unless there was truth in the prophecy of one minister, who, rising at this time before a convention of "Christian Socialists" in Buffalo (a fellowship of those whom Mark Hanna styled "Moral Cranks"), said:

> Some day after the Trusts have, with great labor and difficulty taken the cart up to the top of a long hill, we will relieve them of their labors. We will say, "This is our cart" and take it.

But in the temperament of Theodore Roosevelt the motives were mixed. As a gifted politician he sensed the tremors among the people. Moreover he himself was a descendant of that old mercantile "aristocracy" of New York which had been largely outstripped by newcomers in the hurly-burly of industrial revolution. Everything led him, as his most penetrating biographer, Henry Pringle, has shown, "to be alarmed and irritated at the great industrialists who complacently assured themselves that their power was greater than that of the Federal government." As a municipal reformer, earlier, he had shrilly denounced the predations of Jay Gould and had actually opposed that Mephistophelian financier in the matter of New York's elevated railroads. Now in the recent upheavals, such as the Northern Pacific Panic, he saw chiefly the unbridled hand of Edward Harriman, who was to his mind another Jay Gould. He had written:

> In no other country ... was such power held by the men who had gained these fortunes. . . . The power of the mighty industrial overlords of the country had increased with giant strides ... the government [was] practically impotent. . . . Of all forms of tyranny the least attractive and the most vulgar is the tyranny of mere wealth, the tyranny of a plutocracy.

The new tyrants, whom he styled, in one of his memorable phrases, "malefactors of great wealth," he now secretly prepared to attack. But while fearing the corporations, Roosevelt was admirably suited to step into the crisis of 1901. For him the only course would be the "middle road," since he abhorred simultaneously the socialists, silver-standard people, and all the other demagogues "who raved against the wealth which is ... embodied thrift, foresight and intelligence." Roosevelt moved energetically to curb combinations both of capital and of labor, and to save the social order from fatal dissensions. He had felt the deep currents of discontent, the preparing strife, sooner than the great bankers, because they were perforce too busy at their architecture, and hoped by dealing with the tribunes of the "plain people," the Quays, and Penroses, to spare themselves all further pains in this quarter. Thus, the apparent fact that Roosevelt, new idol of the great middle classes, was acting to avert a deeper, more implacable division in society, which might ultimately annihilate *their* system (as he himself interpreted it), escaped utterly the minds of old Bourbons like Pierpont Morgan and Jim Hill.

January 7, 1902, the State of Minnesota moved to attack the Northern Securities Corporation as a violation of its statutes. The Sherman Anti-Trust Law of 1890 had only once in a decade (in 1899) been used to halt conspiracies in restraint of trade (the Addystone Pipe Case). This move had been awaited. But soon afterward, when President Roosevelt, acting with profound secrecy, ordered his Attorney-General to prosecute the Northern Securities Corporation, on the ground of the Sherman Law, panic broke out in high quarters, where word of his move arrived in February, 1902.

Morgan was at a dinner party at his home, and to all his companions expressed his "surprise" and "disappointment" at the President's action. He had been assured that Mr. Roosevelt would "do the gentlemanly thing." In reality the old banker was infuriated, and forced himself to visit the White House to protest at the secrecy of the government's move against him.

"If we have done anything wrong," said the imperious monarch of banker, in words that have become immortal, "send your man [meaning the Attorney-General] to my man [naming one of his lawyers] and they can fix it up." Roosevelt had demurred; and Philander Knox, yesterday lawyer to Carnegie Steel Company, friend of Henry Frick and Andrew Mellon, cast now in a strange role, asserted that the purpose was not to "fix up" things. Then Morgan, anxious for his steel Trust, had asked whether it was the President's purpose "to attack my other interests," and had been courteously assured that no harm would befall them if they did no wrong.

Roosevelt said to Knox, after Morgan had left: "That is a most illuminating illustration of the Wall Street point of view. Mr. Morgan could not help regarding me as a big rival operator, who either intended to ruin all his interests or else could be induced to come to an agreement to ruin none."

Jim Hill, too, expressed himself with infinite bitterness, exclaiming: "It really seems hard . . . that we should be compelled to fight for our lives against the political adventurers who have never done anything but pose and draw a salary."

In the days of the "gentlemanly" McKinley, there would have been hints or warnings sufficient for measures to be taken in time. But still there was the Supreme Court, which had fought many a battle for the combinations. Would they sustain the "Trust-busting" President? The nation waited for their awful judgment, and Roosevelt himself suffered anxiety, while the monopolists vigorously pleaded their case during weary months. After two years of costly litigation, on March 14, 1904, the order of dissolution came from the Supreme Court, by a close five-to-four vote—Holmes dissenting. Jubilation. Roosevelt had "busted" his Trust, and now the country might go back to "business as usual." The middle-class President had his victory. He could now proceed to attack other judiciously chosen malefactors, one at a time. And the barons had merely their own measures of self-protection to take.

The omnipotent Hill spoke further on this subject, though in private. *"Two certificates of stock are now issued instead of one; they are printed in different colors, and that,"* as the monopolist laughingly said, *"is the main difference."* These are the most trenchant words that have ever been said on the whole Northern Securities affair. "I've made my mark on the surface of the earth," Hill added later, waving his hand toward a map of the United States, "and they can't wipe it out!"

The Supreme Court decision did not "bring the ruin of the country," as some prophesied, but caused fresh disturbance for a time, since it ordered liquidation of the holding company's assets on a pro rata basis. The Rockefeller-Harriman interests protested long and loud, because the securities returned to them were different from those they had put into the holding company, each owner receiving $39.27 of N. P. and $30.17 of Great Northern for his shares of Northern Securities. But eventually they accepted the situation with good grace. The new parcel of securities returned to the Union Pacific group for the old brought a windfall, an immense profit of some $58,000,000 in cash. Thus the wily Harriman, whom Roosevelt detested, wrested victory out of defeat. Then, imperturbably he marched with his great bag of plunder to new investments or conquests which further forged the chains of centralized control. The fact that Harriman or his agents, in the years after 1904, entered the directorate of the Baltimore & Ohio, the Atchison, Topeka & Santa Fe, the Illinois Central, and even the New York Central is in itself a clear commentary on the usefulness of Theodore Roosevelt's crusades.

The sound and the fury were soon over, long ago. In 1904, the largest contributors to the election campaign chest—from which Roosevelt pruriently turned his eyes away—would be Frick, Harriman, Morgan, Stillman, George J. Gould, H. H. Rogers, Archbold, and H. B. Hyde, the notorious head of the Equitable Life Assurance Society. They had all learned, as Mr. Pringle relates, that after furiously advocating reform measures designed to stem radicalism, Roosevelt bestirred himself to conciliate the great industrialists. In this connection, the Rev. W. S. Rainsford, minister of Morgan's St. George's Church and his confidant, said to him: "The time will come when you will get down on your knees and bless Providence for having given us Theodore Roosevelt as our President."[5]

By instruments more devious and impenetrable than ever, the retirement or expropriation of small-scale undertakers, the building of the giant Trusts into solid community of interests" was continued unfalteringly during nearly three decades that followed the battles of Theodore Roosevelt. The unsocial excesses, the periodic impoverishment of consumers, the misdirection and mismanagement of the nation's savings and natural wealth, were to be expiated through lean years (following fat years of "prosperity") through depressions and by way of a World War. Fleeing disastrous competition and price contests, the industrial combinations, like the railroad groups managed by the banker-promoters, continued to form coalitions with each other by far more subtle or masked corporate devices such as lawyers were always willing to furnish.

Had not Theodore Roosevelt furnished a hint that no harm would befall the large combinations if they did no wrong? Hence the "good" corporation came to flourish, fixing its margin of profits evenly, rather than scandalously, high. Like the one presided over by Elbert Gary, it might work collusively to sustain its price structure; it might hold its men working twelve hours a day, and keep spies in its mills to weed out union agitators. But its directors were outwardly virtuous; at board meetings, they were prohibited by Gary from gambling with the $20 gold pieces awarded them for their attendance.

[5]Morgan, a Bourbon to the end, was perennially disgusted with Roosevelt's measures of "regulation" such as actually served to tranquilize a population of consumers. For his part he would have clubbed down all opposition at all cost. Not all of his associates agreed with him however; George W. Perkins for instance expressed himself as friendly to such "reforms" as might allay popular mistrust and preserve the status quo. This view was actually advanced by Theodore Roosevelt, some years afterward when he spoke at a dinner of the Gridiron Club in Washington, at which Pierpont Morgan was present. He pointed seriously to the need of restoring stability and contentment to the masses. And in the course of his address, he turned suddenly and strode toward Morgan—who sat listening impassively—shaking his fist in the race of the financial colossus and shouting theatrically:

"And if you don't let us do this, those who will come after us will rise and bring you to ruin!"

Nevertheless Morgan was unappeased. When Roosevelt, upon retirement from office, went to hunt in Africa, the banker remarked feelingly to a friend: "I hope the first lion he meets does his duty."

What the giant Trusts learned from the era of "muck-raking" and the brandishings of the Big Stick was to move with a superior cunning and discretion about their tasks. Less and less did they act with the tactless arrogance of a Cornelius Vanderbilt or a Harriman, but sought nowadays to propitiate public opinion, hiring "public-relations counselors" who disseminated propaganda of great art, by which a mellower picture of themselves was presented. After so many storms, upheavals and trials which led to the Great Truce of 1901 between the House of Morgan and the House of Rockefeller, a period of comparative harmony ruled in these high quarters. It was shown at last how the national wealth might be peaceably and equitably divided, and conciliation practiced even in the ranks of capitalists. The rivalries and picturesque combats of an earlier, less organized economy grew rare. It seemed in the end, as one commentator writing in the prosperous 1920's observed, that *the rival banking groups sank their jealousies in the face of a common danger. The era of creation and struggle has given way to one of maintenance and conservative mastery.* A well-oiled and scientifically regulated machine seems the financial system of today, in comparison with that of the first decade of the century."

"Scientifically regulated"? Perhaps for a few seasons.

Ever since the turn of the century the form of our economic organization was virtually crystallized; the ownership of the means of production, the method of exploiting labor and natural resources, were fixed. To those who had known the technology of the Chicago slaughterhouses and of the Carnegie Steel Company, a Henry Ford was but a projection of the immediate past. To those whose memories were long enough to recall the era of Frenzied Finance, the Insulls and Van Sweringens of 1929 would be inevitable and repetitious figures of history. The successive periods of plethora and complacency, the intervals of tragic disillusionment, the waves of infantile reform launched by middle-road politicians, the recurrence of public corruption, financial madness and renewed crisis—all this, would seem so much ironical and wearisome historical reiteration of a familiar system, did we not begin to perceive at last in this system all the fatal signs of a shortening rope.

Soon there would be few who hoped that the old economic rulership established by adventurers, plunderers and their children, could minister to the just interests of the masses of citizens, the workers in the mills, the tillers of the land, let alone preserve the population for long. And during long years of industrial lethargy, while grass literally grew upon the floors of magnificent factories, the lesson would be finally driven home of the fearful sabotage practiced by capital upon the energy and intelligence of human society.

For, the second generation of money-masters, the sons of the barons, were weaker, less watchful and more vainglorious than their elders perforce. Extremes of mismanagement and stupidity would make themselves felt, as the more advanced cycles of the industrial revolution were attained and the economic organism became less susceptible of control. The alternations of prosperity and poverty would be more violent and mercurial, speculation and breakdown each more excessive; while the inherent contradictions within the society pressed with increasing intolerable force against the bonds of the old order. Then in the days when the busy workers of our cities were turned into idle and hungry louts, and our once patriotic farmers into rebels and lawbreakers, there would arise hosts of men and women, numerous enough, who knew that "they could no longer live in a world where such things can be. . . .

BIBLIOGRAPHY

The sources of information concerning the great industrialists of the post–Civil War era should have been principally the authenticated statements and memoirs of the leading figures themselves. However, these are full of pitfalls, or are disappointingly meager, or distorted by the spirit of special pleading. Not all of the great barons were articulate; when they were, they wrote of themselves instinctively in the same spirit with which they conducted their important commercial transactions, warily, deceptively, now using exaggeration or now underemphasis: they would be driving bargains, or vaunting themselves, or explaining everything away. And if not they, then their "official biographers," as, for instance, the late Colonel George Harvey, or Miss Ida Tarbell in her reactionary phase, would plead for them as lawyers before the judgment of posterity.

Feeling themselves under fire their life long, they generally carried their profoundest secrets to the grave, maintaining a terrible silence on all-important matters. I know of not one of the business captains who has submitted his private papers and correspondence to the scrutiny of an impartial scholar or historian.

Nevertheless, autobiographical works, despite their literary-historical shortcomings, have been used freely. Because of the vanity or naïveté of their authors such works as Carnegie's "Autobiography" and Rockefeller's "Random Reminiscences," are unconsciously revealing when carefully weighed. Although they invariably picture their authors as innocent, brave, kind, just, generous, and patriotic, they leave us room in many instances to form our own judgments, and interpolate with our own reasons. Other significant documents in this category are Villard's "Memoirs," Charles Francis Adams's "Autobiography," and Lawson's "Frenzied Finance," the last a piece of romantic, self-glorifying "muck-raking," part false and inaccurate, in part tremendously illuminating.

Still other autobiographical works by men who watched from behind the scenes, while by no means wholly trustworthy or accurate, give us rich clues with regard to the real motives or interests of the captains of business enterprise or finance. Such are Clews's extremely long and garrulous "Fifty Years of Wall Street," the memoirs of a direct witness; "They Told Barron" and "More They Told Barron," the "indiscretions," conversations, and sketches of a famous financial reporter, the "Pepys of Wall Street." In the last two, a mass of secretive gossip, hearsay and rumor, there are hundreds of instances when men and events are seen with the veil torn away, which is enough to make the two volumes of Barron's notes one of the most significant contributions to our subject.

The most direct sources are official stenographic government records made by "inquisitorial" committees of Congress or of the various state legislatures before whom the barons were often called. Although the subject of investigation usually speaks under the prompting of his legal counsel, important evidence is taken and authenticated. Such government documents as the following have been specially studied for the present work:

Report of the Committee on Railroads New York State Senate, Jan. 14, 1869 (relative to Jay Gould, Erie and New York Central).
U.S. House Reports, No. 77, 42nd Congress, Third Session, Vol. 2, 1872–73 (the Crédit Mobilier investigation).
Report of Special Committee (Hepburn Committee) of the New York State Assembly on Railroads, Albany, 1879, Vol. I (concerning freight rebates, Standard Oil, etc.).
Congressional Record, Vol. 17, First Session, 49th Congress (on railroads), proceedings of the Mullen Committee.
U.S. Pacific Railway Commission, 1887, Vol. 1, First Session, 50th Congress (on Central Pacific and Union Pacific Railways, with voluminous citations of the "Huntington Letters").
U.S. House of Representatives, Committee on Manufactures, Proceedings, 1888, No. 3112 (concerning Trusts).
U.S. Industrial Commission Report on Trusts, 1899–1900, especially Volumes 9 and 13 (testimony of Schwab, Gates, and officials of coal railroads).
Pujo Committee, Report of the U.S. House of Representatives, February, 1913 (on "The Concentration of Control of Money and Credit").

Many other official records have been cited from secondary sources, from documentary studies such as Haney's compilation, "A Congressional History of Railways," and from those few critical historians who more recently labored in this field. In this category I must do homage to a valued predecessor and a heroic digger in archives, Gustavus Myers, author of "The History of the Great American Fortunes," a monument of research in government and trial records, which narrates in brief from the view of an evolutionary socialist the careers of nearly all the great barons of the period save Rockefeller, Carnegie and Harriman. Lloyd's "Wealth against Commonwealth," a study of the great Trusts, and Ida Tarbell's "History of the Standard Oil" are also notable for their use of voluminous authenticated records cited in this work.

The trend in more recent works has been to both more independent and more realistic studies, reflecting an economic-materialist view of our history. A valuable economic history of the general period is Hacker and Kendrick's "The United States since 1865." A most penetrating view of the period is reflected in Corey's abundantly documented "House of Morgan" and Flynn's "God's Gold: John D. Rockefeller and His Times," both of which have proved invaluable. The most thoughtful and stimulating discussion of the general economic principles in force here were—after Marx's "Capital," and George's "Progress and Poverty"—Hobson's "The Evolution of Modern Capitalism," Turner's "Significance of the American Frontier," Tawney's "Religion and the Rise of Capitalism," Veblen's "Theory of the Leisure Class," "Theory of Business Enterprise," and "Absentee Ownership," Sombart's "The Quintessence of Capitalism," and, most of all, the Beards' "The Rise of American Civilization," of which the second volume, with its superb chapters on "The Second American Revolution," "The Triumph of Business Enterprise," "The Politics of Acquisition and Enjoyment," and "The Gilded Age," has manifestly inspired a host of newer historians to the reinterpretation of our history.

I must also make acknowledgment here of the courtesies extended by the Yale University Library, and especially by Dr. Donald Wing of their staff.

A selective list of works consulted or cited follows:

Adams, C.F., Jr., *Charles Francis Adams 1835-1915; an autobiography*, Houghton Mifflin Company, 1916.
—,and Adams, Henry, *Chapters of Erie*, new ed., Henry Holt & Company, 1886.
Adams, Henry, *The Education of Henry Adams*, Houghton Mifflin Company, 1918.
—,*The Letters of Henry Adams*, Houghton Mifflin Company, 1930.
Allen W. H., *Rockefeller, Giant, Dwarf, Symbol*, Institute for Public Service, New York, 1930.

Bancroft, H. H., *History of the Pacific States*, Bancroft-Whitney Company, San Francisco, 1883–92. 39 vols. Vol. XIX especially.

Barron, C. W., *They Told Barron, Notes of the Late Clarence W. Barron*, Harper & Brothers, 1930.

——, *More They Told Barron*, Harper & Brothers, 1931.

Beard, C. A. and M. R., *The Rise of American Civilization*, Macmillan Company, 1927. 2 vols.

Bowers, Claude, *The Tragic Era*, Houghton Mifflin Company, 1929.

Brandeis, L. D., *Other People's Money and How the Bankers Used It*, Frederick A. Stokes Company, 1932.

Bridge, J. H., *The Inside History of the Carnegie Steel Company*, Aldine Book Co., 1903.

Burr, A. R., *Portrait of a Banker: James Stillman*, Duffield and Company, 1927.

Carnegie, Andrew, *Autobiography*, Houghton Mifflin Company, 1920.

Clark, F. C., *State Railroad Commissions*, American Economics Association, *Publications*, Ser. 1, Vol. 6, No. 6, 1891.

Clews, Henry, *Fifty Years in Wall Street*, Irving Publishing Co., 1908.

Commons, J. R., and others, *History of Labour in the United States*, Macmillan Company, 1921. 2 vols.

Corey, Lewis, *The House of Morgan*, G. Howard Watt, 1930.

Croffut, W. A., *The Vanderbilts, and the Story of Their Fortune*, Belford, Clarke & Co., 1886.

Croly, H. A., *Marcus Alonzo Hanna*, Macmillan Company, 1912.

Daggett, Stuart, *Chapters on the History of the Southern Pacific*, Ronald Press Company, 1922.

Dodd, S. C. T., *Combinations, Their Uses and Abuses, with a History of the Standard Oil Trust*, George F. Nesbitt K Co., 1888. The views of Standard Oil's corporation counsel.

Fitch, J. A., *The Workers*, in *The Pittsburgh Survey*, Russell Sage Foundation, 1911.

Flynn, J. T., *God's Gold: John D. Rockefeller and His Times*, Harcourt, Brace and Company, 1932.

Fuller, R. H., *Jubilee Jim; the Life of Colonel James Fisk, Jr.*, Macmillan Company, 1928.

George, Henry, *Progress and Poverty*, 50th anniversary ed., Robert Schalkenbach Foundation, 1929.

Hacker, L. M., and Kendrick, B. B., *The United Stale since 1865*, F. S. Crofts & Co., 1932.

Halstead, Murat, and Beale, J. F., *Life of Jay Gould; How He Made His Fortune*, Edgewood Publishing Company, 1892.

Haney, Lewis, *A Congressional History of Railways in the United States*, University of Wisconsin, Economics and Political Science Series, Vol. 3, No. 2; Vol. 6, No. 1, 1908–10. 2 vols.

Harvey, G. B. McC., *Henry Clay Frick, the Man*, Charles Scribner's Sons, 1928.

Hedges, J. B., *Henry Villard and the Railways of the Northwest*, Yale University Press, 1930.

Hendrick, B. J., *Life of Andrew Carnegie*, Doubleday, Doran & Company, 1932. 2 vols.

——, *The Age of Big Business*, Yale University Press, 1919.

Hibben, Paxton, *Henry Ward Beecher*, George H. Doran Company, 1927.

Hobson, J. A., *The Evolution of Modern Capitalism*, rev. ed., Charles Scribner's Sons, 1926

Hovey, Carl, *The Life Story of J. P. Morgan*, William Heinemann, London, 1912.

Hubbard, Elbert, "Philip D. Armour" in *Little Journeys to the Homes of the Great Business Men*, Wise & Company, 1928.

Jones, Eliot, *The Trust Problem in the United States*, Macmillan Company, 1921.

Kennan, George, *E. H. Harriman; a Biography*, Houghton Mifflin Company, 1922. 2 vols.

Lawson, T. W., *Frenzied Finance*, in *Everybody's Magazine*, October, 1904, February, 1906.

Lloyd, Henry D., *Wealth Against Commonwealth*, Harper & Brothers, 1894.

Lynch, D. T., *Boss Tweed; the Story of a Grim Generation*, Blue Ribbon Books, 1931.

McAllister, Ward, *Society as I Have Found It*, Cassell Publishing Co., 1890.

McMurry, D. Le C., *Coxey's Army; a Study of the Industrial Army Movement of 1894*, Little, Brown and Company, 1929.

Martin, F. T., *The Passing of the Idle Rich*, Doubleday, Page & Co., 1912.

Marx, Karl, *Capital*, E. P. Dutton & Co., 1930. 2 vols.

Medbery, J. K., *Men and Mysteries of Wall Street*, Osgood, 1870.

Montague, G. H., *Trusts of Today*, McClure, Phillips & Co., 1904.

Moody, John, *The Masters of Capital*, Yale University Press, 1919.

——, *The Railroad Builders*, Yale University Press, 1919.

——, *The Truth about Trusts*, Moody Publishing Co., 1904.

Moore, J. L., *How Members of Congress Are Bribed: An Open Letter*, San Francisco, 1895. On C. P. Huntington.

Muldoon, W. H. ("Mul"), *Mark Hanna's Moral Cranks and Others*, G. F. Spinney Co., 1900. Complaints of Christian Socialists against the trusts.

Myers, Gustavus, *History of the Great American Fortunes*, Charles H. Kerr & Company, 1910. 3 vols.

Nichols, C. W. De L., *The Ultra-Fashionable Peerage of America*, George Harjes, 1904.

Northrop, H. D., *The Life and Achievements of Jay Gould*, National Publishing Co., 1892.

Noyes, A. D., *Forty Years of American Finance*, rev. ed., G. P. Putnam's Sons, 1925.

Oberholtzer, E. P., *Jay Cooke, Financier of the Civil War*, George W. Jacobs & Co., 1907. 2 vols.

O'Connor, Harvey, *Mellon's Millions*, John Day Co., 1933.

Orth, S. F., *The Boss and the Machine*, Yale University Press, 1919.

Paxson, F. L., *The History of the American Frontier, 1763–1893*, Houghton Mifflin Company, 1924.

——, *The Civil War*, Henry Holt & Company, 1911.

Peck, H. T., *Twenty Years of the Republic, 1885–1905*, Dodd, Mead & Company, 1907.

Pringle, H. F., *Theodore Roosevelt*, Harcourt, Brace and Company, 1931.

Pyle, J. G., *The Life of James J. Hill*, Doubleday, Doran and Company, 1917. 2 vols.

Riegel, R. E., *The Story of the Western Railroads*, Macmillan Company, 1926.

Ripley, W. Z., ed., *Railway Problems*, rev. ed., Ginn & Company, 1916.

——, *Trusts, Pools, and Corporations*, rev. ed., Ginn & Company, 1916.

Rockefeller, J. D., *Random Reminiscences of Men and Events*, Doubleday; Page & Co., 1909.

Russell, C. E., *The Greatest Trust in the World*, Ridgway-Thayer Co., 1905 About the beef Trust.

Sakolski, A. M., *The Great American Land Bubble*, Harper & Brothers, 1932.

Seitz, D. C., *The Dreadful Decade ... 1869–1879*, Bobbs-Merrill Company, 1926.

Smith, A. D. H., *Commodore Vanderbilt; an Epic of American Achievement*, Robert M. McBride & Company, 1927.

Sombart, Werner, *The Quintessence of Capitalism*, E. P. Dutton & Co., 1915. Translation of *Der Bourgeois*.

Tarbell, Ida, *The Life of Elbert H. Gary; the Story of Steel*, D. Appleton & Company, 1925.

——, *History of the Standard Oil Company*, reissue, Macmillan Company, 1925. 2 vols. First published in 1904.

Tawney, R. H., *Religion and the Rise of Capitalism*, Harcourt, Brace and Company, 1922.

Turner, F. J., *The Frontier in American History*, Henry Holt & Company. 1920. Especially the first chapter, "The Significance of the American Frontier," first published in 1893.

Van Metre, T. W., *Economic History of the United States*, Henry Holt & Company 1921.

Van Rensselaer, May (Mrs. John King), and Van de Water, F. F., *The Social Ladder*, Henry Holt & Company, 1924.

Veblen, Thorstein, *Absentee Ownership*, Viking Press, 1923.

——, *Theory of Business Enterprise*, Charles Scribner's Sons, 1904.

——, *Theory of the Leisure Class*, Viking Press, 1924.

Villard, Henry, *Memoirs*, Houghton Mifflin Company, 1904. 2 vols.

Warshow R. I., *Jay Gould; the Story of a Fortune*, Greenberg, 1928.

——, *The Story of Wall Street*, Greenberg, 1929.

White, Bouck, *The Book of Daniel Drew*, George H. Doran Company, 1910.

Winkler, John, *Morgan the Magnificent*, Vanguard Press, 1930.

INDEX

Acme Oil Company, 266

Adams, C. F., Jr., 121, 151-52, 155 n., 198, 293, 308-09, 311; cited, 72, 130, 159, 167-68, 309, 311-12, 337-38

Adams, Henry, 121; cited, 4, 37, 75, 148, 150, 155 n., 179, 335, 336, 337, 340, 416

Adams, J. Q., 76-77

Addicks, J. E. O'S., 397

Addystone Pipe Case, 448

Albany & Susquehanna R.R., 138-41, 153 n.

Alberti, cited, 8 n.

Aldrich, N. W., 347

Alexander, J. H., 279

Alexander, Scofield & Co., 119

Allison, W. B., 93

Altman, Benjamin, 345

Amalgamated Association of Iron and Steel Workers. *See* Homestead steel plant, strike at.

Amalgamated Copper Company, 398

American Bridge Company, 383, 418, 421

American Express Company, 43

American Fur Company, 12

American Sheet Steel Corporation 383

American Smelting and Refining Corporation, 400

American Steel & Wire Company, 388, 422, 426, 429

American Steel Hoop Company, 388

American Sugar Refining Company, 350, 381

American Telephone & Telegraph Company, 383

American Tobacco Company, 381, 387, 446

American Union Telegraph Company, 206

Ames, Oakes (and brothers), 78, 79, 92, 164, 355; cited, 93

"Anaconda" (oil, South Improvement Company), 160-61

Anaconda Copper Company, 398

Andrews, Samuel, 110-11

Archbold, John D., 161, 266, 269, 277, 278, 325, 350, 351, 354-55, 357, 360, 385, 450; characteristics of, 318; cited, 358

Arkwright, Richard, 11

Armor plate, defective Carnegie, 391-92

Armour family, 319, 324; Philip D. Armour, 32, 34, 50, 59, 101-02, 284-87, 305

Armstrong investigation, 409

Art and the barons, 330-33, 334 n., 341-46, 391-92

Arthur, Chester A., 244

A. S. Morgan & Co., 263

Associated Press, 208

Astor family, 12, 302, 319, 331

Astor, John Jacob, 11-12, 20, 22

Astor, John Jacob II, 156, 158, 205, 207, 295

Astor, William B., 12, 71

Astor, Mrs. William B., 205, 328-29

Atchison, Topeka & Santa Fe R.R., 220, 225, 313, 376, 380, 450

Atlantic & Great Western R.R., 137

Atlantic & Pacific R.R., 218, 219, 225-26

Atlantic & Pacific (telegraph) Company, 205

Averill, W. J., 302

Axtell, S. B., 356

Backus Mrs. F. M., and Rockefeller, 267

Bacon, Francis, cited, 53

461

Bacon, Robert, 408, 426, 438, 442
Baer, G. F., 373-74, 412, 414; cited ("divine right"), 374
Baker, G. F., 409, 418, 435
Baltimore & Ohio R.R., 106, 163, 182, 268, 272, 293, 295, 365, 376, 380, 403, 413, 422, 450
Balzac, cited, 404
"Banana Belt," Jay Cooke's, 94, 98
Bancroft, H. H., 45; cited, 249
Banking: early American, 28, 35-36, 290; later, 290-91, 400; modern, 404-05; national act for, 290-91. See also names of bankers and banking houses, and National City Bank.
Banks, Gen. N. P., 67
Baring Brothers & Co., 310
Barlow, Gen. S. L. M., 155
Barnard, Judge G. C., 125-26, 153 n., 154
Barron, C. W., cited, 167 n., 239, 245, 257, 288, 311-12, 351-52, 372, 382-83, 384-85, 398 n., 399, 413, 419, 440
Barstow, F. Q., 279
Beard, C. A., 72 n.; and M. R., cited, 52, 75, 167, 306-07, 352, 367
Beecher, Henry Ward, 94, 95, 150, 151; trial of, 156; cited, 350, 364-65
Belden and Speyer, 145-47
Bell, A. G., 178
Belmont, August, 55, 78, 154, 156, 158, 242, 291, 302, 339, 415
Bemis, E. W., dismissed by the University of Chicago, 324
Benefactions by the barons, 11, 19-20, 182, 229-30, 317-18, 319, 322-23, 324
Benton, Thomas, 76
Berenson, Bernard, 344-45
Berkman, Alexander, attempts to kill Frick, 371
Bessemer steel, 90, 107, 254
Bingham, J. A., 93
Black Friday, 40, 145-47, 302
Blacklist, 367
"Blackmail," 14 n., 186, 205-06, 295, 298, 356-57
Blaine, James G., 58, 95, 148, 165, 166, 212, 305, 347, 351
Bond, F. S., 308
Borden, Richard, cited, 364
Boston, Hartford & Erie R.R., 123
Bostwick, J. A., 274, 277

Bourgeoisie, triumph of the, 30, 274
Bowdoin, G. S., 408
Boutwell. A. S., 93, 144-47
Bowers, Claude, cited, 164
Bowles, Samuel, 153; cited, 60
Brandeis, Justice L. D., cited, 405-06 409, 410
Brewster, Benjamin, 277, 299
Bribery, 84, 93, 130, 164, 204, 223, 351-58
Brice, Calvin S., 352
Bridge, J. H., cited, 256
Brooks, James, 164
Brooks, Van Wyck, cited, 151
Brown, Moses and Obadiah, 11
Brown Brothers & Co., 307, 310
Bryan, W. J., 360-61, 376, 446
Bryce, James, Viscount, 244 (cited)
Buffalo, Bradford & Pittsburgh R.R., 123
Burlington R.R. See Chicago, Burlington & Quincy.
Burns, Robert, Carnegie, Garrett, and, 106-07
Burr, A. R., cited, 441
Burrage, A. C., 397-98
Bury, J. B., 337
Butterfield, Gen. Daniel, 143, 144
Byron: Morgan and, 345-46; translation of Goethe cited, 99

California, settlement of, 25-28. See also Gold rush.
California Central R.R., 218
Calvinism, 7
Cambria and Pennsylvania Steel Company, 108
Cameron, J. D., 347
Cameron, Simon, 103
Cammack, Addison, 198, 206, 208, and Travers, 213
Canadian Pacific R.R., 248
"Canon War," 225
Carbines, Morgan deal in, 61-62
Carlyle, Thomas, 23
Carnegie, Andrew, 32, 48, 177, 181, 228, 262, 297, 337, 400, 410; characteristics of, 42, 102, 105, 256-57; early life of, 41-44; early ambition of, 105-06; and Homestead strike, 359, 368-72; and iron, 102-07, 170-71, 397; and oil, 110; and railroads,

93, 296, 411, 413, 422-23; and steel, 107-09, 173, 254-60, 363, 367, 378, 380, 383, 388-94, 403, 406, 418-31; at odds with Frick, 418-20; cited, 42-44, 105-08, 173, 254-59, 263, 296, 336, 351, 369, 371, 378, 380, 389-92, 419-22, 426 n.
Carnegie, Thomas M., 103-04; death of, 255
Carnegie Associates explained, 264
Carnegie companies, 256, 259, 281, 362, 449; become a trust, 389; price of, to United States Steel Corporation, 425
Carr, W. B., 357
Cassatt, A. J., 295, 373, 422
Centennial Exhibition, 1876, 178
Central Pacific R.R., 78-93, 217, 220, 222
Central R.R., Georgia, 313
Charities. See Benefactions.
Chase, Salmon P., 54-56, 58, 95, 166; cited, 165
Chesapeake & Ohio R.R., 228, 301, 413
Chicago & Alton R.R., 308, 402
Chicago & Northwestern R.R., 155, 188
Chicago, Burlington & Quincy R.R., 202, 245, 313, 417, 433-44
Chicago fire, 168
Chicago, Milwaukee & St. Paul R.R., 308, 435
Chicago papers: Post, 97; Tribune, 284
Chicago, St. Paul & Kansas City R.R., 308
Childs, G. W., 167
Choate, J. H., 275, 367, 385
Cisco, J. J., 55, 78
Civil War, 3-4, 50-53, 66-67, 102, 163, 179, 232
Claflin, Tennessee, 182
Clark, Horace F., 72
Clark, M. B., 48, 110-11
Clark, William A., 217, 237, 347, 348-49 (cited), 436 n.
Clark & Dodge, 35, 53
Clemens, S. L. See Twain, Mark.
Cleveland, Grover, 195, 212, 305, 347, 351-52, 359-60, 392, 414-15; cited, 367

Clews, Henry, cited, 18, 19, 64-65, 70, 80, 186, 189, 199, 207, 208, 240, 304-05, 315, 326-27, 332-33, 350, 395-96
Coffin, Charles, 183-85
Coke, 262-63
Coleman, W. T., 107
Colfax, Schuyler, 93, 95, 164
Collins, E. K., 14-16; cited, 15
Colorado Fuel and Iron Company, 325
Colton, David D., 204, 224, 351, 353, 356; cited, 229
Columbia River Line, 239
Combination: first industrial, 115; "vertical," 264. See also Trusts.
Commercial & Financial Chronicle, cited, 311, 313
Commons, J. R., 325, 365
"Community of interest," 307, 402, 422, 442
Comstock Lode, 27-28, 33, 83, 149, 217
Cone, S. J, 228, 356
Conkling, Roscoe, 385; cited, 52
Conspicuous waste by the barons, 58, 134-35, 165-60, 212, 230, 247, 326-33, 445-46
Contract & Finance Company (Huntington), 218
Cooke, Eleutheros, 34
Cooke, Henry D., 54, 96, 357; cited, 164
Cooke, Jay, 32, 47, 48, 80, 164, 177-78, 201, 231, 238, 291, 357; characteristics of, 35-36, 38, 317-18; early life of, 34-37; operations of, 53-58, 66-67, 71, 92, 93-98, 145, 165-70, 237; cited, 35, 36, 37, 50, 53-55, 57, 169
Coolidge, T. Jefferson, 225
Corbin, A. R., 142-48; wife of, 145, 148
Corey, Lewis, cited, 294 312, 373-74, 408, 441
Corey, W. E., 391, 416
Corliss, G. H., 178
"Corsair." See Morgan, J. P.
Corsair (yacht), peace conference on, 298-99
Cotton Oil Trust, 382
Coxey, "Gen." J. S., army of, 359, 376
Coster, C. H., 314, 408

Credit & Finance Corporation (Huntington ring), 87
Crédit Foncier, 98
Crédit Mobilier, 81, 91-93, 98, 148, 163-65, 166, 194, 221, 223, 355
Crocker, Charles, 81-89, 217-29, 353-54
Croffut, C. K., cited, 14, 69 n., 72, 151 n., 184-85, 315, 330, 342
Cudahy, Hammond Company, 285
Cunard, Edward, 71
Custer, Gen. G. A., 165, 217
Czolgosz assassinates McKinley, 445

Dabney & Morgan, 62-63
Daggett, Stuart, cited, 81, 82-83, 218, 226-27, 350
Daly, Marcus, 217, 237, 348, 398
Dante, Rockefeller and Pullman superior to, 324
"Deacon." See White, S. van C.
Debs, Eugene V., 359, 446
Decoration, interior, and the barons, 134, 165-66, 330-33, 346
Deems, Rev. C. F., 182
Defoe, Daniel, cited, 8 n., 17, 39 n.
Delaware & Hudson Canal Company, 138, 302
Delaware, Lackawanna & Western Coal Company, 138
Delaware, Lackawanna & Western R.R., 413
Denver & Rio Grande R.R., 225
Denver Pacific R.R., 194, 197, 199-201
Depew, C. M., 130, 183, 298-99, 308, 347; cited, 187, 274
Dey, P. A., 92
Dickens, Charles, 150
Dillon, Sidney, 198, 241, 257, 337
Distilling and Cattle Feeding Association, 283-84, 351, 381
Diven, A. S., cited, 136
Dix, Morgan, 158
Dodd, S. C. T., 275, 277-78; cited, 278 n.
Dodge, G. M., cited, 23
"Dooley. Mr.," 446
Doubleday, Frank N., 336
Douglas, Stephen A., 76, 77
Drake, E. L., discovers petroleum, 109
Dreiser, Theodore, cited, 386

Drew, Daniel, 312; characteristics of, 18, 19-20, 128-29, 317; early life of, 17-18; and Erie, 18-19, 65-66, 74, 112, 122-33, 137; handkerchief trick of, 19; operations of, 18-20, 59, 63-74, 141; cited, 18, 59, 70, 194, 201
Drew, Robinson & Co., 18
Drexel, Anthony J., 55, 96, 167, 292, 298, 408; death of, 407 n.
Drexel, Mrs. John, cited, 329, 337
Drexel, Morgan & Co., 167, 188, 242, 291, 293-314, 307, 407 n.
Dubuque & Sioux City R.R., 303-04
Dunne, F. P., cited, 446
Durant, Thomas C., 78, 79, 92, 164

Eastman, A. M., 61
Eckert, Gen. T. T., 205-06
Economy. See Thrift.
Edison, Thomas A., 383, 386
Eldridge, J. S., 123
Elkins, Stephen B., 347
Emerson, Ralph Waldo, 43; cited, 23
Empire Transportation Company, 271-72
Entertainment by the barons, 331-32, 334-35, 338-40
Equitable Life Assurance Society, 409, 450
Erie Canal, 328
Erie R.R., 18-19, 63, 107, 117, 136, 121-41, 150, 179, 182, 271, 313, 380; and Drew, 18-19, 65-66, 74, 112, 22-33, 137; and Fisk, 74, 121-41, 153-57, 194; and Gould, 65-66, 74-75, 121-41, 153-59, 194, 201; and Morgan, 121, 138-41, 401, 405, 413; and Vanderbilt, 73 n., 141, 153 n., 157; and the fight for, 121-34
Evarts, William M., 155, 244
Everett, Edward, cited, 60

Fabbri, Egisto, 314, 408
Fahnestock, Harris C., 169
Fair, James G., 347
Farley, J. P., 233, 235
Federal Steel Company, 383, 393, 412, 423, 425, 429
Federalism, 22
Fenton, R. E., 131

Field, Cyrus W., 105, 198, 210-12, 305; cited, 293-94
Field, David Dudley, 157
Field, Stephen J., cited, 359
Fifty-niners, 14, 25-28, 33-34
Finance. See Banking; Short-selling; Stockjobbing; Stock-watering; Trusts.
Fish, Stuyvesant, 303, 401
Fisk, James, Jr. (Jim), 32, 80, 143, 150, 151, 159, 182; characteristics of, 65, 129; early life of, 33, 65; and Erie, 74, 121-41, 153-57, 194; and gold "conspiracy," 144-48; operations of, 59, 65-66, 84, 134-48; assassinated, 156-57; cited, 126, 127, 133-34, 138, 148
Fisk & Belden, 66
Fitch, John, cited, 370-71
Fitzgerald, Gen. Louis, 257
Flagler, Henry M., 112-16, 160, 274, 275, 277, 395, 435; cited, 265
Flower, Roswell P., 418
Flynn, John, cited, 46, 48, 112, 116, 270, 272, 318, 325, 398-99
Foraker, Joseph B., 347, 355, 358, 360
Forbes, J. M., 433
Ford, H. J., cited, 359
Four Hundred, the, 329-33
Fourteenth Amendment, 52
Franklin, Benjamin, 8 n., 9-11, 13, 16, 20, 22; Vanderbilt likened to, 151; cited, 9-10, 330
Free-pass evil, 251-52
Frémont, Gen. J. C., 61, 95, 218
Frick, Henry C., 47, 170, 178, 333, 341, 345, 346, 389-91, 406, 430-31, 449-50; characteristics of, 260-61, 319; early life of, 260-64; and Homestead strike, 368-72; at odds with Carnegie, 418-20; helps Morgan, 428; cited, 343, 351, 371, 389, 427
Frick and Company, 261
Frontier, 6-7, 21-29, 75-81, 216-17, 250-51, 364
Fulton, Robert, 13

Gallatin, Albert, 6, 13
Garfield, James A., 92-93, 148, 164, 350; assassinated, 303; cited, 148
Garrett, John W., 106, 301

Garrison, "Commodore" C.K., 199-200
Gary, Elbert H., 382-83, 393-94, 417, 420, 426-28, 430, 432, 451; cited, 299, 393-94, 423, 427
Gates, Rev. F. T., 321-22, 323, 397
Gates, J. W., 283, 372-73, 383, 387, 421, 422, 424-26, 429, 446; cited, 373, 402, 426
General Electric Company, 383-84, 417
George, Henry, cited, 86 n., 178-79, 208 n.
George Peabody & Co., 45, 59-60
Gladden, Washington, 446
Gladstone, William Ewart, cited, 183-84
Godkin, E. Lawrence, 305 (cited)
Goethe, cited, 99
Gold, dealing in, 58-59, 62, 63; "conspiracy" in, 142-48, 153; Morgan, 414-15
Gold rush, 25; California, 14, 25-28, 33-34; Comstock lode, 27-28, 33, 149; social, 376-33
Goldbugs, 142-48, 376
Golden Spike (Northern Pacific), 244, 245
Goldschmidt, Marcus, 158
Gompers, Samuel, 368; cited, 373
Gould family, 334; George J. Gould, 308, 329, 332, 337, 422, 450
Gould, Jay, 32, 45, 47, 50, 80, 150, 177, 181, 186, 188, 228, 241, 247, 252, 257, 301-05, 308, 330, 337, 338, 343, 356, 357, 386, 395, 447-48; characteristics of, 38, 192-95, 212-13; and Erie, 65-66, 74, 121-41, 153-59, 194, 201; and gold "conspiracy," 141-48; and Western Union, 205-08; other operations of, 59, 63-65, 84, 134-40, 163, 173, 178, 191-215, 225-27, 245, 248-49, 301, 309, 311-12, 355, 365-67, 385, 401, 402, 417; failure of, 214; fortune of, 378; unacceptable socially, 329; cited, 37, 131-32, 136 n., 194, 205, 220 n., 312, 350, 366
Grange (organization), 196, 251-52, 301
Grant, Ulysses S., 58, 62, 67, 80, 244; elected President, 164, 166, 250; as

President, 89, 91, 169, 224, 287-88, 328; and gold "conspiracy," 142-48; supports Southern Pacific bill, 95-96; wife of, 144, 145, 148

Grant, Ulysses S., Jr. (Grant and Ward), 214, 293

"Great Bear." See Drew, Daniel.

Great Northern R.R., 246, 247-48, 311, 313, 379, 416, 432-44, 450

Greeley, Horace, 94, 95, 127, 145, 158, 238; cited, 97, 151 n.

Greenhut, J. B., 352

Grimes, J. W., cited, 67, 79

Gunton, George, praises Rockefeller and Pullman, 324

Hacker, L. M., and Kendrick, B. B., cited, 77 n.

Hadley, Arthur T., 278

Hall, Oakey, 151

Halstead, Murat, cited, 64, 214, 316, 378

Handkerchief trick (Drew), 19

Hanna, M. A. (Mark), 322 n., 347, 358, 387, 445; cited, 353, 360-61, 445, 447

Hanna, Robert, 119

Harkness, Stephen V., 112, 114, 115, 395

Harlan, James, cited, 96

Harlem R.R. See New York & Harlem R.R.

Harriman, E. H., 170, 202, 336, 379-80, 396, 448; characteristics of, 193, 301-02, 323-24, 400-01, 452; early life of, 301; operations of, 178, 230, 301-04, 399-403, 416, 417, 423, 432-44, 450; wife of, 302; cited, 380, 401-02, 432, 435

Harrison, Benjamin, 351, 358

Harte, Bret, 27

Hartford Courant, 97

Harvey, G. B. McC., cited, 62 n., 261, 262, 319, 343, 345, 349, 389, 418, 427, 431

Havemeyer, H. O., 341, 343, 345, 380, 381-82; cited, 350, 381

Hayes, Rutherford B., 95

Haymarket riot, 367

H. C. Frick Coke Company, 260, 418

Hearst: George, 347; William R., 339, 415, 445-46

Hendrick, B. J., cited, 43, 104, 386, 392-93, 425

Hepburn, A. B., 274

Hepburn Committee, 186-87, 251, 267-68, 281, 304

Herbert, H. A., 391

Hewitt, I. L., cited, 119

Hibben, Paxton, cited, 151

Hill, James J., 32-33, 48, 242, 245, 312, 314, 322, 337, 347, 360, 365, 448; characteristics of, 231-32, 236, 301, 311, 313, 320-21; and Morgan, 432-44; operations of, 178, 191, 217, 227, 231-38, 246-49, 406, 416; fortune of, 379; cited, 235-37, 248, 293, 320-21, 351, 360, 379, 416, 433, 434, 435 n., 437-38, 443-44, 449-50

Hill, Samuel, cited, 379

Hoar, G. A., 223; cited, 165

Hobson, J. A., cited, 115 n., 254, 377, 379

Hocking Valley R.R., 313, 413

Hoffman, J. T., 140

Holding company, 92, 382, 443

Holley, Alexander L., 107

Holmes, Justice Oliver Wendell, 449

Homer, Rockefeller and Pullman greater than, 324

Homestead Act, 51-52, 77

Homestead steel plant, 260; strike at the, 359, 368-72, 389, 428

Hopkins, Mark, 81, 82, 87, 217, 229

Houston, E. J., 383-85

Hovey, Carl, cited, 300, 309, 310, 344, 345, 406-07, 411, 415, 416, 439

Hoxie, H. M., 92

Hudson River R.R., 69-70, 72 n., 122

Hughes, Charles E., 409

Huntington, Collis P., 32, 47, 93, 151, 177, 207, 241, 257, 301, 312, 333, 349-50; early life of, 33-34; characteristics of, 221; operations of, 78-91, 178, 191, 194-95, 203-05, 217-31, 245, 248-49, 301, 305, 352-58, 385, 406 432; death of, 403; cited, 79, 84, 204, 218, 222-24, 227, 252, 256, 307, 349, 350-51, 353-54, 355-56, 357

Hyde, H. B., 450

Idealism, American, 7, 28-29

Illinois Central R.R., 23, 301-04, 379-80, 401, 403, 450

Immigrants, 6-7, 21, 97, 234-35, 243, 361-62
Immigration Act, 52
Indians, 34, 89-90, 91, 165, 216-17,
Industrial Commission, 406, 413
Industrial conditions: early, 5; later, 171-73, 361-73
Injunctions (labor), 367
Iron-clad oath (labor), 367
Insull, Samuel, 384
International Harvester Company, 417
Interstate Commerce Act, 306-10, 360, 367, 382
Inventors, 101
Irons, Martin, 366
Irving, Washington, 12

Jackson, Andrew, 5; Vanderbilt likened to, 151
Jackson, Edwin E., Jr., cited, 288
James, Henry, cited, 340, 341
Jay Cooke & Co., 50, 95 96, 143; failure of, 169-70
J. Edgar Thomson Works, 109, 159, 265, 369
Jefferson, Thomas, 4, 5, 6, 13, 17, 28-29
Johnson, Andrew, cited, 80
Joint-stock companies, 16, 114, 253
Jones, Capt. "Billy," 104, 254-58, 391
J. P. Morgan & Co., 290, 404, 407 n., 416, 443-44
Jonson, Ben, cited, 39 n.
Judah, T. D., 82, 86
"Jupiter." See Morgan, J. P.

Kahn, Otto, 333; cited, 380, 432
Kansas Pacific R.R., 63, 163, 194, 197, 199-201
Keene, James R., 198, 205, 206, 208-09, 213-14, 301, 351-52, 430-3, 439; cited, 403
Keats, John, 345
Kelley, W. E. ("Pig Iron"), 93
Kellogg, W. M., cited, 56 n.
Kelly, William, 107
Kennan, George, cited, 302-03
Kerosene, 110
Ketchum, Edward B., son of Morris, 62

Keystone Bridge Company, 103, 105, 107
Kidd, Capt. William, 16
Kidder, Peabody & Co., 307, 310, 407
"Kier's Medicine," 110
King, Mrs. J. Van Rensselaer, cited, 326
Kloman, Andrew, 103-05, 177
Kloman & Company, 103-04
Kloman & Phipps, 105
Knight decision, 382
Knights of Labor, 212, 365-66, 368
Knott, J. P., cited, 98-99
Knox, Philander C., 449
Kuhn, Loeb & Co., 401, 407-08, 437-39, 442 n. 444

Labor organizes, 361-73
Lackawanna R.R. See Delaware, Lackawanna & Western R.R.
La Follette, Robert M., 446
Lake Erie & Mad River R.R., 34
Lake Shore R.R., 122, 186
Lake Superior & Mississippi R.R., 94
Lake Superior Consolidated Ore Mines, 397
Land: a source of wealth, 11-12, 22-25; grants, 51-52; grants to railroads, 23, 52, 77-80, 83, 93-95, 232, 432
Law, George, 68
Lawson, Thomas W., 397-98; cited, 279, 384-85, 396, 398 n.
Lee, Higginson & Co., 407
Lehigh Valley R.R., 313, 413
Leupp, C. M. (Leupp & Lee), 40-41
Life, 446
Life insurance companies, 409
Lincoln, Abraham, 23-24, 32, 51-52, 55, 77; Vanderbilt likened to, 151; cited, 447
Linville, J. H., 103
Literature, the barons and, 106-107, 345-46
Little, Jacob, 17
Livingston, Robert R., 13, 22, 29
Lloyd, H. D., cited, 268, 269, 284, 322, 336-37, 355, 358
Lobbying, 79-80, 143, 223, 245, 305
Lockout, 367, 369
Lodge, Henry Cabot, cited, 337, 37
Los Angeles & San Pedro R.R., 85

Louisville & Nashville R.R., 313
Luttrell, J. K., 357

McAllister, Ward, 329; cited, 329-30
McClellan, Gen. George B., 57
McCormick family, 324
McCormick, Cyrus H., 30, 100-01
McCulloch, Hugh, 95
McDowell, Gen. Irvin, 224
Mackay family, 334; J. W. Mackay, 217
McKinley, William, 322 n., 359, 360-61, 387, 416, 441, 446, 449; assassinated, 445
McLeod, A. A., 411 (cited)
Macy, S. J., 303
Madison, James, 6, 17
Manhattan Elevated Railway Company, 209-12
Manifest destiny, 149, 151
Manitoba R.R. See St. Paul, Minneapolis & Manitoba R.R.
Mansfield, Josie, 129, 135, 153 n., 154, 155-56
Marlborough, Duke of, marries Consuelo Vanderbilt, 340
Marshall, John, 6
Martin, Bradley, 339
Martin, F. T., cited, 337, 339-40, 352
Marx, Karl, cited, 162, 171 n., 181, 192
Materialism, American, 7
Mattoon, A. C., 130, 131
Medbery, J. K., cited, 152
Mellon family, 263-64: Andrew Mellon, 262, 333, 449, (cited) 349; James Mellon, 50, (cited) 59; Judge Thomas Mellon, 43, 262, (cited) 9 n., 50, 60
"Mephistopheles of Wall Street." See Gould, Jay.
Merritt brothers (Rockefeller), 321-22, 397, 428
Mesabi iron, 389-90, 397
Metropolitan Traction Company, 385
Mexican War, 36, 54; land warrants, 23
Michigan Salt Association, 115, 281
Michigan Southern R.R., 122
Miles, Gen. N. A., 217
Miller, Thomas N., 104

Mills family, 334; Mills, D. O., 83, 332-33, 334
Missouri, Kansas & Texas R.R., 191
Missouri Pacific R.R., 194, 199-203, 214, 301, 305, 308, 366
Mitchell J. H., 204
Mitchell John, 373
Money Trust, 314
Monopoly, 161 n., 181, 247, 264, 277, 278, 298, 380, 382
Montague, G. H., cited, 381, 387-88
Moody, John, cited, 91, 163, 192, 297, 307, 380, 388, 395, 399, 400, 410-418
Moore brothers, 383, 387, 400, 418, 421, 424
Morehouse, and Rockefeller, 267-68
Morgan family, 319
Morgan, J. P., 32, 50, 158, 207, 211, 322, 330, 337, 360, 374, 446-52; characteristics of, 63, 193, 294, 319-20, 324, 336, 410, 414-15; early life of, 44-45; and Erie, 121, 138-41, 401, 405, 413; and other railroads, 290-314, 380; reorganizing railroads, 401-23, 432-44; and steel Trust, 388, 393-94, 417-31; other operations of, 59-63, 167, 170, 178, 188, 191, 373, 383; collections of, 342-46; cited, 63, 294, 298-99, 308-09, 313, 344, 373, 394-407, 414, 417, 423, 425-27, 434, 439, 441 ("I owe the public nothing"), 443, 449, 451 n.
Morgan, Junius S., 44, 45, 59-60, 105, 154, 167, 294
Morgan, Harjes & Cie., 441
"Morganization," 294
Morley, John, Viscount, 418
Morris, Ira Nelson, 101-02, 284-87, 352
Morris, Robert, 17, 22, 23, 166; "of Wall Street" (Gould), 57
Morton, Levi P., 55, 156, 291
Motley, John Lothrop. 45
Mousetrap, Jay Gould's, 38
Muldoon, W. H. ("Mul"), cited, 44
Mutual Life Insurance Company, 409
Myers, Gustavus, cited, 14 n., 61, 67, 85-86, 141, 146, 171-72, 297, 333, 340

Napoleon, the barons in the rôle of, 40, 55, 242, 264, 345, 400

"Narrows," economic, 115 n.

Nast, Tom, cartoon on Fisk's death, 155 n., 157

National Biscuit Company, 383

National City Bank, 398-99, 437,

National Cordage Company, 376

National Steel Company, 388

National Transit Company, 276

National Tube Company, 383, 393, 418-23

Nationalism, 22

New Jersey Central R.R., 413

New York & Harlem R.R., 72 n., 122, 183; corner in, 68-70

New York & New England R.R., 412

New York Central R.R., 71-75, 112, 113, 117, 121-34, 137, 150, 151, 161, 177-78, 181-88, 251, 271, 286, 291, 294-99, 302-03, 308, 347, 377-78, 405, 413, 417, 450

New York Elevated Railway Company, 209

New York, New Haven & Hartford R.R., 411-13

New York Life Insurance Company, 409

New York papers: Evening Post, 312; Herald, 97, (cited) 40-41, 144; Sun, 97, (cited) 360, 366, Times, 97, (cited) 140, 159, 198 n., 210; Tribune, cited, 360 (see also Greeley, Horace); World, 97, 194, 205, 208, 209, (cited) 79, 210

Niagara (Vanderbilt's defective ship), 67

Nichols, Rev. C. W. de L., cited, 334

Nickel Plate R.R., 186, 298

Nickerson, Thomas, 225

Noble Order of Knights of Labor, 212, 365-66, 368

Norris, Frank, cited, 249-50

Northern Pacific R.R., 79, 93-98, 165-70, 203, 226, 231-32, 237, 238-49, 291, 293, 301, 311, 313, 379, 380, 405, 416-17, 432-44, 446, 448; completion of original, 244

Northern Securities Corporation: formed, 443-44; dissolved, 446-50

Noyes, A. D., cited, 415

Oberholtzer, E. P., cited, 34, 36, 58, 98, 170

Occidental & Oriental S. S. Co, 226

O'Connor, Harvey, cited, 9 n.

"Octopus": (Huntington railroads), 227; (Frank Norris), 249-50

O'Day, Daniel, 274

Ogdensburg & Lake Champlain R.R., 302-03

Oil: discovered in Pennsylvania, 109; rushes, 25, 44, 110; pipe lines for, 117, 160, 271, 273-77. See also Carnegie, Andrew; Rockefeller, J. D.; Standard Oil Company.

Old Colony Line, 412

Oliver, H. W., 389-90

Omaha Pool, 188-89

Oregon & Transcontinental Company, 243, 247

Oregon Railway and Navigation Company, 239-40

Oregon Steam Navigation Company,

Oswego, Milwaukee & St. Paul R.R., 399

Overholt (Abraham) distillery, 260, 261

Pacific Associates, explained, 81

Pacific Mail Steamship Line, 14, 15, 86 n., 150, 194-95, 204, 226

Pacific R.R.: demand for, 30-31, 52 n., 76, 80-81; bill passed, 78

Panics: 1869 (gold, Black Friday), 40, 145-47, 302; 1884 (Grant & Ward); 1893, 375-77; 1901, 440-41

Parrington, V. L., cited, 29

Patrons of Husbandry. See Grange.

Payne, Henry B., 347, 348, 349, 395

Payne, Oliver H., 119-20, 277, 296, 352

Peabody, George, 59, 290. See also George Peabody & Co.

Peary, R. E., 337

Pennsylvania Blue Stone Company, 136

Pennsylvania Coal Company, 413

Pennsylvania R.R., 43, 64, 102-03, 105, 109, 112, 117, 137, 182, 186, 188, 271, 272, 293, 295-300, 302-03, 308, 313, 314, 365, 373, 392-33 411, 413, 416, 422

Penrose, Boies A., 347, 355, 358, 386, 448

People's Canal system and People's

Railroad proposed, 305
Perham, Josiah, 78, 79
Perkins, C. E., 245
Perkins, George W., 382, 408-09, 451
Philadelphia & Reading Coal and Iron Co. *See* Baer, G. F.
Philadelphia & Reading R.R., 273, 295-90, 300, 313, 380, 411
Philadelphia Ledger, 96, 167
Phillips, Wendell, cited, 223
Phipps, Henry, 103-04, 109, 262, 264, 418, 431
Pinkerton detectives, 367, 370-71
Pioneers. *See* Frontier.
Pipe lines. *See* Oil.
Piper, J. L., 103
Pittsburgh & Lake Erie R.R., 296
Pittsburgh, Chenango & Lake Erie R.R. (later Pittsburgh, Bessemer & Lake Erie), 392-93, 422
Pittsburgh, Fort Wayne & Chicago R.R, 137
Pittsburgh Plan (Rockefeller), 265
Pittsburgh Survey, cited, 362
Platt, Thomas C., 347
Politics, the barons and, 347-58
Pool: "blind" (Villard), 242, 281, 437; Omaha, 188-89; whiskey, 283-84; wire-nail, 283
Pools: early, 115, 258, 282-89; later, 253, 281
Poor's Manual, cited, 292-93
Porter, Gen. Horace, 95, 144, 295
Potts, Col. Joseph D., 271-72, 281
Powderly, Terence V., cited, 366
Pratt, Charles, 266, 277, 278, 318
Pratt, Zadoc, 39-40
Pratt & Rogers, 266
Price, Bonamy, cited, 153
Priest, William, cited, 22
Prince, F. H., cited, 399
Pringle, Henry, cited, 368, 445, 447, 450
Projectors, 7, 33, 38, 77 n., 90; definition of, 39 n.
Public, the: "I owe the public nothing" (Morgan), 441; "The public be dammed! (W. H. Vanderbilt), Public utilities, 109-12, 383-87, 400
Pujo Committee, 409
Pulitzer, Joseph, 339, 415, 445-46
Pullman family, 319, 324; George M.

Pullman, 242, 295, 324
Pullman Company, 363; strike against, 359, 367
Pyle, J. G., cited, 152, 234-35, 237, 246, 321, 379, 433, 437, 442

Quay, Matthew S., 103, 355, 386, 448

Railroads: early American, 30, 43; and the West, 75-78; government aid to, 23, 52, 77-80, 83, 88, 93-95, 232, 432; earnings of, 168-69; Morgan and the, 290-314. *See also* names of roads; Rate wars; Rebates; Strikes.
"Railway Congressmen," 78, 93, 148, 164, 204, 222
Rainsford, Rev. W. S., 450-51
Ramsey, J. H., 138-40
Rate wars: railroad, 182, 189-90, 201-02, 237, 271, 295, 296-97, 310; telegraph, 206
Reading R.R. *See* Philadelphia & Reading R.R.
Rebates by railroads, 113, 117-18, 186-87, 189-90, 228, 251, 253, 265, 282, 286, 392-93, 422; forbidden, 306
"Reckafellow," 390
Religion: in early America, 7-8; of the barons, 19-20, 47-48, 116, 317-32, 374, 439
Rensselaer & Saratoga R.R., 64
Rhodes, J. F., 337
Richellieu, Cardinal, cited, 421
Richmond Terminal Company, 412
Riegel, R. E., cited, 191, 198, 203, 216, 224
Rings (combinations), 253
Riprey, W. Z., cited, 77 n., 282, 283, 381, 402, 446-47
Roberts, George B., 295, 298-99 (cited), 301, 308-10 (cited)
Roberts, W. Milnor, 96
Roberts, Percival, 426
Rockefeller family, 319; Frank Rockefeller, cited, 119; John D., Jr. cited, 427-28
Rockefeller, John D., 32, 45, 50, 59, 170, 172-73, 181, 263, 289, 321-25, 356, 367, 368, 402, 410, 430, 452; early life of, 45-49; characteristics of, 46-48, 111, 193, 265, 275, 318-19,

321-23, 415, 439; and iron, 390, 397, 400, 423, 427-28; and oil, 102, 109-20, 159-63, 237, 264-81, 378, 380, 394-400, 406; and railroads, 416, 422, 433-43, 450; wife of, 48; cited, 46, 47, 49, 113, 266, 270, 275, 318, 325, 372, 378, 390

Rockefeller, William A., 111, 114, 274, 277, 278-79, 296, 336, 383, 395, 398-99, 435, 441, 444

Rockefeller & Andrews, 111

Rockefeller & Clark, 48, 110-11

Rockefeller, Flagler & Andrews, 112, 113-14

Rocky Mountain Coal & Iron Co., 226

Rogers, H. H., 161, 266, 269, 275, 279, 305, 336, 383, 395-99, 450; cited, 279-80, 397 n.

Roosevelt, Theodore, 368; and coal strike, 373-74; and trusts, 445, 447-51; cited, 337, 448, 449, 451 n.

Rossettis, 346

Rothschilds, 12, 95, 154, 291 415

Rourke, C. M., cited, 20

Russell, C. E., cited, 285-86

Rutland & Washington R.R., 64

Ryan, Thomas Fortune, 335, 383, 385-87, 400

Sacramento Valley R.R., 88

Sage, Russell, 178, 198, 206, 209-11, 213, 305, 312, 337; wife of, 362

St. Joseph & Denver R.R., 199

St. Louis & San Francisco R.R., 313

St. Paul & Pacific R.R., 163, 232-35

St. Paul Daily Globe, 360

St. Paul, Minneapolis & Manitoba R.R., 235-38, 242, 247-49

Sampson, Capt. W. T. (later Admiral), 391

Santa Fe R.R. See Atchison, Topeka & Santa Fe R.R.

Sargent, A. A., 349

Saturday Evening Post, 346

Schiff, Jacob, 401-02 (cited), 435, 438-39, 441, 444

Schwab, Charles M., 255, 389, 391, 418-25, 430; cited, 372, 420 n., 425

Scott, Thomas A., 43, 78, 79, 93, 102-03, 104, 112, 161, 163, 177, 194, 203-04, 219-24, 295, 337, 356, 357

Scott, Sir Walter, 345; cited, 62 n.

Seligman Isaac N., 291

Self-made Man, 10, 16, 148, 366

Sellers, Coleman, 178

Selover, Major A. A., 207

Shakespeare: Carnegie and Garrett intimate with, 106-07; Rockefeller and Pullman greater than, 324

Sharon, William, 347

Sharp, Jacob, 385

Sherman, John, 54, 353, 359; cited, 306

Sherman, Gen. William T., cited, 92

Sherman Anti-Trust Law, 359, 381, 382, 448-50

Shipping trade: early American, 5-6, 13; government aid to the, 14 n.; Vanderbilt and the, 13-16, 66-67; Villard and the, 239-40

Shore Line R.R., 412

Short-selling, 17, 102, 141-42, 205, 440; of the dollar, 58, 62, 63

Sibley, Joseph C., 351, 355, 357

Sickles, Gen. Daniel E., 155

"Silver Fox." See Keene, James R.

Silver rush, 25

Sinclair, Upton, 287

Sitting Bull, 244

Slater, Samuel, 11

Slick, Jonathan, or Sam, 20

Smith, Adam, cited, 254

Smith, C. M., 166

Smith, Donald A., 233

Smith, Henry N, 142, 155, 214

Smith, Sidney, 54

Smith, Gould and Martin, 65, 142

Social aspirations of the barons, 326-33

Sombart, Werner, cited, 8 n., 39 n.

South Improvement Company, 115-20, 160-61, 251, 264-65, 275

South Pennsylvania R.R., 296, 298-99

Southard (Vanderbilt agent), 67

Southern Pacific R.R., 85, 95, 204, 218-30, 249, 305, 347, 348, 549-50, 354, 356, 403, 432, 434

Southern R.R., 313, 412

Spanish-American War, 394

Speculation general, 152

Spelman, Laura (Mrs. J. D. Rockefeller), 48

Spencer, Herbert, 105

Speyer & Co., 411

"Sphinx of the Stock Market." *See* Drew, Daniel.

Spies, industrial, 367

Spooner, J. C., cited, 190

Spreckels, Claus, 227

Springfield Republican, 153; cited, 60

Standard Oil Company, 114-20, 163, 189-90, 226, 228, 230, 265-80, 349, 355, 358, 394-403, 423, 447, 452; becomes a trust, 277-78, 381; opposition to, 353; sued for conspiracy in trade, 274; men of the, 185, 259, 304, 382, 406, 433, 437, 441, 442, 446 (*see also* names of the men); political contributions of, 360

Stanford, Leland, 32, 34, 52 n., 79, 81-89, 203, 217-30, 347, 348, 349-50, 354; cited, 219

Stanford, Philip, 83

Stanley Committee, 422

Starbuck, W. H., cited, 239

Steel. *See* Carnegie; trusts, 388; United States Steel Corporation.

Stephen, George (Lord Mount), 233, 235, 236, 248, 301, 434, 435 n,; cited, 245

Steffens, Lincoln, cited, 446

Stevens, Simon, 61

Stewart, A. T., 12, 72 n., 251

Stickney, A. B., 308-09; cited, 309, 312

Stillman, James, 304, 318, 336 (cited), 341, 343, 395-400, 402, 414 (cited), 415, 441, 450

Stock Exchange, New York, 16-17

Stockjobbing, 17, 93, 304

Stock-watering, 18, 207, 233, 388, 417

Stockyards. *See* Union Stock Yards.

Stokes, Edward S., 155; kills Jim Fisk, 156-57

Stoneman, George, cited, 228

Stonington R.R., 65

Strathcona, Lord. *See* Smith, Donald A.

Coal: Morgan controls, 413; strike, 373-74

Strikes: Borden mills, 364; Colorado Fuel & Iron Company, 325; coal, 373-74; Erie, 364; Homestead, 359, 368-72, 389, 428; Pullman Company, 359, 367; railroad, 272, 305, 365-66, 367; Western Union, 367

Sugar Trust. *See* Havemeyer, H. O.

Sullivan & Cromwell, 382

Sutro, Adolph, 217

Sutter, J. A., 25

Sweeney, P. B., 133, 153, 154

Swift, Gustavus F., 284-85

Symonds, J. A., 346

Syndicates, 253

Syracuse University dismisses Commons, 325

Tammany Hall, 385. *See also* Tweed, W. M., and ring.

Tarbell, Ida M., cited, 48-49, 111, 162, 265-66, 267, 269-70, 279, 299, 381, 426

Tariff, protective, 31, 52, 100, 108-09, 348, 381, 420 n.

Tawney, R. H., cited, 7-8

Taylor, Moses, 55, 290, 291

Texas, annexation of, 36

Texas & Pacific R.R., 79, 93, 163, 194, 202, 204, 218-25

Thielsen, H. cited, 241

Thomson, Elihu, 383-85

Thomas, S. G., 389

Thomson, Frank, 295

Thomson, J. Edgar, 43, 48, 103, 104, 109, 112

Thrift, doctrine of, 8, 10; of Carnegie, 42; of Rockefeller, 46-47, 270-71; of Vanderbilt, 185 n.

Tidewater Pipe Line, 273-74, 276-77

Tilden, Samuel J., 347, 359-60, 385; cited, 60, 315-16

Tilton, Libby (Mrs. Theodore), 156

Tocqueville, Alexis de, 7

Train, G. F., 78

Trollope, Anthony, cited, 24

Trusts, 163, 253, 277, 289; growth of, 298, 381-89; opposition to, 358-61, 381-82; Super-Trust, 428. *See also* Standard Oil Company; United Steel Corporation; and other names of Trusts.

Turner, F. J., cited, 21

Twain, Mark, 336; cited, 23-25, 29, 149-50

Tweed, William M. and ring, 68, 69,

84, 125, 130-36, 141, 142, 144, 151, 153-56, 385
"Tycoon." *See* Cooke, Jay.

"Uncle Daniel." *See* Drew, Daniel.
Uncle Jonathan, 20
Union Iron Mills, 105
Union League Club, 62
Union Pacific R.R., 78-93, 98, 163-65, 168, 186, 194, 196-203, 221, 225, 226, 245, 249, 293, 305, 308-09, 311, 380, 401-03, 423, 432-44; completion of, 91
Union Stock Yards, 102, 284-87. *See also* Armour, Philip D.; Morris, Ira Nelson.
United Gas Improvement Company, 400
United Mine Workers, 373
United Pipe Lines, 271
United States Bank, 36
United States Steel Corporation, 397, 417-30, 448
United States Supreme Court decisions, 306, 359, 368, 382, 448, 449
University of Chicago dismisses Bemis, 324

Vacuum Oil Company, 269
Vail, T. N., 383
Vanderbilt family, 302, 311, 313, 314, 319, 331, 334, 373, 401; fortune of, 378; Consuelo Vanderbilt becomes Duchess of Marlborough, 340; Cornelius Vanderbilt, Jr., 15, 331; George Vanderbilt, 333; William K. Vanderbilt, 329, 330; Mrs. William K. Vanderbilt, 331, 340
Vanderbilt, Cornelius, 17-20, 150-51, 161, 170, 181, 184-85, 251, 301, 386, 395; characteristics of, 13, 15, 71-72, 183, 185 n., 452; early life of, 12-16; and Erie, 73 n., 74, 121-34, 140, 141, 153 n., 157; other operations of, 59, 63, 66-74, 84, 112, 113, 118, 177-78, 181-83, 355; unacceptable socially, 329; death of, 183; cited, 13, 15, 16, 70-72, 123, 133, 161, 183-84, 185 n.
Vanderbilt, William H., 161, 207, 251, 257, 291, 330, 333, 336, 341, 342-43, 422; characteristics of, 184-85, 187, 191: early life of, 59; operations of

59, 177-78, 183-91, 205, 206, 295-300, 302-03, 305, 308, 380, 406, 411; cited, 15, ("The public be damned!") 187, 281, 294-95, 296, 377-78
Vandergrift, J. J., 266, 271, 274, 318
Van Syckel's pipe line, 117, 280
Veblen, Thorstein, cited, 29, 80, 180 n., 181, 191, 195, 203, 280, 317, 319, 322 n., 323, 334, 341, 367 n., 370
Villard, Henry, 97, 200, (cited) 201, 293, 301, 335, 402, 433; operations of, 178, 217, 226, 227, 231, 238-52, 281, 401, 436-37; failure of the enterprises of, 247; cited, 201, 238-39, 240, 242, 244, 246-47
Vinci, Leonardo da, cited, 8 n.

Wabash, St. Louis & Pacific R.R., 186, 188, 194, 199, 201-02, 203; decision in case of, *vs.* Illinois, 306
Wage-cutting, 272, 297, 365, 369, 378
Wall Street. *See* Stock Exchange, New York.
"Wall Street Copperheads," 56
Wanamaker family, 319; John Wanamaker, 323
"War chest," 215, 282, 379, 393
Ward, Ferdinand, 214, 293
Ward, Hamilton, Attorney-General N. Y., 209
Ward, L. F., cited, 180
Warden, W. G., 277
Warner, Charles Dudley, cited, 23-24
Washington, George, 9, 22, 29
Watson, P. H., 161
Webster, Daniel, cited, 79 n.
Westbrook, Judge (N.Y. State), 209
West Shore R.R., 186, 295-300
Western Development Company (Huntington), 218-19, 229 n.
Western Maryland R.R., 422
Western Union Telegraph Company, 195, 205-08, 214; strike against, 367
Westinghouse, George, 178, 383-85, 417; cited, 384
Whiskey and the frontier, 27; pool by distillers of, 283-84, 351, 381
White, S. van C. ("Deacon"), 301-02
Whitman, Walt, 346; cited, 76
Whitney, William C., 296, 335-36, 341 347, 352, 383, 385-87, 400

Widener, Peter A. B., 59, 335, 341, 345, 383, 386-87; cited, 386

Wilkerson, Sam, cited, 94-95, 98

Wilson, Henry, 87, 93, 164; cited, 78-79

Winkler, John, cited, 319

Wilson, Woodrow, 62 n.

Wilson & Company, 285

Winkler, John, cited, 436

Wister, Owen, 294

"Wizard." *See* Keene, J. R.

Woerishoffer, Charles T., 214, 240-242

Woodhull, Victoria, 182

Woodruff Palace Car Company, 43-44

Wright, J. H., 314, 408

Yankee Trader, 20-22

Yerkes, Charles T., 168, 335, 383, 386-87

Young Men's Christian Association, 323

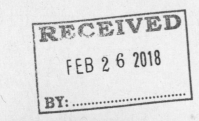